"Why Are All the Black Kids Sitting Together in the Cafeteria?"

And Other Conversations About Race

Also by Beverly Daniel Tatum, Ph.D.

**Assimilation Blues: Black Families in
a White Community**

"Why Are All the Black Kids Sitting Together in the Cafeteria?"

And Other Conversations About Race

Beverly Daniel Tatum, Ph.D.

BASIC
BOOKS

A Member of the Perseus Books Group

Published by Basic Books,
A Member of the Perseus Books Group

All rights reserved. Printed in the United States of America.

No part of this book may be used in any manner whatsoever without written permission except in the case of brief quotations embodied in critical articles and
reviews. For information, address Basic Books, 387 Park Avenue South, New York,
NY 10016.

Designed by Peng Olaguera.

Library of Congress Cataloging-in-Publication Data

Tatum, Beverly Daniel.
    "Why are all the Black kids sitting together in the cafeteria?" and other
conversations about race / Beverly Daniel Tatum. — rev. ed.
      p. cm.
    Includes bibliographical references and index.
    ISBN-10 0-465-08361-7; ISBN-13 978-0-465-08361-9
    1. Afro-Americans—Race identity. 2. Whites—United States—Race identity.
3. Afro-Americans—Psychology. 4. Whites—United States—Psychology.
5. Race awareness—United States. 6. United States—Race relations. I. Title
E185.625.T38   1997
305.8'00973—dc21   97-23119

DHSB   31 30 29 28 27 26 25

To my students,
who will have the courage to go
where no one else will go
and do what no one else will do . . .

and

For my sons,
who will surely know in their hearts how good and
pleasant it is when brothers live together in unity . . .

When I dare to be powerful—
to use my strength in the service of my vision,
then it becomes less and less important
whether I am afraid.

AUDRE LORDE

Contents

Introduction to the Paperback Edition (1999)

Beverly Daniel Tatum

Writing a book is a little like putting a note in a bottle and casting it out to sea. You have no idea where or when it will land, who will receive it, or what impact it will have. You simply send it out with the hope that someone will read its message—and that you might one day receive a reply. I am tremendously grateful that my message reached shore and that so many of my readers have in fact sent messages back to me, via letters, e-mail, and often in person at conferences and workshops. They tell me how useful my book has been in helping them talk to their children, their friends, and their colleagues about the difficult topic of racism. It seems that "Why Are All the Black Kids Sitting Together in the Cafeteria?"—with that provocative question as its title—has served as an entry point, a conversation starter even for those who ordinarily avoid such conversations. And that indeed was an important goal.

I put my message in this bottle not only to respond to commonly asked questions about race and racism but, more important, to help others move beyond fear, beyond anger, beyond denial to a new understanding of what racism is, how it impacts all of us, and ultimately what we can do about it. I wanted to en-courage—literally, to offer courage—to every reader to break the silence about racism more often, and to offer hope that it is worth the effort to do so. I am blessed that so many readers have taken the time to let me know that they have found both courage and hope in these pages.

When I cast my message on the water, I did not know that my action would coincide with President Clinton's call for a national conversation about race or that it would connect me to others whose courage and hope would both humble and inspire me. I never imagined that my message would wash up on the shores of the White House. I was surprised and thrilled when I came home from an afternoon of running errands one November day in 1997 and was greeted by my husband with uncharacteristic agitation. He told me that a member of the President's staff had called *twice* that afternoon looking for me. The caller offered an invitation to participate along with two other authors and a gathering of students and community leaders in President Clinton's first Town Hall meeting on race in Akron, Ohio. That December 3 event was personally very exciting and symbolically very important. As I looked out at the thousands of people gathered in the auditorium, and imagined the millions of people watching the televised event, I thought of my students back at Mount Holyoke College and the need they express for models of antiracist action and leadership. Though there are those who criticized the President's Initiative as "idle talk," I knew it offered hope for my students to see a powerful white man using his power to try to interrupt the cycle of racism. While acts of bigotry like the murders of James Byrd in Texas or of Matthew Shepard in Wyoming are usually well publicized and easy to spot, efforts to oppose bigotry and discrimination often go without notice in the media. In Akron, the power of the Presidency was making visible the work of community activists and concerned citizens participating in the forum who, in their daily lives, were trying to counteract racism. I was delighted to be a part of that process.

Just a few months earlier, in September 1997, I had been invited to participate in a conference commemorating the 40th anniversary of the desegregation of Central High School in Little Rock, Arkansas, a landmark event in civil rights history. This conference, one of the first involving the advisory panel of the President's Initiative on Race, allowed me not only to meet those distinguished panelists but also to hear firsthand the experiences of the "Little Rock Nine." These African American men and women made tremendous personal sacrifices in their youth to create change in their community and I was awed by their courage. I had the opportunity to stand in front of the imposing structure that is Central High School, imagining how frightened those teenagers must have been as they walked through jeering crowds into hostile hallways. Across the street from the school, a new museum commemorating the struggle to desegregate Central High opened on the weekend I was in Little Rock. I was deeply moved when I walked through the exhibit behind an elderly white man, who paused at the museum exit and openly sobbed with what I imagined was both grief and shame about what racism had done to those students and his community. The power of his emotions and of mine reminded me again of how the legacy of racism has damaged all of us and why we all must work to dismantle it.

I tried to explain this point to a radio interviewer I met while traveling on a book tour. A white man in his 50s, he spoke despairingly of the fact that race relations had changed so little in his lifetime. He commented that although there had been progress during the Civil Rights era, since then it seemed that we lost momentum. He noted that segregation still persists, economic inequality has worsened, and racial violence continues to make national headlines. All these statements are true, and the temptation to despair is strong. Yet despair is an act of resignation I am not willing to make, and I urged him not to as well. In response, he pointed to his own racially mixed community as an example. Here was a place, he said, where people of color and white people lived together as neighbors, and yet there was little meaningful interaction across racial lines; no dialogue was taking place. He lamented, "We just don't have the leaders we used to have, we don't have the leaders we need." I paused, and then asked, "Well, if you are interested in dialogue, have you invited anyone to your house to talk about these issues? You are a person who has a sphere of influence. How are you using it to make things different?" As Gandhi once said, we need to "be the change we want to see happen." We are the leaders we have been waiting for.

I began this Introduction with an image of a person standing on the water's edge. I would like to end it with a different image. Several months ago I made a donation to the annual fund of City Year, a national service organization that gives young people the opportunity to spend a year doing service projects in cities across the United States—a kind of urban Peace Corps. As a token of appreciation, I received a mug with a story printed on its side. It read:

> A young girl was walking along a beach. To her amazement, she came upon thousands of starfish. Washed ashore by a storm, they were dying in the hot sun. The girl began to toss starfish back into the sea, one by one. After a while, a man approached her. "Little girl," he asked, "why are you doing this? There are thousands of starfish on the beach. You cannot possibly hope to make a difference!" The girl was discouraged, and dropped the starfish in her hand. But a moment later, she bent down, picked up the starfish again, and tossed it as far as she could into the sea. She turned back to the man. Smiling brightly, she said, "I made a difference to that one!" Inspired, he joined her. A crowd had gathered, and soon others joined in. Before long, there were hundreds of people tossing starfish back into the sea and calling out, "I made a difference to that one!" After a while, their calls subsided. The girl looked up. To her amazement, she saw no starfish on the beach. Each one had been tossed back into the sea.

As this story so beautifully illustrates, each of us has the power to make a difference, and collectively we can create a more just and peaceful society. We can lead by our own example and begin to erase the effects of racism in our communities if that is what we choose to do. I am grateful to hear that so many of my readers are making that choice.

To the new readers of the paperback edition, I hope you too will find in these pages the information and the inspiration you need to join the effort.

Introduction
A Psychologist's Perspective

As a clinical psychologist with a research interest in Black children's racial identity development, I began teaching about racism many years ago when I was asked by the chair of the Black studies department of the large public university where I was a lecturer to teach a course called "Group Exploration of Racism." None of my colleagues, all of whom had been trained in the traditional lecture style of college teaching, wanted to teach the course, which emphasized group interaction and self-revelation. But as a clinical psychologist trained to facilitate emotionally difficult group discussions, I was intrigued by the experiential emphasis implied by the course title, and I took on the challenge.

Aided by a folder full of handouts and course descriptions left behind by the previous instructor, a copy of *White Awareness: Handbook for Anti-Racism Training,*[1] and my own clinical skills as a group facilitator, I constructed a course that seemed to meet the goals outlined in the course catalog. Designed "to provide students with an understanding of the psychological causes and emotional reality of racism as it appears in everyday life," the course incorporated the use of lectures, readings, simulation exercises, group research projects, and extensive class discussion to help students explore the psychological impact of racism on both Whites and people of color.

Though my first efforts were tentative, the results were powerful. The students in my class, most of whom were White, repeatedly described the course in their evaluations as one of the most valuable educational experiences of their college careers. I was convinced that helping students understand the ways in which racism operates in their own lives and what they could do about it was a true calling that I should accept. The freedom to institute the course in the curriculum of the psychology departments in which I would eventually teach became a personal condition of employment. Since 1980, I have taught this course, now called "The Psychology of Racism," to hundreds of students at three different institutions—a large public university, a small coeducational state college, and an elite private college for women.[2] I have also developed a similar course especially for elementary and secondary school teachers and administrators that hundreds of educators have now taken.[3] These experiences, along with the countless parent education workshops I have led and my ongoing research about the experiences of Black adolescents in predominantly White settings, have taught me a lot about the significance of racial identity in the lives of children as well as adults. In fact, my deepening understanding of racial identity development theory has greatly informed my thinking about how best to teach these courses and lead these workshops.

After about ten years of teaching, I decided to share some of what I had learned in an article, "Talking About Race, Learning About Racism: An Application of Racial Identity Development Theory in the Classroom."[4] Published in the Spring 1992 edition of the *Harvard Educational Review,* the article has been read widely by my academic colleagues in the field of education, many of whom tell me that reading about the theoretical framework of racial identity development triggered an "aha" moment for them. Suddenly the racial dynamics in their classrooms and within their own campus communities made sense in a way that they hadn't before. Those who were parents of adolescents of color suddenly had a new lens with which to see the sometimes sudden shifts in their children's behavior both at home and at school. Cross-racial interactions with colleagues took on new meaning. Just as it had for me, an understanding of racial identity development gave them new ways of thinking about old problems and offered them new strategies for facilitating productive dialogue about racial issues.

What concerns me is how little most people outside my particular specialty know about racial identity development. Even those who have studied child psychology are often uninformed about the role of racial or ethnic identity in young people's development. Perhaps given the historical emphasis on the experiences of White, middle-class children in psychological research, this fact should not be surprising. Most introductory psychology or developmental psychology text-books include very little mention, if any, of racial or ethnic identity development. Because racial identity is not seen as salient for White adolescents, it is usually not included in the texts.

One consequence of this omission that should concern all of us is that educators all across the country, most of whom are White, are teaching in racially mixed classrooms, daily observing identity development in process, and are without an important interpretive framework to help them understand what is happening in their interactions with students, or even in their cross-racial interactions with colleagues. Although educators are hungry for this information, too often it has not been made accessible to them, instead confined to scholarly journals and academic volumes.

And if my colleagues in education know little about racial identity development theory, the general public knows even less. Yet whenever I talk about this concept in workshops and public lectures, the response is always the same: "This is *so* helpful. Now I have a better understanding of those interactions, now I see why talking about racism is so hard, now I know what I can do to make it easier."

Kurt Lewin, a famous social psychologist, once said, "There is nothing so practical as a good theory." A theoretical framework that helps us make sense of what we observe in our daily lives is a very valuable resource. What I hope to provide with this book is a helpful understanding of racial identity development from the perspective of a psychologist who has been applying the theory in her teaching, research, and clinical and consulting practice for almost twenty years.

It is a perspective we need now more than ever. Daily news reports tell us of the rising racial tensions in the United States. As our nation becomes more diverse, we need to be able to communicate across racial and ethnic lines, but we seem increasingly less able to do so. New tools are needed. While the insights of sociologists, economists, political scientists, historians, and other social commentators have much to offer, a psychological understanding of cross-racial interactions has been noticeably absent from the public discourse. In the absence of such an understanding, many questions important to our daily lives go unanswered.

I am often asked by parents and educators to address questions about children's understanding of race, racial identity in adolescence, and how to combat racism in daily life. White parents and teachers, in particular, often ask me questions about how to talk to children and other adults about racial issues. They struggle with embarrassment about the topic, the social awkwardness that can result if the "wrong" words are used, the discomfort that comes from breaking a social taboo, the painful possibility of being perceived as racist. Parents of color, too, have questions. They are sometimes unsure about how to talk to their own children about racism, torn between wanting to protect them from the pain of racial realities and wanting to prepare them effectively to cope with a potentially hostile world.

Adults, both White and of color, often hesitate to speak to children about racism for fear they will create problems where perhaps none exist, afraid that they will make "colorblind" children unnecessarily color-conscious. A psychological perspective—informed by developmental psychology in general, racial identity development theory in particular, and the insights of social psychological research—allows me to respond to these questions and others in ways that I hope will add useful clarity to the daily discourse about race.

My audiences often tell me that what they appreciate about my articles and my public presentations is that I make the idea of talking about race and racism less intimidating. I help them to see the importance of dialogue about this issue, and give them the confidence they need to break the silence about race at home, at work, among their friends, and with their children.

I decided to write this book when I received a letter from a school principal in New Jersey. He had heard me speak at a conference the summer before, and wrote to say that I had given the best explanation he had ever heard of why, in racially mixed schools all over the country, Black kids were still sitting together in school cafeterias. He invited me to come to his school and give the same explanation to his staff. The letter came at a particularly busy time in the school year. My desk was covered with student papers to read, there were project deadlines to meet, and I had just returned from a series of speaking engagements with a bad case of laryngitis. I was exhausted, and the idea of traveling to yet another school to give yet another talk on adolescent racial identity development was painful even to contemplate at that time. Yet the request represented a genuine need for information. I thought of the hundreds of times I had been asked the question, "Why are all the Black kids sitting together in the cafeteria?" The tone of voice implied what usually remained unsaid, "And what can we do to solve this problem?" It became apparent to me that it was time to address this question in print, and to bring an understanding of racial identity development to a wider audience.

As the idea for the book percolated in my head, other frequently asked questions came to mind. How do you talk to children about such a painful historical event as slavery? When do children start to notice racial differences? How should I respond to racial jokes? Isn't racism a thing of the past? I thought about the many public conversations I have had with educators, parents, and students, and the private conversations I have had with family and friends. It seemed to me that there was value in making some of these conversations available to others, as I do in my public presentations, as a way of both sharing information and modeling a process of engagement, a way of talking about the legacy of racism in our lives.

At the center of these conversations is an understanding of racial identity, the meaning each of us has constructed or is constructing about what it means to be a White person or a person of color in a race-conscious society. Present also is an understanding of racism. It is because we live in a racist society that racial identity has as much meaning as it does. We cannot talk meaningfully about racial identity without also talking about racism.

All of the conversations in this book are drawn from my own life experience and in the context of my own teaching about racism and racial identity, as well as from my research on Black children and families in predominantly White settings. Because I am a Black woman, these conversations are often framed in the context of Black-White relations. However, one of the lessons I have learned in the years that I have been teaching about racism is that racism is a live issue for other groups of color as well. My Latino, Asian, American Indian, and biracial students have taught me that they have a developing sense of racial/ethnic identity, too, and that all of us need to see our experiences reflected back to us. In that spirit, I have included discussions of the identity development of Latino, Asian, and American Indian adolescents, as well as of the experiences of young people growing up in multiracial families.

In envisioning this book, it was not my intention to write for an academic audience. Instead I wanted to talk to the many parents, educators, and community leaders who would come to one of my presentations on "Talking to Children About Race" or "Interrupting the Cycle of Oppression" or "Understanding Racial Identity Development" if it were held at their children's school or in their town, and to respond to the kinds of questions I often hear these concerned adults ask. I wanted to make this psychological perspective as jargon-free as possible while still maintaining the integrity of the ideas. To the extent that readers find ideas they can use in their daily conversations with colleagues, friends, and family, I have been successful.

James Baldwin wrote, "Not everything that is faced can be changed. But nothing can be changed until it is faced." Talking about racism is an essential part of facing racism and changing it. But it is not the only part. I am painfully aware that people of color have been talking about racism for a long time. Many people of color are tired of talking, frustrated that talk has not lead to enough constructive action or meaningful social change. But in my own work, I have seen the effectiveness of talking about racism and teaching others to do the same. I have seen the impact on individual students who years later have written to me about the changes they are making in their workplaces. I have seen the impact on educators I have worked with who are now transforming their curricula and interacting with students of color in ways that facilitate rather than hinder those children's academic success. I have witnessed the parents who begin to use their own spheres of influence within the community to address racism and other forms of oppression in their own environments. I remain hopeful. It is with this spirit of optimism that I invite my readers to join with me in these conversations about race.

Part I

A Definition of Terms

1

Defining Racism

"Can we talk?"

Early in my teaching career, a White student I knew asked me what I would be teaching the following semester. I mentioned that I would be teaching a course on racism. She replied, with some surprise in her voice, "Oh, is there still racism?" I assured her that indeed there was and suggested that she sign up for my course. Fifteen years later, after exhaustive media coverage of events such as the Rodney King beating, the Charles Stuart and Susan Smith cases, the O. J. Simpson trial, the appeal to racial prejudices in electoral politics, and the bitter debates about affirmative action and welfare reform, it seems hard to imagine that anyone would still be unaware of the reality of racism in our society. But in fact, in almost every audience I address, there is someone who will suggest that racism is a thing of the past. There is always someone who hasn't noticed the stereotypical images of people of color in the media, who hasn't observed the housing discrimination in their community, who hasn't read the newspaper articles about documented racial bias in lending practices among well-known banks, who isn't aware of the racial tracking pattern at the local school, who hasn't seen the reports of rising incidents of racially motivated hate crimes in America—in short, someone who hasn't been paying attention to issues of race. But if you are paying attention, the legacy of racism is not hard to see, and we are all affected by it.

The impact of racism begins early. Even in our preschool years, we are exposed to misinformation about people different from ourselves. Many of us grew up in neighborhoods where we had limited opportunities to interact with people different from our own families.

When I ask my college students, "How many of you grew up in neighborhoods where most of the people were from the same racial group as your own?" almost every hand goes up. There is still a great deal of social segregation in our communities. Consequently, most of the early information we receive about "others"—people racially, religiously, or socioeconomically different from ourselves—does not come as the result of firsthand experience. The secondhand information we do receive has often been distorted, shaped by cultural stereotypes, and left incomplete.

Some examples will highlight this process. Several years ago one of my students conducted a research project investigating preschoolers' conceptions of Native Americans.[1] Using children at a local day care center as her participants, she asked these three- and four-year-olds to draw a picture of a Native American. Most children were stumped by her request. They didn't know what a Native American was. But when she rephrased the question and asked them to draw a picture of an Indian, they readily complied. Almost every picture included one central feature: feathers. In fact, many of them also included a weapon—a knife or tomahawk—and depicted the person in violent or aggressive terms. Though this group of children, almost all of whom were White, did not live near a large Native American population and probably had had little if any personal interaction with American Indians, they all had internalized an image of what Indians were like. How did they know? Cartoon images, in particular the Disney movie *Peter Pan,* were cited by the children as their number-one source of information. At the age of three, these children already had a set of stereotypes in place. Though I would not describe three-year-olds as prejudiced, the stereotypes to which they have been exposed become the foundation for the adult prejudices so many of us have.

Sometimes the assumptions we make about others come not from what we have been told or what we have seen on television or in books, but rather from what we have *not* been told. The distortion of historical information about people of color leads young people (and older people, too) to make assumptions that may go unchallenged for a long time. Consider this conversation between two White students following a discussion about the cultural transmission of racism:

"Yeah, I just found out that Cleopatra was actually a Black woman."

"What?"

The first student went on to explain her newly learned information. The second student exclaimed in disbelief, "That can't be true. Cleopatra was beautiful!"

What had this young woman learned about who in our society is considered beautiful and who is not? Had she conjured up images of Elizabeth Taylor when she thought of Cleopatra? The new information her classmate had shared and her own deeply ingrained assumptions about who is beautiful and who is not were too incongruous to allow her to assimilate the information at that moment.

Omitted information can have similar effects. For example, another young woman, preparing to be a high school English teacher, expressed her dismay that she had never learned about any Black authors in any of her English courses. How was she to teach about them to her future students when she hadn't learned about them herself? A White male student in the class responded to this discussion with frustration in his response journal, writing "It's not my fault that Blacks don't write books." Had one of his elementary, high school, or college teachers ever told him that there were no Black writers? Probably not. Yet because he had never been exposed to Black authors, he had drawn his own conclusion that there were none.

Stereotypes, omissions, and distortions all contribute to the development of prejudice. *Prejudice* is a preconceived judgment or opinion, usually based on limited information. I assume that we all have prejudices, not because we want them, but simply because we are so continually exposed to misinformation about others. Though I have often heard students or workshop participants describe someone as not having "a prejudiced bone in his body," I usually suggest that they look again. Prejudice is one of the inescapable consequences of living in a racist society. Cultural racism—the cultural images and messages that affirm the assumed superiority of Whites and the assumed inferiority of people of color—is like smog in the air. Sometimes it is so thick it is visible, other times it is less apparent, but always, day in and day out, we are breathing it in. None of us would introduce ourselves as "smog-breathers" (and most of us don't want to be described as prejudiced), but if we live in a smoggy place, how can we avoid breathing the air? If we live in an environment in which we are bombarded with stereotypical images in the media, are frequently exposed to the ethnic jokes of friends and family members, and are rarely informed of the accomplishments of oppressed groups, we will develop the negative categorizations of those groups that form the basis of prejudice.

People of color as well as Whites develop these categorizations. Even a member of the stereotyped group may internalize the stereotypical categories about his or her own group to some degree. In fact, this process happens so frequently that it has a name, *internalized oppression*. Some of the consequences of believing the distorted messages about one's own group will be discussed in subsequent chapters.

Certainly some people are more prejudiced than others, actively embracing and perpetuating negative and hateful images of those who are different from themselves. When we claim to be free of prejudice, perhaps what we are really saying is that we are not hate-mongers. But none of us is completely innocent. Prejudice is an integral part of our socialization, and it is not our fault. Just as the preschoolers my student interviewed are not to blame for the negative messages they internalized, we are not at fault for the stereotypes, distortions, and omissions that shaped our thinking as we grew up.

To say that it is not our fault does not relieve us of responsibility, however. We may not have polluted the air, but we need to take responsibility, along with others, for cleaning it up. Each of us needs to look at our own behavior. Am I perpetuating and reinforcing the negative messages so pervasive in our culture, or am I seeking to challenge them? If I have not been exposed to positive images of marginalized groups, am I seeking them out, expanding my own knowledge base for myself and my children? Am I acknowledging and examining my own prejudices, my own rigid categorizations of others, thereby minimizing the adverse impact they might have on my interactions with those I have categorized? Unless we engage in these and other conscious acts of reflection and reeducation, we easily repeat the process with our children. We teach what we were taught. The unexamined prejudices of the parents are passed on to the children. It is not our fault, but it is our responsibility to interrupt this cycle.

Racism: A System of Advantage Based on Race

Many people use the terms *prejudice* and *racism* interchangeably. I do not, and I think it is important to make a distinction. In his book *Portraits of White Racism,* David Wellman argues convincingly that limiting our understanding of racism to prejudice does not offer a sufficient explanation for the persistence of racism. He defines racism as a "system of advantage based on race."[2] In illustrating this definition, he provides example after example of how Whites defend their racial advantage—access to better schools, housing, jobs—even when they do not embrace overtly prejudicial thinking. Racism cannot be fully explained as an expression of prejudice alone.

This definition of racism is useful because it allows us to see that racism, like other forms of oppression, is not only a personal ideology based on racial prejudice, but a *system* involving cultural messages and institutional policies and practices as well as the beliefs and actions of individuals. In the context of the United States, this system clearly operates to the advantage of Whites and to the disadvantage of people of color. Another related definition of racism, commonly used by antiracist educators and consultants, is "prejudice plus power." Racial prejudice when combined with social power—access to social, cultural, and economic resources and decision-making— leads to the institutionalization of racist policies and practices. While I think this definition also captures the idea that racism is more than individual beliefs and attitudes, I prefer Wellman's definition because the idea of systematic advantage and disadvantage is critical to an understanding of how racism operates in American society.

In addition, I find that many of my White students and workshop participants do not feel powerful. Defining racism as prejudice plus power has little personal relevance. For some, their response to this definition is the following: "I'm not really prejudiced, and I have no power, so racism has nothing to do with me." However, most White people, if they are really being honest with themselves, can see that there are advantages to being White in the United States. Despite the current rhetoric about affirmative action and "reverse racism," every social indicator, from salary to life expectancy, reveals the advantages of being White.[3]

The systematic advantages of being White are often referred to as White privilege. In a now well-known article, "White Privilege: Unpacking the Invisible Knapsack," Peggy McIntosh, a White feminist scholar, identified a long list of societal privileges that she received simply because she was White.[4] She did not ask for them, and it is important to note that she hadn't always noticed that she was receiving them. They included major and minor advantages. Of course she enjoyed greater access to jobs and housing. But she also was able to shop in department stores without being followed by suspicious salespeople and could always find appropriate hair care products and makeup in any drugstore. She could send her child to school confident that the teacher would not discriminate against him on the basis of race. She could also be late for meetings, and talk with her mouth full, fairly confident that these behaviors would not be attributed to the fact that she was White. She could express an opinion in a meeting or in print and not have it labeled the "White" viewpoint. In other words, she was more often than not viewed as an individual, rather than as a member of a racial group.

This article rings true for most White readers, many of whom may have never considered the benefits of being White. It's one thing to have enough awareness of racism to describe the ways that people of color are disadvantaged by it. But this new understanding of racism is more elusive. In very concrete terms, it means that if a person of color is the victim of housing discrimination, the apartment that would otherwise have been rented to that person of color is still available for a White person. The White tenant is, knowingly or unknowingly, the beneficiary of racism, a system of advantage based on race. The unsuspecting tenant is not to blame for the prior discrimination, but she benefits from it anyway.

For many Whites, this new awareness of the benefits of a racist system elicits considerable pain, often accompanied by feelings of anger and guilt. These uncomfortable emotions can hinder further discussion. We all like to think that we deserve the good things we have received, and that others, too, get what they deserve. Social psychologists call this tendency a "belief in a just world."[5] Racism directly contradicts such notions of justice.

Understanding racism as a system of advantage based on race is antithetical to traditional notions of an American meritocracy. For those who have internalized this myth, this definition generates considerable discomfort. It is more comfortable simply to think of racism as a particular form of prejudice. Notions of power or privilege do not have to be addressed when our understanding of racism is constructed in that way.

The discomfort generated when a systemic definition of racism is introduced is usually quite visible in the workshops I lead. Someone in the group is usually quick to point out that this is not the definition you will find in most dictionaries. I reply, "Who wrote the dictionary?" I am not being facetious with this response Whose interests are served by a "prejudice only" definition of racism? It is important to understand that the system of advantage is perpetuated when we do not acknowledge its existence.

Racism: For Whites Only?

Frequently someone will say, "You keep talking about White people. People of color can be racist, too." I once asked a White teacher what it would mean to her if a student or parent of color accused her of being racist. She said she would feel as though she had been punched in the stomach or called a "low-life scum." She is not alone in this feeling. The word *racist* holds a lot of emotional power. For many White people, to be called racist is the ultimate insult. The idea that this term might only be applied to Whites becomes highly problematic for after all, can't people of color be "low-life scum" too?

Of course, people of any racial group can hold hateful attitudes and behave in racially discriminatory and bigoted ways. We can all cite examples of horrible hate crimes which have been perpetrated by people of color as well as Whites. Hateful behavior is hateful behavior no matter who does it. But when I am asked, "Can people of color be racist?" I reply, "The answer depends on your definition of racism." If one defines racism as racial prejudice, the answer is yes. People of color can and do have racial prejudices. However, if one defines racism as a system of advantage based on race, the answer is no. People of color are not racist because they do not systematically benefit from racism. And equally important, there is no systematic cultural and institutional support or sanction for the racial bigotry of people of color. In my view, reserving the term *racist* only for behaviors committed by Whites in the context of a White-dominated society is a way of acknowledging the ever-present power differential afforded Whites by the culture and institutions that make up the system of advantage and continue to reinforce notions of White superiority. (Using the same logic, I reserve the word *sexist* for men. Though women can and do have gender-based prejudices, only men systematically benefit from sexism.)

Despite my best efforts to explain my thinking on this point, there are some who will be troubled, perhaps even incensed, by my response. To call the racially motivated acts of a person of color acts of racial bigotry and to describe similar acts committed by Whites as racist will make no sense to some people, including some people of color. To those, I will respectfully say, "We can agree to disagree." At moments like these, it is not agreement that is essential, but clarity. Even if you don't like the definition of racism I am using, hopefully you are now clear about what it is. If I also understand how, you are using the term, our conversation can continue—despite our disagreement.

Another provocative question I'm often asked is "Are you saying all Whites are racist?" When asked this question, I again remember that White teacher's response, and I am conscious that perhaps the question I am really being asked is, "Are you saying all Whites are bad people?" The answer to that question is of course not. However, all White people, intentionally or unintentionally, do benefit from racism. A more relevant question is what are White people as individuals doing to interrupt racism? For many White people, the image of a racist is a hood-wearing Klan member or a name-calling Archie Bunker figure. These images represent what might be called *active racism*, blatant, intentional acts of racial bigotry and discrimination. *Passive racism* is more subtle and can be seen in the collusion of laughing when a racist joke is told, of letting exclusionary hiring practices go unchallenged, of accepting as appropriate the omissions of people of color from the curriculum, and of avoiding difficult race-related issues. Because racism is so ingrained in the fabric of American institutions, it is easily self-perpetuating.[6] All that is required to maintain it is business as usual.

I sometimes visualize the ongoing cycle of racism as a moving walkway at the airport. Active racist behavior is equivalent to walking fast on the conveyor belt. The person engaged in active racist behavior has identified with the ideology of White supremacy and is moving with it. Passive racist behavior is equivalent to standing still on the walkway. No overt effort is being made, but the conveyor belt moves the bystanders along to the same destination as those who are actively walking. Some of the bystanders may feel the motion of the conveyor belt, see the active racists ahead of them, and choose to turn around, unwilling to go to the same destination as the White supremacists. But unless they are walking actively in the opposite direction at a speed faster than the conveyor belt—unless they are actively antiracist—they will find themselves carried along with the others.

So, not all Whites are actively racist. Many are passively racist. Some, though not enough, are actively antiracist. The relevant question is not whether all Whites are racist, but how we can move more White people from a position of active or passive racism to one of active antiracism? The task of interrupting racism is obviously not the task of Whites alone. But the fact of White privilege means that Whites have greater access to the societal institutions in need of transformation. To whom much is given, much is required.

It is important to acknowledge that while all Whites benefit from racism, they do not all benefit equally. Other factors, such as socioeconomic status, gender, age, religious affiliation, sexual orientation, mental and physical ability, also play a role in our access to social influence and power. A White woman on welfare is not privileged to the same extent as a wealthy White heterosexual man. In her case, the systematic disadvantages of sexism and classism intersect with her White privilege, but the privilege is still there. This point was brought home to me in a 1994 study conducted by a Mount Holyoke graduate student, Phyllis Wentworth.[7] Wentworth interviewed a group of female college students, who were both older than their peers and were the first members of their families to attend college, about the pathways that lead them to college. All of the women interviewed were White, from working-class backgrounds, from families where women were expected to graduate from high school and get married or get a job. Several had experienced abusive relationships and other personal difficulties prior to coming to college. Yet their experiences were punctuated by "good luck" stories of apartments obtained without a deposit, good jobs offered without experience or extensive reference checks, and encouragement provided by willing mentors.

While the women acknowledged their good fortune, none of them discussed their Whiteness. They had not considered the possibility that being White had worked in their favor and helped give them the benefit of the doubt at critical junctures. This study clearly showed that even under difficult circumstances, White privilege was still operating.

It is also true that not all people of color are equally targeted by racism. We all have multiple identities that shape our experience. I can describe myself as a light-skinned, well-educated, heterosexual, able-bodied, Christian African American woman raised in a middle-class suburb. As an African American woman, I am systematically disadvantaged by race and by gender, but I systematically receive benefits in the other categories, which then mediate my experience of racism and sexism. When one is targeted by multiple isms—racism, sexism, classism, heterosexism, ableism, anti-Semitism, ageism—in whatever combination, the effect is intensified. The particular combination of racism and classism in many communities of color is life-threatening. Nonetheless, when I, the middle-class Black mother of two sons, read another story about a Black man's unlucky encounter with a White police officer's deadly force, I am reminded that racism by itself can kill.

The Cost of Racism

Several years ago, a White male student in my psychology of racism course wrote in his journal at the end of the semester that he had learned a lot about racism and now understood in a way he never had before just how advantaged he was. He also commented that he didn't think he would do anything to try to change the situation. After all, the system was working in his favor. Fortunately, his response was not typical. Most of my students leave my course with the desire (and an action plan) to interrupt the cycle of racism. However, this young man's response does raise an important question. Why should Whites who are advantaged by racism *want* to end that system of advantage? What are the *costs* of that system to them?

A *Money* magazine article called "Race and Money" chronicled the many ways the American economy was hindered by institutional racism.[8] Whether one looks at productivity lowered by racial tensions in the workplace, or real estate equity lost through housing discrimination, or the tax revenue lost in underemployed communities of color, or the high cost of warehousing human talent in prison, the economic costs of racism are real and measurable.

As a psychologist, I often hear about the less easily measured costs. When I ask White men and women how racism hurts them, they frequently talk about their fears of people of color, the social incompetence they feel in racially mixed situations, the alienation they have experienced between parents and children when a child marries into a family of color, and the interracial friendships they had as children that were lost in adolescence or young adulthood without their ever understanding why. White people are paying a significant price for the system of advantage. The cost is not as high for Whites as it is for people of color, but a price is being paid.[9] Wendell Berry, a White writer raised in Kentucky, captures this psychic pain in the opening pages of his book, *The Hidden Wound:*

> If white people have suffered less obviously from racism than black people, they have nevertheless suffered great- ly; the cost has been greater perhaps than we can yet know. If the white man has inflicted the wound of racism upon black men, the cost has been that he would receive the mirror image of that wound into himself. As the master, or as a member of the dominant race, he has felt little compulsion to acknowledge it or speak of it; the more painful it has grown the more deeply he has hidden it within himself. But the wound is there, and it is a profound disorder, as great a damage in his mind as it is in his society.[10]

The dismantling of racism is in the best interests of everyone.

A Word About Language

Throughout this chapter I have used the term *White* to refer to Americans of European descent. In another era, I might have used the term *Caucasian*. I have used the term *people of color* to refer to those groups in America that are and have been historically targeted by racism. This includes people of African descent, people of Asian descent, people of Latin American descent, and indigenous peoples (sometimes referred to as Native Americans or American Indians).[11] Many people refer to these groups collectively as non-Whites. This term is particularly offensive because it defines groups of people in terms of what they are not. (Do we call women "non-men?") I also avoid using the term *minorities* because it represents another kind of distortion of information which we need to correct. So-called minorities represent the majority of the world's population. While the term *people of color* is inclusive, it is not perfect. As a workshop participant once said, White people have color, too. Perhaps it would be more accurate to say "people of more color," though I am not ready to make that change. Perhaps fellow psychologist Linda James Myers is on the right track. She refers to two groups of people, those of acknowledged African descent and those of unacknowledged African descent, reminding us that we can all trace the roots of our common humanity to Africa.

I refer to people of acknowledged African descent as Black. I know that *African American* is also a commonly used term, and I often refer to myself and other Black people born and raised in America in that way. Perhaps because I am a child of the 1960s "Black and beautiful" era, I still prefer *Black*. The term is more inclusive than *African American,* because there are Black people in the United States who are not African American—Afro-Caribbeans, for example—yet are targeted by racism, and are identified as Black.

When referring to other groups of color, I try to use the terms that the people themselves want to be called. In some cases, there is no clear consensus. For example, some people of Latin American ancestry prefer *Latino,* while others prefer *Hispanic* or, if of Mexican descent, *Chicano*.[12] The terms *Latino* and *Hispanic* are used interchangeably here. Similarly, there are regional variations in the use of the terms *Native American, American Indian,* and *Indian. American Indian* and *Native people* are now more widely used than *Native American,* and the language used here reflects that. People of Asian descent include Pacific Islanders, and that is reflected in the terms *Asian/Pacific Islanders* and *Asian Pacific Americans.* However, when quoting others I use whichever terms they use.

My dilemma about the language to use reflects the fact that race is a social construction.[13] Despite myths to the contrary, biologists tell us that the only meaningful racial categorization is that of human. Van den Berghe defines race as "a group that is socially defined but on the basis of *physical* criteria," including skin color and facial features.[14]

Racial identity development, a central focus of this book, usually refers to the process of defining for oneself the personal significance and social meaning of belonging to a particular racial group. The terms *racial identity* and *ethnic identity* are often used synonymously, though a distinction can be made between the two. An ethnic group is a socially defined group based on *cultural* criteria, such as language, customs, and shared history. An individual might identify as a member of an ethnic group (Irish or Italian, for example) but might not think of himself in racial terms (as White). On the other hand, one may recognize the personal significance of racial group membership (identifying as Black, for instance) but may not consider ethnic identity (such as West Indian) as particularly meaningful.

Both racial and ethnic categories are socially constructed, and social definitions of these categories have changed over time. For example, in his book *Ethnic Identity: The Transformation of White America,* Richard Alba points out that the high rates of intermarriage and the dissolution of other social boundaries among European ethnic groups in the United States have reduced the significance of ethnic identity for these groups. In their place, he argues, a new ethnic identity is emerging, that of European American.[15]

Throughout this book, I refer primarily to racial identity. It is important, however, to acknowledge that ethnic identity and racial identity sometimes intersect. For example, dark-skinned Puerto Ricans may identify culturally as Puerto Rican and yet be categorized racially by others as Black on the basis of physical appearance. In the case of either racial or ethnic identity, these identities remain most salient to individuals of racial or ethnic groups that have been historically disadvantaged or marginalized.

The language we use to categorize one another racially is imperfect. These categories are still evolving as the current debate over Census classifications indicates.[16] The original creation of racial categories was in the service of oppression. Some may argue that to continue to use them is to continue that oppression. I respect that argument. Yet it is difficult to talk about what is essentially a flawed and problematic social construct without using language that is itself problematic. We have to be able to talk about it in order to change it. So this is the language I choose.

2

The Complexity of Identity
"Who am I?"

The concept of identity is a complex one, shaped by individual characteristics, family dynamics, historical factors, and social and political contexts. Who am I? The answer depends in large part on who the world around me says I am. Who do my parents say I am? Who do my peers say I am? What message is reflected back to me in the faces and voices of my teachers, my neighbors, store clerks? What do I learn from the media about myself? How am I represented in the cultural images around me? Or am I missing from the picture altogether? As social scientist Charles Cooley pointed out long ago, other people are the mirror in which we see ourselves.[1]

This "looking glass self" is not a flat one-dimensional reflection, but multidimensional. Because the focus of this book is racial identity in the United States, race is highlighted in these pages. Yet, how one's racial identity is experienced will be mediated by other dimensions of oneself: male or female; young or old; wealthy, middle-class, or poor; gay, lesbian, bisexual, transgender, or heterosexual; able-bodied or with disabilities; Christian, Muslim, Jewish, Buddhist, Hindu, or atheist.

Abigail Stewart and Joseph Healy's research on the impact of historical periods on personality development raises the question, Who is my cohort group?[2] Am I a child of the Depression, a survivor of World War II, the Holocaust, the U.S. internment of Japanese Americans? A product of the segregation of the 1940s and 1950s, or a beneficiary of the Civil Rights era? Did I serve in the Vietnam War, or am I a refugee of it? Did I come of age during the conservatism of the Reagan years? Did I ride the wave of the Women's Movement?

Was I born before or after Stonewall and the emergence of gay activism? What historical events have shaped my thinking?

What has my social context been? Was I surrounded by people like myself, or was I part of a minority in my community? Did I grow up speaking standard English at home or another language or dialect? Did I live in a rural county, an urban neighborhood, a sprawling suburb, or on a reservation?

Who I am (or say I am) is a product of these and many other factors. Erik Erikson, the psychoanalytic theorist who coined the term *identity crisis,* introduced the notion that the social, cultural, and historical context is the ground in which individual identity is embedded. Acknowledging the complexity of identity as a concept, Erikson writes,

> We deal with a process "located" *in the core of the individual* and yet also *in the core of his communal culture.* . . . In psychological terms, identity formation employs a process of simultaneous reflection and observation, a process taking place on all levels of mental functioning, by which the individual judges himself in the light of what he perceives to be the way in which others judge him in comparison to themselves and to a typology significant to them; while he judges their way of judging him in the light of how he perceives himself in comparison to them and to types that have become relevant to him. This process is, luckily, and necessarily, for the most part unconscious except where inner conditions and outer circumstances combine to aggravate a painful, or elated, "identity-consciousness."[3]

Triggered by the biological changes associated with puberty, the maturation of cognitive abilities, and changing societal expectations, this process of simultaneous reflection and observation, the self-creation of one's identity, is commonly experienced in the United

States and other Western societies during the period of adolescence.[4] Though the foundation of identity is laid in the experiences of childhood, younger children lack the physical and cognitive development needed to reflect on the self in this abstract way. The adolescent capacity for self-reflection (and resulting self-consciousness) allows one to ask, "Who am I now?" "Who was I before?" "Who will I become?" The answers to these questions will influence choices about who one's romantic partners will be, what type of work one will do, where one will live, and what belief system one will embrace. Choices made in adolescence ripple throughout the lifespan.

Who Am I? Multiple Identities

Integrating one's past, present, and future into a cohesive, unified sense of self is a complex task that begins in adolescence and continues for a lifetime. The complexity of identity is made clear in a collection of autobiographical essays about racial identity called *Names We Call Home*.[5] The multiracial, multiethnic group of contributors narrate life stories highlighting the intersections of gender, class, religion, sexuality, race, and historical circumstance, and illustrating that "people's multiple identifications defy neat racial divisions and unidimensional political alliances."[6] My students' autobiographical narratives point to a similar complexity, but the less developed narratives of the late adolescents that I teach highlight the fact that our awareness of the complexity of our own identity develops over time. The salience of particular aspects of our identity varies at different moments in our lives. The process of integrating the component parts of our self-definition is indeed a lifelong journey.

Which parts of our identity capture our attention first? While there are surely idiosyncratic responses to this question, a classroom exercise I regularly use with my psychology students reveals a telling pattern. I ask my students to complete the sentence, "I am _____," using as many descriptors as they can think of in sixty seconds. All kinds of trait descriptions are used—friendly, shy, assertive, intelligent, honest, and so on—but over the years I have noticed something else. Students of color usually mention their racial or ethnic group: for instance, I am Black, Puerto Rican, Korean American. White students who have grown up in strong ethnic enclaves occasionally mention being Irish or Italian. But in general, White students rarely mention being White. When I use this exercise in coeducational settings, I notice a similar pattern in terms of gender, religion, and sexuality. Women usually mention being female, while men don't usually mention their maleness. Jewish students often say they are Jews, while mainline Protestants rarely mention their religious identification. A student who is comfortable revealing it publicly may mention being gay, lesbian, or bisexual. Though I know most of my students are heterosexual, it is very unusual for anyone to include their heterosexuality on their list.

Common across these examples is that in the areas where a person is a member of the dominant or advantaged social group, the category is usually not mentioned. That element of their identity is so taken for granted by them that it goes without comment. It is taken for granted by them because it is taken for granted by the dominant culture. In Eriksonian terms, their inner experience and outer circumstance are in harmony with one another, and the image reflected by others is similar to the image within. In the absence of dissonance, this dimension of identity escapes conscious attention.

The parts of our identity that *do* capture our attention are those that other people notice, and that reflect back to us. The aspect of identity that is the target of others' attention, and subsequently of our own, often is that which sets us apart as exceptional or "other" in their eyes. In my life I have been perceived as both. A precocious child who began to read at age three, I stood out among my peers because of my reading ability. This "gifted" dimension of my identity was regularly commented upon by teachers and classmates alike, and quickly became part of my self-definition. But I was also distinguished by being the only Black student in the class, an "other," a fact I grew increasingly aware of as I got older.

While there may be countless ways one might be defined as exceptional, there are at least seven categories of "otherness" commonly experienced in U.S. society. People are commonly defined as other on the basis of race or ethnicity, gender, religion, sexual orientation, socioeconomic status, age, and physical or mental ability. Each of these categories has a form of oppression associated with it: racism, sexism, religious oppression/anti-Semitism,[7] heterosexism, classism, ageism, and ableism, respectively. In each case, there is a group considered dominant (systematically advantaged by the society because of group membership) and a group considered subordinate or targeted (systematically disadvantaged). When we think about our multiple identities, most of us will find that we are both dominant and targeted at the same time. But it is the targeted identities that hold our attention and the dominant identities that often go unexamined.

In her essay, "Age, Race, Class, and Sex: Women Redefining Difference," Audre Lorde captured the tensions between dominant and targeted identities co-existing in one individual. This self-described "forty-nine-year-old Black lesbian feminist socialist mother of two" wrote,

> Somewhere, on the edge of consciousness, there is what I call a *mythical norm*, which each one of us within our hearts knows "that is not me." In america, this norm is usually defined as white, thin, male, young, heterosexual, christian, and financially secure. It is with this mythical norm that the trappings of power reside within society. Those of us who stand outside that power often identify one way in which we are different, and we assume that to be the primary cause of all oppression, forgetting other distortions around difference, some of which we ourselves may be practicing.[8]

Even as I focus on race and racism in my own writing and teaching, it is helpful to remind myself and my students of the other distortions around difference that I (and they) may be practicing. It is an especially useful way of generating empathy for our mutual learning process. If I am impatient with a White woman for not recognizing her White privilege, it may be useful for me to remember how much of my life I spent oblivious to the fact of the daily advantages I receive simply because I am heterosexual, or the ways in which I may take my class privilege for granted.

Domination and Subordination

It is also helpful to consider the commonality found in the experience of being dominant or subordinate even when the sources of dominance or subordination are different. Jean Baker Miller, author of *Toward a New Psychology of Women,* has identified some of these areas of commonality.[9]

Dominant groups, by definition, set the parameters within which the subordinates operate. The dominant group holds the power and authority in society relative to the subordinates and determines how that power and authority may be acceptably used. Whether it is reflected in determining who gets the best jobs, whose history will be taught in school, or whose relationships will be validated by society, the dominant group has the greatest influence in determining the structure of the society.

The relationship of the dominants to the subordinates is often one in which the targeted group is labeled as defective or substandard in significant ways. For example, Blacks have historically been characterized as less intelligent than Whites, and women have been viewed as less emotionally stable than men. The dominant group assigns roles to the subordinates that reflect the latter's devalued status, reserving the most highly valued roles in the society for themselves. Subordinates are usually said to be innately incapable of being able to perform the preferred roles. To the extent that the targeted group internalizes the images that the dominant group reflects back to them, they may find it difficult to believe in their own ability.

When a subordinate demonstrates positive qualities believed to be more characteristic of dominants, the individual is defined by dominants as an anomaly. Consider this illustrative example: Following a presentation I gave to some educators, a White man approached me and told me how much he liked my ideas and how articulate I was. "You know," he concluded, "if I had had my eyes closed, I wouldn't have known it was a Black woman speaking." (I replied, "This is what a Black woman sounds like.")

The dominant group is seen as the norm for humanity. Jean Baker Miller also asserts that inequitable social relations are seen as the model for "normal human relationships." Consequently, it remains perfectly acceptable in many circles to tell jokes that denigrate a particular group, to exclude subordinates from one's neighborhood or work setting, or to oppose initiatives which might change the power balance.

Miller points out that dominant groups generally do not like to be reminded of the existence of inequality. Because rationalizations have been created to justify the social arrangements, it is easy to believe everything is as it should be. Dominants "can avoid awareness because their explanation of the relationship becomes so well integrated *in other terms;* they can even believe that both they and the subordinate group share the same interests and, to some extent, a common experience."[10]

The truth is that the dominants do not really know what the experience of the subordinates is. In contrast, the subordinates are very well informed about the dominants. Even when firsthand experience is limited by social segregation, the number and variety of images of the dominant group available through television, magazines, books, and newspapers provide subordinates with plenty of information about the dominants. The dominant world view has saturated the culture for all to learn. Even the Black or Latino child living in a segregated community can enter White homes of many kinds daily via the media. However, dominant access to information about the subordinates is often limited to stereotypical depictions of the "other." For example, there are many images of heterosexual relations on television, but very few images of gay or lesbian domestic partnerships beyond the caricatures of comedy shows. There are many images of White men and women in all forms of media, but relatively few portrayals of people of color.

Not only is there greater opportunity for the subordinates to learn about the dominants, there is also greater need. Social psychologist Susan Fiske writes, "It is a simple principle: People pay attention to those who control their outcomes. In an effort to predict and possibly influence what is going to happen to them, people gather information about those with power."[11]

In a situation of unequal power, a subordinate group has to focus on survival. It becomes very important for the subordinates to become highly attuned to the dominants as a way of protecting themselves from them. For example, women who have been battered by men often talk about the heightened sensitivity they develop to their partners' moods. Being able to anticipate and avoid the men's rage is important to survival.

Survival sometimes means not responding to oppressive behavior directly. To do so could result in physical harm to oneself, even death. In his essay "The Ethics of Living Jim Crow," Richard Wright describes eloquently the various strategies he learned to use to avoid the violence of Whites who would brutalize a Black person who did not "stay in his place."[12] Though it is tempting to think that the need for such strategies disappeared with Jim Crow laws, their legacy lives on in the frequent and sometimes fatal harassment Black men experience at the hands of White police officers.[13]

Because of the risks inherent in unequal relationships, the subordinates often develop covert ways of resisting or undermining the power of the dominant group. As Miller points out, popular culture is full of folk tales, jokes, and stories about how the subordinate—whether the woman, the peasant, or the sharecropper—outwitted the

Doss."[14] In his essay "I Won't Learn from You," Herbert Kohl identifies one form of resistance, "not-learning," demonstrated by targeted students who are too often seen by their dominant teachers as "others."

> Not-learning tends to take place when someone has to deal with unavoidable challenges to her or his personal and family loyalties, integrity, and identity. In such situations, there are forced choices and no apparent middle ground. To agree to learn from a stranger who does not respect your integrity causes a major loss of self. The only alternative is to not-learn and reject their world.[15]

The use of either strategy, attending very closely to the dominants or not attending at all, is costly to members of the targeted group. Not-learning may mean there are needed skills which are not acquired. Attending closely to the dominant group may leave little time or energy to attend to one's self. Worse yet, the negative messages of the dominant group about the subordinates may be internalized, leading to self-doubt or, in its extreme form, self-hate. There are many examples of subordinates attempting to make themselves over in the image of the dominant group—Jewish people who want to change the Semitic look of their noses, Asians who have cosmetic surgery to alter the shape of their eyes, Blacks who seek to lighten their skin with bleaching creams, women who want to smoke and drink "like a man." Whether one succumbs to the devaluing pressures of the dominant culture or successfully resists them, the fact is that dealing with oppressive systems from the underside, regardless of the strategy, is physically and psychologically taxing.

Breaking beyond the structural and psychological limitations imposed on one's group is possible, but not easily achieved. To the extent that members of targeted groups do push societal limits—achieving unexpected success, protesting injustice, being "uppity"—by their actions they call the whole system into question. Miller writes, they "expose the inequality, and throw into question the basis for its existence. And they will make the inherent conflict an open conflict. They will then have to bear the burden and take the risks that go with being defined as 'troublemakers.'"[16]

The history of subordinate groups is filled with so-called troublemakers, yet their names are often unknown. Preserving the record of those subordinates and their dominant allies who have challenged the status quo is usually of little interest to the dominant culture, but it is of great interest to subordinates who search for an empowering reflection in the societal mirror.

Many of us are both dominant and subordinate. Clearly racism and racial identity are at the center of discussion in this book, but as Audre Lorde said, from her vantage point as a Black lesbian, "There is no hierarchy of oppression." The thread and threat of violence runs through all of the isms. There is a need to acknowledge each other's pain, even as we attend to our own.

For those readers who are in the dominant racial category, it may sometimes be difficult to take in what is being said by and about those who are targeted by racism. When the perspective of the subordinate is shared directly, an image is reflected to members of the dominant group which is disconcerting. To the extent that one can draw on one's own experience of subordination—as a young person, as a person with a disability, as someone who grew up poor, as a woman—it may be easier to make meaning of another targeted group's experience. For those readers who are targeted by racism and are angered by the obliviousness of Whites sometimes described in these pages, it may be useful to attend to your experience of dominance where you may find it—as a heterosexual, as an able-bodied person, as a Christian, as a man—and consider what systems of privilege you may be overlooking. The task of resisting our own oppression does not relieve us of the responsibility of acknowledging our complicity in the oppression of others.

Our ongoing examination of who we are in our full humanity, embracing all of our identities, creates the possibility of building alliances that may ultimately free us all. It is with that vision in mind that I move forward with an examination of racial identity in the chapters to follow. My goal is not to flatten the multidimensional self-reflection we see of ourselves, but to focus on a dimension often neglected and discounted in the public discourse on race.

Part II

Understanding Blackness in a White Context

3

The Early Years

"Is my skin brown because I drink chocolate milk?"

Think of your earliest race-related memory. How old were you? When I ask adults in my workshops this question, they call out a range of ages: "Three," "Five," "Eight," "Thirteen," "Twenty." Sometimes they talk in small groups about what they remember. At first they hesitate to speak, but then the stories come flooding forward, each person's memory triggering another's.

Some are stories of curiosity, as when a light-skinned child wonders why a dark-skinned person's palms are so much lighter than the backs of his hands. Some are stories of fear and avoidance, communicated verbally or nonverbally by parents, as when one White woman describes her mother nervously telling her to roll up the windows and lock the doors as they drove through a Black community. Some are stories of active bigotry, transmitted casually from one generation to the next through the use of racial slurs and ethnic jokes. Some are stories of confusing mixed messages, as when a White man remembers the Black maid who was "just like family" but was not allowed to eat from the family dishes or use the upstairs bathroom. Some are stories of terror, as when a Black woman remembers being chased home from school by a German shepherd, deliberately set loose by its White owner as she passed by. I will often ask audience members, "What do you remember? Something someone said or did? A name-calling incident? An act of discrimination? The casual observation of skin color differences? Were you the observer or the object of observation?"

In large groups, I hesitate to ask the participants to reveal their memories to a crowd of strangers, but I ask instead what emotions are attached to the memories. The participants use such words as *anger, confusion, surprise, sadness, embarassment*. Notice that this list does not include such words as *joy, excitement, delight*. Too often the stories are painful ones. Then I ask, "Did you talk to anyone about what happened? Did you tell anyone how you felt?" It is always surprising to me to see how many people will say that they never discussed these clearly emotional experiences with anyone. Why not? Had they already learned that race was not a topic to be discussed?

If they didn't talk to anyone else about it, how did these three- or five- or eight- or thirteen-year-old children make sense of their experience? Has the confusion continued into adulthood? Are we as adults prepared to help the children we care about make sense of their own race-related observations?

Preschool Conversations

Like many African Americans, I have many race-related memories, beginning when I was quite small. I remember being about three years old when I had an argument with an African American playmate. He said I was "black." "No I'm not," I said, "I'm tan." I now see that we were both right. I am Black, a person of African descent, but tan is surely a more accurate description of my light brown skin than black is. As a three-year-old child who knew her colors, I was prepared to stand my ground. As an adult looking back on this incident, I wonder if I had also begun to recognize, even at three, that in some circles it was better to be tan than to be black. Had I already started internalizing racist messages?

Questions and confusion about racial issues begin early. Though adults often talk about the "colorblindness" of children, the fact is that children as young as three do notice physical differences such as skin color, hair texture, and the shape of one's facial features.[1] Certainly preschoolers talk about what they see, and often they do it in ways that make parents uncomfortable. How should we respond when they do?

My own children have given me many opportunities to think about this question. For example, one winter day, my youngest son, David, observed a White mother helping her brown-skinned biracial daughter put on her boots in the hallway of his preschool. "Why don't they match, Mommy?" he asked loudly. Absentmindedly collecting his things, I didn't quite understand what he was talking about—mismatched socks, perhaps? When I asked, he explained indignantly, "You and I match. They don't match. Mommies and kids are supposed to match."

David, like many three-year-olds (and perhaps some adults), had overgeneralized from his routine observations of White parents with White children, and Black parents, like his own, with Black children. As a psychologist, I recognized this preschool tendency to overgeneralize as a part of his cognitive development, but as a mother standing with her child in the hallway, I was embarrassed, afraid that his comment might have somehow injured the mother-daughter pair standing in the hallway with us. I responded matter-of-factly, "David, they don't have to match. Sometimes parents and kids match, and sometimes they don't."

More often, my children and I have been on the receiving end of a preschooler's questions. The first conversation of this type I remember occurred when my oldest son, Jonathan, was enrolled in a day care center where he was one of few children of color, and the only Black child in his class. One day, as we drove home from the day care center, Jonathan said, "Eddie says my skin is brown because I drink too much chocolate milk. Is that true?"* Eddie was a White three-year-old in Jonathan's class who, like David, had observed a physical difference and was now searching for an explanation.

"No," I replied, "your skin is brown because you have something in your skin called melanin. Melanin is very important because it helps protect your skin from the sun. Eddie has melanin in his skin,

---

* With the exception of my own children's names, all names used in these examples are pseudonyms.

too. Remember when Eddie went to Florida on vacation and came back showing everybody his tan? It was the melanin in his skin that made it get darker. Everybody has melanin, you know. But some people have more than others. At your school, you are the kid with the most!"

Jonathan seemed to understand the idea and smiled at the thought that he was the child with the most of something. I talked more about how much I liked the color of his pecan-colored skin, how it was a perfect blend of my light-brown skin and his father's dark-brown complexion. I wanted to affirm who Jonathan was, a handsome brown-skinned child. I wanted to counter the implication of Eddie's question—that there was perhaps something wrong with brown skin, the result of "too much" chocolate milk.

This process of affirmation was not new. Since infancy I had talked about how much I liked his smooth brown skin and those little curls whenever I bathed him or brushed his hair. I searched for children's books depicting brown-skinned children. When Jonathan was one year old, we gave him a large brown rag doll, complete with curly black hair made of yarn, a Marcus Garvey T-shirt, and an African name. Olayinka, or Olay for short, was his constant companion at home and at the day care center during nap time. Especially because we have lived in predominantly White communities since his birth, I felt it was important to make sure he saw himself reflected positively in as many ways as possible. As many Black families do, I think we provided an important buffer against the negative messages about Blackness offered by the larger society.[2]

But Jonathan continued to think about the color of his skin, and sometimes he would bring it up. One Saturday morning I was cooking pancakes for breakfast, and Jonathan was at my side, eagerly watching the pancakes cook on the griddle. When I flipped the pancakes over, he was excited to see that the cream-colored batter had been transformed into a golden brown. Jonathan remarked, "I love pancakes. They are brown, just like me." On another occasion when we were cooking together, he noticed that I had set some eggs out on the kitchen counter. Some of the eggs were brown, and some of them were white. He commented on the fact that the eggs were not all the same color. "Yes," I said, "they do have different shells. But look at this!" I cracked open a brown egg and emptied its contents into a bowl. Then I cracked open a white egg. "See, they are different on the outside, but the same on the inside. People are the same way. They look different on the outside, but they are the same on the inside."

Jonathan's questions and comments, like David's and Eddie's, were not unusual for a child of his age. Preschool children are very focused on outward appearances, and skin color is the racial feature they are most likely to comment on.[3] I felt good about my ability as a parent to respond to Jonathan's questions. (I was, after all, teaching courses on the psychology of racism and child development. I was not caught completely off guard!) But I wondered about Jonathan's classmates. What about Eddie, the boy with the chocolate milk theory? Had anyone set him straight?

In fact, Eddie's question, "Is your skin brown because you drink too much chocolate milk?" represented a good attempt to make sense of a curious phenomenon that he was observing. All the kids in the class had light skin except for Jonathan. Why was Jonathan's skin different? It didn't seem to be dirt—Jonathan washed his hands before lunch like all the other children did, and there was no change. He did often have chocolate milk in his lunch box—maybe that was it. Eddie's reasoning was first-rate for a three-year-old. The fact that he was asking about Jonathan's skin, rather than speculating about his own, reflected that he had already internalized "Whiteness" as the norm, which it was in that school. His question did not reflect prejudice in an adult sense, but it did reveal confusion. His theory was flawed, and he needed some help.

I decided to ask a staff member how she and the other preschool teachers were handling children's questions about racial differences. She smiled and said, "It really hasn't come up." I was amazed. I knew it had come up; after all, Jonathan had reported the conversations to me. How was it that she had not noticed?

Maybe it was easy not to notice. Maybe these conversations among three-year-olds had taken place at the lunch table or in the sand box, away from the hearing of adults. I suspect, too, that there may have been some selective inattention on the part of the staff. When children make comments to which we don't know how to respond, it may be easier simply not to hear what has just been said or to let it slip from our consciousness and memory. Then we don't have to respond, because it "hasn't come up."

Many adults do not know how to respond when children make race-related observations. Imagine this scenario. A White mother and preschool child are shopping in the grocery store. They pass a Black woman and child, and the White child says loudly, "Mommy, look at that girl! Why is she so dirty?" (Confusing dark skin with dirt is a common misconception among White preschool children.) The White mother, embarassed by her child's comment, responds quickly with a "Ssh!"

An appropriate response might have been: "Honey, that little girl is not dirty. Her skin is as clean as yours. It's just a different color. Just like we have different hair color, people have different skin colors." If the child still seemed interested, the explanation of melanin could be added.[4] Perhaps afraid of saying the wrong thing, however, many parents don't offer an explanation. They stop at "Ssh," silencing the child but not responding to the question or the reasoning underlying it. Children who have been silenced often enough learn not to talk about race publicly. Their questions don't go away, they just go unasked.

I see the legacy of this silencing in my psychology of racism classes. My students have learned that there is a taboo against talking about race, especially in racially mixed settings, and creating enough safety in the class to overcome that taboo is the first challenge for me as an instructor. But the evidence of the internalized taboo is apparent long before children reach college.

When addressing parent groups, I often hear from White parents who tell me with pride that their children are "colorblind." Usually the parent offers as evidence a story of a friendship with a child of color whose race or ethnicity has never been mentioned to the parent. For example, a father reported that his eight-year-old daughter had been talking very enthusiastically about a friend she had made at school. One day when he picked his daughter up from school, he asked her to point out her new friend. Trying to point her out of a large group of children on the playground, his daughter elaborately described what the child was wearing. She never said she was the only Black girl in the group. Her father was pleased that she had not, a sign of her colorblindness. I wondered if, rather than a sign of colorblindness, it was a sign that she had learned not to be so impolite as to mention someone's race.

My White college students sometimes refer to someone as Black in hushed tones, sometimes whispering the word as though it were a secret or a potentially scandalous identification. When I detect this behavior, I like to point it out, saying it is not an insult to identify a Black person as Black. Of course, sometimes one's racial group membership is irrelevant to the conversation, and then there is no need to mention it. But when it is relevant, as when pointing out the only Black girl in a crowd, we should not be afraid to say so.

Blackness, Whiteness, and Painful History

Of course, when we talk to children about racial issues, or anything else, we have to keep in mind each child's developmental stage and cognitive ability to make sense of what we are saying. Preschool children are quite literal in their use of language and concrete in their thinking. They talk about physical differences and other commonly observed cultural differences such as language and style of dress because they are tangible and easy to recognize. They may be confused by the symbolic constructs that adults use.[5]

This point was brought home to me in another conversation with my son Jonathan. As a working mother, I often found trips to the grocery store to be a good opportunity for "quality" time with my then four-year-old. We would stroll the grocery aisles chatting, as he sat in the top part of the grocery cart and I filled the bottom. On such an outing, Jonathan told me that someone at school had said he was Black. "Am I Black?" he asked me. "Yes, you are," I replied. "But my skin is brown," he said. I was instantly reminded of my own preschool "I'm not black, I'm tan" argument on this point. "Yes," I said, "your skin is brown, but *Black* is a term that people use to describe African Americans, just like *White* is used to describe people who came from Europe. It is a little confusing," I conceded, "because Black people aren't really the color black, but different shades of brown." I mentioned different members of our family and the different shades we represented, but I said that we were all African Americans and in that sense could all be called Black.

Then I said, "It's the same with White people. They come in lots of different shades—pink, beige, even light brown. None of them are white like this piece of paper." I held up the white note paper on which my grocery list was written as proof. Jonathan nodded his agreement with my description of Black people as really being varying shades of brown, but hesitated when I said that White people were not really white in color. "Yes they are," he said. I held up the paper again and said, "White people don't really look like this." "Yes, they do," he insisted. "Okay," I said, remembering that children learn from actual experiences. "Let's go find one and see." We were alone in the grocery aisle, but sure enough, when we turned the corner, there was a White woman pushing her cart down the aisle. I leaned over and whispered in Jonathan's ear, "Now, see, she doesn't look like this paper." Satisfied with this evidence, he conceded the point, and we moved on in our conversation. As I discovered, we were just getting started.

Jonathan's confusion about society's "color" language was not surprising or unusual. At the same time that preschoolers are identifying the colors in the crayon box, they are also beginning to figure out racial categorizations. The color-coded language of social categories obviously does not match the colors we use to label objects. People of Asian descent are not really "yellow" like lemons, Native Americans don't really look "red" like apples. I understood the problem and was prepared for this kind of confusion.

What was of most concern to me at that moment was the tone of my son's question. In his tone of voice was the hint that maybe he was not comfortable being identified as Black, and I wondered what messages he was taking in about being African American. I said that if he wanted to, he could tell his classmate that he was African American. I said that he should feel very proud to have ancestors who were from Africa. I was just beginning to talk about ancient African civilizations when he interrupted me. "If Africa is so great, what are we doing here?" he asked.

I had not planned to have a conversation about slavery with my four-year-old in the grocery store that day. But I didn't see how I could answer his question otherwise. Slavery is a topic that makes many of us uncomfortable. Yet the nature of Black-White race relations in the United States have been forever shaped by slavery and its social, psychological, and economic legacies. It requires discussion. But how does one talk to a four-year-old about this legacy of cruelty and injustice?

I began at the beginning. I knew his preschool had discussed the colonial days when Europeans first came to these shores. I reminded him of this and said:

> A long, long time ago, before there were grocery stores and roads and houses here, the Europeans came. And they wanted to build roads and houses and grocery stores here, but it was going to be a lot of work. They needed a lot of really good, strong, smart workers to cut down trees, and build roads, and work on farms, and they didn't have enough. So they went to Africa to get the strongest, smartest workers they could find. Unfortunately they didn't want to pay them. So they kidnapped them and brought them here as slaves. They

made them work and didn't pay them. And that was really unfair.

Even as I told this story I was aware of three things. (1) I didn't want to frighten this four-year-old who might worry that these things would happen to him (another characteristic of four-year old thinking). (2) I wanted him to know that his African ancestors were not just passive victims, but had found ways to resist their victimization. (3) I did not want him to think that all White people were bad. It *is* possible to have White allies.

So I continued:

Now, this was a long, long time ago. You were never a slave. I was never a slave. Grandmommy and Granddaddy were never slaves. This was a really long time ago, and the Africans who were kidnapped did whatever they could to escape. But sometimes the Europeans had guns and the Africans didn't, so it was hard to get away. But some even jumped off the boats into the ocean to try to escape. There were slave rebellions, and many of the Africans were able to escape to freedom after they got here, and worked to help other slaves get free. Now, even though some White people were kidnapping Africans and making them work without pay, other White people thought that this was very unfair, which it was. And those White people worked along with the Black people to bring an end to slavery. So now it is against the law to have slaves.

Jonathan was paying very close attention to my story, and when I declared that slavery had ended a long time ago, he asked, "Well, when they weren't slaves anymore, why didn't they go back to Africa?" Thanks to the African American history classes I took in college, I knew enough to say, "Well, some did. But others might not have been able to because they didn't have enough money, and besides that, by then they had families and friends who were living here and they might have wanted to stay."

"And this is a nice place, too," he declared.

"Yes it is."

Over the next few weeks, an occasional question would come up about my story, and I knew that Jonathan was still digesting what I had said. Though I did not anticipate talking about slavery with my four-year-old, I was glad in retrospect that it was I who had introduced him to the subject, because I was able to put my own spin on this historical legacy, emphasizing both Black resistance to victimization and White resistance to the role of victimizer.

Too often I hear from young African American students the embarrassment they have felt in school when the topic of slavery is discussed, ironically one of the few ways that the Black experience is included in their school curriculum. Uncomfortable with the portrayal of their group as helpless victims—the rebellions and resistance offered by the enslaved Africans are rarely discussed—they squirm uncomfortably as they feel the eyes of White children looking to see their reaction to this subject.

In my professional development work with White teachers they sometimes remark how uncomfortable they, too, are with this and other examples of the painful history of race relations in the United States. As one elementary school teacher said,

> It is hard to tell small children about slavery, hard to explain that Black young men were lynched, and that police turned firehoses on children while other men bombed churches, killing Black children at their prayers. This history is a terrible legacy for all of us. The other day a teacher told me that she could not look into the faces of her students when she taught about these things. It was too painful, and too embarrassing. . . . If we are all uncomfortable, something is wrong in our approach.[6]

Something *is* wrong. While I think it is necessary to be honest about the racism of our past and present, it is also necessary to empower children (and adults) with the vision that change is possible. Concrete examples are critical. For young children these examples can sometimes be found in children's picture books. One of my favorites is Faith Ringgold's *Aunt Harriet's Underground Railroad in the Sky*.[7] Drawing on historical accounts of the Underground Railroad and the facts of Harriet Tubman's life, this story is told from the point of view of a young Black girl who travels back in time and experiences both the chilling realities of slavery and the power of her own resistance and eventual escape.

White people are present in the story both as enemies (slave-owners) and as allies (abolitionists). This dual representation is important for children of color, as well as for White children. I remember a conversation I had a few years ago with a White friend who often talked to her then preschool son about issues of social justice. He had been told over and over the story of Rosa Parks and the Montgomery bus boycott, and it was one of his favorites as a four-year-old. But as he got a little older she began to notice a certain discomfort in him when she talked about these issues. "Are all White people bad?" he asked her. At the age of five, he seemed to be feeling badly about being White. She asked me for some advice. I recommended she begin talking more about what White people had done to oppose injustice. Finding examples of this in children's literature can be a challenge, but one example is Jeanette Winter's book, *Follow the Drinking Gourd*.[8] This too is a story about the Underground Railroad, but it highlights the role of a White man named Peg Leg Joe and other White allies who offer assistance along the escape route, again providing a tangible example of White resistance to injustice.

A Question of Color

All of these preschool questions reflect the beginnings of a developing racial identity. The particular questions my child asked me reflected his early experience as one of few Black children in a predominantly White community. Even in the context of all-Black communities, the color variations in the community, even within families, can lead to a series of skin-color related conversations. For example, it is common to hear a preschool child describe a light-skinned Black person as White, often to the chagrin of the individual so identified. The child's misclassification does not represent a denial of Blackness, only the child's incomplete understanding of the adult world's racial classifications. As preschoolers, my own children have asked me if I was White. When I am misidentified by children as White, I usually reply matter-of-factly, "I am an African American person. We come in all shades of brown, dark brown, medium brown, and sometimes light brown—like me."

The concept of *race constancy*, that one's racial group membership is fixed and will not change, is not achieved until children are six or seven years old. (The same is true of gender constancy.)[9] Just as preschool boys sometimes express a desire to have a baby like Mom when they grow up (and are dismayed when they learn they cannot), young Black children may express a desire to be White. Though such statements are certainly distressing to parents, they do not necessarily mean that the child has internalized a negative self-image. It may, however, reflect a child's growing awareness of White privilege, conveyed through the media. For example, in a study of children's race-related conversations, one five-year-old Black boy reportedly asked, "Do I have to be Black?" To the question of why he asked, he responded, "I want to be chief of paramedics." His favorite TV show at the time featured paramedics and firefighters, all of whom were White.[10]

Though such comments by young children are not necessarily rooted in self-rejection, it is important to consider what messages children are receiving about the relative worth of light or dark skin. The societal preference for light skin and the relative advantage historically bestowed on light-skinned Blacks, often referred to as colorism, manifests itself not only in the marketplace but even within Black families.[11]

A particular form of internalized oppression, the skin-color prejudice found within Black communities is toxic to children and adults. A by-product of the plantation hierarchy, which privileged the light-skinned children of enslaved African women and White slaveowners, a post-slavery class system was created based on color. Historically the Black middle class has been a light-skinned group. But the racially mixed ancestry of many Black people can lead to a great deal of color variation among siblings and extended family members. The internalization of White-supremacist standards of beauty and the desire to maintain what little advantage can be gained in a racist system leads some families to reject darker-skinned members. Conversely, in some families, anger at White oppression and the pain of colorism can lead to resentment toward and rejection of lighter-skinned members. According to family therapist Nancy Boyd-Franklin, family attitudes about skin color are rarely discussed openly, but the messages are often clearly conveyed when some children are favored over others, or when a relative teasingly says, "Whose child are you?" to the child whose skin color varies from other family members. Boyd-Franklin writes,

> All Black people, irrespective of their color, shade, darkness, or lightness, are aware from a very early age that their blackness makes them different from mainstream White America. It sets them apart from White immigrant groups who were not brought here as slaves and who have thus had a different experience in becoming assimilated into mainstream American culture. The struggle for a strong positive racial identity for young Black Afro-American children is clearly made more difficult by the realities of color prejudice.[12]

We need to examine not only our behavior toward our children, but also the language we use around them. Is *black* ever used as a derogatory term to describe others, as in "that black so-and-so?" Is darkness seen as an obstacle to be overcome, as in "She's dark, but she's still pretty," or avoided, as in "Stay out of the sun, you're dark enough already?" Is lightness described as defective, as in "You need some sun, girl?" Do we sing hymns in church on Sunday proclaiming our wish to be washed "white as snow"? Even when our clear desire is to reflect positive images of Blackness to young Black children, our habits of speech may undermine our efforts unless we are intentional about examining the color-coded nature of our language.

Related to questions of color are issues of hair texture, an especially sensitive issue for Black women, young and old. I grew up with the expression "good hair." Though no one in my household used that phrase often, I knew what it meant when I heard it. "Good hair" was straight hair, the straighter the better. I still remember the oohs and ahs of my White elementary school classmates when I arrived at school for "picture day" with my long mane of dark hair resting on my shoulders. With the miracle of a hot comb, my mother had transformed my ordinary braids into what I thought was a glamorous cascade of curls. I received many compliments that day. "How pretty you look," the White teacher said. The truth is I looked pretty every day, but a clear message was being sent both at home and at school about what real beauty was.

I now wear my hair in its natural state of tiny curls. It has been that way for more than twenty-five years. My sons are unfamiliar with Saturday afternoon trips to the beauty parlor, the smell of hot combs and chemical straighteners. Instead they go with me or their father to the Black-owned barber shop where Black men and some women wait their turn for a seat in the barber's chair. I admire their neatly trimmed heads, and they admire mine. I genuinely like the way my short hair looks and feels, and that sends an important message to my sons about how I feel about myself as a Black woman and, by extension, how I feel about them.

Though a woman's choice to straighten her hair is not necessarily a sign of internalized oppression, it does reinforce the notion to an observant child that straight is better. In her book *Sisters of the Yam:*

Black Women and Self Recovery, bell hooks relates a conversation she had with a Black woman frustrated by her daughter's desire for long blond hair, despite the family's effort to affirm their Blackness. Observing the woman's dark skin and straightened hair, she encouraged the mother to examine her own attitudes about skin color and hair texture to see what messages she might be communicating to her child by the way she constructed her own body image.[13]

Countering the images of the dominant culture is a challenge, but it can be done. Finding images that reflect the range of skin tones and hair textures in Black families is an important way to affirm a positive sense of Black identity. A wonderfully illustrated book for children that opposes the prevailing Eurocentric images of beauty is John Steptoe's *Mufaro's Beautiful Daughters: An African Tale*.[14] As the story states on the opening page, "everyone agreed that Manyara and Nyasha are beautiful." These lovely brown-skinned sisters have broad noses and full lips, with hair braided in short cornrows.

Though it is easier than it used to be to find children's picture books depicting Black children authentically rather than as White children painted a darker shade, it may still be hard to find children's books depicting Black children with very dark or very light skin. A medium brown seems to be the color of choice. Decorating one's home with photographs of family and friends who represent a range of skin tones and hair textures is one way to begin to fill this representational gap.

"It's That Stuff Again": Developing a Critical Consciousness

From the time my children were infants, reading has been a shared activity in our family. I have always loved to read, and that love of books has been imparted to my children, who rarely leave home without a book to read on the way. I have worked hard to find good children's literature featuring African Americans and other children of color, but I have also introduced my children to some of the books I liked when I was a child, most of which only included White children.

When Jonathan was just learning to read on his own and had advanced to "chapter books," I introduced him to *The Boxcar Children* series of easy-reading mysteries that I loved as a child.[15] Originally written in the 1940s, these books feature four White children, two boys and two girls, orphaned and homeless, who lived in an abandoned railway car until they were found by their wealthy grandfather. From then on, they traveled with Grandfather and solved mysteries wherever they went.

Reading these volumes again with Jonathan, I had a new perception of them: how sexist they seemed to be. The two girls seemed to spend most of their time on these adventures cooking and cleaning and setting up house while the boys fished, paddled the canoe, and made the important discoveries. After reading several pages of this together, I decided to say something about it to my then seven-year-old son. I asked if he knew what sexism was. He did not, so I explained that it was when girls were treated differently than boys just because they were girls. I said that the girls in this story were being treated differently than the boys, and I pointed out some examples and discussed the unfairness of it. Jonathan wanted to continue the story, and I agreed that we could finish it, despite my new perception. What pleased and surprised me as we continued to read was that Jonathan began to spot the gender bias himself. "Hey Mom," he interrupted me as I read on, "there's that stuff again!"

Learning to spot "that stuff"—whether it is racist, or sexist, or classist—is an important skill for children to develop. It is as important for my Black male children to recognize sexism and other forms of oppression as it is for them to spot racism. We are better able to resist the negative impact of oppressive messages when we see them coming than when they are invisible to us. While some may think it is a burden to children to encourage this critical consciousness, I consider it a gift. Educator Janie Ward calls this child-rearing process "raising resisters."[16] And there are infinite opportunities to do so.

One such opportunity came in the form of a children's book of Bible stories, a gift from a friend. My son and I sat down to read the story of Moses together. We hadn't gotten very far when I said, "You know, something is bothering me about this book." "What is it?" he replied. "You know, this story took place in Egypt, and the people in these pictures do not look much like Egyptians." "Well, what do Egyptians look like?" he asked. We turned to a children's world atlas and found that the photographs of the Egyptians in the atlas had noticeably darker skin and hair than the drawings in the book. Though we did not discard the book, we did discuss the discrepancy.

I do not point out every omission or distortion I notice (and I am sure that a lot go by me unnoticed), and sometimes my children don't agree with my observations. For example, when discussing with them my plans to talk about media stereotyping in this book, I offered the example of the Disney film *The Lion King*. A very popular family film, I was dismayed at the use of ethnically identifiable voices to characterize the hyenas, clearly the undesirables in the film. The Spanish-accented voice of Cheech Marin and the Black slang of Whoopi Goldberg clearly marked the hyenas racially. The little Lion King is warned never to go to the place where the hyenas live. When the evil lion (darker in shade than the good lions) takes over, and the hyenas have access to power, it is not long before they have ruined the kingdom. "There goes the neighborhood!"

My sons, now ten and fourteen, countered that the distinguished Black actor James Earl Jones as the voice of the good lion offset the racial characterizations of the hyenas. I argued that to the target audience of young children, the voice of James Earl Jones would not be identified as a voice of color, while the voices of the hyenas surely would. The racial subtext of the film would be absorbed uncritically by many young children, and perhaps their parents. Whether we agree or not, the process of engaging my children in a critical examination of the books they read, the television they watch, the films they see, and the video games they play is essential.

And despite my best efforts, the stereotypes still creep in. One Saturday afternoon a few years ago, after attending choir rehearsal at a church located in a Black section of a nearby city, my oldest son and

I drove past a Black teenager running down the street. "Why is that boy running?" my son asked. "I don't know," I said absentmindedly. "Maybe he stole something." I nearly slammed on the brakes. "Why would you say something like that?" I said. "Well, you know, in the city, there's a lot of crime, and people steal things," he said. He did not say "Black people," but I knew the cultural images to which he was responding. Now, this neighborhood was very familiar to us. We had spent many Saturdays at choir rehearsal and sat in church next to Black kids who looked a lot like that boy on the street. We had never personally experienced any crime in that location. In fact the one time my car stereo was stolen was when it was parked in a "good neighborhood" in our own small town. I pointed out this contradiction and asked my son to imagine why he, also a Black boy, might be running down the street—in a hurry to get home, late for a bus, on his way to a job at the McDonald's up the street? Then we talked about stereotyping and the images of urban Black boys we see on television and elsewhere. Too often they are portrayed as muggers, drug dealers, or other criminals. My sons know that such images are not an accurate representation of themselves, and I have to help them see that they are also a distorted image of their urban peers.

Children can learn to question whether demeaning or derogatory depictions of other people are stereotypes. When reading books or watching television, they can learn to ask who is doing what in the story line and why, who is in the role of leader and who is taking the orders, who or what is the problem and who is solving it, and who has been left out of the story altogether.[17]

But not only do children need to be able to recognize distorted representations, they also need to know what can be done about them. Learning to recognize cultural and institutional racism and other forms of inequity without also learning strategies to respond to them is a prescription for despair. Yet even preschool children are not too young to begin to think about what can be done about unfairness. The resource book *Anti-Bias Curriculum: Tools for Empowering Young Children,* includes many examples of young children learning to recognize and speak up against unfairness.[18] The book suggests increasing levels of activism for developing children. Two- and three-year-olds are encouraged to use words to express their feelings and to empathize with one another. With adult guidance, four- and five-year-olds are capable of group activism.

Several years ago a group of seven-year-olds in a second-grade class in Amherst, Massachusetts, wrote letters to the state Department of Transportation protesting the signs on the Massachusetts Turnpike depicting a Pilgrim hat with an arrow through it. This sign was certainly a misrepresentation of history, and offensive to American Indians. The children received national recognition for their efforts, and more important, the signs were changed. I am sure the lesson that collective effort can make a difference will be remembered by those children for a long time.

As early childhood educator Louise Derman-Sparks and her colleagues write in *Anti-Bias Curriculum*,

> For children to feel good and confident about themselves, they need to be able to say, "That's not fair," or "I don't like that," if they are the target of prejudice or discrimination. For children to develop empathy and respect for diversity, they need to be able to say, "I don't like what you are doing" to a child who is abusing another child. If we teach children to recognize injustice, then we must also teach them that people can create positive change by working together. . . . Through activism activities children build the confidence and skills for becoming adults who assert, in the face of injustice, "I have the responsibility to deal with it, I know how to deal with it, I will deal with it."[19]

When we adults reflect on our own race-related memories, we may recall times when we did not get the help we needed to sift through the confusing messages we received. The task of talking to our children about racism and other isms may seem formidable. Our children's questions may make us uncomfortable, and we may not have a ready response. But even a missed opportunity can be revisited at another time. It is never too late to say, "I've been thinking about that question you asked me the other day . . ." We have the responsibility, and the resources available, to educate ourselves if necessary so that we will not repeat the cycle of oppression with our children.

4

Identity Development in Adolescence
"Why are all the Black kids sitting together in the cafeteria?"

Walk into any racially mixed high school cafeteria at lunch time and you will instantly notice that in the sea of adolescent faces, there is an identifiable group of Black students sitting together. Conversely, it could be pointed out that there are many groups of White students sitting together as well, though people rarely comment about that. The question on the tip of everyone's tongue is "Why are the Black kids sitting together?" Principals want to know, teachers want to know, White students want to know, the Black students who aren't sitting at the table want to know.

How does it happen that so many Black teenagers end up at the same cafeteria table? They don't start out there. If you walk into racially mixed elementary schools, you will often see young children of diverse racial backgrounds playing with one another, sitting at the snack table together, crossing racial boundaries with an ease uncommon in adolescence. Moving from elementary school to middle school (often at sixth or seventh grade) means interacting with new children from different neighborhoods than before, and a certain degree of clustering by race might therefore be expected, presuming that children who are familiar with one another would form groups. But even in schools where the same children stay together from kindergarten through eighth grade, racial grouping begins by the sixth or seventh grade. What happens?

One thing that happens is puberty. As children enter adolescence, they begin to explore the question of identity, asking "Who am I? Who can I be?" in ways they have not done before. For Black youth, asking "Who am I?" includes thinking about "Who am I ethnically and/or racially? What does it mean to be Black?"

As I write this, I can hear the voice of a White woman who asked me, "Well, all adolescents struggle with questions of identity. They all become more self-conscious about their appearance and more con-cerned about what their peers think. So what is so different for Black kids?" Of course, she is right that all adolescents look at themselves in new ways, but not all adolescents think about themselves in racial terms.

The search for personal identity that intensifies in adolescence can involve several dimensions of an adolescent's life: vocational plans, religious beliefs, values and preferences, political affiliations and beliefs, gender roles, and ethnic identities. The process of exploration may vary across these identity domains. James Marcia described four identity "statuses" to characterize the variation in the identity search process: (1) *diffuse,* a state in which there has been little exploration or active consideration of a particular domain, and no psychological commitment; (2) *foreclosed,* a state in which a commitment has been made to particular roles or belief systems, often those selected by par-ents, without actively considering alternatives; (3) *moratorium,* a state of active exploration of roles and beliefs in which no commitment has yet been made; and (4) *achieved,* a state of strong personal commit-ment to a particular dimension of identity following a period of high exploration.[1]

An individual is not likely to explore all identity domains at once, therefore it is not unusual for an adolescent to be actively exploring one dimension while another remains relatively unexamined. Given the impact of dominant and subordinate status, it is not surprising that researchers have found that adolescents of color are more likely to be actively engaged in an exploration of their racial or ethnic identity than are White adolescents.[2]

Why do Black youths, in particular, think about themselves in terms of race? Because that is how the rest of the world thinks of them. Our self-perceptions are shaped by the messages that we receive from those around us, and when young Black men and women enter adolescence, the racial content of those messages intensifies. A case in point: If you were to ask my ten-year-old son, David, to describe himself, he would tell you many things: that he is smart, that he likes to play computer games, that he has an older brother. Near the top of his list, he would likely mention that he is tall for his age. He would probably not mention that he is Black, though he certainly knows that he is. Why would he mention his height and not his racial group membership? When David meets new adults, one of the first questions they ask is "How old are you?" When David states his age, the inevitable reply is "Gee, you're tall for your age!" It happens so frequently that I once overheard David say to someone, "Don't say it, I know. I'm tall for my age." Height is salient for David because it is salient for others.

When David meets new adults, they don't say, "Gee, you're Black for your age!" If you are saying to yourself, of course they don't, think again. Imagine David at fifteen, six-foot-two, wearing the adolescent attire of the day, passing adults he doesn't know on the sidewalk. Do the women hold their purses a little tighter, maybe even cross the street to avoid him? Does he hear the sound of the automatic door locks on cars as he passes by? Is he being followed around by the security guards at the local mall? As he stops in town with his new bicycle, does a police officer hassle him, asking where he got it, implying that it might be stolen? Do strangers assume he plays basketball? Each of these experiences conveys a racial message. At ten, race is not yet salient for David, because it is not yet salient for society. But it will be.

Understanding Racial Identity Development

Psychologist William Cross, author of *Shades of Black: Diversity in African American Identity,* has offered a theory of racial identity development that I have found to be a very useful framework for understanding what is happening not only with David, but with those Black students in the cafeteria.[3] According to Cross's model, referred to as the psychology of nigrescence, or the psychology of becoming Black, the five stages of racial identity development are *pre-encounter, encounter, immersion/emersion, internalization,* and *internalization-commitment.* For the moment, we will consider the first two stages as those are the most relevant for adolescents.

In the first stage, the Black child absorbs many of the beliefs and values of the dominant White culture, including the idea that it is better to be White. The stereotypes, omissions, and distortions that reinforce notions of White superiority are breathed in by Black children as well as White. Simply as a function of being socialized in a Eurocentric culture, some Black children may begin to value the role models, lifestyles, and images of beauty represented by the dominant group more highly than those of their own cultural group. On the other hand, if Black parents are what I call race-conscious—that is, actively seeking to encourage positive racial identity by providing their children with positive cultural images and messages about what it means to be Black—the impact of the dominant society's messages are reduced.[4] In either case, in the pre-encounter stage, the personal and social significance of one's racial group membership has not yet been realized, and racial identity is not yet under examination. At age ten, David and other children like him would seem to be in the pre-encounter stage. When the environmental cues change and the world begins to reflect his Blackness back to him more clearly, he will probably enter the encounter stage.

Transition to the encounter stage is typically precipitated by an event or series of events that force the young person to acknowledge the personal impact of racism. As the result of a new and heightened awareness of the significance of race, the individual begins to grapple with what it means to be a member of a group targeted by racism. Though Cross describes this process as one that unfolds in late adolescence and early adulthood, research suggests that an examination of one's racial or ethnic identity may begin as early as junior high school.

In a study of Black and White eighth graders from an integrated urban junior high school, Jean Phinney and Steve Tarver found clear evidence for the beginning of the search process in this dimension of identity. Among the forty-eight participants, more than a third had thought about the effects of ethnicity on their future, had discussed the issues with family and friends, and were attempting to learn more about their group. While White students in this integrated school were also beginning to think about ethnic identity, there was evidence to suggest a more active search among Black students, especially Black females.[5] Phinney and Tarver's research is consistent with my own study of Black youth in predominantly White communities, where the environmental cues that trigger an examination of racial identity often become evident in middle school or junior high school.[6]

Some of the environmental cues are institutionalized. Though many elementary schools have self-contained classrooms where children of varying performance levels learn together, many middle and secondary schools use "ability grouping," or tracking. Though school administrators often defend their tracking practices as fair and objective, there usually is a recognizable racial pattern to how children are assigned, which often represents the system of advantage operating in the schools.[7] In racially mixed schools, Black children are much more likely to be in the lower track than in the honors track. Such apparent sorting along racial lines sends a message about what it means to be Black. One young honors student I interviewed described the irony of this resegregation in what was an otherwise integrated environment, and hinted at the identity issues it raised for him.

> It was really a very paradoxical existence, here I am in a
> school that's 35 percent Black, you know, and I'm the
> only Black in my classes. . . . That always struck me as
> odd. I guess I felt that I was different from the other
> Blacks because of that.

In addition to the changes taking place within school, there are changes in the social dynamics outside school. For many parents, puberty raises anxiety about interracial dating. In racially mixed communities, you begin to see what I call the birthday party effect. Young children's birthday parties in multiracial communities are often a reflection of the community's diversity. The parties of elementary school children may be segregated by gender but not by race. At puberty, when the parties become sleepovers or boy-girl events, they become less and less racially diverse.

Black girls, especially in predominantly White communities, may gradually become aware that something has changed. When their White friends start to date, they do not. The issues of emerging sexuality and the societal messages about who is sexually desirable leave young Black women in a very devalued position. One young woman from a Philadelphia suburb described herself as "pursuing White guys throughout high school" to no avail. Since there were no Black boys in her class, she had little choice. She would feel "really pissed off" that those same White boys would date her White friends. For her, "that prom thing was like out of the question."[8]

Though Black girls living in the context of a larger Black community may have more social choices, they too have to contend with devaluing messages about who they are and who they will become, especially if they are poor or working-class. As social scientists Bonnie Ross Leadbeater and Niobe Way point out,

> The school drop-out, the teenage welfare mother, the drug addict, and the victim of domestic violence or of AIDS are among the most prevalent public images of poor and working-class urban adolescent girls. . . . Yet, despite the risks inherent in economic disadvantage, the majority of poor urban adeolescent girls do not fit the stereotypes that are made about them.[9]

Resisting the stereotypes and affirming other definitions of themselves is part of the task facing young Black women in both White and Black communities.

As was illustrated in the example of David, Black boys also face a devalued status in the wider world. The all too familiar media image of a young Black man with his hands cuffed behind his back, arrested for a violent crime, has primed many to view young Black men with suspicion and fear. In the context of predominantly White schools, however, Black boys may enjoy a degree of social success, particularly if they are athletically talented. The culture has embraced the Black athlete, and the young man who can fulfill that role is often pursued by Black girls and White girls alike. But even these young men will encounter experiences that may trigger an examination of their racial identity.

Sometimes the experience is quite dramatic. *The Autobiography of Malcolm X* is a classic tale of racial identity development, and I assign it to my psychology of racism students for just that reason. As a junior high school student, Malcolm was a star. Despite the fact that he was separated from his family and living in a foster home, he was an A student and was elected president of his class. One day he had a conversation with his English teacher, whom he liked and respected, about his future career goals. Malcolm said he wanted to be a lawyer. His teacher responded, "That's no realistic goal for a nigger," and advised him to consider carpentry instead.[10] The message was clear: You are a Black male, your racial group membership matters, plan accordingly. Malcolm's emotional response was typical—anger, confusion, and alienation. He withdrew from his White classmates, stopped participating in class, and eventually left his predominately white Michigan home to live with his sister in Roxbury, a Black community in Boston.

No teacher would say such a thing now, you may be thinking, but don't be so sure. It is certainly less likely that a teacher would use the word *nigger,* but consider these contemporary examples shared by high school students. A young ninth-grade student was sitting in his homeroom. A substitute teacher was in charge of the class. Because the majority of students from this school go on to college, she used the free time to ask the students about their college plans. As a substitute she had very limited information about their academic performance, but she offered some suggestions. When she turned to this young man, one of few Black males in the class, she suggested that he consider a community college. She had recommended four-year colleges to the other students. Like Malcolm, this student got the message.

In another example, a young Black woman attending a desegregated school to which she was bussed was encouraged by a teacher to attend the upcoming school dance. Most of the Black students did not live in the neighborhood and seldom attended the extracurricular activities. The young woman indicated that she wasn't planning to come. The well-intentioned teacher was persistent. Finally the teacher said, "Oh come on, I know you people love to dance." This young woman got the message, too.

Coping with Encounters: Developing an Oppositional Identity

What do these encounters have to do with the cafeteria? Do experiences with racism inevitably result in so-called self-segregation? While certainly a desire to protect oneself from further offense is understandable, it is not the only factor at work. Imagine the young eighth-grade girl who experienced the teacher's use of "you people" and the dancing stereotype as a racial affront. Upset and struggling with adolescent embarrassment, she bumps into a White friend who can see that something is wrong. She explains. Her White friend responds, in an effort to make her feel better perhaps, and says, "Oh, Mr. Smith is such a nice guy, I'm sure he didn't mean it like that. Don't be so sensitive." Perhaps the White friend is right, and Mr. Smith didn't mean it, but imagine your own response when you are upset, perhaps with a spouse or partner. He or she asks what's wrong and you explain why you are offended. Your partner brushes off your complaint, attributing it to your being oversensitive. What happens to your emotional thermostat? It escalates. When feelings, rational or irrational, are invalidated, most people disengage. They not only choose to discontinue the conversation but are more likely to turn to someone who will understand their perspective.

In much the same way, the eighth-grade girl's White friend doesn't get it. She doesn't see the significance of this racial message, but the girls at the "Black table" do. When she tells her story there, one of them is likely to say, "You know what, Mr. Smith said the same thing to me yesterday!" Not only are Black adolescents encountering racism and reflecting on their identity, but their White peers, even when they are not the perpetrators (and sometimes they are), are unprepared to respond in supportive ways. The Black students turn to each other for the much needed support they are not likely to find anywhere else.

In adolescence, as race becomes personally salient for Black youth, finding the answer to questions such as, "What does it mean to be a young Black person? How should I act? What should I do?" is particularly important. And although Black fathers, mothers, aunts, and uncles may hold the answers by offering themselves as role models, they hold little appeal for most adolescents. The last thing many fourteen-year-olds want to do is to grow up to be like their parents. It is the peer group, the kids in the cafeteria, who hold the answers to these questions. They know how to be Black. They have absorbed the stereotypical images of Black youth in the popular culture and are reflecting those images in their self-presentation.

Based on their fieldwork in U.S. high schools, Signithia Fordham and John Ogbu identified a common psychological pattern found among African American high school students at this stage of identity development.[11] They observed that the anger and resentment that adolescents feel in response to their growing awareness of the systematic exclusion of Black people from full participation in U.S. society leads to the development of an oppositional social identity. This oppositional stance both protects one's identity from the psychological assault of racism and keeps the dominant group at a distance. Fordham and Ogbu write:

> Subordinate minorities regard certain forms of behavior and certain activities or events, symbols, and mean-

ings as *not appropriate* for them because those behaviors, events, symbols, and meanings are characteristic of white Americans. At the same time they emphasize other forms of behavior as more appropriate for them because these are *not* a part of white Americans' way of life. To behave in the manner defined as falling within a white cultural frame of reference is to "act white" and is negatively sanctioned.[12]

Certain styles of speech, dress, and music, for example, may be embraced as "authentically Black" and become highly valued, while attitudes and behaviors associated with Whites are viewed with disdain. The peer groups's evaluation of what is Black and what is not can have a powerful impact on adolescent behavior.

Reflecting on her high school years, one Black woman from a White neighborhood described both the pain of being rejected by her Black classmates and her attempts to conform to her peer's definition of Blackness:

> "Oh you sound White, you think you're White," they said. And the idea of sounding White was just so absurd to me. . . . So ninth grade was sort of traumatic in that I started listening to rap music, which I really just don't like. [I said] I'm gonna be Black, and it was just that stupid. But it's more than just how one acts, you know. [The other Black women there] were not into me for the longest time. My first year there was hell.

Sometimes the emergence of an oppositional identity can be quite dramatic, as the young person tries on a new persona almost overnight. At the end of one school year, race may not have appeared to be significant, but often some encounter takes place over the summer and the young person returns to school much more aware of his or her Blackness and ready to make sure that the rest of the world is aware of it, too. There is a certain "in your face" quality that these adolescents can take on, which their teachers often experience as threatening. When a group of Black teens are sitting together in the cafeteria, collectively embodying an oppositional stance, school administrators want to know not only why they are sitting together, but what can be done to prevent it.

We need to understand that in racially mixed settings, racial grouping is a developmental process in response to an environmental stressor, racism. Joining with one's peers for support in the face of stress is a positive coping strategy. What is problematic is that the young people are operating with a very limited definition of what it means to be Black, based largely on cultural stereotypes.

Oppositional Identity Development and Academic Achievement

Unfortunately for Black teenagers, those cultural stereotypes do not usually include academic achievement. Academic success is more often associated with being White. During the encounter phase of racial identity development, when the search for identity leads toward cultural stereotypes and away from anything that might be associated with Whiteness, academic performance often declines. Doing well in school becomes identified as trying to be White. Being smart becomes the opposite of being cool.

While this frame of reference is not universally found among adolescents of African descent, it is commonly observed in Black peer groups. Among the Black college students I have interviewed, many described some conflict or alienation from other African American teens because of their academic success in high school. For example, a twenty-year-old female from a Washington, D.C., suburb explained:

> It was weird, even in high school a lot of the Black students were, like, "Well, you're not really Black." Whether it was because I became president of the sixth-grade class or whatever it was, it started pretty much back

then. Junior high, it got worse. I was then labeled certain things, whether it was "the oreo" or I wasn't really
Black.

Others described avoiding situations that would set them apart
from their Black peers. For example, one young woman declined to
participate in a gifted program in her school because she knew it
would separate her from the other Black students in the school.

In a study of thirty-three eleventh-graders in a Washington, D.C.,
school, Fordham and Ogbu found that although some of the students
had once been academically successful, few of them remained so.
These students also knew that to be identified as a "brainiac" would
result in peer rejection. The few students who had maintained strong
academic records found ways to play down their academic success
enough to maintain some level of acceptance among their Black
peers.[13]

Academically successful Black students also need a strategy to find
acceptance among their White classmates. Fordham describes one
such strategy as *racelessness*, wherein individuals assimilate into the
dominant group by de-emphasizing characteristics that might identify them as members of the subordinate group.[14] Jon, a young man I
interviewed, offered a classic example of this strategy as he described
his approach to dealing with his discomfort at being the only Black
person in his advanced classes. He said, "At no point did I ever think
I was White or did I ever want to be White. . . . I guess it was one of
those things where I tried to de-emphasize the fact that I was Black."
This strategy led him to avoid activities that were associated with
Blackness. He recalled, "I didn't want to do anything that was traditionally Black, like I never played basketball. I ran cross-country. . . . I
went for distance running instead of sprints." He felt he had to show
his White classmates that there were "exceptions to all these stereotypes." However, this strategy was of limited usefulness. When he traveled outside his home community with his White teammates, he
sometimes encountered overt racism. "I quickly realized that I'm

Black, and that's the thing that they're going to see first, no matter how much I try to de-emphasize my Blackness."

A Black student can play down Black identity in order to succeed in school and mainstream institutions without rejecting his Black identity and culture.[15] Instead of becoming raceless, an achieving Black student can become an *emissary,* someone who sees his or her own achievements as advancing the cause of the racial group. For example, social scientists Richard Zweigenhaft and G. William Domhoff describe how a successful Black student, in response to the accusation of acting White, connected his achievement to that of other Black men by saying, "Martin Luther King must not have been Black, then, since he had a doctoral degree, and Malcolm X must not have been Black since he educated himself while in prison." In addition, he demonstrated his loyalty to the Black community by taking an openly political stance against the racial discrimination he observed in his school.[16]

It is clear that an oppositional identity can interfere with academic achievement, and it may be tempting for educators to blame the adolescents themselves for their academic decline. However, the questions that educators and other concerned adults must ask are, How did academic achievement become defined as exclusively White behavior? What is it about the curriculum and the wider culture that reinforces the notion that academic excellence is an exclusively White domain? What curricular interventions might we use to encourage the development of an empowered emissary identity?

An oppositional identity that disdains academic achievement has not always been a characteristic of Black adolescent peer groups. It seems to be a post-desegregation phenomenon. Historically, the oppositional identity found among African Americans in the segregated South included a positive attitude toward education. While Black people may have publicly deferred to Whites, they actively encouraged their children to pursue education as a ticket to greater freedom.[17] While Black parents still see education as the key to upward mobility, in today's desegregated schools the models of success—the teachers, administrators, and curricular heroes—are almost always White.

Black Southern schools, though stigmatized by legally sanctioned segregation, were often staffed by African American educators, themselves visible models of academic achievement. These Black educators may have presented a curriculum that included references to the intellectual legacy of other African Americans. As well, in the context of a segregated school, it was a given that the high achieving students would all be Black. Academic achievement did not have to mean separation from one's Black peers.

The Search for Alternative Images

This historical example reminds us that an oppositional identity discouraging academic achievement is not inevitable even in a racist society. If young people are exposed to images of African American academic achievement in their early years, they won't have to define school achievement as something for Whites only. They will know that there is a long history of Black intellectual achievement.

This point was made quite eloquently by Jon, the young man I quoted earlier. Though he made the choice to excel in school, he labored under the false assumption that he was "inventing the wheel." It wasn't until he reached college and had the opportunity to take African American studies courses that he learned about other African Americans besides Martin Luther King, Malcolm X, and Frederick Douglass—the same three men he had heard about year after year, from kindergarten to high school graduation. As he reflected on his identity struggle in high school, he said:

> It's like I went through three phases. . . . My first phase
> was being cool, doing whatever was particularly cool
> for Black people at the time, and that was like in junior
> high. Then in high school, you know, I thought being
> Black was basically all stereotypes, so I tried to avoid all

of those things. Now in college, you know, I realize that being Black means a variety of things.

Learning his history in college was of great psychological importance to Jon, providing him with role models he had been missing in high school. He was particularly inspired by learning of the intellectual legacy of Black men at his own college:

> When you look at those guys who were here in the Twenties, they couldn't live on campus. They couldn't eat on campus. They couldn't get their hair cut in town. And yet they were all Phi Beta Kappa. . . . That's what being Black really is, you know, knowing who you are, your history, your accomplishments. . . . When I was in junior high, I had White role models. And then when I got into high school, you know, I wasn't sure but I just didn't think having White role models was a good thing. So I got rid of those. And I basically just, you know, only had my parents for role models. I kind of grew up thinking that we were on the cutting edge. We were doing something radically different than everybody else. And not realizing that there are all kinds of Black people doing the very things that I thought we were the only ones doing. . . . You've got to do the very best you can so that you can continue the great traditions that have already been established.

This young man was not alone in his frustration over having learned little about his own cultural history in grade school. Time and again in the research interviews I conducted, Black students lamented the absence of courses in African American history or literature at the high school level and indicated how significant this new learning was to them in college, how excited and affirmed they felt by this newfound knowledge. Sadly, many Black students never get to college, alienated from the process of education long before high school graduation. They may never get access to the information that might have helped them expand their definition of what it means to be Black and, in the process, might have helped them stay in school. Young people are developmentally ready for this information in adolescence. We ought to provide it.

Not at the Table

As we have seen, Jon felt he had to distance himself from his Black peers in order to be successful in high school. He was one of the kids *not* sitting at the Black table. Continued encounters with racism and access to new culturally relevant information empowered him to give up his racelessness and become an emissary. In college, not only did he sit at the Black table, but he emerged as a campus leader, confident in the support of his Black peers. His example illustrates that one's presence at the Black table is often an expression of one's identity development, which evolves over time.

Some Black students may not be developmentally ready for the Black table in junior or senior high school. They may not yet have had their own encounters with racism, and race may not be very salient for them. Just as we don't all reach puberty and begin developing sexual interest at the same time, racial identity development unfolds in idiosyncratic ways. Though my research suggests that adolescence is a common time, one's own life experiences are also important determinants of the timing. The young person whose racial identity development is out of synch with his or her peers often feels in an awkward position. Adolescents are notoriously egocentric and assume that their experience is the same as everyone else's. Just as girls who have become interested in boys become disdainful of their friends still interested in dolls, the Black teens who are at the table can be quite judgmental toward those who are not. "If I think it is a sign of authentic Blackness to sit at this table, then you should too."

The young Black men and women who still hang around with

the White classmates they may have known since early childhood will often be snubbed by their Black peers. This dynamic is particularly apparent in regional schools where children from a variety of neighborhoods are brought together. When Black children from predominantly White neighborhoods go to school with Black children from predominantly Black neighborhoods, the former group is often viewed as trying to be White by the latter group. We all speak the language of the streets we live on. Black children living in White neighborhoods often sound White to their Black peers from across town, and may be teased because of it. This can be a very painful experience, particularly when the young person is not fully accepted as part of the White peer group either.

One young Black woman from a predominantly White community described exactly this situation in an interview. In a school with a lot of racial tension, Terri felt that "the worst thing that happened" was the rejection she experienced from the other Black children who were being bussed to her school. Though she wanted to be friends with them, they teased her, calling her an "oreo cookie" and sometimes beating her up. The only close Black friend Terri had was a biracial girl from her neighborhood.

Racial tensions also affected her relationships with White students. One White friend's parents commented, "I can't believe you're Black. You don't seem like all the Black children. You're nice." Though other parents made similar comments, Terri reported that her White friends didn't start making them until junior high school, when Terri's Blackness became something to be explained. One friend introduced Terri to another White girl by saying, "She's not really Black, she just went to Florida and got a really dark tan." A White sixth-grade "boyfriend" became embarrassed when his friends discovered he had a crush on a Black girl. He stopped telling Terri how pretty she was, and instead called her "nigger" and said, "Your lips are too big. I don't want to see you. I won't be your friend anymore."

Despite supportive parents who expressed concern about her situation, Terri said she was a "very depressed child." Her father would have conversations with her "about being Black and beautiful" and about "the union of people of color that had always existed that I needed to find. And the pride." However, her parents did not have a network of Black friends to help support her.

It was the intervention of a Black junior high school teacher that Terri feels helped her the most. Mrs. Campbell "really exposed me to the good Black community because I was so down on it" by getting Terri involved in singing gospel music and introducing her to other Black students who would accept her. "That's when I started having other Black friends. And I thank her a lot for that."

The significant role that Mrs. Campbell played in helping Terri open up illustrates the constructive potential that informed adults can have in the identity development process. She recognized Terri's need for a same-race peer group and helped her find one. Talking to groups of Black students about the variety of living situations Black people come from and the unique situation facing Black adolescents in White communities helps to expand the definition of what it means to be Black and increases intragroup acceptance at a time when that is quite important.

For children in Terri's situation, it is also helpful for Black parents to provide ongoing opportunities for their children to connect with other Black peers even if that means traveling outside the community they live in. Race-conscious parents often do this by attending a Black church or maintaining ties to Black social organizations such as Jack and Jill. Parents who make this effort often find that their children become bicultural, able to move comfortably between Black and White communities, and able to sit at the Black table when they are ready.

Implied in this discussion is the assumption that connecting with one's Black peers in the process of identity development is important and should be encouraged. For young Black people living in predominantly Black communities, such connections occur spontaneously with neighbors and classmates and usually do not require special encouragement. However, for young people in predominantly

White communities they may only occur with active parental intervention. One might wonder if this social connection is really necessary. If a young person has found a niche among a circle of White friends, is it really necessary to establish a Black peer group as a reference point? Eventually it is.

As one's awareness of the daily challenges of living in a racist society increase, it is immensely helpful to be able to share one's experiences with others who have lived it. Even when White friends are willing and able to listen and bear witness to one's struggles, they cannot really share the experience. One young woman came to this realization in her senior year of high school:

> [The isolation] never really bothered me until about senior year when I was the only one in the class. . . . That little burden, that constant burden of you always having to strive to do your best and show that you can do just as much as everybody else. Your White friends can't understand that, and it's really hard to communicate to them. Only someone else of the same racial, same ethnic background would understand something like that.

When one is faced with what Chester Pierce calls the "mundane extreme environmental stress" of racism, in adolescence or in adulthood, the ability to see oneself as part of a larger group from which one can draw support is an important coping strategy.[18] Individuals who do not have such a strategy available to them because they do not experience a shared identity with at least some subset of their racial group are at risk for considerable social isolation.

Of course, who we perceive as sharing our identity may be influenced by other dimensions of identity such as gender, social class, geographical location, skin color, or ethnicity. For example, research indicates that first-generation Black immigrants from the Caribbean tend to emphasize their national origins and ethnic identities, distancing themselves from U.S. Blacks, due in part to their belief that West Indians are viewed more positively by Whites than those American Blacks whose family roots include the experience of U.S. slavery. To relinquish one's ethnic identity as West Indian and take on an African American identity may be understood as downward social mobility. However, second-generation West Indians without an identifiable accent may lose the relative ethnic privilege their parents experienced and seek racial solidarity with Black American peers in the face of encounters with racism.[19] Whether it is the experience of being followed in stores because they are suspected of shoplifting, seeing people respond to them with fear on the street, or feeling overlooked in school, Black youth can benefit from seeking support from those who have had similar experiences.

An Alternative to the Cafeteria Table

The developmental need to explore the meaning of one's identity with others who are engaged in a similar process manifests itself informally in school corridors and cafeterias across the country. Some educational institutions have sought to meet this need programmatically. Several colleagues and I recently evaluated one such effort, initiated at a Massachusetts middle school participating in a voluntary desegregation program known as the Metropolitan Council for Educational Opportunity (METCO) program.[20] Historically, the small number of African American students who are bussed from Boston to this suburban school have achieved disappointing levels of academic success. In an effort to improve academic achievement, the school introduced a program, known as Student Efficacy Training (SET) that allowed Boston students to meet each day as a group with two staff members. Instead of being in physical education or home economics or study hall, they were meeting, talking about homework difficulties, social issues, and encounters with racism. The meeting was mandatory and at first the students were resentful of missing some of their classes. But the impact was dramatic. Said one young woman,

> In the beginning of the year, I didn't want to do SET at all. It took away my study and it was only METCO students doing it. In the beginning all we did was argue over certain problems or it was more like a rap session and I didn't think it was helping anyone. But then when we looked at records . . . I know that last year out of all the students, sixth through eighth grade, there was, like, six who were actually good students. Everyone else, it was just pathetic, I mean, like, they were getting like Ds and Fs. . . . The eighth grade is doing much better this year. I mean, they went from Ds and Fs to Bs and Cs and occasional As. . . . And those seventh-graders are doing really good, they have a lot of honor roll students in seventh grade, both guys and girls. Yeah, it's been good. It's really good.

Her report is borne out by an examination of school records. The opportunity to come together in the company of supportive adults allowed these young Black students to talk about the issues that hindered their performance—racial encounters, feelings of isolation, test anxiety, homework dilemmas—in the psychological safety of their own group. In the process, the peer culture changed to one that supported academic performance rather than undermined it, as revealed in these two students' comments:

> Well, a lot of the Boston students, the boys and the girls, used to fight all the time. And now, they stopped yelling at each other so much and calling each other stupid.

> It's like we've all become like one big family, we share things more with each other. We tease each other like brother and sister. We look out for each other with homework and stuff. We always stay on top of each other 'cause we know it's hard with African American

students to go to a predominantly White school and try to succeed with everybody else.

The faculty, too, were very enthusiastic about the outcomes of the intervention, as seen in the comments of these two classroom teachers:

This program has probably produced the most dramatic result of any single change that I've seen at this school. It has produced immediate results that affected behavior and academics and participation in school life.

My students are more engaged. They aren't battling out a lot of the issues of their anger about being in a White community, coming in from Boston, where do I fit, I don't belong here. I feel that those issues that often came out in class aren't coming out in class anymore. I think they are being discussed in the SET room, the kids feel more confidence. The kids' grades are higher, the homework response is greater, they're not afraid to participate in class, and I don't see them isolating themselves within class. They are willing to sit with other students happily. . . . I think it's made a very positive impact on their place in the school and on their individual self-esteem. I see them enjoying themselves and able to enjoy all of us as individuals. I can't say enough, it's been the best thing that's happened to the METCO program as far as I'm concerned.[21]

Although this intervention is not a miracle cure for every school, it does highlight what can happen when we think about the developmental needs of Black adolescents coming to terms with their own sense of identity. It might seem counterintuitive that a school involved in a voluntary desegregation program could improve both academic performance and social relationships among students by *separating* the

Black students for one period every day. But if we understand the unique challenges facing adolescents of color and the legitimate need they have to feel supported in their identity development, it makes perfect sense.

Though they may not use the language of racial identity development theory to describe it, most Black parents want their children to achieve an internalized sense of personal security, to be able to acknowledge the reality of racism and to respond effectively to it. Our educational institutions should do what they can to encourage this development rather than impede it. When I talk to educators about the need to provide adolescents with identity-affirming experiences and information about their own cultural groups, they sometimes flounder because this information has not been part of their own education. Their understanding of adolescent development has been limited to the White middle-class norms included in most textbooks, their knowledge of Black history limited to Martin Luther King, Jr., and Rosa Parks. They sometimes say with frustration that parents should provide this kind of education for their children. Unfortunately Black parents often attended the same schools the teachers did and have the same informational gaps. We need to acknowledge that an important part of interrupting the cycle of oppression is constant re-education, and sharing what we learn with the next generation.

5

Racial Identity in Adulthood
"Still a work in progress . . . "

When I was in high school, I did not sit at the Black table in the cafeteria because there were not enough Black kids in my high school to fill one. Though I was naive about many things, I knew enough about social isolation to know that I needed to get out of town. As the child of college-educated parents and an honor student myself, it was expected that I would go on to college. My mother suggested Howard University, my parents' alma mater, but although it was a good suggestion, I had my own ideas. I picked Wesleyan University in Middletown, Connecticut. It was two hours from home, an excellent school, and of particular interest to me was that it had a critical mass of Black and Latino students, most of whom were male. Wesleyan had just gone co-ed, and the ratio of Black male students to Black female students was seven-to-one. I thought it would improve my social life, and it did.

I thrived socially and academically. Since I had decided in high school to be a psychologist, I was a psychology major, but I took a lot of African American studies courses—history, literature, religion, even Black child development. I studied Swahili in hopes of traveling to Tanzania, although I never went. I stopped straightening my hair and had a large Afro à la Angela Davis circa 1970. I happily sat at the Black table in the dining hall every day. I look back on my days at Wesleyan with great pleasure. I maintain many of the friendships I formed there, and I can't remember the name of one White classmate.

I was having what William Cross might call an "immersion experience." I had my racial encounters in high school, so when I got to college I was ready to explore my racial identity and I did it wholeheartedly. The third stage in Cross's model, immersion/emersion is characterized by a strong desire to surround oneself with symbols of one's racial identity, and actively seek out opportunities to learn about one's own history and culture with the support of same-race peers. While anger toward Whites is often characteristic of the encounter phase, during the immersion/emersion phase the developing Black person sees White people as simply irrelevant. This is not to say that anger is totally absent, but that the focus of attention is on self-discovery rather than on White people. If I had spent a lot of time being angry with the White men and women I encountered at Wesleyan, I would remember them. The truth is I wasn't paying much attention to them. My focus was almost exclusively on exploring my own cultural connections.

The Black person in the immersion/emersion phase is energized by the new information he or she is learning—angry perhaps that it wasn't available sooner—but excited to find out that there is more to Africa than Tarzan movies and that there is more to Black history than victimization. In many ways, the person at the immersion/emersion stage is unlearning the internalized stereotypes about his or her own group and is redefining a positive sense of self, based on an affirmation of one's racial group identity.

One emerges from this process into the internalization stage, characterized by a sense of security about one's racial identity. Often the person at this stage is willing to establish meaningful relationships across group boundaries with others, including Whites, who are respectful of this new self-definition. Cross suggests that there are few psychological differences between this fourth stage and the fifth, internalization-commitment. However, by the fifth stage the individual has found ways to translate a personal sense of racial identity into ongoing action expressing a sense of commitment to the concerns of Blacks as a group. Whether at the fourth or fifth stage, the individual is now anchored in a positive sense of racial identity and is prepared to perceive and transcend race.

In my own life, I see these stages clearly. I left Wesleyan anchored in my sense of Blackness. I went off to graduate school at the University of Michigan and quickly became part of an extensive network of Black graduate students, but I did have a few White friends, too. I even remember their names. But there were also White people that I chose not to associate with, people who weren't ready to deal with me in terms of my self-definition. I continue to have a racially mixed group of friends, and I am glad to model that for my children. My choice of research topics throughout my career reflects my concerns about my racial group. I like to think that I both perceive and transcend race, but I am still a work in progress. I know that I revisit the earlier stages of development a lot.

Sometimes I find it helpful to compare this process to learning another language. The best way to learn a second language is to travel to a place where it is spoken and experience complete immersion. Once you have achieved the level of proficiency you need, you can leave. If you worked hard to become conversant, you will of course take pride in your accomplishment and will not want to spend time with people who disparage your commitment to this endeavor. You may choose not to speak this new language all the time, but if you want to maintain your skill, you will need to speak it often with others who understand it.

Though the cultural symbols for this generation are not the same as for mine, the process of racial identity development is the same. Black students practice their "language" in Black student unions and cultural centers and at college dining halls on predominantly White campuses all over the United States.[1] And they should not be discouraged from doing so. Like the Black middle school students from Boston, they need safe spaces to retreat to and regroup in the process of dealing with the daily stress of campus racism.

That life is stressful for Black students and other students of color on predominantly White campuses should not come as a surprise, but it often does. White students and faculty frequently underestimate the power and presence of the overt and covert manifestations of racism on campus, and students of color often come to predominantly White campuses expecting more civility than they find. Whether it is the loneliness of being routinely overlooked as a lab partner in science courses, the irritation of being continually asked by curious classmates about Black hairstyles, the discomfort of being singled out by a professor to give the "Black perspective" in class discussion, the pain of racist graffiti scrawled on dormitory room doors, the insult of racist jokes circulated through campus e-mail, or the injury inflicted by racial epithets (and sometimes beer bottles) hurled from a passing car, Black students on predominantly White college campuses must cope with ongoing affronts to their racial identity.[2] The desire to retreat to safe space is understandable. Sometimes that means leaving the campus altogether.

For example, one young woman I interviewed at Howard University explained why she transferred from a predominantly White college to a historically Black one. Assigned to share a dormitory room with two White girls, both of whom were from rural White communities, she was insulted by the assumptions her White roommates made about her. Conflict erupted between them when she was visited by her boyfriend, a young Black man.

> They put padlocks on their doors and their dressers. And they accused me of drinking all their beers. And I was like, "We don't drink. This doesn't make any sense." So what really brought me to move out of that room was when he left, I came back, they were scrubbing things down with Pine Sol. I was like, "I couldn't live here with you. You think we have germs or something?"

She moved into a room with another Black woman, the first Black roommate pair in the dormitory. The administration had discouraged Black pairings because they didn't want Black students to separate themselves. She and her new roommate got along well, but they became targets of racial harassment.

All of a sudden we started getting racial slurs like "South Africa will strike. Africans go home." And all this other stuff. I knew the girls who were doing it. They lived all the way down the hall. And I don't understand why they were doing it. We didn't do anything to them. But when we confronted them they acted like they didn't know anything. And my friends, their rooms were getting trashed. . . . One day I was asleep and somebody was trying to jiggle the lock trying to get in. And I opened the door and chased this girl down the hallway.

Though she said the college administration handled the situation and the harassers were eventually asked to leave, the stress of these events had taken its toll. At the end of her first year, she transferred to Howard.

While stressful experiences can happen at any college, and social conflicts can and do erupt among Black students at Black colleges as well, there is considerable evidence that Black students at historically Black colleges and universities achieve higher academic performance, enjoy greater social involvement, and aspire to higher occupational goals than their peers do at predominantly White institutions.[3] Drawing on his analysis of data from the National Study on Black College Students, Walter Allen offers this explanation of the difference in student outcomes.

On predominantly White campuses, Black students emphasize feelings of alienation, sensed hostility, racial discrimination, and lack of integration. On historically Black campuses, Black students emphasize feelings of engagement, connection, acceptance, and extensive support and encouragement. Consistent with accumulated evidence on human development, these students, like most human beings, develop best in environments where they feel valued, protected, accepted, and socially connected. The supportive environments of historically Black colleges communicate to Black students that it is safe to take the risks associated with intellectual growth and development. Such environments also have more people who provide Black students with positive feedback, support, and understanding, and who communicate that they care about the students' welfare.[4]

While Allen's findings make a compelling case for Black student enrollment at historically Black colleges, the proportion of Black students entering predominantly White colleges continues to increase. Predominantly White colleges concerned about attracting and keeping Black students need to take seriously the psychological toll extracted from students of color in inhospitable environments and the critical role that cultural space can play. Having a place to be rejuvenated and to feel anchored in one's cultural community increases the possibility that one will have the energy to achieve academically as well as participate in the cross-group dialogue and interaction many colleges want to encourage. If White students or faculty do not understand why Black or Latino or Asian cultural centers are necessary, then they need to be helped to understand.[5]

Not for College Students Only

Once when I described the process of racial identity development at a workshop session, a young Black man stood up and said, "You make it sound like if you don't go to college you have to stay stuck in the encounter stage." It was a good observation. Not every Black person moves through every stage. People of any educational background can get stuck. Identity development does not have to happen in college. Malcolm X had his immersion experience in prison. As he began to read books about Black history and was encouraged by older Black inmates, he began to redefine for himself what it meant to be a Black man. As he said in his autobiography,

> The teachings of Mr. Muhammad stressed how history had been "whitened"—when white men had written history books, the black man had simply been left out. Mr. Muhammad couldn't have said anything that would have struck me much harder. I had never forgotten how when my class, me and all of those whites, had studied seventh-grade United States history back in Mason, the history of the Negro had been covered in one paragraph. . . .
>
> This is one reason why Mr. Muhammad's teachings spread so swiftly all over the United States, among *all* Negroes, whether or not they became followers of Mr. Muhammad. The teachings ring true . . . You can hardly show me a black adult in America—or a white one, for that matter—who knows from the history books anything like the truth about the black man's role. In my own case, once I heard of the "glorious history of the black man," I took special pains to hunt in the library for books that would inform me on details about black history.[6]

Malcolm's period of immersion included embracing the teachings of the Nation of Islam. Though Malcolm X later rejected the Nation's teachings in favor of the more inclusive message of orthodox Islam, his initial response to the Nation's message of Black empowerment and self-reliance was very enthusiastic.

One reason the Nation of Islam continues to appeal to some urban Black youth, many of whom are not in college, is that it offers another expanded, positive definition of what it means to be Black. In particular, the clean-shaven, well-groomed representatives of the Nation that can be seen on city streets emphasizing personal responsibility and Black community development offer a compelling contrast to the pervasive stereotypes of Black men. The hunger for positive expressions of identity can be seen in the response of many Black men to the Nation of Islam's organization of the Million Man March. The march can be understood as a major immersion event for every Black man who was there, and vicariously for those who were not.

Michael Eric Dyson expresses this quite clearly when he writes:

> As I stood at the Million Man March, I felt the powerful waves of history wash over me. There's no denying that this march connected many of the men—more than a million, I believe—to a sense of racial solidarity that has largely been absent since the '60s. I took my son to Washington so that he could feel and see, drown in, even, an ocean of beautiful black brothers.[7]

It was an affirming and definition-expanding event for Black men. And despite the White commentators that continuously offered their opinions about the march on television, it seemed to me that, for the participants, White people were that day irrelevant.

The need for safe space in which to construct a positive self-definition is, of course, also important for Black women. In her book *Black Feminist Thought,* Patricia Hill Collins identifies various ways that Black women have found to create such space in or out of the academy. "One location," she writes, "involves Black women's relationships with one another. In some cases, such as friendships and family interactions, these relationships are informal, private dealings among individuals. In others, . . . more formal organizational ties have nurtured powerful Black women's communities."[8] Whether in the context of mother-daughter relationships, small social networks, Black churches, or Black women's clubs, space is created for resisting stereotypes and creating positive identities.

Though Black churches can sometimes be criticized as purveyors of the dominant ideology, as evidenced in Eurocentric depictions of Jesus and sexist assumptions about the appropriate role of women, it is also true that historically Black churches have been the site for organized resistance against oppression and a place of affirmation for African American adults as well as for children. The National Survey of Black Americans, the largest collection of survey data on Black Americans to date, found very high rates of religious participation among Blacks in general, and among women in particular.[9] The survey respondents clearly indicated the positive role that the churches had played in both community development and psychological and social support.[10] Many Black churches with an Afrocentric perspective are providing the culturally relevant information for which Black adults hunger. For example, in some congregations an informational African American history moment is part of the worship service and Bible study includes a discussion of the Black presence in the Bible. As these examples suggest, there are sources of information within Black communities that will speak to the identity development needs of both young and older adults, but there is still a need for more.

Cycles of Racial Identity Development

The process of racial identity development, often beginning in adolescence and continuing into adulthood, is not so much linear as circular. It's like moving up a spiral staircase: As you proceed up each level, you have a sense that you have passed this way before, but you are not in exactly the same spot. Moving through the immersion stage to internalization does not mean there won't be new encounters with racism, or the recurring need to retreat to the safety of one's same-race peer group, or that identity questions that supposedly were resolved won't need to be revisited as life circumstances change.

In his article "Cycles of Psychological Nigrescence," counseling psychologist Thomas Parham has expanded Cross's model of racial identity development to explore the kind of changes in racial identity that a Black person may experience throughout the life cycle, not just in adolescence or early adulthood.[11] For example, during middle adulthood, that broad span of time between the mid-thirties and the mid-fifties, individuals regardless of race come to terms with new physical, psychological, and social challenges. This period in the life span is characterized by changing bodies (gaining weight, thinning or graying hair, waning energy), increasing responsibilities (including rearing children and grandchildren and caring for aging parents), continuing employment concerns, and often increasing community involvement. In addition, Levinson argues that adults at midlife fluctuate between periods of stability and transition, as they re-examine previous life decisions and commitments and choose to make minor or major changes in their lives.[12] What role does racial identity play for Black adults at midlife?

Parham argues that "the middle-adulthood period of life may be the most difficult time to struggle with racial identity because of one's increased responsibilities and increased potential for opportunities."[13] Those whose work or lifestyle places them in frequent contact with Whites are aware that their ability to "make it" depends in large part on their ability and willingness to conform to those values and behaviors that have been legitimated by White culture. While it is unlikely that the lack of racial awareness that characterizes an adolescent at the pre-encounter stage would be found among a Black adult at midlife, some Black adults may have consciously chosen to retreat from actively identifying with other Blacks. Choosing a "raceless" persona, these adults may have adopted a pre-encounter stance as a way of winning the approval of White friends and co-workers. George Davis and Glegg Watson quote a Black corporate manager describing some Black co-workers who took that path: "Most of them don't know and don't care much about Black culture or any other kind of culture. They won't even speak to you in the hallway when they see you, but they'll speak to the White guy, so they do have a negative racial consciousness."[14]

In terms of childrearing, adults in the pre-encounter stage are likely to de-emphasize their children's racial group membership as well. This attitude is captured in the comment of one father I interviewed who said that his children's peer group was "basically non-Black." Unlike other parents who told me that they felt it was important that their children have Black friends and were regretful when they did not, this father said, "I think it's more important that they have a socioeconomic group than a racial peer group."[15] In this case, class identification seemed more salient than racial identification.

Those adults who have adopted a strategy of racelessness may experience racial encounters in middle adulthood with particular emotional intensity. Because of the increased family responsibilities and financial obligations associated with this stage of life, the stakes are higher and the frustration particularly intense when a promotion is denied, a dream house is unattainable, or a child is racially harassed at school. Journalist Ellis Cose has chronicled many such incidents in his book *The Rage of a Privileged Class*,[16] as have Joe Feagin and Melvin Sikes in *Living with Racism: The Black Middle-Class Experience*.[17] Parham distinguishes between these "achievement-oriented" stresses of the upwardly mobile middle-class and the "survival-related" stresses experienced by poor and working-class Blacks. However, he concludes that despite a person's social status, "if an individual's sense of affirmation is sought through contact with and validation from Whites, then the struggle with one's racial identity is eminent."[18]

The latter survival stress is described by another father I interviewed who is worried not about promotions, but about simply holding on to what he has already achieved:

> Just being Black makes it hard, because people look at you like you're not as good as they are, like you're a second-class citizen, something like that. You got to always look over your shoulder like somebody's always watching you. At my job, I'm the only Black in my department and it seems like they're always watching me, the pressure's always on to perform. You feel like if you miss a day, you might not have a job. So there's that constant

awareness on my part, they can snatch what little you
have, so that's a constant fear, you know, especially when
you have a family to support. . . . So I'm always aware
of what can happen.[19]

The chronically high rates of Black unemployment form the
backdrop for this man's fear. Under such circumstances, he is
unlikely to speak up against the discrimination or racial hostility he
feels.

While some adults struggle (perhaps in vain) to hold on to a
"raceless" persona, other midlife adults express their racial identity
through immersion/emersion attitudes. On the job, they may be open
advocates of institutional change, or because of survival concerns, they
may feel constrained in how they express their anger. One male inter-
viewee, working in a human service agency, fluctuates between being
silent and speaking up:

It's very difficult, and dealing with all the negative problems, and then going back and fighting the administration of the department that you're working in, and
fighting the racism, and squabbling of White males as
well as White females, it's really difficult, and one
becomes programmed to be a little bit hard, but then in
order to survive, you've got to control it, and generally
I stay pretty much out of trouble. It's just like playing a
game in order to survive.[20]

Adults in the immersion/emersion stage are likely to be race-
conscious about their children's socialization experiences, choosing to
live in a Black community. If the demographics of their geographic
area do not permit such a choice, they will, in contrast to "raceless"
parents, actively seek out Black playmates for their children wherever they can find them. One mother explained,

> I'm not opposed to my child interacting with White
> children or kids of any other race, but I want them to
> have a Black peer group just for the sense of common-
> ality, and sharing some of the same experiences, and just
> not losing that identity of themselves.[21]

Though they may work in predominantly White settings, adults
in this stage choose to spend as much of their nonwork time as possible in the company of other Black people.

Individuals who have achieved an internalized racial identity also
usually embrace a race-conscious perspective on childrearing, but
they may also have a multiracial social network. Yet, anchored in an
empowered sense of racial identity, they make clear to others that
their racial identity is important to them, and that they expect it to be
acknowledged. The White person who makes the mistake of saying,
"Gee, I don't think of you as Black" will undoubtedly be corrected.
However, the inner security experienced by adults at this stage often
translates into a style of interaction that is perceived by Whites as less
threatening than that of adults in the immersion/emersion stage.

Some of the recycling that occurs in midlife is precipitated by
observing the racial identity processes of one's children. Parham suggests that "parents may begin to interpret the consequences of their
lifestyle choices (i.e., sending their children to predominantly White
schools, living in predominantly White neighborhoods) through their
children's attitudes and behaviors and become distressed at what they
see and hear from [them]."[22] For example, a Black professor struggling
with guilt over his choice to live in a predominantly White community suggested to his daughter that she should have more Black
friends. She replied, "Why do I have to have Black friends? Just
because I'm Black?" He admitted to himself that he was more concerned about her peer group than she was. When he told her that she
could "pay a price" for having a White social life, she replied, "Well,
Daddy, as you always like to say, nothing is free."[23]

The process of re-examining racial identity can continue even into late adulthood. According to Erikson, the challenge of one's later years is to be able to reflect on one's life with a sense of integrity rather than despair.[24] Although racism continues to impact the lives of the elderly—affecting access to quality health care and adequate pension funds, for example—Black retirees have fairly high levels of morale.[25] Those who approach the end of their lives with a positive, well-internalized sense of racial identity are likely to reflect on life with that sense of integrity intact.

Just as racial identity unfolds over the life span, so do gender, sexual, and religious identities, to name a few. Cross reminds us that "the work of Internalization does not stop with the resolution of conflicts surrounding racial/cultural identity." Referring to the work of his colleague Bailey Jackson, he adds that racial identity development should be viewed as "a process during which a single dimension of a person's complex, layered identity is first isolated, for purposes of revitalization and transformation, and then, at Internalization, reintegrated into the person's total identity matrix."[26] Unraveling and reweaving the identity strands of our experience is a neverending task in a society where important dimensions of our lives are shaped by the simultaneous forces of subordination and domination. We continue to be works in progress for a lifetime.

The Corporate Cafeteria

When I told my sister I was writing a book called *"Why Are All the Black Kids Sitting Together in the Cafeteria?"* she said, "Good, then maybe people will stop asking me about it." My sister spends her time not at a high school or college campus but in a corporate office. Even in corporate cafeterias, Black men and women are sitting together, and for the same reason. As we have seen, even mature adults sometimes need to connect with someone who looks like them and who shares the same experiences.

It might be worth considering here why the question is asked at all. In *A Tale of O,* psychologist Rosabeth Moss Kanter offers some insight. She highlights what happens to the *O,* the token, in a world of *X*s.[27] In corporate America, Black people are still in the *O* position. One consequence of being an *O,* Kanter points out, is heightened visibility. When an *O* walks in the room, the *X*s notice. Whatever the *O* does, positive or negative, stands out because of this increased visibility. It is hard for an *O* to blend in. When several *O*s are together, the attention of the *X*s is really captured. Without the tokens present in the room, the *X*s go about their business, perhaps not even noticing that they are all *X*s. But when the *O* walks in, the *X*s are suddenly self-conscious about their *X*-ness. In the context of race relations, when the Black people are sitting together, the White people notice and become self-conscious about being White in a way that they were not before. In part the question reflects that self-consciousness. What does it say about the White people if the Black people are all sitting together? The White person wonders, "Am *I* being excluded? Are they talking about us? Are my own racial stereotypes and perhaps racial fears being stimulated?"

Particularly in work settings, where people of color are isolated and often in the extreme minority, the opportunity to connect with peers of color are few and far between. White people are often unaware of how stressful such a situation can be. There are many situations where White people say and do things that are upsetting to people of color. For example, a Black woman working in a school system where she was one of few Black teachers—and the only one in her building—was often distressed by the comments she heard her White colleagues making about Black students. As a novice, untenured teacher, she needed support and mentoring from her colleagues but felt alienated from them because of their casually expressed prejudices. When participating in a workshop for educators, she had the chance to talk in a small group made up entirely of Black educators and was able to vent her feelings and ask for help from her more experienced colleagues about how to cope with this situation. Though such opportunities may not occur daily, as in a cafeteria, they are important for psychological survival in such situations.

In fact, some organizations are creating opportunities for these meetings to take place, providing time, space, and refreshments for people of color to get together for networking and support. They find that such activity supports the recruitment, retention, and heightened productivity of their employees. Like the SET program, it is an institutional affirmation of the unique challenges facing employees of color.

A few years ago I was invited to give a speech at the annual meeting of a national organization committed to social justice. All the managers from around the country were there. Just before I was introduced, a Black man made an announcement that there would be a breakfast meeting the next day for all interested people of color in the organization. Though this national organization had a long history, this was the first time that the people of color were going to have a "caucus" meeting. Following the announcement, I was introduced and I gave my talk entitled, "Interrupting the Cycle of Oppression." After a warm round of applause, I asked if there were any questions. Immediately a visibly agitated White woman stood up, and asked, "How would you feel if just before you began speaking a White person had stood up and said there would be a breakfast meeting of all the White people tomorrow?" I replied, "I would say it was a good idea." What I meant by my response is the subject of the next chapter.

Part III

Understanding Whiteness in a White Context

6

The Development of White Identity

"I'm not ethnic, I'm just normal"*

I often begin the classes and workshops I lead by asking participants to reflect on their own social class and ethnic background in small discussion groups. The first question I pose is one that most people of color answer without hesitation: "What is your class and ethnic background?" White participants, however, often pause before responding. On one such occasion a young White woman quickly described herself as middle-class but seemed stumped as to how to describe herself ethnically. Finally, she said, "I'm just normal!" What did she mean? She explained that she did not identify with any particular ethnic heritage, and that she was a lot like the other people who lived in her very homogeneous White middle-class community. But her choice of words was telling. If she is just normal, are those who are different from her "just abnormal"?

Like many White people, this young woman had never really considered her own racial and ethnic group membership. For her, Whiteness was simply the unexamined norm. Because they represent the societal norm, Whites can easily reach adulthood without thinking much about their racial group. For example, one White teacher who was taking a professional development course on racism with me

* Portions of this chapter are taken from two previously published articles: B. D. Tatum, "Teaching White students about racism: The search for White allies and the restoration of hope," *Teachers College Record* 95, no. 4 (1994): 462–76; and B. D. Tatum, "Talking about race, learning about racism: The application of racial identity development theory in the classroom," *Harvard Educational Review* 62, no. 1 (1992): 1–24.

wrote in one of her papers: "I am thirty-five years old and I never really started thinking about race too much until now, and that makes me feel uncomfortable. . . . I just think for some reason I didn't know. No one taught us."[1] There is a lot of silence about race in White communities, and as a consequence Whites tend to think of racial identity as something that other people have, not something that is salient for them. But when, for whatever reason, the silence is broken, a process of racial identity development for Whites begins to unfold.

Counseling psychologist Janet Helms has described this process of development for Whites in her book *Black and White Racial Identity Development: Theory, Research, and Practice.*[2] She assumes, as do I, that in a race-conscious society, racial group membership has psychological implications. The messages we receive about assumed superiority or inferiority shape our perceptions of reality and influence our interactions with others. While the task for people of color is to resist negative societal messages and develop an empowered sense of self in the face of a racist society, Helms says the task for Whites is to develop a positive White identity based in reality, not on assumed superiority. In order to do that each person must become aware of his or her Whiteness, accept it as personally and socially significant, and learn to feel good about it, not in the sense of a Klan member's "White pride," but in the context of a commitment to a just society.

It comes as a surprise to some White people to think about their race in this way. "Of course White people feel good about being White," they say. But that is not my experience with my students or with the people who come to my workshops. Most of the White people I talk to either have not thought about their race and so don't feel anything, or have thought about it and felt guilt and shame. These feelings of guilt and shame are part of the hidden costs of racism.[3]

How can White people achieve a healthy sense of White identity? Helms's model is instructive.[4] For Whites, there are two major developmental tasks in this process, the abandonment of individual racism and the recognition of and opposition to institutional and cultural racism. These tasks occur over six stages: *contact, disintegration, reintegration, pseudo-independent, immersion/emersion,* and *autonomy.*[5]

Abandoning Racism

At the contact stage, the first step in the process, Whites pay little attention to the significance of their racial identity. As exemplified by the "I'm just normal" comment, individuals at this point of development rarely describe themselves as White. If they have lived, worked, or gone to school in predominantly White settings, they may simply think of themselves as being part of the racial norm and take this for granted without conscious consideration of their White privilege, the systematically conferred advantages they receive simply because they are White.

While they have been breathing the "smog" and have internalized many of the prevailing societal stereotypes of people of color, they typically are unaware of this socialization process. They often perceive themselves as color-blind, completely free of prejudice, unaware of their own assumptions about other racial groups. In addition, they usually think of racism as the prejudiced behaviors of individuals rather than as an institutionalized system of advantage benefiting Whites in subtle as well as blatant ways. Peggy McIntosh speaks for many Whites at the contact level when she writes, "I was taught to recognize racism only in individual acts of meanness by members of my group, never in invisible systems conferring unsought racial dominance on my group from birth."[6]

While some Whites may grow up in families where they are encouraged to embrace the ideology of White superiority (children of Klan members, for example), for many Whites this early stage of racial identity development represents the passive absorption of subtly communicated messages. Robert Carter, another racial identity researcher, illustrates this point when he quotes a forty-four-year-old White male who grew up in upstate New York, where he had limited direct contact with Blacks.

There was no one to compare ourselves to. As you would drive through other neighborhoods, I think there was a clear message of difference or even superiority. The neighborhoods were poorer, and it was probably subtle, I don't remember my parents being bigoted, although by today's standards they clearly were. I think there was probably a message of superiority. The underlying messages were subtle. No one ever came out and said, White people are this and Black people are like this. I think the underlying message is that White people are generally good and they're like us, us and them.[7]

These messages may go unchallenged and unexamined for a long time.

However, the next level, disintegration, is marked by a growing awareness of racism and White privilege as a result of personal encounters in which the social significance of race is made visible. For some White people, disintegration occurs when they develop a close friendship or a romantic relationship with a person of color. The White person then sees firsthand how racism can operate. For example, one female college student described her experiences shopping with a Puerto Rican roommate. She couldn't help noticing how her Latina friend was followed around in stores and was asked for more identification than Whites when writing checks. She also saw how her friend's Black boyfriend was frequently asked to show his college ID when he visited their residence hall, while young White men came and went without being questioned. For other White people, disintegration may result from seeing racist incidents such as the police beating of Rodney King or participating in an "unlearning racism" workshop. Certainly being in a classroom where the social consequences of racial group membership are explicitly discussed as part of the course content is likely to trigger the process.

Once the silence is broken, the cycle of racism becomes increasingly visible. For example, in my class I show a very powerful video,

Ethnic Notions,[8] on the dehumanizing images of African Americans in the popular culture from before the Civil War through the twentieth century. The video links the nineteenth-century caricatures of Black physical features, commonly published racial epithets, and the early cinematic portrayals of stupid but happy "darkies," menacing Black "savages," and heavyset, caretaking "mammies," to their updated forms in today's media. After seeing this film, students can't help but notice the pervasiveness of racial stereotyping on television each night. The same programs they used to find entertaining now offend them. They start to notice the racism in the everyday language of family and friends. For example, one White student reported that when she asked her roommate to get her a glass of water, the White roommate jokingly replied, "Do I look Black to you?" Although I had never heard of this expression, it was very familiar to the student. Yet, before then, she had never recognized the association of Blackness with servitude, and the assumed superiority of Whiteness being conveyed in the remark.

This new awareness is characterized by discomfort. The uncomfortable emotions of guilt, shame, and anger are often related to a new awareness of one's personal prejudices or the prejudices within one's family. The following excerpts from the journals of two White students illustrate this point:

> Today was the first class on racism. . . . Before today I didn't think I was exposed to any form of racism. Well, except for my father. He is about as prejudiced as they come.

> It really bothers me that stereotypes exist because it is from them that I originally became uninformed. My grandmother makes all kinds of decisions based on stereotypes—who to hire, who to help out. When I was growing up, the only Black people that I knew were adults [household help], but I admired them just as

much as any other adult. When I expressed these feelings to my parents, I was always told that the Black people that I knew were the exceptions and that the rest of
the race were different. I, too, was taught to be afraid.

Others' parents were silent on the subject of racism, simply
accepting the status quo.

Those whose parents were actively antiracist may feel less guilt,
but often still feel unprepared for addressing racism outside the family, a point highlighted by the comments of this young woman:

Talking with other class members, I realized how
exceptional my parents were. Not only were they not
overtly racist but they also tried to keep society's subtle
racism from reaching me. Basically I grew up believing
that racism was no longer an issue and all people should
be treated as equals. Unfortunately, my parents were not
being very realistic as society's racism did begin to reach
me. They did not teach me how to support and defend
their views once I was interacting in a society without
them as a buffer.

At the disintegration stage, White individuals begin to see how
much their lives and the lives of people of color have been affected
by racism in our society. The societal inequities they now notice
directly contradict the idea of an American meritocracy, a concept
that has typically been an integral part of their belief system. The cognitive dissonance that results is part of the discomfort which is experienced at this point in the process of development. Responses to this
discomfort may include denying the validity of the information that
is being presented, or psychologically or physically withdrawing from
it. The logic is, "If I don't read about racism, talk about racism, watch
those documentaries or special news programs, or spend time with
those people of color, I won't have to feel uncomfortable." (In the case

of my students, this is usually not an option. By the time they have to deal with these emotional responses, it is too late to drop the course.)

If the individual remains engaged, he or she can turn the discomfort into action. Once they have an awareness of the cycle of racism, many people are angered by it and want to interrupt it. Often action comes in the form of educating others—pointing out the stereotypes as they watch television, interrupting the racial jokes, writing letters to the editor, sharing articles with friends and family. Like new converts, people experiencing disintegration can be quite zealous in their efforts. A White woman in her forties who participated in an antiracist professional development course for educators described herself at this stage:

> What it was like for me when I was taking the course [one year ago] and just afterwards, hell, because this dissonance stuff doesn't feel all that great. And trying to put it in a perspective and figure out what to do with it is very hard. . . . I was on the band wagon so I'm not going to be quiet about it. So there was dissonance everywhere. Personally, I remember going home for Thanksgiving, the first Thanksgiving [while taking the course], back to our families . . . and turning to my brother-in-law and saying, "I really don't want you to say that in front of me—I don't want to hear that joke—I am not interested." . . . At every turn it seemed like there, I was *responsible* for saying something. . . . My husband, who I think is a very good, a very liberal person, but who really hasn't been through [this], saying, "You know I think you're taking yourself too seriously here and where is your sense of humor? You have lost your sense of humor." And my saying, "It isn't funny; you don't understand, it just isn't funny to me." Not that he would ever tell a racial joke, but there were these things that would come up and he would just sort of

> look back and say, "I don't understand where you're
> coming from now." So there was a lot of dissonance. . . .
> I don't think anybody was too comfortable with me for
> a while.[9]

My college students have similar experiences with family members and friends. Though they want to step off the cycle of racism, the message from the surrounding White community seems to be, "Get back on!" A very poignant example of this was shared with me by a young White man from a very privileged background. He wrote:

> I realized that it was possible to simply go through life
> totally oblivious to the entire situation or, even if one
> realizes it, one can totally repress it. It is easy to fade
> into the woodwork, run with the rest of society, and
> never have to deal with these problems. So many people I know from home are like this. They have simply
> accepted what society has taught them with little, if any,
> question. My father is a prime example of this. . . . It
> has caused much friction in our relationship, and he
> often tells me as a father he has failed in raising me correctly. Most of my high school friends will never deal
> with these issues and propagate them on to their own
> children. It's easy to see how the cycle continues. I don't
> think I could ever justify within myself simply turning
> my back on the problem. I finally realized that my position in all of these dominant groups gives me power to
> make change occur. . . . It is an unfortunate result often
> though that I feel alienated from friends and family. It's
> often played off as a mere stage that I'm going through.
> I obviously can't tell if it's merely a stage, but I know
> that they say this to take the attention off of the truth
> of what I'm saying. By belittling me, they take the
> power out of my argument. It's very depressing that

being compassionate and considerate are seen as only
phases that people go through. I don't want it to be a
phase for me, but as obvious as this may sound, I look at
my environment and often wonder how it will not be.

The social pressure from friends and acquaintances to collude, to
not notice racism, can be quite powerful.

But it is very difficult to stop noticing something once it has been
pointed out. The conflict between noticing and not noticing generates internal tension, and there is a great desire to relieve it. Relief
often comes through what Helms calls reintegration. At this stage, the
previous feelings of guilt or denial may be transformed into fear and
anger directed toward people of color. The logic is, "If there is a problem with racism, then you people of color must have done something
to cause it. And if you would just change your behavior, the problem
would go away." The elegance of this argument is that it relieves the
White person of all responsibility for social change.

I am sometimes asked if it is absolutely necessary to go through
this phase. Must one blame the victim? Although it is not inevitable,
most White people who speak up against racism will attest to the
temptation they sometimes feel to slip back into collusion and silence.
Because the pressure to ignore racism and to accept the socially sanctioned stereotypes is so strong, and the system of advantage so seductive, many White people get stuck in reintegration thinking. The psychological tension experienced at this stage is clearly expressed by
Connie, a White woman of Italian ancestry who took my course on
the psychology of racism. After reading about the stages of White
identity development, she wrote:

There was a time when I never considered myself a
color. I never described myself as a "White, Italian
female" until I got to college and noticed that people of
color always described themselves by their color/race.
While taking this class, I have begun to understand that

being White makes a difference. I never thought about it before, but there are many privileges to being White. In my personal life, I cannot say that I have ever felt that I have had the advantage over a Black person, but I am aware that my race has the advantage.

I am feeling really guilty lately about that. I find myself thinking: "I didn't mean to be White, I really didn't mean it." I am starting to feel angry toward my race for ever using this advantage toward personal gains. But at the same time I resent the minority groups. I mean, it's not my fault that society has deemed us "superior." I don't feel any better than a Black person. But it really doesn't matter because I am a member of the dominant race. . . . I can't help it . . . and I sometimes get angry and feel like I'm being attacked.

I guess my anger toward a minority group would enter me into the next stage of Reintegration where I am once again starting to blame the victim. This is all very trying for me and it has been on my mind a lot. I really would like to be able to reach the last stage . . . where I can accept being White without hostility and anger. That is really hard to do.

"But I'm an Individual!"

Another source of the discomfort and anger that Whites often experience in this phase stems from the frustration of being seen as a group member, rather than as an individual. People of color learn early in life that they are seen by others as members of a group. For Whites, thinking of oneself only as an individual is a legacy of White privilege. As McIntosh writes, "I can swear, or dress in second hand clothes, or not answer letters, without having people attribute these choices to the bad morals, the poverty, or the illiteracy of my race. . . .

I can do well in a challenging situation without being called a credit to my race. . . . I am never asked to speak for all the people of my racial group."[10] In short, she and other Whites are perceived as individuals most of the time.

The view of oneself as an individual is very compatible with the dominant ideology of rugged individualism and the American myth of meritocracy. Understanding racism as a system of advantage that structurally benefits Whites and disadvantages people of color on the basis of group membership threatens not only beliefs about society but also beliefs about one's own life accomplishments. For example, organizational consultant Nancie Zane writes that senior White male managers "were clearly invested in the notion that their hard work, ingenuity and skills had won them their senior-level positions." As others talked about the systemic racist and sexist barriers to their own achievement, "white men heard it as a condemnation that they somehow didn't 'deserve' their position."[11] If viewing oneself as a group member threatens one's self-definition, making the paradigm shift from individual to group member will be painful.

In the case of White men, both maleness and Whiteness are normative, so acknowledging group status may be particularly difficult. Those White women who have explored their subordinate gender identity have made at least some movement away from the notion of a strictly individual self-definition and may find it easier to grasp the significance of their racial group membership. However, as McIntosh and others have pointed out, understanding one form of oppression does not guarantee recognition of another.

Those Whites who are highly identified with a particular subordinate identity may also struggle with claiming Whiteness as a meaningful group category because they feel far from the White male norm. For example, Jewish people of European ancestry sometimes do not think of themselves as White because for them the term means White Christian.[12] Also, in Nazi Germany, Jews were defined as a distinct, non-Aryan racial group. In the context of an anti-Jewish culture, the salient identity may be the targeted Jewish identity. However, in terms of U.S. racial ideology, Jews of European ancestry are also the beneficiaries of White racial privilege. My White Jewish students often struggle with the tension between being targeted and receiving privilege. In this case, as in others, the reality of multiple identities complicates the process of coming to terms with one particular dimension of identity. For example, one student wrote:

> I am constantly afraid that people will see my assertion
> of my Jewish identity as a denial of whiteness, as a way
> of escaping the acknowledgment of white privilege. I
> feel I am both part of and not part of whiteness. I am
> struggling to be more aware of my white privilege . . .
> but I will not do so at the cost of having my Jewishness
> erased.

Similarly, White lesbians sometimes find it hard to claim privileged status as Whites when they are so targeted by homophobia and heterosexism, often at the hands of other Whites.

These complexities notwithstanding, when White men and women begin to understand that they are viewed as members of a dominant racial group not only by other Whites but also by people of color, they are sometimes troubled, even angered, to learn that simply because of their group status they are viewed with suspicion by many people of color. "I'm an individual, view me as an individual!" For example, in a racially mixed group of educators participating in an antiracist professional development course, a Black man commented about using his "radar" to determine if the group would be a safe place for him. Many of the White people in the room, who believed that their very presence in the course was proof of their trustworthiness, were upset by the comment, initially unprepared to acknowledge the invisible legacy of racism that accompanied any and every interaction they had with people of color.[13] The White people in the course found some comfort in reading Lois Stalvey's memoir, *The*

Education of a WASP, in which she described her own responses to the ways Black people tested her trustworthiness. She writes,

> I could never resent the tests as some white people have told me they do. . . . But to me, the longest tests have always indicated the deepest hurts. We whites would have to be naive to expect that hundreds of years of humiliation can be forgotten the moment we wish it to be. At times, the most poignant part of the test is that black people have enough trust left to give it. Testing implies we might pass the test. It is safer and easier for a black person to turn his back on us. If he does not gamble on our sincerity, he cannot be hurt if we prove false. Testing shows an optimism I doubt I could duplicate if I were black.[14]

Sometimes poorly organized antiracism workshops or other educational experiences can create a scenario that places participants at risk for getting stuck in their anger. Effective consciousness-raising about racism must also point the way toward constructive action. When people don't have the tools for moving forward, they tend to return to what is familiar, often becoming more vigorous in their defense of the racial status quo than they were initially.

As we have seen, many White people experience themselves as powerless, even in the face of privilege. But the fact is that we all have a sphere of influence, some domain in which we exercise some level of power and control. The task for each of us, White and of color, is to identify what our own sphere of influence is (however large or small) and to consider how it might be used to interrupt the cycle of racism.

Defining a Positive White Identity

As a White person's understanding of the complexity of institutional racism in our society deepens, the less likely he or she is to resort to explanations that blame the victim. Instead, deepening awareness usually leads to a commitment to unlearn one's racism, and marks the emergence of the pseudo-independent stage.

Sometimes epitomized by the "guilty White liberal" persona, the pseudo-independent individual has an intellectual understanding of racism as a system of advantage, but doesn't quite know what to do about it. Self-conscious and guilty about one's own Whiteness, the individual often desires to escape it by associating with people of color. Ruth Frankenberg, author of *White Women, Race Matters: The Social Construction of Whiteness*,[15] describes the confusing emotions of this process in an autobiographical essay. "I viewed my racial privilege as total. I remember months when I was terrified to speak in gatherings that were primarily of color, since I feared that anything I did say would be marked by my whiteness, my racial privilege (which in my mind meant the same)."[16] When her friends of color were making casual conversation—chatting about their mothers, for example—she would worry that anything she might say about her own mother would somehow reveal her race privilege, and by the time she had sorted it out mentally, the topic of conversation would have changed. She writes, "In that silence, I tried to 'pass' (as what? as racially unmarked? as exceptional? as the one white girl who could 'hang'?)."[17]

Similarly, a student of mine writes:

> One of the major and probably most difficult steps in identity development is obtaining or finding the consciousness of what it means to be White. I definitely remember many a time that I wished I was not White, ashamed of what I and others have done to the other racial groups in the world. . . . I wanted to pretend I was Black, live with them, celebrate their culture, and deny my Whiteness completely. Basically, I wanted to escape the responsibility that came with identifying myself as "White."

How successful these efforts to escape Whiteness via people of color will be depends in part on the racial identity development of the people of color involved. Remember the Black students at the cafeteria table? If they are in the encounter or immersion/emersion stages, they are not likely to be interested in cultivating White friendships. If a White person reaches out to a Black person and is rebuffed, it may cause the White person to retreat into "blame the victim" thinking. However, even if these efforts to build interracial relationships are successful, the White individual must eventually confront the reality of his or her own Whiteness.

We all must be able to embrace who we are in terms of our racial and cultural heritage, not in terms of assumed superiority or inferiority, but as an integral part of our daily experience in which we can take pride. But, as we see in these examples, for many White people who at this stage have come to understand the everyday reality of racism, Whiteness is still experienced as a source of shame rather than as a source of pride.

Recognizing the need to find a more positive self-definition is a hallmark of the next phase of White racial identity development, the immersion/emersion stage. Bob, a White male student in my racism class, clearly articulated this need.

> I'm finding that this idea of White identity is more important than I thought. Yet White identity seems very hard to pin hole. I seem to have an idea and feel myself understanding what I need to do and why and then something presents itself that throws me into mass confusion. I feel that I need some resources that will help me through the process of finding White identity.

The resource Bob needs most at this point are not people of color, but other Whites who are further along in the process and can help show him the way.

It is at just this point that White individuals intensify their efforts to see their Whiteness in a positive light. Just as Cross describes the period of Black redefinition as a time for Black people to seek new ways of thinking about Blackness, ways that take them beyond the role of victim, White people must seek new ways of thinking about Whiteness, ways that take them beyond the role of victimizer.

The Search for White Allies and the Restoration of Hope

In fact, another role does exist. There is a history of White protest against racism, a history of Whites who have resisted the role of oppressor and who have been allies to people of color. Unfortunately these Whites are often invisible to us. While the names of active racists are easily recalled—past and present Klan leaders and Southern segregationists, for example—the names of White allies are often unknown. I have had the experience of addressing roomfuls of classroom teachers who have been unable to name even one White person who has worked against racism without some prompting from me. If they can't do it, it is likely that their students can't either.

Those who have studied or lived through the Civil Rights era (many of my students have not) may know the names of Viola Liuzzo, James Reeb, or Michael Schwerner, White civil rights workers who were killed for their antiracist efforts. But most people don't want to be martyrs. There is a need to know about White allies who spoke up, who worked for social change, who resisted racism and lived to tell about it. How did these White allies break free from the confines of the racist socialization they surely experienced to claim this identity for themselves? These are the voices that many White people at this stage in the process are hungry to hear.

Biographies of or autobiographies by White individuals who have been engaged in antiracist activities can be very helpful. For example, there is *A Season of Justice,* the autobiography of Morris Dees, the executive director of the Southern Poverty Law Center and a vigorous anti-Klan litigator.[18] There is *Outside the Magic Circle,* the oral history of Virginia Foster Durr, a Southern belle turned civil rights activist.[19] And there is *The Education of a WASP,* the story of Lois Stalvey, a mother struggling to create a nonracist environment for her children.[20] Such books can be an antidote to the feelings of isolation and loneliness that White people often feel at this point. There is comfort in knowing that others have traveled this terrain.

One of the consequences of racism in our society is that those who oppose racism are often marginalized, and as a result, their stories are not readily accessed. Yet having access to these stories makes a difference to those Whites who are looking for ways to be agents of change. White people who are doing this work need to make their stories known to serve as guides for others.

In my class I try to address the lack of knowledge of White role models by providing concrete examples of such people. In addition to assigning reading material, my strategy has been to invite a local White antiracist activist, Andrea Ayvazian, to my class to speak about her own personal journey toward an awareness of racism and her development as a White ally. Students typically ask questions that reflect their fears about social isolation at this phase of development. "Did you lose friends when you started to speak up?" "My boyfriend makes a lot of racist comments. What can I do?" "What do you say to your father at Thanksgiving when he tells those jokes?" These are not just the questions of late adolescents. The mature White teachers I work with ask the same things.

My White students, who often comment about how depressing it is to study racism, typically say that the opportunity to talk with this ally gave them renewed hope. Through her example, they see that the role of the ally is not to help victims of racism, but to speak up against systems of oppression and to challenge other Whites to do the same. One point that Andrea emphasizes in her speaking and writing is the idea that "allies need allies," others who will support their efforts to swim against the tide of cultural and institutional racism.[21] This point was especially helpful for one young woman who had been struggling with feelings of isolation. She wrote:

About being an ally, a positive role model: . . . it enhanced my positive feelings about the difference each individual (me!) can make. I don't need to feel helpless when there is so much I can do. I still can see how easily things can back-up and start getting depressing, but I can also see how it is possible to keep going strong and powerful. One of the most important points she made was the necessity of a support group/system; people to remind me of what I have done, why I should keep going, of why I'm making a difference, why I shouldn't feel helpless. I think our class started to help me with those issues, as soon as I started to let it, and now I've found similar supports in friends and family. They're out there, it's just finding and establishing them—it really is a necessity. Without support, it would be too easy to give up, burn-out, become helpless again. In any endeavor support is important, but when the forces against you are so prevalent and deep-rooted as racism is in this society, it is the only way to keep moving forward.

Participation in White consciousness-raising groups organized specifically for the purpose of examining one's own racism are another way to "keep moving forward." At Mount Holyoke College such a group, White Women Against Racism, was formed following the 1992 acquittal of the Los Angeles police officers involved in the beating of Rodney King. There are similar groups with different names operating formally and informally in local communities around the country.[22] Support groups of this nature help to combat the social isolation that antiracist Whites often experience, and provide places to forge new identities.

I am sometimes asked why such groups need to be made up of Whites only. To many Whites it seems inconceivable that there would be any value in participating in all-White discussions of racism. While of course there is value in cross-racial dialogue, all-White support groups serve a unique function. Particularly when Whites are trying to work through their feelings of guilt and shame, separate groups give White people the "space to speak with honesty and candor rarely possible in racially-mixed groups."[23] Even when Whites feel comfortable sharing these feelings with people of color, frankly, people of color don't necessarily want to hear about it. The following comment, written by a Black woman in my class, illustrates this dilemma:

> Many times in class I feel uncomfortable when White students use the term Black because even if they aren't aware of it they say it with all or at least a lot of the negative connotations they've been taught goes along with Black. Sometimes it just causes a stinging feeling inside of me. Sometimes I get real tired of hearing White people talk about the conditions of Black people. I think it's an important thing for them to talk about, but still I don't always like being around when they do it. I also get tired of hearing them talk about how hard it is for them, though I understand it, and most times I am very willing to listen and be open, but sometimes I can't. Right now I can't.

Though a White person may need to describe the racist things a parent or spouse has said or done, to tell the story to a person of color may reopen that person's wounds. Listening to those stories and problem-solving about them is a job that White people can do for each other.

It is at this stage of redefining Whiteness, immersion/emersion, that the feelings of guilt and shame start to fade. Reflecting on her own White identity development, sociologist Becky Thompson chronicles this process:

> [I understood] that I didn't have to recreate the wheel
> in my own life. I began to actively seek writing by
> white women who have historically stood up against
> racism—Elly Bulkin, Lillian Smith, Sara Evans, Angelina
> Grimke, Ruth Frankenberg, Helen Joseph, Melanie
> Kaye/Kantrowitz, Tillie Olsen, Minnie Bruce Pratt,
> Ruth Seid, Mab Segrest, and others.[24]

She also realized that she needed antiracist White people in her daily life with whom she could share stories and whom she could trust to give her honest feedback. Her experience in a White antiracism group helped her to stop feeling bad because she was White. She writes, "I started seeing ways to channel my energies without trying to leave a piece of my identity behind."

The last stage, autonomy, represents the culmination of the White racial developmental process. At this point, a person incorporates the newly defined view of Whiteness as part of a personal identity. The positive feelings associated with this redefinition energize the person's efforts to confront racism and oppression in daily life. Clayton Alderfer, a White man with many years of personal and professional experience, describes the thinking that characterizes this stage. "We have a more complete awareness of ourselves and of others to the degree that we neither negate the uniqueness of each person, regardless of that person's group memberships, nor deny the ever-present effects of group memberships for each individual."[25]

While autonomy might be described as racial self-actualization, racial identity development never really ends. The person at this level is continually open to new information and new ways of thinking about racial and cultural variables.[26] Helms describes each of the six stages as representing patterns of thinking that predominate at particular points of development. But even when active antiracist thinking predominates, there may still be particular situations that trigger old modes of responding. Whites, like people of color, continue to be works in progress.

A major benefit of this racial identity development process is increased effectiveness in multiracial settings. The White person who has worked through his or her own racial identity process has a deep understanding of racism and an appreciation and respect for the identity struggles of people of color. When we see strong, mutually respectful relationships between people of color and Whites, we are usually looking at the tangible results of both people's identity processes. If we want to promote positive cross-group relations, we need to help young White people engage in the kind of dialogue that precipitates this kind of identity development just as we need to help youth of color achieve an empowered sense of racial and ethnic identity.

Though the process of examining their racial identity can be uncomfortable and even frightening for Whites, those who persist in the struggle are rewarded with an increasingly multiracial and multicultural existence. In our still quite segregated society, this "borderland" is unfamiliar to many Whites and may be hard to envision. Becky Thompson has experienced it, and she writes: "We need to talk about what living in this borderland feels like, how we get there, what sustains us, and how we benefit from it. For me, this place of existence is tremendously exciting, invigorating, and life-affirming."[27] Though it can also be "complicated and lonely," it is also liberating, opening doors to new communities, creating possibilities for more authentic connections with people of color, and in the process, strengthening the coalitions necessary for genuine social change.

7

White Identity and Affirmative Action
"I'm in favor of affirmative action except when it comes to my jobs."

Because of the persistence of residential segregation and the school segregation that often accompanies it, the workplace is one of the few places that the lives of people of color and Whites regularly intersect. Those intersections can sometimes lead to close friendships and serve as a catalyst for Whites to begin to examine their own racial identities. But even when the workplace is only a site of superficial exchanges across color lines, the presence of an affirmative action policy can be enough to draw an individual's attention to his own Whiteness. What will affirmative action mean in my life? Will I get the job I want, or will it go to some "minority"? Will the opportunities I expected still be there for me, or will I be the victim of "reverse racism"?

Even those Whites who have not given much thought to their racial identity have thought about affirmative action. As sociologist Howard Winant writes, assaults on affirmative action policies are "currently at hysterical levels. . . . These attacks are clearly designed to effect ideological shifts, rather than to shift resources in any meaningful way. They represent whiteness as *disadvantage,* something which has few precedents in U.S. racial history." Though there is almost no empirical evidence for this "imaginary white disadvantage," the idea has achieved "widespread popular credence."[1]

In my classes and workshops, the concern about White disadvantage takes the form of questions about affirmative action and "reverse discrimination." Inevitably someone has a story to tell about a friend or relative who was not admitted to the school of her choice, or a parent who lost a coveted promotion because a "less-qualified" person of color took that spot. It is interesting to note that the "less-qualified" person in the story is always a person of color, usually Black, never a White woman.[2] (When these stories are told, I often wonder how the speaker knows so much about the person of color's résumé.)

Whenever possible, I defer the discussion of affirmative action, at least until a basic understanding of racism as a system of advantage has been established. I do this because it is very difficult to have a useful discussion about affirmative action with a person who does not understand the concept of White privilege. If someone uses the phrases "affirmative action" and "reverse racism" in the same sentence, it is usually a sign that a lesson on White privilege is needed. This is not to say that everyone who understands White privilege supports affirmative action policies, but at least that basic understanding assures that all parties in the conversation recognize that there are systematic social inequities operating in our society, and that the playing field is not level. We may have different opinions about how to fix those inequities, but an acknowledgment of the inequities is essential to a productive conversation.

After assigning several readings on the topic of affirmative action, I ask my students to write essays about whether they think it is a good idea and why. If they are opposed to affirmative action, I ask them to propose an alternative approach to dismantling the system of advantage in the arenas of educational and employment opportunity. Several years ago, one young White woman wrote the following sentence in her essay: "I am in favor of affirmative action except when it comes to my jobs." I wrote in response, "Which jobs have your name on them?"

The sense of entitlement conveyed in the statement was striking. Of course, she wanted to get the jobs she applied for, and did not want to lose out to anyone, especially on the basis of race, a factor over which she had no control. Yet she seemed to assume that because she wanted them, they belonged to her. She assumed that she would, of course, be qualified for the job, and would therefore be entitled to it.

What was she assuming about the candidates of color? She did not seem to take into account the possibility that one of them might be as qualified, or more qualified, than she was. The idea that she as a White woman might herself be the recipient of affirmative action was apparently not part of her thinking. While she expressed a desire for equity and justice, she also wanted to maintain her own advantage. She was still sifting through some confused thinking on this issue. She is not alone.

What Is Affirmative Action?

There has been much public debate about affirmative action since its inception, with little attempt to clarify concepts. Politicians' interchangeable use of the terms *affirmative action* and *quotas* have contributed to the confusion, perhaps intentionally. The term *quota* has a repugnant history of discrimination and exclusion. For example, earlier in the twentieth century, quotas were used to limit how many Jews would be admitted to prestigious institutions of higher learning.

But despite common public perceptions, most affirmative action programs do not involve quotas, though they may involve goals. The difference between a goal and a quota is an important one. Quotas, defined here as fixed numerical allocations, are illegal, unless courtordered as a temporary remedy for a well-documented, proven pattern of racially-motivated discrimination. Unlike a quota, goals are voluntary, legal, and may even be exceeded. Goals are not a ceiling meant to limit (as quotas did in the past). Instead, goals provide a necessary target toward which to aim. As any long-range planner knows, goals are necessary in order to chart one's course of action, and to evaluate one's progress. Goals are an essential component of effective affirmative action programs.

The term *affirmative action* was introduced into our language and legal system by Executive Order 11246, signed by President Lyndon Johnson in 1965. This order obligated federal contractors to "take affirmative action to ensure that applicants are employed, and that employees are treated during employment without regard to their race, color, religion, sex, or national origin." As set forth by this order, contractors were to commit themselves to "apply every good faith effort" to use procedures that would result in equal employment opportunity for historically disadvantaged groups. The groups targeted for this "affirmative action" were White women, and men and women of color (specifically defined by the federal government as American Indian/Alaska Natives, Asian or Pacific Islanders, Blacks, and Hispanics). In the 1970s, legislation broadened the protected groups to include persons with disabilities and Vietnam veterans. Though Executive Order 11246 required affirmative action, it did not specify exactly what affirmative action programs should look like.[3]

Given this lack of specificity, it is not surprising that there is great variety in the way affirmative action programs have been developed and implemented around the country.[4] The executive order had as its goal equal employment opportunity. But in practice, because of continuing patterns of discrimination, that goal cannot be reached without positive steps—affirmative actions—to create that equality of opportunity. Consequently, affirmative action can be defined as attempts to make progress toward actual, rather than hypothetical, equality of opportunity for those groups which are currently underrepresented in significant positions in society by explicitly taking into account the defining characteristics—sex or race, for example—that have been the basis for discrimination.[5] These attempts can be categorized as either *process-oriented* or *goal-oriented*.

Process-oriented programs focus on creating a fair application process, assuming that a fair process will result in a fair outcome. If a job opening has been advertised widely, and anyone who is interested has a chance to apply, and all applicants receive similar treatment (i.e., standard interview questions, same evaluation criteria and procedures), the process is presumed to be fair. The search committee can freely choose the "best" candidate knowing that no discrimination has taken place. Under such circumstances, the "best" candidate will sometimes be a person of color, "too good to ignore."[6] In theory, such would seem to be the case, and because process-oriented programs seem consistent with the American ideal of the meritocracy, most people support this kind of affirmative action.[7] At the very least, it is an improvement over the "old boy network" that filled positions before outsiders even had a chance to apply.

Goal-oriented affirmative action also provides an open process. However, when the qualified pool of applicants has been identified, those among the pool who move the organization closer to its diversity hiring goals are favored. If the finalist hired was qualified but not the "best" choice in the eyes of those who don't share the goal, the decision is often criticized as "reverse discrimination."

Though the process-oriented emphasis is more palatable to some than the goal-oriented emphasis, in practice the process-oriented approach is often quite ineffective. Despite the attempts to insure a fair process, search committee after search committee finds the "best" person is yet another member of the dominant group. What goes wrong? Some answers may be found in the research of social psychologist John Dovidio and his colleagues.

Aversive Racism and Affirmative Action

In "Resistance to Affirmative Action: The Implications of Aversive Racism," John Dovidio, Jeffrey Mann, and Samuel Gaertner argue that White opposition to affirmative action programs is largely rooted in a subtle but pervasive form of racism they call "aversive racism." Aversive racism is defined as "an attitudinal adaptation resulting from an assimilation of an egalitarian value system with prejudice and with racist beliefs." In other words, most Americans have internalized the espoused cultural values of fairness and justice for all at the same time that they have been breathing the "smog" of racial biases and stereotypes pervading the popular culture. "The existence, both of almost unavoidable racial biases and of the desire to be egalitarian and racially tolerant, forms the basis of the ambivalence that aversive racists experience."[8]

Pointing to the findings of several impressive research studies, these social psychologists argue that because aversive racists see themselves as nonprejudiced and racially tolerant, they generally do not behave in overtly racist ways. When the norms for appropriate, nondiscriminatory behavior are clear and unambiguous, they "do the right thing," because to behave otherwise would threaten the nonprejudiced self-image they hold. However, Dovidio and his colleagues assert that in situations when it is not clear what the "right thing" is, or if an action can be justified on the basis of some factor other than race, negative feelings toward Blacks will surface. In these ambiguous situations, an aversive racist can discriminate against Blacks without threatening his racially tolerant self-image.

For example, in a study in which White college students were asked to evaluate Black and White people on a simple "good-bad" basis, where choosing *bad* rather than *good* to describe Blacks might clearly indicate bias, the students consistently rated both Blacks and Whites positively. However, when the task was changed slightly to rating Blacks and Whites on a more subtle continuum of goodness, Whites were consistently rated better than Blacks. For instance, when the rating choice was "ambitious–not lazy," Blacks were not rated as more lazy than Whites, but Whites were evaluated as more ambitious than Blacks. Repeated findings of this nature led these researchers to conclude that a subtle but important bias was operating. In the eyes of the aversive racists, Blacks are not worse, but Whites are better.

How might such a bias affect hiring decisions? Would this kind of bias affect how the competence of Black and White candidates might be evaluated? To explore this question, a study was conducted in which White college students were asked to rate college applicants who on the basis of transcript information were strongly qualified, moderately qualified, or weakly qualified. In some cases the applicant was identified as Black, in other cases as White. When the applicant was weakly qualified, there was no discrimination between Black and White applicants. Both were rejected. When the applicant had moderate qualifications, Whites were evaluated slightly better than Blacks, but not significantly so. However, when the applicant had strong qualifications, there was a significant difference between how strong White candidates and strong Black candidates were rated. Though the information that had been provided about the candidates was identical, the Black applicants were evaluated significantly less positively than the White applicants. The subtle bias that Dovidio and his colleagues have identified does not occur at all levels, but it occurs when you might least expect it, when the Black candidate is highly qualified. In this and other similar studies, Blacks could be seen as good, but Whites with the same credentials were consistently rated as better.[9]

The bias was even more apparent when the Black person being rated was in a position superior to the White evaluator. While high-ability White supervisors were accepted by subordinate White raters as being somewhat more intelligent than themselves, White evaluators consistently described high-ability Black supervisors as significantly less intelligent than themselves. So even when the Black supervisor is more competent than the White subordinate, the White again sees the situation as though a Black person less qualified than themselves is being given preferential treatment. The researchers speculate that the bias is accentuated in this scenario because the possibility of being subordinated to a Black person threatens deeply held (though perhaps unconscious) notions of White superiority.[10]

Social psychologists Susan Clayton and Sandra Tangri also discuss the illusory nature of "objective" evaluation, and offer another reason that the pattern of underestimating the abilities of competent Black candidates is so widespread. They suggest that when an evaluator expects a weak performance and sees a strong one, the strong performance is attributed to unstable causes such as luck or effort. Unlike "innate" ability, luck or effort can change and are therefore unreliable. However, strong performances based on ability will probably be repeated. Strong performances attributed to ability (the explanation likely used for White male candidates) are viewed more positively and more often rewarded than performances assumed to be based on luck or an unusual effort.[11]

Dovidio and colleagues conclude:

> The aversive racism framework has important and direct implication for the implementation of affirmative action–type policies. Affirmative action has often been interpreted as "when all things are equal, take the minority person." Our research suggests that even when things are equal, they may not be perceived as equal— particularly when the minority person is well-qualified and the situation has personal relevance to the non-minority person. Because Whites tend to misperceive the competence of Blacks relative to themselves, resistance to affirmative action may appear quite legitimate to the protesters. Insufficient competence, not race, becomes the rationale justifying resistance.[12]

The particular irony is that the more competent the Black person is, the more likely this bias is to occur.

The research that has been discussed here has been framed in terms of Black-White relationships.[13] Of course, affirmative action programs may also involve other people of color as well as White women.[14] Yet the Black-White emphasis in the aversive racism framework seems well placed when we consider that researchers have found that negative attitudes toward affirmative action are expressed most strongly when Blacks are identified as the target beneficiaries. As Audrey Murrell and her colleagues point out, "whereas giving preference based on nonmerit factors is perceived as unfair, giving such preference to Blacks is perceived as more unfair."[15]

Now we can see why affirmative action efforts focusing on the process rather than the outcome are likely to be ineffective. There are too many opportunities for evaluator bias to manifest itself—in the initial recruitment and screening of applicants, in the interview process, and ultimately in the final selection. Competent candidates of color are likely to be weeded out all along the way. Those that make it to the final selection process may in fact be "too good to ignore," but as the research suggests and as I have seen in some of my own search committee experiences, for Black candidates "too good to ignore" can mean too good to hire.

"Not a Prejudiced Bone in Their Bodies": A Case Example

During the first nine years of my teaching career, I taught on two different campuses. In each case, I was the only Black female faculty member throughout my tenure. Though both institutions identified themselves as "equal employment opportunity/affirmative action employers," my experience on search committees in those settings taught me a lot about why there weren't more Black women or many Black men on campus. Black applicants "too good to be ignored" regularly were ignored, sometimes because they were too good. "Can't hire him, he's too good, he won't stay." "She's good, but not exactly what we had in mind." "He gave a brilliant talk, but there's just something about him, I can't quite put my finger on it."

In at least one instance, I thought I could put my finger on it, and did. When I raised questions about racial bias, I was told by the chair of the search committee, "I've known all of these [White] people for years. There's not a prejudiced bone in their bodies." If you've read chapter 1, you know how I feel about that comment. In this particular instance, I replied, "You know, I don't think anyone on the committee would intentionally discriminate, but I know that people feel most comfortable with people like themselves, with the kind of people they've grown up around, that they play golf with. When interacting with someone who doesn't fit that description, there may be a kind of uneasiness that is hard to articulate. So when I sit in a committee meeting, and White people all agree that a Black candidate is well qualified for the position, better than the competing White candidates in fact, but then they say things like, 'I'm not sure if he's the right person for the job,' 'I'm not sure what kind of colleague he'd be, I just didn't feel comfortable with him,' I think we have a problem."

We did have a problem. In this case, rather than offer the Black candidate the position, it was declared a failed search and the position was advertised again the following year. I was not asked to serve on the next search committee, and perhaps not surprisingly, there were no Black candidates in the pool of finalists the second time around. Did the Black candidate recognize the discrimination that I believe occurred, or was it seen as just another rejected application? I don't know. But this case highlighted for me one of the reasons that affirmative action is still needed. As social psychologist Faye Crosby writes,

> Affirmative action is needed to lessen bias in the paid labor force because affirmative action is the only legal remedy in the United States for discrimination that does not require the victims (or someone with a stake in their welfare) to notice their condition and come forward with a grievance on their own behalf. . . . In affirmative action, designated individuals monitor the operations of institutions and so can notice (and correct) injustices in the absence of any complaint. This monitoring role is crucial because an accumulation of studies have shown that it is very difficult to detect discrimination on a case-by-case basis, even when the case involves the self.[16]

When we examine the aggregate data, case after case, hiring decision after hiring decision, the idiosyncracies of particular cases recede and the discriminatory pattern can emerge. Then we can make a change.

Keeping Our Eyes on the Prize: Goal-Oriented Affirmative Action

Though the research on evaluator bias is dismaying, it also points us in the direction of an effective response. Remember that when expectations for appropriate behavior are clearly defined and a biased response can be recognized, Whites are consistently as positive in their behavior toward Blacks as toward Whites. If administrators clearly articulate the organization's diversity goals and the reasons that such goals are in the organization's best interests, the appropriate behavior in the search process should be clear. If we keep our eyes on the prize, we can get past the bias.

Some might say, "Doesn't such an outcome-based focus lead to instances of 'reverse discrimination,' when well-qualified majority-group candidates are rejected in favor of a less qualified candidate from an underrepresented group simply because that candidate meets the diversity goal?" Certainly that could happen, but only in a poorly administered program. When affirmative action programs are functioning appropriately, no one is ever hired who is not qualified for the job. To do so undermines the program and is patently unfair to the newly hired person who has in effect been set up to fail.

In a well-conceived and implemented affirmative action program, the first thing that should be done is to establish clear and meaningful selection criteria. What skills does the person need to function effectively in this environment? How will we assess whether the candidates have these required skills? Will it be on the basis of demonstrated past performance, scores on an appropriate test,[17] the completion of certain educational requirements? Once the criteria have been established, anyone who meets the criteria is considered qualified.

Now we can consider who among these qualified candidates will best help us achieve our organizational goals for diversifying our institution. If one candidate meets the criteria but also has some additional education or experience, it may be tempting to say this candidate is the "best," but this one may not be the one who moves us toward our diversity goal. Because of the systematic advantages that members of the dominant group receive, it is often the case that the person with the extra experience or educational attainment is a person from the majority group. If our eyes are on our organizational goal, we are not distracted by these unasked-for extras. If we need someone who has toured Europe or had a special internship, it should already be part of our criteria. If it is not part of the criteria, it shouldn't be considered.

And if making our organization a more inclusive environment is a goal, then perhaps we should have that goal reflected in our criteria so that whoever is selected can support the organization's goals. Fletcher Blanchard, author of "Effective Affirmative Action Programs," suggests what some of these new criteria might be: the extent and favorability of one's experience working in multicultural settings, the experience of being supervised by managers of color, experience of collaborating in multicultural workgroups, or living in racially-mixed communities, fluency in a second language, or substantial college coursework in the study of multicultural perspectives.[18]

In my own consultation with school systems interested in increasing their faculty of color, we have discussed the need for such new criteria. The number of young people of color entering the teaching profession is still too small to meet the demand. While effective recruiting strategies can increase a school system's likelihood of being able to attract new teachers of color, many White teachers will still be needed to replace retiring teachers in the coming years. Schools concerned about meeting the needs of an increasingly diverse student population should be looking specifically for teachers of all backgrounds with demonstrated experience in working with multiracial populations, with courses on their transcripts like Psychology of Racism; Race, Class, Culture, and Gender in the Classroom; and Foundations of Multicultural Education, to name a few.

Criteria like these are important for all candidates, but they are also criteria which are more likely to be met by candidates of color, because people of color often have more life experience in multiracial settings than many White people do. However, because such criteria are not explicitly race-based, they are also criteria which should withstand the legal assaults that many affirmative action programs have experienced.[19] Should these legal challenges move us into a post–affirmative action age, such criteria will be increasingly important in the search and selection process. Under any circumstance, clarity about organizational goals and qualification criteria will lead to better and more equitable selection decisions.

White Disadvantage Revisited

When the dominant identity of Whiteness goes unexamined, racial privilege also goes unacknowledged. Instead, the achievements that unearned privilege make more attainable are seen as just reward for one's own efforts. The sense of entitlement that comes as the result of privileges given and received without notice goes unchallenged. When that sense of entitlement is threatened, it is most often experienced as an unfair personal penalty rather than as a necessary and impersonal leveling of an uneven field. An understanding of what affirmative action is and is not often changes the perception of White disadvantage, especially when coupled with an understanding of White privilege. For example, Stanley Fish, a White man who understands both privilege and past and present patterns of employment discrimination, explains clearly why he believes affirmative action policies are justified even when such policies cost him a job he wanted.

> Although I was disappointed, I did not conclude that the situation was "unfair," because the policy was obviously not directed at me . . . the policy was not intended to disenfranchise white males. Rather the policy was driven by other considerations, and it was only as a by-product of those considerations—not as the main goal—that white males like me were rejected. Given that the institution in question has a high percentage of minority students, a very low percentage of minority faculty, and an even lower percentage of minority administrators, it made perfect sense to focus on women and minority candidates, and within that

sense, not as the result of prejudice, my whiteness and maleness became disqualifications. I can hear the objection in advance: "What's the difference? Unfair is unfair: you didn't get the job." . . . It is the difference between an unfairness that befalls one as the unintended effect of a policy rationally conceived and an unfairness that is pursued as an end in itself.[20]

Are there reasons to resist such an understanding? Absolutely. Describing interviews with "angry White men" from working-class communities, Michele Fine reveals how these men, displaced from jobs by the flight of capital from their cities, blame their misfortune not on corporate greed but on African Americans. Explains Fine, Black people are psychologically "imported to buffer the pain, protest the loss, and still secure the artificial privilege of whiteness."[21] In a societal context where historically the scapegoating of the "other" has been standard operating procedure, it is easier to do that than critically examine the large structural conditions that have created this situation.

Speaking from her vantage point as a White female psychologist who has studied affirmative action for many years, Faye Crosby comments on this anger: "For those who study affirmative action, the attitudes of angry and frightened White males can provoke some impatience. But to end the impatience and become sympathetic with aspects of the resistance to affirmative action, I need only remember how privilege has blinded me, too."[22] Rather than dismissing with disdain those who suffer the illusion of "imaginary white disadvantage," she urges engagement in dialogue. For those who are fatigued by the effort, she offers a good reason to continue. "[M]y fervent support of affirmative action comes ultimately from being the mother of White boy-men. It is because I want a better world for my children that I bother to fight for affirmative action."[23]

All of us want a better, more peaceful world for our children. If we want peace, we must work for justice. How do we achieve a more just society in the present context of institutional and cultural racism? Goal-oriented affirmative action is but one potentially effective strategy. Serious dialogue about other strategies is needed, and that dialogue needs to be expanded beyond the Black-White paradigm that has shaped discussions of affirmative action. The voices of other disenfranchised groups need to be acknowledged in the process, because as my students continually remind me, "Racism is not just a Black-White thing."

Part IV

Beyond Black and White

8

Critical Issues in Latino, American Indian, and Asian Pacific American Identity Development

"There's more than just Black and White, you know."

"I took a Chicano Studies class my freshman year and that made me very militant."

JUDITH, A CHICANA COLLEGE STUDENT

"There's a certain amount of anger that comes from the past, realizing that my family because they had to assimilate through the generations, don't really know who they are."

DON, AN AMERICAN INDIAN COLLEGE STUDENT

"Being an Asian person, a person of color growing up in this society, I was taught to hate myself. I did hate myself, and I'm trying to deal with it."

KHANH, AN ASIAN AMERICAN COLLEGE STUDENT[1]

Like the African American and European American students I have described, each of the young people quoted above is also engaged in a process of racial or ethnic identity development. Although conversations about race, racism, and racial identity tend to focus on Black–White relations, to do so ignores the experiences of other targeted racial or ethnic groups. When we look at the experiences of Latinos, American Indians, and Asian Pacific Americans in the United States, we can easily see that racial and cultural oppression has been a part of their past and present and that it plays a role in the identity development process for individuals in these groups as well.[2]

Though racial identity models such as that of William Cross were developed with African Americans in mind, the basic tenets of such models can be applied to all people of color who have shared similar patterns of racial, ethnic, or cultural oppression. Psychologist Stanley Sue, an expert in crosscultural counseling, writes, "[I]n the past several decades, Asian Americans, Hispanics, and American Indians have experienced sociopolitical identity transformations so that a 'Third World consciousness' has emerged with cultural oppression as the common unifying force."[3]

In this multiracial context, Jean Phinney's model of adolescent ethnic identity development stands out. Grounded in both an Eriksonian understanding of adolescence and research studies with adolescents from various racial or ethnic groups, Phinney's model is made up of three stages: (1) unexamined ethnic identity, when race or ethnicity is not particularly salient for the individual; (2) ethnic identity search, when individuals are actively engaged in defining for themselves what it means to be a member of their own racial or ethnic group; and (3) achieved ethnic identity, when individuals are able to assert a clear, positive sense of their racial or ethnic identity.[4] Phinney's model shares with both Cross's and Helms's models the ideas that an achieved identity develops over time in a predictable fashion and that encounter experiences often lead to the exploration, examination, and eventual internalization of a positive, self-defined sense of one's own racial or ethnic identity.

While Phinney's work describes the identity process for adolescents of color in general, it is important to continually keep in mind the cultural diversity and wide range of experience represented by the groups known as Latinos, Asian Pacific Americans, and American Indians. Because of this tremendous diversity, it is impossible in the space of one chapter to detail the complexities of the identity process for each group.[5] Therein lies my dilemma. How can I make the experiences of my Latino, Asian, and Native students visible without tokenizing them? I am not sure that I can, but I have learned in teaching about racism that a sincere, though imperfect, attempt to interrupt the oppression of others is usually better than no attempt at all. In that spirit, this chapter is an attempt to interrupt the frequent silence about the impact of racism on these communities of color. It is not an attempt to provide an in-depth discussion of each group's identity development process, an attempt which would inevitably be incomplete. Rather this chapter highlights a few critical issues pertinent to the identity development of each group, particularly in schools, and points the reader to more information.

What Do We Mean When We Say "Latino"?

Latinos, also known as Hispanics, are the second largest and fastest-growing community of color in the United States. There are more than 25 million Latinos residing permanently in the United States. As a result of high birthrates and continuing immigration, the Latino population is expected to surpass the African American population in number early in the twenty-first century, thereby becoming the largest "minority" group in the United States. Over 60 percent of Latinos are of Mexican ancestry, a population that includes U.S.-born Mexican Americans (also known as Chicanos) whose families may have been in the Southwest for many generations as well as recent Mexican immigrants. Approximately 13 percent of Latinos are Puerto Rican, 5 percent are Cuban, and about 20 percent are considered "other Hispanics" by the U.S. Bureau of the Census. The last category includes Dominicans, newly arrived Central Americans (e.g., Nicaraguans, Guatemalecos, and Salvadoreños), and South Americans (e.g., Chileans, Colombians, and Argentinians).[6] Each of these groups is a distinct population with a particular historical relationship to the United States.

In the case of Chicanos, the U.S. conquest and annexation of Mexican territory in 1848 created a situation in which people of Mexican ancestry became subject to White domination. Like African Americans and Native Americans, Mexican Americans were initially incorporated into U.S. society against their will. It was the general feeling among White settlers that Whites and Mexicans were never meant to live together. Segregated schools, segregated housing, and employment discrimination were the result. State legislation in Texas and California outlawing the use of Spanish in the schools was enacted. Though the Mexican population declined immediately after the conquest (due to forced relocations), it increased again during the early twentieth century when U.S. farmers actively encouraged the immigration of Mexicans as an inexpensive source of agricultural labor. Subsequently, political and economic conditions in Mexico have fueled a steady stream of immigrants to the United States.[7]

While most Mexican-origin Latinos are legal residents, people of Mexican descent are often stereotyped as illegal aliens. Most Mexican Americans continue to live in the Southwest in urban areas. According to the most recent census data, Mexican-origin Latinos are the youngest of all Latino subgroups—median age in 1990 was 24.1 as compared to 33.5 for non-Hispanics. Education and family income remain below the U.S. average—only 45 percent of Mexican Americans age 25 and older have completed high school, and approximately 26 percent of all Mexican-origin families live in poverty.[8]

Like the conquered Mexicans, Puerto Ricans did not choose to become U.S. citizens. Puerto Rico became an unincorporated territory of the United States in 1898, ceded by Spain at the conclusion of the Spanish-American War. Puerto Rico, which had struggled to become independent of Spain, did not welcome subjugation by the United States. An active policy of Americanization of the island population was implemented, including attempts to replace Spanish with English as the language of instruction on the island. The attempts to displace Spanish were vigorously resisted by Puerto Rican teachers and students alike. In 1915, resistance to the imposition of English resulted in a student strike at Central High School in San Juan, part of a rising wave of nationalism and calls for independence. Rather than let the Puerto Rican people vote on whether they wanted citizenship, the U.S. Congress passed the Jones Act of 1917, imposing citizenship and the obligation to serve in the U.S. military but denying the right to vote in national elections. In 1951, Puerto Ricans were allowed to vote on whether to remain a territory or to become a commonwealth. Though there were those who urged another option, Puerto Rican independence, commonwealth status was the choice. Commonwealth status allowed Puerto Ricans greater control of their school systems, and Spanish was restored in the schools.[9]

Economic conditions on the island have driven many Puerto Ricans to New York and other Northeastern U.S. cities. Many came in the 1940s and 1950s to work in the factories of the Northeast, but as industry left the region many Puerto Rican workers were displaced. Fluctuating employment conditions have contributed to a pattern of circular migration to and from Puerto Rico which is made easier by U.S. citizenship.

In general, Puerto Ricans have the poorest economic conditions of all Latino groups—the poverty rate is close to 60 percent. Approximately 53 percent of Puerto Rican adults over age 25 have completed high school.[10] A multiracial population descended from European colonizers, enslaved Africans, and the indigenous Taino Indians, a significant number of Puerto Ricans are dark-skinned and may experience more racism and discrimination than lighter-skinned Latino populations.[11]

As a group, Cuban Americans are older and more affluent than other Latinos, reflecting a different immigration history. Although Cuban communities have existed in Florida and New York since the 1870s, Cuban immigration to the United States increased dramatically following the 1959 revolution led by Fidel Castro. The first wave of immigrants were upper-class, light-skinned Cubans who left in the very first days of the revolution. They were able to bring their personal fortunes with them and established businesses in the United States. The second major group left after Castro had been in power for a few months, and were largely middle-class professionals and skilled workers. Though many were unable to bring possessions with them, they received support from the the U.S. government and charitable organizations. The last major group of Cuban immigrants, known as Marielitos, arrived in 1980, having lived most of their lives under a socialist government. Marielitos are typically much poorer, less educated, and darker-skinned than earlier refugees.

On average, Cubans have higher education levels than Mexican Americans and Puerto Ricans. Approximately 17 percent of Cubans over age 25 are college graduates, as compared to less than 10 percent for Chicanos or Puerto Ricans.[12] Because the early Cuban immigrants view themselves as people in exile who might return to Cuba when Castro is no longer in power, they have worked to keep Spanish an integral part of their lives in the United States.[13]

"Other Hispanics," as the U.S. government classifies those Latinos who do not trace their family background to Mexico, Puerto Rico, or Cuba, are an extremely heterogeneous group. They include South Americans as well as Central Americans, well-educated professionals as well as rural farmers, those who immigrated for increased economic opportunities as well as those escaping civil war. Among this category of "other Hispanics," the largest groups are from the Dominican Republic, Colombia, Ecuador, El Salvador, Guatemala, Peru, and Nicaragua.[14]

Although non-Latinos often use *Latino* to refer to a racial group, it is an error to do so. The term *Hispanic* was used by the Bureau of the Census as an ethnic label and not to denote a race, because Hispanics are a racially mixed group, including combinations of European White, African Black, and indigenous American Indian. It is possible for an individual to identify himself or herself as ethnically Hispanic and racially Black or White at the same time.[15] As in African American families, there can be wide color variations in the same family. *Racismo* within Latino communities is akin to colorism in Black American communities, advantaging lighter-skinned individuals.[16] Although a majority of Latinos share the Roman Catholic faith and speak Spanish, not all do. Researchers Gerardo Marín and Barbara VanOss Marín argue that cultural values—not demographic characteristics—help Hispanics self-identify as members of one ethnic group.

All in the Family: Familism in Latino Communities

In particular, the cultural value of *familism,* the importance of the extended family as a reference group and as providers of social support, has been identified as a characteristic shared by most Hispanics independent of their national background, birthplace, dominant language, or any other sociodemographic characteristic.[17]

In a carefully designed comparative study of four groups of adolescents—Mexicans living in Mexico, immigrant Mexicans in the United States, U.S.-born Mexican Americans, and White American adolescents—researchers Carola and Marcelo Suárez-Orozco investigated the nature of familism among the four groups. In particular, they examined perceptions of the degree of emotional and material support provided by the family, the sense of obligation to provide support to one's family, and the degree to which families served as one's reference group (as opposed to peers, for example). They predicted that the three Latino groups would demonstrate more familism than white American adolescents, and that Mexican immigrants would demonstrate the highest level of familism because immigrants frequently turn to the family for support and comfort. They found that the Latino groups were indeed more family-oriented than the White American group, but that there was no significant difference between the three Latino groups. All the adolescents of Mexican ancestry had a strong family orientation that expressed itself in a variety of ways.

For example, achieving in school and at work were considered important by Latino teens because success would allow them to take care of family members. Conversely, White American teens considered education and work as a means of gaining independence from their families. The researchers concluded that "in Mexico the family seems to be a centripetal force; in the United States it is a centrifugal force."[18] Because both immigrant and non-immigrant Latino adolescents expressed this value, the researchers also concluded that familism is related to enduring psychocultural features of the Latino population, not only the stresses of immigration. Similarly, Fabio Sabogal and his colleagues found that Mexican Americans, Central Americans, and Cuban Americans all reported similar attitudes toward the family, this familism standing in contrast to the rugged individualism so often identified with White Anglo-American culture.[19]

In her book *Affirming Diversity,* Sonia Nieto describes a very successful program for Latino youth in a large, urban high school that has recognized the importance of this cultural value and has incorporated it into the classroom structure.[20] The program was infused with a sense of caring and support, and family-like relationships were fostered between the teacher and students, and between the students themselves. Through activities such as peer tutoring and mentoring, a sense of collective responsibility was reinforced. In contrast to the high dropout rates common in many Latino communities, up to 65 percent of the high school graduates of this program have gone on to college. Said one student, "The best thing I like about this class is that we all work together and we all participate and try to help each other. We're family!"[21]

Though familism is not caused by immigration, it is reinforced by it. The ongoing influx of new Latino immigrants and the circular migration of some populations (Puerto Ricans, for example) help to keep cultural values alive in the U.S. communities. The Suárez-Orozcos write,

> For many second- and third-generation Latinos the immigrant past may also *be* the present. . . . Among Latinos the past is not only kept alive through family narratives but unfolds in front of our very eyes as recent arrivals endure anew the cycle of deprivation, hardship, and discrimination that is characteristic of first-generation immigrant life.[22]

In this context, perhaps the most critical task facing the children of immigrants is reconciling the culture of home with the dominant

American culture. Drawing on the work of social identity theorist Tajfel and others, Phinney describes four possible outcomes for coping with this cultural conflict: *assimilation, withdrawal, biculturalism,* and *marginalization.* Assimilation is the attempt to blend into the dominant culture as much as possible, distancing oneself from one's ethnic group. Individuals using this strategy may actively reject the use of Spanish. Withdrawal results in an emphasis on one's ethnic culture and an avoidance of contact with the dominant group. This strategy is seen in highly segregated communities where English is rarely spoken. A bicultural identity incorporates selected aspects of both the home culture and the dominant culture, often achieving bilingual fluency in the process. The bicultural strategy can be a very positive one, but it is not easily achieved. For some the attempt to bridge two worlds may result in alienation from both. Having rejected the "old country" ways of the family, yet unable to find full acceptance in the dominant culture, these adolescents often experience marginalization. These alienated young people, relying on their peers for a sense of community, may be at particular risk for gang membership. School programs, such as the one Nieto describes, that help bridge the gap between the culture of home and the culture of the dominant society can reduce the risks of alienation.[23]

"Who Are You if You Don't Speak Spanish?" Language and Identity Among Latinos

As is suggested above, language is inextricably bound to identity. Language is not only an instrumental tool for communication, but also the carrier of cultural values and attitudes. It is through language that the affect of *mi familia,* the emotions of family life, are expressed. Richard Rodriguez, author of *Hunger of Memory* and critic of bilingual education, describes what happened in his family when the nuns at his parochial school told his Mexican parents to stop using Spanish at home, so their children might learn English more quickly. Gradually, he and his parents stopped speaking to each other. His family was "no longer so close; no longer bound tight by the pleasing and troubling knowledge of our public separateness. . . . The family's quiet was partly due to the fact that as we children learned more and more English, we shared fewer and fewer words."[24] What did it mean to his understanding of familism, and other aspects of ethnic identity when he relinquished his Spanish?

For Jose, a young Puerto Rican man, the answer to this question is clear.

> I think that the only thing that Puerto Ricans preserve
> in this country that is Puerto Rican is the language. If
> we lose that, *we* are lost. I think that we need to preserve
> it because it is the primordial basis of our culture. It is
> the only thing we have to identify ourselves as Puerto
> Rican. If you don't know your language, who are
> you? . . . I believe that being Puerto Rican and speak-
> ing Spanish go hand in hand.[25]

This sentiment was echoed repeatedly by other young Puerto Rican adults who were interviewed by Maria Zavala as part of a study of language and ethnic identity among Puerto Ricans.[26]

However, these young people had also learned that their language was devalued by the dominant culture. Those who had spent their childhoods in the United States in particular recalled feeling ashamed to be bilingual. Said Margarita,

> In school there were stereotypes about the bilingual
> students, big time. [Since] they don't speak "the" lan-
> guage, they don't belong here. That's number one.
> Number two, they were dumb, no matter what. . . .
> Everyone said "that bilingual person," but they didn't
> realize that bilingual means they speak *two* languages. To
> them bilingual was not a good thing. There was a hor-
> rible stigma attached to them and I think I fell in the

trap sometimes of saying "those bilingual people" just
because that was what I was hearing all around me.[27]

A common coping strategy in childhood was to avoid the use of
Spanish in public, a strategy akin to the "racelessness" adopted by
some African American students. Said Cristina, a young woman raised
in the United States, "I remember pretending I didn't know how to
speak Spanish. You know, if you pretended that you were that
American then maybe you would get accepted by the White kids. I
remember trying not to speak Spanish or speaking it with an
[English] accent."[28]

However, avoiding the use of Spanish does not guarantee acceptance by the dominant society. A growing awareness of this reality and
the unfolding process of adolescent identity development led these
students to reclaim their Spanish, a process integral to their exploration of Puerto Rican identity. Cristina, now a college student,
explains:

> I'm a lot more fluent with English. I struggle with
> Spanish and it's something that I've been trying to
> reclaim. I've been reading a lot of literature written by
> Latinos lately, . . . some Puerto Rican history. Before
> [college] I didn't even know it existed. Now I'm read-
> ing and writing more and more in Spanish and I'm
> using it more in conversations with other Puerto
> Ricans. Now I have confidence. I don't feel inferior any
> more. I used to in high school, I did. People don't want
> you to speak Spanish and before I was one of those
> that's very guilty of not speaking it because I didn't
> want to draw attention to me, but now you can't tell me
> not to speak Spanish because for me that's the biggest
> form of oppression. My kids are going to speak Spanish
> and they're going to speak it loud. They're not going to
> go with the whispering stuff. As a matter of fact, if a

White person comes by, we're going to speak it even louder. I am going to ingrain that in them, that you need to be proud of that.[29]

Zavala effectively demonstrates that while these young people are still in the process of exploring identity, the resolution of their feelings about the Spanish language is a central dimension of the identity development process. The linguicism—discrimination based on language use—to which they all had been subjected had been internalized by some, and had to be rejected in order for them to assert a positive sense of identity.

While Zavala's study focused only on Puerto Ricans, sociologist Samuel Betances argues that for Latinos the Spanish language is a unifying theme. He writes, "in essence, the core which links Hispanics/Latinos is language, i.e., the theme of Spanish and English as vital to a healthy membership in both the larger society and in the ever growing emerging ethnic interest group."[30]

Given the strong connection between language and identity it seems very important for educators to think carefully about how they respond to Latino children's use of Spanish at school. As Nieto points out, schools often work hard to strip away the child's native language, asking parents to speak English to their children at home, punishing children with detention for using their native language at school, or even withholding education until children have mastered English.[31] While of course fluency in English is a necessary educational goal, the child's fluency in Spanish need not be undermined in order to achieve it.

There is increasing evidence that the level of proficiency in one's native language has a direct influence on the development of proficiency in the second language. Contrary to common belief, it makes sense to use students' native language to reinforce their acquisition of English. While it is not possible here to review the varieties of bilingual education and the political controversies surrounding them, the positive effects of bilingual education, from lower dropout rates to increased literacy development, have been demonstrated again and again.[32] Bilingual education, in which children are receiving education in content areas in their native language, as well as receiving structured instruction in English, is more effective than English as a second language (ESL) instruction alone, because the children can build on their previous literacy. Research suggests that it takes five to seven years on average to develop the level of English proficiency needed to succeed academically in school. For this reason, late-exit bilingual education programs—in which students remain until they have developed adequate English proficiency for high-level academic work—are particularly effective. Such programs have not only cognitive benefits, but social and emotional ones as well. Students who are encouraged to maintain their Spanish are able to maintain close family ties through their shared use of the language and their parents feel more comfortable with the school environment, increasing the likelihood of parental involvement at school.[33] Nieto and others are quick to point out that bilingual education alone cannot completely reverse the history of school failure that Latino students have experienced. But it does challenge the alienating and emotionally disruptive idea that native language and culture need to be forgotten in order to be successful.

The attempted destruction of an oppressed people's native language has been an issue not only for Latinos, but also for American Indians. In fact, Indian education as carried out by the U.S. government in the nineteenth and early twentieth centuries served as the model for the early Americanization efforts in Puerto Rico.[34] The physical and cultural dislocations visited upon Native Americans still have major implications for the identity development of Indian youth today.

What Do We Mean When We Say "Indian"?

It is conservatively estimated that prior to 1492 there were 3 to 5 million indigenous people in America. Following the disastrous contact with Europeans, the populations were greatly reduced, and by 1850 there were only about 250,000 Indians in North America. Now there are almost 2 million American Indians and Alaska Natives living in the United States.[35] They represent more than 500 different cultural communities federally defined as sovereign entities with which the United States has a government-to-government relationship.[36] In addition there are an estimated 250 Native groups that are not recognized by the U.S. government.

Each of these cultural communities has its own language, customs, religion, economy, historical circumstances, and environment. They range from the very traditional, whose members speak their indigenous language at home, to the mostly acculturated, whose members speak English as their first language. Most Native people identify with their particular ancestral community first, and as American Indians second.[37]

The Native population grew slowly in the first half of the twentieth century, but has grown rapidly in the second half, due to a high birth rate and reduced infant mortality. Another source of the population increase, however, has been the fact that since 1970 a significant number of people have changed their Census identification to American Indian from some other racial category on the Census forms. This shift in self-identification raises the questions, who is an American Indian and how is that category defined?

The answers depend on whom you ask. Each Indian nation sets its own criteria for membership. Some specify a particular percentage of Indian ancestry (varying from one-half to one-sixty-fourth), others do not. Some nations specify native language fluency as a prerequisite for service in their government, others do not. The U.S. government requires one-quarter blood quantum (as indicated on a federal "certificate of Indian blood") in order to qualify for Bureau of Indian Affairs college scholarships. Other federal agencies, such as the Bureau of the Census, rely on self-identification. Declining social discrimination, growing ethnic pride, a resurgence in Indian activism, and the pursuit of sovereign rights may account for the growing numbers of racially mixed U.S. citizens who are now choosing to identify themselves as American Indian.[38]

Despite the stereotypes to the contrary, there is great diversity among this population. K. Tsianina Lomawaima, a professor of American Indian Studies, makes this point very clearly when she writes:

> A fluent member of a Cherokee Baptist congregation living in Tahlequah, Oklahoma, is different from an English-speaking, pow-wow–dancing Lakota born and raised in Oakland, California, who is different from a Hopi fluent in Hopi, English, Navajo, and Spanish who lives on the reservation and supports her family by selling "traditional" pottery in New York, Santa Fe, and Scottsdale galleries. The idea of being generically "Indian" really was a figment of Columbus's imagination.[39]

However, there are general demographic statements that can be made about the American Indian population. Approximately 50 percent live west of the Mississippi River. In fact according to recent Census reports, more than half of the American Indian population lives in just six states: Oklahoma, California, Arizona, New Mexico, Alaska, and Washington. Approximately 50 percent live in urban areas. Only 22 percent of all American Indians (including Alaska Natives) live on reservations and trust lands, with most of the rest living in rural communities nearby.[40]

There are also some shared cultural values that are considered characteristic of American Indian families. For example, as with Latinos (who often share Indian ancestry), extended family and kinship obligations are considered very important. Consequently, group needs are more important than individual needs. Communal sharing with those less fortunate is expected. Traditional Indian culture sees an interdependent relationship between all living things. Just as one seeks harmony with one's human family, so should a person try to be in harmony with nature, rather than dominant over it.[41]

Surviving the Losses

From the beginning of their encounters with Europeans, these and other Indian values were at odds with the individualistic and capitalistic orientation of the White settlers. U.S. government leaders were convinced that changing Indian cultural values were the key to "civilizing" Indians and acquiring Indian-controlled lands.[42]

Following the establishment of reservations, one of the major strategies used to facilitate this cultural conversion was the establishment of off-reservation boarding schools for Indian children. The first such school was the Carlisle Indian School in Carlisle, Pennsylvania, established in 1879. Over the fifty years that followed, thousands of Indian children as young as five were forcibly removed from their families and placed in boarding schools, too far away for their poverty-stricken families to visit. Parental nurturing was replaced with forced assimilation, hard physical labor, harsh discipline, and emotional, physical, and often sexual abuse. Though the U.S. government's practice of removing children from their home environments was reversed in the 1930s, by then several generations of Indian children had lost their traditional cultural values and ways, and yet remained alienated from the dominant American culture.[43]

Further cultural disruptions occurred in the 1940s and 1950s when federal Indian policy shifted again, this time with the goal of terminating the official relationship between the Indian nations and the U.S. government. Many Indians were taken from their homes and relocated in urban areas, in a manner reminiscent of the earlier forced removal to reservations.[44] Unprepared for urban life, the upheaval brought on by the relocation process was devastating to many. Alcoholism, suicide, and homicide increased to epidemic proportions,[45] and continue to be the leading causes of death among American Indians.[46]

The intergenerational impact of these disruptions can be seen in this Native woman's narrative:

> For 500 years, my people have been told in so many ways, "You're no good. You are a savage. Change your ways. You are not civilized. Your ways are heathen and witchery. Your ways are not Christian!" My grandfather gave up his tribal religion and customs. He adopted Christianity. He, my grandmother, and the other people on the reservation did their best to give up the old ways, become farmers, quit hunting, go to church and be "good Indians, civilized Indians." They wept when the federal agents rounded up their children to take them away to boarding school. Some of the children never came home. Some came home to be buried. My grandparents and the people wept again because their children grew up learning alien ways, forgetting their language and customs in schools too far away to visit.
>
> My parents married soon after they came home from the boarding school. They came from different tribes. They left my father's reservation encouraged by the U.S. government and the boarding school system to find jobs in the "real world." . . . The promised jobs never materialized and, stuck between two worlds, the big city and the reservation, the Indian world and the White, my father drank and beat my mother. My mother worked at menial jobs to support us. My life was built on this foundation. I was never parented because my parents, raised in government boarding schools, had nothing to give me. They had lost their languages and retained only traces of their cultures. They had never been parented themselves. Boarding school nurturing was having their mouths washed out with soap for talking Indian and receiving beatings for failing to follow directions.

So this is my legacy and the legacy of many Indians, both reservation and urban. . . . We are survivors of multigenerational loss and only through acknowledging our losses will we ever be able to heal.[47]

The legacy of loss is accompanied by a legacy of resistance. As they had in the past, Native peoples resisted the termination policy, and the policy ended in the 1960s following the election of John F. Kennedy. The Civil Rights era included Native American demands for greater self-determination and the development of a pan-Indian movement based on the assumption that Native American peoples shared a common set of values and interests. In response to Indian activism, the federal government condemned its own destructive policies of the past and increased support for Indian self-determination, passing legislation in the 1980s and 1990s designed to promote Indian-controlled schools, protect American Indian religious freedom, and preserve traditional Indian languages.

But the struggle is not over. On the occasion of the 1992 celebration of the five-hundredth anniversary of Columbus's arrival to the Western Hemisphere, Pulitzer Prize–winning author N. Scott Momaday reflected on the future of Indians in the United States:

The major issues we face now are survival—how to live in the modern world. Part of this is how to remain Indian, how to assimilate without ceasing to be Indian. I think some important strides have been made. Indians remain Indian, and against pretty good odds. They remain Indian and in some situations, by a thread. Their languages are being lost at a tremendous rate, poverty is rampant, as is alcoholism. But still there are Indians, and the traditional world is intact.

It's a matter of identity. It's thinking about who I am. I grew up on Indian reservations, and then I went away from the Indian world and entered a different context. But I continue to think of myself as Indian, I write out of that conviction. I think this is what most Indian people are doing today. They go off the reservations, but they keep an idea of themselves as Indians. That's the trick.[48]

That *is* the trick. Remaining anchored in a positive sense of one's cultural identity in the face of racism is an antidote to alienation and despair. What constructive role can educators play in this process? Next to Latinos, American Indians are least likely to graduate from high school or college.[49] The use of schools as instruments of forced assimilation was education at its worst. What would it look like at its best? How could the identities of Native students be affirmed in school? That is the question to be considered next.

"I" Is for Invisible: Contemporary Images of American Indians in the Curriculum

In her article "Is There an 'Indian' in Your Classroom?" Lee Little Soldier makes the point that teachers might find it hard to determine whether there even are Native American students in their classrooms.[50] Indians often have European names, and because of the high proportion of mixed-heritage individuals, there are wide variations in physical appearance. While some are easily recognized as people of color, others have light skin, light eyes, and brown or blond hair and may be identified by others as White. Those who are products of Black-Indian unions may simply be assumed to be African American. Particularly in those parts of the United States with small Indian populations, many people may be surprised to discover that American Indians still exist at all. For example, American Indian studies professor Donald Andrew Grinde, Jr., describes his history professor's response when he expressed an interest in studying American Indian history: "My advisor told me I needed to focus on an area such as American economic history to secure employment. When I told him

I was an American Indian and thus still wanted to do research in this area, he smiled and murmured, 'I thought that we had killed all of them.'"[51] This perception is not surprising given the absence of contemporary images of American Indians in the popular culture. Native American communities are typically portrayed as people of the past, not of the present or the future. This depiction prevails even in places where there is a large and visible Indian population.

Consider this case example provided by Alaska Native educator Paul Ongtooguk.[52] Describing the high school curriculum he experienced in Nome, Alaska, a community where Alaska Natives outnumbered Whites, but where the school board, faculty, and administration of the school were all White, he writes: "During my four years at Nome-Beltz High School, teachers and students maintained a veil of silence about Alaska Native history and culture except for the disparaging remarks about Alaska Natives as barbaric and ignorant that were part of the hidden curriculum." Teacher expectations of Alaska Natives were low, and in fact, almost half of them dropped out of high school before graduation. Many committed suicide. Those who did graduate were discouraged from attending college and encouraged instead to pursue vocational training. In this context, Ongtooguk struggled to define a positive sense of identity as an Alaska Native adolescent:

> Despite the denigration of Alaska Native societies in schools, in other places in my life there were images that were actually complimentary and admirable. Slowly these conflicting images began to tear at the veil of silence. I rejected the argument of the inferiority of Alaska Natives that was part of the structure of the schools, sensing if not actually realizing that who I was was not shameful but was an inescapable fact and that what was shameful was what members of the white community were saying about Alaska Natives.

He learned about his heritage through the oral histories of the older Alaska Natives he knew, elders who talked about the tremendous difficulties they had endured when Whites took control of Northwest Alaska.

> It seemed remarkable to me, as an adolescent boy, that anybody had survived in that community let alone found a way to sustain a distinctive way of life and maintain a rich and complex culture. I realized then that there were members of the Alaska Native community who were working to create the conditions in which all could have lives with dignity and be well-regarded as human beings. This realization was the result of becoming acquainted with Alaska Native leaders working in the community with Native elders trying to preserve the legacy of our society and introduce the young people to that legacy.

Ongtooguk was one of the few Alaska Natives at his school to graduate and go on to college. His ambition was to become a social studies and history teacher. While in college, he immersed himself in Alaska Native history. To his amazement, he found thousands of volumes in the University of Washington library written by European and American scholars about Alaska Natives. He writes, "Until that time, I had not realized how much of our own history had been written down, how much of our lives had been described, and how important we were as people." When he returned to Northwest Alaska as a certified secondary teacher, he brought with him thirty-six boxes of books and documents about Alaska Natives to share with his new students.

One of the first tasks in his new job was to review a recently implemented "Inupiaq Heritage Curriculum," constructed by White educators and consisting primarily of Native arts and crafts projects.

While the traditional arts and crafts were worthy of study, the curriculum embodied a "museum" perspective whereby the traditional life of Alaska Natives was studied as "an interesting curiosity commemorating the past." Ongtooguk writes,

> The most disturbing picture of Inupiaq culture, then, was of its static nature—something that had happened "back then" rather than something that was happening now. Did this mean that the people living in the region now were like a cast of actors who had run out of lines?

He set out to reconstruct the curriculum to reflect not only traditional life, but transitional life and the modern period.

He explains:

> If, as their teachers commonly implied, being Inupiaq only meant being traditional (or Ipani), then both assimilation and all of modern schooling were essentially cultural genocide in that they moved the students away from things traditional. . . . The course was not intended to turn back the clock, but to allow students to realize that they were the latest inheritors of a society in the midst of dramatic transformation. They needed to know both what was and what is crucial for survival and for leading productive lives within the Inupiaq community.

The inclusion of contemporary life as part of this new Inupiaq studies curriculum was essential if Inupiaq students were to see themselves reflected in the schools and see the Inupiaq identity as having a future, not only a past. They needed a coherent picture of the continuity, conflict, and cultural transformation that had shaped and continued to shape the Inupiaq community. Ongtooguk's reconstructed curriculum was eventually adopted by the Northwest Arctic School

District and has become a model for Yupik studies in several school districts in southwest Alaska.

Such curricular interventions stand in stark contrast to the deculturalization that has been the legacy of American Indian education, reminding us that education does not have to mean alienation. More such interventions are needed if faculty and students, both Indian and White, are to realize that the Native community is not a relic of the past, but a growing community with a future.

Another growing population, which unlike American Indians is usually assumed to have a very bright future, is that of the Asian Pacific American community. The collective image of Asians as the "model minority" in the United States is a pervasive one. Yet like the Latino and American Indian communities, the Asian Pacific American community is not a monolith.

What Do We Mean When We Say "Asian"?

The terms, *Asian, Asian American,* and more inclusively *Asian Pacific American* are often used as a collective reference to the Asian and Pacific Islander populations living in the United States. The U.S. government includes in its definition of Asian, peoples from East Asia (e.g., Chinese, Japanese, Korean), from Southeast Asia (e.g., Vietnamese, Laotian, Burmese), from the Pacific Islands (e.g., Samoan, Guamanian, Fijian), from South Asia (e.g., Indian, Pakistani, Nepali), from West Asia (Iranian, Afghan, Turkish), and from the Middle East (e.g., Iraqi, Jordanian, Palestinian).[53] The Asian Pacific population in the United States has increased from less than 1 million in 1960 to more than 7 million by 1990, now representing about 3 percent of the U.S. population. It includes 43 ethnic groups, including 28 from the Asian continent and 15 from the Pacific Islands. Religious beliefs vary greatly among these groups, and include Buddhism, Islam, Christianity (both Protestant and Catholic), Hinduism, Shintoism, ancestor worship, and animism.[54] Those from communist countries where religion was essentially outlawed may be without any religious tradition.

The most populous Asian Pacific American groups are Chinese (23% of the Asian population in the United States), Filipino (19%), Japanese (12%), Asian Indian (11%), Korean (11%). However, the Vietnamese (presently 9% of the Asian American population) represent the fastest-growing Asian community in the United States. Except for isolated Southeast Asian refugees scattered throughout the country, most Asian Pacific American communities are on the coasts, with about 70 percent of the total population residing in only five states: California, Hawaii, New York, Illinois, and Texas.[55]

In 1960, most Asian Americans were descendants of early Chinese and Japanese immigrants. Changes in immigration policy in 1965 dramatically increased Asian immigration, significantly altering the demographic makeup of the Asian Pacific American community. By 1990, over half of the Asians and Pacific Islanders in the United States were foreign born. As is the case among Latinos, each national group has its own unique immigration history that has shaped its experience in the United States. While it is not possible to review the immigration history of all these groups, the immigration experience of the most populous groups will be briefly summarized here.

The Chinese were the first Asians to immigrate to the United States in large numbers, arriving in California in 1850 as part of the rush for gold. These first arrivals were single men who paid their own way to the California gold fields, hoping to get rich and then return to China. As the gold rush waned, many Chinese did not have enough money to go home. Hired at wages one-third below what whites would have been paid, Chinese men found employment as laborers working on the transcontinental railroad and on California farms. In 1882 immigration was severely restricted by the Chinese Exclusion Act and completely forbidden by the 1924 Immigration Act.[56] Like Blacks and Indians, the Chinese were viewed as a threat to White racial purity. Laws prohibiting marriage between a White person and a "negro, mulatto, or Mongolian" were passed.[57] These laws, combined with immigration restrictions, special taxes directed against the Chinese, and discrimination in housing and employment, limited the growth of the Chinese population. Most of the men did not start families in the United States.

A second wave of Chinese immigration occurred after World War II. In an effort to promote an alliance with China against Japan, the U.S. government repealed the Exclusion Act to allow a few thousand Chinese to enter the country. Chinese scientists and professionals and their families escaping communism were part of this second wave.

A third wave of Chinese immigration occurred after the 1965 Immigration Act (and its 1990 extension). Because racial quotas on immigration were eliminated by this legislation, Chinese immigration dramatically increased, with entire families immigrating at once. Tens of thousands of Chinese have come to the United States every year since passage of the 1965 Immigration act. In addition, the re-establishment of diplomatic relations between the People's Republic of China and the United States provided new immigration opportunities for Chinese students.

In the last thirty years, Chinese immigrants have come not only from China, but also from Hong Kong, Taiwan, Vietnam, Laos, and Cambodia as well as other parts of Asia. Because of the magnitude of this wave of immigration, over half of the Chinese in the United States in 1990 were foreign born. As a consequence of these three phases of immigration, there is great socioeconomic, political, and linguistic diversity within the Chinese American community.[58]

By contrast, more than three-quarters of the people with Japanese ancestry in the United States are American born, descendants of those who came to the U.S. mainland or Hawaii before 1924. These early immigrants were attracted by higher U.S. wages, and because the Japanese government encouraged women to immigrate as well, often as "picture brides" in arranged marriages, Japanese families quickly established themselves. While Japanese workers were welcomed on the plantations of Hawaii, there was considerable anti-Japanese feeling on the West Coast. In 1906 the San Francisco board of education established a separate school for Chinese, Japanese, and Korean children, and the California Alien Land Law prohibited Japanese immigrants and other foreign-born residents from purchasing agricultural land because they were ineligible for citizenship. (The Naturalization Act, passed in 1790, only allowed Whites to become naturalized citizens, so while children born in the United States automatically became citizens, until this law was repealed, their immigrant parents could never be eligible.) As with the Chinese, immigration of Japanese came to a halt with the Immigration Act of 1924.

The Japanese bombing of Pearl Harbor in 1941 certainly intensified anti-Japanese sentiment. In March 1942, Executive Order 9102 established the War Relocation Authority, making it possible to remove 120,000 Japanese Americans from their West Coast homes without a trial or hearing and confine them in internment camps in places as far away as Idaho, Colorado, and Utah.[59] One response to this internment experience was for Japanese American families to encourage their children to become as "American" as possible in an effort to prevent further discrimination. For this reason, as well as their longevity in the United States, Japanese Americans as a group are the most acculturated of the Asian Pacific American communities.

Korean immigration to the United States occurred in three distinct waves, beginning with fewer than 10,000 laborers who arrived between 1903 and 1905. While there were some Korean "picture brides," most male immigrants were unable to start families because of the same antimiscegenation laws that affected the Chinese. Another small group of immigrants came to the United States after World War II and the Korean War. This group included Korean adoptees and war brides. As with the Chinese, the 1965 Immigration Act dramatically increased Korean immigration of entire families, with 30,000 Koreans arriving annually between 1970 and 1990. These Koreans came from a wide range of socioeconomic and educational levels. Most Korean Americans currently living in the United States were part of this post–1965 immigration, thus most are living in families consisting of immigrant parents and American-born or -raised children, families in which differing rates of acculturation may contribute to generational conflicts.[60]

Filipino Americans also experienced a pattern of male immigration to Hawaii, and then the mainland United States, in the early 1900s. Because these men could not establish families, there are few descendants from this wave of immigration. This pattern ended in 1930 when Congress set a Filipino immigration quota of fifty per year. As with Chinese and Koreans, tens of thousands of Filipinos have immigrated annually since 1965. Some Filipino immigrants were quite affluent in the Philippines, while others were extremely poor. In general, because of the U.S. military presence in the Philipines during most of the twentieth century, Filipino immigrants are much more familiar with U.S. culture than most Asian immigrants are.[61]

Southeast Asian refugees are quite different from other Asian immigrant groups in their reasons for coming to the United States and their experiences in their homelands. After the end of the Vietnam War in 1975, a large number of mostly educated Vietnamese arrived. Since 1978, a second group of immigrants, many of them uneducated rural farmers traumatized by the war and its aftermath, came to the United States to escape persecution. This group includes Vietnamese, Chinese Vietnamese, Cambodians, Lao, Hmong, and Mien.[62]

Asian Indians have also experienced a dramatic population growth in the United States. The number of Asian Indians in the United States increased from 800,000 in 1990 to 1 million in 1993. The first immigrants from India were farmers who settled on the West Coast in the 1850s, but like other Asians they encountered a lot of discrimination and did not gain a strong foothold at that time. The contemporary wave of Asian Indian immigration includes many highly educated English-speaking adults and their children. However, newer rural immigrant families are less fluent in English and are having more difficulty adjusting to the American culture.

Arab Americans are a very heterogeneous group that is multicultural, multiracial, and multiethnic. Although "Arab" and "Muslim" are often linked together in the popular culture, many Arabs are Christian, and many Muslims are not Arabs. Some who identify as

Arab may not identify as Asian at all, despite the government's classification system. In fact the first wave of Arab immigrants came to the
United States between 1890 and 1940 from regions now known as
Syria and Lebanon. Ninety percent were Christian and they seem to
have assimilated in their new country with relative ease.

The second wave of Arab immigrants began after World War II.
Most of this group are college graduates or came in pursuit of
higher education. This wave was dominated by Palestinians, Egyptians,
Syrians, and Iraqis, and came to the United States with an Arab identity shaped by Cold War politics and the Arab-Israeli conflict.[63] Many
of this group are Muslims and have been increasingly impacted by
anti-Arab sentiments and "terrorist" stereotyping in the U.S.

The linguistic, religious, and other cultural diversity of these disparate groups, some of whom have long histories of conflict with one
another in Asia—for example, Japan and Korea, Japan and China,
China and Vietnam—gives validity to the question posed by Valerie
Lee, director of the 1992 Asian American Renaissance Conference:
"What do we have in common except for racism and rice?"[64] Social
scientists Kenyon Chan and Shirley Hune argue that racism is quite
enough. Because the treatment of early Asian immigrant communities was so similar and distinctions between them ignored by the
dominant culture, the foundation of a group identity was laid.

> Racial ideologies defined Pacific immigrants as aliens
> ineligible for citizenship, unfair economic competitors,
> and socially unassimilable groups. For the first 100 years
> of "Asian America"—the 1840s to the 1940s—the
> images of each community were racialized and predom-
> inantly negative. The Chinese were called "Mongolians"
> and depicted in the popular press as heathens, gamblers,
> and opium addicts. The Japanese and Koreans were
> viewed as the "yellow peril." Filipinos were derogatori-
> ly referred to as "little brown monkeys," and Asian
> Indians, most of them Sikhs, were called "ragheads."[65]

In the late 1960s, as part of the social transformation of the Civil Rights era, the concept of a panethnic Asian American identity emerged among second- and third-generation Japanese, Chinese, and Filipino American college students. Chan and Hune write:

> Racial identity and ethnic consciousness were funda-
> mentally transformed along with the racial order. The
> polarization of civil rights protests required Asians in
> America to consider their identity, their self-definition,
> and their place in racialized America. They discovered
> that racial quotas and legal inequalities applied to them
> just as they did to other minorities. "Colored" was
> clearly defined as anyone nonwhite.[66]

Consequently, the terms *Asian American* and *Asian Pacific American* emerged as a unifying political construct encompassing all U.S. residents of Asian and Pacific Island ancestry, encouraging individuals to work across ethnic lines for increased economic, political, and social rights. Asian American groups have lobbied for bilingual education, curricular reform, Asian American studies, improved working conditions for garment and restaurant workers, and support for community-based development. They have also opposed media misrepresentations and sought more opportunities for Asian Pacific Americans in theater, film, and television. Racial politics have continued to foster this unifying panethnic identity, though the large influx of new immigrants has changed the character of the Asian American community from the stable third- and fourth-generation community of the 1960s to one now composed largely of newcomers.[67]

Beyond the Myth of the Model Minority

"What do you know about Asians?" a young Chinese American woman asks Mark, a young White man of Italian descent. His response:

I'm going to be honest with you. I completely believed
the stereotype. Asian people are hard workers, they're
really quiet, they get good grades because they have
tons of pressure from their families to get good
grades. . . . Asians are quiet so people can't have a problem with them.[68]

This exchange captures the essence of the current stereotypes
about Asian Pacific Americans. The "model minority" characteriza-
tion is a pervasive one. The first public presentation of this idea is generally credited to a 1966 article by William Petersen entitled "Success
Story, Japanese-American Style." It reviewed the success of Japanese
Americans despite the history of discrimination they had endured. A
similar article describing the success of Chinese Americans appeared
in *U.S. News and World Report* the same year.[69] Both articles used statistics on rising educational attainment and income levels, along with
statistics on low rates of reported crime and mental illness, to demonstrate how Asian cultural values had allowed these groups to succeed
against the odds.[70] Now more than thirty years later, Asian American
youth are routinely depicted in the media as star students (especially
in math and science), supported by industrious, entrepreneurial, and
upwardly mobile parents.

This stereotype might initially seem to be a positive and beneficial one, but it has had some negative effects. In terms of intergroup
relations, it has served to pit Asian Pacific Americans against other
groups targeted by racism. The accusing message to Blacks, Latinos,
and American Indians is "They overcame discrimination—why can't
you?" It has also contributed to White resentment, leading to an
increase in sometimes deadly anti-Asian violence.[71] In addition,
uncritical acceptance of the stereotype has concealed the needs and
problems of those Asians in America who have not experienced such
success.

For example, though the Census reports Asian American families
as having median family incomes higher than all other family groups,

including Whites, this frequently cited statistic obscures several facts: Asian Pacific Americans are better educated, on average, than Whites; they tend to have more family members contributing to the household income than the average White family; and Asian Pacific American families are concentrated in the high-income, high-cost states of California, New York, and Hawaii. When comparing equally qualified individuals, Asian Pacific Americans consistently earn less than Whites. And when the Asian Pacific American community is broken down along ethnic lines, the inaccuracy of the stereotype is even more apparent.

More than 25 percent of Vietnamese Americans live in poverty, as compared to 13 percent of the general population. Poverty rates are even higher for Laotians (35%) and Cambodians (43%). For most Asian Pacific Americans, the average income of native-born individuals is lower than that of recent immigrants, suggesting that some of the Asian American success story may be due to immigration policies that have given priority to highly skilled Asian immigrants.[72]

Similarly a closer examination of the statistics on educational attainment reveal wide variations. The high school completion rates are approximately 35 percent for Cambodians, 36 percent for Laotians, and 58 percent for Vietnamese, well below the overall average of 82 percent for Asian Americans as a group.[73] Because of the widespread attitude that Asians are academically successful, many schools do not monitor or even record the dropout rates among Asian Pacific Americans. Consequently, some school districts do not realize, for example, that as many as half of the female Hmong students in their schools drop out before graduation.[74]

For individual students, the stereotype of success may have negative consequences for the quality of instruction they receive. For example, educator Lisa Delpit reports her observation of a five-year-old Asian American girl in a Montessori kindergarten class dutifully engaged in the task the teacher had assigned, placing a number of objects next to the various numerals printed on a cloth. The child worked quietly without any help from the teacher and when the time was up, she put her work away. Delpit writes, "The only problem was that at the end of the session no numeral had the correct number of objects next to it. The teacher later told me that Cathy, like Asian-American students she had taught previously, was one of the best students in the class." In this case, the stereotype of good Asian students meant Cathy had not received the instruction she needed.[75]

Asian students in America know that their teachers expect them to excel in math and science, and they may be encouraged to pursue those fields at the expense of other academic interests. Educator Valerie Ooka Pang reports that Asian Pacific American students often suffer from communication anxiety, feeling inadequate about their writing and speaking ability. This anxiety may contribute to a student's choice to pursue subject areas, such as math, which require less verbal fluency. In this case, the "model minority" stereotype actually serves to restrict their academic options.[76]

Finding a Voice

Another dimension of the "model minority" stereotype is the notion that Asian Pacific Americans are quiet and content with the status quo. Mitsuye Yamada challenges that stereotype in her classic essay, "Invisibility Is an Unnatural Disaster: Reflections of an Asian American Woman."[77] She recounts her experiences teaching the Asian segment of an ethnic American literature course, discovering that her White students were offended by the angry tone of the Asian American writers. Yamada was puzzled by this response, since her students had not been offended by the Black, Chicano, or Native American writings. When she pressed them for an explanation, they said they understood the anger of Blacks and Chicanos and empathized with the frustrations and sorrows of the American Indians. But the anger of the Asian Americans took them by surprise. Said one student, "It made me angry. *Their* anger made *me* angry, because I didn't even know the Asian Americans felt oppressed. I didn't expect their anger."[78]

The myth of the model minority obscures the reality of racism in the lives of Asian Pacific Americans and encourages their silence about it. One of my Korean American students wrote about this silence: "When racial comments were said around me I would somehow ignore it and pretend that nothing was said. By ignoring comments such as these, I was protecting myself. It became sort of a defense mechanism." While denial is a common coping strategy for dealing with racism, when the experiences are too numerous or too painful to be ignored, the silence is broken. Unfortunately, the voices of Asian Pacific American students often fall on deaf ears.

In his paper "We Could Shape It: Organizing for Asian Pacific American Student Empowerment," Peter Nien-chu Kiang cites examples from urban and suburban schools in Massachusetts in which Asian Pacific American students were frequent victims of racial harassment.[79] For example, Thuy, a Vietnamese immigrant recalled:

> When we pass by them they give you some kind of like a dirty look. . . . They say, "Look at that Chinese girl," and they call like, "Chinks, go back where you belong."[80]

Yet in each case cited by Kiang, school administrators seemed unresponsive. Responding to this indifference, one young Asian American woman said:

> It made me realize even more that . . . no one listens to [Asians]. Like if the African Americans came out and said something, probably the people in the school would have done something, but when the Asians come out, no one really does anything.[81]

Out of this context grew a regional youth conference organized by an ad hoc group of adults and teens who initially gathered to discuss how community resources could support Asian Pacific American students confronting racial harassment at school. The result was the Conference for Asian Pacific American Youth, attended by seven hundred students from fifty area high schools. The conference brought together many Asian Pacific American students who had been isolated in their own schools and created a place for them to see themselves reflected in each other and to explore their identities as Asian Pacific Americans. The power of this process is reflected in Amy's comments. She recalls her first meeting:

> When I first walked in, I swear, I just wanted to turn around and walk right out, I was so intimidated. I've never really been in a room with so many Asian students in my age group. I was like, what am I doing here? And then I started coming to the meetings, and I got more involved in it, and I was like, oh my god, you know this is really cool! Asians are cool! [laughs][82]

Planning for the conference sessions and workshops introduced the student organizers to older generations of Asian Pacific American activists. The topics they discussed ranged from gangs and media stereotypes to interracial dating, civil rights strategies, and curriculum reform. The opportunity to work with Asian adults was very meaningful since there were no Asian Pacific American teachers in most of the schools they represented. For Amy and others the conference planning process was a transformative experience not unlike Paul Ongtooguk's discovery of his Inupiak history. Said Amy, "I've become really proud of who I am and where I come from, and I know that I've become stronger. I'm no longer that silent anymore. . . . I have really found myself."[83]

The process of finding oneself in the face of invisibility, silence, and stereotypes is not an easy one. In her analysis of thirty-nine autobiographical narratives written by Asian American adults, Lucy Tse uncovered their struggle to face and name their oppression, then to affirm a positive sense of their identity as Asian Americans.[84] In commenting on his book *Turning Japanese: Memoirs of a Sansei,* David Mura writes eloquently about why it is so important to do so.[85]

> Many white Americans don't want to deal with these questions and, through much of their lives, have not had to deal with them. In contrast, my memoir explores how, up until my late twenties, I mainly attempted to avoid dealing with my *sansei* identity, and tended to think of myself as a middle-class white person. The result of such an identification, as my memoir makes clear, was self-hatred and self-abuse, a long string of depression, promiscuity, and failed relationships. If I had not become self-conscious about my identity, I might have destroyed myself. What appears to certain white readers as either negligible or a flaw in the book is actually its very lifeline.[86]

Racial Formation and Racial Identity

Asian Pacific Americans, Latinos, and American Indians are disparate groups, but they all share with people of African descent the need for this lifeline. As social scientists Chan and Hune remind us, the racialization of America has never been simply Black and White. Early European settlers used race-based policies towards Native Americans long before Africans were introduced to this continent. The U.S. government applied race-based discriminatory and exclusionary policies to Mexican residents and Chinese settlers in the Western territories immediately upon contact. The social categories we now use are the legacy of those racial formations.[87] Cultural identities are not solely determined in response to racial ideologies, but racism increases the need for a positive self-defined identity in order to survive psychologically.

To find one's racial or ethnic identity, one must deal with negative stereotypes, resist internalizing negative self-perceptions, and affirm the meaning of ethnicity for oneself.[88] If educators and parents wish to foster these positive psychological outcomes for the children in our care, we must hear their voices and affirm their identities at school and at home. And we must interrupt the racism that places them at risk.

These are challenging tasks for all of us, but they may be especially difficult for those who do not fit neatly into standard racial categories. The increasing number of multiracial families (some of whom have been represented in this chapter as Latinos, American Indians, and Asian Pacific Americans) call into question long-held assumptions about these categories. When life experience and societal paradigms collide, what gives way? What does a multiracial heritage mean for identity development? These questions also take us beyond the paradigm of Black and White and will be considered in the next chapter.

9
Identity Development in Multiracial Families
"But don't the children suffer?"

Whenever I give a presentation on the racial identity development of young people of color or White youth, I am inevitably asked, "What about the identity development process for biracial children?" It is a hard question to answer quickly because there are so many contingencies to consider. What racial combination are we talking about: Black-White, White-Asian, Asian-Black, Black–Native American? What does the young person look like: visibly identifiable as Black or Asian, apparently White, or racially ambiguous? What is the family situation? Are both parents actively involved in the child's socialization? If not, what is the racial membership of the primary caregiver? What racial identification have the parents encouraged, and is there agreement between the parents about it? Are the extended families accepting of the parents' union and of their biracial child? Where does the young person live: in a community of color, a predominantly White neighborhood, or one that is racially mixed? Are there other multiracial families in the vicinity, or is being biracial an oddity in that context? Is the racial climate one of harmony or hostility? The answer to each of these questions is relevant to the identity development process for biracial children.

Constructing our identities is a complex process for all of us, but for some it is more complicated than for others. Though theorists have attempted to develop stage-models to describe biracial identity development, there is no clear consensus about which model best accounts for the variation in experience among this population. What may have adequately explained the identity development process of older men and women may not apply so well to children born after 1967, when the Supreme Court overturned the last remaining laws prohibiting interracial marriage of all types.[1] Since that time, a biracial baby boom has occurred. The number of children living in families where one parent is White and the other Black, Asian, or American Indian has tripled, from fewer than 400,000 in 1970 to 1.5 million in 1990.[2] When biracial children living with a single or divorced parent are included, the number is even greater. The changing racial climate since the Civil Rights era has created a new context in which children of interracial unions can define themselves.

The One-Drop Rule: Racial Categorization in the United States

Yet even as the context is changing, the history of racial classification in the United States is an enduring legacy that plays a large role in the identity development process. As discussed in chapter 1, race is a social construction that has little biological meaning. Though populations from particular geographic regions can be distinguished from each other by commonly occurring physical traits such as hair texture, skin tone, facial structure, or blood type, most biologists and physical anthropologists tell us that there is no such thing as a "pure" race. All human populations are "mixed" populations. However, in terms of social realities, boundaries have been clearly drawn in the United States between those who are considered White and those who are considered non-White.

Maria P. P. Root, psychologist and editor of *Racially Mixed People in America,* the first collection of studies on racially mixed persons since the repeal of antimiscegenist laws, points out that there has been little research attention given to mixing between communities of color (e.g., American Indians and Blacks, Filipinos and Native Americans, Latino and Blacks), since these cross-group relationships do not threaten the sanctity of Whiteness.[3] The racial mixes over which there has been the most concern are those between groups that are very socially distant: Blacks and Whites, Japanese and Blacks, and Japanese and Whites.[4] Concerns with maintaining group purity have been part of both White and Asian history. However, in the context of the United States the most vigilant attention to racial purity has been given to the boundary between Whites and Blacks.[5]

Paul Spickard, a scholar who has studied the history of racial categories, writes:

> The most important thing about races was the boundaries between them. If races were pure (or had once been), and if one were a member of the race at the top, then it was essential to maintain the boundaries that defined one's superiority, to keep people from the lower categories from slipping surreptitiously upward. Hence U.S. law took pains to define just who was in which racial category. Most of the boundary drawing came on the border between White and Black.[6]

Physical appearance was an unreliable criterion for maintaining this boundary, because the light-skinned children of White slave masters and enslaved Black women sometimes resembled their fathers more than their mothers. Ancestry, rather than appearance, became the important criterion. In both legal and social practice, anyone with any known African ancestry (no matter how far back in the family lineage) was considered Black, while only those without any trace of known African ancestry were called Whites. Known as the "one-drop rule," this practice solidified the boundary between Black and White.

The use of the one-drop rule was institutionalized by the U.S. Census Bureau in the early twentieth century. Prior to 1920, "pure Negroes" were distinguished from "mulattoes" in the Census count, but in 1920 the mulatto category was dropped and *Black* was defined as any person with known Black ancestry. In 1960, the practice of self-definition began, with heads of household indicating the race of household members. However, the numbers of Black families remained essentially the same, suggesting that the heads of household were using the same one-drop criteria that the Census takers had been using. About 12 percent of the population of the United States self-identifies as Black in the Census. Though it is estimated that 75–90 percent of Black Americans have White ancestors, and about 25 percent have Native American ancestry, the widespread use of the one-drop rule meant that children with one Black parent, regardless of appearance, were classified as Black.[7] The choice of a biracial identity was not a viable option.

For example, Carol Calhoun, a fifty-four-year-old biracial woman interviewed by journalist Lise Funderburg, explained why she identifies herself as Black, even though others often assume she is White based on her physical appearance. Raised by her White mother until she was eight, then adopted by a Black family, Carol stated, "This is the way I was brought up, and this is where I'm comfortable. Had I stayed with my biological mother I might not have, except that in those times, a bastard child, or an illegitimate child of a mixed union, wouldn't have stood a snowball's chance in hell of being white. Not at all."[8]

F. James Davis, author of *Who Is Black? One Nation's Definition*, highlights the fact that no other ethnic population in the United States is defined and counted according to the one-drop rule.

> For example, individuals whose ancestry is one-fourth or less American Indian are not generally defined as Indian unless they want to be. . . . The same implicit rule appears to apply to Japanese Americans, Filipinos, or other peoples from East Asian nations and also to Mexican Americans who have Central American Indian ancestry, as a large majority do. For instance, a person whose ancestry is one-eighth Chinese is not defined as just Chinese, or East Asian, or a member of the mongoloid race. . . . Americans do not insist that an American with a small fraction of Polish ancestry be

classified as a Pole, or that someone with a single remote Greek ancestor be designated Greek, or that someone with any trace of Jewish lineage is a Jew and nothing else.[9]

According to Davis, the one-drop rule applies only to Blacks in the United States, and to no other racial group in any other nation in the world.

In 1983 the one-drop rule was challenged in the Louisiana courts by Susie Guillory Phipps, a woman who had been denied a passport because she had given her race as White on the passport application although her birth certificate designated her race as "colored." The designation had been made by the midwife, presumably based on her knowledge of the family's status in the community; however, the information came as a shock to Phipps, who had always considered herself White. She asked the Louisiana courts to change the classification on her deceased parents' birth certificates to White so that she and her siblings could be legally designated as White. They all appeared to be White, and some were blue-eyed blonds. At the time, Louisiana law indicated that anyone whose ancestry was more than one-thirty-second Black was categorized as Black. In this case, the lawyers for the state claimed to have proof that Phipps was three-thirty-seconds Black, which was more than enough African ancestry to justify her parents' classfication as colored. Consequently, she and her siblings were legally Black. The case was decided in May 1983, and in June the state legislature gave parents the right to designate the race of newborns themselves rather than relying on the doctor or midwife's assessment. In the case of previous misclassification, parents were given the right to change their children's racial designation to White if they could prove the children's Whiteness by a "preponderance of the evidence." But the 1983 statute did not abolish the one-drop rule. In fact, when Phipps appealed her case, the state's Fourth Circuit of Appeals upheld the lower court's decision, concluding that the preponderance of the evidence was that her parents were indeed colored. In 1986, when the case was appealed to the Louisiana Supreme Court, and then to the U.S. Supreme Court, both courts refused to review the decision, in effect leaving the one-drop rule untouched.[10]

It is against this historical backdrop that the contemporary question of biracial identity development must be considered. While it is clear that many people of color (and some Whites) have a multiracial heritage, the term *biracial* is usually used to refer to the offspring of parents from differing racial groups. Though the label can apply to any racial combination, it most often conjures up images of Black-White pairings. The history of racial categorization suggests that the Black-White combination has been the most controversial. For example, researchers report that biracial Asian-White and White-Hispanic children appear to have more acceptance in White communities than biracial Black-White children do.[11] Because most of the limited research on biracial identity has involved Black-White pairings, it is the biracial identity development of children of Black and White parents that I will focus on here.

"But Don't the Children Suffer?"

It is common to hear Black and White adults alike justify their ambivalence toward or outright disapproval of interracial relationships because of their concerns about the hardship the children of these relationships are assumed to suffer. The stereotype of the "tragic mulatto"—as portrayed in the classic film *Imitation of Life,* for example—is one of marginality and maladjustment.[12] This stereotype has been reinforced to some degree by published clinical reports of biracial individuals receiving mental health services. For example, in a survey of social service, mental health, special education, and probation agencies located in the San Francisco area, 60 percent of the responding agencies reported that referrals of biracial adolescents had increased during the past ten years and that this group was overrepresented among their adolescent client population.[13] Such reports may lead to the conclusion that the emotional difficulties being experienced are a direct result of one's biracial status. However, this is not necessarily the case.

Journalist Lise Funderburg interviewed sixty-five biracial adults about their experiences growing up and their current views on race and identity. While some of the adults profiled in her book *Black, White, Other* do seem to fit the "tragic mulatto" stereotype, these individuals also had experienced family disruptions—in some cases, abuse and neglect—as well as other stressful circumstances.[14] In such cases, it seems incorrect to attribute emotional distress to mixed-race heritage alone.

To counter this trend, a carefully designed comparison study of the social adjustment of biracial adolescents was conducted by Ana Mari Cauce and her colleagues at the University of Washington.[15] They compared a group of both Black-White and Asian-White adolescents with a control group of monoracial adolescents who were matched in terms of their gender, age, year in school, family income, family composition, and race of the parent of color. In other words, biracial adolescents with one White parent and one Black parent were matched with adolescents with two Black parents, and Asian-White teens were matched with monoracial Asian Americans. While the researchers could have matched the biracial participants with White adolescents (matching the White parents), they concluded that choosing a control group made up of adolescents of color would also control, in part, for the effects of racial discrimination related to growing up as a person of color in this society. Consequently, any differences found between the two groups would be more likely due to the unique circumstances associated with being biracial than to the more pervasive difficulties facing all people of color.

Forty-four adolescents (half biracial, half control group) participated in interviews of one to two hours, and completed a series of standardized questionnaires designed to assess family relations, peer relations, self-esteem, life stress, and overall psychological adjustment. The results of the comparisons did not suggest significant differences on any of the measures examined. Cauce and her colleagues con-cluded that the biracial adolescents were indistinguishable from ado-lescents of color who were similar to themselves. They wrote:

> Biracial early adolescents appear to be remarkably sim-ilar to other children of color matched on basic demo-graphic variables. This does not mean that the adoles-cents were not experiencing difficulties, either as indi-viduals or as a group. It does imply that to the degree that such difficulties were experienced they were no greater in our sample of biracial adolescents than they were in similar adolescents of color.[16]

For both groups, all measures of psychological adjustment were in the normal range, suggesting that biracial adolescents can be as rea-sonably healthy and happy as other young people are.

Cauce and her colleagues do urge further research, pointing out that their study involved only those who responded to materials advertising a study of adolescents of color. By volunteering to partic-ipate in such a study, they indicated that they considered themselves people of color. These findings might not apply to biracial adolescents who have defined themselves as White or who may be ashamed of their Asian or African American heritage. In addition, the study was conducted in the greater Seattle area, described by the researchers as more tolerant of racial difference than other parts of the country or even than other parts of Washington State.

Though the limitations of this study are important to note, its findings are supported by other studies of biracial teens, which have also found most of these adolescents to be well adjusted with high levels of self-esteem.[17] In a San Francisco study of twelve biracial teenagers, Jewelle Taylor Gibbs and Alice Hines found that nine (75%) of the biracial adolescents in their study appeared to feel positively about themselves and comfortable with their biracial identity. They had learned to incorporate positive aspects of their Black and White racial backgrounds, had established satisfactory peer and social relationships, had achieved a relatively healthy adolescent separation from their parents, and had begun to set appropriate educational and career goals. In short, they were mastering all the major tasks of adolescence. However, three (25%) seemed to be having more difficulty, reporting lower self-esteem and more ambivalence about their biracial status.

Factors associated with positive psychological adjustment in this group were intact families, higher socioeconomic status, attending integrated schools, living in multiracial neighborhoods, having a multicultural social life, and enjoying open, warm relationships with parents. In addition, teens appeared to be better adjusted in families where both parents and adolescents talked about the issues related to biracial identity. As with monoracial Black children, it also helps to have a positive race-consciousness that includes a willingness to talk to children openly about issues related to identity.[18]

While it is clear that biracial children can grow up happy and healthy, it is also clear that particular challenges associated with a biracial identity must be negotiated. One such challenge is embodied in the frequently asked question, "What are you?" While the question may be prompted by the individual's sometimes racially ambiguous appearance, the insistence with which the question is often asked represents society's need to classify its members racially. The existence of the biracial person challenges the rigid boundaries between Black and White, and the questioner may really be asking, "Which side are you on? Where do you stand?" Choosing a standpoint and an identity (or identities) is a lifelong process that manifests itself in different ways at different developmental periods.[19] Drawing on the empirical findings from their own and other studies, counseling psychologists Christine Kerwin and Joseph Ponterotto have identified key transition points as part of a general framework for understanding this complex process.[20] In many ways it overlaps with the experiences of monoracial children of color, but being positioned on the boundary of Black and White has its own unique dimensions.

The Preschool Years

Biracial children, like all children, begin to develop their racial awareness during the preschool years. They notice physical differences between themselves, their parents, and others. Skin color and hair texture are likely to be commented on from an early age. As discussed earlier, these observations can catch parents off guard. Maureen Reddy, the author of *Crossing the Color Line: Race, Parenting, and Culture,* relates her son's efforts to understand both gender and race simultaneously at the age of three.[21] Her son had observed that he and his Black father both had penises, but his White mother did not. Attributing the difference to race rather than gender, he asked, "Why do White people have vaginas?" Such questions reflect the child's efforts to make sense of the world and to create categories, as all children do. The racial awareness of biracial children seems to develop earlier than it does among White children, probably due to their early exposure to different racial groups in the context of their own family. In this regard, their experiences may be similar to monoracial Black children growing up in families where one parent is light-skinned and the other dark.

During the preschool years children are also taught by their parents to label themselves racially. The rigid racial categorization in the United States generally precludes parents of a biracial Black-White child from choosing White as a label. Some parents may intentionally choose Black, recognizing that if the child looks Black, he or she will be treated as such. Emphasizing the child's Black heritage in a positive way may be viewed as a strategy to counteract the devaluing messages of the dominant society.[22] Such a choice may be a point of conflict, however, for the White parent who feels left out by this choice.

If the parents are no longer together, and the custodial parent is White, what meaning will a Black identity have for the child? While it is certainly possible for a White parent to actively promote a positive sense of Blackness—seeking out culturally relevant books and toys, developing a Black or biracial friendship network, seeking out multiracial environments—it may not always be recognized as important to do so. If Blackness is devalued by either parent or within either extended family, if the Black parent is disparaged in front of the child, or if there are no positive ties to a Black community, then it will be very difficult for the child to value his or her Black heritage. There will be no buffer against the negative messages about Blackness in the wider society, posing a threat to the child's developing self-esteem. Of course, it is also important that the White parent not be disparaged in racial terms, but in the context of the wider culture that is less likely to happen because Whiteness is more highly valued.[23]

Increasingly, parents are choosing to teach their children to label themselves as biracial, hoping to affirm both identities. But the concept of "both" is a complex one for preschoolers to understand, simply because of their cognitive immaturity. They may learn the biracial label, with little grasp of its meaning initially, though that will change as they get older. Psychologists Robin Lin Miller and Mary Jane Rotheram-Borus recommend that if parents are going to encourage a biracial identity, they need to provide substantial positive exposure to both racial groups to help the child understand what it means to be a participant in both cultures. Communities with positive intergroup relations provide environmental support for a biracial identity, and communities with high levels of racial tension are more likely to undermine it. The pressure to choose sides in such situations is too great for developing children.[24]

If the child's racial label and look is different from that of the same-sex parent, the child may express a desire for sameness at an early age. For example, if the mother's skin is light and her daughter's is dark, the daughter may wish for lighter skin like Mom's. This wish in itself is not necessarily a sign of low self-esteem but a natural expression of a desire to be identified with the parent. In fact, in the following example, it was the mother that the five-year-old child wished to change, not herself. As a mother and daughter were riding in the car together, the child was playing with a "magic wand." The

White mother asked, "If you really had magic, what would you do?" Without any hesitation, the Black daughter replied, "I would turn your skin brown."[25]

The fact that the child and parent don't match may be a cause for unwanted attention from others who will ask if the child is adopted or assume that the parent is a babysitter. Particularly if the parent appears Black and the child appears White, White adults may even question the parent's right to be with the child. For example, one Black mother of a White-looking child took her infant to a public gathering several weeks after her birth, one of their first outings together. An older White woman saw her carrying the child and asked accusingly, "Where did you get that baby?" While the infant surely doesn't remember this event, similar scenes are repeated during the preschool years and later, heightening the child's awareness of the physical differences between family members.

The child's own physical appearance may be a source of special attention, also beginning in the preschool years. Biracial children sometimes appear quite exotic to others. Frequent comments about one's physical features—"those beautiful light eyes," "that curly hair," "that gorgeous complexion"—may initially be flattering, but then they become objectifying. In her article "Resolving 'Other' Status: Identity Development of Biracial Individuals," Maria Root observes,

> It is the combination of inquisitive looks, longer than passing glances to comprehend unfamiliar racial-ethnic features . . . and comments of surprise to find out that the child is one or the other parent's biological child *along with* disapproving comments and nonverbal communication that begin to convey to the child that this otherness is "undesirable or wrong."[26]

As a preschooler, the child is not equipped to process all of these issues, but they foreshadow conflicts to be resolved later. The challenge for the parent at this stage is to affirm who the child is, regardless of the chosen label. In this sense, the task is the same as it is for any parent. However, the absence of resources—few instances of interracial families in children's books or on television, for example—increases the challenge for parents of biracial children.

Necessity is sometimes the mother of invention. One grandmother, unable to find a doll that matched her biracial grandchild's complexion, made a "Raggedy Ann" style doll for her, choosing fabric of just the right shade. A wonderful book depicting a multiracial family consisting of a White father and a Black mother, *Black, White, Just Right!* was written by a grandmother who wanted her grandchildren to see themselves reflected positively.[27] Given the relatively rapid growth of the biracial population, it would seem that the marketplace should begin to reflect these parenting needs.

Entry into School

The transition from the preschool years to middle childhood is marked not only by entrance into elementary school but also by an understanding of race or ethnicity which is concrete and associated with specific markers—the language one speaks, the foods one eats, the physical characteristics one has. A biracial child now may have a better understanding of what it means to be part of two groups, but his or her monoracial peers may also have learned stereotypic notions of race and ethnicity.[28] For example, Maureen Reddy describes her son's encounter at the beach with a White child who had clearly learned that racial categories were mutually exclusive:

> I noticed eight-year-old Sean standing in waist-deep water with another boy and pointing toward the blanket where Doug and I sat. When I asked him later what that was about, he explained that the (white) boy had asked him if he were black or white—the other child's very first question, before name, age, or invitation to play together! Sean went on, "I said 'both.' The kid said,

'You can't be *both*. Which one are you really?' So I said 'both' again, and told him to look at my parents for proof."[29]

The biracial label Sean had been taught clearly challenged his White playmate's view of the world, and the playmate's response was to challenge the label. Such challenges occur not only on the beach but also at school, and are made not only by peers but also by adults. This kind of challenge is especially likely to occur if the child's label does not match the child's look.

For example, Danielle, the Puerto Rican–looking child of an Irish Catholic mother and an African American father, described such a grade-school incident to Lise Funderburg. Danielle's second-grade teacher asked her students to talk about their family's culture and ethnicity. When Danielle took her turn, she stood up and told the class that she was Irish Catholic. She recalled, "My teacher, in front of the entire classroom, said I didn't know what I was talking about and I needed to sit down and go home and ask my mother. . . . She was a white woman, and she all but laughed at me when I was a *child!* I was *eight years old!*" Danielle, who lived with her Irish Catholic mother and faithfully attended catechism classes, was shocked by her teacher's disbelief and tried to defend herself. But the teacher remained unconvinced until Danielle's irate mother appeared in her classroom the next day, successfully demanding an apology to her daughter.[30]

Conversely, a young biracial child I know who resembles her Irish Catholic father much more than her African American mother becomes frustrated when her peers don't believe her when she talks about her Black heritage. Although she has been taught to think of herself as biracial, she may rarely be asked about her racial background because people simply assume they know what it is. When a biracial child is assumed to be White, discomfort may occur when in the company of the darker-skinned parent. As discussed earlier, adults may question the adult's relationship to the child, and the prejudices of peers, previously unexpressed, may surface.

Consider this example: A biracial child with wiry blond hair and blue eyes is assumed to be White by classmates and teachers, who have only had contact with his White mother. One day his African American father picks him up from school, and his best friend runs away from him, yelling, "I played with a nigger."[31] While Black-appearing biracial children may be teased for their light skin or wavy hair by Black children expressing the color-based prejudices they've learned, there does not seem to be the same shock when the White parent of a dark-skinned child appears.

The importance of the parents' role in helping children make sense of these experiences cannot be overemphasized. Talking about the possibility of such interactions and providing children with appropriate responses they might use in such situations is one way to inoculate children against the stress of this kind of racism. Several of the biracial adults profiled by Funderburg expressed a wish that their parents had prepared them better for the situations they would encounter. Said one, "I thought my parents should have talked to me about it or tried to figure it out, but I don't think they knew themselves, so they just didn't try at all."[32] This respondent, now a parent herself, is being more proactive with her own racially mixed child.

The racial awareness that emerges in the grade-school years continually increases in the years just before puberty. Kerwin and Ponterotto identify preadolescence as a time of building on the knowledge of the previous stage.[33] Changes in the environment—moving from one neighborhood to another, experiencing a different racial mix at school—can trigger new learning, but in many ways these years are just the prelude for the big event, adolescence. During adolescence the question "Who am I?" must be addressed directly, not by the parents, but by the adolescents themselves.

Adolescence: Making Choices

In her doctoral study of the experience of racial self-identification of Black-White biracial adults and the factors affecting their choices of racial identity, Charmaine Wijeyesinghe identified several factors that can significantly impact the process and its outcome. They are biological heritage, sociohistorical context of society, early socialization experiences, culture, ethnic identity and heritage, spirituality, individual awareness of self in relation to race and racism, and physical appearance, as well as other personal social identities such as sexual orientation. These factors can combine in a large number of different ways, leading to a wide range of experience.[34] Other researchers have confirmed this diversity of experience.[35] According to Wijeyesinghe, "identity confusion" is most likely to occur when there is a discrepancy between various factors. For example, in a Black neighborhood one's physical appearance might make a Black self-identification a comfortable one, but one's sexual identity as a gay male would likely threaten one's acceptance in a Black male peer group. On the other hand, anti-Black sentiments among gay White adolescents may be a barrier to acceptance there, complicating both the racial and the sexual identity processes.[36] Sorting through the various factors and finding a way to integrate them into a positive sense of self is the task adolescents of mixed heritage face.

During adolescence many biracial teens feel pressured to choose one racial group over another. As the school cafeteria becomes increasingly divided along racial lines, where does the biracial student choose to sit? If parents have encouraged a Black identification and the young person's physical appearance fits that identity, the initial choice may seem easy. But the narrow definition of Blackness that Black adolescents typically use may leave the Black-identified child with a White parent feeling not quite Black enough. Or if the adolescent is very light-skinned, Black peers who do not know the individual's racial heritage may question his or her presence in their group. Biracial students who choose to sit at the Black table may also become uncomfortable with the anger Black adolescents often express toward Whites. Ironically, as a result of their own encounters with racism, biracial youth often have reason to be angry with White people themselves, which may generate internal conflicts. For example, one Black-looking biracial woman described herself as becoming "very anti-White because of the experiences I had" and feeling guilty about it because her mother was White. "But then," she said, "I would think my mother is the exception to the rule."[37] Fortunately she felt able to talk to her parents about these incidents and could process her feelings about them.

For biracial teens who feel more comfortable among their White peers, perhaps because of their childhood socialization and neighborhood environment, the choice to affiliate primarily with White people has its own complications. While a very light-skinned adolescent whose biracial parentage is not public information might be accepted as White, this kind of "passing" is difficult to do in adolescence. Unlike adults who might choose to blend into the White community, the adolescent is unlikely to be able to effectively break all ties with relatives of color and assume a completely White identity.[38]

Consequently, like monoracial Black adolescents in White communities, biracial teens often become aware of the racial boundaries in their community when they reach dating age. White parents typically view biracial children as non-White and may discourage romantic connections. A young White woman in one of my psychology of racism classes wrote about this parental attitude in her journal. The young woman was dating a very light-skinned biracial man. Her mother's comment about him was that he "got lucky" by having light skin, but because she couldn't be sure that his children would be as light-skinned as he was, her daughter should not take the risk of getting too serious with this young man.

Such parental prejudices notwithstanding, biracial boys seem to have more social options than do girls, particularly if they are actively involved in sports. Participation on a sports team allows boys to maintain cross-racial friendships (assuming the teams are racially mixed) and is often a source of status in the school environment. Biracial girls are often considered beautiful objects of curiosity because of their "exotic" looks, but this attention does not necessarily translate into dating partners. Like monoracial Black girls in White communities,

biracial girls in White communities often become more socially isolated in adolescence. Biracial girls in predominantly Black environments, on the other hand, may be actively sought after by Black boys
(and consequently become objects of resentment by monoracial
Black girls) because of the legacy of colorism in Black communities,
conferring favored status to those with light skin, straight or wavy
hair, and European features.

Though pressures to choose one monoracial identity at the
exclusion of other possible identities are most intense in adolescence,
some young people are able to successfully maintain a multiracial self-
concept even as they affiliate with one group or another. Their identities may seem fluid, and they may describe themselves as biracial in
some contexts and as Black in others. For example, when with White
friends who were making stereotypical references to Black people in
her presence, one young woman responded by asserting her own
Blackness, thereby challenging her friends' generalizations about
Black people. But when Black friends teased her for being White, she
responded with pride in her biracial heritage. In both cases, she was
doing what her parents had taught her to do. She said,

> It was something that was ingrained in me by both my
> mother and father: "You're black *and* you're white. You
> have to accept everything about yourself, otherwise
> you're not going to like yourself. But claim your black
> first, because that's the part of you that needs sticking up
> for most . . . I've had [teasing] from both sides, and I've
> dealt with it the way my parents taught me to. And
> they're right, the black side's the one that almost always
> needs protecting, so I claim it first.[39]

The College and Adult Years

Kerwin and Ponterotto argue that with the development of a more
secure personal identity in early adulthood, it becomes easier to reject

peer pressures and more actively embrace one's bicultural heritage. Even when adults publicly identify themselves as Black, they can still appreciate their multiracial heritage.[40] Jane Lazarre, author of *Beyond the Whiteness of Whiteness: Memoir of a White Mother of Black Sons,* includes a portion of a letter she received from her adult son, Adam, illustrating this kind of resolution:

> Notwithstanding my multicultural consciousness, my racial identity is simply that of a Black man as any other Black man of any combination. I am related to and I relate to others as a Black man. Sometimes I identify with Jewish culture because of you and my Jewish family, but it is never without the footnote of knowing that I am perceived as a Black man who "does a good Jew" instead of a Jew celebrating his own culture. Over the years of growing up, that phenomenon has pulled me further and further from a comfortable, natural identification with Jewish culture. I still retain some, but I am conscious of a different perspective on that part of me now as my age increases and my innocence decreases. When I am in a group of people who are white, Jewish or not, I am a Black man. When I am in a group of people who are Black, I am a Black man. I feel no difference in my identity because my mother is white and Jewish. I only feel, perhaps, a greater familiarity with white people than Blacks who have not been exposed to white family and friends. But that familiarity, or comfort, is not related to a sense of identity.[41]

I assigned Kerwin and Ponterotto's chapter on biracial identity development to students in my psychology of racism course prior to showing a video in class called *Just Black? Multiracial Identity.*[42] In response, a biracial student wrote:

I felt that what Kerwin and Ponterotto described as col-
lege/young adulthood and adulthood were on target as
to where I am right now. I would see myself as between
these stages. I would say that I am no longer rejecting
any part of my heritage, and that I have grown to appreciate both sides of my family, and to be proud of where
I come from. . . . I feel that the video was probably the
single thing that I could identify with more than anything else we did this semester. As I listened to the people speak, I could understand what they were talking
about because so many of their experiences were things
that I experienced throughout my life. . . . It was nice
to see someone in the video whose hair looked just like
mine, and whose features were similar to mine. . . .
What has concerned me has always been encountering
people who would choose the "part" of me that they
were comfortable with—whether it was the fact that I
was half Black, or that I was part White. Right now I
want to learn as much as I can about the experiences of
multiracial people like myself.

Like monoracial students of color, this young woman has a need
to see herself reflected in the curriculum and is expressing a desire to
immerse herself in an examination of a multiracial identity, actively
seeking out others who have shared the experience of growing up in
a multiracial family. Educators interested in fostering the positive
growth and development of all students need to include in their consideration those who define themselves as biracial. As with other racial
identities, the development of a biracial identity is a lifelong process,
and it continues to be influenced by numerous personal, societal, and
environmental factors. What is most significant for the children of
interracial unions ultimately is not what label they claim, but the self-
acceptance they have of their multiracial heritage.

Identity in Adoptive Families Considered

In considering the identity development of children of color adopted by White parents, issues similar to those experienced by nonadopted biracial children emerge.[43] For example, the Black or biracial adoptee may experience the same kind of divided loyalties in adolescence that nonadopted biracial teens do. However, some issues are unique to children adopted into White families. In particular, the absence of an adult of color in the family to serve as a racial role model may make adolescent identity development more difficult. In addition, the identity process is often complicated by the adolescent's questions and feelings about the adoption itself. "Who are my biological parents? What were the circumstances of my birth? Why did my birth mother give me up for adoption?" These questions and the underlying feelings of rejection and abandonment add another layer to the complex process of identity development.

However, as in the case of nonadopted biracial children, the role of the caregivers is critical in easing this process. Race-conscious parents who openly discuss racism, who seek to create a multiracial community of friends and family (perhaps adopting more than one child of color so there will be siblings with a shared experience), who seek out racially-mixed schools, who, in short, take seriously the identity needs of their adopted children of color and try to provide for them increase the likelihood that their adopted children of color will grow to adulthood feeling good about themselves and their adoptive parents.

Consider the case of Alan, a dark-skinned Black male raised by White parents in a predominantly White community. In an interview with me, he remarked that his Black friends were often surprised to learn that his parents were White. How was it possible that a Black guy with White parents could be so "cool"? He attributed his social success to the fact that his parents always sought out integrated neighborhoods and placed him in racially mixed schools. They encouraged his involvement in athletics where he made strong connections with other Black boys. In junior high school, when the identity process often begins to unfold, Alan felt most comfortable with those Black boys. He explained, "Whenever I went out with my [Black] friends or played my sports . . . that's where I liked to be. That's where I found myself." When his parents wanted to leave the city on vacation, he found himself less and less willing to leave his network of Black friends. Their idea of getting away meant social isolation for him. As he got older he realized that he didn't want to go on vacation to a place "where there's three Black people in the whole town."

While it does not seem that he ever rejected his parents in his adolescence, as a young adult he has put some distance between himself and his extended family members. He is the only Black person among a large extended family, and his mother's relatives live in a rural area in a state with a very small Black population. Whenever Alan goes to visit them, he feels very self-conscious, very aware of his visibility in that environment. His parents, respectful of his feelings, do not insist that he accompany them on those family visits. Alan has considered a search for his biological mother but has not yet pursued it. His parents have responded to the possibility in a supportive way.

Alan's experience is contrasted with the experiences of several Korean adoptees I have taught over the years. In all of these cases, the young women grew up in White families that considered their daughters' racial category irrelevant to their childrearing. No particular effort was made to affirm their Korean heritage, beginning with the choice of their first names, which typically reflected the parents' European heritage rather than the children's Korean heritage.

The names themselves often led to encounters with racism. For example, one young woman told me of an experience she had cashing a check. The White male clerk looked at her face and then looked down at the name on the check and asked, "What kind of name is that?" She identified its European origin. The clerk looked dumbfounded and said rudely, "What are you doing with a name like that?!" Such experiences remind these adoptees of their outsider status in White communities.

In one instance, a young woman reported that when she was a child a Korean family friend had offered to take her to Korean cultural events, but that her parents had declined the offers, encouraging instead her complete assimilation into her adoptive culture. Unfortunately, *complete* assimilation was not possible because she did not look the part. Her Asian features continually set her apart, but with no cultural connection to any Asian community she had no one to share these experiences with and no help in learning how to cope with the racism she encountered. In college she began to realize her need for some connection to an Asian community and began to explore how to make those connections. In reflecting on the choices her parents made, she said, "In a way I think my parents messed up and that they taught me to hate what I really was. Maybe if they hadn't ignored my racial heritage so much I would have an easier time accepting that I am an Asian and that I always will be." At least that is the way she believes the world will always see her.

Several years ago I was invited to moderate a panel of adoptive parents who were sharing their experiences with interracial adoption with an audience of prospective parents considering the same option. The White panelists spoke of ways they had tried to affirm the identity of their adopted children of color. One parent, the mother of a Central American adoptee, spoke of how she had become involved in a support group of parents who had adopted Latino children as a way of providing her son with playmates who had a shared experience. She also described her efforts to find Latino adults who might serve as role models for her child. There were very few Latinos in her mostly White community, but she located a Latino organization in a nearby town and began to do volunteer work for it as a way of building a Latino friendship network.

During the question-and-answer period that followed, a White woman stood up and explained that she was considering adopting a Latino child but lived in a small rural community that was entirely White. She was impressed by the mother's efforts to create a Latino network for her child but expressed doubts that she herself could do so. She said she would feel too uncomfortable placing herself in a situation where she would be one of few Whites. She didn't think she could do it.

I thought this was an amazing statement. How could this White adult seriously consider placing a small child in a situation where the child would be in the minority *all* the time, while the idea of spending a few hours as a "minority" was too daunting for her? Had I been the social worker doing the home study in that case, I would not have recommended an interracial placement. The prospective mother was apparently not ready to risk the discomfort required to help a child of color negotiate a racist environment.

The successful adoption of children of color by White parents requires those parents to be willing to experience the close encounters with racism that their children—and they as parents—will have, and to be prepared to talk to their children about them. Ultimately they need to examine their own identities as White people, going beyond the idea of raising a child of color in a White family to a new understanding of themselves and their children as members of a multiracial family.

The creation of well-adjusted multiracial families, whether through adoption or through the union of parents of different racial backgrounds, is clearly possible, but not automatic. Considerable examination of one's own racial identity is required. Adults willing to do the personal work required to confront racism and stretch their own cultural boundaries increase the possibility that they will have the reward of watching their children emerge into adulthood with a positive sense of their identities intact.

Part V

Breaking the Silence

10

Embracing a Cross-Racial Dialogue
"We were struggling for the words."

Some people say there is too much talk about race and racism in the United States. I say that there is not enough. In recent years, news headlines have highlighted the pervasiveness of the problem. There have been race riots in Los Angeles and St. Petersburg, Florida. A thirteen-year-old Black boy was beaten into a coma by White youths who caught him riding his bicycle in their Chicago neighborhood. Anti-immigrant legislation in California has led to the public harassment of Latino citizens. Anti-Asian violence has increased dramatically. Precipitated by the damaging publicity incurred by the release of tape recordings in which Texaco officials used racial slurs to describe Black employees, Texaco agreed to pay $176.1 million to settle a race discrimination lawsuit, the largest such settlement in history.[1] Carl Rowan, a respected Black journalist, authored a book titled *The Coming Race War in America: A Wake-Up Call* in which he warns of the growing threat of White supremacist militia groups plotting to ignite racial conflict.[2]

What is happening here? We need to continually break the silence about racism whenever we can.[3] We need to talk about it at home, at school, in our houses of worship, in our workplaces, in our community groups. But talk does not mean idle chatter. It means meaningful, productive dialogue to raise consciousness and lead to effective action and social change. But how do we start? This is the question my students ask me. "How do I engage in meaningful dialogue about racial issues? How do I get past my fear? How do I get past my anger? Am I willing to take the risk of speaking up? Can I trust that there will be others to listen and support me? Will it make a difference anyway? Is it worth the effort?"

The Paralysis of Fear

Fear is a powerful emotion, one that immobilizes, traps words in our throats, and stills our tongues. Like a deer on the highway, frozen in the panic induced by the lights of an oncoming car, when we are afraid it seems that we cannot think, we cannot speak, we cannot move.

What do we fear? Isolation from friends and family, ostracism for speaking of things that generate discomfort, rejection by those who may be offended by what we have to say, the loss of privilege or status for speaking in support of those who have been marginalized by society, physical harm caused by the irrational wrath of those who disagree with your stance? My students readily admit their fears in their journals and essays. Some White students are afraid of their own ignorance, afraid that because of their limited experience with people of color they will ask a naive question or make an offensive remark that will provoke the wrath of the people of color around them.

"Yes, there is fear," one White woman writes, "the fear of speaking is overwhelming. I do not feel, for me, that it is fear of rejection from people of my race, but anger and disdain from people of color. The ones who I am fighting for." In my response to this woman's comment, I explain that she needs to fight for herself, not for people of color. After all, she has been damaged by the cycle of racism, too, though perhaps this is less obvious. If she speaks because *she* needs to speak, perhaps then it would be less important whether the people of color are appreciative of her comments. She seems to understand my comment, but the fear remains.

Another student, a White woman in her late thirties, writes about her fears when trying to speak honestly about her understanding of racism.

> Fear requires us to be honest with not only others, but with ourselves. Often this much honesty is difficult for many of us, for it would permit our insecurities and

ignorances to surface, thus opening the floodgate to our vulnerabilities. This position is difficult for most of us when [we are] in the company of entrusted friends and family. I can imagine fear heightening when [we are] in the company of those we hardly know. Hence, rather than publicly admit our weaknesses, we remain silent.

These students are not alone in their fear-induced silence. Christine Sleeter, a White woman who has written extensively about multicultural education and antiracist teaching, writes:

> I first noticed White silence about racism about 15 years ago, although I was not able to name it as such. I recall realizing after having shared many meals with African American friends while teaching in Seattle, that racism and race-related issues were fairly common topics of dinner-table conversation, which African Americans talked about quite openly. It struck me that I could not think of a single instance in which racism had been a topic of dinner-table conversation in White contexts. Race-related issues sometimes came up, but not *racism*.[4]

Instead, Sleeter argues, White people often speak in a kind of racial code, using communication patterns with each other that encourage a kind of White racial bonding. These communication patterns include race-related asides in conversations, strategic eye contact, jokes, and other comments that assert an "us-them" boundary. Sleeter observes,

> These kinds of interactions seem to serve the purpose of defining racial lines, and inviting individuals to either declare their solidarity or mark themselves as deviant. Depending on the degree of deviance, one runs the risk

of losing the other individual's approval, friendship and company.[5]

The fear of the isolation that comes from this kind of deviance is a powerful silencer. My students, young and old, often talk about this kind of fear, experienced not only with friends but with colleagues or employers in work settings. For instance, Lynn struggled when her employer casually used racial slurs in conversation with her. It was especially troubling to Lynn because her employer's young children were listening to their conversation. Though she was disturbed by the interaction, Lynn was afraid and then embarrassed by her own silence:

> I was completely silent following her comment. I knew that I should say something, to point out that she was being completely inappropriate (especially in front of her children) and that she had really offended me. But I just sat there with a stupid forced half-smile on my face.

How could she respond to this, she asked? What would it cost her to speak? Would it mean momentary discomfort or could it really mean losing her job? And what did her silence cost her on a personal level?

Because of the White culture of silence about racism, my White students often have little experience engaging in dialogue about racial issues. They have not had much practice at overcoming their inhibitions to speak. They notice that the students of color speak about racism more frequently, and they assume they do so more easily. One White woman observed,

> In our class discussion when White students were speaking, we sounded so naive and so "young" about what we were discussing. It was almost like we were struggling for the words to explain ourselves and were

even speaking much slower than the students of color. The students of color, on the other hand, were extremely well aware of what to say and of what they wanted to express. It dawned on me that these students had dealt with this long before I ever thought about racism. Since last fall, racism has been a totally new concept to me, almost like I was hearing about it for the first time. For these students, however, the feelings, attitudes and terminology came so easily.

This woman is correct in her observation that most of the people of color in that classroom are more fluent in the discourse of racism, and more aware of its personal impact on their lives than perhaps she has been. But she is wrong that their participation is easy. They are also afraid.

I am reminded of an article written by Kirsten Mullen, a Black parent who needed to speak to her child's White teachers about issues of racial insensitivity at his school. She wrote, "I was terrified the first time I brought up the subject of race at my son's school. My palms were clammy, my heart was racing, and I could not have done it without rehearsing in the bathroom mirror."[6] She was afraid, but who would advocate for her son if she didn't? She could not afford the cost of silence.

An Asian American woman in my class writes about the difficulty of speaking:

The process of talking about this issue is not easy. We people of color can't always make it easier for White people to talk about race relations because sometimes they need to break away from that familiar and safe ground of being neutral or silent. . . . I understand that [some are] trying but sometimes they need to take bigger steps and more risks. As an Asian in America, I am always taking risks when I share my experiences of racism; however, the dominant culture expects it of me. They think I like talking about how my parents are laughed at at work or how my older sister is forced to take [cancer-causing] birth control pills because she is on welfare. Even though I am embarrassed and sometimes get too emotional about these issues, I talk about them because I want to be honest about how I feel.

She has fears, but who will tell her story if she doesn't? For many people of color, learning to break the silence is a survival issue. To remain silent would be to disconnect from her own experience, to swallow and internalize her own oppression. The cost of silence is too high.

Sometimes we fear our own anger and frustration, the chance of losing control or perhaps collapsing into despair should our words, yet again, fall on deaf ears. A Black woman writes:

One thing that I struggle with as an individual when it comes to discussions about race is the fact that I tend to give up. When I start to think, "He or she will never understand me. What is the point?" I have practically defeated myself. No human can ever fully understand the experiences and feelings of another, and I must remind myself that progress, although often slow and painful, can be made.

A very powerful example of racial dialogue between a multiracial group of men can be seen in the award-winning video *The Color of Fear*.[7] One of the most memorable moments in the film is when Victor, an African American man, begins to shout angrily at David, a White man, who continually invalidates what Victor has said about his experiences with racism. After viewing the video in my class, several students of color wrote about how much they identified with Victor's anger and how relieved they were to see that it could be expressed without disastrous consequences. An Asian American woman wrote:

> I don't know if I'll ever see a more powerful, moving, on-the-money movie in my life! . . . Victor really said it all. He verbalized all I've ever felt or will feel so eloquently and so convincingly. When he first started speaking, he was so calm and I did not expect anything remotely close to what he exhibited. When he started shouting, my initial reaction was of discomfort. Part of that discomfort stemmed from watching him just going nuts on David. But there was something else that was embedded inside of me. I kept thinking throughout the whole movie and I finally figured it out at the end. Victor's rage and anger was mine as well. Those emotions that I had hoped to keep inside forever and ever because I didn't know if I was justified in feeling that way. I had no words or evidence, solid evidence, to prove to myself or others that I had an absolute RIGHT to scream and yell and be angry for so many things.

The anger and frustration of people of color, even when received in smaller doses, is hard for some White people to tolerate. One White woman needed to vent her own frustrations before she could listen to the frustration and anger of people of color. She wrote:

> Often I feel that because I am White, my feelings are disregarded or looked down upon in racial dialogues. I feel that my efforts are unappreciated. . . . I also realize that it is these feelings which make me want to withdraw from the fight against racism altogether. . . . [However,] I acknowledge the need for White students to listen to minority students when they express anger

against the system which has failed them without taking this communication as a personal attack.

Indeed, this is what one young woman of color hoped for:

> When I'm participating in a cross-racial dialogue, I prefer that the people I'm interacting with understand why I react the way that I do. When I say that I want understanding, it does not mean that I'm looking for sympathy. I merely want people to know why I'm angry and not to be offended by it.

In order for there to be meaningful dialogue, fear, whether of anger or isolation, must eventually give way to risk and trust. A leap of faith must be made. It is not easy, and it requires being willing to push past one's fear. Wrote one student,

> At times it feels too risky . . . but I think if people remain equally committed, it can get easier. It's a very stressful process, but I think the consequences of not exploring racial issues are ultimately far more damaging. . . .

The Psychological Cost of Silence

As a society, we pay a price for our silence. Unchallenged personal, cultural, and institutional racism results in the loss of human potential, lowered productivity, and a rising tide of fear and violence in our society. Individually, racism stifles our own growth and development. It clouds our vision and distorts our perceptions. It alienates us not only from others but also from ourselves and our own experiences.

Jean Baker Miller's paper "Connections, Disconnections and Violations" offers a helpful framework for seeing how this self-alienation takes place.[8] As Miller describes, when we have meaningful experiences, we usually seek to share those experiences with someone else. In doing so, we hope to be heard and understood, to feel validated by the other. When we do not feel heard, we feel invalidated, and a relational disconnection has taken place. We might try again, persisting in our efforts to be heard, or we may choose to disconnect from that person. If there are others available who will listen and affirm us, disconnection from those who won't may be the best alternative. But if disconnection means what Miller calls "condemned isolation," then we will do whatever we have to in order to remain in connection with others. That may mean denying our own experiences of racism, selectively screening things out of our consciousness so that we can continue our relationships with reduced discomfort. As a person of color, to remain silent and deny my own experience with racism may be an important coping strategy in some contexts but it may also lead to the self-blame and self-doubt of internalized oppression.[9]

The consequences are different but also damaging for Whites. As we have seen, many Whites have been encouraged by their culture of silence to disconnect from their racial experiences. When White children make racial observations, they are often silenced by their parents, who feel uncomfortable and unsure of how to respond. With time the observed contradictions between parental attitudes and behaviors, or between societal messages about meritocracy and visible inequities, become difficult to process in a culture of silence. In order to prevent chronic discomfort, Whites may learn not to notice.

But in not noticing, one loses opportunities for greater insight into oneself and one's experience. A significant dimension of who one is in the world, one's Whiteness, remains uninvestigated and perceptions of daily experience are routinely distorted. Privilege goes unnoticed, and all but the most blatant acts of racial bigotry are ignored. Not noticing requires energy. Exactly how much energy is used up in this way becomes apparent with the opportunity to explore those silenced perceptions. It is as though a blockage has been removed and energy is released.

According to Miller, when a relationship is growth-producing, it results in five good things: increased zest, a sense of empowerment, greater knowledge, an increased sense of self-worth, and a desire for more connection. In interviews done with White teachers who were leading discussions with others about racism, there was abundant evidence of these benefits. Said one, "The thing that's happened for me is that I'm no longer afraid to bring [race] up. I look to bring it up; I love bringing it up." This educator now brings these issues up regularly with her colleagues, and they, like she, seem to feel liberated by the opportunity for dialogue. Describing a discussion group in which participants talked about racial issues, she said, "It was such a rich conversation and it just flowed the whole time. It was exciting to be a part of it. Everybody contributed and everybody felt the energy and the desire."

Another participant described the process of sharing the new information she had learned with her adult son, and said, "There's a lot of energy that's going on in all sorts of ways. It feels wonderful." Yet another described her own exploration of racial issues as "renewal at midlife." The increased self-knowledge she experienced was apparent as she says, "I'm continuing to go down the path of discovery for myself about what I think and what I believe and the influences I've had in my life. . . . It impacts me almost every moment of my waking hours." These benefits of self-discovery are made available to them as the silence about racism is broken.

It is important to say that even as good things are generated, the growth process is not painless. One of the White teachers interviewed described the early phase of her exploration of racism as "hell," a state of constant dissonance. Another commented, "I get really scared at some of the things that come up. And I've never been so nervous in my life as I have been facilitating that antiracist study group." A third said, "How do I feel about the fact that I might be influencing large groups of people? Well, in a way, I'm proud of it. I'm scared about it [too] because it puts me out in the forefront. It's a vulnerable position." The fear is still there, but these pioneers are learning to push past it.[10]

Finding Courage for Social Change

Breaking the silence undoubtedly requires courage. How can we find the courage we need? This is a question I ask myself a lot, because I too struggle with fear. I am aware of my own vulnerability even as I write this book. What will writing it mean for my life? Will it make me a target for attack? How will readers respond to what I have to say? Have I really said anything helpful? Silence feels safer, but in the long run, I know that it is not. So I, like so many others, need courage.

I look for it in the lives of others, seeking role models for how to be an effective agent of change. As a person of faith, I find that the Bible is an important source of inspiration for me. It is full of stories of change agents, whose lives inspire me. Moses and Esther are two favorites. Because I am a Black woman, I am particularly interested in the lives of other Black women who have been agents of change. I find strength in learning about the lives of Harriet Tubman, Sojourner Truth, Ida B. Wells, Zora Neale Hurston, Fannie Lou Hamer, Rosa Parks, and Gloria Wade-Gayles, to name a few. I also want to know about the lives of my White allies, past and present: Angelina and Sarah Grimke, Clarence Jordan, Virginia Foster Durr, Lois Stalvey, Mab Segrest, Bill Bradley, and Morris Dees, for example. What about Black men and other men and women of color, Asian, Latino, American Indian? W. E. B. DuBois, Thurgood Marshall, Ronald Takaki, Maxine Hong Kingston, Cesar Chavez, Wilma Mankiller, Joel Spring, Mitsuye Yamada, Nellie Wong? Yes, those examples and many unnamed others are important, too. I am filling in the gaps in my education as quickly as I can.

I have heard many people say, "But I don't know enough! I don't even recognize most of those names. I don't have enough of the facts to be able to speak up about racism or anything else!" They are not alone. We have all been miseducated in this regard. Educating ourselves and others is an essential step in the process of change. Few of us have been taught to think critically about issues of social injustice. We have been taught not to notice or to accept our present situation as a given, "the way it is." But we can learn the history we were not taught, we can watch the documentaries we never saw in school, and we can read about the lives of change agents, past and present. We can discover another way. We are surrounded by a "cloud of witnesses" who will give us courage if we let them.

Do you feel overwhelmed by the task? When my students begin to recognize the pervasiveness of racism in the culture and our institutions, they begin to despair, feeling powerless to effect change. Sometimes I feel overwhelmed, too. The antidote I have found is to focus on my own sphere of influence. I can't fix everything, but some things are within my control. While many people experience themselves as powerless, everyone has some sphere of influence in which they can work for change, even if it is just in their own personal network of family and friends. Ask yourself, "Whose lives do I affect and how? What power and authority do I wield in the world? What meetings do I attend? Who do I talk to in the course of a day?" Identify your strengths and use them.

If you are a parent, what conversations have you had with your children about these issues? What books are sitting on their bookshelves? Do you know what discussions are taking place at your child's school? If you are a teacher, what dialogue is taking place in your classroom? Regardless of your subject matter, there are ways to engage students in critical thinking about racism which are relevant to your discipline. Have you considered what they might be? If you like to write letters to friends, have you written any letters to the editor, adding to the public discourse about dismantling racism? Have you written to broadcasters protesting programming which reinforces racial stereotypes? If you are an extrovert, have you used your people skills to gather others together for dialogue about racism? If you are an athlete, what language and behavior do you model in the locker room? If you are a board member, what questions do you raise at the meetings? Who sits on the board with you? What values and perspectives are represented there? If you are an employer, who is missing from your work force? What are you doing about it?

"What if I make a mistake?" you may be thinking. "Racism is a volatile issue, and I don't want to say or do the wrong thing." In nearly twenty years of teaching and leading workshops about racism, I have made many mistakes. I have found that a sincere apology and a genuine desire to learn from one's mistakes are usually rewarded with forgiveness. If we wait for perfection, we will never break the silence. The cycle of racism will continue uninterrupted.

We all want to "do the right thing," but each of us must determine what our own right thing is. The right thing for me, writing this book, may not be the right thing for you. Parker Palmer offers this wisdom about doing the "right thing": "Right action requires only that we respond faithfully to our own inner truth and to the truth around us . . . If an action is rightly taken, taken with integrity, its outcomes will achieve whatever is possible—which is the best that anyone can do."[11]

You may be saying, "I *am* a change agent. I am always the one who speaks up at the meetings, but I'm tired. How do I keep going?" This is an important question, because a genuine commitment to interrupting racism is a long-term commitment. How can we sustain ourselves for the long haul? One thing I have learned is that we need a community of support. We all need community to give us energy, to strengthen our voices, and to offer constructive criticism when we stray off course. We need to speak up against racism and other forms of oppression, but we do not have to speak alone. Look for like-minded others. Organize a meeting for friends or colleagues concerned about racial issues. Someone else will come. Attend the meetings others have organized. Share your vision. Others will be drawn to you. Your circle of support does not have to be big. It may be only two or three other people with whom you can share the frustrations of those meetings and the joys of even the smallest victories. Even those who seem to be solo warriors have a support network somewhere. It is essential. If you don't have such a network now, start thinking about how to create one. In the meantime, learn more about that cloud of witnesses. Knowing that history can sustain you as well.

We all have a sphere of influence. Each of us needs to find our own sources of courage so that we will begin to speak. There are many problems to address, and we cannot avoid them indefinitely. We cannot continue to be silent. We must begin to speak, knowing that words alone are insufficient. But I have seen that meaningful dialogue can lead to effective action. Change is possible. I remain hopeful.

Continuing the Conversation

In the years since the publication of this book, I have received many e-mail messages from readers interested in having a conversation with me. Some found it hard to believe that being White was still an advantage in the United States and asked me to offer more statistical evidence than they found in the book to support this assertion. Fortunately, the National Research Council, an institution chartered by Congress for the sole purpose of providing research to inform public policy, has made that task easy. The council recently issued a two-volume compendium of up-to-date data and authoritative analysis on the state of race relations in America today.[1] Among the statistical conclusions reported in *America Becoming: Racial Trends and Their Consequences* are these:

> First, race and Hispanic origin continue to be defining characteristics for many Americans. They are correlated with educational and economic opportunities, with health status, and with where people live and who they live next to. The magnitude of these differences, especially for Blacks and Hispanics, is extremely significant on average, suggesting that these disparities are widely experienced. Relative to the White and Asian population, the Black population on average has only two-fifths as many college graduates, three-fourths as much earnings, and only slightly more than one-half as much income. The Hispanic population fares even worse. Although we do not have as much comparable information for American Indians and Alaska Natives, their data tends to be closer to those of Blacks and Hispanics than to those of Whites. Whatever their causes, these are substantial differentials; they shape our life opportunities

and they shape our opinions about and behaviors toward each other . . . race continues to be a salient predictor of well-being in American society.[2]

As the quote suggests, these data do not tell us why disparities exist, only that they do. So, some might ask, how do we know it is racism that is fueling these differences in life opportunities, and not simply the result of lifestyle choices made by individuals within these groups?

Not surprisingly, there are racial differences in perceptions of discrimination and its causes. In a review of national survey data about racial attitudes, Lawrence D. Bobo reported that Whites tend to minimize the contemporary persistence of patterns of discrimination, whereas Blacks, Latinos, and, to a lesser extent, Asians perceive these patterns in most areas of their lives. Further, people of color are much more likely to attribute these problems to racial bias; Whites are more likely to attribute them, to the extent they acknowledge them, to the level of individual effort or cultural values within the disadvantaged groups.[3]

Sorting out the role racism plays in complex social problems is not easy. An example of this complexity is the discussion of racial disparities in the criminal justice system. A statistic frequently cited is that approximately one-third of Black males in their twenties are under the control of the criminal justice system, either in jail, on parole, or on probation. A particularly sharp increase in the rates of Black male incarceration began in the mid-1980s, coinciding with the implementation of stiff federal and state laws aimed at the control of crack cocaine (the less expensive and powerfully addictive form of cocaine commonly available in inner-city communities). As Harvard Law professor Randall Kennedy has explained:

A federal statute enacted in 1986 criminalizes the distribution of crack cocaine with unusual severity. Under that law, a person convicted of possession with intent to distribute 50 grams or more of crack must be sentenced to no fewer than 10 years in prison; by striking contrast, a person has to be convicted of possession with intent to distribute at least 5,000 grams of powder cocaine before being subject to a mandatory minimum of 10 years—a 100:1 ratio in terms of intensity of punishment. Moreover, under a federal statute enacted in 1988, a person merely possessing 1 to 5 grams of crack cocaine is subject to a mandatory minimum sentence of 5 years in prison, which makes crack the only drug for which there exists a mandatory minimum penalty for a first offense of simple possession.[4]

The racial disparity embedded in this particular law becomes apparent when we also note that in 1992, more than 90 percent of the defendants convicted for crack cocaine offenses nationwide were Black, while approximately 5 percent were White. Conversely, 45 percent of those convicted for powder cocaine offenses were White, and only 21 percent were Black.[5] Did racial bias play a role in the enactment of these laws? Attempts to eliminate this sentencing disparity through legislative changes have failed. Would the response of our predominantly White body of lawmakers be different if 90 percent of crack users were White? Or is there something about the destructiveness of crack cocaine in urban communities that justifies the stiffness of these penalties? If cocaine (in either powder or crack form) is harmful, why should there be such a discrepancy in severity of punishment? Regardless of how one explains this and other racial disparities, the conclusion of the National Research Council analysts that "race continues to be a salient predictor of well-being in American society" seems well founded.

Some readers thanked me for taking the discussion of race beyond simply a Black-White framework. We can see from the preceding data about incarceration rates that dichotomizing the analysis of racial problems in our society in Black-White terms is a persistent trend in social science. However, researchers increasingly are recognizing the need to collect data on other groups of color, thereby broadening our understanding of racial dynamics in the United States. This more inclusive trend is important because by 2050 a dramatic shift in the racial distribution of our population will have occurred. Michael Omi noted this in his essay "The Changing Meaning of Race": "Demographically the nation is becoming less White and the dominant Black-White paradigm of race relations is challenged by the dramatic growth and increasing visibility of Hispanics and Asians."[6]

There are approximately 265 million people in the United States—1 percent American Indians, 3 percent Asians, 11 percent Latinos (Hispanics), 12 percent Black, and 73 percent White. By 2050, Whites are projected to make up only 53 percent of the population. As a consequence of both immigration and birthrate patterns, the size of the Latino and Asian population will increase significantly, and by 2010, Latinos are expected to surpass African Americans as the largest racial/ethnic group of color. Although the Asian population is smaller than either of these groups, it is expected to increase in number more rapidly than any other group.[7]

The dynamics of racism in the United States have always extended beyond Black-White relations, but that reality has not been acknowledged. The growing presence of Latinos and Asian and Pacific Islanders underscores the need for a broadening of conversations about race in our society. Frank Wu's book *Yellow: Race in America Beyond Black and White*[8] is one important contribution to that conversation, and the collaborative effort of Lani Guinier and Gerald Torres in *The Miner's Canary: Enlisting Race, Resisting Power, Transforming Democracy*[9] is another.

One college student wrote to me to ask why I had said in Chapter 5 that although I maintain many of the friendships I made with students of color in college, I didn't remember the names of my White classmates. "Why would you say something of that nature? Are you proud of the fact that you can't remember their names?" the student asked me. I appreciated the question, and was sorry my statement could be misinterpreted as a declaration of pride. It was really just a statement of fact, reflecting how immersed I was in a network of

Black and Latino friends and simultaneously uninterested in White social networks. In 2000 I attended my twenty-fifth class reunion and had the opportunity to talk about this experience with one of my Black friends, June, and a White classmate, Cynthia, who reintroduced herself to me at the event. As Cynthia commented, "There were many of us whose paths did not cross much, and we each built our own networks." Although June, Cynthia, and I shared the same campus and were part of a diverse college community, our social groups were very often—intentionally or unintentionally—racially or ethnically defined. Indeed, my path and June's crossed frequently, outside of the classroom, but we rarely encountered White students. Twenty-five years later, has the situation on college campuses changed?

One thing is certainly different: Our college communities have become much more diverse. According to Deborah Wilds and Reginald Wilson of the American Council on Education, college enrollment among students of color has increased by 22.2 percent since 1991 and by 61.3 percent since 1986.[10] Today, students of color represent approximately one-fourth of those participating in higher education in the United States. Although geographically isolated campuses still struggle to increase the diversity of their student body, almost all colleges and universities have felt the impact of the changing demographics in the United States.

However, the schools and communities from which many of these students come remain socially segregated. More than forty-five years after the landmark U.S. Supreme Court *Brown v. Board of Education* decision, school segregation in the United States persists. In fact, it has been on the rise since the early 1990s. There is a strong relationship between racial segregation and concentrated poverty. National data show that most segregated African American and Latino schools are dominated by poor children, but that 96 percent of White schools have middle-class majorities.[11] Such segregation cuts children of color off from educational and employment networks of opportunity.

Segregation and inequality are strongly self-perpetuating, yet the ideal of democratic education is to create an environment in which such patterns can be interrupted. The first step in interrupting this cycle of inequity is mutual engagement. We will not be able to effectively dismantle systems of oppression—systems of inequity—without working in coalition with one another across lines of difference. Yet because of persistent residential and school segregation, the opportunities young people in the United States have had to interact with those racially, ethnically, or religiously different from them have typically been quite limited. This lack of direct experience means that what one learns about the "other" is based on secondhand information, information too often conveyed in the form of media stereotypes or parental prejudices. Exactly who the "other" is varies, depending on where students have grown up and what their life experience has been. But we can be sure that all members of our campus populations have come to college with stereotypes and prejudices about other segments of the student body. Such preconception is unavoidable when there is so much misinformation circulating. And these biases are a barrier to meaningful engagement across lines of difference.

Why does engagement matter? It should be clear that diversity is not the end in itself. It is not *just* about being friends. It *is* about being allies and becoming effective agents of change. To work effectively as an agent of change in a pluralistic society, it is necessary to be able to connect with people different from oneself. Most students do not come with this capacity for connection already developed, yet it is a capacity that can be developed. In the context of the self-perpetuating nature of inequity, meaningful engagement is an important step, a prerequisite for the transformative education we need for a more just society.

Increasingly, faculty, students, and administrators alike are recognizing the importance of engagement across difference as an essential dimension of preparing the next generation for effective participation in a pluralistic world.[12] This focus on diversity is supported by a growing body of empirical research demonstrating the educational benefits of learning in a diverse community.[13] After analyzing national data drawn from nearly 200 colleges and universities as well as data specific to the University of Michigan, social psychologist Patricia Gurin concluded that students who experienced the most racial and ethnic diversity in and out of their classrooms benefited most in terms of both "learning outcomes" and "democracy outcomes." In learning outcomes, these students showed the greatest engagement in active thinking processes, growth in intellectual engagement and motivation, and growth in intellectual and academic skills. In democracy outcomes, they showed the most engagement during college in various forms of citizenship and the most involvement with people from different races and cultures, and they were the most likely to acknowledge that group differences are compatible with the interests of the broader community. These results persisted beyond graduation. Students with the most diversity experiences during college had the most cross-racial friends, neighbors, and work associates nine years after they entered college.[14]

The benefits of engaging diversity are compelling, but are enough students taking advantage of these formal and informal learning opportunities? Are students learning to negotiate across lines of difference, lines defined not only by race but also by class, ethnicity, gender, sexual orientation, or religion? Or are they still building their own homogeneous networks, operating in circles that rarely intersect, and failing to engage meaningfully with those whose backgrounds differ from their own?

The popular perception is that the latter situation is more common, particularly in reference to race. Newspapers and magazines regularly feature stories about the dilemma of so-called self-segregation on college campuses, a reality reflected in the title of this book. Despite this perception, there is some evidence that students desire more cross-group interaction than a quick glance at the cafeteria may indicate.

In a recent study of friendship groups within a diverse campus community, researcher Anthony Lising Antonio found that more than 90 percent of the 638 third-year students he surveyed reported that students predominantly cluster by race and ethnicity, but almost half (46 percent) described their own friendship groups as racially and ethnically mixed. Clearly, these students did not view their behavior as the norm. They still perceived segregation as the rule, a perception reinforced by the fact that African American students were the most likely to report racially or ethnically homogeneous friendship groups, and one in three White students also reported having racially homogeneous friendship groups.[15] The pattern of social isolation of both Black and White students is a visible symbol of the continuing legacy of past and present systems of inequity.

This pattern is also an expression of different goals for interracial contact. In a study of Berkeley undergraduates, Troy Duster and his associates found that most students express interest in more interracial experiences, yet how that interest is engaged varies along racial lines. White students wanted to make friends with African Americans, but they wanted to do so in informal settings, and were less likely to want to participate in special programs, courses, or activities that structure interethnic contacts. In contrast, African Americans were far more likely to want special programs and activities and were less interested in developing cross-racial friendships and social activities. Both groups wanted interracial experiences but on different terms. Duster concluded, "The task is to provide all students with a range of safe environments and options where they can explore and develop terms that they find comfortable. In the absence of such opportunities, the tendencies remain for each group to see the others from a distance, in terms of images, stereotypes, stories, and myths that are not informed by direct contact and experience."[16]

We know, empirically and experientially, that the challenge of educating a diverse student body that will be ready to live and work together in an increasingly complex and pluralistic society requires us to interrupt patterns of social isolation. We must provide opportunities for students to practice, opportunities to understand multiple perspectives as well as individual ones during the college years. How, then, can we create campus environments in which engagement across lines of difference is perceived as the norm rather than the exception? How can we maximize the learning opportunities created by the diversity of our communities?

In the years since the first publication of this book, I have tried to answer these questions in very practical terms. In 1998 I became intrigued by an administrative opportunity to translate the theory about which I had written into practice. Could we create a model, a transformative environment in which young people could explore and expand their understanding of what justice means? Could we create an environment that truly prepared them to take their place as agents of change? With a vision like that in mind, I left full-time teaching to become dean of Mount Holyoke College.

My administrative role bridged the world of the classroom and the world beyond the classroom where students are engaged as part of a residential learning community. As dean, I had to assess how the cocurricular life on campus reinforced and supported our curricular goals as an educational institution. As a psychologist, I have spent most of my professional life studying identity and its role in student development, and it was exciting to be able to spend the better part of every day exploring these issues in a pragmatic way.

I called our task the ABCs—we sought to affirm identity, build community, and cultivate leadership in a way that would prepare our students for the twenty-first century. This simple mnemonic device provided the outline for three critical dimensions of effective learning environments, not only during the college years but also through all levels of education. "A," affirming identity, refers to the idea that students need to see themselves reflected in the environment around them—in the curriculum, in the faculty and staff, and in the faces of their classmates—to avoid feelings of invisibility or marginality that can undermine student success. "B," building community, highlights the importance of creating a sense of belonging to a larger, shared campus community. The goals of affirming identity and building community are often perceived as being contradictory, but they are in fact complementary. Students who feel that their needs for affirmation have been met are more willing and able to engage with others across lines of difference. Learning to build community is both a challenge and a benefit of being part of a diverse learning community.

"C," cultivating leadership, refers to the fact that leadership in the twenty-first century requires not only the ability to think critically and speak and write effectively but also the ability to interact effectively with others in a pluralistic context. The development of each of these abilities requires opportunities to practice. Intergroup interaction is an area that has too often been neglected in the lives of students, and they need structured opportunities to practice the requisite skills.

Translating the ABCs into action required my staff and me routinely to ask each other important questions: Who is reflected in each staff member's area and the relevant programs? Who is left out? What opportunities exist for building community, for encouraging dialogue across difference? How are students involved so that they are honing leadership skills in a diverse context?

There were many examples of the ABCs in action at Mount Holyoke; an especially clear one involved not racial diversity but religious diversity. My colleague and friend, Rev. Dr. Andrea Ayvazian, worked hard to put the ABCs into practice. To better understand and respond to the needs of her diverse constituents, she created an advisory board of thirty students, representing all the faith traditions on campus. Among them were Protestants, Catholics, Buddhists, Jews, Muslims, Baha'is, Unitarians, Hindus, and Native American and other Earth-based traditions, as well as a group of what she called "unaffiliated seekers."

As the students began to meet regularly with the dean of religious life, tensions rose around the issue of religious space on campus. Christians were privileged because there was a large Christian chapel in the center of campus, a symbol of the institution's religious roots. Attached to the large chapel was a smaller chapel, also clearly intended for Christian worship. The Christian students could easily see themselves reflected in the campus architecture, but the other faith traditions were missing from the picture.

It was clear that the institution did not have the resources to construct additional worship space. Instead the dean and the advisory board proposed converting the small chapel to an interfaith sanctuary. How could this nineteenth-century chapel with stained-glass windows and bolted-down wooden pews be transformed into space suitable for Muslims who need room to pray prostrate, for Hindus who need visible icons, or for Buddhists who want to sit in a circle on meditation cushions?

The answer was simple: Remove the pews. This "simple" solution was certainly controversial. Comments like "They're ruining the small chapel," "This diversity stuff has gone too far," and "What will the alumnae say?" could be heard around campus. The dialogue that ensued was not always smooth, but it built community among those engaged in it, and the multifaith advisory board learned a great deal about leadership. The students were out in front talking to their peers about why the change was necessary. It was an excellent opportunity for them to experience the kind of leadership needed in a pluralistic community with multiple needs and limited resources, where sharing is required. The e-mail exchanges in the campus chat room were exciting to read as students challenged each other to confront their biases and acknowledge their (in this case) Christian privilege.

Eventually the physical transformation was completed. The pews were replaced with a beautiful oriental rug in the open space, ready to accommodate the Muslim prayerful or the Buddhist chanters seated in a circle on their small round cushions. The Christians used attractive stackable chairs, arranged in pewlike rows during Sunday services but lined up against the walls when not in use. Hindu icons were enclosed in a movable cabinet, not visible to those who would find the images unacceptable in their worship space, but easily accessible when needed by the Hindu students. In addition, a Torah was housed in a lovely wooden ark available for Jewish student use, and a small collection of sacred texts from each of the faith traditions was assembled in a corner of the room. Every faith tradition is represented in some way in the space. The result is breathtaking—a beautiful space that is frequently in use, a tangible manifestation of the ABCs in action, and a powerful symbol of the social transformation we seek in a pluralistic society.

My transformation as a college administrator has continued. On August 1, 2002, I began my tenure as president of Spelman College in Atlanta, Georgia. Founded in 1881, only sixteen years after the end of legalized slavery, by two White missionaries for the purpose of educating Black women, Spelman College is the oldest and most successful historically Black women's college in the United States.

I am now frequently asked why a "diversity expert" like me would choose to lead such a "homogeneous" institution. Of course, the question is based on a flawed assumption. Although 97 percent of our students are racially categorized as Black, the campus environment is not homogeneous. Spelman students come from all regions of the United States, and many foreign countries, from predominantly White suburban and rural communities as well as urban Black ones. All parts of the African diaspora are represented, and the diversity of experience and perspectives among these young women creates many opportunities for important dialogue. As I discussed in response to the question "Why are all the Black kids sitting together in the cafeteria?" within-group dialogue can often be as important, and sometimes more important, than between-group dialogue. And, even in the context of a historically Black college, it is possible to create opportunities for both. Meanwhile, the intellectual and social empowerment that comes to those who have been historically oppressed, when they are given the opportunity to stand in the center of campus life rather than on the margins, is evident in the accomplishments of graduates of historically Black colleges and universities. I am honored to participate in that process for young women at Spelman.

Although the context of my work has shifted from a traditionally White college to a historically Black one, the ABC questions remain relevant. At every institution, we must ask ourselves, "How do we create and sustain school environments that affirm identity, build community, and cultivate leadership in a way that supports the learning of all students?" The young people we are educating will graduate on the edge of a new frontier. We as educators are naturally inclined to teach the way we were taught, but relying on the lessons of the past will not necessarily take us where we want to go. How will we get there?

A few years ago, I had a dream that illuminated the difficulty of the task we are undertaking. In the dream I was driving a car along a road, when suddenly I found myself driving not on a road but on a pile of rocks. I exclaimed in surprise, "What happened to the road?" A voice answered, "There is no road." When I awakened, it occurred to me that my dream held the perfect metaphor for what we as multicultural educators are trying to do. We live in a time when there is no clear path to where we are trying to go. Yet many of us have a vision of where we would like to be, a vision of schools where all students have the opportunity and the encouragement to achieve at a high standard. It is a vision of multiethnic communities characterized by equitable and just group relations rather than the present deeply ingrained power hierarchies that systematically advantage some and systematically disadvantage others. It is a vision of education that not only should foster intellectual development by providing students the tools of critical thinking, speaking, writing, and quantitative reasoning, but also should provide all students the skills and experiences necessary for effective participation in a diverse society. An understanding of racial identity development, for both White students and students of color, is one important tool in building the road, because it gives us a better understanding of the complex dynamics operating in our daily interactions with one another. Enhanced understanding leads to enhanced cooperation, and this project must be a collaborative effort across racial lines if it is to be successful.

I write this epilogue humbly knowing that our "road" is still under construction. In 1903, W.E.B. DuBois wrote in the foreword to his classic text, *The Souls of Black Folk*, the oft-quoted line, "The problem of the Twentieth Century is the problem of the color line."[17] One hundred years later, his statement regrettably still rings true. It is incumbent upon all of us to engage in the dialogue and take the collective action needed to create a more just and equitable world for all. That is the task of this century. I hope you will join me in that effort.

Appendix
Getting Started
Resources for the Next Step

At the end of my workshops or other presentations, participants often ask me where they can go for more information about racism and racial identity. I have tried to answer that question throughout this book, but this appendix highlights several resources, some of which have not been cited elsewhere, that may be useful as starting points for those who want a better understanding of racism, its historical roots, and most important, what we can do about it. I have also included a list of resources particularly useful for educators interested in antiracist education, and a list of multicultural children's books, which may be helpful to parents.

What It Is: Resources Dealing with Contemporary Racism

Bell, D. *Faces at the bottom of the well: The permanence of racism.* New York: Basic Books, 1992.

> In this powerful and provocative book, legal scholar Derrick Bell uses fictional as well as historical accounts to show how our legal system has been structured to advantage White people systematically. Disturbing and inspiring, it makes clear why interrupting the cycle of racism is so important.

Feagin, J. R., and M. P. Sikes. *Living with racism: The Black middle-class experience.* Boston: Beacon Press, 1994.

> Based on the testimony of more than two hundred Black respondents, this book captures the continuing significance of racism in the daily lives of men and women of African descent in the United States.

Hacker, A. *Two nations: Black and White, separate, hostile, unequal.* New York: Charles Scribner's Sons, 1992.

> Because of what Hacker calls the "particular reluctance" of the dominant White community to absorb people of African descent, he focuses primarily on the racial inequalities between Blacks and Whites in this statistical analysis of racism in America.

Rothenberg, P. S. (Ed.). *Race, class, and gender: An integrated study,* 3d ed. New York: St. Martin's Press, 1995.

> This collection of essays provides a multiracial perspective on racism, sexism, and classism in the United States. An excellent text for courses on racism, it is also a great primer for any interested adult reader.

Williams, P. J. *The alchemy of race and rights: Diary of a law professor.* Cambridge: Harvard University Press, 1991.

> In this highly acclaimed autobiographical essay, the author reflects on the intersection of race, gender, and class from her perspective as an African American woman and legal scholar.

Lucasiewicz, M. (Producer). *True colors* [Video]. Northbrook, IL: MTI Film & Video, 1991.

> ABC News correspondent Diane Sawyer follows two discrimination testers, one Black and one White, as they shop at a local mall and a car dealership, and as they look for employment and housing. This 19-minute video clearly illustrates the concept of White privilege.

Reid, F. (Producer/Director). *Skin deep: College students confront racism* [Video]. San Francisco, CA: Resolution/California Newsreel, 1995.

> This 53-minute video chronicles the journey of a multiracial group of college students as they examine their own attitudes about race and ethnicity, and confront each other's. This video vividly illustrates students of color and White students at different stages of racial identity and demonstrates the possibility of growth as a result of dialogue.

Wah, L. M. (Producer/Director). *The color of fear* [Video]. Oakland, CA: Stir-Fry Productions, 1994.

> This 90-minute film captures a multiracial group of eight men engaged in intense and riveting dialogue about racism. This powerful film makes clear why cross-racial dialogue is so hard and why it is so necessary.

How It Happened: Resources Providing a Historical Perspective

Loewen, J. W. *Lies my teacher told me: Everything your American history textbook got wrong.* New York: Simon & Schuster, 1995.

> After surveying twelve leading high school history text-books, Loewen concluded that none of them accurately represented the reality of racism in U.S. history. He corrects the record.

Spring, J. *Deculturalization and the struggle for equality: A brief history of the education of dominated cultures in the United States,* 2d ed. New York: McGraw-Hill, 1997.

> In fewer than 125 pages, the author provides a lot of very useful information about the historical impact of racism on the education of people of color.

Takaki, R. *A different mirror: A history of multicultural America.* Boston: Little, Brown, 1993.

> Beginning with the colonization of the New World and ending with the Los Angeles riots of 1992, this book recounts U.S. history from the perspective of people of color and marginalized White immigrants.

Hampton, H. (Producer). *Eyes on the prize I: America's civil rights years, 1954–65* [Video]. Alexandria, VA: PBS Video, 1986.

Hampton, H. (Producer). *Eyes on the prize II: America at the racial cross-roads, 1965–85* [Video]. Alexandria, VA: PBS Video, 1990.

> Combined, this fourteen-volume set of videos provides a comprehensive look at a critical thirty-year period in the

race relations between Blacks and Whites in the United States.

Riggs, M. (Producer/Director). *Ethnic notions* [Video]. San Francisco: Resolution/California Newsreel, 1986.

> This powerful video traces the history of anti-Black stereotypes in U.S. popular culture from the 1820s to the 1960s, examining the social context that gave rise to these pernicious images.

What We Can Do About It? Resources for Taking Action

Barndt, J. *Dismantling racism: The continuing challenge to White America.* Minneapolis: Augsburg Fortress Press, 1991.

> Joseph Barndt is a White minister who has been involved in working against racism for many years. He offers a clear analysis of individual as well as institutional racism. Barndt brings an explicitly Christian perspective to his discussion of dismantling racism.

Bartlett, J. W. *The future is ours: A handbook for student activists in the 21st century.* New York: Henry Holt, 1996.

> A guide to grassroots organizing, this book is full of practical advice for moving from individual thought to collective action for meaningful social change.

Ford, C. *We can all get along: Fifty steps you can take to help end racism at home, at work, in your community.* New York: Dell, 1994.

> As the title promises, this book offers fifty concrete actions a person can take, working individually or with others, to interrupt the cycle of racism. Each step is accompanied by a list of resources relevant to the particular suggestion.

Hopson, D. P., and D. S. Hopson with T. Clavin. *Raising the rainbow generation: Teaching your children to be successful in a multicultural society.* New York: Simon & Schuster, 1993.

A guide for parents who want to teach their children respect for all others and how to combat bias and negative racial attitudes when they encounter them. It includes a useful listing of good multicultural children's books and where to purchase them.

Kivel, P. *Uprooting racism: How White people can work for racial justice.* Philadelphia: New Society, 1996.

Written by a White Jewish man, this book features discussions of affirmative action, immigration issues, institutional racism, political correctness, and the meaning of Whiteness. It is multiracial in its focus, and includes self-assessment checklists and other exercises to raise consciousness about racism. Though it is clearly intended for a White audience, it would be of interest to people of color as well.

Lewis, B. *The kid's guide to social action.* Minneapolis: Free Spirit, 1991.

Though not specifically focused on racism, this book clearly outlines step-by-step strategies for social action: letter writing, speechmaking, surveying, fundraising, getting media coverage, etc. Designed by a teacher for kids to use, adults will learn some things, too.

Mathias, B., and M. A. French. *Forty ways to raise a nonracist child.* New York: HarperCollins, 1996.

A biracial team of authors presents parents with practical, developmentally appropriate suggestions for interrupting the cycle of racism with their children.

Reddy, M. T. (Ed.). *Everyday acts against racism: Raising children in a multiracial world.* Seattle: Seal Press, 1996.

In this empowering book, a multiracial group of mothers and teachers look at the effects of racism on their children and communities, and suggest concrete ways all of us can work to end racial divisions and inequity.

Study Circles Resource Center. *Can't we all just get along? A manual for discussion programs on racism and race relations.* Pomfret, CT: Study Circles Resource Center, 1994.

This guide, designed to foster cross-racial dialogue, provides a brief introduction to the issue, an overview of how study circles work, as well as materials for five possible discussion sessions.

Brandon, L. *How to prevent a nuclear war* [16mm film]. New York: New Day Films, 1987.

This 32-minute film presents a series of vignettes featuring a diverse group of individuals who describe their own efforts at social action. Though the topic is disarmament, the strategies they use could apply to any social issue, including racism. It is a very upbeat film that leaves the viewer feeling that change is possible.

Not in our town [Video]. Oakland, CA: California Working Group.

This 27-minute video chronicles the community-wide response to hate crimes in Bozeman, Montana, and clearly illustrates the power of working together.

Anti-Racism Education: Resource Guides Especially for Educators

Adams, M., L. A. Bell, and P. Griffin (Eds.). *Teaching for diversity and social justice: A sourcebook.* New York: Routledge, 1997.

This sourcebook provides a conceptual framework for understanding oppression, many illustrative examples for designing classroom and workshop activities for adult learners, and a useful list of print and video resources.

Banks, J. *Teaching strategies for ethnic studies,* 6th ed. Boston: Allyn & Bacon, 1997.

This latest edition of a classic text by the "father of multicultural education" is full of resource information for making one's curriculum more inclusive.

Bigelow, B., L. Christensen, S. Karp, B. Miner, and B. Peterson. *Rethinking our classrooms: Teaching for equity and justice*. Milwaukee: Rethinking Schools, 1994.

> This thought-provoking collection includes creative teaching ideas and compelling classroom examples of ways teachers can promote critical thinking and social justice while they build academic skills. A great resource that is very inexpensive when purchased in bulk. Superintendents should get a copy for every teacher in their district.

Derman-Sparks, L., and the ABC Task Force. *Anti-bias curriculum: Tools for empowering young children*. Washington, DC: National Association for the Education of Young Children, 1989.

> Known as the "red book" among preschool teachers, this is an invaluable resource for thinking about how to do antiracist education with young children.

Lee, E. *Letters to Marcia: A teacher's guide to anti-racist education*. Toronto, Ontario: Cross Cultural Communication Centre, 1985.

> This small but wise book is organized around three related aspects of school life: community, curriculum, and support services for students. Full of practical suggestions, it would be of use to both classroom teachers, administrators, and staff developers.

Nieto, S. *Affirming diversity: The sociopolitical context of multicultural education*, 2d ed. White Plains, NY: Longman, 1996.

> Though not focused on practical strategies per se, this book clearly identifies what the issues of concern are when we seek to "affirm diversity" in our schools. Through well-placed questions, the author encourages reflection on our own educational practice throughout the book and does include a helpful resource guide.

Ramsey, P. *Teaching and learning in a diverse world: Multicultural education for young children*. New York: Teachers College Press, 1985.

> This book specifically addresses both the importance of

doing multicultural, antiracist education in mostly White classrooms, and provides strategies for doing it.

Schniedewind, N., and E. Davidson. *Open minds to equality: A sourcebook of learning activities to affirm diversity and promote equity*, 2d ed. Boston: Allyn & Bacon, 1997.

A much-needed resource for elementary and secondary educators who are interested in promoting critical thinking in their classrooms and social change in their communities. It provides a helpful framework for understanding the isms, practical hands-on strategies to combat them, and a hopeful vision that the effort will be worth it.

Teaching Tolerance is a magazine, published twice a year by the Southern Poverty Law Center, which provides teachers at all levels with resources and ideas for promoting interracial and multicultural understanding in the classroom. Free to educators, it can be obtained by sending a written request to Teaching Tolerance, 400 Washington Avenue, Montgomery, AL 36104.

Multicultural Books for Children and Adolescents: A Selected Guide for Parents

The number of good multicultural books for children and young adults is increasing rapidly. Many of them depict children of varying backgrounds engaged in daily activities with their families and friends, and are not specifically related to issues of oppression. This list, however, features only books that address stereotypes, omissions, and distortions in some specific way. It includes just a few of the books that my own children have enjoyed or books that have often been recommended to me by classroom teachers who are committed to antiracist education. The list is roughly divided between books for young children and books for adolescents.

Books for Younger Children

Brenner, B. *Wagon wheels*. Illustrated by D. Bolognese. New York: Harper & Row, 1978.

> Based on a true story, this is an exciting, easy-to-read early "chapter book" about a Black pioneer family in the 1870s. The main characters are three brothers whose courage and care for one another are the key to the family's survival on the frontier. A great antidote to the myth of the Whites-only westward expansion.

Garza, C. L., and H. Rohmer. *Family pictures/Cuadros de familia*. Illustrations by C. L. Garza. San Francisco: Children's Book Press, 1990.

> The Mexican American author–illustrator's memories of her childhood in rural southern Texas convey the customs of her family and community. The book also introduces young readers and their parents to the art work of this well-known artist of Mexican American descent.

Grimes, N. *Meet Danitra Brown*. Illustrated by F. Cooper. New York: Scholastic, 1984.

> This beautifully illustrated book deals with friendship between two Black girls, and addresses the issue of colorism in an empowering way.

Herrera, J. F. *Calling the doves/El canto de las palomas*. Illustrated by E. Simmons. San Francisco: Children's Book Press, 1995.

> Mexican American poet Juan Felipe Herrera captures wonderful images of his childhood in a closeknit family of migrant farmworkers. The text is in English and Spanish and the illustrations are spectacular.

Hoffman, M. *Amazing Grace*. Illustrated by C. Birch. New York: Dial Books for Young Readers, 1991.

> A classmate tells Grace she can't play Peter Pan in the school play because she is Black. With the help of her sup-

portive family, Grace discovers that with determination and preparation, she can do anything.

Hubbard, J. (Ed.). *Shooting back from the reservation: A photographic view of life by Native American youth.* New York: New Press, 1994.

This photographic essay features photographs taken by young Native people and includes their own written commentary, allowing the reader to glimpse the world the way these young people see it. The photographers range in age from seven to eighteen.

Langstaff, J. (Ed). *What a morning! The Christmas story in Black spirituals.* Illustrated by A. Bryan. New York: Macmillan, 1987.

If you are tired of Eurocentric nativity scenes, this is the book for you. This is the Christmas story told with and through Black spirituals. It includes vocal and piano arrangements.

Mochizuki, K. *Passage to freedom: The Sugihara story.* Illustrated by D. Lee. New York: Lee & Low Books, 1997.

This story, told through the eyes of Hiroki Sugihara, the five-year-old son of the Japanese consul to Lithuania, is about one man's singlehanded efforts to help Jewish refugees escaping from the Nazis, going against his government's orders in the process. Another great example of the power of one person to make a difference.

Nikola-Lisa, W. *Bein' with you this way.* Illustrated by M. Bryant. New York: Lee & Low Books, 1995.

This book features great multiracial illustrations of children playing together in a city playground. The narrative verse explores physical differences in a celebratory way.

Ringgold, F. *Aunt Harriet's Underground Railroad in the sky.* Illustrated by F. Ringgold. New York: Crown, 1992.

This tribute to Harriet Tubman by an internationally known artist is told through the eyes of two Black children, eight-year-old Cassie and her brother, Be Be, who magically travel back in time to the days of slavery. This book is an excellent vehicle for discussing slavery with young children.

Ringgold, F. *Dinner at Aunt Connie's house.* Illustrated by F. Ringgold. New York: Crown, 1993.

While Melody and her cousin Lonnie are playing hide-and-seek in Aunt Connie's house, they hear strange voices. To their suprise, they find that Aunt Connie has twelve beautiful portraits of famous African American women, and the paintings can speak. A delightful introduction to Black women's history.

Ringgold, F. *Tar Beach.* Illustrated by F. Ringgold. New York: Crown, 1991.

Another great book by Faith Ringgold featuring eight-year-old Cassie and her brother, Be Be. Set in Harlem in 1939, Cassie, who is of African and Native American ancestry, lies on the roof of her building, her "tar beach," and dreams of flying over the city. Based on her "story-quilt" of the same name, this book will not only entertain young children but will introduce older children and adults to the artwork of this internationally known African American artist.

Rosen, M. J. *Elijah's angel.* Illustrated by A. B. L. Robinson. San Diego: Harcourt Brace, 1992.

Set during the season of Chanukah and Christmas, this moving story is about the friendship between a young Jewish boy and an eighty-year-old African American barber and woodcarver who create a path of understanding between the Jewish and Christian religions. The story is a fictionalized incident in the life of a real person, Elijah Pierce, a renowned folk artist who lived in Columbus, Ohio.

Steptoe, J. *Mufaro's beautiful daughters.* Illustrated by J. Steptoe. New York: Scholastic, 1987.

This African folktale features a man and his two beautiful daughters, one who is kind and humble and the other who is mean and arrogant. In the Cinderella-like plot, the sisters compete to be chosen as the wife of the nearby king. This book affirms an Afrocentric vision of beauty, but also emphasizes the greater importance of good character.

Winter, J. *Follow the drinking gourd*. Illustrated by J. Winter. New York: Knopf, 1988.

This story about the Underground Railroad highlights the role of a White man named Peg Leg Joe who hired himself out to plantation owners and used the opportunity to tell enslaved Africans about the escape route to the North. A good example of White ally behavior for young White children and children of color to learn about.

Books for Young Adults (6th Grade and Up)

Alvarez, J. *How the Garcia girls lost their accents.* New York: Plume, 1991.

This novel deals with multiple issues of identity (i.e., race, class, gender) and assimilation for an immigrant family from the Dominican Republic. Recommended for high school readers and older.

Carson, B., with C. Murphey. *Gifted hands: The Ben Carson story*. Grand Rapids, MI: Zondervan, 1990.

This is the autobiography of Ben Carson, once a quick-tempered adolescent headed for trouble, now the extraordinary African American neurosurgeon who has become world famous for successfully performing very difficult operations. A great role model book for young Black men especially.

Cisneros, S. *The house on Mango Street*. New York: Random House, 1994.

This collection of interrelated vignettes tells the story of Esperanza Cordero, a young girl growing up in the Latino section of Chicago. A classic coming-of-age story featuring a Chicana heroine.

Haley, A., and Malcolm X. *The autobiography of Malcolm X.* New York: Grove, 1965.

Many young people I have interviewed have talked about how powerfully they were affected by this book. Malcolm's story conveys insight into a particular period in U.S. history but also one Black man's process of racial identity development.

McKissack, F. and C. Patricia. *Sojourner Truth: Ain't I a woman?* New York: Scholastic, 1992.

This biography chronicles the life and times of Sojourner Truth, preacher, abolitionist, and activist for the rights of both Blacks and women. Born a slave named Isabella, she changed her name to Sojourner Truth after being freed in 1827. Although she couldn't read, she could quote the Bible word for word, and was a powerful speaker, the essence of empowerment.

Myers, W. D. *Fallen Angels.* New York: Scholastic, 1988.

Walter Dean Myers has written many good books for young adults. This one deals with the Vietnam War from the perspective of a young Black soldier.

Parks, R., with G. F. Reed. *Dear Mrs. Parks: A dialogue with today's youth.* New York: Lee & Low Books, 1996.

A collection of letters exchanged between Rosa Parks and children all over the country, on subjects ranging from the Montgomery Bus Boycott to the Million Man March. Throughout, she challenges young people to become a force for positive change in the society.

Uchida, Y. *The invisible thread.* New York: Simon & Schuster, 1991.

This powerful memoir of a Japanese American girl who was held with her family in a U.S. internment camp brings this episode in U.S. history to life for her readers.

Collections of Short Stories for Older Readers

Augenbraum, H., and I. Stavans. *Growing up Latino: Memoirs and stories.* Boston: Houghton Mifflin, 1993.

David, J. (Ed.). *Growing up Black: From the slave days to the present.* New York: Avon, 1992.

Hong, M. (Ed.). *Growing up Asian American: An anthology.* New York: Morrow, 1993.

Lopez, T. A. (Ed.). *Growing up Chicano/a: An anthology.* New York: Morrow, 1993.

Riley, P. (Ed.). *Growing up Native American: An anthology.* New York: Morrow, 1993.

> I often spot good books in the multicultural section of progressive bookstores. For more structured guidance, consider these resource guides:

AACP, Inc. *Asian American Books for all Ages.* Catalogue available from AACP, Inc., 234 Main St., P.O. Box 1587, San Mateo, CA 94401.

Day, F. A. *Latina and Latino voices in literature for children and teenagers.* Portsmouth, NH: Heinemann, 1997.

Miller-Lachman, L. (Ed.). *Our family, our friends, our world: An annotated guide to significant multicultural books for children and teenagers.* New Providence, NJ: R. R. Bowker, 1992.

Slapin, B., and D. Seale. *Through Indian eyes: The Native experience in books for children.* Philadelphia: New Society, 1987.

Reader Discussion Guide

About the Author

Beverly Daniel Tatum is president of Spelman College in Atlanta, Georgia. Prior to her appointment at Spelman, she was acting president of Mount Holyoke College (Massachusetts), its dean, and—for thirteen years—professor of psychology and education. She has also maintained a private consulting practice.

A renowned authority on the psychology of racism, race relations in the classroom, and racial identity development in adolescents and young adults, Dr. Tatum participated in President Clinton's "Dialogue on Race." She speaks extensively throughout the country and conducts numerous workshops with students, educators, and parents. She has published articles in *Harvard Educational Review*, *Sojourner*, *Women's Studies Quarterly*, and other journals. Her first book, *Assimilation Blues: Black Families in a White Community*, was published in 1987.

A fourth-generation educator, Dr. Tatum earned her B.A. degree in psychology from Wesleyan University and her M.A. and Ph.D. degrees in clinical psychology from the University of Michigan. Before her appointment at Mount Holyoke, she taught at Westfield State College (Massachusetts) and the University of California at Santa Barbara. In 1996 she received a Carnegie Corporation grant for a two-year demonstration project in the Northampton, Massachusetts, school system. "*Why Are All the Black Kids Sitting Together in the Cafeteria? And Other Conversations About Race*" first exploded on the national scene in 1997.

Dr. Tatum lives in Atlanta, Georgia.

About the Book

Walk into any racially mixed high school and you will find Black youths seated together in the cafeteria. You will also see White, Latino,

Asian Pacific, American Indian, and other ethnically distinct kids clustered together in their own groups. The same phenomenon can be observed in college dining halls, faculty lounges, and corporate cafeterias. Is this self-segregation a problem we should try to fix, or a coping strategy we should support? How can we get past our reluctance to talk about racial issues?

Whites are afraid of using the wrong words or of being perceived as racist. People of color are wary of exposing themselves and their children to painful social and institutional realities. But the costs—obvious and hidden—of racism afflict every one of us. We have waited too long to begin the conversation.

Beverly Daniel Tatum, distinguished educator, scholar, and authority on the psychology of racism and the development of racial and ethnic identity, presents compelling evidence that open and honest talk about our racial identities, whatever they may be, is essential to promoting understanding across racial and ethnic divides. Drawing on real-life examples, scholarly studies, the latest research, and interviews with children and adults of all ethnic groups, she provides us in *"Why Are All the Black Kids Sitting Together in the Cafeteria?"* with an innovative framework for thinking and talking about race.

Now with a fifth-anniversary epilogue by the author, *"Why Are All the Black Kids Sitting Together in the Cafeteria?"* has helped thousands of students, parents, educators, politicians, and cultural leaders to begin their participation in a national conversation about race. Tatum offers clear, accessible definitions of such terms as *racism, prejudice, antiracism, racial identity,* and *target groups* and details the processes by which our attitudes about race, and about racial identity, develop. She also explains the role that "affinity groups" of racially, ethnically, and culturally similar people can play in combating racism. For people of color, these groups can function as modes of connection and empowerment. For Whites, they can be a means of becoming conscious of racial privilege and of developing an antiracist consciousness and commitment.

In an interview with *FamilyEducation.com,* Tatum said, "This is all about preparing kids for leadership in the twenty-first century.

Everyone pays a price for racism. Racism harms White people as well as people of color, particularly in terms of the rising tide of fear and violence that exists when people don't know how to cross racial boundaries." Tatum is optimistic. "Each of us has the power to make a difference," she notes, "and collectively we can create a more just and peaceful society."

For Discussion

1. Tatum writes, "We need to understand that in racially mixed settings, racial grouping is a developmental process in response to an environmental stressor." (p. 62) Why is connecting with one's ethnic or racial peers important in the process of identity development, and why should it be encouraged? (69) What are the primary advantages and disadvantages of such peer groups?

2. How successful has Tatum's book been in increasing your understanding of "the role of racial or ethnic identity in young people's development" (xv) and of "what racism is, how it impacts all of us, and . . . what we can do about it"? (ix) To what extent is an understanding of racial identity development important for every member of every ethnic group?

3. What benefits might accrue from talking about racism and encouraging others to do the same? How might such conversations be advantageous for all of us as individuals, for the ethnic groups to which we belong, and for American society? How might each of us effectively and consistently "break the silence about racism whenever we can"? (193) What fears might hinder us from doing so?

4. What distortions, deficiencies, assumptions, historical and cultural omissions, and stereotypes have affected your attitudes toward ethnic groups other than your own? What distortions, deficiencies, and stereotypes do you see influencing children, adolescents, and adults today? What corrective actions might we engage in?

5. In what ways and to what extent is David Wellman's definition of *racism*—a "system of advantage based on race"—accurate in

relation to the United States? In what ways might it lead to an understanding "of how racism operates in American society"? (8) How important is it that any definition of *racism* include the elements of advantage, privilege, and power? To what degree is Tatum justified in basing the bulk of her discussion on Wellman's definition?

6. Why do you agree or disagree with Tatum's arguments concerning whether people of color can be racist?

7. In what ways do Whites in America benefit—intentionally or unintentionally, knowingly or unknowingly—from racism? "Why should Whites who are advantaged by racism *want* to end that system of advantage?" Tatum asks. "What are the *costs* of that system to them?" (13) How does she answer those questions? How would you answer them?

8. How does Tatum distinguish between *active racism* and *passive racism*? What examples does she present to illustrate the two kinds of racism and the distinctions between them? What examples of each can you cite from your observation and experience? How do you usually respond to the two kinds?

9. In what ways are language and habits of speech important to any discussion of racism—particularly with children—as well as to racial and ethnic identity development? In what ways do our habitual ways of speaking reflect our attitudes toward and behavior relating to racism? In what ways is language of particular importance among Latinos, Native Americans, Asian Pacific Americans, and other specific ethnic and immigrant groups in the United States?

10. What do you learn about yourself by applying to your life Tatum's discussion of the development of self-identity and of racial identity? To what degree has her presentation increased your understanding of yourself and of the factors that contributed to the shaping of your identity?

11. What strategies of resisting or undermining the power of the dominant group have evolved in the United States? Which are observable today? To what degree might some of those strategies, covert or not, actually have contributed to the continuation of racism

and repression? What have been the costs of these strategies to members of targeted groups?

12. In what ways might we help children, and assist or encourage others in helping children, understand their race-related observations, experiences, and feelings? How might we draw on our own experiences to do so?

13. Tatum notes that "Black-White race relations in the United States have been forever shaped by slavery and its social, psychological, and economic legacies." (39) In what ways is this so? What indications of these legacies are observable today? How might we best address those legacies, individually and institutionally, and regardless of our ethnicities, with our children?

14. Why does Tatum see skin-color prejudice within Black communities and Black families as particularly harmful and distressing? What are its origins and its potential consequences? What other forms of "internalized oppression" does Tatum identify, among Blacks and other groups, and what consequences does she link to them?

15. Why might it be essential, in terms of interracial understanding, to engage children "in a critical examination of the books they read, the television they watch, the films they see, and the video games they play" (48) and their other activities? How might we teach children "to question whether demeaning or derogatory depictions of other people are stereotypes" and to learn how to respond to racial stereotypes and other forms of inequity? (49)

16. How useful or effective in understanding racial identity development do you find William Cross's stages of racial identity development and Tatum's explanation of them? (54ff) What examples of each stage can you cite from your experience and observation? Are the same five stages applicable or appropriate vis-à-vis other ethnic groups, including Whites? How useful or effective do you find Janet Helms's and Jean Phinney's models vis-à-vis a multicultural context?

17. How would you describe the emergence and function of "oppositional social identity" among African American and other high-school students of color? (60) In what ways does this phenomenon

serve the individual and group needs of students in relationship to the dominant White culture? What questions must educators and other concerned adults address when confronted with instances of oppositional identity? (64)

18. How does Tatum describe "the critical role that cultural space can play" for children, adolescents, and adults of color? In what ways can establishment of cultural space be fostered and encouraged, and in what ways might the possible drawbacks of cultural space be avoided?

19. What characterizes the onset and process of racial identity development among Whites, according to Tatum and counseling psychologist Janet Helms? If you are White, to what degree do you see your life as illustrative of that process and its six stages? In what ways is the process similar to, and in what ways different, from the process as experienced by people of color? (94ff) "How can White people achieve a healthy sense of White identity?" Tatum asks. How does she answer that question, and how would you answer it?

20. What elements and representations of institutional and cultural racism are observable today in the entertainment and news media and in our schools, corporations, government, and other institutions? How might both people of color and Whites call attention to these instances, work for their elimination, and establish nonracist and antiracist representations and behavior?

21. Tatum draws attention to the "history of White protest against racism, a history of Whites who have resisted the role of oppressor and who have been allies to people of color." (108) With what specifics of that history are you familiar? What might be the benefits of your learning more about that history? In what ways has that history provided, and might it now provide, models of thought, action, and cooperation for everyone?

22. How does affirmative action, in theory and in practice, and people's attitudes toward it fit into Tatum's discussion of racism in America? What are the salient arguments in support of affirmative action and in opposition to it? Given the context of historical and present-day institutional racism in the United States, which arguments

carry the greater force *at this time*? How might goal-oriented affirmative action help us to "achieve a more just society in the present context of institutional and cultural racism"? (127–28)

23. What situations, problems, and possibilities appear to be unique to multiethnic and biracial families and the children in those families? In what ways is the process of racial identity development for those children similar to, and in what ways different from, the process experienced by children who claim a single racial or ethnic heritage?

24. How might we explain the apparent social need in America to classify people racially? Is the phenomenon of racial classification unique to the United States, or does it exist (or has it existed) elsewhere?

25. How helpful toward an understanding of the development and choice of biracial identity are the factors identified by Charmaine Wijeyesinghe as significant in the process and outcome involved? How might discrepancies among the factors result in "identity confusion"? (182) To what extent might these factors be helpful in understanding racial identity development in members of monoracial or monoethnic groups?

26. Tatum frequently refers to "the White culture of silence about racism." (196) How successful is she in illustrating and explaining that culture of silence and its consequences for Whites and people of color? What are some of those consequences? What are some of the personal and social costs of silence? What examples of the White culture of silence about racism can you cite from your experience and observation? How might we explain that culture?

27. How does fear in relation to racism and race- and ethnic-related issues affect the attitudes of behavior of everyone? How might we all overcome the fears that prevent us from speaking openly and honestly about racism and other race-related issues?

28. Why does Tatum contend that there is no such thing as being passively antiracist? What arguments does she present to support that contention? Why is it not enough to be antiracist in our thoughts and

behavior? What can *you* do to combat racism and work toward its elimination in the United States? What have you done or failed to do?

29. Why *do* all the Black kids, and all the Asian and Latino and Indian and American Indian and biracial and other kids of color, and corporate employees of color sit together in the cafeteria and elsewhere? What is positive about the phenomenon, and what is problematic? What alternatives does Tatum suggest? What additional alternatives can you suggest?

Written by Hal Hager, Hal Hager & Associates, Somerville, New Jersey

Notes

Introduction

1. J. H. Katz, *White awareness: Handbook for anti-racism training* (Norman: University of Oklahoma Press, 1978).

2. For more information about the Psychology of Racism course, see B. D. Tatum, "Talking about race, learning about racism: An application of racial identity development theory in the classroom," *Harvard Educational Review* 62, no. 1 (1992): 1–24.

3. For a description of the professional development course for educators, see S. M. Lawrence and B. D. Tatum, "White educators as allies: Moving from awareness to action," pp. 333–42 in M. Fine, L. Weis, L. C. Powell, and L. M. Wong (Eds.), *Off White: Readings on race, power, and society* (New York: Routledge, 1997).

4. B. D. Tatum, "Talking about race, learning about racism: An application of racial identity development theory in the classroom," *Harvard Educational Review* 62, no. 1 (1992): 1–24.

Chapter 1

1. C. O'Toole, "The effect of the media and multicultural education on children's perceptions of Native Americans" (senior thesis, Department of Psychology and Education, Mount Holyoke College, South Hadley, MA, May 1990).

2. For an extended discussion of this point, see David Wellman, *Portraits of White racism* (Cambridge: Cambridge University Press, 1977), ch. 1.

3. For specific statistical information, see R. Farley, "The common destiny of Blacks and Whites: Observations about the social and economic status of the races," pp. 197–233 in H. Hill and J. E. Jones, Jr. (Eds.), *Race in America: The struggle for equality* (Madison: University of Wisconsin Press, 1993).

4. P. McIntosh, "White privilege: Unpacking the invisible knapsack," *Peace and Freedom* (July/August 1989): 10–12.

5. For further discussion of the concept of "belief in a just world," see M. J. Lerner, "Social psychology of justice and interpersonal attraction," in

T. Huston (Ed.), *Foundations of interpersonal attraction* (New York: Academic Press, 1974).

6. For a brief historical overview of the institutionalization of racism and sexism in our legal system, see "Part V: How it happened: Race and gender issues in U.S. law," in P. S. Rothenberg (Ed.), *Race, class, and gender in the United States: An integrated study,* 3d ed. (New York: St. Martin's Press, 1995).

7. P. A. Wentworth, "The identity development of non-traditionally aged first-generation women college students: An exploratory study" (master's thesis, Department of Psychology and Education, Mount Holyoke College, South Hadley, MA, 1994).

8. W. L. Updegrave, "Race and money," *Money* (December 1989): 152–72.

9. For further discussion of the impact of racism on Whites, see B. Bowser and R. G. Hunt (Eds.), *Impacts of racism on White Americans* (Thousand Oaks, CA: Sage, 1981); P. Kivel, *Uprooting racism: How White people can work for racial justice* (Philadelphia: New Society Publishers, 1996); and J. Barndt, *Dismantling racism: The continuing challenge to White America* (Minneapolis: Augsburg Press, 1991).

10. W. Berry, *The hidden wound* (San Francisco: North Point Press, 1989), pp. 3–4.

11. It is important to note here that these groups are not necessarily mutually exclusive. For example, people of Latin American descent may have European, African, and Native American ancestors. The politics of racial categorization has served to create artificial boundaries between groups with shared ancestry.

12. It is difficult to know which is the preferred term to use because different subgroups have different preferences. According to Amado Padilla, younger U.S.-born university-educated individuals of Mexican ancestry prefer *Chicano(a)* to *Mexican American* or *Hispanic.* On the other hand, *Latino* is preferred by others of Mexican ancestry or other Latin American origin. Those of Cuban ancestry may prefer *Cuban American* to *Latino,* whereas recent immigrants from Central America would rather be identified by their nationality (e.g., *Guatematecos* or *Salvadoreños*). A. Padilla (Ed.), *Hispanic psychology* (Thousand Oaks, CA: Sage, 1995).

13. For an expanded discussion of the social construction of race, see M. Omi and H. Winant, *Racial formation in the United States,* 2d ed. (New York: Routledge, 1994).

14. P. L. Van den Berghe, *Race and racism* (New York: Wiley, 1967).

15. See R. Alba, *Ethnic identity: The transformation of White America* (New Haven: Yale University Press, 1990).

16. For a discussion of the census classification debate and the history of racial classification in the United States, see L. Wright, "One drop of blood," *The New Yorker* (July 25, 1994): 46–55.

Chapter 2

1. See C. Cooley, *Human nature and the social order* (New York: Scribner, 1922). George H. Mead expanded on this idea in his book, *Mind, self, and society* (Chicago: University of Chicago Press, 1934).

2. A. J. Stewart and J. M. Healy, "Linking individual development and social changes," *American Psychologist* 44, no. 1 (1989): 30–42.

3. E. H. Erikson, *Identity, youth, and crisis* (New York: W. W. Norton, 1968), p. 22.

4. For a discussion of the Western biases in the concept of the self and individual identity, see A. Roland, "Identity, self, and individualism in a multicultural perspective," pp. 11–23 in E. P. Salett and D. R. Koslow (Eds.), *Race, ethnicity, and self: Identity in multicultural perspective* (Washington, DC: National MultiCultural Institute, 1994).

5. B. Thompson and S. Tyagi (Eds.), *Names we call home: Autobiography on racial identity* (New York: Routledge, 1996).

6. Ibid., p. xi.

7. *Anti-Semitism* is a term commonly used to describe the oppression of Jewish people. However, other Semitic peoples (Arab Muslims, for example) are also subject to oppressive treatment on the basis of ethnicity as well as religion. For that reason, the terms *Jewish oppression* and *Arab oppression* are sometimes used to specify the particular form of oppression under discussion.

8. A. Lorde, "Age, race, class, and sex: Women redefining difference," pp. 445–51 in P. Rothenberg (Ed.), *Race, class, and gender in the United States: An integrated study,* 3d ed. (New York: St. Martin's Press, 1995), p. 446.

9. J. B. Miller, "Domination and subordination," pp. 3–9 in *Toward a new psychology of women* (Boston: Beacon Press, 1976).

10. Ibid., p. 8.

11. S. T. Fiske, "Controlling other people: The impact of power on stereotyping," *American Psychologist* 48, no. 6 (1993): 621–28.

12. R. Wright, "The ethics of living Jim Crow" (1937), reprinted in P. Rothenberg (Ed.), *Race, class, and gender in the United States: An integrated study,* 3d ed. (New York: St. Martin's Press, 1995).

13. An article in the popular weekly magazine *People* chronicled the close encounters of famous Black men with White police officers. Despite their fame, these men were treated as potential criminals. Highlighted in the article is the story of Johnny Gammage, who was beaten to death by White police officers following a routine traffic stop in Pittsburgh. T. Fields-Meyer, "Under suspicion," *People* (January 15, 1996): 40–47.

14. Miller, "Domination and subordination," p. 10.

15. H. Kohl, "I won't learn from you: Confronting student resistance," pp. 134–35 in *Rethinking our classrooms: Teaching for equity and justice* (Milwaukee: Rethinking Our Schools, 1994), p. 134.

16. Miller, "Domination and subordination," p. 12.

Chapter 3

1. For an in-depth discussion of preschool children's recognition and understanding of racial differences, see L. Derman-Sparks, C. T. Higa, and B. Sparks, "Children, race, and racism: How race awareness develops," *Interracial Books for Children* 11, no. 3–4 (1980): 3–9.

2. For an expanded discussion of the role of Black families in the positive socialization of their children, see B. D. Tatum, *Assimilation blues: Black families in a White community* (Northampton, MA: Hazel-Maxwell, 1992).

3. See "Is multicultural education appropriate for young children?" in P. G. Ramsey, *Teaching and learning in a diverse world: Multicultural education for young children* (New York: Teachers College Press, 1985), ch. 2.

4. For other examples of good responses to preschoolers' questions, send for the helpful brochure, "Teaching Young Children to Resist Bias: What Parents Can Do," available from the National Association for the Education of Young Children, 1509 16th Street, N.W., Washington, DC, 20036–1426 (1–800–424–2460). The flyers are very inexpensive and can be ordered in bulk to be given to parents at school meetings and other educational forums. They are also available in Spanish.

5. In terms of Piaget's model of cognitive development, preschool children are considered to be in the preoperational stage. For more information about

the preoperational stage as it relates to children's understanding of racial and other forms of difference, see Ramsey, *Teaching and learning in a diverse world.* For a clear discussion of the cognitive characteristics of children at various stages of development, see B. J. Wadsworth, *Piaget's theory of cognitive and affective development: Foundations of constructivism,* 5th ed. (White Plains, NY: Longman, 1996).

6. S. Lawrence and B. D. Tatum, "Teachers in transition: The impact of anti-racist professional development on classroom practice," *Teachers College Record* (Fall 1997).

7. F. Ringgold, *Aunt Harriet's underground railroad in the sky* (New York: Crown, 1992).

8. J. Winter, *Follow the drinking gourd* (New York: Dragonfly Books, 1988).

9. See Derman-Sparks, Higa, and Sparks, "Children, race, and racism," p. 6.

10. Ibid.

11. For a more in-depth discussion of the impact of colorism, see K. Russell, M. Wilson, and R. H. Sacks, *The color complex* (San Diego: Harcourt Brace Jovanovich, 1992).

12. N. Boyd-Franklin, *Black families in therapy: A multisystems approach* (New York: Guilford, 1989), p. 34.

13. b. hooks, *Sisters of the yam: Black women and self-recovery* (Boston: South End Press, 1993), p. 95.

14. J. Steptoe, *Mufaro's beautiful daughters: An African tale* (New York: Scholastic, 1989).

15. The first book in this series by Gertrude Chandler Warner is *The Boxcar Children* (Niles, IL: Albert Whitman), published in 1942. Other books in the series include *Surprise Island, The Yellow House Mystery, Mystery Ranch,* and many others.

16. J. V. Ward, "Raising resisters: The role of truth telling in the psychological development of African-American girls," in B. J. R. Leadbeater and N. Way (Eds.), *Urban girls: Resisting stereotypes, creating identities* (New York: New York University Press, 1996).

17. For a useful set of guidelines for analysis of media, see Council on Interracial Books for Children, "Ten quick ways to analyze children's books for racism and sexism," pp. 14–15 in *Rethinking our classrooms* (Milwaukee: Rethinking Schools, 1994).

18. L. Derman-Sparks and the ABC Task Force, *Anti-bias curriculum: Tools for empowering young children* (Washington, DC: National Association for the Education of Young Children, 1989).

19. Ibid., p. 77.

Chapter 4

1. J. Marcia, "Development and validation of ego identity status," *Journal of Personality and Social Psychology* 3 (1966): 551–58.

2. For a review of the research on ethnic identity in adolescents, see J. Phinney, "Ethnic identity in adolescents and adults: Review of research," *Psychological Bulletin* 108, no. 3 (1990): 499–514. See also "Part I: Identity development" in B. J. R. Leadbeater and N. Way (Eds.), *Urban girls: Resisting stereotypes, creating identities* (New York: New York University Press, 1996).

3. W. E. Cross, Jr., *Shades of Black: Diversity in African-American identity* (Philadelphia: Temple University Press, 1991).

4. For an expanded discussion of "race-conscious" parenting, see in B. D. Tatum, *Assimilation blues,* ch. 6.

5. J. S. Phinney and S. Tarver, "Ethnic identity search and commitment in Black and White eighth graders," *Journal of Early Adolescence* 8, no. 3 (1988): 265–77.

6. See B. D. Tatum, "African-American identity, academic achievement, and missing history," *Social Education* 56, no. 6 (1992): 331–34; B. D. Tatum, "Racial identity and relational theory: The case of Black women in White communities," in *Work in progress, no. 63* (Wellesley, MA: Stone Center Working Papers, 1992); B. D. Tatum, "Out there stranded? Black youth in White communities," pp. 214–33 in H. McAdoo (Ed.), *Black families,* 3d ed. (Thousand Oaks, CA: Sage, 1996).

7. For an in-depth discussion of the negative effects of tracking in schools, see J. Oakes, *Keeping track: How schools structure inequality* (New Haven: Yale University Press, 1985).

8. For further discussion of the social dynamics for Black youth in White communities, see Tatum, "Out there stranded?"

9. Leadbeater and Way, *Urban girls,* p. 5.

10. A. Haley and Malcolm X, *The autobiography of Malcolm X* (New York: Grove Press, 1965), p. 36.

11. S. Fordham and J. Ogbu, "Black student's school success: Coping with the burden of 'acting White,'" *Urban Review* 18 (1986): 176–206.

12. Ibid., p. 181.

13. For an expanded discussion of the "trying to be White" phenomenon, see Fordham and Ogbu, "Black students' school success," and S. Fordham, "Racelessness as a factor in Black students' school success: Pragmatic strategy or Pyrrhic victory?" *Harvard Educational Review* 58, no. 1(1988): 54–84.

14. Fordham, "Racelessness as a factor in Black students' school success." See also S. Fordham, *Blacked out: Dilemmas of race, identity, and success at Capital High* (Chicago: University of Chicago Press, 1996).

15. For further discussion of this point, see R. Zweigenhaft and G. W. Domhoff, *Blacks in the White establishment? A study of race and class in America* (New Haven: Yale University Press, 1991), p. 155.

16. Ibid.

17. Ibid., p. 156.

18. C. Pierce, "Mundane extreme environment and its effects on learning," in S. G. Brainard (Ed.), *Learning disabilities: Issues and recommendations for research* (Washington, DC: National Institute of Education, 1975).

19. See M. C. Waters, "The intersection of gender, race, and ethnicity in identity development of Caribbean American teens," in B. J. R. Leadbeater and N. Way (Eds.), *Urban girls: Resisting stereotypes, creating identities* (New York: New York University Press, 1996).

20. The Metropolitan Council for Educational Opportunity (METCO) program was established in 1966 under the state's Racial Imbalance Law passed by the Massachusetts General Court in 1965. METCO was established to provide (1) the opportunity for an integrated public school education for urban Black children and other children of color from racially imbalanced schools in Boston by placing them in suburban schools, (2) a new learning experience for suburban children, and (3) a closer understanding and cooperation between urban and suburban parents and other citizens in the Boston metropolitan area. Thirty-four suburban communities participate in the METCO program.

21. For a more complete description of the program and its evaluation, see B. D. Tatum, P. C. Brown, P. Elliott, and T. Tatum, "Student efficacy training: An evaluation of one middle school's programmatic response to the Eastern Massachusetts Initiative" (presented at the American Educational Research Association Annual Meeting, April 9, 1996, New York).

Chapter 5

1. Approximately 75 percent of all Black college students attend predominantly White colleges. For a discussion of Black college attendance and retention at White colleges in comparison to historically Black colleges, see W. R. Allen, "The color of success: African-American college student outcomes at predominantly White and historically Black public colleges and universities," *Harvard Educational Review* 62, no. 1 (1992): 26–44.

2. For a detailed account and many more examples of campus racism, see J. R. Feagin and M. P. Sikes, *Living with racism: The Black middle-class experience* (Boston: Beacon Press, 1994), ch. 3.

3. Many researchers have reported similar findings. For more information, see J. Fleming, *Blacks in college* (San Francisco: Jossey-Bass, 1984). See also W. R. Allen, E. G. Epp, and N. Z. Haniff (Eds.), *College in Black and White: African American students in predominantly White and in historically Black public universities* (Albany: State University of New York Press, 1991).

4. W. R. Allen, "The color of success," pp. 39–40. The National Study of Black College Students (NSBCS) surveyed more than twenty-five hundred Black college students attending a total of sixteen public universities (eight predominantly White and eight historically Black) about their college experiences and outcomes.

5. For a discussion of White students' responses to learning about the racial identity development process of students of color, see B. D. Tatum, "Talking about race, learning about racism."

6. Haley and Malcolm X, *The autobiography of Malcolm X,* p. 174.

7. M. E. Dyson, *Race rules: Navigating the color line* (Boston: Beacon Press, 1996), p. 151.

8. P. H. Collins, *Black feminist thought: Knowledge, consciousness, and the politics of empowerment* (London: HarperCollins Academic, 1990), p. 96.

9. The National Survey of Black Americans (NSBA) was the first in a series of major research projects undertaken by social scientists at the Institute for Social Research at the University of Michigan to collect and analyze high-quality national survey data on the social, psychological, economic, and political behaviors of Black Americans. The NSBA and the major studies that followed it are all part of the Program for Research on Black Americans (PRBA) at the Institute for Social Research. The PRBA has involved thou-

sands of Black participants in both face-to-face and telephone interviews. The findings of the PRBA are reported in J. Jackson (Ed.), *Life in Black America* (Thousand Oaks, CA: Sage, 1991).

10. See R. J. Taylor and L. M. Chatters, "Religious life," pp. 105–23 in J. Jackson (Ed.), *Life in Black America* (Thousand Oaks, CA: Sage, 1991).

11. T. A. Parham, "Cycles of psychological nigrescence," *The Counseling Psychologist* 17, no. 2 (1989): 187–226.

12. D. Levinson, *The seasons of a man's life* (New York: Knopf, 1978).

13. Parham, "Cycles of psychological nigrescence," p. 202.

14. G. Davis and G. Watson, *Black life in corporate America: Swimming in the mainstream* (New York: Anchor Press, 1982), p. 51.

15. Tatum, *Assimilation blues.*

16. E. Cose, *The rage of a privileged class* (New York: HarperCollins, 1993).

17. Feagin and Sikes, *Living with racism.*

18. Parham, "Cycles of psychological nigrescence," p. 196.

19. Tatum, *Assimilation blues,* p. 99.

20. Ibid., p. 108.

21. Ibid., p. 79.

22. Parham, "Cycles of psychological nigrescence," p. 204.

23. G. Early, *Lure and loathing: Essays on race, identity, and the ambivalence of assimilation* (New York: Penguin, 1993), p. xxiii.

24. See E. Erikson, *Childhood and society* (New York: W. W. Norton, 1950), ch. 8.

25. R. C. Gibson, "Retirement," pp. 179–98 in J. S. Jackson (Ed.), *Life in Black America* (Thousand Oaks, CA: Sage, 1991).

26. W. E. Cross, "The psychology of nigrescence: Revising the Cross model," pp. 93–122 in J. G. Ponterotto, J. M. Casas, L. A. Suzuki, and C. M. Alexander (Eds.), *Handbook of multicultural counseling* (Thousand Oaks, CA: Sage, 1995), p. 116.

27. The concept of tokenism is explored in R. M. Kanter, *Men and women of the corporation* (New York: Basic Books, 1977). See also *A tale of O* [video] (Cambridge, MA: Goodmeasure, 1979); and R. M. Kanter with B. A. Stein, *A tale of O* (New York: Harper Colophon, 1980). Video conceived by R. M. Kanter; produced by B. A. Stein.

Chapter 6

1. S. M. Lawrence and B. D. Tatum, "White educators as allies," p. 333.

2. J. E. Helms (Ed.), *Black and White racial identity: Theory, research, and practice* (Westport, CT: Greenwood, 1990).

3. Paul Kivel makes the point that working-class Whites are more likely to feel angry and less likely to feel guilty than their middle-class counterparts. See P. Kivel, *Uprooting racism*.

4. There are other models of White racial identity development, most notably those of Rita Hardiman and Joseph Ponterotto. Though there are some differences, there are considerable similarities across these models. Helms's model is emphasized here because it is the most commonly cited of the White identity models and is the one most often used in empirical investigations of White racial identity. For a summary of Hardiman's model, see R. Hardiman, "White racial identity development in the United States," ch. 6 in E. P. Salett and D. R. Koslow (Eds.), *Race, ethnicity, and self: Identity in multicultural perspectives* (Washington, DC: National Multicultural Institute, 1994). For a discussion of Ponterotto's model and its relationship to the others, see J. G. Ponterotto and P. B. Pedersen, *Preventing prejudice: A guide for counselors and educators* (Thousand Oaks, CA: Sage, 1993).

5. Janet Helms has changed her terminology from *stages* to *statuses* in describing this six-part model. For stylistic reasons, the term *stages* is retained here. Helms discusses the change in terminology in her article, "An update of Helms's White and people of color racial identity models," pp. 181–98 in J. G. Ponterotto, J. M. Casas, L. A. Suzuki, and C. M. Alexander (Eds.), *Handbook of multicultural counseling* (Thousand Oaks, CA: Sage, 1995).

6. McIntosh, "White privilege," p. 12.

7. R. Carter, "Is White a race? Expressions of White racial identity," in M. Fine, L. Weis, L. C. Powell, and L. M. Wong (Eds.), *Off White: Readings on race, power, and society* (New York: Routledge, 1997), p. 201.

8. M. Riggs (Producer/Director), *Ethnic notions* [Video] (San Francisco: Resolution/California Newsreel, 1986).

9. This interview was conducted by my graduate student, Elizabeth Knaplund, as part of a study we conducted on the relational impact of antiracist activity on the lives of White women. See B. D. Tatum and E. G. Knaplund, "Outside the circle: The relational implications for White women

working against racism," *Work in progress, no. 78* (Wellesley, MA: Stone Center Working Paper Series, 1996).

10. McIntosh, "White privilege," p. 11.

11. See N. Zane, "Interrupting historical patterns: Bridging race and gender gaps between senior White men and other organizational groups," pp. 343–53 in M. Fine, L. Weis, L. C. Powell, and L. M. Wong (Eds.), *Off White: Readings on race, power, and society* (New York: Routledge, 1997), p. 349.

12. Jews are a multiracial group, including Jews of African descent. For a helpful discussion of the complexity of Jewish racial identity, see M. Kaye/Kantrowitz, "Jews in the U.S.: The rising costs of Whiteness," pp. 121–38 in B. Thompson and S. Tyagi (Eds.), *Names we call home: Autobiography on racial identity* (New York: Routledge, 1996).

13. Lawrence and Tatum, "White educators as allies."

14. L. Stalvey, *The education of a WASP* (Madison: University of Wisconsin Press, [1970] 1989), p. 151.

15. R. Frankenberg, *White women, race matters: The social construction of Whiteness* (Minneapolis: University of Minnesota Press, 1993).

16. R. Frankenberg, "'When we are capable of stopping, we begin to see': Being White, seeing Whiteness," pp. 3–17 in B. Thompson and S. Tyagi (Eds.), *Names we call home: Autobiography on racial identity* (New York: Routledge, 1996), p. 14.

17. Ibid.

18. M. Dees with S. Fiffer, *A season of justice: A lawyer's own story of victory over America's hate groups* (New York: Touchstone, 1991).

19. H. F. Barnard (Ed.), *Outside the magic circle: The autobiography of Virginia Foster Durr* (Tuscaloosa: University of Alabama Press, 1985). An excerpt of this oral history can also be found in A. Colby and W. Damon, *Some do care: Contemporary lives of moral commitment* (New York: Free Press, 1992).

20. Stalvey, *The education of a WASP.*

21. A. Ayvazian, "Interrupting the cycle of oppression: The role of allies as agents of change," *Fellowship* (January/February 1995): 7–10.

22. For an example of such a group in process, see B. Thompson and White Women Challenging Racism, "Home/Work: Antiracism activism and the meaning of Whiteness," pp. 354–66 in M. Fine, L. Weis, L. C. Powell, and L. M. Wong (Eds.), *Off White: Readings on race, power, and society* (New York: Routledge, 1997).

23. For a discussion of the value of "Whites only" support groups, see B. Thompson, "Time traveling and border crossing: Reflections on White identity," pp. 104–5 in B. Thompson and S. Tyagi (Eds.), *Names we call home: Autobiography on racial identity* (New York: Routledge, 1996).

24. Ibid., p. 104.

25. C. P. Alderfer, "A White man's perspective on the unconscious process within Black-White relations in the United States," pp. 201–29 in E. J. Trickett, R. Watts, and D. Birman (Eds.), *Human diversity* (San Francisco: Jossey-Bass, 1994), p. 202.

26. Helms, *Black and White racial identity*, p. 66.

27. Ibid., p. 105.

Chapter 7

1. H. Winant, "Behind blue eyes: Whiteness and contemporary U.S. racial politics," pp. 40–53 in M. Fine, L. Weis, L. C. Powell, and L. M. Wong (Eds.), *Off white: Readings on race, power, and society* (New York: Routledge, 1997), p. 42.

2. Jennifer Eberhardt and Susan Fiske report similar conversations in their classrooms. See J. Eberhardt and S. Fiske, "Affirmative action in theory and practice: Issues of power, ambiguity, and gender versus race," *Basic and Applied Social Psychology* 15, no. 1/2 (1994): 201–20.

3. For more information about the history of affirmative action, see F. A. Holloway, "What is affirmative action?" and D. A. Taylor, "Affirmative action and presidential executive orders," both in F. A. Blanchard and F. Crosby (Eds.), *Affirmative action in perspective* (New York: Springer-Verlag, 1989).

4. F. Crosby, "Understanding affirmative action," *Basic and Applied Social Psychology* 15 no. 1/2 (1994): 13–41.

5. T. Mullen, "Affirmative action," pp. 244–66 in S. McLean and N. Burrows (Eds.), *The legal relevance of gender* (Atlantic Highlands, NJ: Humanities Press International, 1988).

6. I have borrowed this phrase from Stephen Carter, who argues that when candidates of color are "too good to ignore" affirmative action programs should be unnecessary. See S. Carter, *Reflections of an affirmative action baby* (New York: Basic Books, 1991).

7. For a discussion of the American preference for process-oriented affirmative action, see R. Nacoste, "Opportunities yes, but no guarantees:

Procedural goals and resistance to affirmative action" (presented at the Eastern Psychological Association Annual Meeting, Buffalo, NY, April 23, 1988).

8. J. F. Dovidio, J. Mann, and S. L. Gaertner, "Resistance to affirmative action: The implications of aversive racism," pp. 83–102 in F. A. Blanchard and F. J. Crosby (Eds.), *Affirmative action in perspective* (New York: Springer-Verlag, 1989), p. 86.

9. For more information about this study, see B. B. Kline and J. F. Dovidio, "Effects of race, sex, and qualifications on predictions of a college applicant's performance" (presented at the annual meeting of the Eastern Psychological Association, Baltimore, April 1982).

10. For a more detailed description of these studies, see J. F. Dovidio and S. L. Gaertner, "The effects of sex, status, and ability on helping behavior," *Journal of Applied Social Psychology* 13 (1983): 191–205.

11. For more information, see S. D. Clayton and S. S. Tangri, "The justice of affirmative action," pp. 177–92 in F. A. Blanchard and F. J. Crosby (Eds.), *Affirmative action in perspective* (New York: Springer-Verlag, 1989).

12. Dovidio, Mann, and Gaertner, "Resistance to affirmative action," p. 92.

13. For a discussion of how the concept of aversive racism might apply to discriminatory treatment of Hispanics, see J. F. Dovidio, S. L. Gaertner, P. A. Anastasio, and R. Sanitioso, "Cognitive and motivational bases of bias: Implications of aversive racism for attitudes toward Hispanics," pp. 75–106 in S. B. Knouse, P. Rosenfeld, and A. L. Culbertson (Eds.), *Hispanics in the workplace* (Newbury Park, CA: Sage, 1992).

14. For a discussion of affirmative action as it relates to other groups, see G. E. Curry (Ed.), *The affirmative action debate* (Reading, MA: Addison-Wesley, 1996), ch. 5.

15. A. J. Murrell, B. L. Dietz-Uhler, J. F. Dovidio, S. L. Gaertner, and C. Drout, "Aversive racism and resistance to affirmative action: Perceptions of justice are not necessarily color blind," *Basic and Applied Social Psychology* 15, no. 1/2 (1994): 81.

16. Crosby, "Understanding affirmative action," p. 24.

17. Of course the evaluation of scores on such standardized tests as the SAT and the GRE must be done with the understanding that the predictive validity of such tests varies among racial and gender groups. For an interesting investigation of the impact of racial variables on test performance, see

C. Steele and J. Aronson, "Stereotype threat and the intellectual test performance of African Americans," *Journal of Personality and Social Psychology* 69, no. 5 (1995): 797–811.

18. F. J. Blanchard, "Effective affirmative action programs," pp. 193–207 in F. A. Blanchard and F. J. Crosby (Eds.), *Affirmative action in perspective* (New York: Springer-Verlag, 1989).

19. In May 1995, the U.S. Court of Appeals for the Fourth Circuit invalidated a scholarship program for Black students at the University of Maryland at College Park. In June 1995, the Supreme Court's decision in *Adarand Constructors Inc. v. Pena* restricted the use of preferences based on race or ethnicity in federal programs. In July 1995, the University of California Board of Regents voted to prohibit the use of racial and gender preferences in admissions and hiring. In March 1996, the U.S. Court of Appeals for the Fifth Circuit barred the University of Texas Law School from considering race in its admission process in any way. The law school, like many colleges and universities, had considered racial/ethnic minority group membership as an admissions factor in its efforts to create a more diverse student body. However, the appeals court ruled that "any consideration of race or ethnicity by the law school for the purpose of achieving a diverse student body is not a compelling interest." The Supreme Court has declined to hear an appeal. For more information, see "Appeals court bars racial preference," *Chronicle of Higher Education* (March 29, 1996): A26–36.

20. S. Fish, "Reverse racism, or how the pot got to call the kettle black?" *Atlantic Monthly* (November 1993): 136.

21. M. Fine, "Witnessing Whiteness," pp. 57–65 in M. Fine, L. Weis, L. C. Powell, and L. M. Wong (Eds.), *Off White: Readings on race, power, and society* (New York: Routledge, 1997).

22. F. Crosby, "Confessions of an affirmative action mama," pp. 179–86 in M. Fine, L. Weis, L. C. Powell, and L. M. Wong (Eds.), *Off White: Readings on race, power, and society* (New York: Routledge, 1997), p. 185.

23. Ibid., p. 184.

Chapter 8

1. The statements quoted here are taken from F. Reid (Producer/Director), *Skin deep: College students confront racism* [Video] (San Francisco: Resolution/ California Newsreel, 1995).

2. An excellent source for a multicultural history of these and other groups in the United States is R. Takaki, *A different mirror: A history of multicultural America* (Boston: Little, Brown, 1993).

3. Stanley Sue, as quoted in M. J. Casas and S. D. Pytluk, "Hispanic identity development: Implications for research and practice," in J. G. Ponterotto, J. M. Casas, L. A. Suzuki, and C. M. Alexander (Eds.), *Handbook of multicultural counseling* (Thousand Oaks, CA: Sage, 1995), p. 165.

4. J. Phinney, "A three-stage model of ethnic identity development in adolescence," pp. 61–79 in M. E. Bernal and G. P. Knight (Eds.), *Ethnic identity: Formation and transmission among Hispanics and other minorities* (Albany: State University of New York Press, 1993).

5. An excellent source for detailed discussions of identity development for these and other groups is J. G. Ponterotto, J. M. Casas, L. A. Suzuki, and C. M. Alexander (Eds.), *Handbook of multicultural counseling* (Thousand Oaks, CA: Sage, 1995).

6. For more demographic information, see G. Marín and B. V. Marín, *Research with Hispanic populations* (Newbury Park, CA: Sage, 1991).

7. For more information, see J. Spring, *Deculturalization and the struggle for equality: A brief history of the education of dominated cultures in the United States,* 2d ed. (New York: McGraw-Hill, 1997), ch. 5.

8. C. Suárez-Orozco and M. Suárez-Orozco, *Transformations: Immigration, family life, and achievement motivation among Latino adolescents* (Stanford, CA: Stanford University Press, 1995), p. 50.

9. See Spring, *Deculturalization and the struggle for equality,* ch. 3.

10. Bureau of the Census, *We the Americans: Our education* (Washington, DC: Government Printing Office, 1993).

11. B. B. Hess, E. W. Markson, and P. J. Stein, "Racial and ethnic minorities: An overview," in P. S. Rothenberg (Ed.), *Race, class, and gender in the United States: An integrated study,* 3d ed. (New York: St. Martin's Press, 1995).

12. Bureau of the Census, *We the Americans,* p. 5.

13. Marín and Marín, *Research with Hispanic populations,* p. 10.

14. Ibid., p. 11.

15. While in the context of U.S. society those with any African ancestry were legally categorized as Black, that was not the case in Latin American countries. The Spanish colonizers, who traveled without female companionship, formed sexual liaisons with indigenous Indian women and enslaved

African women. The Spaniards often baptized and gave their names to the children of their unions, sometimes marrying the mothers. Consequently, racial categorizations were less rigid than in the United States. For more information about categorizations of Hispanics in the U.S., see Marín and Marín, *Research with Hispanic populations*.

16. For a discussion of *racismo* in Latino communities, see L. Comas-Diaz, "LatiNegra," pp. 167–90 in M. P. P. Root (Ed.), *The multiracial experience: Racial borders as the new frontier* (Thousand Oaks, CA: Sage, 1996).

17. Marín and Marín, *Research with Hispanic populations,* p. 2.

18. Suárez-Orozco and Suárez-Orozco, *Transformations,* p. 136.

19. See Ibid., ch. 4.

20. S. Nieto, *Affirming diversity: The sociopolitical context of multicultural education,* 2d ed. (White Plains, NY: Longman, 1996).

21. Ibid., p. 147.

22. Suárez-Orozco and Suárez-Orozco, *Transformations,* p. 52.

23. For further discussion of these four options and their connection to Tajfel's social identity theory, see J. S. Phinney, B. T. Lochner, and R. Murphy, "Ethnic identity development and psychological adjustment in adolescence," pp. 53–72 in A. R. Stiffman and L. E. Davis (Eds.), *Ethnic issues in adolescent mental health* (Newbury Park, CA: Sage, 1990).

24. R. Rodriguez, *Hunger of memory: The education of Richard Rodriguez* (New York: Bantam, 1982), p. 23.

25.M. Zavala, "Who are you if you don't speak Spanish? The Puerto Rican dilemma" (presented at the American Educational Research Association Annual Meeting, New York, April 1996).

26. M. Zavala, "A bridge over divided worlds: An exploration into the nature of bilingual Puerto Rican youths' ethnic identity development" (master's thesis, Mount Holyoke College, South Hadley, MA, 1995).

27. Zavala, "Who are you if you don't speak Spanish?" p. 9.

28. Ibid.

29. Ibid., p. 11.

30. S. Betances, "African-Americans and Hispanic/Latinos: Eliminating barriers to coalition building" (presented at the Ethnic Diversity Roundtable, Chicago Urban Policy Institute and the Joint Center for Political and Economic Studies, April 15, 1994).

31. Nieto, *Affirming diversity,* ch. 6.

32. For a review of this literature, see C. E. Moran and K. Hakuta, "Bilingual education: Broadening research perspectives," pp. 445–62 in J. Banks and C. M. Banks (Eds.), *Handbook of research on multicultural education* (New York: Simon & Schuster, 1995).

33. Nieto, *Affirming diversity,* p. 200.

34. See Spring, *Deculturalization and the struggle for equality.*

35. Bureau of the Census, *We, the First Americans* (Washington, DC: Government Printing Office, 1993).

36. Although the different cultural communities (Cherokee, Navajo, Chippewa, etc.) are frequently referred to as tribes, Native American scholar Ward Churchill argues persuasively that this term has pejorative connotations of "primitivism" that are highly problematic. For that reason, the terms *nations* and *peoples* are used here instead. For a discussion of this issue, see W. Churchill, "Naming our destiny: Toward a language of American Indian liberation" pp. 291–357 in *Indians are us? Culture and genocide in Native North America* (Monroe, ME: Common Courage Press, 1994).

37. R. D. Herring, "Native American Indian identity: A people of many peoples," pp. 170–97 in E. P. Salett and D. R. Koslow (Eds.), *Race, ethnicity, and self: Identity in multicultural perspective* (Washington, DC: National MultiCultural Institute, 1994).

38. C. M. Snipp, "American Indian studies," pp. 245–58 in J. Banks and C. M. Banks (Eds.), *Handbook on research on multicultural education* (New York: Simon & Schuster, 1995).

39. K. T. Lomawaima, "Educating Native Americans," pp. 331–47 in J. Banks and C. M. Banks (Eds.), *Handbook on research on multicultural education* (New York: Simon & Schuster, 1995).

40. Bureau of the Census, *We, the First Americans.*

41. C. T. Sutton and M. A. Broken Nose, "American Indian families: An overview," pp. 31–44 in M. McGoldrick, J. Giordano, and J. K. Pearce (Eds.), *Ethnicity and family therapy,* 2d ed. (New York: Guilford, 1996).

42. Spring, *Deculturalization and the struggle for equality,* p. 12.

43. N. Tafoya and A. DelVecchio, "Back to the future: An examination of the Native American Holocaust experience," pp. 45–54 in M. McGoldrick, J. Giordano, and J. K. Pearce (Eds.), *Ethnicity and family therapy* (New York: Guilford, 1996).

44. Spring, *Deculturalization and the struggle for equality,* 100–104.

45. Sutton and Broken Nose, "American Indian families," p. 34.

46. Snipp, "American Indian studies," p. 251.

47. Tafoya and Del Vecchio, "Back to the future," p. 46.

48. N. S. Momaday, "Confronting Columbus again," in P. Nabokov (Ed.), *Native American testimony: A chronicle of Indian-White relations from prophecy to the present, 1492–1992* (New York: Viking, 1991), p. 438.

49. Nieto, *Affirming diversity,* p. 13.

50. L. Little Soldier, "Is there an 'Indian' in your classroom? Working successfully with urban Native American students," *Phi Delta Kappan* (April 1997): 650–53.

51. D. A. Grinde, Jr., "Place and kinship: A Native American's identity before and after words," pp. 63–72 in B. Thompson and S. Tyagi (Eds.), *Names we call home: Autobiography on racial identity* (New York: Routledge, 1996), p. 66.

52. P. Ongtooguk, "Their silence about us: The absence of Alaska Natives in the curriculum" (presented at the American Educational Research Association Annual Meeting, Atlanta, GA, April 1993).

53. T. Tsugawa, "Asian Pacific American demographics" (presented at the METCO Directors Association Conference, Boston, MA, March 28, 1997).

54. E. Lee, "Asian American families: An overview," pp. 227–48 in M. McGoldrick, J. Giordano, and J. K. Pearce (Eds.), *Ethnicity and family therapy,* 2d ed. (New York: Guilford, 1996).

55. L. Uba, *Asian Americans: Personality patterns, identity, and mental health* (New York: Guilford, 1994), p. 3.

56. Spring, *Deculturalization and the struggle for equality,* p. 74.

57. Takaki, *A different mirror,* p. 205.

58. Uba, *Asian Americans,* p. 5.

59. W. T. Matsui, "Japanese families," pp. 268–80 in M. McGoldrick, J. Giordano, and J. K. Pearce (Eds.), *Ethnicity and family therapy,* 2d ed. (New York: Guilford, 1996).

60. B. C. Kim, "Korean families," pp. 281–94 in M. McGoldrick, J. Giordano, and J. K. Pearce (Eds.), *Ethnicity and family therapy,* 2d ed. (New York: Guilford, 1996).

61. Uba, *Asian Americans,* p. 7.

62. Lee, "Asian American families," p. 228.

63. N. Abudabbeh, "Arab families," pp. 333–46 in M. McGoldrick, J. Giordano, and J. K. Pearce (Eds.), *Ethnicity and family therapy*, 2d ed. (New York: Guilford, 1996).

64. D. Mura, "A shift in power, a sea change in the arts: Asian American constructions," pp. 183–204 in K. Aguilar–San Juan (Ed.), *The state of Asian America: Activism and resistance in the 1990s* (Boston: South End Press, 1994).

65. K. Chan and S. Hune, "Racialization and panethnicity: From Asians in America to Asian Americans," pp. 205–33 in W. D. Hawley and A. W. Jackson (Eds.), *Toward a common destiny: Improving race and ethnic relations in America* (San Francisco: Jossey-Bass, 1995), p. 210.

66. Ibid., p. 215.

67. Ibid., p. 218.

68. Reid, *Skin deep.*

69. W. Petersen, "Success Story, Japanese-American Style," *New York Times Magazine* (January 9, 1966): 20-21, 33, 36, 40-41, 43. "Success Story of One Minority in the U.S.," *U.S. News and World Report* (December 26, 1966): 73-78.

70. Chan and Hune, "Racialization and panethnicity," p. 222.

71. A case in point is the 1982 murder of Vincent Chin, who was beaten to death by two White autoworkers who blamed U.S. unemployment on the Japanese. Chin, a Chinese American, was mistaken for a Japanese national. For more information on anti-Asian violence, see Chan and Hune, "Racialization and panethnicity," p. 220.

72. T. H. Wang and F. H. Wu, "Beyond the model minority myth," pp. 191–97 in G. E. Curry (Ed.), *The affirmative action debate* (Reading, MA: Addison-Wesley, 1996).

73. Chan and Hune, "Racialization and panethnicity," p. 226.

74. W. Walker-Moffat, *The other side of the Asian American success story* (San Francisco: Jossey-Bass, 1995), p. 22.

75. L. Delpit, *Other people's children: Cultural conflict in the classroom* (New York: New Press, 1995), p. 171.

76. V. O. Pang, "Asian Pacific American students: A diverse and complex population," pp. 412–24 in J. Banks and C. M. Banks (Eds.), *Handbook on research on multicultural education* (New York: Simon & Schuster, 1995).

77. M. Yamada, "Invisibility is an unnatural disaster: Reflections of an Asian American woman," pp. 35–40 in C. Moraga and G. Anzaldua (Eds.), *This*

bridge called my back: Writings by radical women of color (New York: Kitchen Table Press, 1981).

78. Ibid., p. 35.

79. P. N. Kiang, *We could shape it: Organizing for Asian Pacific American student empowerment* [occasional paper] (Boston: University of Massachusetts Institute for Asian American Studies, 1996).

80. Ibid., p. 6.

81. Ibid., p. 12.

82. Ibid., p. 15.

83. Ibid., p. 16.

84. L. Tse, "Finding a place to be: Asian Americans in ethnic identity exploration," *Adolescence* (in press).

85. *Sansei* means third-generation Japanese American. See D. Mura, *Turning Japanese: Memoirs of a sansei* (New York: Atlantic Monthly Press, 1991).

86. Mura, "A shift in power," p. 187.

87. Chan and Hune, "Racialization and panethnicity," p. 208.

88. Phinney, "A three-stage model."

Chapter 9

1. For a state-by-state summary of the laws forbidding interracial marriages, see P. R. Spickard, *Mixed blood: Intermarriage and ethnic identity in twentieth-century America* (Madison: University of Wisconsin Press, 1989), pp. 374–75.

2. Wright, "One drop of blood," pp. 46–55.

3. M. P. P. Root (Ed.), *Racially mixed people in America* (Thousand Oaks, CA: Sage, 1992).

4. This chapter will be focused primarily on biracial Black-White identity development. For information regarding Black-Japanese identity, see C. C. I. Hall, "The ethnic identity of racially mixed people: A study of Black-Japanese" (doctoral dissertation, University of California, Los Angeles, 1980). For information regarding Asian-White experiences, see G. K. Kich, "The developmental process of asserting a biracial, bicultural identity," pp. 304–17 in M. P. P. Root (Ed.), *Racially mixed people in America* (Thousand Oaks, CA: Sage, 1992).

5. M. P. P. Root, "Within, between, and beyond race," pp. 3–11 in M. P. P. Root (Ed.), *Racially mixed people in America* (Thousand Oaks, CA: Sage, 1992).

6. P. R. Spickard, "The illogic of American racial categories," pp. 12–23 in

M. P. P. Root (Ed.), *Racially mixed people in America* (Thousand Oaks, CA: Sage, 1992), p. 15.

7. See F. J. Davis, *Who is Black? One nation's definition* (University Park: Pennsylvania State University Press, 1991), chs. 1 and 2.

8. L. Funderberg, *Black, White, other: Biracial Americans talk about race and identity* (New York: Quill, 1994), p. 186.

9. Davis, Who is Black? p. 12.

10. For more details, see Davis, *Who is Black?* pp. 10–11.

11. See C. K. Bradshaw, "Beauty and the beast: On racial ambiguity," in M. P. P. Root (Ed.), *Racially mixed people in America* (Thousand Oaks, CA: Sage, 1992), p. 81. See also C. Kerwin and J. G. Ponterotto, "Biracial identity development: Theory and research," pp. 199–217 in J. G. Ponterotto, J. M. Casas, L. A. Suzuki, and C. M. Alexander (Eds.), *Handbook of multicultural counseling* (Thousand Oaks, CA: Sage, 1995).

12. *Imitation of Life* was released in 1934 and remade in 1959. It follows the lives of two women, one White and one Black, and their daughters. The Black mother is heartbroken when her light-skinned daughter disavows her and chooses to pass for White.

13. J. T. Gibbs, "Biracial adolescents," pp. 322–50 in J. T. Gibbs, L. N. Huang, and Associates (Eds.), *Children of color: Psychological interventions with minority youth* (San Francisco: Jossey-Bass, 1989).

14. The "Self Portrait" of Michael Tyron Ackley is a particularly compelling example of emotional distress caused not by biracial heritage but by familial abuse. See Funderberg, *Black, White, other*, pp. 137–49.

15. A. M. Cauce, Y. Hiraga, C. Mason, T. Aguilar, N. Ordonez, and N. Gonzales, "Between a rock and a hard place: Social adjustment of biracial youth," pp. 207–22 in M. P. P. Root (Ed.), *Racially mixed people in America* (Thousand Oaks, CA: Sage, 1992).

16. Ibid., p. 220.

17. For a review of this literature, see J. T. Gibbs and A. M. Hines, "Negotiating ethnic identity: Issues for Black-White biracial adolescents," pp. 223–38 in M. P. P. Root (Ed.), *Racially mixed people in America* (Thousand Oaks, CA: Sage, 1992). See also L. D. Field, "Piecing together the puzzle: Self-concept and group identity in biracial Black/White youth," pp. 211–26 in M. P. P. Root (Ed.), *The multiracial experience: Racial borders as the new frontier* (Thousand Oaks, CA: Sage, 1996).

18. Gibbs and Hines, "Negotiating ethnic identity," p. 237.

19. For an additional discussion of this lifelong process, see M. P. P. Root, "Resolving 'other' status: Identity development of biracial individuals," pp. 185–205 in L. S. Brown and M. P. P. Root (Eds.), *Diversity and complexity in feminist therapy* (New York: Haworth Press, 1989).

20. Kerwin and Ponterotto, "Biracial identity development."

21. See M. T. Reddy, *Crossing the color line: Race, parenting, and culture* (New Brunswick, NJ: Rutgers University Press, 1994), ch. 3.

22. R. L. Miller and M. J. Rotheram-Borus, "Growing up biracial in the United States," pp. 143–69 in E. P. Salett and D. R. Koslow (Eds.), *Race, ethnicity, and self: Identity in multicultural perspective* (Washington, DC: National Multicultural Institute, 1994).

23. Even when White people are demeaned as "nigger lovers," it is the association with Blackness that is the source of the insult, not Whiteness itself.

24. Miller and Rotheram-Borus, "Growing up biracial in the United States," p. 156.

25. Reddy, *Crossing the color line,* p. 61.

26. Root, "Resolving 'other' status," p. 190.

27. M. Davol, *Black, White, just right!* (Morton Grove, IL: A. Whitman, 1993).

28. Miller and Rotheram-Borus, "Growing up biracial in the United States."

29. Reddy, *Crossing the color line,* p. 77.

30. Funderburg, *Black, White, other,* p. 44.

31. Miller and Rotheram-Borus, "Growing up biracial in the United States," p. 143.

32. Funderburg, *Black, White, other,* p. 367.

33. Kerwin and Ponterotto, "Biracial identity development," p. 212.

34. C. Wijeyesinghe, "Towards an understanding of the racial identity of biracial people: The experience of racial self-identification of African-American/Euro-American adults and the factors affecting their choices of racial identity" (doctoral dissertation, University of Massachusetts, Amherst, 1992), *Dissertation Abstracts International* 53, no. 11A.

35. See Funderburg, *Black, White, other,* and the research of psychologist Trude Cooke (personal communication).

36. Monoracial Black youth who are identified as gay, lesbian, or bisexual may experience similar conflicts.

37. Funderburg, *Black, White, other,* p. 39.

38. For a history of the phenomenon of light-skinned Blacks passing as White, see Spickard, *Mixed blood.*

39. Funderburg, *Black, White, other,* p. 315.

40. Kerwin and Ponterotto, "Biracial identity development," p. 210.

41. J. Lazarre, *Beyond the Whiteness of Whiteness: Memoir of a White mother of Black sons* (Durham, NC: Duke University Press, 1996), p. 63.

42. F. W. Twine, J. F. Warren, and F. F. Martin, *Just Black?* [Video] (New York: Filmakers Library, 1991).

43. The placement of children of color in White adoptive families continues to be a controversial issue. Organizations such as the National Association of Black Social Workers and the Child Welfare League of America have argued that within-race placements are preferable to transracial adoptions and that the latter should only be considered when efforts at within-race placements have been unsuccessful. For a review of the controversy, see R. G. McRoy and C. C. I. Hall, "Transracial adoptions: In whose best interest?" pp. 63–78 in M. P. P. Root (Ed.), *The multiracial experience: Racial borders as the new frontier* (Thousand Oaks, CA: Sage, 1996).

Chapter 10

1. S. Walsh, "Texaco settles race suit," *Washington Post* (November 16, 1996).

2. C. A. Rowan, *The coming race war in America: A wake-up call* (Boston: Little, Brown, 1996).

3. In the same way, we need to break the silence about sexism, anti-Semitism, heterosexism and homophobia, classism, ageism, and ableism. In my experience, once we learn to break the silence about one ism, the lessons learned transfer to other isms.

4. C. Sleeter, "White racism," *Multicultural Education* (Spring 1994): 6.

5. Ibid., p. 8.

6. K. Mullen, "Subtle lessons in racism," *USA Weekend* (November 6–8, 1992): 10–11.

7. L. M. Wah (Producer/director), *The color of fear* [Video] (Oakland, CA: Stir-Fry Productions, 1994).

8. J. B. Miller, "Connections, disconnections, and violations," *Work in Progress, No. 33* (Wellesley, MA: Stone Center Working Paper Series, 1988).

9. B. D. Tatum, "Racial identity and relational theory: The case of Black

women in White communities," *Work in Progress, No. 63* (Wellesley, MA: Stone Center Working Paper Series, 1992).

10. An in-depth discussion of the relational implications of working against racism for these female educators can be found in Tatum and Knaplund, "Outside the circle."

11. P. Palmer, *The active life: Wisdom for work, creativity, and caring* (New York: HarperCollins, 1990), p. 115.

Epilogue

1. N. J. Smelser, W. J. Wilson, and F. Mitchell (Eds.), *America becoming: Racial trends and their consequences,* 2 vols. (Washington, DC: National Academy Press, 2001).

2. R. M. Blank, "An overview of trends in social and economic well-being, by race," pp. 21–39 in N. J. Smelser, W. J. Wilson, and F. Mitchell (Eds.), *America becoming: Racial trends and their consequences,* vol. 1 (Washington, DC: National Academy Press, 2001).

3. L. D. Bobo, "Racial attitudes and relations at the close of the twentieth century," pp. 264–301 in N. J. Smelser, W. J. Wilson, and F. Mitchell (Eds.), *America becoming: Racial trends and their consequences,* vol. 1 (Washington, DC: National Academy Press, 2001).

4. R. Kennedy, "Racial trends in the administration of criminal justice," p. 15 in N. J. Smelser, W. J. Wilson, and F. Mitchell (Eds.), *America becoming: Racial trends and their consequences,* vol. 2 (Washington, DC: National Academy Press, 2001).

5. Ibid., p. 15.

6. R. Kennedy, "Racial Trends in the administration of criminal justice," p. 15 in N. J. Smelse, W. J. Wilson, and F. Mitchell, (Eds.) *America becoming: Racial trends and their consequences,* vol. 2. (Washington, D.C.: National Academy Press, 2001.)

7. G. D. Sandefur, M. Martin, J. Eggerling-Boeck, S. E. Mannon, and A. M. Meier, "An overview of racial and ethnic demographic trends," pp. 40–95 in N. J. Smelser, W. J. Wilson, and F. Mitchell (Eds.), *America becoming: Racial trends and their consequences,* vol. 1 (Washington, DC: National Academy Press, 2001).

8. Frank Wu, *Yellow: Race in America beyond Black and White* (New York: Basic Books, 2001).

9. L. Guinier and G. Torres, *The miner's canary: Enlisting race, resisting power, transforming democracy* (Cambridge, MA: Harvard University Press, 2002).

10. D. J. Wilds and R. Wilson, *Sixteenth annual status report on minorities in higher education, 1997–98* (Washington, DC: American Council on Education, 1998).

11. G. Orfield, S. E. Eaton, and the Harvard Project on School Desegregation, *Dismantling desegregation: The quiet reversal of* Brown v. Board of Education (New York: New Press, 1996).

12. American Association of Colleges and Universities, *American pluralism and the college curriculum* (Washington, DC: AACU, 1995).

13. S. Hurtado, "Reaffirming educators' judgment: Educational value of diversity," *Liberal Education* 85, 2 (1999): 24–31.

14. P. Gurin, Expert report of Patricia Gurin, in legal brief "The compelling need for diversity in higher education," presented in *Gratz et al. V. Bollinger et al.* and *Grutter et al. v. Bollinger et al.* (Washington, DC: Wilmer, Cutler, and Pickering, 1999).

15. A. L. Antonio, "Racial diversity and friendship groups in college: What the research tells us," *Diversity Digest* 3, 4 (1999): 6–7, 16.

16. T. Duster, "The diversity of the University of California at Berkeley: An emerging reformulation of competence in an increasingly multicultural world," in B. W. Thompson and S. Tyagi (Eds.), *Beyond a dream deferred: Multicultural education and the politics of excellence* (Minneapolis: University of Minnesota Press, 1993).

17. W. E. B. Dubois, *The souls of Black folk* (originally published 1903; New York: Signet Classics, 1969), p. xi.

Bibliography

Abudabbeh, N. "Arab families." Pp. 333–46 in M. McGoldrick, J. Giordano, and J. K. Pearce (Eds.), *Ethnicity and family therapy*, 2d ed. New York: Guilford Press, 1996.

Alba, A. *Ethnic identity: The transformation of White America*. New Haven: Yale University Press, 1990.

Alderfer, C. P. "A White man's perspective on the unconscious process within Black-White relations in the United States." Pp. 201–29 in E. J. Trickett, R. Watts, and D. Birman (Eds.), *Human diversity*. San Francisco: Jossey-Bass, 1994.

Allen, W. R. "The color of success: African-American college student outcomes at predominantly White and historically Black public colleges and universities." *Harvard Educational Review* 62, no. 1 (1992): 26–44.

Allen, W. R., E. G. Epp, and N. Z. Haniff (Eds.). *College in Black and White: African American students in predominantly White and in historically Black public universities*. Albany: State University of New York Press, 1991.

"Appeals court bars racial preference." *Chronicle of Higher Education* (March 29, 1996): A26–36.

Ayvazian, A. "Interrupting the cycle of oppression: The role of allies as agents of change." *Fellowship* (January/February 1995): 7–10.

Barnard, H. F. (Ed.). *Outside the magic circle: The autobiography of Virginia Foster Durr*. Tuscaloosa: University of Alabama Press, 1985.

Barndt, J. *Dismantling racism: The continuing challenge to White America*. Minneapolis: Augsburg Press, 1991.

Berry, W. *The hidden wound*. San Francisco: North Point Press, 1989.

Betances, S. "African-Americans and Hispanic/Latinos: Eliminating barriers to coalition building." Paper presented at the Ethnic Diversity Roundtable, Chicago Urban Policy Institute and the Joint Center for Political and Economic Studies, April 15, 1994.

Blanchard, F. J. "Effective affirmative action programs." Pp. 193–207 in F. A. Blanchard and F. J. Crosby (Eds.), *Affirmative action in perspective*. New York: Springer-Verlag, 1989.

Bowser, B., and R. G. Hunt (Eds.). *Impacts of racism on White Americans.* Thousand Oaks, CA: Sage, 1981.

Boyd-Franklin, N. *Black families in therapy: A multisystems approach.* New York: Guilford, 1989.

Bradshaw, C. K. "Beauty and the beast: On racial ambiguity." Pp. 77–88 in M. P. P. Root (Ed.), *Racially mixed people in America.* Thousand Oaks, CA: Sage, 1992.

Bureau of the Census. *We the Americans: Our education.* Washington, DC: Government Printing Office, 1993.

Bureau of the Census. *We, the First Americans.* Washington, DC: Government Printing Office, 1993.

Carter, R. "Is White a race? Expressions of White racial identity." Pp. 198–209 in M. Fine, L. Weis, L. C. Powell, and L. M. Wong (Eds.), *Off White: Readings on race, power, and society.* New York: Routledge, 1997.

Carter, S. *Reflections of an affirmative action baby.* New York: Basic Books, 1991.

Casas, M. J., and S. D. Pytluk. "Hispanic identity development: Implications for research and practice." Pp. 155–180 in J. G. Ponterotto, J. M. Casas, L. A. Suzuki, and C. M. Alexander (Eds.), *Handbook of multicultural counseling.* Thousand Oaks, CA: Sage, 1995.

Cauce, A. M., Y. Hiraga, C. Mason, T. Aguilar, N. Ordonez, and N. Gonzales. "Between a rock and a hard place: Social adjustment of biracial youth." Pp. 207–22 in M. P. P. Root (Ed.), *Racially mixed people in America.* Thousand Oaks, CA: Sage, 1992.

Chan, K., and S. Hune. "Racialization and panethnicity: From Asians in America to Asian Americans." Pp. 205–33 in W. D. Hawley and A. W. Jackson (Eds.), *Toward a common destiny: Improving race and ethnic relations in America.* San Francisco: Jossey-Bass, 1995.

Churchill, W. *Indians are us? Culture and genocide in Native North America.* Monroe, ME: Common Courage Press, 1994.

Clayton, S. D., and S. S. Tangri. "The justice of affirmative action." Pp. 177–92 in F. A. Blanchard and F. J. Crosby (Eds.), *Affirmative action in perspective.* New York: Springer-Verlag, 1989.

Colby, A., and W. Damon. *Some do care: Contemporary lives of moral commitment.* New York: Free Press, 1992.

Collins, P. H. *Black feminist thought: Knowledge, consciousness, and the politics of empowerment.* London: HarperCollins Academic, 1990.

Comas-Diaz, L. "LatiNegra." Pp. 167–90 in M. P. P. Root (Ed.), *The multiracial experience: Racial borders as the new frontier.* Thousand Oaks, CA: Sage, 1996.

Cooley, C. *Human nature and the social order.* New York: Scribner, 1922.

Cose, E. *The rage of a privileged class.* New York: HarperCollins, 1993.

Crosby, F. "Confessions of an affirmative action mama." Pp. 179–86 in M. Fine, L. Weis, L. C. Powell, and L. M. Wong (Eds.), *Off White: Readings on race, power, and society.* New York: Routledge, 1997.

Crosby, F. "Understanding affirmative action." *Basic and Applied Social Psychology* 15, nos. 1 and 2 (1994): 13–41.

Cross, W. E. "The psychology of Nigrescence: Revising the Cross model." Pp. 93–122 in J. G. Ponterotto, J. M. Casas, L. A. Suzuki, and C. M. Alexander (Eds.), *Handbook of multicultural counseling.* Thousand Oaks, CA: Sage, 1995.

Cross, W. E., Jr. *Shades of Black: Diversity in African-American identity.* Philadelphia: Temple University Press, 1991.

Curry, G. E. (Ed.). *The affirmative action debate.* Reading, MA: Addison-Wesley, 1996.

Davis, F. J. *Who is Black? One nation's definition.* University Park: Pennsylvania State University Press, 1991.

Davis, G., and G. Watson. *Black life in corporate America: Swimming in the mainstream.* New York: Anchor Press, 1982.

Davol, M. *Black, white, just right!* Morton Grove, IL: A. Whitman, 1993.

Dees, M., with S. Fiffer. *A season of justice: A lawyer's own story of victory over America's hate groups.* New York: Touchstone Books, 1991.

Delpit, L. *Other people's children: Cultural conflict in the classroom.* New York: New Press, 1995.

Derman-Sparks, L., and the ABC Task Force. *Anti-bias curriculum: Tools for empowering young children.* Washington, DC: National Association for the Education of Young Children, 1989.

Derman-Sparks, L, C. T. Higa, and B. Sparks. "Children, race, and racism: How race awareness develops." *Interracial Books for Children* 11, no. 3–4 (1980): 3–9.

Dovidio, J. F., and S. L. Gaertner. "The effects of sex, status, and ability on helping behavior." *Journal of Applied Social Psychology* 13 (1983): 191–205.

Dovidio, J. F., S. L. Gaertner, P. A. Anastasio, and R. Sanitioso. "Cognitive and motivational bases of bias: Implications of aversive racism for attitudes toward Hispanics." Pp. 75–106 in S. B. Knouse, P. Rosenfeld, and A. L. Culbertson (Eds.), *Hispanics in the workplace*. Newbury Park, CA: Sage, 1992.

Dovidio, J. F., J. Mann, and S. L. Gaertner. "Resistance to affirmative action: The implications of aversive racism." Pp. 83–102 in F. A. Blanchard and F. J. Crosby (Eds.), *Affirmative action in perspective*. New York: Springer-Verlag, 1989.

Dyson, M. E. *Race rules: Navigating the color line*. Boston: Beacon Press, 1996.

Early, G. *Lure and loathing: Essays on race, identity, and the ambivalence of assimilation*. New York: Penguin, 1993.

Eberhardt, J., and S. Fiske. "Affirmative action in theory and practice: Issues of power, ambiguity, and gender versus race." *Basic and Applied Social Psychology* 15, nos. 1 and 2 (1994): 201–20.

Erikson, E. "Eight Ages of Man." In *Childhood and Society*. New York: W. W. Norton, 1950.

Erikson, E. H. *Identity, youth, and crisis*. New York: W. W. Norton, 1968.

Farley, R. "The common destiny of Blacks and Whites: Observations about the social and economic status of the races." Pp. 197–233 in H. Hill and J. E. Jones, Jr. (Eds.), *Race in America: The struggle for equality*. Madison: University of Wisconsin Press, 1993.

Feagin, J. R., and M. P. Sikes. *Living with racism: The Black middle-class experience*. Boston: Beacon Press, 1994.

Field, L. D. "Piecing together the puzzle: Self-concept and group identity in biracial Black/White youth." Pp. 211–26 in M. P. P. Root (Ed.), *The multiracial experience: Racial borders as the new frontier*. Thousand Oaks, CA: Sage, 1996.

Fine, M. "Witnessing Whiteness." Pp. 57–65 in M. Fine, L. Weis, L. C. Powell, and L. M. Wong (Eds.), *Off White: Readings on race, power, and society*. New York: Routledge, 1997.

Fish, S. "Reverse racism, or how the pot got to call the kettle black?" *The Atlantic Monthly* (November 1993): 128–36.

Fiske, S. T. "Controlling other people: The impact of power on stereotyping." *American Psychologist* 48, no. 6 (1993): 621–28.

Fleming, J. *Blacks in college*. San Francisco: Jossey-Bass, 1984.

Fordham, S. *Blacked out: Dilemmas of race, identity, and success at Capital High*. Chicago: University of Chicago Press, 1996.

Fordham, S. "Racelessness as a factor in Black students' school success: Pragmatic strategy or Pyrrhic victory?" *Harvard Educational Review* 58, no. 1 (1988): 54–84.

Fordham, S., and J. Ogbu. "Black student's school success: Coping with the burden of 'acting White.'" *Urban Review* 18 (1986): 176–206.

Frankenberg, R. "'When we are capable of stopping, we begin to see': Being White, seeing Whiteness." Pp. 3–17 in B. Thompson and S. Tyagi (Eds.), *Names we call home: Autobiography on racial identity*. New York: Routledge, 1996.

Frankenberg, R. *White women, race matters: The social construction of Whiteness.* Minneapolis: University of Minnesota Press, 1993.

Funderberg, L. *Black, White, Other: Biracial Americans talk about race and identity.* New York: Quill, 1994.

Gibbs, J. T. "Biracial adolescents." Pp. 322–50 in J. T. Gibbs, L. N. Huang, and Associates (Eds.), *Children of color: Psychological interventions with minority youth.* San Francisco: Jossey-Bass, 1989.

Gibbs, J. T., and A. M. Hines. "Negotiating ethnic identity: Issues for Black–White biracial adolescents." Pp. 223–38 in M. P. P. Root (Ed.), *Racially mixed people in America.* Thousand Oaks, CA: Sage, 1992.

Gibson, R. C. "Retirement." Pp. 179–98 in J. S. Jackson (Ed.), *Life in Black America.* Thousand Oaks, CA: Sage, 1991.

Grinde, D. A., Jr. "Place and kinship: A Native American's identity before and after words." Pp. 63–72 in B. Thompson and S. Tyagi (Eds.), *Names we call home: Autobiography on racial identity.* New York: Routledge, 1996.

Haley, Alex, and Malcolm X. *The autobiography of Malcolm X.* New York: Grove Press, 1965.

Hall, C. C. I. "The ethnic identity of racially mixed people: A study of Black-Japanese." Doctoral dissertation, University of California, Los Angeles, 1980.

Hardiman, R. "White racial identity development in the United States." In E. P. Salett and D. R. Koslow (Eds.), *Race, ethnicity, and self: Identity in multicultural perspectives.* Washington, DC: National Multicultural Institute, 1994.

Helms, J. E. (Ed.). *Black and White racial identity: Theory, research, and practice.* Westport, CT: Greenwood, 1990.

Helms, J. E. "An update of Helms's White and people of color racial identity models." Pp. 181–98 in J. G. Ponterotto, J. M. Casas, L. A. Suzuki, and C. M. Alexander (Eds.), *Handbook of multicultural counseling*. Thousand Oaks, CA: Sage, 1995.

Herring, R. D. "Native American Indian identity: A people of many peoples." Pp. 170–97 in E. P. Salett and D. R. Koslow (Eds.), *Race, ethnicity, and self: Identity in multicultural perspective*. Washington, DC: National MultiCultural Institute, 1994.

Hess, B. B., E. W. Markson, and P. J. Stein. "Racial and ethnic minorities: An overview." In P. S. Rothenberg (Ed.), *Race, class, and gender in the United States: An integrated study*, 3d ed. New York: St. Martin's Press, 1995.

Holloway, F. A. "What is affirmative action?" Pp. 9–19 in F. A. Blanchard and F. Crosby (Eds.), *Affirmative action in perspective*. New York: Springer-Verlag, 1989.

hooks, b. *Sisters of the yam: Black women and self recovery*. Boston: South End Press, 1993.

Jackson, J. (Ed.). *Life in Black America*. Thousand Oaks, CA: Sage, 1991.

Kanter, R. M. *Men and women of the corporation*. New York: Basic Books, 1977.

Kaye/Kantrowitz, M. "Jews in the U.S.: The rising costs of Whiteness." Pp. 121–38 in B. Thompson and S. Tyagi (Eds.), *Names we call home: Autobiography on racial identity*. New York: Routledge, 1996.

Katz, J. H. *White awareness: Handbook for anti-racism training*. Norman: University of Oklahoma Press, 1978.

Kerwin, C., and J. G. Ponterotto. "Biracial identity development: Theory and research." Pp. 199–217 in J. G. Ponterotto, J. M. Casas, L. A. Suzuki, and C. M. Alexander (Eds.), *Handbook of multicultural counseling*. Thousand Oaks, CA: Sage, 1995.

Kiang, P. N. *We could shape it: Organizing for Asian Pacific American student empowerment*. (Occasional Paper.) Boston: University of Massachusetts Institute for Asian American Studies, 1996.

Kich, G. K. "The developmental process of asserting a biracial, bicultural identity." Pp. 304–17 in M. P. P. Root (Ed.), *Racially mixed people in America*. Thousand Oaks, CA: Sage, 1992.

Kim, B. C. "Korean families." Pp. 281–94 in M. McGoldrick, J. Giordano, and J. K. Pearce (Eds.), *Ethnicity and family therapy*, 2d ed. New York: Guilford, 1996.

Kivel, P. *Uprooting racism: How White people can work for racial justice.* Philadelphia: New Society Publishers, 1996.

Kline, B. B., and J. F. Dovidio. "Effects of race, sex, and qualifications on predictions of a college applicant's performance." Presented at the annual meeting of the Eastern Psychological Association, Baltimore, April 1982.

Kohl, H. "I won't learn from you: Confronting student resistance." Pp. 134–35 in *Rethinking our classrooms: Teaching for equity and justice.* Milwaukee: Rethinking Our Schools, 1994.

Lawrence, S., and B. D. Tatum. "Teachers in transition: The impact of anti-racist professional development on classroom practice." *Teachers College Record* (Fall 1997).

Lawrence, S. M., and B. D. Tatum. "White educators as allies: Moving from awareness to action." Pp. 333–42 in M. Fine, L. Weis, L. C. Powell, and L. M. Wong (Eds.), *Off White: Readings on race, power, and society.* New York: Routledge, 1997.

Lazarre, J. *Beyond the Whiteness of Whiteness: Memoir of a White mother of Black sons.* Durham, NC: Duke University Press, 1996.

Lee, E. "Asian American families: An overview." Pp. 227–48 in M. McGoldrick, J. Giordano, and J. K. Pearce (Eds.), *Ethnicity and family therapy,* 2d ed. New York: Guilford, 1996.

Lerner, M. J. "Social psychology of justice and interpersonal attraction." In T. Huston (Ed.), *Foundations of interpersonal attraction.* New York: Academic Press, 1974.

Levinson, D. *The seasons of a man's life.* New York: Knopf, 1978.

Little Soldier, L. "Is there an 'Indian' in your classroom? Working successfully with urban Native American students." *Phi Delta Kappan* (April 1997): 650–53.

Lomawaima, K. T. "Educating Native Americans." Pp. 331–47 in J. Banks and C. M. Banks (Eds.), *Handbook of research on multicultural education.* New York: Simon & Schuster, 1995.

Lorde, A. "Age, race, class, and sex: Women redefining difference." Pp. 445–51 in P. Rothenberg (Ed.), *Race, class, and gender in the United States: An integrated study,* 3d ed. New York: St. Martin's Press, 1995.

Marcia, J. "Development and validation of ego identity status." *Journal of Personality and Social Psychology* 3 (1966): 551–58.

Marín, G., and B. V. Marín. *Research with Hispanic populations.* Newbury Park, CA: Sage, 1991.

Matsui, W. T. "Japanese families." Pp. 268–80 in M. McGoldrick, J. Giordano, and J. K. Pearce (Eds.), *Ethnicity and family therapy,* 2d ed. New York: Guilford, 1996.

McIntosh, P. "White privilege: Unpacking the invisible knapsack." *Peace and Freedom* (July/August 1989): 10–12.

McRoy, R. G., and C. C. I. Hall. "Transracial adoptions: In whose best interest?" Pp. 63–78 in M. P. P. Root (Ed.), *The multiracial experience: Racial borders as the new frontier.* Thousand Oaks, CA: Sage, 1996.

Mead, G. H. *Mind, self, and society.* Chicago: University of Chicago Press, 1934.

Miller, J. B. "Connections, disconnections, and violations." *Work in Progress, No. 33.* Wellesley, MA: Stone Center Working Paper Series, 1988.

Miller, J. B. "Domination and subordination." Pp. 3–12 in *Toward a new psychology of women.* Boston: Beacon Press, 1976.

Miller, R. L., and M. J. Rotheram-Borus. "Growing up biracial in the United States." Pp. 143–69 in E. P. Salett and D. R. Koslow (Eds.), *Race, ethnicity, and self: Identity in multicultural perspective.* Washington, DC: National Multicultural Institute, 1994.

Momaday, N. S. "Confronting Columbus again." Pp. 436–39 in P. Nabokov (Ed.), *Native American testimony: A chronicle of Indian-White relations from prophecy to the present, 1492–1992.* New York: Viking, 1991.

Moran, C. E., and K. Hakuta. "Bilingual education: Broadening research perspectives." Pp. 445–62 in J. Banks and C. M. Banks (Eds.), *Handbook of research on multicultural education.* New York: Simon & Schuster, 1995.

Mullen, K. "Subtle lessons in racism." *USA Weekend* (November 6–8, 1992): 10–11.

Mullen, T. "Affirmative action." Pp. 244–66 in S. McLean and N. Burrows (Eds.), *The legal relevance of gender.* Atlantic Highlands, NJ: Humanities Press International, 1988.

Mura, D. "A shift in power, a sea change in the arts: Asian American constructions." Pp. 183–204 in K. Aguilar–San Juan (Ed.), *The state of Asian America: Activism and resistance in the 1990s.* Boston: South End Press, 1994.

Mura, D. *Turning Japanese: Memoirs of a sansei.* New York: Atlantic Monthly Press, 1991.

Murrell, A. J., B. L. Dietz-Uhler, J. F. Dovidio, S. L. Gaertner, and C. Drout. "Aversive racism and resistance to affirmative action: Perceptions of justice are not necessarily color blind." *Basic and Applied Social Psychology* 15, nos. 1 and 2 (1994): 71–86.

Nacoste, R. "Opportunities yes, but no guarantees: Procedural goals and resistance to affirmative action." Paper presented at the Eastern Psychological Association Annual Meeting, Buffalo, NY, April 23, 1988.

Nieto, S. *Affirming diversity: The sociopolitical context of multicultural educationm,* 2d ed. White Plains, NY: Longman, 1996.

Oakes, J. *Keeping track: How schools structure inequality.* New Haven: Yale University Press, 1985.

Omi, M., and H. Winant. *Racial formation in the United States,* 2d ed. New York: Routledge, 1994.

Ongtooguk, P. "Their silence about us: The absence of Alaska Natives in the curriculum." Paper presented at the American Educational Research Association Annual Meeting, Atlanta, Georgia, April 1993.

O'Toole, C. "The effect of the media and multicultural education on children's perceptions of Native Americans." Senior thesis presented to the Department of Psychology and Education, Mount Holyoke College, South Hadley, MA, May 1990.

Padilla, A. (Ed.). *Hispanic psychology.* Thousand Oaks, CA: Sage, 1995.

Palmer, P. *The active life: Wisdom for work, creativity, and caring.* New York: HarperCollins, 1990.

Pang, V. O. "Asian Pacific American students: A diverse and complex population." Pp. 412–24 in J. Banks and C. M. Banks (Eds.), *Handbook on research on multicultural education.* New York: Simon & Schuster, 1995.

Parham, T. A. "Cycles of psychological nigrescence." *The Counseling Psychologist* 17, no. 2 (1989): 187–226.

Petersen, W. "Success story, Japanese-American style." *New York Times Magazine* (January 9, 1966): 20-21, 33, 36, 38, 40-41, 43.

Phinney, J. "Ethnic identity in adolescents and adults: Review of research." *Psychological Bulletin* 108, no. 3 (1990): 499–514.

Phinney, J. "A three-stage model of ethnic identity development in adolescence." Pp. 61–79 in M. E. Bernal and G. P. Knight (Eds.), *Ethnic identity: Formation and transmission among Hispanics and other minorities.* Albany: State University of New York Press, 1993.

Phinney, J. S., B. T. Lochner, and R. Murphy. "Ethnic identity development and psychological adjustment in adolescence." Pp. 53–72 in A. R. Stiffman and L. E. Davis (Eds.), *Ethnic issues in adolescent mental health*. Newbury Park, CA: Sage, 1990.

Phinney, J. S., and S. Tarver. "Ethnic identity search and commitment in Black and White eighth graders." *Journal of Early Adolescence* 8, no. 3 (1988): 265–77.

Pierce, C. "Mundane extreme environment and its effects on learning." In S. G. Brainard (Ed.), *Learning disabilities: Issues and recommendations for research*. Washington, DC: National Institute of Education, 1975.

Ponterotto, J. G., J. M. Casas, L. A. Suzuki, and C. M. Alexander (Eds.), *Handbook of multicultural counseling*. Thousand Oaks, CA: Sage, 1995.

Ponterotto, J. G., and P. B. Pedersen. *Preventing prejudice: A guide for counselors and educators*. Thousand Oaks, CA: Sage, 1993.

Ramsey, P. *Teaching and learning in a diverse world: Multicultural education for young children*. New York: Teachers College Press, 1985.

Reddy, M. T. *Crossing the color line: Race, parenting, and culture*. New Brunswick, NJ: Rutgers University Press, 1994.

Reid, M. (Producer/Director). *Skin deep: College students confront racism* [Video]. San Francisco, CA: Resolution/California Newsreel, 1995.

Riggs, M. (Producer/Director). *Ethnic Notions* [Video]. San Francisco, CA: Resolution/California Newsreel, 1986.

Ringgold, F. *Aunt Harriet's underground railroad in the sky*. New York: Crown, 1992.

Rodriguez, R. *Hunger of memory: The education of Richard Rodriguez*. New York: Bantam, 1982.

Roland, A. "Identity, self, and individualism in a multicultural perspective." Pp. 11–23 in E. P. Salett and D. R. Koslow (Eds.), *Race, ethnicity, and self: Identity in multicultural perspective*. Washington, DC: National MultiCultural Institute, 1994.

Root, M. P. P. (Ed.). *Racially mixed people in America*. Thousand Oaks, CA: Sage, 1992.

Root, M. P. P. "Resolving 'other' status: Identity development of biracial individuals." Pp. 185–205 in L. S. Brown and M. P. P. Root (Eds.), *Diversity and complexity in feminist therapy*. New York: Haworth Press, 1989.

Root, M. P. P. "Within, between, and beyond race." Pp. 3–11 in M. P. P. Root (Ed.), *Racially mixed people in America*. Thousand Oaks, CA: Sage, 1992.

Rothenberg, P. S. (Ed.). *Race, class, and gender in the United States: An integrated study,* 3d ed. New York: St. Martin's Press, 1995.

Rowan, C. A. *The coming race war in America: A wake-up call.* Boston: Little, Brown, 1996.

Russell, K., M. Wilson, and R. H. Sacks. *The color complex.* San Diego: Harcourt Brace Jovanovich, 1992.

Sleeter, C. "White racism." *Multicultural Education* (Spring 1994): 5–8, 39.

Snipp, C. M. "American Indian studies." Pp. 245–58 in J. Banks and C. M. Banks (Eds.), *Handbook on research on multicultural education.* New York: Simon & Schuster, 1995.

Spickard, P. R. "The illogic of American racial categories." Pp. 12–23 in M. P. P. Root (Ed.), *Racially mixed people in America.* Thousand Oaks, CA: Sage, 1992.

Spickard, P. R. *Mixed blood: Intermarriage and ethnic identity in twentieth-century America.* Madison: University of Wisconsin Press, 1989.

Spring, J. *Deculturalization and the struggle for equality: A brief history of the education of dominated cultures in the United States,* 2d ed. New York: McGraw-Hill, 1997.

Stalvey, L. *The education of a WASP.* Madison: University of Wisconsin Press, [1970] 1989.

Steele, C., and J. Aronson. "Stereotype threat and the intellectual test performance of African Americans." *Journal of Personality and Social Psychology* 69, no. 5 (1995): 797–811.

Steptoe, J. *Mufaro's beautiful daughters: An African tale.* New York: Scholastic, 1989.

Stewart, A. J., and J. M. Healy. "Linking individual development and social changes." *American Psychologist* 44, no. 1 (1989): 30–42.

Suárez-Orozco, C., and M. Suárez-Orozco. *Transformations: Immigration, family life, and achievement motivation among Latino adolescents.* Stanford, CA: Stanford University Press, 1995.

"Success story of one minority in the U.S." *U.S. News and World Report* (December 26, 1966): 73-78.

Sutton, C. T., and M. A. Broken Nose. "American Indian families: An overview." Pp. 31–44 in M. McGoldrick, J. Giordano, and J. K. Pearce (Eds.), *Ethnicity and family therapy,* 2d ed. New York: Guilford, 1996.

Tafoya, N., and A. Del Vecchio. "Back to the future: An examination of the Native American Holocaust experience." Pp. 45–54 in M. McGoldrick,

J. Giordano, and J. K. Pearce (Eds.), *Ethnicity and family therapy*. New York: Guilford, 1996.

Takaki, R. *A different mirror: A history of multicultural America*. Boston: Little, Brown, 1993.

Tatum, B. D. "African-American identity, academic achievement, and missing history." *Social Education* 56, no. 6 (1992): 331–34.

Tatum, B. D. *Assimilation blues: Black families in a White community*. Northampton, MA: Hazel-Maxwell, 1992.

Tatum, B. D. "Out there stranded? Black youth in white communities." Pp. 214–33 in H. McAdoo (Ed.), *Black Families,* 3d ed. Thousand Oaks, CA: Sage, 1996.

Tatum, B. D. "Racial identity and relational theory: The case of Black women in White communities." *Work in Progress, No. 63*. Wellesley, MA: Stone Center Working Papers, 1992.

Tatum, B. D. "Talking about race, learning about racism: An application of racial identity development theory in the classroom." *Harvard Educational Review* 62, no. 1 (1992): 1–24.

Tatum, B. D. "Teaching White students about racism: The search for White allies and the restoration of hope." *Teachers College Record* 95, no. 4 (1994): 462–76.

Tatum, B. D., P. C. Brown, P. Elliott, and T. Tatum. "Student efficacy training: An evaluation of one middle school's programmatic response to the Eastern Massachusetts Initiative." Paper presented at the American Educational Research Association Annual Meeting, New York, April 9, 1996.

Tatum, B. D., and E. G. Knaplund. "Outside the circle: The relational implications for White women working against racism." *Work in Progress, No. 78*. Wellesley, MA: Stone Center Working Paper Series, 1996.

Taylor, D. "Affirmative action and Presidential executive orders." Pp. 21–29 in F. A. Blanchard and F. Crosby (Eds.), *Affirmative action perspective*. New York: Springer-Verlag, 1989.

Taylor, R. J., and L. M. Chatters. "Religious life." Pp. 105–23 in J. Jackson (Ed.), *Life in Black America*. Thousand Oaks, CA: Sage, 1991.

Thompson, B. "Time traveling and border crossing: Reflections on White identity." Pp. 93–109 in B. Thompson and S. Tyagi (Eds.), *Names we call home: Autobiography on racial identity*. New York: Routledge, 1996.

Thompson, B., and S. Tyagi (Eds.). *Names we call home: Autobiography on racial identity.* New York: Routledge, 1996.

Thompson, B., and White Women Challenging Racism. "Home/Work: Antiracism activism and the meaning of Whiteness." Pp. 354–66 in M. Fine, L. Weis, L. C. Powell, and L. M. Wong (Eds.), *Off White: Readings on race, power, and society.* New York: Routledge, 1997.

Tse, L. "Finding a place to be: Asian Americans in ethnic identity exploration." *Adolescence* (in press).

Tsugawa, T. "Asian Pacific American demographics." Presented at the METCO Directors Association Conference, Boston, MA, March 28, 1997.

Twine, F. W., J. F. Warren, and F. F. Martin. *Just Black?* [Video]. New York: Filmakers Library, 1991.

Uba, L. *Asian Americans: Personality patterns, identity, and mental health.* New York: Guilford, 1994.

"Under suspicion." *People* (January 15, 1996): 40–47.

Updegrave, W. L. "Race and money." *Money* (December 1989): 152–72.

Van den Berghe, P. L. *Race and racism.* New York: Wiley, 1967.

Wadsworth, B. J. *Piaget's theory of cognitive and affective development: Foundations of constructivism,* 5th ed. White Plains, NY: Longman, 1996.

Wah, L. M. (Producer/Director). *The color of fear* [Video]. Oakland, CA: Stir-Fry Productions, 1994.

Walker-Moffat, W. *The other side of the Asian American success story.* San Francisco: Jossey-Bass, 1995.

Walsh, S. "Texaco settles race suit." *Washington Post* (November 16, 1996).

Wang, T. H., and F. H. Wu. "Beyond the model minority myth." Pp. 191–207 in G. E. Curry (Ed.), *The affirmative action debate.* Reading, MA: Addison-Wesley, 1996.

Ward, J. V. "Raising resisters: The role of truth telling in the psychological development of African-American girls." In B. J. R. Leadbeater and N. Way (Eds.), *Urban Girls: Resisting stereotypes, creating identities.* New York: New York University Press, 1996.

Waters, M. C. "The intersection of gender, race, and ethnicity in identity development of Caribbean American teens." In B. J. R. Leadbeater and N. Way (Eds.), *Urban girls: Resisting stereotypes, creating identities.* New York: New York University Press, 1996.

Wellman, D. *Portraits of white racism.* Cambridge: Cambridge University Press, 1977.

Wentworth, P. A. "The identity development of non-traditionally aged first-generation women college students: An exploratory study." Master's thesis, Department of Psychology and Education, Mount Holyoke College, South Hadley, MA, 1994.

Wijeyesinghe, C. "Towards an understanding of the racial identity of bi-racial people: The experience of racial self-identification of African-American/Euro-American adults and the factors affecting their choices of racial identity." Doctoral dissertation, University of Massachusetts, Amherst, 1992. *Dissertation Abstracts International,* 53, 11A.

Winant, H. "Behind blue eyes: Whiteness and contemporary U.S. racial politics." Pp. 40–53 in M. Fine, L. Weis, L. C. Powell, and L. M. Wong (Eds.), *Off white: Readings on race, power, and society.* New York: Routledge, 1997.

Winter, J. *Follow the drinking gourd.* New York: Dragonfly Books, 1988.

Wright, L. "One drop of blood." *The New Yorker* (July 25, 1994): 46–55.

Wright, R. "The ethics of living Jim Crow." Reprinted in P. Rothenberg (Ed.), *Race, class, and gender in the United States: An integrated study,* 3d ed. New York: St. Martin's Press, 1995.

Yamada, M. "Invisibility is an unnatural disaster: Reflections of an Asian American woman." Pp. 35–40 in C. Moraga and G. Anzaldua (Eds.), *This bridge called my back: Writings by radical women of color.* New York: Kitchen Table Press, 1981.

Zane, N. "Interrupting historical patterns: Bridging race and gender gaps between senior White men and other organizational groups." Pp. 343–53 in M. Fine, L. Weis. L. C. Powell, and L. M. Wong (Eds.), *Off White: Readings on race, power, and society.* New York: Routledge, 1997.

Zavala, M. "A bridge over divided worlds: An exploration into the nature of bilingual Puerto Rican youths' ethnic identity development." Master's thesis, Mount Holyoke College, South Hadley, MA, 1995.

Zavala, M. "Who are you if you don't speak Spanish? The Puerto Rican dilemma." Presented at the annual meeting of the American Educational Research Association, New York, April 1996.

Zweigenhaft, R., and G. W. Domhoff. *Blacks in the White establishment? A study of race and class in America.* New Haven: Yale University Press, 1991.

Acknowledgments

Though I am the sole author of this book, I did not write it alone. Throughout the process, I have been surrounded by family and friends who have supported me in countless ways, and I am deeply grateful.

It has been informed by the invaluable conversations I have had with my students and the many people who have attended my workshops. Though I no longer remember all of their names, I do remember their questions, the newspaper clippings and magazine articles they sent my way, the books and videos they recommended, and the encouragement I received in those settings.

Many of those workshops were shared with my colleague and friend Andrea Ayvazian. I am sure the influence of our years of association is felt in this book in very important ways. I especially thank her for the "knitting" lessons needed during the course of the book's writing.

Long before I began writing in earnest, I shared my vision of the book with my fellow "dreamers," Sherry Turner and Phyllis Brown. I know they have held the vision with me, and I am deeply grateful. A special thank-you to Phyllis for being there whenever and wherever I needed something, a true "sistah" if there ever was one. Chanise is so lucky to have such a wonderful auntie.

When I decided I needed an agent, Dr. Margaret Woodbury pointed me in the right direction and fellow author and friend, Elinor Lipman, confirmed the lead. Thanks to Meg and Ellie for steering me toward just the right person, Faith Childs. I thank Faith for her confidence in this project and her skill at finding just the right editor for me.

I said I wanted an editor who "gets it," and in Gail Winston I found one. Gail deserves a lot of the credit for expanding my vision of what this book could and should be. Though I didn't know where I would find the time to write more chapters, it is a much better book as a result. I am very grateful for her insightful suggestions.

The early chapters of the book were written while I was on retreat at Wisdom House Retreat Center in Litchfield, Connecticut. Thanks to the staff for their unobtrusive hospitality.

Several people talked to me when I was stuck on a particular section, located resources, or read particular chapters and took the time to give me oral and sometimes written feedback that was a real gift to me. Thanks to Elizabeth Carr, Ricki Kantrowitz, Elizabeth Knaplund, Joan Rasool, Janet Crosby, Poppy Milner, Beverly Hollis, Lisa Pickron, Christine Trufant, Hank Van Putten, Carroll Blake, Manuel Fernandez, Milena Uribe, Elsie Irizarry, Zowie Banteah, Sara Burgdorf, Nicole Moodie, Kira Hudson, Sung Park, Michael Feldstein, Sandra Lawrence, Eileen Rakouskas, Tracey Tsugawa, Thao Mee Xiong, and Paula Elliott. A special thank-you to Judith Mullins, who not only read but listened in just the right way at just the right time. It made a difference.

I am grateful also to some other very special readers: my friend and former pastor, Rev. Dr. Edward P. Harding, Jr., whose encouraging e-mail often lifted my spirits; my brother-in-law, Matthew Keenan, who asked good questions; my sister, Patricia Daniel Keenan, whose praise for the book means a lot to me; and my parents, Robert and Catherine Daniel, who taught me to treat people the way I want to be treated. I know they are "pleased but not surprised" at what their daughter has accomplished. Though my brothers, Eric and Kevin, were not readers, I know they are supporters, and I thank them for that.

My sons, Jonathan and David, have graciously allowed me to share their stories and even more generously allowed me privacy in my office while I was writing and patience when I was tired and grouchy. I truly hope they will read this book with pride in what they have helped to produce.

Travis Tatum, my husband, has been my most faithful supporter throughout the many years of our marriage, and certainly during the year I wrote this book. He read every page multiple times, made suggestions, offered encouragement, stayed up late to keep me company, made pancakes on request, did double-duty parenting when I and my computer had become inseparable—in all these ways and more, he has truly been my "labor coach." We often joked about when the "baby" would be delivered and we celebrated when the 3 lb. manuscript was in the mail. As author, I am the mother of this baby, but Travis truly is the father. It has been a pleasure to share parenting with him.

Clearly I have many people to thank, but in addition, I have been continually sustained by the still, small voice I hear when I listen carefully. Not by might, not by power, but by Spirit alone was I able to finish this book in the time available to me. I felt continually blessed as I wrote it. I hope it is a blessing to those who read it.

Index

Ableism, 13, 22

Academic achievement, 62–65

Adolescence, 20, 52–74, 83, 132–33, 181–84

Adoptive families, 187–90

Affirmative action, 114–28

Affirming Diversity (Nieto), 138

African American history, 39–41, 65–67, 80–81

African Americans. *See* Black Americans

Afro-Caribbeans, 15, 70–71

Age, 12, 22

"Age, Race, Class, and Sex: Women Redefining Difference" (Lorde), 22

Ageism, 13, 22

AIDS, 57

Alaska Natives, 117, 144–45, 150–52, 164

Alba, Richard, 16

Alderfer, Clayton, 112

Allen, Walter, 79–80

American Indians. *See* Native Americans

Amherst (Massachusetts), 50

Anti-Bias Curriculum: Tools for Empowering Young Children, 50–51

Anti-Semitism, 13, 21, 103–4

Arab Americans, 153, 157–158. *See also* Asian Americans

Arab-Israeli conflict, 158

Arizona, 145

Asian American Renaissance Conference, 158

Asian Americans, 15–16, 80, 117, 203; and adoptive families, 189; and identity development, 131–32, 153-159, 165; and Latinos, 154, 160; and mixed-race families, 168; and the myth of the model minority, 159-165; and the one-drop rule, 168–72; and talking about race relations, 197–99; violence against, 193

Asian Pacific Americans. *See* Asian Americans

Aunt Harriet's Underground Railroad in the Sky (Ringgold), 42

Autobiography of Malcolm X (Malcolm X), 58–59, 80–81

Ayvazian, Andrea, 109–10

Beauty, standards of, 44

Berry, Wendell, 14

Betances, Samuel, 142

Beyond the Whiteness of Whiteness: Memoir of a White Mother of Black Sons (Lazarre), 185

Bible, 48, 83

Biculturalism, 139

Black Americans, 31–92

Black and White Racial Identity Development: Theory, Research, and Practice (Helms), 94

Black Feminist Thought (Collins), 82

first fiction

*f*IRST *f*ICTION

An Anthology of the First

Published Stories by

Famous Writers

Introduction by

Jane Smiley

EDITED BY KATHY KIERNAN

AND MICHAEL M. MOORE

Little, Brown and Company

Boston New York Toronto London

Permission to reprint the stories can be found starting on p. 450.

FIRST EDITION

Library of Congress Cataloging-in-Publication Data
First fiction: an anthology of the first published stories by famous writers /
edited by Kathy Kiernan and Michael Moore ; introduction by Jane
Smiley. — 1st ed.
    p.   cm.
    ISBN 0-316-49203-5 (hc)
    ISBN 0-316-49204-3 (pb)
    1. Short stories, American.   2. Short stories, English.
I. Kiernan, Kathy.   II. Moore, Michael, 1962–   .
PS648.S5F55   1994
813'.0108—dc20   94-4343

10 9 8 7 6 5 4 3 2 1

RRD-VA

Designed by Barbara Werden

Published simultaneously in Canada by
Little, Brown & Company (Canada) Limited

PRINTED IN THE UNITED STATES OF AMERICA

ACKNOWLEDGMENTS

With thanks to Ebie Briskin, Tracy Brown, Monica Elias, Howard Frisch, Michael Mahana, Barney Rosset, Jen Stein, Greg Tobin, Bill Van Parys, Alice van Straalen, and Maron Waxman

K.K.
M.M.M.

CONTENTS

||||≡

A FEW YEARS ago a book searcher sent us a copy of a short story anthology called *Firsts of the Famous,* published in 1962 as a paperback original by Ballantine Books. It was edited by Whit Burnett, one of the founding editors of *Story* magazine, and it contained the first stories published by such *Story* discoveries as Norman Mailer, Carson McCullers, Truman Capote, and Nelson Algren. "*Story* was its own legend and young writers in the late 1930s and the years of the Second World War used to dream of appearing in its pages," Norman Mailer once said. Our book searcher thought we might be interested in reprinting the book; instead, we decided to redo it.

There were primarily two reasons for our decision. First, many of the writers Burnett included in *Firsts of the Famous* have lapsed into semi-obscurity in the years since it was published. Second, Burnett was not in every case very rigorous about whether the story he included was actually the writer's first published story. He acknowledged, for example, that John Cheever's "Homage to Shakespeare," reprinted in *Firsts of the Famous,* was not really Cheever's first. He was incorrect about Tennessee Williams's "The Field of Blue Children," which *Story* had published in 1939, eleven years after "The Vengeance of Nitocris" appeared in *Weird Tales.* And he admitted that Truman Capote's "My Side of the Matter" appeared in *Story* shortly after "Miriam" was published in *Mademoiselle,* yet he chose to include "My Side" anyway because it had been accepted before "Miriam." Burnett did not include poet and novelist Charles Bukowski in *Firsts of the Famous,* although his first pub-

lished work appeared in the March–April 1944 issue of *Story*. In 1962 Bukowski remained an obscure post office worker, eighteen years after his first appearance in print.

In reviving Burnett's idea, we have included authors' first professionally published stories only; that is, we have not included juvenilia or fiction written for school publications, though many of these writers did make their first sales while still in college or, in a few cases, high school. Some of these stories have never before been reprinted anywhere. Some have been reprinted in the authors' collections or in other anthologies, some in an altered form. In each case, we have tried to include the version of the story as it first appeared in the magazine that originally published it.

Evidence shows that like *Story*, some publications were more quicksighted than others in spotting talent. The *New Yorker* published five of our first-time writers: Shirley Jackson, Harold Brodkey, John Updike, Mark Helprin, and David Leavitt. *Smart Set*, a literary magazine edited by H. L. Mencken and George Jean Nathan from 1914 through 1923, was the first to feature F. Scott Fitzgerald and Dorothy Parker. And *Accent*, a magazine published out of the University of Illinois at Urbana, discovered both Flannery O'Connor and Grace Paley. *Mademoiselle* can claim as discoveries both Truman Capote and Joyce Carol Oates, the latter of whom won its 1959 College Fiction contest.

In selecting authors, we have tried to focus on those who have produced an impressive body of short stories, even though their chief renown may have come from writing other forms of literature. There were some we would have liked to include that, for various reasons, we could not. J. D. Salinger will not permit his first story, which was published in *Story*, to be reprinted. (It was a glaring omission from *Firsts of the Famous*.) In the case of a few authors, the bibliographic information either proved too difficult to track down or was so contradictory we could not accurately determine which story appeared first. One first story, "The Red Pony," by John Steinbeck, which appeared in two parts in the November and December 1933 issues of *The North American Review* and was later published as a book in 1945, is simply too long to include here. And in some cases, we did not feel comfortable calling what we found a story. Here, for example, is John O'Hara's "The Alumnae Bulletin":

"Look, here it says May Fisher has married that kid after all. Why, he's seven years younger than she. Yes, he is. He was in prep school some-where when I met him and that was at least four years ago. . . . Beth Mooney has another baby, I see. Great work. That's the fourth, isn't it? Hmm? Well, the third's pretty good. . . . Lord and TAY-lor! Look at this! 'Nanny Wolcott is engaged to Prentiss Arthur Cook.' Isn't that the awful creature she had up at Lake Placid two years ago? The one that wore two fraternity pins all the time? . . . 'The Evanston Alumnae met at the home of Martha Stetson Himmelbach last month.' I wonder whether Polly Jones was there. Remember how Hod Himmelbach and Polly were? . . . Marian Hand has published another book of poems. She'll be worse than ever. . . . Here's a fat one: 'Members of '22 are asked to write to Pauline Diefenderfer. She is at 18 Rue Ouitt, Paris, France. She writes a daily fashion cable for American department stores.' In other words, Pau-line is in Paris and doesn't care who knows it. . . . Well I'm turning in. I wonder what anybody reads this stuff in the *Bulletin* for, anyway."

The *New Yorker* published this piece on May 5, 1928, and rapidly fol-lowed up with a handful of stories of similar length. O'Hara then began a series of fifteen slightly longer stories about the Orange County After-noon Delphian Society, which the *New Yorker* alternated with fourteen stories about the Hagedorn & Brownmiller Paint & Varnish Company. We felt that, despite O'Hara's later achievements, the first of these stories would be unsatisfying to readers, but that we could not simply choose a later story and maintain the integrity of our criterion. Such is also the case with Dashiell Hammett. His first story appeared in *Smart Set*'s October 1922 issue. It is reprinted below in its entirety:

When the boy was six months old Paulette Key acknowledged that her hopes and efforts had been futile, that the baby was indubitably and irremediably a replica of its father. She could have endured the physical resemblance, but the duplication of Harold Key's stupid obstinacy — unmistakable in the fixity of the child's inarticulate demands for its food, its toys — was too much for Paulette. She knew she could not go on living with *two* such natures! A year and a half of Harold's domination had not subdued her entirely. She took the little boy to church, had him christened Don, sent him home by his nurse, and boarded a train for the West.

Whit Burnett wrote in his introduction to *Firsts of the Famous*, "Some stories read as well today as they did when they were first written, having admirably stood the test of time. Others are available not only for the story itself but as an early indication of how and where the author of this 'first' was to go later in his career." We feel as Burnett did and have tried to remain true to this spirit. We hope we have provided readers with an interesting and enjoyable collection, valuable not only for the undeniable pleasure of these stories, but also as a testament to the keen judgments of the magazine editors who enabled these talented writers to get their first taste of professionalism.

KATHY KIERNAN
MICHAEL M. MOORE

INTRODUCTION

ALTHOUGH I ALWAYS advise my students, to their disbelief, not to rush into print too quickly, I do clearly remember how long the takeoff seemed when I was their age, and my career kept lumbering down the runway year after year, never lifting even an inch off the ground. I kept the rejection slips (none of them letters as yet) taped above the kitchen sink for all to see. I can't remember my professed reasons for displaying them anymore, but the effect was beneficial. As I did the dishes every day, I got inured to the words and stopped trying to read anything positive into them. A rejection slip is simply a business letter, not a comprehensive personal judgment.

Yeah, right.

What I most clearly remember about the earliest stages of my writing career is how hungry I was to get beyond myself, to get somewhere far enough away from myself that I could look at my work and understand it. Though I longed for praise from both editors and teachers, I also knew that even if I got praise, I would be as little able to understand that as I would criticism. I wanted to be both myself and the teacher or editor; along with my own deep investment in my work, I yearned for the benefit of their experience, which I imagined as a simple and instinctive sense of how my work fit into the context of other unpublished work. I knew that there was something to be known about my stories that others easily knew and that I absolutely could not know. The frustration drove me wild.

Talent, hard work, willpower, determination. It felt literally like I was standing in my boots and trying to lift myself off the ground by my own

bootstraps. If telling stories takes both wisdom and technique, then I had little of either. When I look at my early work now, both unpublished and published, I can feel again how ignorance felt — both my unwisdom (the characters try to compensate for their thinness by acting arbitrarily) and clumsiness (no scenes last long enough to develop more than one or two shadings). I felt like I was pressing myself hard into a blank wall, hoping that the wall would dissolve and reveal a wide, new landscape, but knowing there would be none of that — nothing sudden or miraculous or magic. The only real hope was the removal of ignorance stone by stone, or even grain by grain, an operation that took, at least for me, far longer than I ever suspected it would.

Every prepublication writer is certain that what separates her from Virginia Woolf, say, or Alice Munro, is merely a veil that publication will rip away. If the editor would only *allow* himself to see, why, then he *would* see, and then *everyone* would see. It's that simple. One's darling story is clearly only a bit less accomplished than, say, *David Copperfield.* It's either the editor's incompetence or his willful blindness that prevents him from recognizing that.

Education begins with publication. First, there are the stories published with yours — your peers'. You are a *Redbook* writer, and your friend is a *New Yorker* writer. That is sobering. But then you realize that you could have been something else — you could have been someone paid only in copies. Second, there is the sight of your work in print. Now that it looks like real literature, much about it is less amorphous than it was in manuscript. The sentimental convention is that print seems to confer respectability, but actually print is unforgiving. It says to the writer, "You repeated. You echoed someone else. You forgot some things entirely. I have been put to better use by others." Third, your little story, which is the pinnacle of your effort to date, is surrounded by a sea of others. It is hard to resist the disappointment that accompanies the elation of first publication — you have strained and strained to bring forth a mouse, a fly, a mote. Now you are published, but so, it seems, is every other literate person on the face of the earth.

Back to work. The unlooked-for bonus of publication is that it shows you what you really want to do, which is get back to that word processor and re-engage with your work. As pale as it is, your published story

reminds you of the surging vivid joys and pains you felt when you were writing it.

ALL the reasons that a writer shouldn't rush too quickly into print are on display in this collection, and the main one is the embarrassing revelation of youth. Young writers write about youth as if it were worthy of consideration, or maybe what I mean is they write about it as if they, being young, actually know more about youth than just how to demonstrate it. I find John Updike's and Philip Roth's stories especially disconcerting in this regard. Two realists, well known and widely admired for the care and insight they bring to the dissection of the lives of adults, Roth and Updike here follow the accepted realist precept, which is to write about what you know. The result, in Updike's "Friends from Philadelphia," is a characteristic Updike story — assured narrative voice, sharp dialogue, self-confident and insensitive female character, smart but self-effacing male character — except that the man and the woman are teenagers, still subject to the authority of their parents, as yet unmarried to one another. The protagonist is not yet stunned, and rendered eloquent, as so many later Updike fathers seem to be, by the arrival of children on the scene. Roth's milieu is already present in "The Day It Snowed" as well — the big, crowded, talkative Jewish family, the adults who are preoccupied with their own concerns while trying to shield the confused child from the knowledge of death. Of course they succeed only in terrifying him. Sydney, sensitive but restlessly inquisitive, prefigures later Roth protagonists. What is clumsy, what betrays the writer's unsureness, is the sort of melodrama that Roth the realist later gives up in favor of wit and irony.

Not every realist in this collection starts out as one. Surely one of the strangest artifacts the editors have unearthed is Tennessee Williams's "The Vengeance of Nitocris," published when Williams was seventeen years old. Williams takes ancient Egypt as his scene, and concocts a florid, bloodthirsty sacrifice, pitting Nitocris, the "tall and . . . majestically handsome" sister of the pharoah against the priests of the god Osiris. The set piece involves gluttony, drunkenness, lechery, slaves, and a "monstrous deed." Forms of torture abound. Perhaps the story reveals more about what the teenaged Williams liked to read than it portends

about his future work, but it is undeniably visual, dramatic, and full of passion.

Some of these stories show more about the times in which they were published than the writers who wrote them. It is, after all, the special burden of a first-time author that he or she has to appeal purely to an editor's taste. Editors, like readers in general, have to be trained to understand and appreciate an author's work, but a first-time author has no familiarity to bank on. The stories by Graham Greene ("The End of the Party") and E. M. Forster ("Albergo Empedocle") appealed to contemporary editorial tastes for uncanny effects and trick endings. Greene's story, a tale of twin boys who are forced to play hide-and-seek at a birthday party, still offers an authentic chill. "Albergo Empedocle," which climaxes with the "madness" of the main character, seems strangely premodern and naive. David Leavitt's "Territory" appeals to our contemporary taste for the careful exploration of family relationships; like many stories of the 1980s, "Territory" offers less a plot than a situation — a grown son, Neil, brings his lover, Wayne, home to meet his mother, Barbara. Everyone is uneasily polite, and Wayne's visit becomes the occasion for Neil of an extended reflection upon his sexuality and his feelings for his mother. It is one of the longest, if not the longest, in this volume, although also one of the least dramatic. Possibly in fifty years Leavitt's story will seem as clearly an example of a genre as Greene's and Forster's do today. And then there is Mary McCarthy's "Cruel and Barbarous Treatment," a tale of a sophisticated woman who tires of her lover just as she is getting rid of her husband, which seems of all these stories to have aged the most — it reads the way the old Anita Loos movie *The Women* looks. The bitter and judgmental narrative tone, the shallow motives of the woman, and the sympathetic portrayal of both the husband and the lover are as far out of fashion today as it is possible to get.

Sometimes a first-time author can put his or her main distinguishing characteristic — extreme youth — to positive use, offering an editor what you might call rookie benefits. Who better to satisfy the curiosity of the old about the real life of the young than one of the young themselves? Ernest Hemingway's famous story "in our time," which now seems fragmentary, must have struck everyone at the time as the authen-

tic voice of the First World War. John Cheever's "Expelled" is so different from all of Cheever's mature work that it could have been written by
a different person. The teenaged Cheever has none of his later luminous
style, which irresistibly and unforgettably bodies forth the natural world.
But he is a true and unvarnished seventeen-year-old, with a sharp eye
for adult foibles and an ear neatly attuned to the combination of pomposity, self-delusion, and hypocrisy that often constitutes the manner in
which adults communicate with adolescents.

It is not possible to read these stories as they were first read. We must
read them through the lens of our knowledge of each writer's later work,
and because all of these writers have produced later work that is vividly
idiosyncratic as well as technically accomplished, many of these stories
don't provide the satisfaction that the names of their authors promise.
But there's a lesson in that, too. Prepublished writers almost always think
that publication is the great, even the only, hurdle standing between
their obscurity and their fame, but, at least in America, I think the biggest hurdle comes later, at the point where a writer finds the voice and
the subject of his or her maturity. A friend of my early writing days, who
had both a Boy Wonder reputation and a reputation for pure brazen
charm, once buttonholed Joseph Heller in an elevator and asked him for
writing advice. Heller told him not to begin his first novel until he was
thirty. My friend, who was twenty-three, and I (twenty-six) agreed on
the impossibility of this — in the first place, if we waited that long, we
might die first, and in the second place, what were we supposed to do in
the meantime? — but Heller's advice was sound. It is not that there are
no second acts in American lives (or writing careers); it is that the machinery of publication and publicity doesn't know how to accommodate
the inevitable evolution of an author's work as it becomes more idiosyncratic and complex. If an author is already mature enough to express
idiosyncrasy and complexity when he or she first achieves notice, then
the promotional machinery can (creaking and complaining and vaguely
misrepresenting) make something of that. But if, as with F. Scott Fitzgerald, whose story, "Babes in the Woods," is possibly the fluffiest in this
volume, the work thickens and darkens from an earlier simple clarity,
the author will not only get no help in finding his voice, but he will even
encounter resistance. He or she has now become not only his or her

own investment, but the publishing house's investment. Investments are supposed to pay off, and unknown quantities of complexity and idiosyncrasy have unknown dividends.

Were I now a prepublished author reading this book, I might profitably follow the example of Isaac Bashevis Singer, who was forty-nine at the publication of "Gimpel the Fool." I would follow his example, that is, if I wanted my story to be a great one — to speak with a voice of ageless wisdom and authority, to present a coherent philosophy, to make fresh use of traditional forms and materials. Though I have read Singer's story four or five times, though I have taught it and discussed it and appreciated it, it still offers new rewards with each new reading. Singer's technique of presenting Gimpel through his own testimony and also through the testimony of the villagers, which he reports with all apparent ingenuousness, gives him many layers of innocence and wisdom — he is the fool that he reports himself to be, but he also knows more about the workings of the world than any of those who feel superior to him. "Gimpel the Fool" is a masterpiece.

But so, I think, is Carson McCullers's "Wunderkind," published when the author was nineteen. What I find remarkable about the story is the narrator's extraordinary sympathy for the hopes of her teacher, which she feels she can no longer fulfill. The world of the music school is presented in exquisite sensory detail — "Notes she had been practicing falling over each other like a handful of marbles dropped downstairs," "Heime always seemed to smell of corduroy pants and the food he had eaten and rosin" — so that when she flees at the end, her complicated sense of both loss and escape is utterly specific. Frances's experience does not make her wise, as Gimpel's does, but it does bring her, and the reader, to a remarkable pitch of feeling.

Of course, other stories in this volume succeed as well, and are as interesting in their own right as they are as examples of early work. James Baldwin's "Previous Condition," Chester B. Himes's "Crazy in the Stir," Nelson Algren's "So Help Me," and Alice Walker's "To Hell with Dying" all stand on their own as depictions of situations and aspects of American life that don't find their way into literary magazines often enough. These authors don't seem to be looking inward for something to write about, but rather seeking a way to wrestle important themes and new voices into literary form. "Previous Condition," in particular, is

timeless in its evocation of American racism and of the inescapable bind Peter, the protagonist, lives in. A mature writer is one who has found a way to depict the outer and the inner lives (or, you might say, the personal and political lives) in balance, so that both are revealed as the story progresses. Some young writers begin more focused on the inner life, some more focused on the outer. The evidence of these stories, I think, is that the world as a subject holds up better in the long run than the self does.

BUT there is nothing like the moment of first acceptance. It is one of those moments that fixes itself in your memory and returns each time you think of it, as clear in some ways as the present moment. When *Redbook* wrote me that they were interested in publishing "And Baby Makes Three" (which I called "Her Kind Nursery," a quote from *King Lear,* until the editor insisted on a more readily understandable title), I had just gone to Iceland on a Fulbright grant. We were still in the first week of orientation (which must explain my memory of bright sunshine so close to suppertime). When the Fulbright officer handed me the letter that had been forwarded from home, my gaze, of course, riveted on the big red "Redbook." A letter! No fatal Self-Addressed Stamped Envelope, but guaranteed good news.

The good news, of course, was typical: Very interested . . . would I consider changes? . . . of course they weren't making any promises . . . here were some suggestions . . . they would be glad to read the story again. Not an acceptance, but more than a rejection.

It's hard to describe the size of the disparity between my elation at this minimal recognition of my work and the indifference of those around me, who were far more interested in socializing and getting ready to dine than they were in speculating upon the greatness that I was now convinced lay before me like a superhighway. I had the sense to keep my feelings largely to myself, but to this day I remember the bright, sunny whiteness of that sheet of paper, and the crisp blackness of the type. I can still draw the shape of those five paragraphs as they appeared on the page, though I can't remember what changes were requested, or which ones I complied with. I had no principles — if there were ones I didn't comply with, it was out of a failure of imagination, not for the sake of the story's integrity.

I remember the money part, which came later, when I was back in the States for Christmas. Whether *Redbook* would even buy the story remained in question for four or five months. I was in New York for almost a month without hearing from them before I dared to call and, very tentatively and respectfully, ask whether they had had a chance to reconsider —

"Oh," caroled the editor. "Why, yes! We were going to call you very soon and make an offer!"

I exchanged a glance with my friend, an experienced freelance journalist who had been coaching me to ask for $750 or even $850.

"What would be your offer?" I tried to sound businesslike and cagey. "How about $1,250?"

There was a silence while I appeared to be considering but was actually communicating numbers on my fingers to my friend, whose eyebrows rose, pleased and impressed. She nodded. I said, "That would be fine, I think."

We spent a sizable portion of the money feasting with friends at a restaurant in the Village named Alfredo's, the first time I had ever had the wherewithal to pick up the check for ten diners. The meal was delicious and full of things like fresh mozzarella and balsamic vinegar that I had never heard of before.

In the world of art, of course, it is gauche to bring up the money, but the money, either its presence or absence, often turns out to press a writer with repeated and lifelong challenges. First publication is also a writer's first entrance into the world of literary commerce. While readers often forget this, writers seldom do.

Now "And Baby Makes Three" strikes me as surpassingly ignorant. I not only knew little of writing, but I also knew very little of child raising. The baby at the center of the story is not a baby I would recognize after three babies of my own. But yes, it is a true Jane Smiley story, and it predicts my future work, just as most of the others in this volume predict the later work of their authors. Much about it embarrasses me now, but I rather like the audacity of naming my unsympathetic female character "Jane," and I am still amazed at how much the artwork looks like me, though the artist never saw me. Had I been the editor at *Redbook,* I wouldn't have bought it. But maybe despite all the things a writer eventually learns, what she never learns is who she is among the others,

how she fits in, what she has to offer that others seem to want or not want, who she is as "a writer" in contrast to how she experiences herself.

What is clear from this volume, though, and worth cherishing, is the astonishing uniqueness of even the most tentative of these voices, and the multiplicity of settings and subjects the authors have chosen. In the end, what I think is valuable about fiction is not "greatness" but individuality, the way we are invited each time we pick up a story or a novel to remember that every consciousness is a whole world.

JANE SMILEY

first fiction

So Help Me

Wanting to be a writer but unable to find work after he graduated from the University of Illinois in 1931, Nelson Algren stole a typewriter; he was caught and served four months in jail. The idea for his first story came to Algren the following summer during his travels by boxcar around southern Texas, where he picked grapefruit when he could find the work. In Rio Hondo, Algren and a friend came across an abandoned gas station and persuaded the agent to let them fix up the place and reopen it. Business was slow at the station, but Algren became fascinated with the migrant workers and transients ("fruit bums") whom he met. As Bettina Drew wrote in *Nelson Algren: A Life on the Wild Side*, "So Help Me" reflects the lives of these people, "evoking an entire world of outcast people with its own customs and values."

Returning to Chicago, Algren submitted four stories to *Story*. Burnett immediately published "So Help Me" in the August 1933 issue and paid Algren twenty dollars. A Vanguard editor saw it and paid Algren one hundred dollars for a novel in the works, then called *The Gods Gather*, published in 1935 under the title *Somebody in Boots*.

NOW PERHAPS YOU will think that I am just lying to you, and maybe you will even think that Luther really wanted to get rid of the Jew kid so's we would oney have two ways to split instead of three, but you know, Mr. Breckenridge, guys like me can't never get away with bull like that to big-league lawyers like yourself, so you can just taken my word for it Fort didn't really mean to hurt the Jew kid a-tall, and that's the truth so help me.

I seen this Jew high-school kid first in New Orleans on the Desire street wharf luggin' along a bran' new leathern suitcase almost as big as hisself. He come up to me and axes where can he find the shipping steward please, so I judged he was lookin' for a job, and figgerin' to save him trouble I told him they ain't no use lookin' for work around here Bub. You think he took my word for it, Mr. Breckenridge? No, he has to go off and see the steward for hisself. Well, soons he finds out he comes back and sets down on the wharf and commences lookin' scared-like into the fog over the river. I pulls over to him, figgerin' that any bird with rags as dressy as his'n might have a little extra cash handy, so I axed him for a handout, and he look at me like he never seen me befo', and then hand me a dime and look out into the fog over the river again.

I had a hunch I could wrangle a meal out of him if I just hung on a minute, so I settled down again easy-like and ax him has he worked on the big boats befo', 'though I seen he ain't. He just says no, and don't seem anxious to get acquainted a-tall. That made me stubborn, so I just set still, and in a couple of minutes it began to drizzle, and he picks up his suitcase to go, so I got up too and went with him, makin' small talk all the while just to see where he was a-stayin' at. He walked down Tchoupitoulas and turned on Poeyfarre until we got to the Circle, and there he flop down on a bench, and I seen he did not know where to go, even though he had money in his pocket.

We just set there under a space under a tree lookin' up at Lee with water runnin' down his back. A dollar-woman come by and give us the eye, and the Jew kid turn to me and axes do I know the lady, and I says no o'course not. Then he axes why did she look at you so funny then, and now perhaps you will think that I am just lyin' to you, Mr. Breckenridge, but that Jew didn't know what that chip wanted a-tall. I explained, gentle-like, on account him bein' so young and all, but do you think I could get him to believe he coulda bought that girl? Not him — he hadda see for hisself.

So I took him through the district and he seen I wasn't just lyin' to him. He looked a little scared and worried when we come back to the Circle. When we set down again he remarks he wouldn't never spend no dollar of his that way, and I tol' him he could get most of them for six-bits if he jewed them a little. He gimme a look when I says to jew them,

but he didn't let on he was one, so how was I to know? O' course I wouldn't never have picked up with him if I'd knowed.

We got a mite friendly then, and I tol' him I was goin' down to the Rio Grande Valley, 'cause it come into my head just then how nice and warm it was in the Valley while we was sittin' shiverin' in the rain in the Circle. He ax me what I am goin' to do in the Valley, and I thought quick and says I am going to pick oranges and make three-four dollars a day doing so, and I looked at him sideways to see would he swaller that, and he did, hook, line, and sinker. So I tol' him some more about the Valley. Then I waited a minute and says casual-like maybe you would like to come along, and he say yes he would. So we shaken hands on it, and he let me sleep on the floor of his room that night and in the morning I got breakfast off him also.

After breakfast, we walken down to the Soup line yards to wait for a freight through to Houston, and they was about twenty fellas and some niggers there already. All the while we was waitin' the Jew kid kep' throwin' out hints how it might be better we should hitch-hike it, so I seen he was a mite scared, and ax him ain't he never rid a freight befo' though I seen he ain't. He says no he hasn't never. So I says well I ain't never hitch-hiked and ain't aimin' to start now, so that left the gate wide open for him to blow, but he just set still and get that scared look all over his mush again. Right then I surmised he musta somewhere got the idea they was somethin' to see in the Valley.

Some of the fellas was cookin' somethin' by the side o' the track, an' I walked over casual-like to see was it Mulligan, when who do my eyes light on but Luther Morgan what I palled with on the state farm at Wetumpka. I yelled how are you Fort old pal, on account Luther was in Fort Myers so long, and he was glad to see me too. I called the kid over and axed him to shake hands with my old pal Fort Morgan, so they shook hands and Fort had a bottle of bay rum and he give me a shot but didn't offer the kid none cause he oney had a mite left for hisself. I don't think the Jew kid wanted one anyhow. It begin to gimme a pain just to look at that goddam scared lookin' puss o' his. I like a boy with guts.

Well, Fort finished the bay and tried to bum two-bits from the kid for another bottle, but the kid said no and walked away from him. Fort went off a little after that, and he musta gone clean back to Canal street,

'cause he was gone a couple of hours and when he come back he had five cans of Sterno in his pockets and another bottle of bay. He was pretty wobbly and when he seen the kid right away he wants to roll him, and pick up a rock as big as your head to do it with. If ever I seen a scared sheenie in my life it was that Jew kid sittin' on his shiny new leathern suitcase shakin' all over like a leaf. He was so scared that even the niggers over to the side laugh a little. I got Luther quieted down a bit, and he pull out a whole handful of silver and heave it all over the yards. I oney got a Canadian dime out of it, but the Jew kid didn't get nothin' a-tall.

We heard the freight whistlin' just then, and the fellas began to pick theirselves up — all exceptin' Fort. Fort has made up his mind he ain't goin' to hop nothin' but blind baggage on a silk manifest, and I couldn't convince him that there weren't no manifest due on the Soup line before November anyhow, and even that one would be goin' the other way. But all he would say was I will wait here till November then and if it is going the other way I will go the other way too. There isn't any reasoning with Luther when he is in that frame of mind, so I took two of the cans of Sterno and eighteen cents he had in his watch pocket, and dragged him over to the side out of the way of the brakeman.

Then the freight pull up about a hundred yards down the track and the kid says hurry let's get on, like he thought they wouldn't be no seats left if we was late, so I says what's the rush — why go way down there when it will certainly come up here? It'll save you draggin' that suitcase which I surmise is pretty heavy? So we waited till it drag up to hop it.

Now perhaps you will think I am just lyin' to you, Mr. Breckenridge, but so help me it's the truth — it musta been about two a.m. and we was crossin' some river — musta been the Atchafalay' — when the Jew kid sit up straight real suddent and yell "We're cut apart! — cut apart! — cut apart!" just like that. Well, just for a second he give me 'nawful turn 'cause I thought we was really cut in two and running wild, but soon's I got myself together I knew we wasn't, and I tol' him to lay down and quit yellin' like he was nuts. I seen guys in the army get excited in their sleep, but this Jew was the worst thing ever — he jump up and head straight for the open door. Now the Atchafalay' may not be so wide as the Mississippi but it's just as deep, and I set him down befo' he got hisself all wet. In the morning he don't remember nothin' of what he say

the night befo'. I woulda tol' him to go back home, that I had decided to go to Salt Lake City instead, but I kep' wonderin' about that leathern suitcase of his.

When we got to Houston we had a chance to catch a hot shot clear down to the Valley, 'though we had to walk two miles out of town to hop it — but what do you think that damn snot done when it pull up and I was shovin' him into the blind, suitcase and all? He back out quick like a crawfish and say he thought he'd rather hop a freight. I says o.k. Meet me by the depot in San Juan. And the train pulls out. I never expected to see him again.

I got down to San Juan just as it was gettin' light, and I guess that Sterno didn't do me no good 'cause I got off on the depot side and the brakeman called me a son-of-a-bitch and I yelled back, You yellow Mexican bastard you, oney I said it in Mex, and he run after me and give me one on the side of the head that did not even sting on account I got so much Sterno in me.

I walked downtown and seen a young punk in puttees lookin' for guys to pick oranges, and I thought hell with that noise. I tried it oncet in Florida and worked all day and oney made thirty-nine cents, and so I said none o' that for me I come down here to keep warm not to work.

Well, I'd been in San Juan almost two days and had clean forgot all about the Jew kid, Mr. Breckenridge, and was settin' on the packin' shed platform sunnin' myself, thinkin' maybe Fort would drag in, when I seen the Jew kid.

He was settin' top a refrigerator car pert as you please, with his hat smashed in and his clothes all over spots, but the suitcase shiny as ever. He weren't down-hearted a-tall though — happiest I'd ever saw him, and wants to go to work right away pickin' oranges and make three-four dollars a day. So I tol' him the oranges wasn't ripe quite yet and he begin to look worried again. Then he ax me where was I stayin' and I says I guess maybe I will rent myself a tourist cabin and if you wish to stay with me I shall pleased to have you and will surely get you a job three-four dollars a day. He agrees, so we start for the tourist camp and on the way I tell him, casual-like, I got no ready cash but can get forty-five, fifty dollars, from my brother Bryan what is in Apalachicola on Tuesday, so he can put up his wrist-watch for security I will speak to the landlady at the camp just to give it to me, but he back up quick like a crawfish at

that and say no not on your life the wrist-watch is a gift from his girl in Cincinnati so I said tell me all about it, because I needed time to think how am I going to get this wrist-watch.

So we set down on the curb in front of the gas station and that was when he told me he was a Jew and he had a girl in Cincinnati where he come from who wasn't no Jew a-tall. He had sewed her up but his pa wouldn't let him marry her on account she ain't no Jew and her folks is very poor on top of it. Her pa said the kid must marry her or pay him a lot o' dough or go to jail, but the girl herself she wasn't even sore at him, and he liked her a lot also and woulda married her but he didn't have no money to marry on and was still in high school. So he was just about nuts not knowin' what should he do, 'cause his old man won't help him. He decides he must quit school and get hisself a job immediately so's he could get married before the baby was born, but he couldn't find no job in Cincinnati nowhere, and then he read in the paper they was men needed in Las Vegas to work on the Boulder Dam. So he tol' the girl he would go there and get a job and he would send for her, and that made them both very happy, oney when he got to Las Vegas he learns there is oney eight jobs left and there is 4,500 other fellas what had snuck in in front of him. Then he was ashamed to go home and say he can't find no job so he hitch-hiked to New Orleans to try to ship out, and that was how I met up with him.

Just as he finished tellin' me I thought of a good idea, and I says come down to the telegraph office with me, David, I wish to send a telegram to my brother Bryan in Apalachicola, so we went down and I axed Bryan for forty dollars and gave it to the kid to read, and had the charges reversed. I knew Bryan would pay for the telegram since he would not know from who it was before he opened it. He would cuss me out when he read it o'course, and would tear it up immediately and would wonder was I nuts or what. We hung around the office until we found out it was accepted, and the Jew kid was convinced I was not just lying to him that I had a brother Bryan in Apalachicola. He give the woman the wrist-watch, and we taken a cabin and also get some groceries off her. I had not slept on a mattress for quite some time, and so before we turned in I said to myself, Homer, tonight at least you shall sleep better than you have since you was sprung from Wetumpka.

Now maybe you will think I am just lying to you, Mr. Breckenridge,

but do you know I did not get scarcely twenty minutes rest that night? First I laid awake a long time wonderin' it is certainy very peculiar that this Jew should not even open his suitcase to see what is inside it, and I do not approve of wiliness in any of its many forms. He was breathin' deep, and I got to thinkin' maybe should I open it myself, when all of a suddent he give one unholy shriek, sit straight up, grabs tight hold of the side of the bed, and begins that nut line about bein' cut apart again. "Cut apart!" he yells, "Cut in two! Thy blood is not my blood! — We're cut apart!" and the moonlight was on his face like I seen it on the dead faces at Cantigny, and his eyes was bright and staring straight ahead. My hair, if I had any, woulda stood up then, 'cause he begin to get up slow, wavin' those skinny arms like they was white snakes, like he was tryin' to push somethin' away from in front o' him, and didn't have no strength to do it. I got my hooks in him then and set him down hard, and he went back to sleep arguin' somethin' fierce with somebody. So I couldn't sleep much after that, bein' afraid he might get up again and decide to do a little cuttin' apart on his own.

By the time it is morning I had decided to shake him, suitcase or no suitcase, but Fort showed up that day, and that made me change my mind.

I got a job for the kid pickin' oranges with a gang of Mexicans, but did not go along myself on account I wish to see what is it inside the suitcase. I dived for it soon's he was gone, but do you know what, Mr. Breckenridge? — He'd locken it and taken the key with him! Naturally I was pretty sore at such suspicions tactics behind my back as it were, because I am a proud man by nature and a direct descendant of Edmund Ruffin on my mother's side. I went off to the freight depot feeling bad, and set down just to sun myself a bit, and reflected when would my luck change.

It was about noon when Fort come in. I was still settin' on the depot platform, and the noise of the engine waken me, and when I sat up the first thing I seen was Fort. I kidded him a bit about waitin' for the silk manifest and we had a good laugh together over it, and I commenced to feel better. I tol' him I was stayin' with the Jew kid until he would get wise about the telegram, so Fort axes me what have I been doin' for groceries and I tol' him I have been getting those on credit also. Then he remarks that he is hungry and is in great need of tobacco, so we

strolled over to the camp, and Fort waited outside, and the woman still thought it was my watch, so she give me two packs of tobacco and a bag of stale tortillas.

About 6:30 I seen the kid comin' down the road and walked down to meet him, on account I want to tell him Fort is sleepin' on his cot. His shirt was tore almost in two and the backs of his hands was all scratches and he has a scratch on the side of his neck which one look tol' me is goin' to come a tropical sore very shortly. He was all streaked with dried sweat, but was not appearing worried, so I ax him how much has he earned, and he says seventy-six cents, at which I supposed he was just lyin' to me, Mr. Breckenridge, because only a Mexican can earn that much in a day. I woulda done it myself if I'd oney knowed they was payin' that much. Then I remarked, casual-like, that Fort was inside and might as well stay with us until I got my money, which would probly be tomorrow. I seen he didn't like that, but then I figgered what can he do about it if he says anything to hurt my feelings again I shall simply refuse to redeem his watch.

At first Fort and the kid did not have very much to say to each other, but after supper Luther showen him the place back of his ear where he was shot at Cantigny and let him feel the steel plate there and that broke the ice and Fort showen him the marks on his left leg too which he got in a job upstate, but which he tells the kid he got also at Cantigny.

Fort made out on the floor that night, and the kid didn't raise no rumpus, and I didn't say nothin' to Fort 'cause I thought maybe the boy is ashamed of it so I will not antagonize him by telling Luther. I can see now all right I shoulda give Fort a hint, but how was I to know?

In the morning early the Jew goes off to pick some more oranges but Fort and me didn't get up in time and I took to reflectin' it would certainly be a fine thing when the boy got paid on Saturday night because the woman in the store was already actin' very independent, as 'though she was becoming reluctant to extend our credit much further and was not after all a person who had firm faith in human nature. Then I went down to the store and learned my reflectin' was just about correct, because she gave me what I axed for and then said I couldn't never have any more until I paid up. We sat around smokin' awhile after that and Fort thought that the kid must have tellen her it was not my watch at all

but his watch which was a present to him from somebody in Cincinnati. If I'd thought Luther was right I would certainly have grab that suitcase and taken it on the lam right then and there, oney I wasn't sure, and they was Saturday night to look forwards to. The kid come back just as it was getting dark out, and reports he had earned sixty-nine cents more, so now we have $1.45 coming from the Magic Valley Fruit Exchange.

Well, it was oney Friday morning, and our credit weren't no good, and all we had left was old bread and coffee. The kid tried to get them to advance his $1.45, but they wouldn't do it and he went off to work looking worried again. But they wasn't really nothin' to worry about.

Fort tried to panhandle a few nickels in the afternoon, but all the places tol' him he would have to go to the relief station in Alamo or starve. So I copped a half-dozen grapefruit seconds from the packing house, and that was all we had for supper, and by morning we have all three of us decide we would go to Alamo to the relief station there.

Now I suppose you will think that I am just lying to you, Mr. Breckenridge, but do you know, that when we got to the Station that kid would not go inside? He backed out quick like a crawfish. Of course we couldn't bring nothin' out to him, so I guess he musta been pretty hungry when we got back to San Juan. I didn't ax him. But he went to bed lookin' kinda white soon's we got home, and laid with his face to the wall. He give me a pain just to look at him. I like a boy with guts.

Fort and me went back to Alamo again in the afternoon an' when we come back he was still in bed and axes me will I go down to the Exchange and collect his money for him and buy some groceries on the way back. I didn't want Fort along on account Fort is very avaricious, but he come anyhow, and we got the $1.45, and right away he wanted to buy mescal, but I put my foot down on that. I came straight out for tequila or nothing at all. We got a big pint for $1.00 and give the Mex girl who fetched it two-bits because she had to go clear to the other end of town to get it. After we killed it we still had 20 cents left but I got to thinking of the kid how maybe he was gettin' sick and all, and I stopped in the Jitney Jungle and bought a quart of milk. After all it was his money even if he was a Jew. When I was buyin' the milk I seen Fort starin' at the cash register, and when we got outside he says, tryin' to be casual-like, let us walk about a bit, Homer, that tequila has give me a

headache. I guessed what was on his mind and says perhaps we should better take the milk home first and then walk about a bit, I believe our baby is hungry; but Fort says no we should first walk about a bit.

So when we got a ways out of town he propositions me we should hoist the Jitney Jungle and I axes him where can we get a couple rods, and he says we oney need one, Homer, and I got that, and he pull a roscoe off his hip. That surprised me somewhat because I had been completely unaware Fort was packin' a rod on his person, but nevertheless it does not convince me and I says it is all very well for you to say one roscoe is enough when you are carryin' it but what about me? So then he says I can have the roscoe if I wish to be selfish and greedy, but he will get a long cut short for hisself. I am again taken by surprise by this remark about a long cut short for hisself and I says perhaps you already have the long cut short? And he says no, but he knows where he can get one at for three dollars anytime. I says that is very encouraging but where is this place where for three dollars you can get a long cut short anytime? And he told me it is the same place where at we bought the tequila.

I began to get very interested and I ax him what he is going to use for money to get the long cut short, and where he is going to get a car, and several other things he could not answer right off. I reminded him he could never get out of the Valley without a good car, and he got peeved and says he will pull the job alone if I have lost my guts. I told him not to get sore, because I was with him the same as always, and I axed him who will grab the oday? And Luther answer that one so quick I seen he musta been thinkin' about the hoist for a couple days at least. The Jew will grab the oday he says, like it is all settled.

Then we was back in town, almost to the camp, and we shut up.

Now will you believe me, Mr. Breckenridge, but we hadn't no sooner turned the corner into the camp when I stumbled against a old hitching post and dropped that milk right out of my hand and busted it? That was very strong tequila, Homer, Fort says, and then we was inside the cabin. He was still in bed, but he was curled up double, and all the bed clothes was messed up and when he seen me his eyes look like a wolf's, and then he seen I got no groceries, and he moans and turns his face to the wall.

I says do not take it so hard, kid, they would not give me the money

and Fort and I been arguin' with them ever since, and now it is too late to get it, the cashier has went home. Sometimes I think pretty fast so now I said let me take your suitcase down to the pawnshop, David, and I will get enough groceries for to last us until I get my money from Bryan, my brother in Apalachicola. He says I do not believe you have a brother anywhere, but take the suitcase and get me something to eat with it and come back right away I am very hungry. Fort tried to come with me again, but I stopped him in time. Why should I have to split everything with that mug? He has very deceptive ways anyhow.

I taken the suitcase to the pawnshop and they was two gray suits in it, almost new, a pair of shoes, some shirts and b.v.d.'s, and a heavy blue wool sweater with a large white "B" sewed on the front of it. I got three dollars for the clothes and three for the suitcase and I spent two dollars for groceries in the Jitney Jungle just like I tole the kid I would, and I got a pint of mescal for seventy-five cents which I drunk right away, and then I held out three for the long cut short and took to reflectin' how it was oney two days ago that I was thinking my luck wasn't going to change.

On my way back I seen a new Chrysler I knowed belong to the druggist on the corner, and in front of it a big elephant ears was standin'. It was almost nine I guess when I got back, and the kid was lookin' so scared it give me a turn just to look at him — more scared than hungry now, and I knowed somethin' had been goin' on. It was in the air. Fort was sittin' nex' to him on the bed when I come in, but got up quick and sat down at the table when I come in. I didn't say nothin'. I just fixed us up some stew, and the kid dragged hisself out o' bed in his dirty underwear, but didn't eat much a-tall. Nobody said much until we finished eatin' and then Fort cough a little and announces to me that the kid wanted to come in with us on the hoist real bad, and I was a little surprised I did not know Fort was going to proposition him so quick, so I figger to myself he musta squeezed the Jew.

After that the ice was broke and the oney important question left was when to pull it. Fort musta forgot about that telegram I have sent because he suggests nex' Saturday night, which is a full week away, and I says no to that right away, and when I said it the mescal in me bubbled a little, and I began to hope Fort would argue about it. So I says real emphatic Tuesday or Wednesday. I was thinkin' too, that we had to have

the kid, and if we waited a week he would certainy crawfish. Fort says to me, Homer I am surprised at you, you know very well there won't be no mokoy in the pot on Tuesday or Wednesday, Saturday night is the only night, you should know that. So I says tonight is Saturday night, and Fort got up an' put on his coat, an' the kid set up a howl about his wrist-watch, an' Fort give him a look, an' he shut up like a oyster.

We all three of us went down to the Mex bootlegger an' give him three bucks for the long cut short, an' I took it an' beat it down the alley to the garage back of the drug store, an' the druggist was just puttin' the Chrysler up for the night, an' I hopped in with him and give him direction, an' he seen I meant business an' was scared as the devil, but he got me in front of the Jitney Jungle without hittin' nothin'. Fort an' the kid was waitin' in front, an' I made the druggist change places with me easy-like. Then Fort an' the Jew went inside, I heard Fort start barkin' an' I seen him shove the kid. Then the kid grab about half the money, whirls an' tears for the door droppin' bills all over the place, an' Fort give him the shoulder, an' he went back an' taken it all then. I'd thought he'd break his neck comin' out, he come so fast, but Fort back out slow until he got through the door. Then he turn so quick he even surprised me, and in two leaps he was inside the car and we was goin' fast. Fort threw the druggist out when I turned the corner into the highway to McAllen, an' about a minute after they got started behind us, an' I give her every-thing she got.

I never seen Fort so nervous befo' in all my life. He wanted to stick to the main road right through McAllen an' shoot it out if they was waitin' for us there, but I didn't say nothin' 'cause I know it don't pay to argue with Fort when he is nervous and has liquor inside him on top of it. I just turned up the first side-road I seen, run twenty feet into a orange grove, an' lit out for the tracks. They come right behind me, the Jew breathin' hard, an' we wasn't a minute too soon. The bulls from McAllen come by a-tearin' an' turn up the orange grove road. I was scared then, an' Fort started cussin' out the warden at Wetumpka under his breath. If they'd gone forty feet further they woulda seen the car an' knowed we was hidin' close by, but they didn't, an' went back to the highway and tear out for San Juan again.

We waited there by the tracks real quiet-like, an' it musta been about 11:30 a string of empties headed for San Anton' come along, an' we

hoppen it. Fort was sure that they was going to stop us in McAllen an' search for us, an' wouldn't quit fingerin' the trigger of that long for a minute. The Jew kid don't say nothin' but look so almighty goddam scared I didn't know whether to laugh or kick his ugly little face in with my heel. I like a boy with guts.

They didn't look for us in McAllen, an' we got through Falfurrias o.k. I figgered we was out of the Valley then an' didn't have to worry no more so long as we got out of sight before we hit San Anton'. But Fort kep' mumblin' he ain't goin' back to breakin' rock again no matter what happen, an' I dozed off a-listenin' to his blabberin', an' so I wasn't wide awake when it started, Mr. Breckenridge, an' it was all over in a second, an' so I cannot say rightly just what did happen. I oney know I heard that yell from the corner, "We're cut apart — cut apart! an' he then he jump up an' say, "Thy blood is not my blood!" an' make straight for Fort.

Well now you-all can't blame Luther in a way. He was jumpy in the first place, an' him and the kid hadn't never clicked much anyhow, an' maybe he'd squeezed the kid a mite to make him come along, an' o' course he didn't know the Jew was asleep. He jes' heard that yell an' seen him comin', an' the long was in his hand. I guess that Jew never knew what hit him. He jes' doubled up, stretched out, made a gurgly sound in his neck, an' that was all. O' course we had to clear then, but even then they'd never gotten me if Luther hadn't pointed an' on top of that tryin' to make you-all believe it was me had the long all the time.

Now maybe you will think that I am just lying to you, Mr. Breckenridge, and maybe you will even think I really wanted to get rid of the Jew kid so's we could split oney two ways instead of three, but you know guys like me can't never get away with bull like that to big-league lawyers like yourself, Mr. Breckenridge, so you can just taken my word for it I didn't mean to really hurt the Jew. So help me.

MARGARET ATWOOD

The War in the Bathroom

Born in 1939 in Ottawa, Canada, Atwood began writing comic books and novels at the age of five. Three years later she suddenly stopped — perhaps, she suggests, because her older brother, who also wrote, stopped — but started again when she was sixteen. Her first professional short story was published in *Alphabet* on November 8, 1964. Six years before, while an undergraduate, a very short story called "The Glass Slippers" had appeared in *Acta Victoriana,* a student publication of Victoria University at the University of Toronto. Until her first novel, *The Edible Woman,* was published in 1969, Atwood was known primarily as a poet; her collection *The Circle Game* won the Governor General's Award for poetry in 1966. "The War in the Bathroom" has previously appeared only in the Canadian edition of Atwood's first story collection, *Dancing Girls and Other Stories.*

MONDAY

LATE THIS AFTERNOON she moved out of the old place into the new one. The moving was accomplished with a minimum of difficulty: she managed to get everything into the two suitcases and was able to carry them herself for the three blocks that separate the old place from the new one. She only had to stop and rest twice. She is quite strong for her age. A man came along and offered to help her, rather a pleasant-looking man, but I have told her never to accept help from strangers.

I think the German woman was glad to see her go. She always regarded her with a certain amount of suspicion. She stood on the wooden porch in her slippers, watching, her arms in their gray ravelled sweater-sleeves folded across her fat stomach, her slip hanging an inch below the

16

figured cotton housedress she always wore. I, for one, have always disliked the German woman. I had become tired of seeing that certain things in the room had been moved (though she took pains to set them back in the approximate proper spot, she was never quite meticulous enough), and I had begun to suspect lately that she was looking at the mail: the envelopes had greasy thumbprints, and it is still too cold for the postmen to go without their gloves. The new place has a landlord instead of a landlady; I think, on the whole, I prefer them.

When she reached the new place she got the keys from an old man who lives in the ground-floor front room. He answered the doorbell; the landlord was out, but had told him she was to be expected. An agreeable old man with white hair and a benevolent smile. She took the suitcases up the narrow staircase to the second floor, one at a time. She has spent what was left of the day arranging the room. This room is smaller than the old one, but at least it is clean. She put the clothes into the cupboard and some of them into the bureau. There are no shelves so she will have to keep the saucepan, the cup, the plate, the silverware, and the coffee pot in one of the bureau drawers. However there is a small table, and I decided that the teapot may be left on it, even between mealtimes. It has a decorative pattern.

She made up the bed with the sheets and blankets that the landlord had provided. The room has a northern exposure and will be chilly. Fortunately there is an electric heater in the room. She has always been partial to warmth, although I myself have never been overly conscious of temperature. A compensation: the room is the one next to the bathroom, which will be handy.

The Notebook will be kept on the table, beside the teapot.

Tomorrow she must go outside for some groceries, but now she will go to bed.

TUESDAY

She was lying in bed this morning trying to get back to sleep. I was looking at the clock and agreeing with her that indeed the mattress was thin and quite hard, harder even than the one at the old place. It was almost nine and I told her to reach out and shut off the clock before the alarm went off.

Someone came up the front stairs, slowly, with a limping step, and

went into the bathroom, closing and locking the door. I have discovered that the walls are not thick and noises tend to carry. She was about to turn over and sleep again when the person in the bathroom began to cough violently. Then there was a sound of clearing and spitting and the toilet being flushed. I am sure I know who it was: it must be the old man from downstairs. The poor man must have a cold. He stayed in the bathroom exactly half an hour though, which is rather long; and he managed to make a number of unpleasant noises. I can see that the room beside the bathroom may have its disadvantages and I am beginning to realize why the landlord was willing to rent it so cheaply.

I finally persuaded her to get up and close the window (I have always felt fresh air to be necessary for one's health, although she is not fond of it) and turn on the electric heater. She began to go back to bed but I told her to put on the clothes: she had to go shopping, there was nothing to eat. She went into the bathroom, none too soon because there were other footsteps approaching. I thought that the bathroom could have been cleaner; however, this morning she just washed in the basin. Plenty of hot water at any rate.

She went back into the room and put on her coat and overshoes. I told her she had better put on the scarf too as I had noted frost on the storm window. She picked up the purse and went out of the room, locking the door behind her. The bathroom door was closed as she went by; the light showed through the transom. When she reached the bottom of the stairs the old man was in the hall, sorting out the mail on the small dark table that stands near the front door. He was wearing his bathrobe; below it his striped pyjamas went down, then his thin ankles and maroon-leather bedroom slippers. He smiled beautifully and said good morning. I told her to nod and smile back.

She closed the front door behind her and took the gloves out of her pocket and put them on. She made her way down the porch steps, carefully, since they were icy. I have often noticed that it is much less dangerous for her to go up steps than to go down them.

She walked along the street towards the place, a few blocks along, where I knew there was a store. I gloated over the houses on the street as she passed them, fondling them, placing them in order: red brick houses, double houses mostly, like the one that the room is in, with twin

wooden porches. The houses near the old place had been bigger. I had been on this street before, of course (it was not far from the old place), but now I could regard this street for the first time as mine, as part of the new territory through which I could trace out pathways and my own familiar routes. These trees were mine. This sidewalk was mine. When the snow melted and the trees blossomed, the damp earth and the new leaves and the spring water running in the gutters would be mine.

She turned on to a main street with cars moving on it and walked a block and turned and walked two more blocks until she reached the store. There had been another store nearer to the old place. I had never been in this particular store.

She went in the glass doors and through the turnstile. Then she hesitated: she did not know whether to take a pushcart or a wire basket. She felt that the pushcarts are easier, wire baskets are heavy to carry; but I said she wouldn't be buying that much and pushcarts get in the way and slow things up so she finally took a basket.

I always have to watch how much she spends. She would like to buy steak and mushrooms, of course, and olives and pies and pork roasts. Her old habits are hard to break. But I insist that she get things that are cheap and nourishing. It is, after all, the middle of the month, and the government cheque will not come for some time. After the rent has been paid there is not a great quantity of money left for other things. I must remember to have her make out a change-of-address card. She dislikes wieners but I made her buy a package of six. They have a lot of protein for the money. She got bread, and butter (I draw the line at margarine) and a quart of milk and some packaged soups, they are nice on a cold day, and some tea and eggs and several small tins of baked beans. She wanted some ice cream but I told her to get a package of frozen peas instead.

The check-out girl was rude to her simply because some of the things got mixed up with those of the woman ahead. Also I suspect she would have tried to short-change if she had dared. I wonder if it is worthwhile walking the extra distance to the old store?

She carried the parcel back easily enough and put the milk and the eggs and the frozen peas into the refrigerator, which is in the ground-floor hallway. The refrigerator has a peculiar odour. Perhaps the landlord

should be told to clean it. She then went upstairs and got some water from the bathroom and made herself a cup of coffee on the one-burner hotplate (the coffee came in the suitcase along with the sugar and the salt and the pepper) and ate some bread and butter. While she was eating, someone went into the bathroom; not the old man this time, but a woman. She must talk to herself; at any rate I distinguished two voices, one high and querulous, the other an urgent whisper: most curious. The walls are thin but I could not quite hear what she was saying.

When the footsteps had gone out she took the cup and spoon into the bathroom and washed them in the basin. Then she lay down and had a nap. I felt she deserved it after all the walking she had done. It was suppertime when she woke up. She opened one of the cans of beans. When the cheque comes she must buy a new can-opener.

After I finish this I will do a little reading in the Bible (the lighting in this room is better than I would have expected) and then she will go to bed. Note: tomorrow she must take a bath.

WEDNESDAY

This appears to be a daily occurrence. At nine o'clock exactly I was again awakened by the old man limping into the bathroom. He has a most rending cough. It sounds as though he is vomiting. Perhaps it would be possible for her to change the position of the bed so that her head is farther away from the wall. But when I consider the size and shape of the room I can see that there is only one place for it. Really it is annoying. Somehow when she coughs herself it is quite different from listening to someone else cough. If he keeps on coughing like that he will soon cough up everything inside him. I suppose I should feel sorry. Again this morning he stayed in the bathroom for half an hour.

Later, when she had got up and put on the clothes, she went downstairs to get the milk from the refrigerator. The old man had arranged the letters on the hall table: one letter in each corner of the table, and one in the centre. I must remember to have her fill out a change-of-address card.

Several times during the morning the woman with the two voices came into the bathroom. She seemed to be emptying pails or saucepans of water into the basin. Again I could hear the high voice and the harsh

whisper. Talking to oneself is a bad habit. When she went in to wash the cup and plate after lunch, she found a potato peeling caught in the drain.

Later in the afternoon I told her that she must take a bath. She would like to have avoided it because the bathroom tends to be chilly, but I keep telling her that cleanliness and good health necessarily go together. She locked the door and I had her kneel beside the bathtub so that I could inspect it thoroughly. I found a small hair, and some lint around the drain.

At the old place there was only one other person who used the same bathroom, a working girl who used to wash her stockings and leave them on the towel-rack. There is something repugnant about sharing the bathroom with other people. She always feels that the toilet seat is warmer than it ought to be, and I must say that I find even the thought of brushing one's teeth in the same basin used by total strangers disagreeable. I told her that someday soon she would have a bathroom of her own again, but I think she did not believe me. I must have her get a fresh bottle of antiseptic: the present one is almost empty.

The water was hot and she had a pleasant bath, though it was not as leisurely as it might have been. There were anxious footsteps walking outside the door, several times. It would certainly help if the landlord would install another bathroom; perhaps there is space for one in the basement.

Of course I had her clean the bathtub thoroughly after using it. The landlord has provided a sponge for this purpose, as well as a can of cleanser, which indicates that he, at least, has the right idea. Today also she washed out the underwear and hung it over the electric heater to dry.

THURSDAY

This morning it rained, which, I can see from the window, has melted the snow in the backyard considerably. If it continues warm she will have to start keeping the butter in the refrigerator; thus far the cupboard has been quite cool enough for it.

The old man is becoming intolerable. I am beginning to sense a certain aggressiveness about his activities in the bathroom. I feel that he does not want her in this house: he is trying to make her leave. This time he gargled, making a most repulsive sound. He must be discouraged; he

must be made to understand that I cannot put up with it for long. She needs her sleep and must have peace. I am sure it would be possible for him to do that sort of thing in his own room, out of earshot.

I had her leave a note for the landlord about the smell in the refrigerator, but by suppertime, although the note was gone from the table, the refrigerator had still not been cleaned. Some people are quite difficult.

The woman with two voices continues to be active. Today she had a bath. I am beginning to think that she is actually two people, there was such a lot of splashing in the tub; but I can distinguish only one set of footsteps going in and coming out. The whispering voice becomes more violent, almost hysterical. The other voice remains formless.

The food supply is running low. Today she finished the frozen peas and the milk. Soon she will have to go to the store again, but I hope that it will be on a day when it is not raining. The overshoes are none too solid, and I agree with her that wet feet are unpleasant as well as being bad for the health.

FRIDAY

She passed the old man on the stairs today. After his nine o'clock ritual, an even nastier one than usual this morning, he had the gall to smile, as though he is not even aware that I live next to the bathroom (although he must have heard her walking down the hall). There was something malevolent beneath the innocence of his smile. I told her not to smile back: she frowned and closed her mouth more tightly. He must not be encouraged to think that he can continue to get away with it.

Today I found a piece of cooked macaroni stuck in the drain. That is the doing of the woman with two voices. Perhaps she is a foreigner. Whatever she is, she is obviously not a neat person.

SATURDAY

Today she went to the store again, before lunch. I thought she could do without the scarf, as the sun was out. The streets are almost clear of snow now but there will doubtless be another storm before spring. As she walked I thought about the old man. Clearly something must be done soon. I cannot relay a message through the landlord: he is evidently untrustworthy. The refrigerator still has not been cleaned. If she begins to

keep the butter in the refrigerator I know it will pick up the smell. The windowsill may be cool enough.

She bought more milk and another package of wieners, and a tin of tunafish for variety (although the latter was quite expensive). She bought also a quarter of a pound of cheese and a package of brown rice. One must regulate one's vitamins. When the cheque comes she will be able to get some oranges. This time she went through a different check-out counter and there was no trouble.

I thought that it would not do to talk to him in person. He would only take offence, or pretend that he did now know she was being awakened, or that no one had any right to question what he did in the bathroom. He will have some evasive answer and will continue to behave in the same way every morning. I kept thinking about the time: he is always so punctual. I wonder what would happen if his pattern were to be interrupted? Everyone else in the house seems to regard the half hour between nine and nine-thirty as his; at least, no one is ever in the bathroom just before nine. Certainly it would let him know that I know, and that it will be difficult for him to continue. He will not be allowed to drive her out.

When she was going up the steps I thought I saw him looking out from behind the Venetian blind in the front window. Is he trying to keep track of her movements?

This afternoon I decided that I had to know about the woman with two voices. She went into the bathroom about mid-afternoon, and there were loud splashing noises. I strained, trying to tell the separate voices apart, but they seemed to overlap. I told her that she had to wait behind the door and open it quickly as soon as she heard the key being turned in the bathroom lock. She managed to time it just right. I was able to confront the woman as she was coming out. I know now that there are two women. The one that whispers is an old lady, very thin, with small dark eyes that are like holes in her head. She was wrapped in a blanket and was being carried by the other woman; her legs and her crooked bare feet dangled from the blanket. When she saw me she nodded and grinned. The other woman is heavy set and muscular, with a round vacuous face. She stood in the doorway and stared until the old woman said something to her in a sharp whisper and prodded her with a twisted hand. Then she turned and carried the old woman down the hall, plod-

ding on her thick feet, replying in a high whine that had no words in it all. The old woman's head looked over her shoulder, grinning, until they disappeared around the corner of the hall.

I told her to close the door. She was upset so I let her lie down for a short rest. I will never allow her to live like that.

After supper I thought about the old man again. I had her sit up later than usual so that I could listen for the clock of the church on the corner strike the hour. I set the alarm exactly.

SUNDAY

The alarm went off at twenty minutes to nine. I had allowed for the usual five to ten minutes that it takes to urge her out of bed. She put on the dressing gown and the slippers that I had her leave on the chair, ready, the night before, and shut the window and collected the things together: soap, toothbrush, bath towel, nail brush, Notebook, antiseptic bottle, room key, and the clock. At ten minutes to nine she went out of the room, locking the door, and went into the bathroom and turned the key carefully in the lock. She cleaned the bathtub and disinfected it and ran the bathwater till the tub was quite full. I thought how pleasant it was that the sound of running water drowned out all the noises from the rest of the house. It is a true luxury to make noises that the outside people have to listen to while being unable to hear any that they may make in return. I thought, this bathroom is mine now. It is my territory; I can go into it and out of it whenever I please. It is the only place where I am safe.

She placed the clock and the Notebook on the floor and lay back in the warm water. I told her not to be disturbed.

At nine o'clock exactly I heard his limping steps coming down the hall; she smiled. The footsteps paused outside the door, shuffled hesitantly, then began to pace back and forth. The clock ticked. I told her to make some splashing noises. At twenty minutes past nine the footsteps began to jig up and down impatiently outside. Then he knocked on the door. I told her not to say anything; she put her hand over her mouth to keep from laughing out loud.

The knocking increased to a pounding. He was hammering on the door with both fists. "Let me in," he shouted, pleading. His voice was

frantic. I pictured his thin legs in the striped pyjamas, and the bathrobe and the maroon slippers.

At nine-thirty the pounding stopped. He made a choking noise, an inarticulate sound of rage and despair, and the footsteps limped away down the hall. Urgently, almost running. She smiled and swirled some of the water over her stomach. She keeps her figure remarkably well.

The footsteps went down two or three stairs; then there was a crash and a thumping sound and a wail of pain that faded into silence. I could hear other doors being opened.

She made a movement to get out of the bathtub, but I told her to stay where she was. She lay in the bathtub, staring at her pink toes floating on the surface of the water, while I listened. I knew the bathroom door was securely locked.

For the time being I have won.

JAMES BALDWIN

Previous Condition

Born in 1924 in Harlem, the oldest of a large family, James Baldwin started writing as a boy, usually on paper bags because money was so scarce. Unusually bright, he attended DeWitt Clinton High in the Bronx and after graduation laid railroad track and worked as an elevator operator and a waiter while living and writing in Greenwich Village. He first gained attention with two nonfiction pieces — "The Harlem Ghetto: Winter 1948," a controversial essay about the racial scene, published in the February 1948 issue of *Commentary,* and a scathing review of *Raintree County* in *New Leader* in 1948, written before but published after author Ross Lockridge's suicide. His first published piece of fiction, the lush and elegant "Previous Condition," appeared in the October 1948 issue of *Commentary* with this note: "It heralds, we think, an important new talent on the literary scene." A month after the story appeared, Baldwin moved to Paris, where he spent most of the rest of his life.

I WOKE UP shaking, alone in my room. I was clammy cold with sweat; under me the sheet and the mattress were soaked. The sheet was gray and twisted like a rope. I breathed like I had been running.

I couldn't move for the longest while. I just lay on my back, spread-eagled, looking up at the ceiling, listening to the sounds of people getting up in other parts of the house, alarm clocks ringing and water splashing and doors opening and shutting and feet on the stairs. I could tell when people left for work: the hall-door way downstairs whined and shuffled as it opened and gave a funny kind of double slam as it closed. One thud and then a louder thud and then a little final click. While the

26

door was open I could hear the street sounds too, horses' hoofs and delivery wagons and people in the streets and big trucks and motor cars screaming on the asphalt.

I had been dreaming. At night I dreamt and woke up in the morning trembling, but not remembering the dream, except that in the dream I had been running. I could not remember when the dream — or dreams — had started; it had been long ago. For long periods maybe, I would have no dreams at all. And then they would come back, every night, I would try not to go to bed, I would go to sleep frightened and wake up frightened and have another day to get through with the nightmare at my shoulder. Now I was back from Chicago, busted, living off my friends in a dirty furnished room downtown. The show I had been with had folded in Chicago. It hadn't been much of a part — or much of a show either, to tell the truth. I played a kind of intellectual Uncle Tom, a young college student working for his race. The playwright had wanted to prove he was a liberal, I guess. But, as I say, the show had folded and here I was, back in New York and hating it. I knew that I should be getting another job, making the rounds, pounding the pavement. But I didn't. I couldn't face it. It was summer. I seemed to be fagged out. And every day I hated myself more. Acting's a rough life, even if you're white. I'm not tall and I'm not good looking and I can't sing or dance and I'm not white; so even at the best of times I wasn't in much demand.

THE room I lived in was heavy ceilinged, perfectly square, with walls the color of chipped dry blood. Jules Weissman, a Jewboy, had got the room for me. It's a room to sleep in, he said, or maybe to die in but God knows it wasn't meant to live in. Perhaps because the room was so hideous it had a fantastic array of light fixtures: one on the ceiling, one on the left wall, two on the right wall, and a lamp on the table beside my bed. My bed was in front of the window through which nothing ever blew but dust. It was a furnished room and they'd thrown enough stuff in it to furnish three rooms its size. Two easy chairs and a desk, the bed, the table, a straight-backed chair, a bookcase, a cardboard wardrobe; and my books and my suitcase, both unpacked; and my dirty clothes flung in a corner. It was the kind of room that defeated you. It had a fireplace, too, and a heavy marble mantelpiece and a great gray mirror above the

mantelpiece. It was hard to see anything in the mirror very clearly — which was perhaps just as well — and it would have been worth your life to have started a fire in the fireplace.

Well, you won't have to stay here long, Jules told me the night I came. Jules smuggled me in, sort of, after dark, when everyone had gone to bed.

Christ, I hope not.

I'll be moving to a big place soon, Jules said. You can move in with me. He turned all the lights on. Think it'll be all right for a while? He sounded apologetic, as though he had designed the room himself.

Oh, sure. D'you think I'll have any trouble?

I don't think so. The rent's paid. She can't put you out.

I didn't say anything to that.

Sort of stay undercover, Jules said. You know.

Roger, I said.

I had been living there for three days, timing it so I left after everyone else had gone, coming back late at night when everyone else was asleep. But I knew it wouldn't work. A couple of the tenants had seen me on the stairs, a woman had surprised me coming out of the john. Every morning I waited for the landlady to come banging on the door. I didn't know what would happen. It might be all right. It might not be. But the waiting was getting me.

The sweat on my body was turning cold. Downstairs a radio was tuned in to the Breakfast Symphony. They were playing Beethoven. I sat up and lit a cigarette. Peter, I said, don't let them scare you to death. You're a man, too. I listened to Ludwig and I watched the smoke rise to the dirty ceiling. Under Ludwig's drums and horns I listened to hear footsteps on the stairs.

I'd done a lot of traveling in my time. I'd knocked about through St. Louis, Frisco, Seattle, Detroit, New Orleans, worked at just about everything. I'd run away from my old lady when I was about sixteen. She'd never been able to handle me. You'll never be nothin' *but* a bum, she'd say. We lived in an old shack in a town in New Jersey in the nigger part of town, the kind of houses colored people live in all over the US. I hated my mother for living there. I hated all the people in my neighborhood. They went to church and they got drunk. They were nice to the

white people. When the landlord came around they paid him and took his crap.

THE first time I was ever called nigger I was seven years old. It was a little white girl with long black curls. I used to leave the front of my house and go wandering by myself through town. This little girl was playing ball alone and as I passed her the ball rolled out of her hands into the gutter.

I threw it back to her.

Let's play catch, I said.

But she held the ball and made a face at me.

My mother don't let me play with niggers, she told me.

I did not know what the word meant. But my skin grew warm. I stuck my tongue out at her.

I don't care. Keep your old ball. I started down the street.

She screamed after me: Nigger, nigger, nigger!

I screamed back: Your mother was a nigger!

I asked my mother what a nigger was.

Who called you that?

I heard somebody say it.

Who?

Just somebody.

Go wash your face, she said. You dirty as sin. Your supper's on the table.

I went to the bathroom and splashed water on my face and wiped my face and hands on the towel.

You call that clean? my mother cried. Come here, boy!

She dragged me back to the bathroom and began to soap my face and neck.

You run around dirty like you do all the time, everybody'll call you a little nigger, you hear? She rinsed my face and looked at my hands and dried me. Now. Go on and eat your supper.

I didn't say anything. I went to the kitchen and sat down at the table. I remember I wanted to cry. My mother sat down across from me.

Mama, I said. She looked at me. I started to cry.

She came around to my side of the table and took me in her arms.

Baby, don't fret. Next time somebody calls you nigger you tell them you'd rather be your color than be lowdown and nasty like some white folks is.

We formed gangs when I was older, my friends and I. We met white boys and their friends on the opposite sides of fences and we threw rocks and tin cans at each other.

I'd come home bleeding. My mother would slap me and scold me and cry.

Boy, you wanna get killed? You wanna end up like your father?

My father was a bum and I had never seen him. I was named for him: Peter.

I was always in trouble; truant officers, welfare workers, everybody else in town.

You ain't never gonna be nothin' *but* a bum, my mother said.

By and by older kids I knew finished school and got jobs and got married and settled down. They were going to settle down and bring more black babies into the world and pay the same rents for the same old shacks and it would go on and on —

When I was sixteen I ran away. I left a note and told Mama not to worry, I'd come back one day and I'd be all right. But when I was twenty-two she died. I came back and put my mother in the ground. Everything was like it had been. Our house had not been painted and the porch floor sagged and there was somebody's raincoat stuffed in the broken window. Another family was moving in.

Their furniture was stacked along the walls and their children were running through the house and laughing and somebody was frying pork chops in the kitchen. The oldest boy was tacking up a mirror.

LAST year Ida took me driving in her big car and we passed through a couple of towns upstate. We passed some crumbling houses on the left. The clothes on the line were flying in the wind.

Are people living there? asked Ida.

Just darkies, I said.

Ida passed the car ahead, banging angrily on the horn. D'you know you're becoming paranoiac, Peter?

All right. All right. I know a lot of white people are starving too.

You're damn right they are. I know a little about poverty myself.

Ida had come from the kind of family called shanty Irish. She was raised in Boston. She's a very beautiful woman who married young and married for money — so now I can afford to support attractive young men, she'd giggle. Her husband was a ballet dancer who was forever on the road. Ida suspected that he went with boys. Not that I give a damn, she said, as long as he leaves me alone. When we met last year she was thirty and I was twenty-five. We had a pretty stormy relationship but we stuck. Whenever I got to town I called her, whenever I was stranded out of town I'd let her know. We never let it get too serious. She went her way and I went mine.

In all this running around I'd learned a few things. Like a prizefighter learns to take a blow or a dancer learns to fall, I'd learned how to get by. I'd learned never to be belligerent with policemen, for instance. No matter who was right, I was certain to be wrong. What might be accepted as just good old American independence in someone else would be insufferable arrogance in me. After the first few times I realized that I had to play smart, to act out the role I was expected to play. I only had one head and it was too easy to get it broken. When I faced a policeman I acted like I didn't know a thing. I let my jaw drop and I let my eyes get big. I didn't give him any smart answers, none of the crap about my rights. I figured out what answers he wanted and I gave them to him. I never let him think he wasn't king. If it was more than routine, if I was picked up on suspicion of robbery or murder in the neighborhood I looked as humble as I could and kept my mouth shut and prayed. I took a couple of beatings but I stayed out of prison and I stayed off chain gangs. That was also due to luck, Ida pointed out once. Maybe it would've been better for you if you'd been a little less lucky. Worse things have happened than chain gangs. Some of them have happened to you.

There was something in her voice. What are you talking about? I asked.

Don't lose your temper. I said maybe.

You mean you think I'm a coward?

I didn't say that, Peter.

But you meant that. Didn't you?

No. I didn't mean that. I didn't mean anything. Let's not fight.

There are times and places when a Negro can use his color like a

shield. He can trade on the subterranean Anglo-Saxon guilt and get what he wants that way; or some of what he wants. He can trade on his nuisance value, his value as forbidden fruit; he can use it like a knife, he can twist it and get his vengeance that way. I knew these things long before I realized that I knew them and in the beginning I used them, not knowing what I was doing. Then when I began to see it, I felt betrayed. I felt beaten as a person. I had no honest place to stand.

This was the year before I met Ida. I'd been acting in stock companies and little theaters; sometimes fairly good parts. People were nice to me. They told me I had talent. They said it sadly, as though they were thinking, What a pity, he'll never get anywhere. I had got to the point where I resented praise and I resented pity and I wondered what people were thinking when they shook my hand. In New York I met some pretty fine people; easygoing, hard-drinking, flotsam and jetsam; and they liked me; and I wondered if I trusted them; if I was able any longer to trust anybody. Not on top, where all the world could see, but underneath where everybody lives.

SOON I would have to get up. I listened to Ludwig. He shook the little room like the footsteps of a giant marching miles away. On summer evenings (and maybe we would go this summer) Jules and Ida and I would go up to the Stadium and sit beneath the pillars on the cold stone steps. There it seemed to me the sky was far away; and I was not myself, I was high and lifted up. We never talked, the three of us. We sat and watched the blue smoke curl in the air and watched the orange tips of cigarettes. Every once in a while the boys who sold popcorn and soda pop and ice cream climbed the steep steps chattering; and Ida shifted slightly and touched her blue-black hair; and Jules scowled. I sat with my knee up, watching the lighted half-moon below, the black-coated, straining conductor, the faceless men beneath him moving together in a rhythm like the sea. There were pauses in the music for the rushing, calling, halting piano. Everything would stop except the climbing soloist; he would reach a height and everything would join him, the violins first and then the horns; and then the deep blue bass and the flute and the bitter trampling drums; beating, beating and mounting together and stopping with a crash like daybreak. When I first heard the *Messiah* I

was alone; my blood bubbled like fire and wine; I cried; like an infant crying for its mother's milk; or a sinner running to meet Jesus.

Now below the music I heard footsteps on the stairs. I put out my cigarette. My heart was beating so hard I thought it would tear my chest apart. Someone knocked on the door.

I thought: Don't answer. Maybe she'll go away.

But the knocking came again, harder this time.

Just a minute, I said. I sat on the edge of the bed and put on my bathrobe. I was trembling like a fool. For Christ's sake, Peter, you've been through this before. What's the worst thing that can happen? You won't have a room. The world's full of rooms.

When I opened the door the landlady stood there, red-and-white-faced and hysterical.

Who are you? I didn't rent this room to you.

My mouth was dry. I started to say something.

I can't have no colored people here, she said. All my tenants are complainin'. Women afraid to come home nights.

They ain't gotta be afraid of me, I said. I couldn't get my voice up; it rasped and rattled in my throat; and I began to be angry. I wanted to kill her. My friend rented this room for me, I said.

Well, I'm sorry, he didn't have no right to do that, I don't have nothin' against you, but you gotta get out.

Her glasses blinked, opaque in the light on the landing. She was frightened to death. She was afraid of me but she was more afraid of losing her tenants. Her face was mottled with rage and fear, her breath came rushed and little bits of spittle gathered at the edges of her mouth; her breath smelled bad, like rotting hamburger on a July day.

You can't put me out, I said. This room was rented in my name. I started to close the door, as though the matter was finished: I live here, see, this is my room, you can't put me out.

You get outa my house! she screamed. I got the right to know who's in my house! This is a white neighborhood, I don't rent to colored people. Why don't you go on uptown, like you belong?

I can't stand niggers, I told her. I started to close the door again but she moved and stuck her foot in the way. I wanted to kill her. I watched her stupid, wrinkled frightened white face and I wanted to take a club,

a hatchet, and bring it down with all my weight, splitting her skull down the middle where she parted her iron-grey hair.

Get out of the door, I said. I want to get dressed.

But I knew that she had won, that I was already on my way. We stared at each other. Neither of us moved. From her came an emanation of fear and fury and something else. You maggot-eaten bitch, I thought. I said evilly, You wanna come in and watch me? Her face didn't change, she didn't take her foot away. My skin prickled, tiny hot needles punctured my flesh. I was aware of my body under the bathrobe; and it was as though I had done something wrong, something monstrous, years ago, which no one had forgotten and for which I would be killed.

If you don't get out, she said, I'll get a policeman to put you out.

I grabbed the door to keep from touching her. All right. All right. You can have the goddamn room. Now get out and let me dress.

She turned away. I slammed the door. I heard her going down the stairs. I threw stuff into my suitcase. I tried to take as long as possible but I cut myself while shaving because I was afraid she would come back upstairs with a policeman.

JULES was making coffee when I walked in.

Good morning, good morning! What happened to you?

No room at the inn, I said. Pour a cup of coffee for the notorious son of man. I sat down and dropped my suitcase on the floor.

Jules looked at me. Oh. Well. Coffee coming up.

He got out the coffee cups. I lit a cigarette and sat there. I couldn't think of anything to say. I knew that Jules felt bad and I wanted to tell him that it wasn't his fault.

He pushed coffee in front of me and sugar and cream.

Cheer up, baby. The world's wide and life — life, she is very long.

Shut up. I don't want to hear any of your bad philosophy.

Sorry.

I mean, let's not talk about the good, the true, and the beautiful.

All right. But don't sit there holding on to your table manners. Scream if you want to.

Screaming won't do any good. Besides I'm a big boy now.

I stirred my coffee. Did you give her a fight? Jules asked.

I shook my head. No.

Why the hell not?

I shrugged; a little ashamed now. I couldn't have won it. What the hell.

You might have won it. You might have given her a couple of bad moments.

Goddamit to hell, I'm sick of it. Can't I get a place to sleep without dragging it through the courts? I'm goddamn tired of battling every Tom, Dick, and Harry for what everybody else takes for granted. I'm tired, man, tired! Have you ever been sick to death of something? Well, I'm sick to death. And I'm scared. I've been fighting so goddamn long I'm not a person any more. I'm not Booker T. Washington. I've got no vision of emancipating anybody. I want to emancipate myself. If this goes on much longer, they'll send me to Bellevue, I'll blow my top, I'll break somebody's head. I'm not worried about that miserable little room. I'm worried about what's happening to me, *to me,* inside. I don't walk the streets, I crawl. I've never been like this before. Now when I go to a strange place I wonder what will happen, will I be accepted, if I'm accepted, can I accept? —

Take it easy, Jules said.

Jules, I'm beaten.

I don't think you are. Drink your coffee.

Oh, I cried, I know you think I'm making it dramatic, that I'm paranoiac and just inventing trouble! Maybe I think so sometimes, how can I tell? You get so used to being hit you find you're always waiting for it. Oh, I know, you're Jewish, you get kicked around, too, but you can walk into a bar and nobody *knows* you're Jewish and if you go looking for a job you'll get a better job than mine! How can I say what it feels like? I don't know. I know everybody's in trouble and nothing is easy, but how can I explain to you what it feels like to be black? when I don't understand it and don't want to and spend all my time trying to forget it? I don't want to hate anybody — but now maybe, I can't love anybody either — are we friends? can we be really friends?

We're friends, Jules said, don't worry about it. He scowled. If I wasn't Jewish I'd ask you why you don't live in Harlem. I looked at him. He raised his hand and smiled — But I'm Jewish, so I didn't ask you. Ah Peter, he said, I can't help you — take a walk, get drunk, we're all in this together.

I stood up. I'll be around later. I'm sorry.

Don't be sorry. I'll leave my door open. Bunk here for a while.

Thanks, I said.

I felt that I was drowning; that hatred had corrupted me like cancer in the bone.

I SAW Ida for dinner. We met in a restaurant in the Village, an Italian place in a gloomy cellar with candles on the tables.

It was not a busy night, for which I was grateful. When I came in there were only two other couples on the other side of the room. No one looked at me. I sat down in a corner booth and ordered a Scotch old-fashioned. Ida was late and I had three of them before she came.

She was very fine in black, a high-necked dress with a pearl choker; and her hair was combed page-boy style, falling just below her ears.

You look real sweet, baby.

Thank you. It took fifteen extra minutes but I hoped it would be worth it.

It was worth it. What're you drinking?

Oh — what're you drinking?

Old-fashioneds.

She sniffed and looked at me. How many?

I laughed. Three.

Well, she said, I suppose you had to do something. The waiter came over. We decided on one Manhattan and one lasagna and one spaghetti with clam sauce and another old-fashioned for me.

Did you have a constructive day, sweetheart? Find a job?

Not today, I said. I lit her cigarette. Metro offered me a fortune to come to the coast and do the lead in *Native Son* but I turned it down. Type casting, you know. It's so difficult to find a decent part.

Well, if they don't come up with a decent offer soon tell them you'll go back to Selznick. *He'll* find you a part with guts — the very *idea* of offering you *Native Son*! I wouldn't stand for it.

You ain't gotta tell me. I told them if they didn't find me a decent script in two weeks I was through, that's all.

Now that's talking, Peter my lad.

The drinks came and we sat in silence for a minute or two. I finished

half of my drink at a swallow and played with the toothpicks on the table. I felt Ida watching me.

Peter, you're going to be awfully drunk.

Honeychile, the first thing a southern gentleman learns is how to hold his liquor.

That myth is older than the rock of ages. And anyway you come from Jersey.

I finished my drink and snarled at her: that's just as good as the South.

Across the table from me I could see that she was readying herself for trouble: her mouth tightened slightly, setting her chin so that the faint cleft showed: What happened to you today?

I resented her concern; I resented my need. Nothing worth talking about, I muttered, just a mood.

And I tried to smile at her, to wipe away the bitterness.

Now I know something's the matter. Please tell me.

It sounded trivial as hell: You know the room Jules found for me? Well, the landlady kicked me out of it today.

God save the American republic, Ida said. D'you want to waste some of my husband's money? We can sue her.

Forget it. I'll end up with lawsuits in every state in the union.

Still, as a gesture —

The devil with the gesture. I'll get by.

The food came. I didn't want to eat. The first mouthful hit my belly like a gong. Ida began cutting up lasagna.

Peter, she said, try not to feel so badly. We're all in this together the whole world. Don't let it throw you. What can't be helped you have to learn to live with.

That's easy for you to say, I told her.

She looked at me quickly and looked away. I'm not pretending that it's easy to do, she said.

I didn't believe that she could really understand it; and there was nothing I could say. I sat like a child being scolded, looking down at my plate, not eating, not saying anything. I wanted her to stop talking, to stop being intelligent about it, to stop being calm and grown-up about it; good Lord, none of us has ever grown up, we never will.

It's no better anywhere else, she was saying. In all of Europe there's

famine and disease, in France and England they hate the Jews —
nothing's going to change, baby, people are too empty-headed, too
empty-hearted — it's always been like that, people always try to destroy
what they don't understand — and they hate almost everything because
they understand so little —

I BEGAN to sweat in my side of the booth. I wanted to stop her voice. I
wanted her to eat and be quiet and leave me alone. I looked around for
the waiter so I could order another drink. But he was on the far side of
the restaurant, waiting on some people who had just come in; a lot of
people had come in since we had been sitting there.

Peter, Ida said, Peter please don't look like that.

I grinned: the painted grin of the professional clown. Don't worry,
baby, I'm all right. I know what I'm going to do. I'm gonna go back to
my people where I belong and find me a nice, black nigger wench and
raise me a flock of babies.

Ida had an old maternal trick; the grin tricked her into using it now.
She raised her fork and rapped me with it across the knuckles. Now, stop
that. You're too old for that.

I screamed and stood up screaming and knocked the candle over:
Don't *do* that, you bitch, don't *ever* do that!

She grabbed the candle and set it up and glared at me. Her face had
turned perfectly white: Sit down! Sit *down!*

I fell back into my seat. My stomach felt like water. Everyone was
looking at us. I turned cold, seeing what they were seeing: a black boy
and a white woman, alone together. I knew it would take nothing to
have them at my throat.

I'm sorry, I muttered, I'm sorry, I'm sorry.

The waiter was at my elbow. Is everything all right, Miss?

Yes, quite, thank you. She sounded like a princess dismissing a slave.
I didn't look up. The shadow of the waiter moved away from me.

Baby, Ida said, forgive me, please forgive me.

I stared at the table cloth. She put her hand on mine, brightness and
blackness.

Let's go, I said, I'm terribly sorry.

She motioned for the check. When it came she handed the waiter a
ten dollar bill without looking. She picked up her bag.

Shall we go to a nightclub or a movie or something?

No, honey, not tonight. I looked at her. I'm tired, I think I'll go on over to Jules' place. I'm gonna sleep on his floor for a while. Don't worry about me. I'm all right.

She looked at me steadily. She said: I'll come see you tomorrow?

Yes, baby, please.

The waiter brought the change and she tipped him. We stood up; as we passed the tables (not looking at the people) the ground under me seemed falling, the doorway seemed impossibly far away. All my muscles tensed; I seemed ready to spring; I was waiting for the blow.

I put my hands in my pockets and we walked to the end of the block. The lights were green and red, the lights from the theater across the street exploded blue and yellow, off and on.

Peter?

Yes?

I'll see you tomorrow?

Yeah. Come by Jules'. I'll wait for you.

Goodnight darling.

Goodnight.

I started to walk away. I felt her eyes on my back. I kicked a bottle-top on the sidewalk.

God save the American republic.

I DROPPED into the subway and got on an uptown train, not knowing where it was going and not caring. Anonymous, islanded people surrounded me, behind newspapers, behind make-up, fat, fleshy masks and flat eyes. I watched the empty faces. (No one looked at me.) I looked at the ads, unreal women and pink-cheeked men selling cigarettes, candy, shaving cream, night gowns, chewing gum, movies, sex; sex without organs, drier than sand and more secret than death. The train stopped. A white boy and a white girl got on. She was nice, short, svelte. Nice legs. She was hanging on his arm. He was the football type, blonde, ruddy. They were dressed in summer clothes. The wind from the doors blew her print dress. She squealed, holding the dress at the knees and giggled and looked at him. He said something I didn't catch and she looked at me and the smile died. She stood so that she faced him and had her back to me. I looked back at the ads. Then I hated them. I wanted to do

something to make them hurt, something that would crack the pink-cheeked mask. The white boy and I did not look at each other again. They got off at the next stop.

I wanted to keep on drinking. I got off in Harlem and went to a rundown bar on Seventh Avenue. My people, my people. Sharpies stood on the corner, waiting. Women in summer dresses pranced by on wavering heels. Click clack. Click clack. There were white mounted policemen in the streets. On every block there was another policeman on foot. I saw a black cop.

God save the American republic.

The juke box was letting loose with "Hamps' Boogie." The place was jumping. I walked over to the man.

Rye, I said.

I was standing next to somebody's grandmother. Hello papa. What you puttin' down?

Baby, you can't pick it up, I told her. My rye came and I drank.

Nigger, she said, you must think you's somebody.

I didn't answer. She turned away, back to her beer, keeping time to the juke box, her face sullen and heavy and aggrieved. I watched her out of the side of my eye. She had been good looking once, pretty even, before she hit the bottle and started crawling into too many beds. She was flabby now, flesh heaved all over in her thin dress. I wondered what she'd be like in bed; then I realized that I was a little excited by her, I laughed and set my glass down.

The same, I said. And a beer chaser.

The juke box was playing something else now, something brassy and commercial which I didn't like. I kept on drinking, listening to the voices of my people, watching the faces of my people. (God pity us, the terrified republic.) Now I was sorry to have angered the woman who still sat next to me, now deep in conversation with another, younger woman. I longed for some opening, some sign, something to make me part of the life around me. But there was nothing except my color. A white outsider coming in would have seen a young Negro drinking in a Negro bar, perfectly in his element, in his place, as the saying goes. But the people here knew differently, as I did. I didn't seem to have a place.

So I kept on drinking by myself, saying to myself after each drink, Now I'll go. But I was afraid; I didn't want to sleep on Jules' floor; I

didn't want to go to sleep. I kept on drinking and listening to the juke box. They were playing Ella Fitzgerald, "Cow-Cow Boogie."

Let me buy you a drink, I said to the woman.

She looked at me, startled, suspicious, ready to blow her top.

On the level, I said. I tried to smile. Both of you.

I'll take a beer, the young one said.

I was shaking like a baby. I finished my drink.

Fine, I said. I turned to the bar.

Baby, said the old one, what's your story?

The man put three beers on the counter.

I got no story, Ma, I said.

The State of Grace

For most of his career Harold Brodkey's reputation rested on his short fiction — and the anticipation surrounding publication of his long-delayed novel, for years called *A Party of Animals*. The appearance of excerpts from the work-in-progress, finally published in 1991 as *The Runaway Soul*, helped keep Brodkey fresh in the minds of critics and readers, who applauded his first book, *First Love and Other Sorrows* (Dial Press, 1957). Eight of the nine short stories in that collection first appeared in the *New Yorker*. *Mademoiselle* published the ninth in July 1956, along with a brief sketch of Brodkey, which noted, "His first collection . . . was contracted for after only three of his stories had been published — and he's just twenty-five." The first of those three, "The State of Grace," appeared in the *New Yorker* on November 11, 1954.

THERE IS A certain shade of red brick — a dark, almost melodious red, sombre and riddled with blue — that is my childhood in St. Louis. Not the real childhood, but the false one that extends from the dawning of consciousness until the day that one leaves home for college. That one shade of red brick and green foliage is St. Louis in the summer (the winter is just a gray sky and a crowded school bus and the wet footprints on the brown linoleum floor at school), and that brick and a pale sky is spring. It's also loneliness and the queer, self-pitying wonder that children whose families are having catastrophes feel.

I can remember that brick best on the back of our apartment house; it was on all the apartment houses on that block, and also on the apartment house where Edward lived — Edward was a small boy I took care

42

of on the evenings when his parents went out. As I came up the street from school, past the boulevard and its ugliness (the vista of shoe-repair shops, dime stores, hairdressers', pet shops, the Tivoli Theatre, and the closed Piggly Wiggly, about to be converted into a Kroger's), past the place where I could see the Masonic Temple, built in the shape of some Egyptian relic, and the two huge concrete pedestals flanking the boulevard (what they supported I can't remember, but on both of them, in brown paint, was a large heart and the information that someone named Erica loved someone named Peter), past the post office, built in W.P.A. days of yellow brick and chrome, I hurried toward the moment when at last, on the other side, past the driveway of the garage of the Castlereagh Apartments, I would be at the place where the trees began, the apartment houses of dark-red brick, and the empty stillness.

In the middle of that stillness and red brick was my neighborhood, the terribly familiar place where I was more comfortably an exile than anywhere else. There were two locust trees that were beautiful to me — I think because they were small and I could encompass them (not only with my mind and heart but with my hands as well). Then came an apartment house of red brick (but not quite the true shade) where a boy I knew lived, and two amazingly handsome brothers, who were also strong and kind, but much older than I and totally uninterested in me. Then came an alley of black macadam and another vista, which I found shameful but drearily comfortable, of garages and ashpits and telephone poles and the backs of apartment houses — including ours — on one side, the backs of houses on the other. I knew many people in the apartments but none in the houses, and this was the ultimate proof, of course, to me of how miserably degraded I was and how far sunken beneath the surface of the sea. I was on the bottom, looking up through the waters, through the shifting bands of light — through, oh, innumerably more complexities than I could stand — at a sailboat driven by the wind, some boy who had a family and a home like other people.

I was thirteen, and six feet tall, and I weighed a hundred and twenty-five pounds. Though I fretted wildly about my looks (my ears stuck out and my hair was like wire), I also knew I was attractive; girls had smiled at me, but none whom I might love and certainly none of the seven or eight goddesses in the junior high school I attended. Starting in about second grade, I always had the highest grades — higher than anybody

who had ever attended the schools I went to — and I terrified my class-mates. What terrified them was that so far as they could see, it never took any effort; it was like legerdemain. I was never teased, I was never tormented; I was merely isolated. But I was known as "the walking en-cyclopedia," and the only way I could deal with this was to withdraw. Looking back, I'm almost certain I could have had friends if I'd made the right overtures, and that it was not my situation but my forbidding pride that kept them off; I'm not sure. I had very few clothes, and all that I had had been passed to me from an elder cousin. I never was able to wear what the other boys wore.

Our apartment was on the third floor. I usually walked up the back stairs, which were mounted outside the building in a steel framework. I preferred the back stairs — it was a form of rubbing at a hurt to make sure it was still there — because they were steep and ugly and had gar-bage cans on the landings and wash hanging out, while the front door opened off a court where rosebushes grew and the front stairs were made of some faintly yellow local marble that was cool and pleasant to the touch and to the eye. When I came to our back door, I would open the screen and call out to see if my mother was home. If she was not home, it usually meant that she was visiting my father, who had been dying in the hospital for four years and would linger two more before he would come to terms with death. As far as I know, that was the only sign of character he ever showed in his entire life, and I suppose it was consid-erable, but I hoped, and even sometimes prayed, that he would die — not only because I wouldn't have to visit the hospital again, where the white-walled rooms were filled with odors and sick old men (and a tan-gible fear that made me feel a falling away inside, like the plunge into the unconscious when the anesthetic is given), but because my mother might marry again and make us all rich and happy once more. She was still lovely then, still alight with the curious incandescence of physical beauty, and there was a man who had loved her for twenty years and who loved her yet and wanted to marry her. I wished so hard my father would die, but he just wouldn't. If my mother was home, I braced myself for unpleasantness, because she didn't like me to sit and read; she hated me to read. She wanted to drive me outdoors, where I would become an athlete and be like other boys and be popular. It filled her with rage when I ignored her advice and opened a book; once, she rushed up to

me, her face suffused with anger, took the book (I think it was "Pride and Prejudice"), and hurled it out the third-story window. At the time, I sat and tried to sneer, thinking she was half mad, with her exaggerated rage, and so foolish not to realize that I could be none of the things she thought I ought to be. But now I think — perhaps wistfully — that she was merely desperate, driven to extremes in her anxiety to save me. She felt — she knew, in fact — that there was going to come a moment when, like an acrobat, I would have to climb on her shoulders and on the shoulders of all the things she had done for me, and leap out into a life she couldn't imagine (and which I am leading now), and if she wanted to send me out wrapped in platitudes, in an athletic body, with a respect for money, it was because she thought that was the warmest covering.

But when I was thirteen, I only wondered how anyone so lovely could be so impossible. She somehow managed it so that I hated her far more than I loved her, even though in the moments before sleep I would think of her face, letting my memory begin with the curving gentleness of her eyelids and circle through all the subtle interplay of shadows and hollows and bones, and the half-remembered warmth of her chest, and it would seem to me that this vision of her, always standing in half light (as probably I had seen her once when I was younger, and sick, perhaps, though I don't really remember), was only as beautiful to me as the pattern in an immeasurably ancient and faded Persian rug. In the vision, as in the rug, I could trace the lines in and out and experience some unnamed pleasure, but it had almost no meaning, numbed as I was by the problems of being her son.

Being Jewish also disturbed me, because it meant I could never be one of the golden people — the blond athletes, with their easy charm. If my family had been well off, I might have felt otherwise, but I doubt it.

My mother had a cousin whom I called Aunt Rachel, and we used to go and see her three or four times a year. I hated it. She lived in what was called the Ghetto, which was a section of old houses in downtown St. Louis with tiny front porches and two doors, one to the upstairs and one to the downstairs. Most people lived in them only until they could move to something better; no one had ever liked living there. And because of that, the neighborhood had the quality of being blurred; the grass was never neat, the window frames were never painted, no one

cared about or loved the place. It was where the immigrants lived when they arrived by train from New York and before they could move up-town to the apartments near Delmar Boulevard, and eventually to the suburbs — to Clayton, Laclede, and Ladue. Aunt Rachel lived down-stairs. Her living room was very small and had dark-yellow wallpaper, which she never changed. She never cleaned it, either, because once I made a mark on it, to see if she would, and she didn't. The furniture was alive and frightening; it was like that part of the nightmare where it gets so bad that you decide to wake up. I always had to sit on it. It bulged in great curves of horsehair and mohair, and it was dark purple and maroon and dark green, and the room had no light in it anywhere. Somewhere on the other side of the old, threadbare satin draperies that had been bought out of an old house was fresh air and sunshine, but you'd never know it. It was as much like a peasant's hut as Aunt Rachel could man-age, buying furniture in cut-rate furniture stores. And always there were the smells — the smell of onion soup and garlic and beets. It was the only place where I was ever rude to my mother in public. It was always full of people whom I hardly ever knew, but who knew me, and I had to perform. My mother would say, "Tell the people what your last report card was," or "Recite them the poem that Miss Huntington liked so well." That was when the feeling of unreality was strongest. Looking back now, I think that what frightened me was their fierce urgency; I was to be rich and famous and make all their tribulations worth while. But I didn't want that responsibility. Anyway, if I were going to be what they wanted me to be, and if I had to be what I was, then it was too much to expect me to take them as they were. I had to go beyond them and despise them, but first I had to be with them — and it wasn't fair.

It was as if my eyelids had been propped open, and I had to see these things I didn't want to see. I felt as if I had taken part in something shameful, and therefore I wasn't a nice person. It was like my first sexual experiences: What if anyone knew? What if everyone found out? . . . How in hell could I ever be gallant and carefree?

I had read too many books by Englishmen and New Englanders to want to know anything but graceful things and erudite things and the look of white frame houses on green lawns. I could always console myself by thinking my brains would make me famous (brains were good for something, weren't they?), but then my children would have good child-

hoods — not me. I was irrevocably deprived, and it was the irrevocable-
ness that hurt, that finally drove me away from any sensible adjustment
with life to the position that dreams had to come true or there was no
point in living at all. If dreams came true, then I would have my childhood in one form or another, someday.

IF my mother was home when I came in from school, she might say
that Mrs. Leinberg had called and wanted me to baby-sit, and I would
be plunged into yet another of the dilemmas of those years. I had to
baby-sit to earn money to buy my lunch at school, and there were times,
considering the dilemma I faced at the Leinbergs', when I preferred not
eating, or eating very little, to baby-sitting. But there wasn't any choice;
Mother would have accepted for me, and made Mrs. Leinberg promise
not to stay out too late and deprive me of my sleep. She would have a
sandwich ready for me to eat, so that I could rush over in time to let Mr.
and Mrs. Leinberg go out to dinner. Anyway, I would eat my sandwich
reading a book, to get my own back, and then I would set out. As I
walked down the back stairs on my way to the Leinbergs', usually swinging on the railings by my arms to build up my muscles, I would think
forlornly of what it was to be me, and wish things were otherwise, and I
did not understand myself or my loneliness or the cruel deprivation the
vista down the alley meant.

There was a short cut across the back yards to the apartment house
where the Leinbergs lived, but I always walked by my two locust trees
and spent a few moments loving them; so far as I knew, I loved nothing else.

Then I turned right and crossed the street and walked past an apartment house that had been built at right angles to the street, facing a
strange declivity that had once been an excavation for still another apartment house, which had never been built, because of the depression. On
the other side of the declivity was a block of three apartment houses,
and the third was the Leinbergs'. Every apartment in it had at least eight
rooms, and the back staircase was enclosed, and the building had its own
garages. All this made it special and expensive, and a landmark in the
neighborhood.

Mr. Leinberg was a drug manufacturer and very successful. I thought
he was a smart man, but I don't remember him at all well (I never looked

at men closely in those days but always averted my head in shyness and embarrassment; they might guess how fiercely I wanted to belong to them) and I could have been wrong. Certainly the atmosphere then, during the war years — it was 1943 — was that everyone was getting rich; everyone who could work, that is. At any rate, he was getting rich, and it was only a matter of time before the Leinbergs moved from that apartment house to Laclede or Ladue and had a forty-thousand-dollar house with an acre or so of grounds.

Mrs. Leinberg was very pretty; she was dark, like my mother, but not as beautiful. For one thing, she was too small; she was barely five feet tall, and I towered over her. For another, she was not at all regal. But her lipstick was never on her teeth, and her dresses were usually new, and her eyes were kind. (My mother's eyes were incomprehensible; they were dark stages where dimly seen mob scenes were staged and all one ever sensed was tumult and drama, and no matter how long one waited, the lights never went up and the scene never was explained.) Mrs. Leinberg would invite me to help myself in the icebox, and then she would write down the telephone number of the place where she was going to be. "Keep Edward in the back of the apartment, where he won't disturb the baby," she would tell me. "If the baby does wake up, pick her up right away. That's very important. I didn't pick Edward up, and I'll always regret it." She said that every time, even though I could see Edward lurking in the back hallway, waiting for his parents to leave so he could run out and jump on me and our world could come alive again. He would listen, his small face — he was seven — quite blank with hurt and the effort to pierce the hurt with understanding.

Mrs. Leinberg would say, "Call me if she wakes up." And then, placatingly, to her husband, "I'll just come home to put her back to sleep, and then I'll go right back to the party —" Then, to me, "But she almost always sleeps, so don't worry about it."

"Come on, Greta. He knows what to do," Mr. Leinberg would say impatiently.

I always heard contempt in his voice — contempt for his wife, for Edward, and for me. I would be standing by the icebox looking down on the two little married people. Edward's father had a jealous and petulant mouth. "Come on, Greta," it would say impatiently, "We'll be back by eleven," it would say to me.

"Edward goes to bed at nine," Mrs. Leinberg would say, her voice high and birdlike, but tremulous with confusion and vagueness. Then she would be swept out the front door, so much prettily dressed matchwood, in her husband's wake. When the door closed, Edward would come hurtling down the hall and tackle my knees if I was staring after his parents, or, if I was facing him, leap onto my chest and into my arms.

"What shall we play tonight?"

He would ask that and I would have to think. He trembled with excitement, because I could make up games wonderful to him — like his daydreams, in fact. Because he was a child, he trusted me almost totally, and I could do anything with him. I had that power with children until I was in college and began at last to be like other people.

In Edward's bedroom was a large closet; it had a rack for clothes, a washstand, a built-in table, and fifteen or twenty shelves. The table and shelves were crowded with toys and games and sports equipment. I owned a Monopoly board I had inherited from my older sister, an old baseball glove (which was so cheap I never dared use it in front of my classmates, who had real gloves signed by real players), and a collection of postcards. The first time I saw that closet, I practically exploded with pleasure; I took down each of the games and toys and played with them, one after another, with Edward. Edward loved the fact that we never played a game to its conclusion but would leap from game to game after only a few moves, until the leaping became the real game and the atmosphere of laughter the real sport.

It was comfortable for me in the back room, alone in the apartment with Edward, because at last I was chief; and not only that, I was not being seen. There was no one there who could see through me, or think of what I should be or how I should behave; and I have always been terrified of what people thought of me, as if what they thought was a hulking creature that would confront me if I should turn a wrong corner.

There were no corners. Edward and I would take his toy pistols and stalk each other around the bed. Other times, we were on the bed, the front gun turret of a battleship sailing to battle the Japanese fleet in the Indian Ocean. Edward would close his eyes and roll with pleasure when I went "Boom! Boom! BOOOOM!"

"It's sinking! It's sinking, isn't it?"

"No, stupid. We only hit its funnel. We have to shoot again. Boom, Boom —"

Edward's fingers would press his eyelids in a spasm of ecstasy; his delirious, taut, little boy's body would fall backward on the soft pillows and bounce, and his back would curve; the excited breathy laughter would pour out like so many leaves spilling into spring, so many lilacs thrusting into bloom.

Under the bed, in a foxhole (Edward had a Cub Scout hat and I had his plastic soldier helmet), we turned back the yellow hordes from Guadalcanal. Edward dearly loved to be wounded. "I'm hit!" he'd shriek. "I'm hit!" He'd press his hand against his stomach and writhe on the wooden floor. "They shot me in the guts —"

I didn't approve of his getting wounded so soon, because then the scene was over; both his and my sense of verisimilitude didn't allow someone to be wounded and then get up. I remember how pleased he was when I invented the idea that after he got wounded, he could be someone else; so, when we crawled under the bed, we would decide to be eight or twelve or twenty Marines, ten each to get wounded, killed, or maimed as we saw fit, provided enough survived so that when we crawled out from under the bed we could charge the Japanese position under the dining-room table and leave it strewn with corpses.

Edward was particularly good at the detective game, which was a lot more involved and difficult. In that, we would walk into the kitchen, and I would tell him that we had received a call about a murder. Except when we played Tarzan, we never found it necessary to be characters. However, we always had names. In the detective game, we were usually Sam and Fred. We'd get a call telling us who was murdered, and then we'd go back to the bedroom and examine the corpse and question the suspects. I'd fire questions at an empty chair. Sometimes Edward would get tired of being my sidekick and he'd slip into the chair and be the quaking suspect. Other times, he would prowl around the room on his hands and knees with a magnifying glass while I stormed and shouted at the perpetually shifty suspect: "Where were you, Mrs. Eggnogghead [giggles from Edward], at ten o'clock, when Mr. Eggnogghead [laughter, helpless with pleasure, from Edward] was slain with the cake knife?"

"Hey, Fred! *I found bloodstains.*" Edward's voice would quiver with a creditable imitation of the excitement of radio detectives.

"Bloodstains! Where, Sam? This may be the clue that breaks the case."

Edward could sustain the *commedia dell' arte* for hours if I wanted him to. He was a precocious and delicate little boy, quivering with the malaise of being unloved. When we played, his child's heart would come into its own, and the troubled world where his vague hungers went unfed and mothers and fathers were dim and far away — too far away ever to reach in and touch the sore place and make it heal — would disappear, along with the world where I was not sufficiently muscled or sufficiently gallant to earn my own regard. (What ever had induced my mother to marry that silly man, who'd been unable to hang on to his money? I could remember when we'd had a larger house and I'd been happy; why had she let it get away?) It angered me that Edward's mother had so little love for him and so much for her daughter, and that Edward's father should not appreciate the boy's intelligence — he thought Edward was a queer duck, and effeminate. I could have taught Edward the manly postures. But his father didn't think highly of me: I was only a baby-sitter, and a queer duck too. Why, then, should Edward be more highly regarded by his father than I myself was? I wouldn't love him or explain to him.

That, of course, was my terrible dilemma. His apartment house, though larger than mine, was made of the same dark-red brick, and I wouldn't love him. It was shameful for a boy my age to love a child anyway. And who was Edward? He wasn't as smart as I'd been at his age, or as fierce. At his age, I'd already seen the evil in people's eyes, and I'd begun the construction of my defenses even then. But Edward's family was more prosperous, and the cold winds of insecurity (*Where will the money come from?*) hadn't shredded the dreamy chrysalis of his childhood. He was still immersed in the dim, wet wonder of the folded wings that might open if someone loved him; he still hoped, probably, in a butterfly's unthinking way, for spring and warmth. How the wings ache, folded so, waiting; that is, they ache until they atrophy.

So I was thirteen and Edward was seven and he wanted me to love him, but he was not old enough or strong enough to help me. He could not make his parents share their wealth and comfort with me, or force them to give me a place in their home. He was like most of the people I knew — eager and needful of my love; for I was quite remarkable and

made incredible games, which were better than movies or than the heart could hope for. I was a dream come true. I was smart and virtuous (no one knew that I occasionally stole from the dime store) and fairly attractive, maybe even very attractive. I was often funny and always interesting. I had read everything and knew everything and got unbelievable grades. Of course I was someone whose love was desired. Mother, my teachers, my sister, girls at school, other boys — they all wanted me to love them.

But I wanted them to love me first.

None of them did. I was fierce and solitary and acrid, marching off the little mile from school, past the post office, all yellow brick and chrome, and my two locust trees (water, water everywhere and not a drop to drink), and there was no one who loved me first. I could see a hundred cravennesses in the people I knew, a thousand flaws, a million weaknesses. If I had to love first, I would love only perfection. Of course, I could help heal the people I knew if I loved them. No, I said to myself, why should I give them everything when they give me nothing?

How many hurts and shynesses and times of walking up the back stairs had made me that way? I don't know. All I know is that Edward needed my love and I wouldn't give it to him. I was only thirteen. There isn't much you can blame a boy of thirteen for, but I'm not thinking of the blame; I'm thinking of all the years that might have been — if I'd only known then what I know now. The waste, the God-awful waste.

Really, that's all there is to this story. The boy I was, the child Edward was. That and the terrible desire to suddenly turn and run shouting back through the corridors of time, screaming at the boy I was, searching him out, and pounding on his chest: Love him, you damn fool, love him.

CHARLES BUKOWSKI

Aftermath of a Lengthy Rejection Slip

The following note accompanied Charles Bukowski's first story in the March–April 1944 issue of *Story:*

> Charles Bukowski was born in Andernach, Germany, 1920. His father was California-born, of Polish parentage, and served with the American Army of Occupation in the Rhineland, where he met the author's mother. He was brought to America at the age of two. He attended Los Angeles City College for a couple of years and in the two and one-half years since then he has been a clerk in the postoffice, a stockroom boy for Sears Roebuck, a truck-loader nights in a bakery. He is now working as a package-wrapper and box-filler in the cellar of a ladies' sportswear shop.

In Bukowski's 1975 novel *Factotum,* he describes the experience of his first publication (calling *Story*'s Whit Burnett "Clay Gladmore"): "Gladmore returned many of my things with personal rejections. True, most of them weren't very long but they did seem kind and they were encouraging. . . . So I kept him busy with four or five stories a week." On the subject of his first sale, Bukowski wrote, "I got up from the chair still holding my acceptance slip. MY FIRST. Never had the world looked so good, so full of promise." Upon seeing the story in print, however, Bukowski's ebullience disappeared. "Aftermath" had been placed in the end notes, and he felt Burnett had published it only as a curiosity. Feeling humiliated, Bukowski never again submitted anything to *Story,* and he cut back on his writing. It wasn't until the late 1950s that he resumed writing for publication.

I WALKED AROUND outside and thought about it. It was the longest one I ever got. Usually they only said, "Sorry, this did not quite make the grade" or "Sorry, this didn't quite work in." Or more often, the regular printed rejection form.

But this was the longest, the longest ever. It was from my story "My Adventures in Half a Hundred Rooming Houses." I walked under a lamppost, took the little slip out of my pocket and reread it —

Dear Mr. Bukowski:

Again, this is a conglomeration of extremely good stuff and other stuff so full of idolized prostitutes, morning-after vomiting scenes, misanthropy, praise for suicide etc. that it is not quite for a magazine of any circulation at all. This is, however, pretty much a saga of a certain type of person and in it I think you've done an honest job. Possibly we will print you sometime, but I don't know exactly when. That depends on you.

Sincerely yours,
Whit Burnett

Oh, I knew the signature: the long "h" that twisted into the end of the "W," and the beginning of the "B" which dropped halfway down the page.

I put the slip back in my pocket and walked on down the street. I felt pretty good.

Here I had only been writing two years. Two short years. It took Hemingway ten years. And Sherwood Anderson, he was forty before he was published.

I guess I would have to give up drinking and women of ill-fame, though. Whiskey was hard to get anyhow and wine was ruining my stomach. Millie though — Millie, that would be harder, much harder. . . . But Millie, Millie, we must remember art. Dostoievsky, Gorki, for Russia, and now America wants an Eastern-European. America is tired of Browns and Smiths. The Browns and the Smiths are good writers but there are too many of them and they all write alike. America

wants the fuzzy blackness, impractical meditations and repressed desires of an Eastern-European.

Millie, Millie, your figure is just right: it all pours down tight to the hips and loving you is as easy as putting on a pair of gloves in zero weather. Your room is always warm and cheerful and you have record albums and cheese sandwiches that I like. And Millie, your cat, remember? Remember when he was a kitten? I tried to teach him to shake hands and to roll over, and you said a cat wasn't a dog and it couldn't be done. Well, I did it, didn't I, Millie? The cat's big now and he's been a mother and had kittens. We've been friends a long time. But it's going to have to go now, Millie: cats and figures and Tschaikowsky's 6th Symphony. America needs an Eastern-European. . . .

I found I was in front of my rooming house by then and I started to go in. Then I saw a light on in my window. I looked in: Carson and Shipkey were at the table with somebody I didn't know. They were playing cards and in the center sat a huge jug of wine. Carson and Shipkey were painters who couldn't make up their minds whether to paint like Salvador Dali or Rockwell Kent, and they worked at the shipyards while trying to decide.

Then I saw a man sitting very quietly on the edge of my bed. He had a mustache and a goatee and looked familiar. I seemed to remember his face. I had seen it in a book, a newspaper, a movie, maybe. I wondered.

Then I remembered.

When I remembered, I didn't know whether to go in or not. After all, what did one say? How did one act? With a man like that it was hard. You had to be careful not to say the wrong words, you had to be careful about everything.

I decided to walk around the block once first. I read someplace that that helped when you were nervous. I heard Shipkey swearing as I left and I heard somebody drop a glass. That wouldn't help me any.

I decided to make up my speech ahead of time. "Really, I'm not a very good speaker at all. I'm very withdrawn and tense. I save it all and put it in words on paper. I'm sure you'll be disappointed in me, but it's the way I've always been."

I thought that would do it and when I finished my block's walk I went right into my room.

I could see that Carson and Shipkey were rather drunk, and I knew

they wouldn't help me any. The little card player they had brought with them was also bad off, except he had all the money on his side of the table.

The man with the goatee got up off the bed. "How do you do, sir?" he asked.

"Fine, and you?" I shook hands with him. "I hope you haven't been waiting too long?" I said.

"Oh no."

"Really," I said, "I'm not a very good speaker at all —"

"Except when he's drunk, then he yells his head off. Sometimes he goes to the square and lectures and if nobody listens to him he talks to the birds," said Shipkey.

The man with the goatee grinned. He had a marvelous grin. Evidently a man of understanding.

The other two went on playing cards, but Shipkey turned his chair around and watched us.

"I'm very withdrawn and tense," I continued, "and —"

"Past tense or circus tents?" yelled Shipkey.

That was very bad, but the man with the goatee smiled again and I felt better.

"I save it all and put it in words on paper and —"

"Nine-tenths or pretense?" yelled Shipkey.

" — and I'm sure you'll be disappointed in me, but it's the way I've always been."

"Listen, mister!" yelled Shipkey wobbling back and forth in his chair. "Listen, you with the goatee!"

"Yes?"

"Listen, I'm six feet tall with wavy hair, a glass eye and a pair of red dice."

The man laughed.

"You don't believe me then? You don't believe I have a pair of red dice?"

Shipkey, when intoxicated always wanted, for some reason, to make people believe he had a glass eye. He would point to one eye or the other and maintain it was a glass eye. He claimed the glass eye was made for him by his father, the greatest specialist in the world, who had, unfortunately, been killed by a tiger in China.

Suddenly Carson began yelling, "I saw you take that card! Where did you get it? Give it here, *here!* Marked, *marked!* I thought so! No wonder you've been winning! So! *So!*"

Carson rose up and grabbed the little card player by the tie and pulled up on it. Carson was blue in the face with anger and the little card player began to turn red as Carson pulled up on the tie.

"What's up, ha! Ha! What's up! What's goin' on?" yelled Shipkey. "Lemme see, ha? Gimme tha dope!"

Carson was all blue and could hardly speak. He hissed the words out of his lips with a great effort and held up on the tie. The little card player began to flop his arms about like a great octopus brought to the surface.

"He crossed us!" hissed Carson. "Crossed us! Pulled one from under his sleeve, sure as the Lord! Crossed us, I tell you!"

Shipkey walked behind the little card player and grabbed him by the hair and yanked his head back and forth. Carson remained at the tie.

"Did you cross us, huh? Did you! Speak! Speak!" yelled Shipkey pulling at the hair.

The little card player didn't speak. He just flopped his arms and began to sweat.

"I'll take you someplace where we can get a beer and something to eat," I said to the man with the goatee.

"Come on! Talk! Give out! You can't cross us!"

"Oh, that won't be necessary," said the man with the goatee.

"Rat! Louse! Fish-faced pig!"

"I insist," I said.

"Rob a man with a glass eye, will you? *I'll* show you, fish-faced pig!"

"That's very kind of you, and I am a little hungry, thanks," said the man with the goatee.

"Speak! Speak, fish-faced pig! If you don't speak in two minutes, in just two minutes, I'll cut your heart out for a doorknob!"

"Let's leave right away," I said.

"All right," said the man with the goatee.

ALL the eating places were closed at that time of the night and it was a long ride into town. I couldn't take him back to my room, so I had to take a chance on Millie. She always had plenty of food. At any rate, she *always* had cheese.

I was right. She made us cheese sandwiches with coffee. The cat knew me and leaped into my lap.

I put the cat on the floor.

"Watch, Mr. Burnett," I said.

"Shake hands!" I said to the cat. "Shake hands!"

The cat just sat there.

"That's funny, it always used to do it," I said. "Shake hands!"

I remembered Shipkey had told Mr. Burnett that I talked to birds.

"Come on now! Shake hands!"

I began to feel foolish.

"Come *on!* Shake hands!"

I put my head right down by the cat's head and put everything I had into it.

"Shake hands!"

The cat just sat there.

I went back to my chair and picked up my cheese sandwich.

"Cats are funny animals, Mr. Burnett. You can never tell. Millie, put on Tschaikowsky's 6th for Mr. Burnett."

We listened to the music. Millie came over and sat in my lap. She just had on a negligee. She dropped down against me. I put my sandwich to the side.

"I want you to notice," I said to Mr. Burnett, "the section which brings forth the marching movement in this symphony. I think it's one of the most beautiful movements in all music. And besides its beauty and force, its structure is perfect. You can feel intelligence at work."

The cat jumped up into the lap of the man with the goatee. Millie laid her cheek against mine, put a hand on my chest. "Where ya been, baby boy? Millie's missed ya, ya know."

The record ended and the man with the goatee took the cat off his lap, got up and turned the record over. He should have found record #2 in the album. By turning it over we would get the climax rather early. I didn't say anything, though, and we listened to it end.

"How did you like it?" I asked.

"Fine! Just fine!"

He had the cat on the floor.

"Shake hands! Shake hands!" he said to the cat.

The cat shook hands.

"Look," he said, "I can make the cat shake hands."

"Shake hands!"

The cat rolled over.

"No, shake *hands!* Shake *hands!*"

The cat just sat there.

He put his head down by the cat's head and talked into its ear. "Shake hands!"

The cat stuck its paw right into his goatee.

"Did you see? I made him shake hands!" Mr. Burnett seemed pleased.

Millie pressed tight against me. "Kiss me, baby boy," she said, "kiss me."

"No."

"Good Lord, ya gone off ya nut, baby boy? What's eatin' at ya? Sompin's botherin' ya tonight, I can tell! Tell Millie all about ut! Millie'd go ta hell for ya, baby boy, ya know that. Whats'a matter, huh? Ha?"

"Now I'll get the cat to roll over," said Mr. Burnett.

Millie wrapped her arms tight around me and peered down into my upward eye. She looked very sad and motherish and smelled like cheese. "Tell Millie what's eatin' ya up, baby boy."

"Roll over!" said Mr. Burnett to the cat.

The cat just sat there.

"Listen," I said to Millie, "see that man over there?"

"Yeah, I see him."

"Well, that's Whit Burnett."

"Who's that?"

"The magazine editor. The one I send my stories to."

"Ya mean the one who sends you those little tiny notes?"

"Rejection slips, Millie."

"Well, he's mean. I don't like him."

"Roll over!" said Mr. Burnett to the cat. The cat rolled over. "Look!" he yelled. "I made the cat roll over! I'd like to buy this cat! It's marvelous!"

Millie tightened her grip about me and peered down into my eye. I was quite helpless. I felt like a still live fish on ice in a butcher's counter on Friday morning.

"Listen," she said, "I can get him ta print one a ya stories. I can get him ta print *alla* them!"

"Watch me make the cat roll over!" said Mr. Burnett.

"No, no, Millie, you don't understand! Editors aren't like tired business men. Editors have *scruples!*"

"Scruples?"

"Scruples."

"Roll over!" said Mr. Burnett.

The cat just sat there.

"I know all about ya *scruples!* Don't ya worry about scruples! Baby boy, I'll get him ta print *alla* ya stories!"

"Roll over!" said Mr. Burnett to the cat. Nothing happened.

"No, Millie, I won't have it."

She was all wound around me. It was hard to breathe and she was rather heavy. I felt my feet going to sleep. Millie pressed her cheek against mine and rubbed a hand up and down my chest. "Baby boy, ya got nothin' to say!"

Mr. Burnett put his head down by the cat's head and talked into its ear. "Roll over!"

The cat stuck its paw right into his goatee.

"I think this cat wants something to eat," he said.

With that, he got back into his chair. Millie went over and sat on his knee.

"Where'd ya get tha cute little goaty?" she asked.

"Pardon me," I said, "I'm going to get a drink of water."

I went in and sat in the breakfast nook and looked down at the flower designs on the table. I tried to scratch them off with a fingernail.

It was hard enough to share Millie's love with the cheese salesman and the welder. Millie with the figure right down to the hips. Damn, damn.

I kept sitting there and after a while I took my rejection slip out of my pocket and read it again. The places where the slip was folded were beginning to get brown with dirt and torn. I would have to stop looking at it and put it between book pages like a pressed rose.

I began to think about what it said. I always had that trouble. In college, even, I was drawn to the fuzzy blackness. The short story instructress took me to dinner and a show one night and lectured to me on the beauties of life. I had given her a story I had written in which I, as the main character, had gone down to the beach at night on the sand

and began meditating on the meaning in Christ, on the meaning in death, on the meaning and fullness and rhythm in all things. Then in the middle of my meditations, along walks a bleary-eyed tramp kicking sand in my face. I talk to him, buy him a bottle and we drink. We get sick. Afterward we go to a house of ill-fame.

After the dinner, the short story instructress opened her purse and brought forth my story of the beach. She opened it up about halfway down, to the entrance of the bleary-eyed tramp and the exit of meaning in Christ.

"Up to here," she said, "up to here, this was very good, in fact, beautiful."

Then she glared up at me with that glare that only the artistically intelligent who have somehow fallen into money and position can have. "But pardon me, pardon me very much," she tapped at the bottom half of my story, "just what the *hell* is *this* stuff doing in here?"

I couldn't stay away any longer. I got up and walked into the front room.

Millie was all wrapped around him and peering down into his upward eye. He looked like a fish on ice.

Millie must have thought I wanted to talk to him about publishing procedures.

"Pardon me, I have to comb my hair," she said and left the room.

"Nice girl, isn't she, Mr. Burnett?" I asked.

He pulled himself back into shape and straightened his tie. "Pardon me," he said, "why do you keep calling me 'Mr. Burnett'?"

"Well, aren't you?"

"I'm Hoffman. Joseph Hoffman. I'm from the Curtis Life Insurance Company. I came in response to your postcard."

"But I didn't send a postcard."

"We received one from you."

"I never sent any."

"Aren't you Andrew Spickwich?"

"Who?"

"Spickwich. Andrew Spickwich, 3631 Taylor Street."

Millie came back and wound herself around Joseph Hoffman. I didn't have the heart to tell her.

I closed the door very softly and went down the steps and out into the street. I walked part way down the block and then I saw the lights go out.

I ran like hell toward my room hoping that there would be some wine left in that huge jug on the table. I didn't think I'd be that lucky, though, because I am too much a saga of a certain type of person: fuzzy blackness, impractical meditations and repressed desires.

Miriam

The first story Truman Capote ever sold was "My Side of the Matter." *Story* bought it and Whit Burnett included it in *Firsts of the Famous.* It was not, however, the first of Capote's stories to appear in print. After a stint as a copyboy at the *New Yorker,* where, try as he might, he couldn't get any of the editors to take his work seriously, Capote submitted several stories to *Mademoiselle,* including the previously sold "My Side of the Matter." *Mademoiselle* accepted "Miriam" and beat *Story* into print by running it in June 1945. Capote was just twenty years old and, as Gerald Clarke writes in *Capote,* his waiflike charm and precocious talent quickly made him the darling of the New York literary set. Mary Louise Aswell, fiction editor for *Harper's Bazaar,* told Clarke, "I saw 'Miriam' in *Mademoiselle,* and I said, 'This is somebody we've got to get." She was successful, publishing "A Tree of Night" in October 1945. In a 1947 *Life* magazine profile of up-and-coming writers that included Gore Vidal and Jean Stafford among others, it was Capote who received the most prominent treatment, even though he was the only one who had yet to publish a book. (His first, *Other Voices, Other Rooms,* was published by Random House in 1948.) On the strength of "Miriam" and Capote's other stories that appeared in the fall of 1945, Herschell Brickell, editor of the annual *O. Henry Memorial Award Prize Stories,* accurately predicted, "Capote will take his place among the best short-story writers of the rising generation."

FOR SEVERAL YEARS, Mrs. H. T. Miller had lived alone in a pleasant apartment (two rooms with kitchenette) in a remodeled brownstone near the East River. She was a widow: Mr. H. T. Miller had left a reasonable amount of insurance. Her interests were narrow, she had no friends to speak of, and she rarely journeyed farther than the corner grocery. The other people in the house never seemed to notice her: her clothes were matter-of-fact, her hair iron-gray, clipped and casually waved; she did not use cosmetics, her features were plain and inconspicuous, and on her last birthday she was sixty-one. Her activities were seldom spontaneous: she kept the two rooms immaculate, smoked an occasional cigarette, prepared her own meals and tended a canary.

Then she met Miriam. It was snowing that night. Mrs. Miller had finished drying the supper dishes and was thumbing through an afternoon paper when she saw an advertisement of a picture playing at a neighborhood theater. The title sounded good, so she struggled into her beaver coat, laced her galoshes and left the apartment, leaving one light burning in the foyer: she found nothing more disturbing than a sensation of darkness.

The snow was fine, falling gently, not yet making an impression on the pavement. The wind from the river cut only at street crossings. Mrs. Miller hurried, her head bowed, oblivious as a mole burrowing a blind path. She stopped at a drugstore and bought a package of peppermints.

A long line stretched in front of the box office; she took her place at the end. There would be (a tired voice groaned) a short wait for all seats. Mrs. Miller rummaged in her leather handbag till she collected exactly the correct change for admission. The line seemed to be taking its own time and, looking around for some distraction, she suddenly became conscious of a little girl standing under the edge of the marquee.

Her hair was the longest and strangest Mrs. Miller had ever seen: absolutely silver-white, like an albino's. It flowed waistlength in smooth, loose lines. She was thin and fragilely constructed. There was a simple, special elegance in the way she stood with her thumbs in the pockets of a tailored plum-velvet coat.

Mrs. Miller felt oddly excited, and when the little girl glanced toward her, she smiled warmly. The little girl walked over and said, "Would you care to do me a favor?"

"I'd be glad to, if I can," said Mrs. Miller.

"Oh, it's quite easy. I merely want you to buy a ticket for me; they won't let me in otherwise. Here, I have the money." And gracefully she handed Mrs. Miller two dimes and a nickel.

They went into the theater together. An usherette directed them to a lounge; in twenty minutes the picture would be over.

"I feel just like a genuine criminal," said Mrs. Miller gaily, as she sat down. "I mean that sort of thing's against the law, isn't it? I do hope I haven't done the wrong thing. Your mother knows where you are, dear? I mean she does, doesn't she?"

The little girl said nothing. She unbuttoned her coat and folded it across her lap. Her dress underneath was prim and dark blue. A gold chain dangled about her neck, and her fingers, sensitive and musical-looking, toyed with it. Examining her more attentively, Mrs. Miller decided the truly distinctive feature was not her hair, but her eyes; they were hazel, steady, lacking any childlike quality whatsoever and, because of their size, seemed to consume her small face.

Mrs. Miller offered a peppermint. "What's your name, dear?"

"Miriam," she said, as though, in some curious way, it were information already familiar.

"Why, isn't that funny — my name's Miriam, too. And it's not a terribly common name either. Now, don't tell me your last name's Miller!"

"Just Miriam."

"But isn't that funny?"

"Moderately," said Miriam, and rolled the peppermint on her tongue.

Mrs. Miller flushed and shifted uncomfortably. "You have such a large vocabulary for such a little girl."

"Do I?"

"Well, yes," said Mrs. Miller, hastily changing the topic to: "Do you like the movies?"

"I really wouldn't know," said Miriam. "I've never been before."

Women began filling the lounge; the rumble of the newsreel bombs

exploded in the distance. Mrs. Miller rose, tucking her purse under her arm. "I guess I'd better be running now if I want to get a seat," she said. "It was nice to have met you."

Miriam nodded ever so slightly.

IT snowed all week. Wheels and footsteps moved soundlessly on the street, as if the business of living continued secretly behind a pale but impenetrable curtain. In the falling quiet there was no sky or earth, only snow lifting in the wind, frosting the window glass, chilling the rooms, deadening and hushing the city. At all hours it was necessary to keep a lamp lighted, and Mrs. Miller lost track of the days: Friday was no different from Saturday and on Sunday she went to the grocery: closed, of course.

That evening she scrambled eggs and fixed a bowl of tomato soup. Then, after putting on a flannel robe and cold-creaming her face, she propped herself up in bed with a hot-water bottle under her feet. She was reading the *Times* when the doorbell rang. At first she thought it must be a mistake and whoever it was would go away. But it rang and rang and settled to a persistent buzz. She looked at the clock: a little after eleven; it did not seem possible, she was always asleep by ten.

Climbing out of bed, she trotted barefoot across the living room. "I'm coming, please be patient." The latch was caught; she turned it this way and that way and the bell never paused an instant. "Stop it," she cried. The bolt gave way and she opened the door an inch. "What in heaven's name?"

"Hello," said Miriam.

"Oh . . . why, hello," said Mrs. Miller, stepping hesitantly into the hall. "You're that little girl."

"I thought you'd never answer, but I kept my finger on the button; I knew you were home. Aren't you glad to see me?"

Mrs. Miller did not know what to say. Miriam, she saw, wore the same plum-velvet coat and now she had also a beret to match; her white hair was braided in two shining plaits and looped at the ends with enormous white ribbons.

"Since I've waited so long, you could at least let me in," she said.

"It's awfully late. . . ."

Miriam regarded her blankly. "What difference does that make? Let

me in. It's cold out here and I have on a silk dress." Then, with a gentle gesture, she urged Mrs. Miller aside and passed into the apartment.

She dropped her coat and beret on a chair. She was indeed wearing a silk dress. White silk. White silk in February. The skirt was beautifully pleated and the sleeves long; it made a faint rustle as she strolled about the room. "I like your place," she said. "I like the rug, blue's my favorite color." She touched a paper rose in a vase on the coffee table. "Imitation," she commented wanly. "How sad. Aren't imitations sad?" She seated herself on the sofa, daintily spreading her skirt.

"What do you want?" asked Mrs. Miller.

"Sit down," said Miriam. "It makes me nervous to see people stand."

Mrs. Miller sank to a hassock. "What do you want?" she repeated.

"You know, I don't think you're glad I came."

For a second time Mrs. Miller was without an answer; her hand motioned vaguely. Miriam giggled and pressed back on a mound of chintz pillows. Mrs. Miller observed that the girl was less pale than she remembered; her cheeks were flushed.

"How did you know where I lived?"

Miriam frowned. "That's no question at all. What's your name? What's mine?"

"But I'm not listed in the phone book."

"Oh, let's talk about something else."

Mrs. Miller said, "Your mother must be insane to let a child like you wander around at all hours of the night — and in such ridiculous clothes. She must be out of her mind."

Miriam got up and moved to a corner where a covered bird cage hung from a ceiling chain. She peeked beneath the cover. "It's a canary," she said. "Would you mind if I woke him? I'd like to hear him sing."

"Leave Tommy alone," said Mrs. Miller, anxiously. "Don't you dare wake him."

"Certainly," said Miriam. "But I don't see why I can't hear him sing." And then, "Have you anything to eat? I'm starving! Even milk and a jam sandwich would be fine."

"Look," said Mrs. Miller, rising from the hassock, "look — if I make some nice sandwiches will you be a good child and run along home? It's past midnight, I'm sure."

"It's snowing," reproached Miriam. "And cold and dark."

"Well, you shouldn't have come here to begin with," said Mrs. Miller, struggling to control her voice. "I can't help the weather. If you want anything to eat you'll have to promise to leave."

Miriam brushed a braid against her cheek. Her eyes were thoughtful, as if weighing the proposition. She turned toward the bird cage. "Very well," she said, "I promise."

How old is she? Ten? Eleven? Mrs. Miller, in the kitchen, unsealed a jar of strawberry preserves and cut four slices of bread. She poured a glass of milk and paused to light a cigarette. *And why has she come?* Her hand shook as she held the match, fascinated, till it burned her finger. The canary was singing; singing as he did in the morning and at no other time. "Miriam," she called, "Miriam, I told you not to disturb Tommy." There was no answer. She called again; all she heard was the canary. She inhaled the cigarette and discovered she had lighted the cork-tip end and — oh, really, she mustn't lose her temper.

She carried the food in on a tray and set it on the coffee table. She saw first that the bird cage still wore its night cover. And Tommy was singing. It gave her a queer sensation. And no one was in the room. Mrs. Miller went through an alcove leading to her bedroom: at the door she caught her breath.

"What are you doing?" she asked.

Miriam glanced up and in her eyes there was a look that was not ordinary. She was standing by the bureau, a jewel case opened before her. For a minute she studied Mrs. Miller, forcing their eyes to meet, and she smiled. "There's nothing good here," she said. "But I like this." Her hand held a cameo brooch. "It's charming."

"Suppose — perhaps you'd better put it back," said Mrs. Miller, feeling suddenly the need of some support. She leaned against the door frame; her head was unbearably heavy; a pressure weighted the rhythm of her heartbeat. The light seemed to flutter defectively. "Please, child — a gift from my husband . . ."

"But it's beautiful and I want it," said Miriam. "*Give it to me.*"

As she stood, striving to shape a sentence which would somehow save the brooch, it came to Mrs. Miller there was no one to whom she might turn; she was alone; a fact that had not been among her thoughts for a

long time. Its sheer emphasis was stunning. But here in her own room in the hushed snow-city were evidences she could not ignore or, she knew with startling clarity, resist.

MIRIAM ate ravenously, and when the sandwiches and milk were gone, her fingers made cobweb movements over the plate, gathering crumbs. The cameo gleamed on her blouse, the blonde profile like a trick reflection of its wearer. "That was very nice," she sighed, "though now an almond cake or a cherry would be ideal. Sweets are lovely, don't you think?"

Mrs. Miller was perched precariously on the hassock, smoking a cigarette. Her hair net had slipped lopsided and loose strands straggled down her face. Her eyes were stupidly concentrated on nothing and her cheeks were mottled in red patches, as though a fierce slap had left permanent marks.

"Is there a candy — a cake?"

Mrs. Miller tapped ash on the rug. Her head swayed slightly as she tried to focus her eyes. "You promised to leave if I made the sandwiches," she said.

"Dear me, did I?"

"It was a promise and I'm tired and I don't feel well at all."

"Mustn't fret," said Miriam, "I'm only teasing."

She picked up her coat, slung it over her arm, and arranged her beret in front of a mirror. Presently she bent close to Mrs. Miller and whispered, "Kiss me good night."

"Please — I'd rather not," said Mrs. Miller.

Miriam lifted a shoulder, arched an eyebrow. "As you like," she said, and went directly to the coffee table, seized the vase containing the paper roses, carried it to where the hard surface of the floor lay bare, and hurled it downward. Glass sprayed in all directions and she stamped her foot on the bouquet.

Then slowly she walked to the door, but before closing it she looked back at Mrs. Miller with a slyly innocent curiosity.

MRS. Miller spent the next day in bed, rising once to feed the canary and drink a cup of tea; she took her temperature and had none, yet her dreams were feverishly agitated; their unbalanced mood lingered even as

she lay staring wide-eyed at the ceiling. One dream threaded through the others like an elusively mysterious theme in a complicated symphony, and the scenes it depicted were sharply outlined, as though sketched by a hand of gifted intensity: a small girl, wearing a bridal gown and a wreath of leaves, led a gray procession down a mountain path, and among them there was unusual silence till a woman at the rear asked, "Where is she taking us?" "No one knows," said an old man marching in front. "But isn't she pretty?" volunteered a third voice, "Isn't she like a frost flower . . . so shining and white?"

Tuesday morning she woke up feeling better; harsh slats of sunlight, slanting through Venetian blinds, shed a disrupting light on her unwholesome fancies. She opened the window to discover a thawed, mild-as-spring day; a sweep of clean new clouds crumpled against a vastly blue, out-of-season sky; and across the low line of roof-tops she could see the river and smoke curving from tug-boat stacks in a warm wind. A great silver truck plowed the snow-banked street, its machine sound humming in the air.

After straightening the apartment, she went to the grocer's, cashed a check and continued to Schrafft's where she ate breakfast and chatted happily with the waitress. Oh, it was a wonderful day — more like a holiday — and it would be so foolish to go home.

She boarded a Lexington Avenue bus and rode up to Eighty-sixth Street; it was here that she had decided to do a little shopping.

She had no idea what she wanted or needed, but she idled along, intent only upon the passers-by, brisk and preoccupied, who gave her a disturbing sense of separateness.

It was while waiting at the corner of Third Avenue that she saw the man: an old man, bowlegged and stooped under an armload of bulging packages; he wore a shabby brown coat and a checkered cap. Suddenly she realized they were exchanging a smile: there was nothing friendly about this smile, it was merely two cold flickers of recognition. But she was certain she had never seen him before.

He was standing next to an El pillar, and as she crossed the street he turned and followed. He kept quite close; from the corner of her eye she watched his reflection wavering on the shopwindows.

Then in the middle of the block she stopped and faced him. He

stopped also and cocked his head, grinning. But what could she say? Do? Here, in broad daylight, on Eighty-sixth Street? It was useless and, despising her own helplessness, she quickened her steps.

Now Second Avenue is a dismal street, made from scraps and ends; part cobblestone, part asphalt, part cement; and its atmosphere of desertion is permanent. Mrs. Miller walked five blocks without meeting anyone, and all the while the steady crunch of his footfalls in the snow stayed near. And when she came to a florist's shop, the sound was still with her. She hurried inside and watched through the glass door as the old man passed; he kept his eyes straight ahead and didn't slow his pace, but he did one strange, telling thing: he tipped his cap.

"Six white ones, did you say?" asked the florist. "Yes," she told him, "white roses." From there she went to a glassware store and selected a vase, presumably a replacement for the one Miriam had broken, though the price was intolerable and the vase itself (she thought) grotesquely vulgar. But a series of unaccountable purchases had begun, as if by prearranged plan: a plan of which she had not the least knowledge or control.

She bought a bag of glazed cherries, and at a place called the Knickerbocker Bakery she paid forty cents for six almond cakes.

Within the last hour the weather had turned cold again; like blurred lenses, winter clouds cast a shade over the sun, and the skeleton of an early dusk colored the sky; a damp mist mixed with the wind and the voices of a few children who romped high on mountains of gutter snow seemed lonely and cheerless. Soon the first flake fell, and when Mrs. Miller reached the brownstone house, snow was falling in a swift screen and foot tracks vanished as they were printed.

The white roses were arranged decoratively in the vase. The glazed cherries shone on a ceramic plate. The almond cakes, dusted with sugar, awaited a hand. The canary fluttered on its swing and picked at a bar of seed.

At precisely five the doorbell rang. Mrs. Miller *knew* who it was. The hem of her housecoat trailed as she crossed the floor. "Is that you?" she called.

"Naturally," said Miriam, the word resounding shrilly from the hall. "Open this door."

"Go away," said Mrs. Miller.

"Please hurry . . . I have a heavy package."

"Go away," said Mrs. Miller. She returned to the living room, lighted a cigarette, sat down, and calmly listened to the buzzer; on and on and on. "You might as well leave. I have no intention of letting you in."

Shortly the bell stopped. For possibly ten minutes Mrs. Miller did not move. Then, hearing no sound, she concluded Miriam had gone. She tiptoed to the door and opened it a sliver; Miriam was half-reclining atop a cardboard box with a beautiful French doll cradled in her arms.

"Really, I thought you were never coming," she said peevishly. "Here, help me get this in, it's awfully heavy."

It was not spell-like compulsion that Mrs. Miller felt, but rather a curious passivity; she brought in the box, Miriam the doll. Miriam curled up on the sofa, not troubling to remove her coat or beret, and watched disinterestedly as Mrs. Miller dropped the box and stood trembling, trying to catch her breath.

"Thank you," she said. In the daylight she looked pinched and drawn, her hair less luminous. The French doll she was loving wore an exquisite powdered wig and its idiot glass eyes sought solace in Miriam's. "I have a surprise," she continued. "Look into my box."

Kneeling, Mrs. Miller parted the flaps and lifted out another doll; then a blue dress which she recalled as the one Miriam had worn that first night at the theater; and of the remainder she said, "It's all clothes. Why?"

"Because I've come to live with you," said Miriam, twisting a cherry stem. "Wasn't it nice of you to buy me the cherries. . . ?"

"But you can't! For God's sake go away — go away and leave me alone!"

". . . and the roses and the almond cakes? How really wonderfully generous. You know, these cherries are delicious. The last place I lived was with an old man; he was terribly poor and we never had good things to eat. But I think I'll be happy here." She paused to snuggle her doll closer. "Now, if you'll just show me where to put my things . . ."

Mrs. Miller's face dissolved into a mask of ugly red lines; she began to cry, and it was an unnatural, tearless sort of weeping, as though, not

having wept for a long time, she had forgotten how. Carefully she edged backward till she touched the door.

SHE fumbled through the hall and down the stairs to a landing below. She pounded frantically on the door of the first apartment she came to; a short, red-headed man answered and she pushed past him. "Say, what the hell is this?" he said. "Anything wrong, lover?" asked a young woman who appeared from the kitchen, drying her hands. And it was to her that Mrs. Miller turned.

"Listen," she cried, "I'm ashamed behaving this way but — well, I'm Mrs. H. T. Miller and I live upstairs and . . ." She pressed her hands over her face. "It sounds so absurd. . . ."

The woman guided her to a chair, while the man excitedly rattled pocket change. "Yeah?"

"I live upstairs and there's a little girl visiting me, and I suppose that I'm afraid of her. She won't leave and I can't make her and — she's going to do something terrible. She's already stolen my cameo, but she's about to do something worse — something terrible!"

The man asked, "Is she a relative, huh?"

Mrs. Miller shook her head. "I don't know who she is. Her name's Miriam, but I don't know for certain who she is."

"You gotta calm down, honey," said the woman, stroking Mrs. Miller's arm. "Harry here'll tend to this kid. Go on, lover." And Mrs. Miller said, "The door's open — 5A."

After the man left, the woman brought a towel and bathed Mrs. Miller's face. "You're very kind," Mrs. Miller said. "I'm sorry to act like such a fool, only this wicked child . . ."

"Sure, honey," consoled the woman. "Now, you better take it easy."

Mrs. Miller rested her head in the crook of her arm; she was quiet enough to be asleep. The woman turned a radio dial; a piano and a husky voice filled the silence and the woman, tapping her foot, kept excellent time. "Maybe we oughta go up too," she said.

"I don't want to see her again. I don't want to be anywhere near her."

"Uh huh, but what you shoulda done, you shoulda called a cop."

Presently they heard the man on the stairs. He strode into the room frowning and scratching the back of his neck. "Nobody there," he said, honestly embarrassed. "She musta beat it."

"Harry, you're a jerk," announced the woman. "We been sitting here the whole time and we woulda seen . . ." she stopped abruptly, for the man's glance was sharp.

"I looked all over," he said, "and there just ain't nobody there. Nobody, understand?"

"Tell me," said Mrs. Miller, rising, "tell me, did you see a large box? Or a doll?"

"No, ma'am, I didn't."

And the woman, as if delivering a verdict, said, "Well, for cryin out loud. . . ."

Mrs. Miller entered her apartment softly; she walked to the center of the room and stood quite still. No, in a sense it had not changed: the roses, the cakes, and the cherries were in place. But this was an empty room, emptier than if the furnishings and familiars were not present, lifeless and petrified as a funeral parlor. The sofa loomed before her with a new strangeness: its vacancy had a meaning that would have been less penetrating and terrible had Miriam been curled on it. She gazed fixedly at the space where she remembered setting the box and, for a moment, the hassock spun desperately. And she looked through the window; surely the river was real, surely snow was falling — but then, one could not be certain witness to anything: Miriam, so vividly *there* — and yet, where was she? Where, where?

As though moving in a dream, she sank to a chair. The room was losing shape; it was dark and getting darker and there was nothing to be done about it; she could not lift her hand to light a lamp.

Suddenly, closing her eyes, she felt an upward surge, like a diver emerging from some deeper, greener depth. In times of terror or immense distress, there are moments when the mind waits, as though for a revelation, while a skein of calm is woven over thought; it is like a sleep, or a supernatural trance; and during this lull one is aware of a force of quiet reasoning: well, what if she had never really known a girl named Miriam? that she had been foolishly frightened on the street? In the end, like everything else, it was of no importance. For the only thing she had lost to Miriam was her identity, but now she knew she had found again the person who lived in this room, who cooked her own meals,

who owned a canary, who was someone she could trust and believe in: Mrs. H. T. Miller.

Listening in contentment, she became aware of a double sound: a bureau drawer opening and closing: she seemed to hear it long after completion — opening and closing. Then gradually, the harshness of it was replaced by the murmur of a silk dress and this, delicately faint, was moving nearer and swelling in intensity till the walls trembled with the vibration and the room was caving under a wave of whispers. Mrs. Miller stiffened and opened her eyes to a dull, direct stare.

"Hello," said Miriam.

RAYMOND CARVER

Furious Seasons

The man who would be acclaimed as the most significant short story writer of his generation was born in 1939 in Oregon, and grew up in Yakima, Washington. Carver married at nineteen and had two children by the age of twenty. He attended Chico State College by day, where he studied writing under John Gardner, and worked to support his family at night. His first story was published in the Winter 1960–61 issue of *Selection,* a Chico State College literary magazine. "Furious Seasons" appears in slightly different form in the 1992 Carver collection *No Heroics, Please,* where it was called "truly arresting" in a *New York Times* book review. In her introduction to *No Heroics, Please,* Tess Gallagher, Carver's widow, talks about the story:

> It represents perhaps the path not taken, since the borrowed devices — flashbacks and stream of consciousness — will seldom appear in his future work. . . . It was a particularly interesting story for me to reread since it shows that Ray hadn't yet adopted two principles of short fiction which later became laws to him: clarity and purposefulness of expression. But the movement in this story is seamless, held together by that hum of tension he later mastered. . . . I believe Ray would be glad if some young or even middle-aged writer, reading his beginning efforts . . . felt they could do as well or better, or certainly no worse.

The version of the story here is from the collection *Furious Seasons and Other Stories,* published in 1977.

That duration which maketh Pyramids
pillars of snow, and all that's past a moment.

Sir Thomas Browne

RAIN THREATENS. ALREADY the tops of the hills across the valley
are obscured by the heavy gray mist. Quick shifting black clouds with
white furls and caps are coming from the hills, moving down the valley
and passing over the fields and vacant lots in front of the apartment
house. If Farrell lets go his imagination he can see the clouds as black
horses with flared white manes and, turning behind, slowly, inexorably,
black chariots, here and there a white-plumed driver. He shuts the
screen door now and watches his wife step slowly down the stairs. She
turns at the bottom and smiles, and he opens the screen and waves. In
another moment she drives off. He goes back into the room and sits
down in the big leather chair under the brass lamp, laying his arms
straight out along the sides of the chair.

It is a little darker in the room when Iris comes out of her bath
wrapped in a loose white dressing gown. She pulls the stool out from
under the dresser and sits down in front of the mirror. With her right
hand she takes up a white plastic brush, the handle inset with imitation
pearl, and begins combing out her hair in long, sweeping, rhythmical
movements, the brush passing down through the length of the hair with
a faint squeaking noise. She holds her hair down over the one shoulder
with her left hand and makes the long, sweeping, rhythmical movements
with the right. She stops once and switches on the lamp over the mirror.
Farrell takes up a glossy picture magazine from the stand beside the chair
and reaches up to turn on the lamp, fumbling against the parchment-
like shade in his hunt for the chain. The lamp is two feet over his right
shoulder and the brown shade crackles as he touches it.

It is dark outside and the air smells of rain. Iris asks if he will close
the window. He looks up at the window, now a mirror, seeing himself
and, behind, Iris sitting at the dresser watching him, with another,
darker Farrell staring into another window beside her. He has yet to
call Frank and confirm the hunting trip for the next morning. He turns

the pages. Iris takes down the brush from her hair and taps it on the dresser edge.

"Lew," she says, "you know I'm pregnant?"

Under the lamp light the glossy pages are open now to a halftone, two page picture of a disaster scene, an earthquake, somewhere in the Near East. There are five almost fat men dressed in white, baggy pants standing in front of a flattened house. One of the men, probably the leader, is wearing a dirty white hat that hangs down over one eye giving him a secret, malevolent look. He is looking sideways at the camera, pointing across the mess of blocks to a river or a neck of the sea on the far side of the rubble. Farrell closes the magazine and lets it slide out of his lap as he stands. He turns out the light and then, before going on through to the bathroom, asks: "What are you going to do?" The words are dry, hurrying like old leaves into the dark corners of the room and Farrell feels at the same instant the words are out that the question has already been asked by someone else, a long time ago. He turns and goes into the bathroom.

It smells of Iris; a warm, moist odor, slightly sticky; New Spring talc and King's Idyll cologne. Her towel lies across the back of the toilet. In the sink she has spilled talcum. It is wet now and pasty and makes a thick yellow ring around the white sides. He rubs it out and washes it into the drain.

He is shaving. By turning his head, he can see into the living room. Iris in profile sitting on the stool in front of the old dresser. He lays down the razor and washes his face, then picks up the razor again. At this moment he hears the first few drops of rain spatter against the roof. . . .

After a while he turns out the light over the dresser and sits down again in the big leather chair, listening to the rain. The rain comes in short, fluttery swishes against his window. The soft fluttering of a white bird.

His sister has caught it. She keeps it in a box, dropping in flowers for it through the top, sometimes shaking the box so they can hear it fluttering its wings against the sides until one morning she shows him, holding out the box, there is no fluttering inside. Only a lumpy, scraping sound the bird makes as she tilts the box from one side to the other.

When she gives it to him to get rid of he throws box and all into the river, not wanting to open it for it has started to smell funny. The cardboard box is — eighteen inches long and six inches wide and four inches deep, and he is sure it is a Snowflake cracker box because this is what she used for the first few birds.

He runs along the squashy bank following. It is a funeral boat and the muddy river is the Nile and it will soon run into the ocean but before that the boat will burn up and the white bird will fly out and into his father's fields someplace where he will hunt out the bird in some thick growth of green meadow grass, eggs and all. He runs along the bank, the brush whipping his pants, and once a limb hits him on the ear, and it still hasn't burned. He pulls loose some rocks from the bank and begins throwing them at the boat. And then the rain begins; huge, gusty, spattering drops that belt the water, sweeping across the river from one shore to the other.

FARRELL had been in bed for a number of hours now, how long he could not be sure. Every so often he raised up on one shoulder, careful not to disturb his wife, and peered across to her nightstand trying for a look at the clock. Its side was turned a little too much in his direction and raising as he does on one shoulder, being as careful as possible, he could see only that the yellow hands say 3:15 or 2:45. Outside the rain came against his window. He turned on his back, his legs spread wide under the sheet barely touching his wife's left foot, listening to the clock on the nightstand. He pulled down into the quilts again and then because it was too hot and his hands were sweating, he threw back the close covers, twisting his fingers into the sheet, crushing it between his fingers and knotting it against his palms until they felt dry.

Outside the rain came in clouds, lifting up in swells against the faint yellow outside light like myriads of tiny yellow insects coming furiously against his window, spitting and rippling. He turned over and slowly began working himself closer to Lorraine until her smooth back touched his chest. For a moment he held her gently, carefully, his hand lying in the hollow of her stomach, his fingers slipped under the elastic band of her underpants, the fingertips barely touching the stiff, brush-like hair below. An odd sensation then, like slipping into a warm bath and feeling

himself a child again, the memories flooding back. He moved his hand and pulled away, then eased out of bed and walked to the streaming window.

It was a huge, foreign dream night outside. The street lamp a gaunt, scarred obelisk running up into the rain with a faint yellow light holding to its point. At its base the street was black, shiny. Darkness swirled and pulled at the edges of the light. He could not see the other apartments and for a moment it was as if they'd been destroyed, like the houses in the picture he'd been looking at a few hours ago. The rain appeared and disappeared against the window like a dark veil opened and closed. Down below it flooded at the curbs. Leaning closer until he could feel the cold drafts of air on his forehead from the bottom of the window, he watched his breath make a fog. He had read some place and it seemed he could remember looking at some picture once, perhaps *National Geographic,* where groups of brown-skinned people stood around their huts watching the frosted sun come up. The caption said they believed the soul was visible in the breath, that they were spitting and blowing into the palms of their hands, offering their souls to God. His breath disappeared while he watched until only a tiny circle, a dot remained, then nothing. He turned away from the window for his things.

He fumbled in the closet for his insulated boots, his hands tracing the sleeves of each coat until he found the rubber slick waterproof. He went to the drawer for socks and long underwear, then picked up his shirt and pants and carried the armload through the hallway into the kitchen before turning on the light. He dressed and pulled on his boots before starting the coffee. He would have liked to turn on the porchlight for Frank but somehow it didn't seem good with Iris out there in bed. While the coffee perked he made sandwiches and when it had finished he filled a thermos, took a cup down from the cupboard, filled it, and sat down near the window where he could watch the street. He smoked and drank the coffee and listened to the clock on the stove, squeaking. The coffee slopped over the cup and the brown drops ran slowly down the side onto the table. He rubbed his fingers through the wet circle across the rough table top.

He is sitting at the desk in his sister's room. He sits in the straight-backed chair on a thick dictionary, his feet curled up beneath the seat of the chair, the heels of his shoes hooked on the rung. When he leans too

heavily on the table one of the legs picks up from the floor and so he has had to put a magazine under the leg. He is drawing a picture of the valley he lives in. At first he meant to trace a picture from one of his sister's schoolbooks, but after using three sheets of paper and having it still not turn out right, he has decided to draw his valley and his house. Occasionally he stops drawing and rubs his fingers across the grainy surface of the table.

Outside the April air is still damp and cool, the coolness that comes after the rain in the afternoon. The ground and the trees and the mountains are green and steam is everywhere, coming off the troughs in the corral, from the pond his father made, and out of the meadow in slow, pencil-like columns, rising off the river and going up over the mountains like smoke. He can hear his father shouting to one of the men and he hears the man swear and shout back. He puts his drawing pencil down and slips off the chair. Down below in front of the smokehouse he sees his father working with the pulley. At his feet there is a coil of brown rope and his father is hitting and pulling on the pulley bar trying to swing it out and away from the barn. On his head he wears a brown wool army cap and the collar of his scarred leather jacket is turned up exposing the dirty white lining. With a final blow at the pulley he turns around facing the men. Two of them, big, red-faced Canadians with greasy flannel hats, dragging the sheep toward his father. Their fists are balled deep into the wool and one of them has his arms wrapped around the front legs of the sheep. They go toward the barn, half dragging, half walking the sheep on its hind legs like some wild dance. His father calls out again and they pin the sheep against the barn wall one of the men straddling the sheep, forcing its head back and up toward his window. Its nostrils are dark slits with little streams of mucus running down into its mouth. The ancient, glazed eyes stare up at him for a moment before it tries to bleat, but the sound comes out a sharp squeaking noise as his father cuts it off with a quick, sweeping thrust of the knife. The blood gushes out over the man's hands before he can move. In a few moments they have the animal up on the pulley. He can hear the dull crank-crank-crank of the pulley as his father winds it even higher. The men are sweating now but they keep their jackets fastened up tight.

Starting right below the gaping throat his father opens up the brisket and belly while the men take the smaller knives and begin cutting the

pelt away from the legs. The gray guts slide out of the steaming belly and tumble onto the ground in a thick coil. His father grunts and scoops them into a box saying something about bear. The red-faced men laugh. He hears the chain in the bathroom rattle and then the water gurgling into the toilet. A moment later he turns toward the door as footsteps approach. His sister comes into the room, her body faintly steaming. For an instant she is frozen there in the doorway with the towel around her hair one hand holding the ends together and the other on the doorknob. Her breasts are round and smooth-looking, the nipples like the stems of the warm porcelain fruit on the living room table. She drops the towel and it slides down pulling at her neck, touching across her breasts and then heaping up at her feet. She smiles, slowly puts the hand to her mouth and pulls the door shut. He turns back to the window, his toes curling up in his shoes.

FARRELL sat at the table sipping his coffee, smoking again on an empty stomach. Once he heard a car in the street and got up quickly out of the chair, walking to the porch window to see. It started up the street in second then slowed in front of his house, taking the corner carefully, water churning half up to its hubs, but it went on. He sat down at the table again and listened to the electric clock on the stove, squeaking. His fingers tightened around the cup. Then he saw the lights. They came bobbing down the street out of the darkness; two close-set signal lanterns on a narrow prow, the heavy white rain falling across the lights, pelting the street ahead. It splashed down the street, slowed, then eased in under his window.

He picked up his things and went out on the porch. Iris was there, stretched out under the twisted pile of heavy quilts. Even as he hunted for a reason for the action, as if he were detached somehow, crouched on the other side of her bed watching himself go through this, at the same time knowing it was over, he moved toward her bed. Irresistibly he bent down over her figure, as if he hung suspended, all senses released except that of smell, he breathed deeply for the fleeting scent of her body, bending until his face was against her covers he experienced the scent again, for just an instant, and then it was gone. He backed away, remembered his gun, then pulled the door shut behind him. The rain whipped into his face. He felt almost giddy clutching his gun and hold-

ing on to the banister, steadying himself. For a minute, looking down over the porch to the black, ripply sidewalk, it was as though he were standing alone on a bridge someplace, and again the feeling came, as it had last night, that this had already happened, knowing then that it would happen again, just as he somehow knew now. "Christ!" The rain cut at his face, ran down his nose and onto his lips. Frank tapped the horn twice and Farrell went carefully down the wet, slippery stairs to the car.

"Regular downpour, by God!" Frank said. A big man, with a thick quilted jacket zipped up to his chin and a brown duck-bill cap that made him look like a grim umpire. He helped move things around in the back seat so Farrell could put his things in.

Water ran up against the gutters, backed up at the drains on the corners and now and then they could see where it had flooded over the curbs and into a yard. They followed the street to its end and then turned right onto another street that would take them to the highway.

"This is going to slow us down some, but Jesus think what it's going to do to them geese!"

Once again Farrell let go and saw them, pulling them back from that one moment when even the fog had frozen to the rocks and so dark it could as well have been midnight as late afternoon when they started. They come over the bluff, flying low and savage and silent, coming out of the fog suddenly, spectrally, in a swishing of wings over his head and he is jumping up trying to single out the closest, at the same moment pushing forward his safety, but it is jammed and his stiff, gloved finger stays hooked into the guard, pulling against the locked trigger. They all come over him, flying out of the fog across the bluff and over his head. Great strings of them calling down to him. This was the way it happened three years ago.

He watched the wet fields fall under their lights and then sweep beside and then behind the car. The windshield wipers squeaked back and forth.

Iris pulls her hair down over the one shoulder with her left hand while the other wields the brush. Rhythmically the brush makes its sweeping movement through the length of the hair with a faint squeaking noise. The brush rises quickly again to the side of the head and repeats the movement and the sound. She has just told him she is pregnant.

Lorraine has gone to a shower. He has still to call Frank and confirm the hunting trip. The glossy picture of the magazine he holds in his lap is open to the scene of a disaster. One of the men in the picture, evidently the leader, is pointing over the disaster scene to a body of water.

"What are you going to do?" He turns and goes on through to the bathroom. Her towel hangs over the back of the toilet and the bathroom smells of New Spring talc and King's Idyll cologne. There is a yellow pasty ring of talcum powder in the sink that he must rub out with water before he shaves. He can look through to the living room where she sits combing her hair. When he has washed his face and dried, just after he has picked up the razor again, the first raindrops strike the roof.

He looked at the clock on the dashboard but it had stopped.

"What time is it?"

"Don't pay any attention to that clock there," Frank said, lifting his thumb off the wheel to indicate the big glowing yellow clock protruding from the dash. "It's stopped. It's six-thirty. Did your wife say you had to be home at a certain time?" He smiled.

Farrell shook his head but Frank would not be able to see this. "No. Just wondered what time it was." He lit a cigarette and slumped back in his seat, watching the rain sweep into the car lights and splash against the window.

They are driving down from Yakima to get Iris. It started to rain when they hit the Columbia River highway and by the time they got through Arlington, it was a torrent.

It is like a long sloping tunnel, and they are speeding down the black road with the thick matted trees close overhead and the water cascading against the front of the car. Lorraine's arm extends along the back of the seat, her hand resting lightly on his left shoulder. She is sitting so close that he can feel her left breast rise and fall with her breathing. She has just tried to dial something on the radio, but there is too much static.

"She can fix up the porch for a place to sleep and keep her things," Farrell says, not taking his eyes off the road. "It won't be for long."

Lorraine turns toward him for a moment leaning forward a little in the seat, placing her free hand on his thigh. With her left hand she squeezes her fingers into his shoulder then leans her head against him. After a while she says: "You're all mine, Lew. I hate to think of sharing you even for a little while with anybody. Even your own sister."

The rain lets up gradually and often there are no trees at all over their heads. Once Farrell sees the moon, a sharp, stark yellow crescent, shining through the mist of gray clouds. They leave the woods and the road curves and they follow it into a valley that opens onto the river below. It has stopped raining and the sky is a black rug with handfuls of glistening stars strewn about.

"How long will she stay?" Lorraine asks.

"A couple of months. Three at the most. The Seattle job will be open for her before Christmas." The ride has made his stomach a little fluttery. He lights a cigarette. The gray smoke streams out of his nose and is immediately pulled out through the wing window.

The cigarette began to bite the tip of his tongue and he cracked the window and dropped it out. Frank turned off the highway and onto a slick blacktop that would take them to the river. They were in the wheat country now, the great fields of harvested wheat rolling out toward the dimly outlined hills beyond and broken every so often by a muddy, churned-looking field glimmering with little pockets of water. Next year they would be in plant and in the summer the wheat would stand as high as a man's waist, hissing and bending when the wind blew.

"It's a shame," Frank said, "all this land without grain half the time with half the people in the world starving." He shook his head. "If the government would keep its fingers off the farm we'd be a damn sight better off."

The pavement ended in a jag of cracks and chuckholes and the car bounced onto the rubbery, black pitted road that stretched like a long black avenue toward the hills.

"Have you ever seen them when they harvest, Lew?"

"No."

The morning grayed. Farrell saw the stubble fields turned into a cheat-yellow as he watched. He looked out the window at the sky where gray clouds rolled and broke into massive, clumsy chunks. "The rain's going to quit."

They came to the foot of the hills where the fields ended, then turned and drove along at the edge of the fields following the hills until they came to the head of the canyon. Far below at the very bottom of the stone-ribbed canyon lay the river, its far side covered by a bank of fog.

"It's stopped raining," Farrell said.

Frank backed the car into a small, rocky ravine and said it was a good enough place. Farrell took out his shotgun and leaned it against the rear fender before taking out his shell bag and extra coat. Then he lifted out the paper sack with the sandwiches and his hand closed tightly around the warm, hard thermos. They walked away from the car without talking and along the ridge before starting to drop down into one of the small valleys that opened into the canyon. The earth was studded here and there with sharp rocks or a black, dripping bush.

The ground sogged under his feet, pulled at his boots with every step, and made a sucking noise when he released them. He carried the shell bag in his right hand, swinging it like a sling, letting it hang down by its strap from his hand. A wet breeze off the river blew against his face. The sides of the low bluffs overlooking the river down below were deeply grooved and cut back into the rock, leaving table-like projections jutting out, marking the high water lines for thousands of years past. Piles of naked white logs and countless pieces of driftwood lay jammed onto the ledge like cairns of bones dragged up onto the cliffs by some giant bird. Farrell tried to remember where the geese came over three years ago. He stopped on the side of a hill just where it sloped into the canyon and leaned his gun on a rock. He pulled bushes and gathered rocks from nearby and walked down toward the river after some of the driftwood to make a blind.

He sat on his raincoat with his back against a hard shrub, his knees drawn up to his chin, watching the sky whiten and then blue a little and the clouds run with the wind. Geese were gabbling somewhere in the fog on the other side of the river. He rested and smoked and watched the smoke whip out of his mouth. He waited for the sun.

It is four in the afternoon. The sun has just gone behind the gray, late afternoon clouds leaving a dwarfed half-shadow that falls across the car following him as he walks around to open the door for his wife. They kiss.

Iris and he will be back for her in an hour and forty-five minutes, exactly. They are going by the hardware store and then to the grocery. They will be back for her at 5:45. He slides in behind the wheel again and in a moment, seeing his chance, eases out into the traffic. On the way out of town he must stop and wait for every red light, finally turning left onto the secondary, hitting the gas so hard that they both lean back

a little in the seat. It is 4:20. At the forks they turn onto the blacktop, orchards on both sides of the road. Over the tops of the trees, the low brown hills and beyond, the blue-black mountains crowned with white. From the close rows of trees, shadows, blackening into the shoulders, creep across the pavement in front of the car. New boxes are jumbled together in white piles at the end of each orchard row and up against the trees or pushed into the limbs, some leaning in the crotches, are the ladders. He slows the car and stops, pulling off onto the shoulder close enough to one of the trees so that all Iris has to do is open her door and she can reach the limb. It scrapes against the door as she releases it. The apples are heavy and yellow, and sweet juice spurts into his teeth as he bites into one.

The road ends and they follow the dust covered hardtrack right up to the edge of the hills where the orchards stop. He can still go farther, though, by turning onto the bank road that follows the irrigation canal. The canal is empty now and the steep dirt banks are dry and crumbling. He has shifted the car into second. The road is steeper, driving is more difficult and slower. He stops the car under a pine tree outside a water gate where the canal comes down out of the hills to slide into a circular, cement trough. Iris lays her head in his lap. It is nearly dark. The wind is blowing through the car and once he hears the tops of the trees creaking.

He gets out of the car to light a cigarette, walking to the rim of the hill overlooking the valley. The wind has strengthened; the air is colder. The grass is sparse under his feet and there are a few flowers. The cigarette makes a short, twisting red arc as it spins down into the valley. It is six o'clock.

THE cold was bad. The dead numbness of the toes, the cold slowly working its way up into the calves of his legs and setting in under his knees. His fingers too, stiff and cold even though they were balled into his pockets. Farrell waited for the sun. The huge clouds over the river turned, breaking up, shaping and reshaping while he watched. At first he barely noticed the black line against the lowest clouds. When it crossed into sight he thought it was mosquitos, close up against his blind, and then it was a far-off dark rent between cloud and sky that moved closer while he watched. The line turned toward him then and

spread out over the hills below. He was excited but calm, his heart beating in his ears urging him to run, yet his movements slow and ponderous as if heavy stones hung to his legs. He inched up on his knees until his face pressed into the brush wall and turned his eyes toward the ground. His legs shook and he pushed his knees into the soft earth. The legs grew suddenly numb and he moved his hand and pushed it into the ground up over his fingers, surprised at its warmth. Then the soft gabble of geese over his head and the heavy, whistling push of wings. His finger tightened around the trigger. The quick, rasping calls; the sharp upward jerk of ten feet as they saw him. Farrell was on his feet now, pulling down on one goose before swinging to another, then again quickly onto a closer one, following it as it broke and cut back over his head toward the river. He fired once, twice, and the geese kept flying, clamoring, split up and out of range, their low forms melting into the rolling hills. He fired once more before dropping back to his knees inside the blind. Somewhere on the hill behind him and a little to the left he heard Frank shooting, the reports rolling down through the canyon like sharp whip snaps. He felt confused to see more geese getting off the river, stringing out over the low hills and rising up the canyon, flying in V formations for the top of the canyon and the fields behind. He reloaded carefully, pushing the green, ribbed #2's up into the breech, pumping one of the shells into the chamber with a hollow, cracking sound. Yet six shells would do the job better than three. He quickly loosened the plug from the underbarrel of the gun and dropped the coil spring and the wooden plug into his pocket. He heard Frank shoot again, and suddenly there was a flock gone by he hadn't seen. As he watched them he saw three more coming in low and from the side. He waited until they were even with him, swinging across the side of the hill thirty yards away, their heads swinging slowly, rhythmically, right to left, the eyes black and glistening. He raised to one knee, just as they passed him, giving them a good lead, squeezing off an instant before they flared. The one nearest him crumpled and dived straight into the ground. He fired again as they turned, seeing the goose stop it as if it had run into a wall, flailing against the wall trying to get over it before turning over, head downward, wings out, to slowly spiral down. He emptied his gun at the third goose even when it was probably out of range, seeing it stop the charge on the fifth shot, its tail jerking hard and settling down, but its wings still beating.

For a long time he watched it flying closer and closer to the ground before it disappeared into one of the canyons.

Farrell laid the two geese on their backs inside the blind and stroked their smooth white undersides. They were Canadian geese, honkers. After this it didn't matter too much that the geese that flew came over too high or went out someplace else down the river. He sat against the shrub and smoked, watching the sky whirl by over his head. Sometime later, perhaps in the early afternoon, he slept.

When he woke he was stiff, cold and sweating and the sun was gone, the sky a thickening gray pall. Somewhere he could hear geese calling and going out, leaving those strange sharp echoes in the valleys, but he could see nothing but wet, black hills that ended in fog where the river should have been. He wiped his hand over his face and began to shiver. He stood up. He could see the fog rolling up the canyon and over the hills, closing off and hemming in the land, and he felt the breath of the cold damp air around him, touching his forehead and cheeks and lips. He broke through the blind getting out and started running up the hill.

He stood outside the car and pressed the horn in a continual blast until Frank ran up and jerked his arm away from the window.

"What's the matter with you? Are you crazy or something?"

"I have to go home, I tell you!"

"*Jesus* Christ! Well, *Jesus* Christ! Get in then, get in!"

They were quiet then but for Farrell's asking twice the time before they were out of the wheat country. Frank held a cigar between his teeth, never taking his eyes from the road. When they ran into the first drifting patches of fog he switched on the car lights. After they turned onto the highway the fog lifted and layered somewhere in the dark over the car, and the first drops of rain began hitting the windshield. Once three ducks flew in front of the car lights and pitched into a puddle beside the road. Farrell blinked.

"Did you see that?" Frank asked.

Farrell nodded.

"How do you feel now?"

"Okay."

"You get any geese?"

Farrell rubbed the palms of his hands together, interlacing his fingers, finally folding them into his lap. "No, I guess not."

"Too bad. I heard you shooting." He worked the cigar to the other side of his mouth and tried to puff, but it had gone cold. He chewed on it for a minute then laid it in the ashtray and glanced at Farrell.

"Course it's none of my affair, but if it's something you're worried about at home. . . . My advice is not to take it too seriously. You'll live longer. No gray hairs like me." He coughed, laughed. "I know, I used to be the same way. I remember. . . ."

Farrell is sitting in the big leather chair under the brass lamp watching Iris comb out her hair. He is holding a magazine in his lap whose glossy pages are open to the scene of a disaster, an earthquake, somewhere in the Near East. Except for the small light over the dresser it is dark in the room. The brush moves quickly through her hair in long, sweeping, rhythmical movements, causing a faint squeaking noise in the room. He has yet to call Frank and confirm the hunting trip for the next morning. There is a cold, moist air coming in through the window from the outside. She is tapping the brush against the edge of the dresser. "Lew," she says, "you know I'm pregnant?"

Her bathroom smell sickens him. Her towel lies across the back of the toilet. In the sink she has spilled talcum. It is wet now and pasty and makes a thick, yellow ring around the white sides. He rubs it out and washes it into the drain.

He is shaving. By turning his head he can see into the living room. Iris in profile sitting on the stool in front of the old dresser. She is combing her hair. He lays down the razor and washes his face, then picks up the razor again. At this moment he hears the first few drops of rain spatter against the roof. . . .

He carries her out to the porch, turns her face to the wall, and covers her up. He goes back into the bathroom, washes his hands, and stuffs the heavy, blood-soaked towel into the clothes hamper. After a while he turns out the light over the dresser and sits down again in his chair by the window, listening to the rain.

Frank laughed. "So it was nothing, nothing at all. We got along fine after that. Oh, the usual bickering now and then but when she found out just who was running the show, everything was all right." He gave Farrell a friendly rap on the knee.

They drove into the outskirts of town, past the long line of motels with their blazing red, blinking, neon lights, past the cafes with steamy

windows the cars clustered in front, and past the small businesses, dark and locked until the next day. Frank turned right at the next light, then left, and now they were on Farrell's street. Frank pulled in behind a black and white car that had SHERIFF'S OFFICE painted in small white letters across the trunk. In the lights of their car they could see another glass inside the car inset with a wire screen making the back seat into a cage. Steam rose from the hood of their car and mixed with the rain.

"Could be he's after you, Lew." He started to open the door, then chuckled. "Maybe they've found out you were hunting with no license. Come on, I'll turn you in myself."

"No. You go on Frank. That's all right. I'll be all right. Wait a minute, let me get out!"

"Christ, you'd really think they were after you! Wait a minute, get your gun." He rolled down the window and passed out the shotgun to Farrell. "Look's like the rain's never going to let up. See you."

"Yeah."

Upstairs all the lights of his apartment were turned on and blurred figures stood frieze-like at the windows looking down through the rain. Farrell stood behind the sheriff's car holding on to the smooth, wet tail fin. Rain fell on his bare head and worked its way down under his collar. Frank drove a few yards up the street and stopped, looking back. Farrell holding on to the tail fin, swaying a little, with the fine impenetrable rain coming down around him. The gutter water rushed over his feet, swirled frothing into a great whirlpool at the drain on the corner and rushed down to the center of the earth.

||≣

Expelled

In his essay on John Cheever for the *Dictionary of Literary Biography,* Robert A. Morace writes, "Although Cheever has referred to ["Expelled"] slightingly as 'the reminiscences of a sorehead,' his story is neither plaintive nor amateurish and in many ways anticipates the style that has since become Cheever's hallmark." As evidence, Morace notes both the story's episodic, rather than linear, narrative structure, and its central conflict between the decorum required by social imperatives and the longings of the narrator, "the first in a long line of displaced persons who make up Cheever's fiction," to break free.

When he was seventeen, Cheever was expelled from Thayer Academy in Massachusetts for smoking. That event occasioned both the end of his formal education and the beginning of his literary career. "Expelled" (by "Jon" Cheever) was published in the *New Republic* on October 1, 1930, when Cheever was eighteen. Six years would pass before he published a second story and thirteen years before the publication of his first collection, *The Way Some People Live.* "Expelled" has never before appeared in any anthology or collection, although the *New Republic* reprinted it, along with the following original editors' note, in its July 19–26, 1982, issue, on the occasion of Cheever's death:

Teachers often write brilliant things about their pupils, but it is very seldom that pupils of preparatory-school age are able to return the compliment. John Cheever is an exception. Last spring he was expelled from an academy in Massachusetts at the end of his junior year. In the following sketches, written at the age of seventeen, he reproduces the atmosphere of an institution where education is served out dry in cakes, like pemmican. —THE EDITORS

IT DIDN'T COME all at once. It took a very long time. First I had a skirmish with the English department and then all the other departments. Pretty soon something had to be done. The first signs were cordialities on the part of the headmaster. He was never nice to anybody unless he was a football star, or hadn't paid his tuition or was going to be expelled. That's how I knew.

He called me down to his office with the carved chairs arranged in a semicircle and the brocade curtains resting against the vacant windows. All about him were pictures of people who had got scholarships at Harvard. He asked me to sit down.

"Well, Charles," he said, "some of the teachers say you aren't getting very good marks."

"Yes," I said, "that's true." I didn't care about the marks.

"But Charles," he said, "you know the scholastic standard of this school is very high and we have to drop people when their work becomes unsatisfactory." I told him I knew that also. Then he said a lot of things about the traditions, and the elms, and the magnificent military heritage from our West Point founder.

It was very nice outside of his room. He had his window pushed open halfway and one could see the lawns pulling down to the road behind the trees and the bushes. The gravy-colored curtains were too heavy to move about in the wind, but some papers shifted around on his desk. In a little while I got up and walked out. He turned and started to work again. I went back to my next class.

The next day was very brilliant and the peach branches were full against the dry sky. I could hear people talking and a phonograph playing. The sounds came through the peach blossoms and crossed the room. I lay in bed and thought about a great many things. My dreams had been thick. I remembered two converging hills, some dry apple trees and a broken blue egg cup. That is all I could remember.

I put on knickers and a soft sweater and headed toward school. My hands shook on the wheel. I was like that all over.

Through the cloudy trees I could see the protrusion of the new tower. It was going to be a beautiful new tower and it was going to cost a great

deal of money. Some thought of buying new books for the library instead of putting up a tower, but no one would see the books. People would be able to see the tower five miles off when the leaves were off the trees. It would be done by fall.

When I went into the building the headmaster's secretary was standing in the corridor. She was a nice sort of person with brown funnels of hair furrowed about a round head. She smiled. I guess she must have known.

THE COLONEL

Every morning we went up into the black chapel. The brisk headmaster was there. Sometimes he had a member of the faculty with him. Sometimes it was a stranger.

He introduced the stranger, whose speech was always the same. In the spring life is like a baseball game. In the fall it is like football. That is what the speaker always said.

The hall is damp and ugly with skylights that rattle in the rain. The seats are hard and you have to hold a hymnbook in your lap. The hymnbook often slips off and that is embarrassing.

On Memorial Day they have the best speaker. They have a mayor or a Governor. Sometimes they have a Governor's second. There is very little preference.

The Governor will tell us what a magnificent country we have. He will tell us to beware of the Red menace. He will want to tell us that the goddam foreigners should have gone home a hell of a long time ago. That they should have stayed in their own goddam countries if they didn't like ours. He will not dare say this though.

If they have a mayor the speech will be longer. He will tell us that our country is beautiful and young and strong. That the War is over, but that if there is another war we must fight. He will tell us that war is a masculine trait that has brought present civilization to its fine condition. Then he will leave us and help stout women place lilacs on graves. He will tell them the same thing.

One Memorial Day they could not get a Governor or a mayor. There was a colonel in the same village who had been to war and who had a chest thick with medals. They asked him to speak. Of course he said he would like to speak.

He was a thin colonel with a soft nose that rested quietly on his face. He was nervous and pushed his wedding ring about his thin finger. When he was introduced he looked at the audience sitting in the uncomfortable chairs. There was silence and the dropping of hymnbooks like the water spouts in the aftermath of a heavy rain.

He spoke softly and quickly. He spoke of war and what he had seen. Then he had to stop. He stopped and looked at the boys. They were staring at their boots. He thought of the empty rooms in the other buildings. He thought of the rectangles of empty desks. He thought of the curtains on the stage and the four Windsor chairs behind him. Then he started to speak again.

He spoke as quickly as he could. He said war was bad. He said that there would never be another war. That he himself should stop it if he could. He swore. He looked at the young faces. They were all very clean. The boys' knees were crossed and their soft pants hung loosely. He thought of the empty desks and began to whimper.

The people sat very still. Some of them felt tight as though they wanted to giggle. Everybody looked serious as the clock struck. It was time for another class.

People began to talk about the colonel after lunch. They looked behind them. They were afraid he might hear them.

It took the school several weeks to get over all this. Nobody said anything, but the colonel was never asked again. If they could not get a Governor or a mayor they could get someone besides a colonel. They made sure of that.

MARGARET COURTWRIGHT

Margaret Courtwright was very nice. She was slightly bald and pulled her pressed hair down across her forehead. People said that she was the best English teacher in this part of the country, and when boys came back from Harvard they thanked her for the preparation she had given them. She did not like Edgar Guest, but she did like Carl Sandburg. She couldn't seem to understand the similarity. When I told her people laughed at Galsworthy she said that people used to laugh at Wordsworth. She did not believe people were still laughing at Wordsworth. That was what made her so nice.

She came from the West a long time ago. She taught school for so

long that people ceased to consider her age. After having seen twenty-seven performances of "Hamlet" and after having taught it for sixteen years, she became a sort of immortal. Her interpretation was the one accepted on college-board papers. That helped everyone a great deal. No one had to get a new interpretation.

When she asked me for tea I sat in a walnut armchair with grapes carved on the head and traced and retraced the arms on the tea caddy. One time I read her one of my plays. She thought it was wonderful. She thought it was wonderful because she did not understand it and because it took two hours to read. When I had finished, she said, "You know that thing just took right hold of me. Really it just swept me right along. I think it's fine that you like to write. I once had a Japanese pupil who liked to write. He was an awfully nice chap until one summer he went down to Provincetown. When he came back he was saying that he could express a complete abstraction. Fancy . . . a complete abstraction. Well, I wouldn't hear of it and told him how absurd it all was and tried to start him off with Galsworthy again, but I guess he had gone just too far. In a little while he left for New York and then Paris. It was really too bad. One summer in Provincetown just ruined him. His marks fell down . . . he cut classes to go to symphony. . . ." She went into the kitchen and got a tray of tarts.

The pastries were flaky and covered with a white coating that made them shine in the dead sunlight. I watched the red filling burst the thin shells and stain the triangles of bright damask. The tarts were good. I ate most of them.

She was afraid I would go the way of her Japanese pupil. She doubted anyone who disagreed with Heine on Shakespeare and Croce on expression.

One day she called me into her antiseptic office and spoke to me of reading Joyce. "You know, Charles," she said, "this sex reality can be quite as absurd as a hypercritical regard for such subjects. You know that, don't you? Of course, you do." Then she went out of the room. She had straight ankles and wore a gold band peppered with diamond chips on her ring finger. She seemed incapable of carrying the weight of the folds in her clothing. Her skirt was askew, either too long in front or hitching up on the side. Always one thing or the other.

When I left school she did not like it. She was afraid I might go too

near Provincetown. She wished me good luck and moved the blotter back and forth on her desk. Then she returned to teaching "Hamlet."

Late in February Laura Driscoll got fired for telling her history pupils that Sacco and Vanzetti were innocent. In her farewell appearance the headmaster told everyone how sorry he was that she was going and made it all quite convincing. Then Laura stood up, told the headmaster that he was a damned liar, and waving her fan-spread fingers called the school a hell of a dump where everyone got into a rut.

Miss Courtwright sat closely in her chair and knew it was true. She didn't mind much. Professor Rogers with his anti-feminization movement bothered her a little, too. But she knew that she had been teaching school for a long time now and no movement was going to put her out of a job overnight — what with all the boys she had smuggled into Harvard and sixteen years of "Hamlet."

LAURA DRISCOLL

History classes are always dead. This follows quite logically, for history is a dead subject. It has not the death of dead fruit or dead textiles or dead light. It has a different death. There is not the timeless quality of death about it. It is dead like scenery in the opera. It is on cracked canvas and the paint has faded and peeled and the lights are too bright. It is dead like old water in a zinc bathtub.

"We are going to study ancient history this year," the teacher will tell the pupils. "Yes, ancient history will be our field.

"Now of course, this class is not a class of children any longer. I expect the discipline to be the discipline of well bred young people. We shall not have to waste any time on the scolding of younger children. No. We shall just be able to spend all our time on ancient history.

"Now about questions. I shall answer questions if they are important. If I do not think them important I shall not answer them, for the year is short, and we must cover a lot of ground in a short time. That is, if we all coöperate and behave and not ask too many questions we shall cover the subject and have enough time at the end of the year for review.

"You may be interested in the fact that a large percentage of this class was certified last year. I should like to have a larger number this year. Just think, boys: wouldn't it be fine if a very large number — a number larger than last year — was certified? Wouldn't that be fine? Well, there's

no reason why we can't do it if we all coöperate and behave and don't ask too many questions.

"You must remember that I have twelve people to worry about and that you have only one. If each person will take care of his own work and pass in his notebook on time it will save me a lot of trouble. Time and trouble mean whether you get into college or not, and I want you all to get into college.

"If you will take care of your own little duties, doing what is assigned to you and doing it well, we shall all get along fine. You are a brilliant-looking group of young people, and I want to have you all certified. I want to get you into college with as little trouble as possible.

"Now about the books. . . ."

I do not know how long history classes have been like this. One time or another I suppose history was alive. That was before it died its horrible fly-dappled unquivering death.

Everyone seems to know that history is dead. No one is alarmed. The pupils and the teachers love dead history. They do not like it when it is alive. When Laura Driscoll dragged history into the classroom, squirming and smelling of something bitter, they fired Laura and strangled the history. It was too tumultous. Too turbulent.

In history one's intellect is used for mechanical speculation on a probable century or background. One's memory is applied to a list of dead dates and names. When one begins to apply one's intellect to the mental scope of the period, to the emotional development of its inhabitants, one becomes dangerous. Laura Driscoll was terribly dangerous. That's why Laura was never a good history teacher.

She was not the first history teacher I had ever had. She is not the last I will have. But she is the only teacher I have ever had who could feel history with an emotional vibrance — or, if the person was too oblique, with a poetic understanding. She was five feet four inches tall, brown-haired, and bent-legged from horseback riding. All the boys thought Laura Driscoll was a swell teacher.

She was the only history teacher I have ever seen who was often ecstatical. She would stand by the boards and shout out her discoveries on the Egyptian cultures. She made the gargoylic churnings of Chartres in a heavy rain present an applicable meaning. She taught history as an interminable flood of events viewed through the distortion of our own

immediacy. She taught history in the broad-handed rhythms of Haupt-
mann's drama, in the static melancholy of Egypt moving before its own
shadow down the long sand, in the fluted symmetry of the Doric culture. She taught history as a hypothesis from which we could extract the
evaluation of our own lives.

She was the only teacher who realized that, coming from the West,
she had little business to be teaching these children of New England.

"I do not know what your reaction to the sea is," she would say. "For
I have come from a land where there is no sea. My elements are the
fields, the sun, the plastic cadence of the clouds and the cloudlessness.
You have been brought up by the sea. You have been coached in the
cadence of the breakers and the strength of the wind.

"My emotional viewpoints will differ from yours. Do not let me impose my perceptions upon you."

However, the college-board people didn't care about Chartres as long
as you knew the date. They didn't care whether history was looked at
from the mountains or the sea. Laura spent too much time on such trivia
and all of her pupils didn't get into Harvard. In fact, very few of her
pupils got into Harvard, and this didn't speak well for her.

While the other members of the faculty chattered over Hepplewhite
legs and Duncan Phyfe embellishments, Laura was before five-handed
Siva or the sexless compassion glorious in its faded polychrome. Laura
didn't think much of America. Laura made this obvious and the faculty
heard about it. The faculty all thought America was beautiful. They
didn't like people to disagree.

However, the consummation did not occur until late in February.
It was cold and clear and the snow was deep. Outside the windows
there was the enormous roaring of broken ice. It was late in February
that Laura Driscoll said Sacco and Vanzetti were undeserving of their
treatment.

This got everyone all up in the air. Even the headmaster was dis-
concerted.

The faculty met.

The parents wrote letters.

Laura Driscoll was fired.

"Miss Driscoll," said the headmaster during her last chapel at the
school, "has found it necessary to return to the West. In the few months

that we have had with us, she has been a staunch friend of the academy, a woman whom we all admire and love and who, we are sure, loves and admires the academy and its elms as we do. We are all sorry Miss Driscoll is leaving us. . . ."

Then Laura got up, called him a damned liar, swore down the length of the platform and walked out of the building.

No one ever saw Laura Driscoll again. By the way everyone talked, no one wanted to. That was all late in February. By March the school was quiet again. The new history teacher taught dates. Everyone carefully forgot about Laura Driscoll.

"She was a nice girl," said the headmaster, "but she really wasn't made for teaching history. . . . No, she really wasn't a born history teacher."

FIVE MONTHS LATER

The spring of five months ago was the most beautiful spring I have ever lived in. The year before I had not known all about the trees and the heavy peach blossoms and the tea-colored brooks that shook down over the brown rocks. Five months ago it was spring and I was in school.

In school the white limbs beyond the study hall shook out a greenness, and the tennis courts became white and scalding. The air was empty and hard, and the vacant wind dragged shadows over the road. I knew all this only from the classrooms.

I knew about the trees from the window frames. I knew the rain only from the sounds on the roof. I was tired of seeing spring with walls and awnings to intercept the sweet sun and the hard fruit. I wanted to go outdoors and see the spring. I wanted to feel and taste the air and be among the shadows. That is perhaps why I left school.

In the spring I was glad to leave school. Everything outside was elegant and savage and fleshy. Everything inside was slow and cool and vacant. It seemed a shame to stay inside.

But in a little while the spring went. I was left outside and there was no spring. I did not want to go in again. I would not have gone in again for anything. I was sorry, but I was not sorry over the fact that I had gone out. I was sorry that the outside and the inside could not have been open to one another. I was sorry that there were roofs on the classrooms and trousers on the legs of the instructors to insulate their contacts. I

was not sorry that I had left school. I was sorry that I left for the reasons that I did.

If I had left because I had to go to work or because I was sick it would not have been so bad. Leaving because you are angry and frustrated is different. It is not a good thing to do. It is bad for everyone.

Of course it was not the fault of the school. The headmaster and faculty were doing what they were supposed to do. It was just a preparatory school trying to please the colleges. A school that was doing everything the colleges asked it to do.

It was not the fault of the school at all. It was the fault of the system — the noneducational system, the college-preparatory system. That was what made the school so useless.

As a college-preparatory school it was a fine school. In five years they could make raw material look like college material. They could clothe it and breed it and make it say the right things when the colleges asked it to talk. That was its duty.

They weren't prepared to educate anybody. They were members of a college-preparatory system. No one around there wanted to be educated. No sir.

They presented the subjects the colleges required. They had math, English, history, languages and music. They once had had an art department but it had been dropped. "We have enough to do," said the headmaster, "just to get all these people into college without trying to teach them art. Yes sir, we have quite enough to do as it is."

Of course there were literary appreciation and art appreciation and musical appreciation, but they didn't count for much. If you are young, there is very little in Thackeray that is parallel to your own world. Van Dyke's "Abbé Scaglia" and the fretwork of Mozart quartets are not for the focus of your ears and eyes. All the literature and art that holds a similarity to your life is forgotten. Some of it is even forbidden.

Our country is the best country in the world. We are swimming in prosperity and our President is the best president in the world. We have larger apples and better cotton and faster and more beautiful machines. This makes us the greatest country in the world. Unemployment is a myth. Dissatisfaction is a fable. In preparatory school America is beautiful. It is the gem of the ocean and it is too bad. It is bad because people

believe it all. Because they become indifferent. Because they marry and reproduce and vote and they know nothing. Because the tempered newspaper keeps its eyes ceilingwards and does not see the dirty floor. Because all they know is the tempered newspaper.

But I will not say any more. I do not stand in a place where I can talk.

And now it is August. The orchards are stinking ripe. The tea-colored brooks run beneath the rocks. There is sediment on the stone and no wind in the willows. Everyone is preparing to go back to school. I have no school to go back to.

I am not sorry. I am not at all glad.

It is strange to be so very young and to have no place to report to at nine o'clock. That is what education has always been. It has been laced curtseys and perfumed punctualities.

But now it is nothing. It is symmetric with my life. I am lost in it. That is why I am not standing in a place where I can talk.

The school windows are being washed. The floors are thick with fresh oil.

Soon it will be time for the snow and the symphonies. It will be time for Brahms and the great dry winds.

\|\|≣

Landing in Luck

William Faulkner was enrolled at the University of Mississippi as a returning veteran when his first short story, "Landing in Luck," was published by the *Mississippian* on November 26, 1919. He was twenty-two years old, and he still used the family spelling of his surname, Falkner. In his two-volume biography of the author, Joseph Blotner notes a common thread between Faulkner's first story and his more mature works: "Faulkner had obviously drawn upon the triad he would often cite later in life as the artist's sources: observation, imagination, and experience." Frederick Karl, in another biography of Faulkner, puts a slightly different spin on the inspiration for "Landing in Luck": "It is . . . a fantasy version of his own situation, in which World War I's end thwarted his desire to fly."

It took Faulkner six more years to get another story published in a major periodical. *The Double Dealer,* an influential southern weekly that, according to Karl, was established partly in response to H. L. Mencken's remark that the south was a cultural wasteland, published "New Orleans" in 1925. The next story that Faulkner succeeded in publishing was "A Rose for Emily," which *Forum* ran in 1930. By this time, Faulkner had already published four novels, including *The Sound and the Fury.* Soon afterward, the *Saturday Evening Post* published another story, "Thrift," for which it paid Faulkner $750, more than he had been paid for any of his novels to date.

THE MACHINE LEVELLED off and settled on the aerodrome. It turned and taxied back and stopped, headed into the wind again, its engine running idle. The instructor in the forward cockpit faced about and raised his goggles.

"Fairish," he said, "not so bad. How many hours have you had?"

Cadet Thompson, a "barracks ace," who had just made a fairly creditable landing, assumed an expression of assured confidence.

"Seven hours and nine minutes, sir."

"Think you can — hold that stick back, will you? — think you can take her round alone?"

"Yes, sir," he answered as he had answered at least four times a day for the last three days, with the small remaining part of his unconquered optimism in his voice. The instructor climbed slowly out onto the lower wing, then to the ground, stretching his legs. He got a cigarette from his clothes after a fashion resembling sleight-of-hand.

"You've got to solo some day. The C. O. gave us all a raggin' last night. It's chaps like you that give this stage such a name for inefficiency. Here you have had seven hours, and yet you never know if you are goin' to land on this aerodrome or down at Borden. And then you always pick a house or another machine to land on. What ever brought you to think you could fly? Swear I don't know what to do with you. Let you try it and break your neck, or recommend you for discharge. Get rid of you either way, and a devilish good thing, too."

A silence hung heavily about Thompson's unhappy head. The instructor, sucking his cigarette, stared off across the aerodrome, where other wild and hardy amateurs took off, landed and crashed. A machine descended tail high, levelled off too soon and landed in a series of bumps like an inferior tennis ball.

"See that chap there? He's probably had half your time but he makes landings alone. But you, you cut your gun and sit up there like a blind idiot and when you condescend to dive the bus, you try your best to break our necks, yours and mine too; and I'll say right now, that's somethin' none of you rockin' chair aviators is goin' to do. Well, it's your neck

or my reputation, now. Take her off, and what ever you do, keep your nose down."

Thompson pulled down his goggles. He had been angry enough to kill his officer for the better part of a week, so added indignities rested but lightly upon him. He was a strange mixture of fear and pride as he opened the throttle wide and pushed the stick forward — fear that he would wreck the machine landing, and pride that he was on his own at last. He was no physical coward, his fear was that he would show himself up before his less fortunate friends to whom he had talked largely of spins and side slips and gliding angles.

All-in-all, he was in no particularly safe frame of mind for his solo flight. He gained speed down the field. The tail was off the ground now and Thompson, more or less nervous, though he had taken the machine off like a veteran with the instructor aboard, pulled the stick back before the machine had gained speed sufficient to rise. It lurched forward and the tail sank heavily, losing more speed. He knew that he had gone too far down the field and should turn back and take off again, so he closed the throttle. When the noise of the engine ceased he heard the instructor shouting at him, and the splutter of a motor cycle. Sending after him, were they? Cadet Thompson was once more cleanly angry. He jerked the throttle open.

His subconscious mind had registered a cable across the end of the field, and he had flown enough to know that it was touch and go as to whether he would clear it. He was afraid of rising too soon again and he knew that he would not stop in time were he to close the throttle now. So, his eyes on the speed indicator, he pulled the stick back. The motion at once became easier and he climbed as much as he dared.

A shock; he closed his eyes, expecting to go over and down on his back in the road below. When nothing happened he ventured a frightened hurried glance. Below him was the yellow of a wheat field and the aerodrome far to the rear.

So the cable had broken! Must have, for here he was still going forward. His altimeter showed two hundred feet. Thompson felt like shouting. Now he'd show 'em what flying was. Rotten, was he? He'd pull a perfect landing and walk up to that officer and tell him just what kind of a poor fish he was.

"Blasted Englishman," he said, "thinks he's the only man in this wing who can really fly. Bet if he'd a' hit that cable he'd a' been on his back in that road right now. Wish t'hell he was."

He made his turn carefully. Below at the edge of the aerodrome stood the ambulance, its crew gaping foolishly at him. "Like fish," he thought, "like poor fish." He leaned out of his cockpit and gestured pleasantly at them, a popular gesture known to all peoples of the civilized world.

Eight hundred feet. "High enough," he decided, and made another circle, losing height. He picked his spot on the field. "Now," he thought, cut the throttle and pushed the stick forward. He found a good gliding angle, wires singing, engine idle and long flames wrapping back from the exhausts. The field was filled with people running about and flapping their arms. Another machine rose to meet him. He opened the throttle and closed it again, a warning. "Why'n the hell don't they get off and lemme land?" he wondered.

The other machine passed him in a long bank, its occupants shouting at him; one of them carried something to which he gestured and pointed frantically. Thompson came out of his dive. They circled again and he saw that the object was about the size and shape of a wheel? A wheel from the landing gear of a machine. What kind of a joke was this? Why had they brought a wheel up to show him? He'd seen lots of wheels. Had two on his machine — on his machine — wheels? Then Thompson remembered the cable. He had stripped a wheel on that cable, then. There was nothing else it could mean. His brain assimilated this fact calmly. Having lost a wheel, he had nothing to land on. Therefore it were quite pointless to bother about landing, immediately, anyway. So he circled off and climbed, followed cautiously by the other machine, like two strange dogs meeting.

"Sir," said an orderly, entering the mess where the C. O. and three lesser lights were playing bridge, "sir, the Flight Commander, B Flight, reports that a cadet is abaht to crash."

"'Crash?'" repeated the C. O.

"Out 'ere, sir. Yes, sir, 'e 'assn't got no landing gear."

"'No landing gear?' What's this? What's this?"

"Yes, sir. 'E wiped it orf a-taking orf, sir. 'E's abaht out of petrol and the Flight Commander says 'e'll be a'coming down soon, sir."

"My word," said the C. O., going to the door and closely followed by the others.

"There 'e is, sir, that's 'im in front."

"My word," said the C. O. again and went off toward the hangars at a very good gait.

"What's this? What's this?" Approaching the group of officers.

"Cadet Thompson, sir," volunteered one, "Mr. Bessing's cadet. Oh, Bessing!"

Bessing came over, lifting his feet nervously.

"What's all this, Mr. Bessing?" The C. O. watched him narrowly. An instructor gets a bad name when his cadet crashes, he is responsible for the cadet's life as well as the machine.

"Rotten take off, sir. He tried to rise too soon, and when he failed, instead of comin' back and tryin' again, he carried right on. Struck that cable and lost his right wheel and he's been sittin' up there ever since. We sent another chap up to pull him up a bit. He's almost out of petrol and he'll have to come down soon."

"H-m. Didn't sent him up too soon, did you, Mr. Bessing?"

"Chap's had seven hours, sir," he protested, and produced Thompson's card.

The C. O. studied it a moment, then returned it.

"Wharton, sir?" He helped the C. O. to a light and lit a cigarette for himself.

"Good lad, good lad," said the C. O., shading his eyes as he stared into the sky. "Something in you people at this wing, though. Cadets and officers both. N. C. O.'s got it, too. G. O. C. gave me a jolly raggin' not a fortnight ago. Do something. Do something, swear I will."

The drone from the engines above suddenly ceased. Thompson was out of petrol at last. The two machines descended in a wide spiral, and they on the earth stood watching him as he descended, as utterly beyond any human aid as though he were on another planet.

"Here they come," Bessing muttered half aloud. "If he only remembers to land on his left wing — the fool, oh, the blind, bounding fool!"

For Thompson's nerve was going as he neared the earth. The temptation was strong to kick his rudder over and close his eyes. The machine descended, barely retaining headway. He watched the approaching

ground utterly unable to make any pretence of levelling off, paralyzed; his brain had ceased to function, he was all staring eyes watching the remorseless earth. He did not know his height, the ground rushed past too swiftly to judge, but he expected to crash any second. Thompson's fate was on the laps of the Gods.

The tail touched, bounded, scraped again. The left wing was low and the wing tip crumpled like paper. A tearing of fabric, a strut snapped, and he regained dominion over his limbs, but too late to do anything — were there anything to be done. The machine struck again, solidly, slewed around and stood on its nose.

Bessing was the first to reach him.

"Lord, Lord!" he was near weeping from nervous tension. "Are you all right? Never expected you'd come through, never expected it! Didn't think to see you alive! Don't ever let anyone else say you can't fly. Comin' out of that was a trick many an old flyer couldn't do! I say, are you all right?"

Hanging face downward from the cockpit, Cadet Thompson looked at Bessing, surprised at the words of this cold, short tempered officer. He forgot the days of tribulation and insult in this man's company, and his recent experience, and his eyes filled with utter adoration. Then he became violently ill.

That night Thompson sat gracefully on a table in the writing room of a down town hotel, tapping a boot with his stick and talking to sundry companions.

"— and so, when my petrol gave out, I knew it was up to me. I had already thought of a plan — I thought of several, but this one seemed the best — which was to put my tail down first and then drop my left wing, so the old bus wouldn't turn over and lie down on me. Well, it worked just as I had doped it out, only a ditch those fool A. M.'s had dug right across the field, mind you, tripped her up and she stood on her nose. I had thought of that, too, and pulled my belt up. Bessing said — he's a pretty good scout —"

"Ah-h-h —" they jeered him down profanely.

"Look at the nerve he's got, will you?"

"He' —"

"Ah, we know you! Why, the poor bum crashed on his solo, and listen at the line he's giving us!"

"Well, Bessing said —"

"Bessing said! Bessing said! Go tell the G.O.C. what Bessing said!"

"Dammit, don't I know what Bessing said? Ask him! That's all. You're a bunch of poor hams that think you can fly! Why, I got an hour and a half solo time. You poor fish. Ask Bessing! there's a guy that knows what's what."

He flung out of the room. They watched him with varying expressions.

"Say," spoke one, a cadet but recently enlisted and still in ground school: "D'you think he really did all that? He must be pretty good."

"That guy? That guy fly? He's so rotten they can't discharge him. Every time he goes up they have to get a gun and shoot him down. He's the 'f' out of flying. Biggest liar in the R.A.F."

Thompson passed through again, with Bessing, and his arm was through the officer's. He was deep in discussion evidently, but he looked up in time to give them a cheerfully condescending:

"Hello, you chaps."

Babes in the Woods

The first incarnation of "Babes in the Woods" appeared in May 1917 in the *Nassau Literary Magazine,* where Fitzgerald published numerous stories, plays, poems, and humor pieces as an undergraduate at Princeton. Many of them were incorporated into his first novel, *This Side of Paradise* (1920), as well as into *Tales of the Jazz Age* (1922). "Babes in the Woods," according to Matthew J. Bruccoli, appeared in *Paradise* as the first encounter between Amory Blaine and Isabelle. It was a revision of this story that Fitzgerald sold to *Smart Set* in mid-1919 for thirty dollars, his first sale. (He used the money to buy white flannel pajamas and a present for future wife Zelda Sayre, whom he was dating.) At just about the time *Smart Set,* under the co-editorship of H. L. Mencken and George Jean Nathan, published "Babes in the Woods" in September 1919, Fitzgerald sold *This Side of Paradise* to Maxwell Perkins at Scribners.

The original version of "Babes in the Woods" appears in *The Apprentice Fiction of F. Scott Fitzgerald,* edited by John Kuehl. The substantially rewritten *Smart Set* version included here has never before been reprinted.

I

SHE PAUSED AT the top of the staircase. The emotions of divers of spring-boards, leading ladies on opening nights, and lumpy, be-striped young men on the day of the Big Game, crowded through her. She felt as if she should have descended to a burst of drums or to a discordant blend of gems from "Thaïs" and "Carmen." She had never been so wor-

ried about her appearance, she had never been so satisfied with it. She had been sixteen years old for six months.

"Isabelle!" called Elaine, her cousin, from the doorway of the dressing-room.

"I'm ready." She caught a slight lump of nervousness in her throat.

"I've had to send back to the house for another pair of slippers — it'll be just a minute."

Isabelle started toward the dressing-room for a last peek at a mirror, but something decided her to stand there and gaze down the stairs. They curved tantalizingly and she could just catch a glimpse of two pairs of masculine feet in the hall below.

Pump shod in uniform black they gave no hint of identity, but eagerly she wondered if one pair were attached to Stephen Palms. This young man, as yet unmet, had taken up a considerable part of her day — the first day of her arrival.

Going up in a machine from the station Elaine had volunteered, amid a rain of questions and comment, revelation and exaggeration —

"You remember Stephen Palms; well he is simply mad to see you again. He's stayed over a day from college and he's coming tonight. He's heard *so* much about you —"

It had pleased her to know this. It put them on more equal terms, although she was accustomed to stage her own romances with or without a send-off.

But following her delighted tremble of anticipation came a sinking sensation which made her ask:

"How do you mean he's heard about me? What sort of things?"

Elaine smiled — she felt more or less in the capacity of a show-woman with her more exotic cousin.

"He knows you're good-looking and all that." She paused — "I guess he knows you've been kissed."

Isabelle had shuddered a bit under the fur robe. She was accustomed to be followed by this, but it never failed to arouse in her the same feeling of resentment; yet — in a strange town it was an advantage.

She was a "speed," was she? Well, let them find out! She wasn't quite old enough to be sorry nor nearly old enough to be glad.

Out of the window Isabelle watched the high-piled snow glide by in

the frosty morning. It was ever so much colder here than in Baltimore, she had not remembered; the glass of the side door was iced and the windows were shirred with snow in the corners.

Her mind played still with one subject: Did *he* dress like that boy there who walked so calmly down what was evidently a bustling business street, in moccasins and winter-carnival costume? How very *western!* Of course he wasn't that way; he went to college, was a freshman or something.

Really she had no distinct idea of him. A two year back picture had not impressed her except by the big eyes, which he had probably grown up to by now.

However, in the last two weeks, when her Christmas visit to Elaine had been decided on, he had assumed the proportions of a worthy adversary. Children, the most astute of matchmakers, plot and plan quickly, and Elaine had cleverly played a correspondence sonata to Isabelle's excitable temperament. Isabelle was, and had been for some time, capable of very strong, if very transient, emotions.

They drew up at a white stone building, set back from the snowy street. Mrs. Hollis greeted her warmly and her various younger cousins were produced from the corners where they skulked politely. Isabelle met them quite tactfully. At her best, she allied all with whom she came in contact, except older girls and some women. All the impressions that she made were conscious. The half dozen girls she renewed acquaintance with that morning were all rather impressed — and as much by her direct personality as by her reputation.

Stephen Palms was an open subject of conversation. Evidently he was a bit light of love. He was neither popular nor unpopular. Every girl there seemed to have had an affair with him at some time or other, but no one volunteered any really useful information. He was going to "fall for her" . . .

Elaine had issued that statement to her young set and they were retailing it back to Elaine as fast as they set eyes on Isabelle. Isabelle resolved, that if necessary, she would force herself to like him — she owed it to Elaine — even though she were terribly disappointed. Elaine had painted him in such glowing colors — he was good-looking, had a "line" and was properly inconstant.

In fact, he summed up all the romance that her age and environment

led her to desire. Were those his dancing shoes that "shimmied" tentatively around the soft rug below?

All impressions, and in fact all ideas, were terribly kaleidoscopic to Isabelle. She had that curious mixture of the social and artistic temperaments, found so often in two classes, society girls and actresses. Her education, or rather her sophistication, had been absorbed from the boys who had dangled from her favor, her tact was instinctive and her capacity for love affairs was limited only by the number of boys she met. Flirt smiled from her large, black-brown eyes and figured in her intense physical magnetism.

So she waited at the head of the stairs at the Country Club that evening while slippers were fetched. Just as she was getting impatient Elaine came out of the dressing-room beaming with her accustomed good nature and high spirits, and together they descended the broad stairs while the nervous searchlight of Isabelle's mind flashed on two ideas. She was glad she had high color tonight and she wondered if he danced well.

Downstairs, in the Club's great room, the girls she had met in the afternoon surrounded her for a moment, looking unbelievably changed by the soft yellow light; then she heard Elaine's voice repeating a cycle of names and she found herself bowing to a sextet of black and white and terrible stiff figures.

The name Palms figured somewhere, but she did not place him at first. A confused and very juvenile moment of awkward backings and bumpings, and all found themselves arranged talking to the persons they least desired to.

Isabelle maneuvered herself and Duncan Collard, a freshman from Harvard with whom she had once played hopscotch, to a seat on the stairs. A reference, supposedly humorous, to the past was all she needed.

What Isabelle could do socially with one idea was remarkable. First, she repeated it rapturously in an enthusiastic contralto with a trace of a Southern accent; then she held it off at a distance and smiled at it — her wonderful smile; then she delivered it in variations and played a sort of mental catch with it, all this in the nominal form of dialogue.

Duncan was fascinated and totally unconscious that this was being done, not for him, but for the eyes that glistened under the shining, carefully watered hair, a little to her left. As an actor even in the fullest flush of his own conscious magnetism gets a lasting impression of most

of the people in the front row, so Isabelle sized up Stephen Palms. First, he was light, and from her feeling of disappointment, she knew that she had expected him to be dark and of pencil slenderness. For the rest, a faint flush and a straight romantic profile, the effect set off by a close-fitting dress suit and a silk ruffled shirt of the kind that women still delight in on men, but men were just beginning to get tired of.

Stephen was just quietly smiling.

"Don't *you* think so?" she said suddenly, turning to him innocent eyed.

He nodded and smiled — an expectant, waiting smile.

Then there was a stir and Elaine led the way over to their table.

Stephen struggled to her side and whispered:

"You're my dinner partner — Isabelle."

Isabelle gasped — this was rather right in line. But really she felt as if a good speech had been taken from the star and given to a minor character — she mustn't lose the leadership a bit. The dinner table glittered with laughter at the confusion of getting places and then curious eyes were turned on her, sitting near the head.

She was enjoying this immensely, and Duncan Collard was so engrossed with the added sparkle of her rising color that he forgot to pull out Elaine's chair and fell into a dim confusion. Stephen was on the other side, full of confidence and vanity, looking at her most consciously. He began directly and so did Duncan.

"I've heard a lot about you since you wore braids —"

"Wasn't it funny this afternoon —"

Both stopped.

Isabelle turned to Stephen shyly.

Her face was always enough answer for anyone, but she decided to speak.

"How — who from?"

"From everybody — for all the years since you've been away."

She blushed appropriately.

On her right, Duncan was hors-de-combat already although he hadn't quite realized it.

"I'll tell you what I remembered about you all these years," Stephen continued.

She leaned slightly toward him and looked modestly at the celery before her.

Duncan sighed — he knew Stephen and the situations that Stephen was born to handle. He turned to Elaine and asked her if she was going away to school next year.

II

Isabelle and Stephen were distinctly not innocent, nor were they otherwise. Moreover, amateur standing had very little value in the game they were beginning — they were each playing a part that they might play for years. They had both started with good looks and excitable temperaments, and the rest was the result of certain accessible popular novels, and dressing-room conversation culled from a slightly older set.

When Isabelle's eyes, wide and innocent, proclaimed the ingenue most, Stephen was proportionately less deceived. He waited for the mask to drop off, but at the same time he did not question her right to wear it.

She, on her part, was not impressed by his studied air of blasé sophistication. She had lived in a larger city and had slightly an advantage in range. But she accepted his pose. It was one of a dozen little conventions of this kind of affair. He was aware that he was getting this particular favor now because she had been coached. He knew that he stood for merely the best thing in sight, and that he would have to improve his opportunity before he lost his advantage.

So they proceeded, with an infinite guile that would have horrified the parents of both.

After the half dozen little dinners were over the dance began. Everything went smoothly — boys cut in on Isabelle every few feet and then squabbled in the corners with: "You might let me get more than an *inch!*" and "She didn't like it either — she told me so next time I cut in."

It was true — she told everyone so, and gave every hand a parting pressure that said, "You know that your dances are *making* my evening."

But time passed, two hours of it, and the less subtle beaux had better learn to focus their pseudo-passionate glances elsewhere, for eleven o'clock found Isabelle and Stephen sitting on a leather lounge in a little

den off the reading room. She was conscious that they were a handsome pair and seemed to belong distinctly on this leather lounge while lesser lights fluttered and chattered downstairs. Boys who passed the door looked in enviously — girls who passed only laughed and frowned, and grew wise within themselves.

They had now reached a very definite stage. They had traded ages and accounts of their lives since they had met last. She had listened to much that she had heard before. He was a freshman at college and was on his class hockey team. He had learned that some of the boys she went with in Baltimore were "terrible speeds" and came to parties intoxicated — most of them were twenty or so, and drove alluring Stutzes. A good half of them seemed to have flunked out of various boarding schools and colleges, but some of them bore sporting names that made him look at her admiringly.

As a matter of fact, Isabelle's closer acquaintance with the colleges was chiefly through older cousins. She had bowing acquaintances with a lot of young men who thought she was "a pretty kid" and "worth keeping an eye on." But Isabelle strung the names into a fabrication of gaiety that would have dazzled a Viennese nobleman. Such is the power of young contralto voices on leather sofas.

I have said that they had reached a very definite stage — nay more, a very critical stage. Stephen had stayed over a day to see her and his train left at twelve-eighteen that night. His trunk and suitcase awaited him at the station and his watch was already beginning to hang heavy in his pocket.

"Isabelle," he said suddenly, "I want to tell you something."

They had been talking lightly about "that funny look in her eyes," and on the relative attractions of dancing and sitting out, and Isabelle knew from the change in his manner exactly what was coming — indeed, she had been wondering how soon it would come.

Stephen reached above their heads and turned out the electric light, so they were in the dark except for the glow from the red lamps that fell through the door from the reading room. Then he began:

"I don't know — I don't know whether or not you know what you — what I'm going to say. Lordy, Isabelle — this sounds like a line, but it isn't."

"I know," said Isabelle softly.

"We may never meet again like this — I have darned hard luck sometimes."

He was leaning away from her on the other arm of the lounge, but she could see his black eyes plainly in the dark.

"You'll see me again — silly." There was just the slightest emphasis on the last word — so that it became almost a term of endearment.

He continued a bit huskily:

"I've fallen for a lot of people — girls — and I guess you have, too — boys, I mean — but honestly you —" He broke off suddenly and leaned forward, chin on his hands, a favorite and studied gesture. "Oh, what's the use? You'll go your way and I suppose I'll go mine."

Silence for a moment. Isabelle was quite stirred — she wound her handkerchief into a tight ball and, by the faint light that streamed over her, dropped it deliberately on the floor. Their hands touched for an instant, but neither spoke. Silences were becoming more frequent and more delicious. Outside another stray couple had come up and were experimenting on the piano in the next room. After the usual preliminary of "chopsticks," one of them started "Babes in the Woods" and a light tenor carried the words into the den —

> *"Give me your hand,*
> *I'll understand,*
> *We're off to slumberland."*

Isabelle hummed it softly and trembled as she felt Stephen's hand close over hers.

"Isabelle," he whispered, "you know I'm mad about you. You *do* give a darn about me?"

"Yes."

"How much do you care — do you like anyone better?"

"No." He could scarcely hear her, although he bent so near that he felt her breath against his cheek.

"Isabelle, I'm going back to college for six long months and why shouldn't we — if I could only just have one thing to remember you by —"

"Close the door."

Her voice had just stirred so that he half wondered whether she had spoken at all.

As he swung the door softly shut, the music seemed quivering just outside.

"Moonlight is bright,
Kiss me good night."

What a wonderful song, she thought — everything was wonderful tonight, most of all this romantic scene in the den with their hands clinging and the inevitable looming charmingly close.

The future vista of her life seemed an unending succession of scenes like this, under moonlight and pale starlight, and in the backs of warm limousines and in low, cosy roadsters stopped under sheltering trees — only the boy might change, and this one was so nice.

"Isabelle!"

His whisper blended in the music and they seemed to float nearer together.

Her breath came faster.

"Can't I kiss you, Isabelle?"

Lips half parted, she turned her head to him in the dark.

Suddenly the ring of voices, the sound of running footsteps surged toward them.

Like a flash Stephen reached up and turned on the light and when the door opened and three boys, the wrathy and dance-craving Duncan among them, rushed in, he was turning over the magazines on the table, while she sat without moving, serene and unembarrassed, and even greeted them with a welcoming smile. But her heart was beating wildly and she felt somehow as if she had been deprived.

It was evidently over. There was a clamor for a dance, there was a glance that passed between them, on his side despair, on hers regret, and then the evening went on, with the reassured beaux and the eternal cutting in.

At quarter to twelve Stephen shook hands with her gravely, in a small crowd assembled to wish him good-speed.

For an instant he lost his poise and she felt slightly unnecessary, when a satirical voice from a concealed wit on the edge of the company cried:

"Take her outside, Stephen."

As he took her hand he pressed it a little and she returned the pressure as she had done to twenty hands that evening — that was all.

At two o'clock, back at Hollis', Elaine asked her if she and Stephen had had a "time" in the den. Isabelle turned to her quietly. In her eyes was the light of the idealist, the inviolate dreamer of Joan-like dreams.

"No!" she answered. "I don't do that sort of thing any more — he asked me to, but I said 'No.'"

As she crept into bed she wondered what he'd say in his special delivery tomorrow. He had such a good-looking mouth — would she ever —?

"Fourteen angels were watching o'er them," sang Elaine sleepily from the next room.

"Damn!" muttered Isabelle as she explored the cold sheets cautiously. "Damn!"

Albergo Empedocle

After graduating from King's College, Cambridge, in 1901, E. M. Forster traveled in Italy with his mother for a year. While abroad, Forster, nicknamed "the taupe" for his colorless persona by his college friend Lytton Strachey, formulated the ideas for his novels *Where Angels Fear to Tread* and *A Room with a View*. In April 1903 he traveled to Greece, the inspiration for "Albergo Empedocle," his first published story. It appeared in *Temple Bar* in December 1903, a few months before what is generally but erroneously reported to be his first piece of fiction, "The Story of a Panic." Forster himself disclaimed "Albergo Empedocle," perhaps because he thought it was not very good and wanted "Story," published in *The Independent Review* in the spring of 1904, to be remembered as his first.

THE LAST LETTER I had from Harold was from Naples.

"We've just come back from Pompeii," he wrote. "On the whole it's decidedly no go and very tiring. What with the smells and the beggars and the mosquitoes we're rather off Naples altogether, and we've changed our plans and are going to Sicily. The guide-books say you can run through it in no time; only four places you have to go to, and very little in them. That suits us to a T. Pompeii and the awful Museum here have fairly killed us — except of course Mildred, and perhaps Sir Edwin.

"Now why don't you come too? I know you're keen on Sicily, and we all would like it. You would be able to spread yourself no end with your archaeology. For once in my life I should have to listen while you jaw.

You'd enjoy discussing temples, gods, etc., with Mildred. She's taught me a lot, but of course it's no fun for her, talking to us. Send a wire; I'll stand the cost. Start at once and we'll wait for you. The Peaslakes say the same, especially Mildred.

"My not sleeping at night, and my headaches are all right now, thanks very much. As for the blues, I haven't had any since I've been engaged, and don't intend to. So don't worry any more. Yours,

"HAROLD.

"Dear Tommy, if you aren't an utter fool you'll let me pay your ticket out."

I did not go. I could just have managed it, but Sicily was then a very sacred name to me, and the thought of running through it in no time, even with Harold, deterred me. I went afterwards, and as I am well acquainted with all who went then, and have had circumstantial information of all that happened, I think that my account of the affair will be as intelligible as anyone's.

I am conceited enough to think that if I had gone, the man I love most in the world would not now be in an asylum.

CHAPTER I.

The Peaslake party was most harmonious in its composition. Four out of the five were Peaslakes, which partly accounted for the success, but the fifth, Harold, seemed to have been created to go with them. They had started from England soon after his engagement to Mildred Peaslake, and had been flying over Europe for two months. At first they were a little ashamed of their rapidity, but the delight of continual custom-house examinations soon seized them, and they had hardly learnt what "Come in," and "Hot water, please," were in one language, before they crossed the frontier and had to learn them in another.

But, as Harold truly said, "People say we don't see things properly, and are globe-trotters, and all that, but after all one travels to enjoy oneself, and no one can say that we aren't having a ripping time."

Every party, to be really harmonious, must have a physical and an intellectual centre. Harold provided one, Mildred the other. He settled whether a mountain had to be climbed or a walk taken, and it was his

fists that were clenched when a porter was insolent, or a cabman tried to overcharge. Mildred, on the other hand, was the fount of information. It was she who generally held the "Baedeker" and explained it. She had been expecting her Continental scramble for several years, and had read a fair amount of books for it, which a good memory often enabled her to reproduce.

But they all agreed that she was no dry encyclopaedia. Her appetite for facts was balanced by her reverence for imagination.

"It is imagination," she would say, "that makes the past live again. It sets the centuries at naught."

"Rather!" was the invariable reply of Harold, who was notoriously deficient in it. Recreating the past was apt to give him a headache, and his thoughts obstinately returned to the unromantic present, which he found quite satisfactory. He was fairly rich, fairly healthy, very much in love, very fond of life, and he was content to worship in Mildred those higher qualities which he did not possess himself.

These two between them practically ran the party, and both Sir Edwin and Lady Peaslake were glad that the weight of settling or explaining anything should be lifted off their shoulders. Sir Edwin sometimes held the "Baedeker," but his real function was the keeping of a diary in which he put down the places they went to, the people they met, and the times of the trains. Lady Peaslake's department was packing, hotels, and the purchasing of presents for a large circle of acquaintance. As for Lilian, Mildred's sister, whatever pleased other people pleased her. Altogether it was a most delightful party.

They were however just a little subdued and quiet during that journey from Palermo to Girgenti. They had done Palermo in even less time than "Baedeker" had allowed for it, and such audacity must tell on the most robust of tourists. Furthermore they had made an early start, as they had to get to Girgenti for lunch, do the temples in the afternoon, and go on the next morning to Syracuse.

It was no wonder that Lady Peaslake was too weary to look out of the window, and that Harold yawned when Mildred explained at some length how it was that a Greek temple came to be built out of Greece.

"Poor boy! you're tired," she said, without bitterness, and without surprise.

Harold blushed at his impoliteness.

"We really do too much," said Lady Peaslake. "I never bought that Sicilian cart for Mrs. Popham. It would have been the very thing. She will have something out of the way. If a thing's at all ordinary she will hardly say thank you. Harold, would you try at Girgenti? Mind you beat them down. Four francs is the outside."

"Certainly, Lady Peaslake." His method of purchasing for her, was to pay whatever was asked, and to make good the difference out of his own pocket.

"Girgenti will produce more than Sicilian carts," said Mildred, smoothing down the pages of the guide book. "In Greek times it was the second city of the island, wasn't it? It was famous for the ability, wealth, and luxury of its inhabitants. You remember, Harold, it was called Acragas."

"Acragas, Acragas," chanted Harold, striving to rescue one word from the chaos. The effect was too much for him, and he gave another yawn.

"Really, Harold!" said Mildred, laughing. "You're very much exhausted."

"I've scarcely slept for three nights," he replied in rather an aggrieved voice.

"Oh, my dear boy! I'm very sorry. I had no idea."

"Why did not you tell me?" said Sir Edwin. "We would have started later. Yes, I see you do look tired."

"It's so queer. It's ever since I've been in Sicily. Perhaps Girgenti will be better."

"Have you never slept since Naples?"

"Oh, I did sleep for an hour or so last night. But that was because I used my dodge."

"Dodge!" said Sir Edwin, "whatever do you mean!"

"You know it, don't you? You pretend you're someone else, and then you go asleep in no time."

"Indeed I do not know it," said Sir Edwin emphatically.

Mildred's curiosity was aroused. She had never heard Harold say anything unexpected before, and she was determined to question him.

"How extremely interesting! How very interesting! I don't know it either. Who do you imagine yourself to be?"

"Oh, no one — anyone. I just say to myself, 'That's someone lying

awake. Why doesn't he go to sleep if he's tired?' Then he — I mean I — do, and it's all right."

"But that is a very wonderful thing. Why didn't you do it all three nights?"

"Well, to tell the truth," said Harold, rather confused, "I promised Tommy I'd never do it again. You see, I used to do it, not only when I couldn't sleep, but also when I was in the blues about something — or nothing — as one is, I don't know why. It doesn't get rid of them, but it kind of makes me so strong that I don't care for them — I can't explain. One morning Tommy came to see me, and I never knew him till he shook me. Naturally he was horribly sick, and made me promise never to do it again."

"And why have you done it again?" said Sir Edwin.

"Well, I did hold out two nights. But last night I was so dead tired, I couldn't think what I wanted to — of course you understand that: it's rather beastly. All the night I had to keep saying '*I*'m lying awake, *I*'m lying awake, *I*'m lying awake,' and it got more and more difficult. And when it was almost time to get up, I made a slip and said, 'He's lying awake' — and then off I went."

"How very, very interesting," said Mildred, and Lilian cried that it was a simply splendid idea, and that she should try it next time she had the toothache.

"Indeed, Lilian," said her mother, "I beg you'll do no such thing."

"No, indeed," said Sir Edwin, who was looking grave. "Harold, your friend was quite right. It is never safe to play tricks with the brain. I must say I'm astonished: you of all people!"

"Yes," said Harold, looking at a very substantial hand. "I'm such a stodgy person. It is odd. It isn't brain or imagination or anything like that. I simply pretend."

"It is imagination," said Mildred in a low determined voice.

"Whatever it is, it must stop," said Sir Edwin. "It's a dangerous habit. You must break yourself of it before it is fully formed."

"Yes. I promised Tommy. I shall try again to-night," said Harold, with a pitiful little sigh of fatigue.

"I'll arrange to have a room communicating with yours. If you can't sleep to-night, call me."

"Thanks very much, I'm sure not to do it if you're near. It only works

when one's alone. Tommy stopped it by taking rooms in the same house, which was decent of him."

The conversation had woke them up. The girls were quiet, Lilian being awed, and Mildred being rather annoyed with her parents for their want of sympathy with imagination. She felt that Harold had so little, that unless it was nourished it would disappear. She crossed over to him, and managed to say in a low voice,

"You please me very much. I had no idea you were like this before. We live in a world of mystery."

Harold smiled complacently at the praise, and being sure that he could not say anything sensible, held his tongue. Mildred at once began to turn his newly found powers to the appreciation of Girgenti.

"Think," she said, "of the famous men who visited her in her prime. Pindar, Aeschylus, Plato — and as for Empedocles, of course he was born there."

"Oh!"

"The disciple, you know, of Pythagoras, who believed in the transmigration of souls."

"Oh!"

"It's a beautiful idea, isn't it, that the soul should have several lives."

"But, Mildred darling," said the gentle voice of Lady Peaslake, "we know that it is not so."

"Oh, I didn't mean that, mamma. I only said it was a beautiful idea."

"But not a true one, darling."

"No."

Their voices had sunk into that respectful monotone which is always considered suitable when the soul is under discussion. They all looked awkward and ill at ease. Sir Edwin played tunes on his waistcoat buttons, and Harold blew into the bowl of his pipe. Mildred, a little confused at her temerity, passed on to the terrible sack of Acragas by the Romans. Whereat their faces relaxed, and they regained their accustomed spirits.

"But what are dates?" said Mildred. "What are facts, or even names of persons? They carry one a very little way. In a place like this one must simply feel."

"Rather," said Harold, trying to fix his attention.

"You must throw yourself into a past age if you want to appreciate it thoroughly. To-day you must imagine you are a Greek."

"Really, Mildred," said Sir Edwin, "you're almost too fanciful."

"No, father, I'm not. Harold understands. He must forget all these modern horrors of railways and Cook's tours, and think that he's living over two thousand years ago, among palaces and temples. He must think and feel and act like a Greek. It's the only way. He must — well, he must *be* a Greek."

"The sea! the sea!" interrupted Harold. "How absolutely ripping! I swear I'll put in a bathe!"

"Oh, you incorrigible boy!" said Mildred, joining in the laugh at the failure of her own scheme. "Show me the sea, then."

They were still far away from it, for they had hardly crossed the watershed of the island. It was the country of the mines, barren and immense, absolutely destitute of grass or trees, producing nothing but cakes of sallow sulphur, which were stacked on the platform of every wayside station. Human beings were scanty, and they were stunted and dry, mere withered vestiges of men. And far below at the bottom of the yellow waste was the moving living sea, which embraced Sicily when she was green and delicate and young, embraces her now, when she is brown and withered and dying.

"I see something more interesting than the sea," said Mildred. "I see Girgenti."

She pointed to a little ridge of brown hill far beneath them, on the summit of which a few grey buildings were huddled together.

"Oh, what a dreadful place!" cried poor Lady Peaslake. "How uncomfortable we are going to be."

"Oh dearest mother, it's only for one night. What are a few drawbacks, when we are going to see temples! Temples, Greek temples! Doesn't the word make you thrill?"

"Well, no dear, it doesn't. I should have thought the Pesto ones would have been enough. These can't be very different."

"I consider you are a recreant party," said Mildred in a sprightly voice. "First it's Harold, now it's you. I'm the only worthy one among you. To-day I mean to be a Greek. What hotel do we go to?"

Lady Peaslake produced her note-book and said, "Grand Hotel des Temples. Recommended by Mr. Dimbleby. Ask for a back room, as those have the view."

But at the Girgenti railway station, the man from the Temples told

them his hotel was full, and Mildred, catching sight of the modest omnibus of the "Albergo Empedocle," suggested that they should go there,
because it sounded so typical.

"You remember what the doctrine of Empedocles was, Harold?"

The wretched Harold had forgotten.

Sir Edwin was meanwhile being gently urged into the omnibus by
the man from the "Empedocle."

"We know nothing about it, absolutely nothing. Are you — have you
clean beds?"

The man from the "Empedocle" raised his eyes and hands to Heaven,
so ecstatic was his remembrance of the purity of the blankets, the spot-
lessness of the sheets. At last words came, and he said, "The beds of the
Empedocle! They are celestial. One spends one night there, and one
remembers it for ever!"

CHAPTER II.

Sir Edwin and Lady Peaslake were sitting in the temple of Juno Lacinia
and leaning back on a Doric column — which is a form of architecture
neither comfortable as a cushion nor adequate as a parasol. They were
as cross as it was possible for good-tempered people to be. Their lunch
at the dirty hotel had disagreed with them, and the wine that was included with it had made them heavy. The drive to the temples had jog-
gled them up and one of the horses had fallen down. They had been
worried to buy flowers, figs, shells, sulphur crystals, and new-laid an-
tiquities, they had been pestered by the beggars and bitten by the fleas.
Had they been Sicilian born they would have known what was the matter, and lying down on the grass, on the flowers, on the road, on the
temple steps — on anything, would have sunk at once into that marvellous mid-day sleep which is fed by light and warmth and air. But
being northern born they did not know — nor could they have slept if
they had.

"Where on earth are Harold and Mildred?" asked Lady Peaslake. She
did not want to know, but she was restless with fatigue.

"I can't think why we couldn't all keep together," said Sir Edwin.

"You see, papa," said Lilian, "Mildred wants to see the temples that
have tumbled down as well as these, and Harold is taking her."

"He's a poor guide," said Sir Edwin. "Really, Lilian, I begin to think

that Harold is rather stupid. Of course I'm very fond of him, he's a thoroughly nice fellow, honest as the day, and he's good-looking and well made — I value all that extremely — but after all brains are something. He is so slow — so lamentably slow — at catching one's meaning."

"But, father dear," replied Lilian, who was devoted to Harold, "he's tired."

"I am tired, too, but I can keep my wits about me. He seems in a dream; when the horse fell he never attempted to get down and sit on its head. It might have kicked us to pieces. He's as helpless as a baby with beggars. He's too idle to walk properly; three times he trod on my toes, and he fell up the temple steps and broke your camera. He's blind, he's deaf — I may say he's dumb, too. Now this is pure stupidity, and I believe that stupidity can be cured just like anything else, if you make the effort."

Lilian continued the defence, and repeated that he had hardly slept for three nights.

"Ridiculous. Why can't he sleep? It's stupidity again. An effort is needed — that is all. He can cure it if he chooses."

"He does know how to cure it," said Lilian, "but you thought — and so did he — that —"

She produced an explosion of ill-temper in her father, which was quite unprecedented.

"I'm very much annoyed with him. He has no right to play tricks with his brain. And what's more I am annoyed with Mildred, too."

"Oh, father!"

"She encourages him in his silliness — makes him think he's clever. I'm extremely annoyed, and I shall speak to them both, as soon as I get the opportunity."

Lilian was surprised and pained. Her father had never blamed anyone so strongly before. She did not know — indeed, he did not know himself — that neither the indigestion nor the heat, nor the beggars, nor the fleas were the real cause of his irritation. He was annoyed because he failed to understand.

Mildred he could pardon; she had merely been indiscreet, and as she had gone in for being clever when quite a child, such things were to be expected from her. Besides, he shrewdly guessed that, although she might sometimes indulge in fancies, yet when it came to action she

could be trusted to behave in a thoroughly conventional manner. Thank heaven! she was seldom guilty of confusing books with life.

But Harold did not escape so easily, for Sir Edwin absolutely failed to understand him, for the first time. Hitherto he had believed that he understood him perfectly. Harold's character was so simple; it consisted of little more than two things, the power to love and the desire for truth, and Sir Edwin, like many a wiser thinker, concluded that what was not complicated could not be mysterious. Similarly, because Harold's intellect did not devote itself to the acquisition of facts or to the elaboration of emotions, he had concluded that he was stupid. But now, just because he could send himself to sleep by an unexplained device, he spied a mystery in him, and was aggrieved.

He was right. There was a mystery, and a great one. Yet it was trivial and unimportant in comparison with the power to love and the desire for truth — things which he saw daily, and, because he had seen daily, ignored.

His meditations took shape, and he flung this challenge at the unknown: "I'll have no queerness in a son-in-law!" He was sitting in a Doric temple with a sea of gold and purple flowers tossing over its ruins, and his eyes looked out to the moving, living sea of blue. But his ears caught neither the echo of the past nor the cry of the present, for he was suddenly paralysed with the fear that after all he had not done so well for his daughter as he hoped.

Meanwhile, Mildred, at the other end of the line of temples, was concentrated on the echoes of the past. Harold was even more inattentive to them than usual. He was very sleepy, and would only say that the flowers were rather jolly and that the sea looked in prime condition if only one could try it. To the magnificence and pathos of the ruined temple of Zeus he was quite dead. He only valued it as a chair.

"Suppose you go back and rest in the carriage?" said Mildred, with a shade of irritation in her voice.

He shook his head and sat yawning at the sea, thinking how wonderfully the water would fizz up over his body and how marvellously cold would be the pale blue pools among the rocks. Mildred endeavoured to recall him to higher pleasures by reading out of her "Baedeker."

She turned round to explain something and he was gone.

At first she thought it was a mild practical joke, such as they did not

disdain to play on each other; then that he had changed his mind and gone back to the carriage. But the custodian at the gate said that no one had gone out, and she returned to search the ruins.

The temple of Zeus — the third greatest temple of the Greek world — has been overthrown by an earthquake, and now resembles a ruined mountain rather than a ruined building. There is a well-made path, which makes a circuit over the mass, and is amply sufficient for all rational tourists. Those who wish to see more have to go mountaineering over gigantic columns and pilasters, and squeeze their way through passes of cut stone.

Harold was not on the path, and Mildred was naturally annoyed. Few things are more vexatious for a young lady than to go out with an escort and return without. It argues remissness on her own part quite as much as on that of her swain.

Having told the custodian to stop Harold if he tried to come out, she began a systematic hunt. She saw an enormous block of stone from which she would get a good view of the chaos, and wading through the gold and purple flowers that separated her from it, scrambled up.

On its further side were two fallen columns, lying close together, and the space that separated them had been silted up and was covered with flowers. On it, as on a bed, lay Harold, fast asleep, his cheek pressed against the hot stone of one of the columns, and his breath swaying a little blue iris that had rooted in one of its cracks.

The indignant Mildred was about to wake him, but seeing the dark line that still showed beneath his eyes, stayed her voice. Besides, he looked so picturesque, and she herself, sitting on the stone watching him, must look picturesque, too. She knew that there was no one to look at her, but from her mind the idea of a spectator was never absent for a moment. It was the price she had paid for becoming cultivated.

Sleep has little in common with death, to which men have compared it. Harold's limbs lay in utter relaxation, but he was tingling with life, glorying in the bounty of the earth and the warmth of the sun, and the little blue flower bent and fluttered like a tree in a gale. The light beat upon his eyelids and the grass leaves tickled his hair, but he slept on, and the lines faded out of his face as he grasped the greatest gift that the animal life can offer. And Mildred watched him, thinking what a picture might be made of the scene.

Then her meditation changed. "What a wonderful thing is sleep! How I would like to know what is passing through his brain as he lies there. He looks so peaceful and happy. Poor boy! when he is awake he often looks worried. I think it is because he can't follow the conversation, though I try to make it simple, don't I? Yet some things he sees quite quickly. And I'm sure he has lots of imagination, if only he would let it come out. At all events I love him very much, and I believe I shall love him more, for it seems to me that there will be more in him than I expected."

She suddenly remembered his "dodge" for going to sleep, and her interest and her agitation increased.

"Perhaps, even now, he imagines himself to be someone else. What a marvellous idea! What will he say if he wakes? How mysterious everything is if only one could realise it. Harold, of all people, who seemed so ordinary — though, of course, I love him. But I am going to love him more."

She longed to reach him in his sleep, to guide the course of his dreams, to tell him that she approved of him and loved him. She had read of such a thing. In accordance with the advice of the modern spiritualistic novel she pressed her hands on her temples and made a mental effort. At the end of five minutes she had a slight headache and had effected nothing. He had not moved, he had not even sighed in his sleep, and the little blue flower still bent and fluttered, bent and fluttered in the regular onslaught of his breath.

The awakening, when it did come, found her thoughts unprepared. They had wandered to earthly things, as thoughts will do at times. At the supreme moment, she was wondering whether her stockings would last till she got back to England. And Harold, all unobserved, had woken up, and the little blue flower had quivered and was still. He had woken up because he was no longer tired, woken up to find himself in the midst of beautiful flowers, beautiful columns, beautiful sunshine, with Mildred, whom he loved, sitting by him. Life at that moment was too delicious for him to speak.

Mildred saw all the romance melting away: he looked so natural and so happy: there was nothing mysterious about him after all. She waited for him to speak.

Ten minutes passed, and still he had not spoken. His eyes were fixed

steadily upon her, and she became nervous and uncomfortable. Why would he not speak? She determined to break the silence herself, and at last, in a tremulous voice, called him by his name.

The result was overwhelming, for his answer surpassed all that her wildest flights of fancy had imagined, and fulfilled beyond all dreaming her cravings for the unimagined and the unseen.

He said, "I've lived here before."

Mildred was choking. She could not reply.

He was quite calm. "I always knew it," he said, "but it was too far down in me. Now that I've slept here it is at the top. I've lived here before."

"Oh, Harold!" she gasped.

"Mildred!" he cried, in sudden agitation, "are you going to believe it — that I have lived before — lived such a wonderful life — I can't remember it yet — lived it here? It's no good answering to please me."

Mildred did not hesitate a moment. She was carried away by the magnificence of the idea, the glory of the scene and the earnest beauty of his eyes, and in an ecstasy of rapture she cried, "I do believe."

"Yes," said Harold, " you do. If you hadn't believed now you never would have. I wonder what would have happened to me."

"More, more!" cried Mildred, who was beginning to find her words. "How could you smile! how could you be so calm! O marvellous idea! that your soul has lived before! I should run about, shriek, sing. Marvellous! overwhelming! How can you be so calm! The mystery! and the poetry, oh, the poetry! How can you support it? Oh, speak again!"

"I don't see any poetry," said Harold. "It just has happened, that's all. I lived here before."

"You are a Greek! You have been a Greek! Oh, why do you not die when you remember it."

"Why should I? I might have died if you hadn't believed me. It's nothing to remember."

"Aren't you shattered, exhausted?"

"No: I'm awfully fit. I know that you must have believed me now or never. Remembering has made me so strong. I see myself to the bottom now."

"Marvellous! marvellous!" she repeated.

He leapt up on to the stone beside her. "You've believed me. That's

the only thing that's marvellous. The rest's nothing." He flung his arms round her, and embraced her — an embrace very different from the decorous peck by which he had marked the commencement of their engagement. Mildred, clinging to him, murmured, "I do believe you," and they gazed without flinching into each other's eyes.

Harold broke the silence, saying, "How very happy life is going to be."

But Mildred was still wrapped in the glamour of the past. "More! more!" she cried, "tell me more! What was the city like — and the people in it? Who were you?"

"I don't remember yet — and it doesn't matter."

"Harold, keep nothing from me! I will not breathe a word. I will be silent as the grave."

"I shall keep nothing. As soon as I remember things, I will tell them. And why should you tell no one? There's nothing wrong."

"They would not believe."

"I shouldn't mind. I only minded about you."

"Still — I think it is best a secret. Will you agree?"

"Yes — for you may be right. It's nothing to do with the others. And it wouldn't interest them."

"And think — think hard who you were."

"I do just remember this — that I was a lot greater then than I am now. I'm greater now than I was this morning, I think — but then!"

"I knew it! I knew it from the first! I have known it always. You have been a king — a king! You ruled here when Greece was free!"

"Oh! I don't mean that — at least I don't remember it. And was I a Greek?"

"A Greek!" she stammered indignantly. "Of course you were a Greek, a Greek of Acragas."

"Oh, I daresay I was. Anyhow it doesn't matter. To be believed! Just fancy! you've believed me. You needn't have, but you did. How happy life is!"

He was in an ecstacy of happiness in which all time except the present had passed away. But Mildred had a tiny thrill of disappointment. She reverenced the past as well.

"What do you mean then, Harold, when you say you were greater?"

"I mean I was better, I saw better, heard better, thought better."

"Oh, I see," said Mildred fingering her watch. Harold, in his most

prosaic manner, said they must not keep the carriage waiting, and they regained the path.

The tide of rapture had begun to ebb away from Mildred. His generalities bored her. She longed for detail, vivid detail, that should make the dead past live. It was of no interest to her that he had once been greater.

"Don't you remember the temples?"

"No."

"Nor the people?"

"Not yet."

"Don't you at all recollect what century you lived in?"

"How on earth am I to know!" he laughed.

Mildred was silent. She had hoped he would have said the fifth B.C. — the period in which she was given to understand that the Greek race was at its prime. He could tell her nothing; he did not even seem interested, but began talking about Mrs. Popham's present.

At last she thought of a question he might be able to answer. "Did you also love better?" she asked in a low voice.

"I loved very differently." He was holding back the brambles to prevent them from tearing her dress as he spoke. One of the thorns scratched him on the hand. "Yes, I loved better too," he continued, watching the little drops of blood swell out.

"What do you mean? Tell me more."

"I keep saying I don't know any more. It is fine to remember that you've been better than you are. You know, Mildred, I'm much more worth you than I've ever been before. I do believe I am fairly great."

"Oh!" said Mildred, who was getting bored.

They had reached the temple of Concord, and he retrieved his tactlessness by saying, "After all I'm too happy to go back yet. I love you too much. Let's rest again."

They sat down on the temple steps, and at the end of ten minutes Mildred had forgotten all her little disappointments, and only remembered this mysterious sleep, and his marvellous awakening. Then, at the very height of her content, she felt, deep down within her, the growth of a new wonder.

"Harold, how is it you can remember?"

"The lid can't have been put on tight last time I was sent out."

"And that," she murmured, "might happen to anyone."

"I should think it has — to lots. They only want reminding."

"It might happen to me."

"Yes."

"I too," she said slowly, "have often not been able to sleep. Oh, Harold, is it possible?"

"What?"

"That I have lived before."

"Of course it is."

"Oh, Harold, I too may remember."

"I hope you will. It's wonderful to remember a life better than this one. I can't explain how happy it makes you: there's no need to try or to worry. It'll come if it is coming."

"Oh, Harold! I am remembering!"

He grasped her hands crying, "Remember only what is good. Remember that you were greater than you are now! I would give my life to help you."

"You have helped me," she cried, quivering with excitement. "All fits together. I remember all. It is not the first time I have known you. We have met before. Oh, how often have I dimly felt it. I felt it when I watched you sleeping — but then I didn't understand. Our love is not new. Here in this very place when there was a great city full of gorgeous palaces and snow-white marble temples, full of poets and music, full of marvellous pictures, full of sculptures of which we can hardly dream, full of noble men and noble thoughts, bounded by the sapphire sea, covered by the azure sky, here in the wonderful youth of Greece did I speak to you and know you and love you. We walked through the marble streets, we led solemn sacrifices, I armed you for the battle, I welcomed you from the victory. The centuries have parted us, but not for ever. Harold; I too have lived at Acragas!"

Round the corner swept the Peaslakes' carriage, full of excited occupants. He had only time to whisper in her ear, "No Mildred darling, you have not."

CHAPTER III.

There was a dirty little sitting room in the Albergo Empedocle, and Mildred was sitting there after dinner waiting for her father. He had met

some friends at the temples, and he and she had agreed to pay them a visit. It was a cold night, and the room smelt of mustiness and lamp oil. The only other occupant was a stiff-backed lady who had found a three-year-old number of *Home Chat*. Lady Peaslake, Lilian, and Harold were all with Sir Edwin, hunting for the key of his Gladstone bag. Till it was found he could not go out with her, for all his clean collars were inside.

Mildred was thoroughly miserable. After long torture she had confessed to herself that she was self-deceived. She had never lived in Acragas. She remembered nothing. All her glowing description was pure imagination, the result of sentimental excitement. For instance she had spoken of "snow-white marble temples." That was nonsense, sheer nonsense. She had seen the remains of those temples, and they were built of porous stone, not marble. And she remembered now that the Sicilian Greeks always covered their temples with coloured stucco. At first she had tried to thrust such objections away and to believe that she had found a truth to which archaeology must yield. But what pictures or music did she remember? When had she buckled on Harold's armour, and what was it like? Was it probable that they had led a sacrifice together? The visions, always misty, faded away. She had never lived in Acragas.

But that was only the beginning of her mortification. Harold had proved her wrong. He had seen that she was a shifty, shallow hypocrite. She had not dared to be alone with him since her exposure. She had never looked at him and had hardly spoken. He seemed cheerful, but what was he thinking? He would never forgive her.

Had she only realised that it is only hypocrites who cannot forgive hypocrisy, whereas those who search for truth are too conscious of the maze to be hard on others — then the bitter flow of her thoughts might have been stopped and the catastrophe averted. But it was not conceivable to her that she should forgive — or that she should accept forgiveness, for to her forgiveness meant a triumph of one person over another.

So she went still further towards sorrow. She felt that Harold had scored off her, and she determined to make the score as little as she could. Was he really as sincere as he had seemed? Sincere he might be, but he might be self-deceived even as she was. That would explain all. He too had been moved by the beauty of the scene, by its wonderful

associations. Worn out he had fallen asleep, and, conscious perhaps that she was in a foolish sympathetic state, had indulged in a fit of imagination on awaking. She had fallen in with it, and they had encouraged each other to fresh deeds of folly. All was clear. And how was she to hide it from her father?

Each time she re-stated the question it took a more odious form. Even though she believed Harold had been as foolish as herself, she was still humiliated before him, for her folly had been revealed, and his had not. The last and worst thought pressed itself upon her. Was he really as simple as he seemed? Had he not been trying to deceive her? He had been so careful in speaking of his old life: would only say that he had been "greater," "better" — never gave one single detail by which archaeology might prove him wrong. It was very clever of him. He had never lost his head once. Jealous of her superior acquirements, he had determined to put her to ridicule. He had laid a cunning bait and she had swallowed it. How cleverly he had lured her on to make the effort of recollection! How patiently he had heard her rapturous speech, in order that he might prove her silly to the core! How diabolically worded was his retort — "No, Mildred darling, you have not lived at Acragas." It implied, "I will be kind to you and treat you well when you are my wife, but recollect that you are silly, emotional, hypocritical: that your pretensions to superiority are gone for ever; that I have proved you inferior to me, even as all women are inferior to all men. Dear Mildred, you are a fool!"

"Intolerable! intolerable!" she gasped to herself, "if only I could expose him! I never dreamt it of him! I was never on my guard!"

Harold came quickly into the room, and she was at once upon the defensive. He told her that her father was ready and she got up to go, her ears aching in expectation of some taunt. It came — a very subtle one. She heard him say, "Kiss me before you go," and felt his hands grasp her elbows.

"No!" she said, shrinking from his touch, and frowning towards the stiff-backed lady, who sat a little stiffer.

"You'll have to," was his reply, and catching hold of her — he was very strong — he lifted her right above his head, and broke the feathers in her hat against the ceiling. He never completed his embrace, for she

shrieked aloud, inarticulate with passion, and the voice of Sir Edwin was heard saying "Come, come, Harold, my boy, — come, come!"

He set her down, and white with rage she hissed at him, "I never thought I should live to find you both charlatan and cad," and left the room.

Had she stayed, she would have been gratified at the prompt effect of her rebuke. Harold stood where she left him, dumb with misery, and then, without further warning, began to cry. He cried without shame or restraint, not even turning his head or covering his face with his hands, but letting the tears run down his cheeks till they caught in his moustache, or dropped on to the floor. Sir Edwin, not unmoved, stood before him for a moment, stammering as he tried to think of something that should both rebuke and console.

But the world has forgotten what to say to men of twenty-four who cry. Sir Edwin followed his daughter, giving a despairing look at Lady Peaslake and Lilian as he departed.

Lady Peaslake took up the line of behaving as if nothing had happened, and began talking in a high voice about the events of the day. Harold did not attempt to leave the room, but still stood near the table, sobbing and gulping for breath.

Lilian, moved by a more human impulse, tremulously asked him why he cried, and at this point the stiff-backed lady, who had sat through everything, gathered up her skirts as if she had seen a beetle, and slipped from the room.

"I cry because I'm unhappy: because Mildred's angry with me."

"Er — er," said Lady Peaslake, "I'm sure that it would be Mildred's wish that you should stop."

"I thought at dinner," he gasped, "that she was not pleased. Why? Why? Nothing had happened. Nothing but happiness, I mean. The best way, I thought, of showing I love her is to kiss her, and that will make her understand again. You know, she understood everything."

"Oh yes," said Lady Peaslake. "Look," she added to divert him, "how do you like my new embroidery?"

"It's hideous — perfectly hideous!" was his vigorous reply.

"Well, here is a particular gentleman!" said good-natured Lady Peaslake. "Why, it's Liberty!"

"Frightful," said Harold. He had stopped crying. His face was all

twisted with pain, but such a form of expressing emotion is fairly suitable for men, and Lady Peaslake felt easier.

But he returned to Mildred. "She called me a cad and a charlatan."

"Oh, never mind!" said Lilian.

"I may be a cad. I never did quite see what a cad is, and no one ever quite explained to me. But a charlatan! Why did she call me a charlatan? I can't quite see what I've done."

He began to walk up and down the little room. Lady Peaslake gently suggested a stroll, but he took no notice and kept murmuring "Charlatan."

"Why are pictures like this allowed!" he suddenly cried. He had stopped in front of a coloured print in which the martyrdom of St. Agatha was depicted with all the fervour that incompetence could command.

"It's only a saint," said Lady Peaslake, placidly raising her head.

"How disgusting — and how ugly!"

"Yes, very. It's Roman Catholic."

He turned away shuddering, and began his everlasting question — "Why did she call me a charlatan?"

Lady Peaslake felt compelled to say — "You see, Harold, you annoyed her, and when people are annoyed they will say anything. I know it by myself."

"But a charlatan! I know for certain that she understands me. Only this afternoon I told her —"

"Oh, yes," said Lady Peaslake.

"Told her that I had lived before — lived here over two thousand years ago, she thinks."

"Harold! my dear Harold! what nonsense are you talking?" Lady Peaslake had risen from her chair.

"Over two thousand years ago, when the place had another name."

"Good heavens; he is mad!"

"Mildred didn't think so. It's she who matters. Lilian, do you believe me?"

"No," faltered Lilian, edging towards the door.

He smiled, rather contemptuously.

"Now, Harold," said Lady Peaslake, "go and lie down, there's a good boy. You want rest. Mildred will call you charlatan with reason if you say

such silly, such wicked things — good gracious me! He's fainting! Lilian! water from the dining-room! Oh, what has happened? We were all so happy this morning."

The stiff-backed lady re-entered the room, accompanied by a thin little man with a black beard.

"Are you a doctor?" cried Lady Peaslake.

He was not, but he helped them to lay Harold on the sofa. He had not really fainted, for he was talking continually.

"You might have killed me," he said to Lady Peaslake, "you have said such an awful thing. You mean she thinks I never lived before. I know you're wrong, but it nearly kills me if you even say it. I have lived before — such a wonderful life. You will hear — Mildred will say it again. She won't like talking about it, but she'll say it if I want her to. That will save me from — from — from being a charlatan. Where is Mildred?"

"Hush!" said the little man.

"I have lived before — I have lived before, haven't I? Do you believe me?"

"Yes," said the little man.

"You lie," said Harold. "Now I've only to see people and I can tell. Where is Mildred?"

"You must come to bed."

"I don't speak or move till she comes."

So he lay silent and motionless on the sofa, while they stood around him whispering.

Mildred returned in a very different mood. A few questions from her father, followed by a few grave words of rebuke, had brought her to a sober mind. She was terribly in fault; she had nourished Harold's insanity first by encouraging it, then by rebuffing it. Sir Edwin severely blamed her disordered imagination, and bade her curb it; its effects might be disastrous, and he told her plainly that unless Harold entirely regained his normal condition he would not permit the marriage to take place. She acknowledged her fault, and returned determined to repair it; she was full of pity and contrition, but at the same time she was very matter-of-fact.

He heard them return and rushed to meet her, and she rushed to meet him. They met in the long passage, where it was too dark to see each other's faces.

"Harold," she said hurriedly, "I said two dreadful words to you. Will you forgive me?"

She tried to touch him, but he pushed her off with his arm, and said — "Come to the light."

The landlord appeared with a lamp. Harold took it and held it up to Mildred's face.

"Don't!" she said feebly.

"Harold!" called Lady Peaslake. "Come back!"

"Look at me!" said Harold.

"Don't!" said Mildred and shut her eyes.

"Open your eyes!"

She opened them, and saw his. Then she screamed and called out to her father — "Take him away! I'm frightened. He's mad! He's mad!"

Harold said quite calmly, "This is the end."

"Yes," said Sir Edwin, nervously taking the lamp, "now it's bed-time."

"If you think I'm mad," said Harold, "I am mad. That's all it means."

"Go to bed, Harold, to please me."

"Six people say I'm mad. Is there no one, no one, no one who understands?" He stumbled up the passage as if he were blind, and they heard him calling "Tommy."

In the sitting-room he caught his foot in the carpet and fell. When they picked him up, he was murmuring — "Harold can't stand up against six. What is Harold? Harold. Harold. Harold. Who is Harold?"

"Stop him!" cried the little man. "That's bad! He mustn't do that."

They shook him and tried to overtalk him, but he still went on. "What is Harold? Six letters. H.A.R.O.L.D. Harold. Harold. Harold."

"He's fainted again!" cried Lady Peaslake. "Oh, what has happened?"

"It's a sunstroke," said Sir Edwin. "He caught it through sleeping in the sun this afternoon. Mildred has told me all about it."

They took him up and carried him to his room.

As they were undressing him, he revived, and began to talk in a curious, thick voice.

"I was the last to go off the sofa, wasn't I? I counted five go — the wisest first — and I counted ten kinds of wine for certain before I slipped. Your conjurers are poor — but I liked the looks of the flute-girl."

"Go away, dears," said Lady Peaslake. "It's no good our stopping."

"Yes, I liked the flute-girl; is the porter I gave you last week a success?"

"Yes," said the little man, whose cue it was always to agree.

"Well, he'd better help carry me home, I don't want to walk. Nothing elaborate, you know. Just four porters for the litter, and half a dozen to carry the lights. That won't put you out."

"I'm afraid you must stop here for the night."

"Very well, if you can't send me back. Oh, the wine! the wine! I have got a head."

"What is he saying?" asked Mildred through the door.

"Is that the flute-girl?" said Harold, raising an interested eye.

Sir Edwin laid hold of him, but he was quite passive, and did not attempt to move. He allowed himself to be undressed, but did not assist them, and when his pyjamas were handed to him, he laughed feebly and asked what they were for.

"I want to look out of the window." They took him to it, hoping that the fresh air would recall his wits, and held him tight in case he tried to leap out. There was no moon, and the expanse of trees and fields was dark and indistinguishable.

"There are no lights moving in the streets," said Harold. "It must be very late. I forgot the windows were so high. How odd that there are no lights in the streets!"

"Yes, you're too late," said the little man. "You won't mind sleeping here. It's too far to go back."

"Too far — too far to go back," he murmured. "I am so sleepy, in this room I could sleep for ever. Too far — too far — oh, the wine!"

They put him into the bed, and went off at once, and his breathing was calm and very regular.

"A sunstroke," whispered Sir Edwin. "Perhaps a good night's rest — I shall sit up."

But next morning Harold had forgotten how to put on his clothes, and when he tried to speak he could not pronounce his words.

CHAPTER IV.

They had a terrible scene with him at the Girgenti railway station next morning when the train came in. However they got him on to it at last, and by the evening he was back at Palermo and had seen the English

doctor. He was sent back to England with a keeper, by sea, while the Peaslakes returned by Naples, as soon as Mildred's health permitted.

Long before Harold reached the asylum his speech had become absolutely unintelligible: indeed by the time he arrived at it, he hardly ever uttered a sound of any kind. His case attracted some attention, and some experiments were made, which proved that he was not unfamiliar with Greek dress, and had some knowledge of the alphabet.

But he was quite blank when spoken to, either in ancient or modern Greek, and when he was given a Greek book, he did not know what to do with it, and began tearing out the pages.

On these grounds the doctors have concluded that Harold merely thinks he is a Greek, and that it is his mania to behave as he supposes that a Greek behaved, relying on such elementary knowledge as he acquired at school.

But I firmly believe that he has been a Greek — nay, that he is a Greek, drawn by recollection back into his previous life. He cannot understand our speech because we have lost his pronunciation. And if I could look at the matter dispassionately — which I cannot — I should only rejoice at what has happened. For the greater has replaced the less, and he is living the life he knew to be greater than the life he lived with us. And I also believe, that if things had happened otherwise, he might be living that greater life among us, instead of among friends of two thousand years ago, whose names we have never heard. That is why I shall never forgive Mildred Peaslake as long as I live.

Most certainly he is not unhappy. His own thoughts are sweet to him, and he looks out of the window hour after hour and sees things in the sky and sea that we have forgotten. But of his fellow-men he seems utterly unconscious. He never speaks to us, nor hears us when we speak. He does not know that we exist.

So at least I thought till my last visit. I am the only one who still goes to see him: the others have given it up. Last time, when I entered the room, he got up and kissed me on the cheek. I think he knows that I understand him and love him: at all events it comforts me to think so.

The End of the Party

Determining which story was Graham Greene's first proved to be difficult. According to most reference books and biographies, it was "Proof Positive," which won a *Manchester Guardian* ghost story contest in 1930. However, bibliographies relating to Greene do not list this story as ever having appeared in the *Guardian*. Instead they identify "The End of the Party," which appeared in *The London Mercury* in January 1931, as Greene's first published story.

Greene was born in 1904 in Hertfordshire, England, the son of a headmaster. He attended Balliol College, Oxford, and worked as a copy editor on the *London Times* from 1926 to 1930. Greene published his first work, a book of verse called *Babbling April,* in 1925, and the first of his twenty-four novels, *The Man Within,* in 1929. Like a few other writers in this collection, Greene found it easier to break into print in book form than in periodicals.

PETER MORTON WOKE with a start to face the first light. Rain tapped against the glass. It was January the fifth.

He looked across a table on which a night-light had guttered into a pool of water, at the other bed. Francis Morton was still asleep, and Peter lay down again with his eyes on his brother. It amused him to imagine it was himself whom he watched, the same hair, the same eyes, the same lips and line of cheek. But the thought palled, and the mind went back to the fact which lent the day importance. It was the fifth of January. He could hardly believe a year had passed since Mrs Henne-Falcon had given her last children's party.

Francis turned suddenly upon his back and threw an arm across his

face, blocking his mouth. Peter's heart began to beat fast, not with pleasure now but with uneasiness. He sat up and called across the table, 'Wake up.' Francis's shoulders shook and he waved a clenched fist in the air, but his eyes remained closed. To Peter Morton the whole room seemed to darken, and he had the impression of a great bird swooping. He cried again, 'Wake up,' and once more there was silver light and the touch of rain on the windows. Francis rubbed his eyes. 'Did you call out?' he asked.

'You are having a bad dream,' Peter said. Already experience had taught him how far their minds reflected each other. But he was the elder, by a matter of minutes, and that brief extra interval of light, while his brother still struggled in pain and darkness, had given him self-reliance and an instinct of protection towards the other who was afraid of so many things.

'I dreamed that I was dead,' Francis said.

'What was it like?' Peter asked.

'I can't remember,' Francis said.

'You dreamed of a big bird.'

'Did I?'

The two lay silent in bed facing each other, the same green eyes, the same nose tilting at the tip, the same firm lips, and the same premature modelling of the chin. The fifth of January, Peter thought again, his mind drifting idly from the image of cakes to the prizes which might be won. Egg-and-spoon races, spearing apples in basins of water, blind man's buff.

'I don't want to go,' Francis said suddenly. 'I suppose Joyce will be there . . . Mabel Warren.' Hateful to him, the thought of a party shared with those two. They were older than he. Joyce was eleven and Mabel Warren thirteen. Their long pigtails swung superciliously to a masculine stride. Their sex humiliated him, as they watched him fumble with his egg, from under lowered scornful lids. And last year . . . he turned his face away from Peter, his cheeks scarlet.

'What's the matter?' Peter asked.

'Oh, nothing. I don't think I'm well. I've got a cold. I oughtn't to go to the party.' Peter was puzzled. 'But Francis, is it a bad cold?'

'It will be a bad cold if I go to the party. Perhaps I shall die.'

'Then you mustn't go,' Peter said, prepared to solve all difficulties

with one plain sentence, and Francis let his nerves relax, ready to leave everything to Peter. But though he was grateful he did not turn his face towards his brother. His cheeks still bore the badge of a shameful memory, of the game of hide and seek last year in the darkened house, and of how he had screamed when Mabel Warren put her hand suddenly upon his arm. He had not heard her coming. Girls were like that. Their shoes never squeaked. No boards whined under the tread. They slunk like cats on padded claws.

When the nurse came in with hot water Francis lay tranquil leaving everything to Peter. Peter said, 'Nurse, Francis has got a cold.'

The tall starched woman laid the towels across the cans and said, without turning, 'The washing won't be back till tomorrow. You must lend him some of your handkerchiefs.'

'But, Nurse,' Peter asked, 'hadn't he better stay in bed?'

'We'll take him for a good walk this morning,' the nurse said. 'Wind'll blow away the germs. Get up now, both of you,' and she closed the door behind her.

'I'm sorry,' Peter said. 'Why don't you just stay in bed? I'll tell mother you felt too ill to get up.' But rebellion against destiny was not in Francis's power. If he stayed in bed they would come up and tap his chest and put a thermometer in his mouth and look at his tongue, and they would discover he was malingering. It was true he felt ill, a sick empty sensation in his stomach and a rapidly beating heart, but he knew the cause was only fear, fear of the party, fear of being made to hide by himself in the dark, uncompanioned by Peter and with no night-light to make a blessed breach.

'No, I'll get up,' he said, and then with sudden desperation, 'But I won't go to Mrs Henne-Falcon's party. I swear on the Bible I won't.' Now surely all would be well, he thought. God would not allow him to break so solemn an oath. He would show him a way. There was all the morning before him and all the afternoon until four o'clock. No need to worry when the grass was still crisp with the early frost. Anything might happen. He might cut himself or break his leg or really catch a bad cold. God would manage somehow.

He had such confidence in God that when at breakfast his mother said, 'I hear you have a cold, Francis,' he made light of it. 'We should have heard more about it,' his mother said with irony, 'if there was not a

party this evening,' and Francis smiled, amazed and daunted by her ignorance of him. His happiness would have lasted longer if, out for a walk that morning, he had not met Joyce. He was alone with his nurse, for Peter had leave to finish a rabbit-hutch in the woodshed. If Peter had been there he would have cared less; the nurse was Peter's nurse also, but now it was as though she were employed only for his sake, because he could not be trusted to go for a walk alone. Joyce was only two years older and she was by herself.

She came striding towards them, pigtails flapping. She glanced scornfully at Francis and spoke with ostentation to the nurse. 'Hello, Nurse. Are you bringing Francis to the party this evening? Mabel and I are coming.' And she was off again down the street in the direction of Mabel Warren's home, consciously alone and self-sufficient in the long empty road. 'Such a nice girl,' the nurse said. But Francis was silent, feeling again the jump-jump of his heart, realizing how soon the hour of the party would arrive. God had done nothing for him, and the minutes flew.

They flew too quickly to plan any evasion, or even to prepare his heart for the coming ordeal. Panic nearly overcame him when, all unready, he found himself standing on the doorstep, with coat-collar turned up against a cold wind, and the nurse's electric torch making a short trail through the darkness. Behind him were the lights of the hall and the sound of a servant laying the table for dinner, which his mother and father would eat alone. He was nearly overcome by the desire to run back into the house and call out to his mother that he would not go to the party, that he dared not go. They could not make him go. He could almost hear himself saying those final words, breaking down for ever the barrier of ignorance which saved his mind from his parents' knowledge. 'I'm afraid of going. I won't go. I daren't go. They'll make me hide in the dark, and I'm afraid of the dark. I'll scream and scream and scream.' He could see the expression of amazement on his mother's face, and then the cold confidence of a grown-up's retort.

'Don't be silly. You must go. We've accepted Mrs Henne-Falcon's invitation.' But they couldn't make him go; hesitating on the doorstep while the nurse's feet crunched across the frost-covered grass to the gate, he knew that. He would answer: 'You can say I'm ill. I won't go. I'm afraid of the dark.' And his mother: 'Don't be silly. You know there's

nothing to be afraid of in the dark.' But he knew the falsity of that reasoning; he knew how they taught also that there was nothing to fear in death, and how fearfully they avoided the idea of it. But they couldn't make him go to the party. 'I'll scream. I'll scream."

'Francis, come along.' He heard the nurse's voice across the dimly phosphorescent lawn and saw the yellow circle of her torch wheel from tree to shrub. 'I'm coming,' he called with despair; he couldn't bring himself to lay bare his last secrets and end reserve between his mother and himself, for there was still in the last resort a further appeal possible to Mrs Henne-Falcon. He comforted himself with that, as he advanced steadily across the hall, very small, towards her enormous bulk. His heart beat unevenly, but he had control now over his voice, as he said with meticulous accent, 'Good evening, Mrs Henne-Falcon. It was very good of you to ask me to your party.' With his strained face lifted towards the curve of her breasts, and his polite set speech, he was like an old withered man. As a twin he was in many ways an only child. To address Peter was to speak to his own image in a mirror, an image a little altered by a flaw in the glass, so as to throw back less a likeness of what he was than of what he wished to be, what he would be without his unreasoning fear of darkness, footsteps of strangers, the flight of bats in dusk-filled gardens.

'Sweet child,' said Mrs Henne-Falcon absentmindedly, before, with a wave of her arms, as though the children were a flock of chickens, she whirled them into her set programme of entertainments: egg-and-spoon races, three-legged races, the spearing of apples, games which held for Francis nothing worse than humiliation. And in the frequent intervals when nothing was required of him and he could stand alone in corners as far removed as possible from Mabel Warren's scornful gaze, he was able to plan how he might avoid the approaching terror of the dark. He knew there was nothing to fear until after tea, and not until he was sitting down in a pool of yellow radiance cast by the ten candles on Colin Henne-Falcon's birthday cake did he become fully conscious of the imminence of what he feared. He heard Joyce's high voice down the table, 'After tea we are going to play hide and seek in the dark.'

'Oh, no,' Peter said, watching Francis's troubled face, 'don't let's. We play that every year.'

'But it's in the programme,' cried Mabel Warren. 'I saw it myself. I looked over Mrs Henne-Falcon's shoulder. Five o'clock tea. A quarter to

six to half past, hide and seek in the dark. It's all written down in the programme.'

Peter did not argue, for if hide and seek had been inserted in Mrs Henne-Falcon's programme, nothing which he could say would avert it. He asked for another piece of birthday cake and sipped his tea slowly. Perhaps it might be possible to delay the game for a quarter of an hour, allow Francis at least a few extra minutes to form a plan, but even in that Peter failed, for children were already leaving the table in twos and threes. It was his third failure, and again he saw a great bird darken his brother's face with its wings. But he upbraided himself silently for his folly, and finished his cake encouraged by the memory of that adult refrain, 'There's nothing to fear in the dark.' The last to leave the table, the brothers came together to the hall to meet the mustering and impatient eyes of Mrs Henne-Falcon.

'And now,' she said, 'we will play hide and seek in the dark.'

Peter watched his brother and saw the lips tighten. Francis, he knew, had feared this moment from the beginning of the party, had tried to meet it with courage and had abandoned the attempt. He must have prayed for cunning to evade the game, which was now welcomed with cries of excitement by all the other children. 'Oh, do let's.' 'We must pick sides.' 'Is any of the house out of bounds?' 'Where shall home be?'

'I think,' said Francis Morton, approaching Mrs Henne-Falcon, his eyes focused unwaveringly on her exuberant breasts, 'it will be no use my playing. My nurse will be calling for me very soon.'

'Oh, but your nurse can wait, Francis,' said Mrs Henne-Falcon, while she clapped her hands together to summon to her side a few children who were already straying up the wide staircase to upper floors. 'Your mother will never mind.'

That had been the limit of Francis's cunning. He had refused to believe that so well-prepared an excuse could fail. All that he could say now, still in the precise tone which other children hated, thinking it a symbol of conceit, was, 'I think I had better not play.' He stood motionless, retaining, though afraid, unmoved features. But the knowledge of his terror, or the reflection of the terror itself, reached his brother's brain. For the moment, Peter Morton could have cried aloud with the fear of bright lights going out, leaving him alone in an island of dark surrounded by the gentle lappings of strange footsteps. Then he remem-

bered that the fear was not his own, but his brother's. He said impulsively to Mrs Henne-Falcon, 'Please, I don't think Francis should play. The dark makes him jump so.' They were the wrong words. Six children began to sing, 'Cowardy cowardy custard,' turning torturing faces with the vacancy of wide sunflowers towards Francis Morton.

Without looking at his brother, Francis said, 'Of course I'll play. I'm not afraid, I only thought . . .' But he was already forgotten by his human tormentors. The children scrambled round Mrs Henne-Falcon, their shrill voices pecking at her with questions and suggestions. 'Yes, anywhere in the house. We will turn out all the lights. Yes, you can hide in the cupboards. You must stay hidden as long as you can. There will be no home.'

Peter stood apart, ashamed of the clumsy manner in which he had tried to help his brother. Now he could feel, creeping in at the corners of his brain, all Francis's resentment of his championing. Several children ran upstairs, and the lights on the top floor went out. Darkness came down like the wings of a bat and settled on the landing. Others began to put out the lights at the edge of the hall, till the children were all gathered in the central radiance of the chandelier, while the bats squatted round on hooded wings and waited for that, too, to be extinguished.

'You and Francis are on the hiding side,' a tall girl said, and then the light was gone, and the carpet wavered under his feet with the sibilance of footfalls, like small cold draughts, creeping away into corners.

'Where's Francis?' he wondered. 'If I join him he'll be less frightened of all these sounds.' 'These sounds' were the casing of silence: the squeak of a loose board, the cautious closing of a cupboard door, the whine of a finger drawn along polished wood.

Peter stood in the centre of the dark deserted floor, not listening but waiting for the idea of his brother's whereabouts to enter his brain. But Francis crouched with fingers on his ears, eyes uselessly closed, mind numbed against impressions, and only a sense of strain could cross the gap of dark. Then a voice called 'Coming', and as though his brother's self-possession had been shattered by the sudden cry, Peter Morton jumped with his fear. But it was not his own fear. What in his brother was a burning panic was in him an altruistic emotion that left the reason unimpaired. 'Where, if I were Francis, should I hide?' And because he

was, if not Francis himself, at least a mirror to him, the answer was immediate. 'Between the oak bookcase on the left of the study door, and the leather settee.' Between the twins there could be no jargon of telepathy. They had been together in the womb, and they could not be parted.

Peter Morton tiptoed towards Francis's hiding-place. Occasionally a board rattled, and because he feared to be caught by one of the soft questers through the dark, he bent and untied his laces. A tag struck the floor and the metallic sound set a host of cautious feet moving in his direction. But by that time he was in his stockings and would have laughed inwardly at the pursuit had not the noise of someone stumbling on his abandoned shoes made his heart trip. No more boards revealed Peter Morton's progress. On stockinged feet he moved silently and unerringly towards his object. Instinct told him he was near the wall, and, extending a hand, he laid the fingers across his brother's face.

Francis did not cry out, but the leap of his own heart revealed to Peter a proportion of Francis's terror. 'It's all right,' he whispered, feeling down the squatting figure until he captured a clenched hand. 'It's only me. I'll stay with you.' And grasping the other tightly, he listened to the cascade of whispers his utterance had caused to fall. A hand touched the bookcase close to Peter's head and he was aware of how Francis's fear continued in spite of his presence. It was less intense, more bearable, he hoped, but it remained. He knew that it was his brother's fear and not his own that he experienced. The dark to him was only an absence of light; the groping hand that of a familiar child. Patiently he waited to be found.

He did not speak again, for between Francis and himself was the most intimate communion. By way of joined hands thought could flow more swiftly than lips could shape themselves round words. He could experience the whole progress of his brother's emotion, from the leap of panic at the unexpected contact to the steady pulse of fear, which now went on and on with the regularity of a heart-beat. Peter Morton thought with intensity, 'I am here. You needn't be afraid. The lights will go on again soon. That rustle, that movement is nothing to fear. Only Joyce, only Mabel Warren.' He bombarded the drooping form with thoughts of safety, but he was conscious that the fear continued. 'They are beginning to whisper together. They are tired of looking for us. The lights will go on soon. We shall have won. Don't be afraid. That was only someone on the stairs. I believe it's Mrs Henne-Falcon. Listen. They are

feeling for the lights.' Feet moving on a carpet, hands brushing a wall, a curtain pulled apart, a clicking handle, the opening of a cupboard door. In the case above their heads a loose book shifted under a touch. 'Only Joyce, only Mabel Warren, only Mrs Henne-Falcon,' a crescendo of reassuring thought before the chandelier burst, like a fruit-tree, into bloom.

The voices of the children rose shrilly into the radiance. 'Where's Peter?' 'Have you looked upstairs?' 'Where's Francis?' but they were silenced again by Mrs Henne-Falcon's scream. But she was not the first to notice Francis Morton's stillness, where he had collapsed against the wall at the touch of his brother's hand. Peter continued to hold the clenched fingers in an arid and puzzled grief. It was not merely that his brother was dead. His brain, too young to realize the full paradox, wondered with an obscure self-pity why it was that the pulse of his brother's fear went on and on, when Francis was now where he had always been told there was no more terror and no more darkness.

Because of the Waters of the Flood

Mark Helprin is widely known not only for his fiction, but also for fictionalizing various details and circumstances of his own life. He claims to have embarked upon a writing career at age seventeen, in a hotel room in Paris: "I got up, sat at a table, and began to write on a blotter. I wrote a description of the Hagia Sophia in Istanbul," a cathedral-mosque he had never seen. "In the morning I looked at the blotter. It was like a real writer had written the passage. I said to my-self: 'I can do this. *I* did that.'"

According to one account, Helprin had submitted "about fifty" stories before selling one; according to another, twelve. It is verifiably true, though, that Helprin was only twenty-one and still an under-graduate at Harvard when he sold his first story. "Because of the Waters of the Flood" appeared in the September 27, 1969, issue of the *New Yorker* and was reprinted, along with nineteen others, in Hel-prin's first book, *A Dove of the East and Other Stories* (Knopf, 1975).

JETS FROM AIRFIELDS in Nevada trailed fine white lines across the sky. At the head of white columns, the planes themselves looked like silver ticks. When she looked up, there was a roundness of light as if she were seeing through glass or a lens, but she was only looking through her eyes. All her life the B-52s had left their smoke trails above her. It was almost a part of nature, akin to the rising of the moon, or setting of the sun.

They were miles from Tippet, a town of about thirty-five, and Tippet was miles from anywhere else. You could pull in two or three country-music stations. Sheep grazed in the lower depressions of the mountains

and drank from clear pools, near gray porous rocks. In summer Henry made a fire, and lining his sheep up one by one he pulled off the ticks and cast them into the flame. Always the air was cool and deep. Around the house was no argument, no lawn — just pine trees, wind, and a view of mountains. Winter was hard and sometimes it snowed late in June, though only at night. They were high up where the air was thin. They didn't waste it. Stories were therefore short, expressions clipped, and Agnes had a habit of giving long looks without saying a word, during which her mouth was slightly smiling and her eyebrows slightly raised. When she looked this way, everyone knew she was good-natured and wanted to kiss her and twirl, eyes closed, with so much in reserve.

She cooked. Steam swirled upward around the spoon as she looked into the pot, her body arched away from the stove. The kitchen was full of windows. Through them was miraculous blue and white of mountains, hanging aeriel ice, and sky.

And her face. Her face was an extremely beautiful face. When she laughed you did not laugh at her face nor did she become less pretty. When she was angry it was the same. The eyes were blue. There was a mirror in the hall, surrounded by a frame of grayish-white tin. When she looked at herself in the mirror she saw the blue eyes, shining out, and the simple blond hair, energetic. "Bong Bong," she said as she patted her hair into place and went to the porch to wait for Henry.

She was wearing a loose white dress held together at the neck by a button which said, "All the Way with Alf Landon." The wind blew her hair. She settled her eyes to stare into the valley, past the rocks, past the sheep that looked like moving cylinders of cream or cloud, past the pools and pines, to the road where Henry would be coming. She picked up a knife and stuck it into the chopping block on which it had been lying. She loved Henry, and had doused everything to marry him. Those are the only marriages that work — where you say to hell with it, and hurt three or four dozen people, and tell fifty more to go to hell, and then move out to Nevada or Alaska, or Brazil. If you don't do that, you're not really married. She was married to Henry. Henry tried to tell their parents about how to marry.

"Why?" said their parents.

"Because," said Henry, "if you love you make no concessions — none at all. And in the beginning this is especially true. And Agnes and

I are angry at concessions — little ones, big ones. We want to start clean. I love Agnes. We bought a sheep ranch."

The pot was boiling over. She went in and turned off the heat. It was a simple principle: if the pot boils over, turn off the heat. She always thought passionately that to think is somehow dispassionate. Henry said she was right and drove her in his car up the mountain to their house with the whitening tin-framed mirror where they saw themselves in dusty silver and wondered what was the toughest road they knew.

She went back to her chair on the porch. She led an orchestra with the spoon, and sang several songs. Henry was a hard worker, very strong for his size, and he made up stories. He never went anywhere without adventures. He once had wept in her lap at the top of a mountain. She kissed her hands, ran them down her breast, and said a prayer, for she believed in God, as did Henry — in His power, and that He made everything. That is really why they told everyone to go to hell, for they needed no one, and saw that no one believed.

She prayed to God, surveying His hills and rising high above them, glancing at green pines, and turning humorous circles in heaven. She loved God, and she loved Henry. God made her shake like a true priest, and although she was quiet she was thundering at the hills for His sake, and for Henry's sake.

Henry came up the mountain in the wooden station wagon. There were books on the seat next to him, and groceries in the back. He was driving to music. She could see by the way he moved his head from side to side and was rhythmically intent on making the car sway gracefully up and down turns, through the cool sunshine air.

HE pulled up and left the radio on. He got out of the car and walked around the front to face Agnes, who was on the porch, as still as a branch.

He was dark-haired and had a wide smile. He wore a bulky olive Navy N-1 jacket, denim pants, and brown leather boots. She looked at him and remembered what she had looked like in the mirror — tan, her nose a little shiny, in a white dress and crown of blond, with blue eyes sadly piercing the leaded glass darkened from age in the mountains.

They were still, and the wind ceased. "Well," she said, and raised her eyebrows slightly.

"I told them that I wouldn't go," he said. "That I wouldn't go to prison either, that we both would go into the mountains and fight there to the death, on the little point, for what we believed. And when I said it, I meant it. We're right, aren't we Agnes."

"Yes."

"Then they met for about ten minutes. When they came out, the psychiatrist took me aside and told me I was not fit for military service."

Agnes lifted the sheets of her dress, floated down the steps, twirled in slow motion over millions of particles of white dust, circled dizzy around Henry while he laughed and leaned back and looked at her blue sparkling eyes. "We're both crazy," he said. "Aren't we?"

"Yes," said Agnes, "and we're free." And they sat on the wooden steps of the porch and said that the day was especially fine.

"Why," Henry said, "do you have that spoon so tightly in your hand?"

And Agnes began to cry.

in our time

It should be a simple matter to peg the first published short story of a writer whose long and illustrious career has been so well documented as Ernest Hemingway's, but conflicting information abounds. In his preface to *The Short Stories of Ernest Hemingway,* Hemingway says that "Up in Michigan" was the first story he wrote. Carlos Baker, in his biography of Hemingway, cites "My Old Man" as the author's first to appear in print. And *Benet's Reader's Encyclopedia* names *Three Stories and Ten Poems,* which included both "Up in Michigan" and "My Old Man," as Hemingway's first published work.

In fact, the first adult work of fiction published by Hemingway, was "in our time," included in the Spring 1923 "Exiles" issue of Margaret Anderson and Jane Heap's *The Little Review,* guest edited by Ezra Pound. It is reprinted here as it originally appeared. This story, along with its title, was recycled twice in the next two years. It became chapters one through six of Hemingway's second book, also titled *in our time,* a thirty-two-page limited edition published in Paris in the spring of 1924. Later the material that comprises this story was reprinted as untitled inter-chapters in Hemingway's first book to be published in the United States, *In Our Time: Stories by Ernest Hemingway* (Boni & Liveright, 1925).

When Hemingway heard that Edmund Wilson had read the "Exiles" issue of *The Little Review,* he sent Wilson a review copy of *in our time.* Wilson, in his October 1924 *Dial* review, which helped establish Hemingway's literary reputation, said, "His prose is of the first distinction. . . . He is showing you what life is, too proud to simplify," and he called him "strikingly original." Wilson's only criticism was of the lowercase title: "This device, which used to be rather effective when the modernists first used it . . . , has now grown common and a bore."

EVERYBODY WAS DRUNK. The whole battery was drunk along the road in the dark. We were going to the Champagne. The lieutenant kept riding his horse out into the fields and saying to him, "I'm drunk I tell you, mon vieux. Oh I am so soused." We went along the road all night in the dark and the adjutant kept riding up alongside my kitchen and saying, "You must put it out. It is dangerous. It will be observed." We were fifty kilometers from the front but the adjutant worried about the fire in my kitchen. It was funny going along that road. That was when I was a kitchen corporal.

THE first matador got the horn through his sword hand and the crowd hooted him on his way to the infirmary. The second matador slipped and the bull caught him through the belly and he hung onto the horn with one hand and held the other tight against the place, and the bull rammed him wham against the barrera and the horn came and he lay in the sand; and then got up like crazy drunk and tried to slug the men carrying him away and yelled for a new sword, but he fainted. The kid came out and had to kill five bulls because you can't have more than three matadors and the last bull he was so tired he couldn't get the sword in. He couldn't hardly lift his arm. He tried eight times and the crowd was quiet because it was a good bull and it looked like him or the bull and then he finally made it. He sat down in the sand and puked and they held a cape over him while the crowd come down the barrera into the bull ring.

MINARETS stuck up in the rain out of Adrianople across the mud flats. The carts were jammed for thirty miles along the Karagatch road. Water buffalo and cattle were hauling carts through the mud. No end and no beginning. Just carts loaded with everything they owned. The old men and women, soaked through, walked along keeping the cattle moving. The Maritza was running yellow almost up to the bridge. Carts were jammed solid on the bridge with camels bobbing along through them. Greek cavalry rode hard on the procession. Women and kids were in the carts crouched with mattresses, mirrors, sewing machines, bundles, sacks

158

of things. There was a woman having a kid with a young girl holding a blanket over her and crying. Scared sick looking at it. It rained all through the evacuation.

WE were in a garden at Mons. Young Buckley came in with his patrol from across the river. The first German I saw climbed up over the garden wall. We waited till he got one leg over and then potted him. He had so much equipment on and looked awfully surprised and fell down into the garden. Then three more came over further down the wall. We shot them. They all came just like that.

MONS (TWO)

It was a frightfully hot day. We'd jammed an absolutely perfect barricade across the bridge. It was simply priceless. A big old wrought iron grating from the front of a house. Too heavy to lift and you could shoot through it and they would have to climb over it. It was absolutely topping. They tried to get over it and we potted them from forty yards. They rushed it and officers came out alone and worked on it. It was an absolutely perfect obstacle. Their officers were very fine. We were frightfully put out when we heard the flank had gone and we had to fall back.

THEY shot the six cabinet ministers at half past six in the morning against the wall of a hospital. There were pools of water in the courtyard. There were wet dead leaves on the paving of the courtyard. It rained hard. All the shutters of the hospital were nailed shut. One of the ministers was sick with typhoid. Two soldiers carried him downstairs and out into the rain. They tried to hold him up against the wall but he sat down in a puddle of water. The other five stood very quietly against the wall. Finally the officer told the soldiers it was no good trying to make him stand up. When they fired the first volley he was sitting down in the water with his head on his knees.

CHESTER B. HIMES

Crazy in the Stir

"Crazy in the Stir" appeared in the August 1934 issue of *Esquire.* The note that introduced its author read:

> Chester B. Himes is known as No. 59623 in Columbus, where he is serving a twenty-year sentence in the Ohio State Penitentiary. His story, "Crazy in the Stir," is the first convict writing to appear in our pages. It will be followed in an early issue by another by this same author, "To What Red Hell?"

Born in 1909 in Missouri, Himes was enrolled at Ohio State University when he was arrested and jailed for armed robbery in 1928. He began to write while in prison, where he witnessed the prison fire of 1930. It killed 320 inmates and became the subject of his second story, "To What Red Hell?" After being paroled in 1936, Himes moved to Los Angeles, where he worked in defense plants and for the Federal Writers' Project. He published his first novel, *If He Hollers, Let Him Go,* in 1945, and in 1953 left the United States to live in Europe, where his work was highly regarded.

THE STAINED, SQUASHED cigaret hanging from Red's tight lips glowed, a tiny spark in the yellow glare that spilled from the enameled reflector at the ceiling. Smoke dribbled from his mouth and nostrils, eddied upward around the cardboard sign that hung from the light by a string — "SPITTING ON THE FLOOR AND WALL FORBIDDEN."

Red put his hands palms downward on the gray blanket that was

stretched out on the table and stood up, straddling the low, wooden bench. He spit the cigaret from his lips. It broke up, scattered tobacco flakes over the pasteboard poker chips piled in the center of the blanket.

The other six men in the game looked at him, looked away. He swung away from the game, moved down the aisle. The hard heels of his prison brogues made clumping sounds on the concrete floor. His tall, slim frame jerked stiffly as he walked. His hair was wild flame above his set, white face. His greenish-gray eyes were hot slits. Men walking up and down the aisle for exercise looked at his face, got out of his way.

Broke again! God, what the hell was the matter with him? Sitting in that trim game all day. Card crazy! Couldn't even see the spots on the cards after ten hours play; the hands all ran together in his mind. Four dollars and sixty cents, the last of that fin his sister had slipped him on her last visit. A poker fit! No more smoking for a month: no more gambling! Jesus, the joint was getting on his nerves!

He wheeled, strode back down the aisle, his hickory-striped shirt felt moldy; his long, prison underwear crawled on his skin; his prison-fit trousers chafed him. Even his shoes felt slimy to his feet.

A steady hum of noise swirled about his ears. Air thick with the odor of tobacco fumes and unwashed bodies clogged in his nostrils. Faces drifted in front of his gaze; faces all stamped with that queer docility common to prisoners. Rows of bunks were ugly in his mind. Steel bars formed a grilled background for his thoughts.

Five years! Jesus, he was tired of it — tired! — *tired!* The unvarying monotony: Up at six; breakfast at seven; walk at eight; dinner at eleven; walk at one; supper at three; back in the dormitory; lights out at nine; then gnawing silence until six; the same thing over the next day. Gray uniforms! Gray caps! Gray weather! Gray faces! Angles, stone, brick, bars — all alike! Even the convicts looked alike. You knew what a guy was going to say before he said it. An endless cycle, as unvarying as eternity. An endless chain of days, beginning at six, ending at nine. You knew what breakfast would be before you got to the dining room, and then you didn't want it; the same with dinner and supper. Days! Days! All alike! No change! *Dead days!*

Red turned again, started back down the aisle. A fellow touched his arm. "Wanta buy some oranges, Red? Two for a nickel."

Red stopped, looked at the fellow blankly. "Hunh?"

"Wanta buy some oranges, two for a nickel?" the fellow repeated.

"Where are they?" Red asked.

The fellow said: "I'll get 'em next Sunday. But I need the nickel now. I gotta do something."

Red's expression changed. He wasn't annoyed. He contemplated hitting the fellow in the mouth. No, on the neck just below that mole. A swift chop to the jaw with his left, cross a hard right to his neck, watch his eyes pop out in his face.

He leaned forward on the balls of his feet, his body tensed. He said: "No, pal, I don't wanta buy any oranges." His voice was weary.

The fellow said: "O.K." and turned away.

Red stood stock still. He heard the fellow speaking to another convict — "Wanta buy some oranges, Smith? . . ." He shook himself like a dog coming up out of a pond. His lips stretched. He shoulda bust the mugg one just for the hell of it. Wonder why he hadn't. Five years ago he'd a knocked him sprawling. But now — after five years of discipline . . .

His laugh was ragged. His jerking gaze lighted on the placid features of the guard sitting to a table at the far end of the dormitory next to the door. Stinging resentment flooded his mind. The complacent bastard. Sitting there chewing his plug with the unruffled indifference of a Mississippi goat while a hundred convicts with a thousand years roamed the floors around him. A hundred men caged like animals in a circus. He wasn't guarding a bunch of convicts, desperate men. Not him! He was just a fat, ex-wrestler earning five dollars a day the easiest way he knew how.

His feet carried him in that direction. Wonder what the fat slob would say if he just walked up and bust him one in his blank face? Jesus, that was an idea. The "hole" for thirty days. Damn the "hole!" Solitary confinement with the "red-shirt" desperadoes, perhaps. Hell, that would be a change anyway.

His pace accelerated.

Wonder if he'd have the nerve? Nerve? That wasn't it. It was just breaking through the shell of discipline.

He stopped in front of the guard's table. The guard didn't even look up from the Detective Story Magazine he was reading. He tensed him-

self, planted his feet to deliver the blow. And then . . . He just couldn't do it, just couldn't do it, that was all.

He wheeled away.

Prison etiquette. Guards might hit convicts just for the hell of it. But a convict never hit a guard just for the hell of it. It just wasn't done.

His muscles jerked like the muscles of a freshly slain sheep. Nuts! He was going nuts! He wanted to scream.

He bumped into the corner of a bed and the scattered visions before his eyes crystallized into definite objects with shapes and names:

Two rows of double-decked beds, a table down the center of a concrete floor, backless benches paralleling the tables. White walls grayed with dust in the background; dirty windows showing black bars through their translucent grayness; iron joists holding up a low, concrete ceiling:

Dirty duffel bags, hanging from the bedframes, chunked into fat unshapeliness with the convict's personal belongings. Coats, shoes, towels, mirrors, hanging from hooks or from the bedframes. Pictures of loved ones in fatuous poses stuck about in prominent view:

Men reading, studying, drawing, playing cards, playing musical instruments, making beaded bags, making inlaid jewel boxes, typewriting, talking, laughing, cursing; men coming in and out from between the beds with the sliding, sidewise motion of crabs. Faces with different featuring, different expressions, but all masked with an indefinable sameness:

Noises! A million noises! The noises of the men — shoe heels clumping, yells, curses, laughter, singing; the noises of the dormitory — radiators clanking, leaking steam pipes hissing, iron beds scraping on the concrete floor; the alien noises seeping in through an open window — the far-away whistle of a locomotive, the sharp bleat of a melody horn from a passing car on the highway, the distant wail of a police siren. Confusion!

Heat rolled up from the base of Red's brain.

He moved down into "Black Bottom," down at the far end of the dormitory next to the latrine where the Negroes bunked. He would see what the hell they were doing, the black, stolid animals.

Georgia Skin . . . A group of black faces . . . Cards spinning face-upward in the yellow glare . . . Soft, intense curses rising like thick

smoke . . . A black boy strumming a uke, feet patting time . . . Another cutting a step . . . A circle of swaying bodies . . . Hands clapping in rhythmic beat . . . Animated faces . . .

Chiselers! Petty larceny! Most of 'em in for stealing a ham or strong-arming some hunky laborer. Some in for carving up their women. The days passed and they didn't know it. Time meant nothing to them.

A voice came out from between two beds — "Oh, de little black train's a'coming; Oh, de little black train's a'coming . . ."

A chunky black man and a lean yellow one were sitting side by side on a bed with a Bible between them chanting the repetitious drone.

Red thought: Probably in for rape, both of 'em. Singing to a white man's idea of God. Don't know what the hell it's all about. Don't wanta know. Just an emotional release, a substitute for sex.

He turned away disgusted. His face was streaked with unrest. He wanted to break something in his hands; he'd like to see a man die; like to see the blood coming out of his mouth. Anything to get away from the damned monotony, the damned sameness day after day.

His feet were heavy. His mouth was sour. He bit his bottom lip, moistened his lips with his tongue. Wasn't there something he could do? Wasn't there something in the whole damn prison that a man could do when he got the jitters? Read? Hell, he'd tried that. Just so many words running together before his eyes. Gambling — but he was broke.

He took a package of Bull Durham tobacco from his pocket and rolled a cigaret. The tobacco tasted like so much straw. Damn!

He went over to a window and looked out into the yard. Search lights illuminated the yard in sketchy brilliance. Buildings loomed dark and ugly. A prison guard turned the corner of the big red-brick chapel, making his rounds. Scared grass covered the ground. A lone star peeped through the branches of a tree. The sky was a black blanket; the lone star a scintillating jewel.

And then the years began rushing in parade through his mind. Years in the Bronx alleys where he had been born — narrow streets, dirty gutters, filth, penury — but even at that he had been able to see the sky. Years on the street corners at night, selling papers to the world that went by under the stars. Years of schooling with a mob of young thieves when a right angle meant escape from a copper's bullet. Years overseas in narrow trenches — cooty-ridden, cramped with the damp, unwashed

bodies of thousands of men — but the sky had been wide and big and shell-lit above him. Years in the Marines — Nicaragua, China, long expanses of blue water — the world for a parade ground. Years when he had roamed free, hoboing over the country, working here and there — a girl or two, casual friends, a little money now and then, no responsibilities . . . Free! *Free!*

Places and years and space — *space!* Years colored with the red of adventure, lived beneath a broad expanse of sky, where a man could breathe . . . Not in a tomb like this . . .

He caught himself quoting: "Long years ago we lived, felt dawn, saw sunset glow . . ." Hell! Why hadn't he got it there, on Flander's Field? Not even a scratch. And now — rotting in a lousy prison.

He felt stifled. A wet towel steamed on the radiator at his side. The vapor caught in his nostrils. He couldn't breathe. He opened the window. The cool, damp air blew against the hot haze of his mind. He breathed deeply. Even the air from the yard seemed to have a prison tang, but it was a relief from the stale air inside.

His mind whirled as he stared into the night. His thoughts ran together. But there was no pity in the black heavens.

God! He wanted to scream out to all eternity . . .

Somebody picked a clear melody on a mandolin at his side. A voice crooned a tentative note; he listened to the words: "Sometimes I wonder while I spend the lonely nights . . ."

He turned toward the voice. A lad with a babyish face was sitting in a cane-bottomed chair with the mandolin in his lap. "Like that one — Star Dust?" the lad asked.

Red nodded. A cute kid, he thought. Wonder what he's in for? Reminded him of a girl he had once known. Lessee, her name was some queer name. Leone! That was it — Leone! In Sacramento. And there was that other girl in Nicaragua, when he was in the Marines. He had forgotten her name, but her face lingered in his memory, like — like the tune you remembered in the middle of the night for years afterward. Where had he read that?

He listened to the lad's voice again, a different song now. He noticed that the lad had white, even teeth. And then the tune of the song formed words in the turmoil of his mind — "*Let me hold you in my arms tonight, Leone.*"

He caught a fleeting, crystal clear view of his life in its prison perspective. Maggots crawled in his mind. He said in a low, deliberate voice: "Damn the God who created me for an existence like this."

The lad with the mandolin looked startled. Red felt ashamed. What was he damning God for? It was his own damn fault that he was here. If he had stopped when he missed the guy the first time; if he had just stopped and put the gat back in his pocket. But he hadn't. He had emptied it in the guy's guts. But then the fellow had called him a name that a man couldn't take.

His fingers splayed, stiffened, as his thoughts went back. The bastard wouldn't call another man a name like that.

He turned abruptly, squeezed between a bed on his way back to the center aisle.

He heard a soft voice saying: "Don't, don't now! Somebody'll see . . ." He looked down into a bed that was curtained on one side. An older man sat beside a good-looking youth. The youth's face looked rouged and powdered.

Then the youth's bold gaze met Red's hot stare and his eyes seemed to ask: "Well, what's it to you?"

Wonder if he could learn indifference that way? Red thought. Wonder if it'd make his time easier, make him forget space and the sky and the freight whistles on the Arizona desert of an Autumn night. His mind thickened. He smiled one-sidedly.

Then he moved on out into the aisle. Let people go to hell their own way. That was tolerance. The thought was bitter amusement in his mind.

He circled in the aisles. His eyes caught pictures but his mind gave them no significance:

A prizefighter prancing in the areaway at the front end of the dormitory, showing off his muscles: A deaf convict studying a law course: A half-blind man with thick lens glasses, head thrown back, walking fast up and down the floor: A sleeping Negro brushing at a fly crawling over his face: A blunt-fingered man carving an inlaid jewel box: A timetable sticking from the pocket on a lifer's bed: A negro porter shining shoes: A slim, bald man in purple shorts stamping a crease in his pants stretched out on the floor.

A phrase caught his ear as he passed a bed — "That ain't Miriam

Hopkins, that's, er-er, that's . . ." He shot a quick glance between the beds. Two gray-haired men were poring over a Movie Magazine.

He moved on down the aisle, stopped by a pillar, leaned against it and rolled a cigaret. His face was blunt. A sudden voice in his ear startled him — "*I didn't go to do it!* . . ." He dropped the cigaret from nerveless fingers, whirled around the pillar. The voice trailed to a jumbled mutter. A sleeping convict turned over in his upper bunk, brushed his hand across his face.

Red's "Damn!" was salty. He didn't go to do it. Talking about it in his sleep. He just oughtn'ta done it, the lousy rat. That was all.

He went over to his own bed. His mind felt dead. It cost him a conscious effort to raise his hands. He felt that if he heard another word distinctly he would scream.

He picked up a magazine and began thumbing the pages. He couldn't even see the pictures. He flung the magazine down, cursed under his breath.

He got out into the aisle again, began moving fast. Hot blood was screaming in his head. His eyes were glassy, unseeing. Hate was a knife in his mind; he hated everything, everybody.

He bumped into a fellow, wheeled, knocked him to his knees. He heard a voice saying: "Get the hack, some of youse guys. Red's on the rampage."

He turned toward the voice. Gray legs scuttled down the aisle in the direction of the guard's desk. He moved the other way.

And then . . . What the hell? His pace slowed. Was he afraid of the screw? He turned half around, turned back. No-o-o, not scared — but you didn't borrow trouble with the guards.

His quick stride carried him fast. Figures brushed past his vision. His red-rimmed eyes made pictures. He found himself down in Black Bottom again.

The darkies had a "strut" on . . . Instruments clanging . . . A saxophone wailing. Red looked for the saxophone, saw a black boy blowing a hair comb. Slender bodies swaying to the hot rhythm . . . Feet shuffling, patting . . . A brown boy bucking a step, cap pulled low over his eyes . . . White teeth gleaming in black faces . . . Yellow faces were ivory masks in the shadowed corners . . . Soft voices were a steady beat of sound . . . *Laughter!*

The noise bubbled like hot tar in Red's mind.

But what the hell? The darkies were happy, they laughed. Nothing could hurt them. The days passed . . .

He moved on down to the latrine, got a drink of water at the fountain, leaned against the wall and rolled a cigaret, tossed the empty tobacco sack on the floor.

A crowd was grouped in a noisy discussion — a latrine discussion. He heard words — "That guy Dillinger's got guts, thassall! Just guts! Take a hunka wood and bluff his way out of that jail . . ."

His eyes located the speaker: A beardless youth trying to talk bass out of the side of his mouth.

Another voice took the subject away from him — "Naw-w-w! He had that woman bought. Look what he did to them feds. Say, listen, that baby was sweet on him anyway, but them feds now . . ."

Red's gaze shifted. The complacent, know-it-all voice got on his nerves. He saw a sunburned face, scraggly hair. A farmer! A lousy farmer! Stole a chicken and just got to town.

And then a Negro's voice — "Ah'll bet ma life 'gainst a copper cent dat w'en dey ketch day guy dere'll be . . ."

Red said: "Make it even money."

Everybody stopped talking and stared at him. He met their stares, spat on the floor.

He heard a voice say: "Nuts!"

Dillinger! he was thinking. Just a kill-crazy bum driven by jittery prison years. He'd done his bit: didn't want to go back. Couldn't blame him.

He moved down to the other end of the latrine, took three rapid drags from his cigaret. He could feel the smoke way down in the bottom of his lungs. His skin was tight on his face.

But it was quiet down here. He tried to relax. And then sound creeped into his mind. A broken commode leaked with a monotonous gurgle. The skin crawled on his face like the skin of a snake's belly.

He moved back out into Black Bottom.

A wail rose above the laughter, poignant, stirring with the anguish of a race that has learned to suffer — "*All-l-lll night lo-o-ooo-OOONG, ah set'n, ma cel-l-ll an' mo-o-o-aaa-AAANNNnnn!*"

The muscles tightened all over his body. His right eye began jumping in his head. His smile was twisted, terrible. Red chaos was his mind.

Crazy! He was going *crazy!* He couldn't stand it anymore. *God! God in heaven, he couldn't stand it.*

Visions lost all sense of perspective. Steel bars closed in upon him from all ungodly angles. He groped forward.

And then the lights flashed . . . And flashed again . . . It was bedtime.

SHIRLEY JACKSON

||≣

After You, My Dear Alphonse

If any writer could claim to have penned the most famous American short story of the twentieth century, it would be Shirley Jackson. "The Lottery," first published in the *New Yorker* in 1948, generated the largest volume of mail ever received by the magazine, much of it vituperative and indignant in tone. "The Lottery" was the tenth story Jackson published in the *New Yorker,* for which her husband, Stanley Hyman, was a staff writer. It is perhaps the most effective example of her talent for exposing the unattractive aspects of middle-class social attitudes, but that talent is also very much on display in her first published story, "After You, My Dear Alphonse," which the *New Yorker* ran in its January 16, 1943, issue.

||≣

MRS. WILSON WAS just taking the gingerbread out of the oven when she heard Johnny outside talking to someone.

"Johnny," she called, "you're late. Come in and get your lunch."

"Just a minute, Mother," Johnny said. "After you, my dear Alphonse."

"After *you*, my dear Alphonse," another voice said.

"No, after *you*, my dear Alphonse," Johnny said.

Mrs. Wilson opened the door. "Johnny," she said, "you come in this minute and get your lunch. You can play after you've eaten."

Johnny came in after her, slowly. "Mother," he said, "I brought Boyd home for lunch with me."

"Boyd?" Mrs. Wilson thought for a moment. "I don't believe I've met Boyd. Bring him in, dear, since you've invited him. Lunch is ready."

"Boyd!" Johnny yelled. "Hey, Boyd, come on in!"

"I'm coming. Just got to unload this stuff."

"Well, hurry, or my mother'll be sore."

"Johnny, that's not very polite to either your friend or your mother," Mrs. Wilson said. "Come sit down, Boyd."

As she turned to show Boyd where to sit, she saw he was a Negro boy, smaller than Johnny but about the same age. His arms were loaded with split kindling wood. "Where'll I put this stuff, Johnny?" he asked.

Mrs. Wilson turned to Johnny. "Johnny," she said, "what did you make Boyd do? What is that wood?"

"Dead Japanese," Johnny said mildly. "We stand them in the ground and run over them with tanks."

"How do you do, Mrs. Wilson?" Boyd said.

"How do you do, Boyd? You shouldn't let Johnny make you carry all that wood. Sit down now and eat lunch, both of you."

"Why shouldn't he carry the wood, Mother? It's his wood. We got it at his place."

"Johnny," Mrs. Wilson said, "go on and eat your lunch."

"Sure," Johnny said. He held out the dish of scrambled eggs to Boyd. "After you, my dear Alphonse."

"After *you,* my dear Alphonse," Boyd said.

"After *you,* my dear Alphonse," Johnny said. They began to giggle.

"Are you hungry, Boyd?" Mrs. Wilson asked.

"Yes, Mrs. Wilson."

"Well, don't you let Johnny stop you. He always fusses about eating, so you just see that you get a good lunch. There's plenty of food here for you to have all you want."

"Thank you, Mrs. Wilson."

"Come on, Alphonse," Johnny said. He pushed half the scrambled eggs on to Boyd's plate. Boyd watched while Mrs. Wilson put a dish of stewed tomatoes beside his plate.

"Boyd don't eat tomatoes, do you, Boyd?" Johnny said.

"*Doesn't* eat tomatoes, Johnny. And just because you don't like them, don't say that about Boyd. Boyd will eat *anything.*"

"Bet he won't," Johnny said, attacking his scrambled eggs.

"Boyd wants to grow up and be a big strong man so he can work hard," Mrs. Wilson said. "I'll bet Boyd's father eats stewed tomatoes."

"My father eats anything he wants to," Boyd said.

"So does mine," Johnny said. "Sometimes he doesn't eat hardly anything. He's a little guy, though. Wouldn't hurt a flea."

"Mine's a little guy, too," Boyd said.

"I'll bet he's strong, though," Mrs. Wilson said. She hesitated. "Does he . . . work?"

"Sure," Johnny said. "Boyd's father works in a factory."

"There, you see?" Mrs. Wilson said. "And he certainly has to be strong to do that — all that lifting and carrying at a factory."

"Boyd's father doesn't have to," Johnny said. "He's a foreman."

Mrs. Wilson felt defeated. "What does your mother do, Boyd?"

"My mother?" Boyd was surprised. "She takes care of us kids."

"Oh. She doesn't work, then?"

"Why should she?" Johnny said through a mouthful of eggs. "You don't work."

"You really don't want any stewed tomatoes, Boyd?"

"No, thank you, Mrs. Wilson," Boyd said.

"No, thank you, Mrs. Wilson, no, thank you, Mrs. Wilson, no thank you, Mrs. Wilson," Johnny said. "Boyd's sister's going to work, though. She's going to be a teacher."

"That's a very fine attitude for her to have, Boyd." Mrs. Wilson restrained an impulse to pat Boyd on the head. "I imagine you're all very proud of her?"

"I guess so," Boyd said.

"What about all your other brothers and sisters? I guess all of you want to make just as much of yourselves as you can."

"There's only me and Jean," Boyd said. "I don't know yet what I want to be when I grow up."

"We're going to be tank drivers, Boyd and me," Johnny said. "Zoom." Mrs. Wilson caught Boyd's glass of milk as Johnny's napkin ring, suddenly transformed into a tank, plowed heavily across the table.

"Look, Johnny," Boyd said. "Here's a foxhole. I'm shooting at you."

Mrs. Wilson, with the speed born of long experience, took the gingerbread off the shelf and placed it carefully between the tank and the foxhole.

"Now eat as much as you want to, Boyd," she said. "I want to see you get filled up."

"Boyd eats a lot, but not as much as I do," Johnny said. "I'm bigger than he is."

"You're not much bigger," Boyd said. "I can beat you running."

Mrs. Wilson took a deep breath. "Boyd," she said. Both boys turned to her. "Boyd, Johnny has some suits that are a little too small for him, and a winter coat. It's not new, of course, but there's lots of wear in it still. And I have a few dresses that your mother or sister could probably use. Your mother can make them over into lots of things for all of you, and I'd be very happy to give them to you. Suppose before you leave I make up a big bundle and then you and Johnny can take it over to your mother right away . . ." Her voice trailed off as she saw Boyd's puzzled expression.

"But I have plenty of clothes, thank you," he said. "And I don't think my mother knows how to sew very well, and anyway I guess we buy about everything we need. Thank you very much, though."

"We don't have time to carry that old stuff around, Mother," Johnny said. "We got to play tanks with the kids today."

Mrs. Wilson lifted the plate of gingerbread off the table as Boyd was about to take another piece. "There are many little boys like you, Boyd, who would be very grateful for the clothes someone was kind enough to give them."

"Boyd will take them if you want him to, Mother," Johnny said.

"I didn't mean to make you mad, Mrs. Wilson," Boyd said.

"Don't think I'm angry, Boyd. I'm just disappointed in you, that's all. Now let's not say anything more about it."

She began clearing the plates off the table, and Johnny took Boyd's hand and pulled him to the door. "'Bye, Mother," Johnny said. Boyd stood for a minute, staring at Mrs. Wilson's back.

"After you, my dear Alphonse," Johnny said, holding the door open.

"Is your mother still mad?" Mrs. Wilson heard Boyd ask in a low voice.

"I don't know," Johnny said. "She's screwy sometimes."

"So's mine," Boyd said. He hesitated. "After *you*, my dear Alphonse."

Territory

David Leavitt is one of a small handful of recent writers whose reputation was made by his short fiction. *Family Dancing* (Knopf, 1984) received widespread acclaim and nominations for the best fiction award from the National Book Critics Circle and PEN. Included in *Family Dancing* is Leavitt's first published story, "Territory," which itself attracted attention because it was one of the few stories published in the *New Yorker* that dealt openly with homosexuality. Leavitt was a twenty-one-year-old undergraduate at Yale when he sold "Territory" to the magazine, which published it on May 31, 1982.

NEIL'S MOTHER, Mrs. Campbell, sits on her lawn chair behind a card table outside the food co-op. Every few minutes, as the sun shifts, she moves the chair and table several inches back so as to remain in the shade. It is a hundred degrees outside, and bright white. Each time someone goes in or out of the co-op a gust of air-conditioning flies out of the automatic doors, raising dust from the cement.

Neil stands just inside, poised over a water fountain, and watches her. She has on a sun hat, and a sweatshirt over her tennis dress; her legs are bare, and shiny with cocoa butter. In front of her, propped against the table, a sign proclaims "MOTHERS, FIGHT FOR YOUR CHILDREN'S RIGHTS — SUPPORT A NON-NUCLEAR FUTURE." Women dressed exactly like her pass by, notice the sign, listen to her brief spiel, finger pamphlets, sign petitions or don't sign petitions, never give money. Her weary eyes are masked by dark glasses. In the age of Reagan, she has declared, keeping up the causes of peace and justice is a futile, tiresome, and unrewarding effort; it is therefore an effort fit only for mothers to

keep up. The sun bounces off the window glass through which Neil watches her. His own reflection lines up with her profile.

LATER that afternoon, Neil spreads himself out alongside the pool and imagines he is being watched by the shirtless Chicano gardener. But the gardener, concentrating on his pruning, is neither seductive nor seducible. On the lawn, his mother's large Airedales — Abigail, Lucille, Fern — amble, sniff, urinate. Occasionally, they accost the gardener, who yells at them in Spanish.

After two years' absence, Neil reasons, he should feel nostalgia, regret, gladness upon returning home. He closes his eyes and tries to muster the proper background music for the cinematic scene of return. His rhapsody, however, is interrupted by the noises of his mother's trio — the scratchy cello, whining violin, stumbling piano — as she and Lillian Havalard and Charlotte Feder plunge through Mozart. The tune is cheery, in a Germanic sort of way, and utterly inappropriate to what Neil is trying to feel. Yet it *is* the music of his adolescence; they have played it for years, bent over the notes, their heads bobbing in silent time to the metronome.

It is getting darker. Every few minutes, he must move his towel so as to remain within the narrowing patch of sunlight. In four hours, Wayne, his lover of ten months and the only person he has ever imagined he could spend his life with, will be in this house, where no lover of his has ever set foot. The thought fills him with a sense of grand terror and curiosity. He stretches, tries to feel seductive, desirable. The gardener's shears whack at the ferns; the music above him rushes to a loud, premature conclusion. The women laugh and applaud themselves as they give up for the day. He hears Charlotte Feder's full nasal twang, the voice of a fat woman in a pink pants suit — odd, since she is a scrawny, arthritic old bird, rarely clad in anything other than tennis shorts and a blouse. Lillian is the fat woman in the pink pants suit; her voice is thin and warped by too much crying. Drink in hand, she calls out from the porch, "Hot enough!" and waves. He lifts himself up and nods to her.

The women sit on the porch and chatter; their voices blend with the clink of ice in glasses. They belong to a small circle of ladies all of whom, with the exception of Neil's mother, are widows and divorcées. Lillian's husband left her twenty-two years ago, and sends her a check every

month to live on; Charlotte has been divorced twice as long as she was married, and has a daughter serving a long sentence for terrorist acts committed when she was nineteen. Only Neil's mother has a husband, a distant sort of husband, away often on business. He is away on business now. All of them feel betrayed — by husbands, by children, by history.

Neil closes his eyes, tries to hear the words only as sounds. Soon, a new noise accosts him: his mother arguing with the gardener in Spanish. He leans on his elbows and watches them; the syllables are loud, heated, and compressed, and seem on the verge of explosion. But the argument ends happily; they shake hands. The gardener collects his check and walks out the gate without so much as looking at Neil.

He does not know the gardener's name; as his mother has reminded him, he does not know most of what has gone on since he moved away. Her life has gone on, unaffected by his absence. He flinches at his own egoism, the egoism of sons.

"Neil! Did you call the airport to make sure the plane's coming in on time?"

"Yes," he shouts to her. "It is."

"Good. Well, I'll have dinner ready when you get back."

"Mom —"

"What?" The word comes out in a weary wail that is more of an answer than a question.

"What's wrong?" he says, forgetting his original question.

"Nothing's wrong," she declares in a tone that indicates that everything is wrong. "The dogs have to be fed, dinner has to be made, and I've got people here. Nothing's wrong."

"I hope things will be as comfortable as possible when Wayne gets here."

"Is that a request or a threat?"

"Mom —"

Behind her sunglasses, her eyes are inscrutable. "I'm tired," she says. "It's been a long day. I . . . I'm anxious to meet Wayne. I'm sure he'll be wonderful, and we'll all have a wonderful, wonderful time. I'm sorry. I'm just tired."

She heads up the stairs. He suddenly feels an urge to cover himself; his body embarrasses him, as it has in her presence since the day she saw

him shirtless and said with delight, "Neil! You're growing hair under your arms!"

Before he can get up, the dogs gather round him and begin to sniff and lick at him. He wriggles to get away from them, but Abigail, the largest and the stupidest, straddles his stomach and nuzzles his mouth. He splutters and, laughing, throws her off. "Get away from me, you goddam dogs," he shouts, and swats at them. They are new dogs, not the dog of his childhood, not dogs he trusts.

He stands, and the dogs circle him, looking up at his face expectantly. He feels renewed terror at the thought that Wayne will be here so soon: Will they sleep in the same room? Will they make love? He has never had sex in his parents' house. How can he be expected to be a lover here, in this place of his childhood, of his earliest shame, in this household of mothers and dogs?

"Dinnertime! Abbylucyferny, Abbylucyferny, dinnertime!" His mother's litany disperses the dogs, and they run for the door.

"Do you realize," he shouts to her, "that no matter how much those dogs love you they'd probably kill you for the leg of lamb in the freezer?"

NEIL was twelve the first time he recognized in himself something like sexuality. He was lying outside, on the grass, when Rasputin — the dog, long dead, of his childhood — began licking his face. He felt a tingle he did not recognize, pulled off his shirt to give the dog access to more of him. Rasputin's tongue tickled coolly. A wet nose started to sniff down his body, toward his bathing suit. What he felt frightened him, but he couldn't bring himself to push the dog away. Then his mother called out, "Dinner," and Rasputin was gone, more interested in food than in him.

It was the day after Rasputin was put to sleep, years later, that Neil finally stood in the kitchen, his back turned to his parents, and said, with unexpected ease, "I'm a homosexual." The words seemed insufficient, reductive. For years, he had believed his sexuality to be detachable from the essential him, but now he realized that it was part of him. He had the sudden, despairing sensation that though the words had been easy to say, the fact of their having been aired was incurably damning. Only then, for the first time, did he admit that they were true, and he shook and wept in regret for what he would not be for his mother,

for having failed her. His father hung back, silent; he was absent for that moment as he was mostly absent — a strong absence. Neil always thought of him sitting on the edge of the bed in his underwear, captivated by something on television. He said, "It's O.K., Neil." But his mother was resolute; her lower lip didn't quaver. She had enormous reserves of strength to which she only gained access at moments like this one. She hugged him from behind, wrapped him in the childhood smells of perfume and brownies, and whispered, "It's O.K., honey." For once, her words seemed as inadequate as his. Neil felt himself shrunk to an embarrassed adolescent, hating her sympathy, not wanting her to touch him. It was the way he would feel from then on whenever he was in her presence — even now, at twenty-three, bringing home his lover to meet her.

All through his childhood, she had packed only the most nutritious lunches, had served on the PTA, had volunteered at the children's library and at his school, had organized a successful campaign to ban a racist history textbook. The day after he told her, she located and got in touch with an organization called the Coalition of Parents of Lesbians and Gays. Within a year, she was president of it. On weekends, she and the other mothers drove their station wagons to San Francisco, set up their card tables in front of the Bulldog Baths, the Liberty Baths, passed out literature to men in leather and denim who were loath to admit they even had mothers. These men, who would do violence to each other, were strangely cowed by the suburban ladies with their informational booklets, and bent their heads. Neil was a sophomore in college then, and lived in San Francisco. She brought him pamphlets detailing the dangers of bathhouses and back rooms, enemas and poppers, wordless sex in alleyways. His excursion into that world had been brief and lamentable, and was over. He winced at the thought that she knew all his sexual secrets, and vowed to move to the East Coast to escape her. It was not very different from the days when she had campaigned for a better playground, or tutored the Hispanic children in the audiovisual room. Those days, as well, he had run away from her concern. Even today, perched in front of the co-op, collecting signatures for nuclear disarmament, she was quintessentially a mother. And if the lot of mothers was to expect nothing in return, was the lot of sons to return nothing?

* * *

DRIVING across the Dumbarton Bridge on his way to the airport, Neil thinks, I have returned nothing; I have simply returned. He wonders if she would have given birth to him had she known what he would grow up to be.

Then he berates himself: Why should he assume himself to be the cause of her sorrow? She has told him that her life is full of secrets. She has changed since he left home — grown thinner, more rigid, harder to hug. She has given up baking, taken up tennis; her skin has browned and tightened. She is no longer the woman who hugged him and kissed him, who said, "As long as you're happy, that's all that's important to us."

The flats spread out around him; the bridge floats on purple and green silt, and spongy bay fill, not water at all. Only ten miles north, a whole city has been built on gunk dredged up from the bay.

He arrives at the airport ten minutes early, to discover that the plane has landed twenty minutes early. His first view of Wayne is from behind, by the baggage belt. Wayne looks as he always looks — slightly windblown — and is wearing the ratty leather jacket he was wearing the night they met. Neil sneaks up on him and puts his hands on his shoulders; when Wayne turns around, he looks relieved to see him.

They hug like brothers; only in the safety of Neil's mother's car do they dare to kiss. They recognize each other's smells, and grow comfortable again. "I never imagined I'd actually see you out here," Neil says, "but you're exactly the same here as there."

"It's only been a week."

They kiss again. Neil wants to go to a motel, but Wayne insists on being pragmatic. "We'll be there soon. Don't worry."

"We could go to one of the bathhouses in the city and take a room for a couple of aeons," Neil says. "Christ, I'm hard up. I don't even know if we're going to be in the same bedroom."

"Well, if we're not," Wayne says, "we'll sneak around. It'll be romantic."

They cling to each other for a few more minutes, until they realize that people are looking in the car window. Reluctantly, they pull apart. Neil reminds himself that he loves this man, that there is a reason for him to bring this man home.

He takes the scenic route on the way back. The car careers over foothills, through forests, along white four-lane highways high in the mountains. Wayne tells Neil that he sat next to a woman on the plane who was once Marilyn Monroe's psychiatrist's nurse. He slips his foot out of his shoe and nudges Neil's ankle, pulling Neil's sock down with his toe.

"I have to drive," Neil says. "I'm very glad you're here."

There is a comfort in the privacy of the car. They have a common fear of walking hand in hand, of publicly showing physical affection, even in the permissive West Seventies of New York — a fear that they have admitted only to one another. They slip through a pass between two hills, and are suddenly in residential Northern California, the land of expensive ranch-style houses.

As they pull into Neil's mother's driveway, the dogs run barking toward the car. When Wayne opens the door, they jump and lap at him, and he tries to close it again. "Don't worry. Abbylucyferny! Get in the house, damn it!"

His mother descends from the porch. She has changed into a blue flower-print dress, which Neil doesn't recognize. He gets out of the car and halfheartedly chastises the dogs. Crickets chirp in the trees. His mother looks radiant, even beautiful, illuminated by the headlights, surrounded by the now quiet dogs, like a Circe with her slaves. When she walks over to Wayne, offering her hand, and says, "Wayne, I'm Barbara," Neil forgets that she is his mother.

"Good to meet you, Barbara," Wayne says, and reaches out his hand. Craftier than she, he whirls her around to kiss her cheek.

Barbara! He is calling his mother Barbara! Then he remembers that Wayne is five years older than he is. They chat by the open car door, and Neil shrinks back — the embarrassed adolescent, uncomfortable, unwanted.

So the dreaded moment passes and he might as well not have been there. At dinner, Wayne keeps the conversation smooth, like a captivated courtier seeking Neil's mother's hand. A faggot son's sodomist — such words spit into Neil's head. She has prepared tiny meatballs with fresh coriander, fettuccine with pesto. Wayne talks about the street people in New York; El Salvador is a tragedy; if only Sadat had lived; Phyllis Schlafly — what can you do?

"It's a losing battle," she tells him. "Every day I'm out there with my card table, me and the other mothers, but I tell you, Wayne, it's a losing battle. Sometimes I think us old ladies are the only ones with enough patience to fight."

Occasionally, Neil says something, but his comments seem stupid and clumsy. Wayne continues to call her Barbara. No one under forty has ever called her Barbara as long as Neil can remember. They drink wine; he does not.

Now is the time for drastic action. He contemplates taking Wayne's hand, then checks himself. He has never done anything in her presence to indicate that the sexuality he confessed to five years ago was a reality and not an invention. Even now, he and Wayne might as well be friends, college roommates. Then Wayne, his savior, with a single, sweeping gesture, reaches for his hand, and clasps it, in the midst of a joke he is telling about Saudi Arabians. By the time he is laughing, their hands are joined. Neil's throat contracts; his heart begins to beat violently. He notices his mother's eyes flicker, glance downward; she never breaks the stride of her sentence. The dinner goes on, and every taboo nurtured since childhood falls quietly away.

She removes the dishes. Their hands grow sticky; he cannot tell which fingers are his and which Wayne's. She clears the rest of the table and rounds up the dogs.

"Well, boys, I'm very tired, and I've got a long day ahead of me tomorrow, so I think I'll hit the sack. There are extra towels for you in Neil's bathroom, Wayne. Sleep well."

"Good night, Barbara," Wayne calls out. "It's been wonderful meeting you."

They are alone. Now they can disentangle their hands.

"No problem about where we sleep, is there?"

"No," Neil says. "I just can't imagine sleeping with someone in this house."

His leg shakes violently. Wayne takes Neil's hand in a firm grasp and hauls him up.

LATER that night, they lie outside, under redwood trees, listening to the hysteria of the crickets, the hum of the pool cleaning itself. Redwood

leaves prick their skin. They fell in love in bars and apartments, and this is the first time that they have made love outdoors. Neil is not sure he has enjoyed the experience. He kept sensing eyes, imagined that the neighborhood cats were staring at them from behind a fence of brambles. He remembers he once hid in this spot when he and some of the children from the neighborhood were playing sardines, remembers the intoxication of small bodies packed together, the warm breath of suppressed laughter on his neck. "The loser had to go through the spanking machine," he tells Wayne.

"Did you lose often?"

"Most of the time. The spanking machine never really hurt — just a whirl of hands. If you moved fast enough, no one could actually get you. Sometimes, though, late in the afternoon, we'd get naughty. We'd chase each other and pull each other's pants down. That was all. Boys and girls together!"

"Listen to the insects," Wayne says, and closes his eyes.

Neil turns to examine Wayne's face, notices a single, small pimple. Their lovemaking usually begins in a wrestle, a struggle for dominance, and ends with a somewhat confusing loss of identity — as now, when Neil sees a foot on the grass, resting against his leg, and tries to determine if it is his own or Wayne's.

From inside the house, the dogs begin to bark. Their yelps grow into alarmed falsettos. Neil lifts himself up. "I wonder if they smell something," he says.

"Probably just us," says Wayne.

"My mother will wake up. She hates getting waked up."

Lights go on in the house; the door to the porch opens.

"What's wrong, Abby? What's wrong?" his mother's voice calls softly.

Wayne clamps his hand over Neil's mouth. "Don't say anything," he whispers.

"I can't just —" Neil begins to say, but Wayne's hand closes over his mouth again. He bites it, and Wayne starts laughing.

"What was that?" Her voice projects into the garden. "Hello?" she says.

The dogs yelp louder. "Abbylucyferny, it's O.K., it's O.K." Her voice is soft and panicked. "Is anyone there?" she asks loudly.

The brambles shake. She takes a flashlight, shines it around the garden. Wayne and Neil duck down; the light lands on them and hovers for a few seconds. Then it clicks off and they are in the dark — a new dark, a darker dark, which their eyes must readjust to.

"Let's go to bed, Abbylucyferny," she says gently. Neil and Wayne hear her pad into the house. The dogs whimper as they follow her, and the lights go off.

ONCE before, Neil and his mother had stared at each other in the glare of bright lights. Four years ago, they stood in the arena created by the headlights of her car, waiting for the train. He was on his way back to San Francisco, where he was marching in a Gay Pride Parade the next day. The train station was next door to the food co-op and shared its parking lot. The co-op, familiar and boring by day, took on a certain mystery in the night. Neil recognized the spot where he had skidded on his bicycle and broken his leg. Through the glass doors, the brightly lit interior of the store glowed, its rows and rows of cans and boxes forming their own horizon, each can illuminated so that even from outside Neil could read the labels. All that was missing was the ladies in tennis dresses and sweatshirts, pushing their carts past bins of nuts and dried fruits.

"Your train is late," his mother said. Her hair fell loosely on her shoulders, and her legs were tanned. Neil looked at her and tried to imagine her in labor with him — bucking and struggling with his birth. He felt then the strange, sexless love for women which through his whole adolescence he had mistaken for heterosexual desire. She was regal, a figure to be worshipped, and he understood why homosexuals worship old movie stars — Joan Crawford and Greta Garbo and Judy Garland.

A single bright light approached them; it preceded the low, haunting sound of the whistle. Neil kissed his mother, and waved goodbye as he ran to meet the train. It was an old train, with windows tinted a sort of horrible lemon-lime. It stopped only long enough for him to hoist himself on board, and then it was moving again. He hurried to a window, hoping to see her drive off, but the tint of the window made it possible for him to make out only vague patches of light — street lamps, cars, the co-op.

He sank into the hard, green seat. The train was almost entirely

empty; the only other passenger was a dark-skinned man wearing blue-jeans and a leather jacket. He sat directly across the aisle from Neil, next to the window. He had rough skin and a thick mustache. Neil discovered that by pretending to look out the window he could study the man's reflection in the lemon-lime glass. It was only slightly hazy — the quality of a bad photograph. Neil felt his mouth open, felt sleep closing in on him. Hazy red and gold flashes through the glass pulsed in the face of the man in the window, giving the curious impression of muscle spasms. It took Neil a few minutes to realize that the man was staring at him, or, rather, staring at the back of his head — staring at his staring. The man smiled as though to say, I know exactly what you're staring at, and Neil felt the sickening sensation of desire rise in his throat.

Right before they reached the city, the man stood up and sat down in the seat next to Neil's. The man's thigh brushed deliberately against his own. Neil's eyes were watering; he felt sick to his stomach. Taking Neil's hand, the man said, "Why so nervous, honey? Relax."

Neil woke up the next morning with the taste of ashes in his mouth. He was lying on the floor, without blankets or sheets or pillows. Instinctively, he reached for his pants, and as he pulled them on came face to face with the man from the train. His name was Luis; he turned out to be a dog groomer. His apartment smelled of dog.

"Why such a hurry?" Luis said.

"The parade. The Gay Pride Parade. I'm meeting some friends to march."

"I'll come with you," Luis said. "I think I'm too old for these things, but why not?"

Neil did not want Luis to come with him, but he found it impossible to say so. Luis looked older by day, more likely to carry diseases. He dressed again in a torn T-shirt, leather jacket, bluejeans. "It's my everyday apparel," he said, and laughed. Neil buttoned his pants, aware that they had been washed by his mother the day before. Luis possessed the peculiar combination of hypermasculinity and effeminacy which exemplifies faggotry. Neil wanted to be rid of him, but Luis's mark was on him, he could see that much. They would become lovers whether Neil liked it or not.

They joined the parade midway. Neil hoped he wouldn't meet any-

one he knew; he did not want to have to explain Luis, who clung to him. The parade was full of shirtless men with oiled, muscular shoulders. Neil's back ached. There were floats carrying garishly dressed prom queens and cheerleaders, some with beards, some actually looking like women. Luis said, "It makes me proud, makes me glad to be what I am." Neil supposed that by darting into the crowd ahead of him he might be able to lose Luis forever, but he found it difficult to let him go; the prospect of being alone seemed unbearable.

Neil was startled to see his mother watching the parade, holding up a sign. She was with the Coalition of Parents of Lesbians and Gays; they had posted a huge banner on the wall behind them proclaiming "OUR SONS AND DAUGHTERS, WE ARE PROUD OF YOU." She spotted him; she waved, and jumped up and down.

"Who's that woman?" Luis asked.

"My mother. I should go say hello to her."

"O.K.," Luis said. He followed Neil to the side of the parade. Neil kissed his mother. Luis took off his shirt, wiped his face with it, smiled.

"I'm glad you came," Neil said.

"I wouldn't have missed it, Neil. I wanted to show you I cared."

He smiled, and kissed her again. He showed no intention of introducing Luis, so Luis introduced himself.

"Hello, Luis," Mrs. Campbell said. Neil looked away. Luis shook her hand, and Neil wanted to warn his mother to wash it, warned himself to check with a V.D. clinic first thing Monday.

"Neil, this is Carmen Bologna, another one of the mothers," Mrs. Campbell said. She introduced him to a fat Italian woman with flushed cheeks, and hair arranged in the shape of a clamshell.

"Good to meet you, Neil, good to meet you," said Carmen Bologna. "You know my son, Michael? I'm so proud of Michael! He's doing so well now. I'm proud of him, proud to be his mother I am, and your mother's proud, too!"

The woman smiled at him, and Neil could think of nothing to say but "Thank you." He looked uncomfortably toward his mother, who stood listening to Luis. It occurred to him that the worst period of his life was probably about to begin and he had no way to stop it.

A group of drag queens ambled over to where the mothers were

standing. "Michael! Michael!" shouted Carmen Bologna, and embraced
a sticklike man wrapped in green satin. Michael's eyes were heavily dosed
with green eyeshadow, and his lips were painted pink.

Neil turned and saw his mother staring, her mouth open. He
marched over to where Luis was standing, and they moved back into the
parade. He turned and waved to her. She waved back; he saw pain in her
face, and then, briefly, regret. That day, he felt she would have traded
him for any other son. Later, she said to him, "Carmen Bologna really
was proud, and, speaking as a mother, let me tell you, you have to be
brave to feel such pride."

Neil was never proud. It took him a year to dump Luis, another year
to leave California. The sick taste of ashes was still in his mouth. On the
plane, he envisioned his mother sitting alone in the dark, smoking. She
did not leave his mind until he was circling New York, staring down at
the dawn rising over Queens. The song playing in his earphones would
remain hovering on the edges of his memory, always associated with her
absence. After collecting his baggage, he took a bus into the city. Boys
were selling newspapers in the middle of highways, through the windows of stopped cars. It was seven in the morning when he reached
Manhattan. He stood for ten minutes on East Thirty-fourth Street,
breathed the cold air, and felt bubbles rising in his blood.

Neil got a job as a paralegal — a temporary job, he told himself.
When he met Wayne a year later, the sensations of that first morning
returned to him. They'd been up all night, and at six they walked across
the Park to Wayne's apartment with the nervous, deliberate gait of
people aching to make love for the first time. Joggers ran by with their
dogs. None of them knew what Wayne and he were about to do, and
the secrecy excited him. His mother came to mind, and the song, and
the whirling vision of Queens coming alive below him. His breath solidified into clouds, and he felt happier than he had ever felt before in
his life.

THE second day of Wayne's visit, he and Neil go with Mrs. Campbell
to pick up the dogs at the dog parlor. The grooming establishment is
decorated with pink ribbons and photographs of the owner's champion
pit bulls. A fat, middle-aged woman appears from the back, leading the

newly trimmed and fluffed Abigail, Lucille, and Fern by three leashes. The dogs struggle frantically when they see Neil's mother, tangling the woman up in their leashes. "Ladies, behave!" Mrs. Campbell commands, and collects the dogs. She gives Fern to Neil and Abigail to Wayne. In the car on the way back, Abigail begins pawing to get on Wayne's lap.

"Just push her off," Mrs. Campbell says. "She knows she's not supposed to do that."

"You never groomed Rasputin," Neil complains.

"Rasputin was a mutt."

"Rasputin was a beautiful dog, even if he did smell."

"Do you remember when you were a little kid, Neil, you used to make Rasputin dance with you? Once you tried to dress him up in one of my blouses."

"I don't remember that," Neil says.

"Yes. I remember," says Mrs. Campbell. "Then you tried to organize a dog beauty contest in the neighborhood. You wanted to have runners-up — everything."

"A dog beauty contest?" Wayne says.

"Mother, do we have to —"

"I think it's a mother's privilege to embarrass her son," Mrs. Campbell says, and smiles.

When they are about to pull into the driveway, Wayne starts screaming, and pushes Abigail off his lap. "Oh, my God!" he says. "The dog just pissed all over me."

Neil turns around and sees a puddle seeping into Wayne's slacks. He suppresses his laughter, and Mrs. Campbell hands him a rag.

"I'm sorry, Wayne," she says. "It goes with the territory."

"This is really disgusting," Wayne says, swatting at himself with the rag.

Neil keeps his eyes on his own reflection in the rearview mirror and smiles.

At home, while Wayne cleans himself in the bathroom, Neil watches his mother cook lunch — Japanese noodles in soup. "When you went off to college," she says, "I went to the grocery store. I was going to buy you ramen noodles, and I suddenly realized you weren't going

to be around to eat them. I started crying right then, blubbering like an idiot."

Neil clenches his fists inside his pockets. She has a way of telling him little sad stories when he doesn't want to hear them — stories of dolls broken by her brothers, lunches stolen by neighborhood boys on the way to school. Now he has joined the ranks of male children who have made her cry.

"Mama, I'm sorry," he says.

She is bent over the noodles, which steam in her face. "I didn't want to say anything in front of Wayne, but I wish you had answered me last night. I was very frightened — and worried."

"I'm sorry," he says, but it's not convincing. His fingers prickle. He senses a great sorrow about to be born.

"I lead a quiet life," she says. "I don't want to be a disciplinarian. I just don't have the energy for these — shenanigans. Please don't frighten me that way again."

"If you were so upset, why didn't you say something?"

"I'd rather not discuss it. I lead a quiet life. I'm not used to getting woken up late at night. I'm not used —"

"To my having a lover?"

"No, I'm not used to having other people around, that's all. Wayne is charming. A wonderful young man."

"He likes you, too."

"I'm sure we'll get along fine."

She scoops the steaming noodles into ceramic bowls. Wayne returns, wearing shorts. His white, hairy legs are a shocking contrast to hers, which are brown and sleek.

"I'll wash those pants, Wayne," Mrs. Campbell says. "I have a special detergent that'll take out the stain."

She gives Neil a look to indicate that the subject should be dropped. He looks at Wayne, looks at his mother; his initial embarrassment gives way to a fierce pride — the arrogance of mastery. He is glad his mother knows that he is desired, glad it makes her flinch.

Later, he steps into the back yard; the gardener is back, whacking at the bushes with his shears. Neil walks by him in his bathing suit, imagining he is on parade.

* * *

THAT afternoon, he finds his mother's daily list on the kitchen table:

> TUESDAY
> 7:00-breakfast
> Take dogs to groomer
> Groceries (?)
>
> Campaign against Draft-4-7
>
> Buy underwear
> Trios-2:00
> Spaghetti
> Fruit
> Asparagus if sale
> Peanuts
> Milk
>
> Doctor's Appointment (make)
> Write Cranston/Hayakawa
> re disarmament
>
> Handi-Wraps
> Mozart
> Abigail
> Top Ramen
> Pedro

Her desk and trash can are full of such lists; he remembers them from the earliest days of his childhood. He had learned to read from them. In his own life, too, there have been endless lists — covered with check marks and arrows, at least one item always spilling over onto the next day's agenda. From September to November, "Buy plane ticket for Christmas" floated from list to list to list.

The last item puzzles him: Pedro. Pedro must be the gardener. He observes the accretion of names, the arbitrary specifics that give a sense of his mother's life. He could make a list of his own selves: the child, the adolescent, the sleazy-faggot son, and finally the good son, settled, relatively successful. But the divisions wouldn't work; he is today and will always be the child being licked by the dog, the boy on the floor with

Luis; he will still be everything he is ashamed of. The other lists — the lists of things done and undone — tell their own truth: that his life is measured more properly in objects than in stages. He knows himself as "jump rope," "book," "sunglasses," "underwear."

"Tell me about your family, Wayne," Mrs. Campbell says that night, as they drive toward town. They are going to see an Esther Williams movie at the local revival house: an underwater musical, populated by mermaids, underwater Rockettes.

"My father was a lawyer," Wayne says. "He had an office in Queens, with a neon sign. I think he's probably the only lawyer in the world who had a neon sign. Anyway, he died when I was ten. My mother never remarried. She lives in Queens. Her great claim to fame is that when she was twenty-two she went on 'The $64,000 Question.' Her category was mystery novels. She made it to sixteen thousand before she got tripped up."

"When I was about ten, I wanted you to go on 'Jeopardy,'" Neil says to his mother. "You really should have, you know. You would have won."

"You certainly loved 'Jeopardy,'" Mrs. Campbell says. "You used to watch it during dinner. Wayne, does your mother work?"

"No," he says. "She lives off investments."

"You're both only children," Mrs. Campbell says. Neil wonders if she is ruminating on the possible connection between that coincidence and their "alternative life style."

The movie theatre is nearly empty. Neil sits between Wayne and his mother. There are pillows on the floor at the front of the theatre, and a cat is prowling over them. It casts a monstrous shadow every now and then on the screen, disturbing the sedative effect of water ballet. Like a teen-ager, Neil cautiously reaches his arm around Wayne's shoulder. Wayne takes his hand immediately. Next to them, Neil's mother breathes in, out, in, out. Neil timorously moves his other arm and lifts it behind his mother's neck. He does not look at her, but he can tell from her breathing that she senses what he is doing. Slowly, carefully, he lets his hand drop on her shoulder; it twitches spasmodically, and he jumps, as if he had received an electric shock. His mother's quiet breathing is broken by a gasp; even Wayne notices. A sudden brightness on the screen illuminates the panic in her eyes, Neil's arm frozen above her,

about to fall again. Slowly, he lowers his arm until his fingertips touch her skin, the fabric of her dress. He has gone too far to go back now; they are all too far.

Wayne and Mrs. Campbell sink into their seats, but Neil remains stiff, holding up his arms, which rest on nothing. The movie ends, and they go on sitting just like that.

"I'm old," Mrs. Campbell says later, as they drive back home. "I remember when those films were new. Your father and I went to one on our first date. I loved them, because I could pretend that those women underwater were flying — they were so graceful. They really took advantage of Technicolor in those days. Color was something to appreciate. You can't know what it was like to see a color movie for the first time, after years of black-and-white. It's like trying to explain the surprise of snow to an East Coaster. Very little is new anymore, I fear."

Neil would like to tell her about his own nostalgia, but how can he explain that all of it revolves around her? The idea of her life before he was born pleases him. "Tell Wayne how you used to look like Esther Williams," he asks her.

She blushes. "I was told I looked like Esther Williams, but really more like Gene Tierney," she says. "Not beautiful, but interesting. I like to think I had a certain magnetism."

"You still do," Wayne says, and instantly recognizes the wrongness of his comment. Silence and a nervous laugh indicate that he has not yet mastered the family vocabulary.

When they get home, the night is once again full of the sound of crickets. Mrs. Campbell picks up a flashlight and calls the dogs. "Abbylucyferny, Abbylucyferny," she shouts, and the dogs amble from their various corners. She pushes them out the door to the back yard and follows them. Neil follows her. Wayne follows Neil, but hovers on the porch. Neil walks behind her as she tramps through the garden. She holds out her flashlight, and snails slide from behind bushes, from under rocks, to where she stands. When the snails become visible, she crushes them underfoot. They make a wet, cracking noise, like eggs being broken.

"Nights like this," she says, "I think of children without pants on, in hot South American countries. I have nightmares about tanks rolling down our street."

"The weather's never like this in New York," Neil says. "When it's hot, it's humid and sticky. You don't want to go outdoors."

"I could never live anywhere else but here. I think I'd die. I'm too used to the climate."

"Don't be silly."

"No, I mean it," she says. "I have adjusted too well to the weather."

The dogs bark and howl by the fence. "A cat, I suspect," she says. She aims her flashlight at a rock, and more snails emerge — uncountable numbers, too stupid to have learned not to trust light.

"I know what you were doing at the movie," she says.

"What?"

"I know what you were doing."

"What? I put my arm around you."

"I'm sorry, Neil," she says. "I can only take so much. Just so much."

"What do you mean?" he says. "I was only trying to show affection."

"Oh, affection — I know about affection."

He looks up at the porch, sees Wayne moving toward the door, trying not to listen.

"What do you mean?" Neil says to her.

She puts down the flashlight and wraps her arms around herself. "I remember when you were a little boy," she says. "I remember, and I have to stop remembering. I wanted you to grow up happy. And I'm very tolerant, very understanding. But I can only take so much."

His heart seems to have risen into his throat. "Mother," he says, "I think you know my life isn't your fault. But for God's sake, don't say that your life is my fault."

"It's not a question of fault," she says. She extracts a Kleenex from her pocket and blows her nose. "I'm sorry, Neil. I guess I'm just an old woman with too much on her mind and not enough to do." She laughs halfheartedly. "Don't worry. Don't say anything," she says. "Abbylucyferny, Abbylucyferny, time for bed!"

He watches her as she walks toward the porch, silent and regal. There is the pad of feet, the clinking of dog tags as the dogs run for the house.

H E was twelve the first time she saw him march in a parade. He played the tuba, and as his elementary-school band lumbered down the streets of their then small town she stood on the sidelines and waved. After-

ward, she had taken him out for ice cream. He spilled some on his red uniform, and she swiped at it with a napkin. She had been there for him that day; she had been there for him every day.

Somewhere over Iowa, a week later, Neil remembers this scene, remembers other days, when he would find her sitting in the dark, crying. She had to take time out of her own private sorrow to appease his anxiety. "It was part of it," she told him later. "Part of being a mother."

"The scariest thing in the world is the thought that you could unknowingly ruin someone's life," Neil tells Wayne. "Or even change someone's life. I hate the thought of having such control. I'd make a rotten mother."

"You're crazy," Wayne says. "You have this great mother, and all you do is complain. I know people whose mothers have disowned them."

"Guilt goes with the territory," Neil says.

"Why?" Wayne asks, perfectly seriously.

Neil doesn't answer. He lies back in his seat, closes his eyes, imagines he grew up in a house in the mountains of Colorado, surrounded by snow — endless white snow on hills. No flat places, and no trees; just white hills. Every time he has flown away, she has come into his mind, usually sitting alone in the dark, smoking. Today she is outside at dusk, skimming leaves from the pool.

"I want to get a dog," Neil says.

Wayne laughs. "In the city? It'd suffocate."

The hum of the airplane is druglike, dazing. "I want to stay with you a long time," Neil says.

"I know." Imperceptibly, Wayne takes his hand.

"It's very hot there in the summer, too. You know, I'm not thinking about my mother now."

"It's O.K."

For a moment, Neil wonders what the stewardess or the old woman on the way to the bathroom will think, but then he laughs and relaxes.

Later, the plane makes a slow circle over New York City, and on it two men hold hands, eyes closed, and breathe in unison.

URSULA K. LE GUIN

April in Paris

The daughter of Theodora Kroeber, Le Guin began writing when she was still a child. In her preface to "April in Paris" in *The Wind's Twelve Quarters,* a collection of her short fiction, Le Guin says, "I had been writing poetry and fiction ever since my brother Ted, tired of having an illiterate five-year-old sister around, taught me to read," and she refers to "April in Paris" as perhaps the thirtieth or fortieth story she had written. Despite her early start as a writer, Le Guin did not sell her first story until she was thirty-two years old. Cele Goldsmith Lalli bought it for *Fantastic,* which published it in 1962. According to Le Guin, "April in Paris" was the first genre story — "recognizably fantasy or science fiction" — she had written since 1942, when she submitted an Origin-of-Life-on-Earth story to *Astounding,* which rejected it. "At age twelve," she said, "I was very pleased to get a genuine printed rejection slip, but by the age of thirty-two I was very pleased to get a check."

PROFESSOR BARRY PENNYWITHER sat in a cold, shadowy garret and stared at the table in front of him, on which lay a book and a bread-crust. The bread had been his dinner, the book has been his lifework. Both were dry. Dr. Pennywither sighed, and then shivered. Though the lower-floor apartments of the old house were quite elegant, the heat was turned off on April 1st, come what may; it was now April 2nd, and sleeting. If Dr. Pennywither raised his head a little he could see from his window the two square towers of Notre Dame de Paris, vague and soaring in the dusk, almost near enough to touch: for the Island of Saint-Louis, where he lived, is like a little barge being towed downstream

194

behind the Island of the City, where Notre Dame stands. But he did not raise his head. He was too cold.

The great towers sank into darkness. Dr. Pennywither sank into gloom. He stared with loathing at his book. It had won him a year in Paris — publish or perish, said the Dean of Faculties, and he had published, and been rewarded with a year's leave from teaching, without pay. Munson College could not afford to pay unteaching teachers. So on his scraped-up savings he had come back to Paris, to live again as a student in a garret, to read fifteenth-century manuscripts at the Library, to see the chestnuts flower along the avenues. But it hadn't worked. He was forty, too old for lonely garrets. The sleet would blight the budding chestnut flowers. And he was sick of his work. Who cared about his theory, the Pennywither Theory, concerning the mysterious disappearance of the poet François Villon in 1463? Nobody. For after all his Theory about poor Villon, the greatest juvenile delinquent of all time, was only a theory and could never be proved, not across the gulf of five hundred years. Nothing could be proved. And besides, what did it matter if Villon died on Montfaucon gallows or (as Pennywither thought) in a Lyons brothel on the way to Italy? Nobody cared. Nobody else loved Villon enough. Nobody loved Dr. Pennywither, either; not even Dr. Pennywither. Why should he? An unsocial, unmarried, underpaid pedant, sitting here alone in an unheated attic in an unrestored tenement trying to write another unreadable book. "I'm unrealistic," he said aloud with another sigh and another shiver. He got up and took the blanket off his bed, wrapped himself in it, sat down thus bundled at the table, and tried to light a Gauloise Bleue. His lighter snapped vainly. He sighed once more, got up, fetched a can of vile-smelling French lighter fluid, sat down, rewrapped his cocoon, filled the lighter, and snapped it. The fluid had spilled around a good bit. The lighter lit, so did Dr. Pennywither, from the wrists down. "Oh hell!" he cried, blue flames leaping from his knuckles, and jumped up batting his arms wildly, shouting "Hell!" and raging against Destiny. Nothing ever went right. What was the use? It was then 8:12 on the night of April 2nd, 1961.

A MAN sat hunched at a table in a cold, high room. Through the window behind him the two square towers of Notre Dame loomed in the Spring dusk. In front of him on the table lay a hunk of cheese and a

huge, iron-latched, handwritten book. The book was called (in Latin)
On the Primacy of the Element Fire over the Other Three Elements. Its
author stared at it with loathing. Nearby on a small iron stove a small
alembic simmered. Jehan Lenoir mechanically inched his chair nearer
the stove now and then, for warmth, but his thoughts were on deeper
problems. "Hell!" he said finally (in Late Mediaeval French), slammed
the book shut, and got up. What if his theory was wrong? What if water
were the primal element? How could you prove these things? There
must be some way — some method — so that one could be sure, absolutely sure, of one single fact! But each fact led into others, a monstrous
tangle, and the Authorities conflicted, and anyway no one would read
his book, not even the wretched pedants at the Sorbonne. They smelled
heresy. What was the use? What good this life spent in poverty and
alone, when he had learned nothing, merely guessed and theorized? He
strode about the garret, raging, and then stood still. "All right!" he said
to Destiny. "Very good! You've given me nothing, so I'll take what I
want!" He went to one of the stacks of books that covered most of the
floor-space, yanked out a bottom volume (scarring the leather and bruis-
ing his knuckles when the overlying folios avalanched), slapped it on the
table and began to study one page of it. Then, still with a set cold look
of rebellion, he got things ready: sulfur, silver, chalk. . . . Though the
room was dusty and littered, his little workbench was neatly and handily
arranged. He was soon ready. Then he paused. "This is ridiculous," he
muttered, glancing out the window into the darkness where now one
could only guess at the two square towers. A watchman passed below
calling out the hour, eight o'clock of a cold clear night. It was so still he
could hear the lapping of the Seine. He shrugged, frowned, took up the
chalk and drew a neat pentagram on the floor near his table, then took
up the book and began to read in a clear but self-conscious voice: "Haere, haere, audi me . . ." It was a long spell, and mostly nonsense. His
voice sank. He stood bored and embarrassed. He hurried through the
last words, shut the book, and then fell backwards against the door, gap-
mouthed, staring at the enormous, shapeless figure that stood within the
pentagram, lit only by the blue flicker of its waving, fiery claws.

BARRY Pennywither finally got control of himself and put out the fire
by burying his hands in the folds of the blanket wrapped around him.

Unburned but upset, he sat down again. He looked at his book. Then he stared at it. It was no longer thin and grey and titled *The Last Years of Villon: an Investigation of Possibilities.* It was thick and brown and titled *Incantatoria Magna.* On his table? A priceless manuscript dating from 1407 of which the only extant undamaged copy was in the Ambrosian Library in Milan. He looked slowly around. His mouth dropped slowly open. He observed a stove, a chemist's workbench, two or three dozen heaps of unbelievable leatherbound books, the window, the door. His window, his door. But crouching against his door was a little creature, black and shapeless, from which came a dry rattling sound.

Barry Pennywither was not a very brave man, but he was rational. He thought he had lost his mind, and so he said quite steadily, "Are you the Devil?"

The creature shuddered and rattled.

Experimentally, with a glance at invisible Notre Dame, the professor made the sign of the Cross.

At this the creature twitched; not a flinch, a twitch. Then it said something, feebly, but in perfectly good English — no, in perfectly good French — no, in rather odd French: "Mais vous estes de Dieu," it said.

Barry got up and peered at it. "Who are you?" he demanded, and it lifted up a quite human face and answered meekly, "Jehan Lenoir."

"What are you doing in my room?"

There was a pause. Lenoir got up from his knees and stood straight, all five foot two of him. "This is *my* room," he said at last, though very politely.

Barry looked around at the books and alembics. There was another pause. "Then how did I get here?"

"I brought you."

"Are you a doctor?"

Lenoir nodded, with pride. His whole air had changed. "Yes, I'm a doctor," he said. "Yes, I brought you here. If Nature will yield me no knowledge, then I can conquer Nature herself, I can work a miracle! To the Devil with science, then. I was a scientist —" he glared at Barry. "No longer! They call me a fool, a heretic, well by God I'm worse! I'm a sorcerer, a black magician, Jehan the Black! Magic works, does it? Then science is a waste of time. Ha!" he said, but he did not really look

triumphant. "I wish it hadn't worked," he said more quietly, pacing up and down between folios.

"So do I," said the guest.

"Who are you?" Lenoir looked up challengingly at Barry, though there was nearly a foot difference in their heights.

"Barry A. Pennywither, I'm a professor of French at Munson College, Indiana, on leave in Paris to pursue my studies of Late Mediaeval Fr —" He stopped. He had just realized what kind of accent Lenoir had. "What year is this? What century? Please, Dr. Lenoir —" The Frenchman looked confused. The meanings of words change, as well as their pronunciations. "Who rules this country?" Barry shouted.

Lenoir gave a shrug, a French shrug (some things never change). "Louis is king," he said. "Louis the Eleventh. The dirty old spider."

They stood staring at each other like wooden Indians for some time. Lenoir spoke first. "Then you're a man?"

"Yes. Look, Lenoir, I think you — your spell — you must have muffed it a bit."

"Evidently," said the alchemist. "Are you French?"

"No."

"Are you English?" Lenoir glared. "Are you a filthy Goddam?"

"No. No. I'm from America. I'm from the — from your future. From the twentieth century A.D." Barry blushed. It sounded silly, and he was a modest man. But he knew this was no illusion. The room he stood in, his room, was new. Not five centuries old. Unswept, but new. And the copy of Albertus Magnus by his knee was new, bound in soft supple calfskin, the gold lettering gleaming. And there stood Lenoir in his black gown, not in costume, at home. . . .

"Please sit down, sir," Lenoir was saying. And he added, with the fine though absent courtesy of the poor scholar, "Are you tired from the journey? I have bread and cheese, if you'll honor me by sharing it."

THEY sat at the table munching bread and cheese. At first Lenoir tried to explain why he had tried black magic. "I was fed up," he said. "Fed up! I've slaved in solitude since I was twenty, for what? For knowledge. To learn some of Nature's secrets. They are not to be learned." He drove his knife half an inch into the table, and Barry jumped. Lenoir was a thin little fellow, but evidently a passionate one. It was a fine face, though

pale and lean: intelligent, alert, vivid. Barry was reminded of the face of a famous atomic physicist, seen in newspaper pictures up until 1953. Somehow this likeness prompted him to say, "Some are, Lenoir; we've learned a good bit, here and there. . . ."

"What?" said the alchemist, skeptical but curious.

"Well, I'm no scientist —"

"Can you make gold?" He grinned as he asked.

"No, I don't think so, but they do make diamonds."

"How?"

"Carbon — coal, you know — under great heat and pressure, I believe. Coal and diamond are both carbon, you know, the same element."

"Element?"

"Now as I say, I'm no —"

"Which is the primal element?" Lenoir shouted, his eyes fiery, the knife poised in his hand.

"There are about a hundred elements," Barry said coldly, hiding his alarm.

Two hours later, having squeezed out of Barry every dribble of the remnants of his college chemistry course, Lenoir rushed out into the night and reappeared shortly with a bottle. "O my master," he cried, "to think I offered you only bread and cheese!" It was a pleasant burgundy, vintage 1477, a good year. After they had drunk a glass together Lenoir said, "If somehow I could repay you . . ."

"You can. Do you know the name of the poet François Villon?"

"Yes," Lenoir said with some surprise, "but he wrote only French trash, you know, not in Latin."

"Do you know how or when he died?"

"Oh, yes; hanged at Montfaucon here in '64 or '65, with a crew of no-goods like himself. Why?"

Two hours later the bottle was dry, their throats were dry, and the watchman had called three o'clock of a cold clear morning. "Jehan, I'm worn out," Barry said, "you'd better send me back." The alchemist was too polite, too grateful, and perhaps also too tired to argue. Barry stood stiffly inside the pentagram, a tall bony figure muffled in a brown blanket, smoking a Gauloise Bleue. "Adieu," Lenoir said sadly. "Au revoir," Barry replied. Lenoir began to read the spell backwards. The candle flickered, his voice softened. "Me audi, haere, haere," he read, sighed,

had never really expected to be listened to. They had merely wanted to learn.

So they were happy for the first time in their lives; so happy, in fact, that certain desires always before subjugated to the desire for knowledge, began to awaken. "I don't suppose," Barry said one night across the table, "that you ever thought much about marrying?"

"Well, no," his friend answered, doubtfully. "That is, I'm in minor orders . . . and it seemed irrelevant. . . . "

"And expensive. Besides, in my time, no self-respecting woman would want to share my kind of life. American women are so damned poised and efficient and glamorous, terrifying creatures. . . ."

"And women here are little and dark, like beetles, with bad teeth," Lenoir said morosely.

They said no more about women that night. But the next night they did; and the next; and on the next, celebrating the successful dissection of the main nervous system of a pregnant frog, they drank two bottles of Montrachet '74 and got soused. "Let's invoke a woman, Jehan," Barry said in a lascivious bass, grinning like a gargoyle.

"What if I raised a devil this time?"

"Is there really much difference?"

They laughed wildly, and drew a pentagram. "Haere, haere," Lenoir began; when he got the hiccups, Barry took over. He read the last words. There was a rush of cold, marshy-smelling air, and in the pentagram stood a wild-eyed being with long black hair, stark naked, screaming.

"Woman, by God," said Barry.

"Is it?"

It was. "Here, take my cloak," Barry said, for the poor thing now stood gawping and shivering. He put the cloak over her shoulders. Mechanically she pulled it round her, muttering, "Gratias ago, domine."

"Latin!" Lenoir shouted. "A woman speaking Latin?" It took him longer to get over that shock than it did Bota to get over hers. She was, it seemed, a slave in the household of the Sub-Prefect of North Gaul, who lived on the smaller island of the muddy island town called Lutetia. She spoke Latin with a thick Celtic brogue, and did not even know who was emperor in Rome in her day. A real barbarian, Lenoir said with scorn. So she was, an ignorant, taciturn, humble barbarian with tangled hair, white skin, and clear grey eyes. She had been waked from a sound

sleep. When they convinced her that she was not dreaming, she evidently assumed that this was some prank of her foreign and all-powerful master the Sub-Prefect, and accepted the situation without further question. "Am I to serve you, my masters?" she inquired timidly but without sullenness, looking from one to the other.

"Not me," Lenoir growled, and added in French to Barry, "Go on; I'll sleep in the store-room." He departed.

Bota looked up at Barry. No Gauls, and few Romans, were so magnificently tall; no Gauls and no Romans ever spoke so kindly. "Your lamp" (it was a candle, but she had never seen a candle) "is nearly burnt out," she said. "Shall I blow it out?"

FOR an additional two sols a year the landlord let them use the store-room as a second bedroom, and Lenoir now slept alone again in the main room of the garret. He observed his friend's idyll with a brooding, unjealous interest. The professor and the slave-girl loved each other with delight and tenderness. Their pleasure overlapped Lenoir in waves of protective joy. Bota had led a brutal life, treated always as a woman but never as a human. In one short week she bloomed, she came alive, evincing beneath her gentle passiveness a cheerful, clever nature. "You're turning out a regular Parisienne," he heard Barry accuse her one night (the attic walls were thin). She replied, "If you knew what it is for me not to be always defending myself, always afraid, always alone . . ."

Lenoir sat up on his cot and brooded. About midnight, when all was quiet, he rose and noiselessly prepared the pinches of sulfur and silver, drew the pentagram, opened the book. Very softly he read the spell. His face was apprehensive.

In the pentagram appeared a small white dog. It cowered and hung its tail, then came shyly forward, sniffed Lenoir's hand, looked up at him with liquid eyes and gave a modest, pleading whine. A lost puppy . . . Lenoir stroked it. It licked his hands and jumped all over him, wild with relief. On its white leather collar was a silver plaque engraved, "Jolie. Dupont, 36 rue de Seine, Paris VIe."

Jolie went to sleep, after gnawing a crust, curled up under Lenoir's chair. And the alchemist opened a book again and read, still softly, but this time without self-consciousness, without fear, knowing what would happen.

* * *

EMERGING from his store-room-bedroom-honeymoon in the morning, Barry stopped short in the doorway. Lenoir was sitting up in bed, petting a white puppy, and deep in conversation with the person sitting on the foot of the bed, a tall red-haired woman dressed in silver. The puppy barked. Lenoir said, "Good morning!" The woman smiled wondrously.

"Jumping Jesus," Barry muttered (in English). Then he said, "Good morning. When are you from?" The effect was Rita Hayworth, sublimated — Hayworth plus the Mona Lisa, perhaps?

"From Altair, about seven thousand years from now," she said, smiling still more wondrously. Her French accent was worse than that of a football-scholarship freshman. "I'm an archaeologist. I was excavating the ruins of Paris III. I'm sorry I speak the language so badly; of course we know it only from inscriptions."

"From Altair? The star? But you're human — I think —"

"Our planet was colonized from Earth about four thousand years ago — that is, three thousand years from now." She laughed, most wondrously, and glanced at Lenoir. "Jehan explained it all to me, but I still get confused."

"It was a dangerous thing to try it again, Jehan!" Barry accused him. "We've been awfully lucky, you know."

"No," said the Frenchman. "Not lucky."

"But after all it's black magic you're playing with — Listen — I don't know your name, madame."

"Kislk," she said.

"Listen, Kislk," Barry said without even a stumble, "your science must be fantastically advanced — is there any magic? Does it exist? Can the laws of Nature really be broken, as we seem to be doing?"

"I've never seen nor heard of an authenticated case of magic."

"Then what goes on?" Barry roared. "Why does that stupid old spell work for Jehan, for us, that one spell, and here, nowhere else, for nobody else, in five — no, eight — no, fifteen thousand years of recorded history? Why? Why? And where did that damn puppy come from?"

"The puppy was lost," Lenoir said, his dark face grave. "Somewhere near this house, on the Île Saint-Louis."

"And I was sorting potsherds," Kislk said, also gravely, "in a house-

site, Island 2, Pit 4, Section D. A lovely Spring day, and I hated it. Loathed it. The day, the work, the people around me." Again she looked at the gaunt little alchemist, a long, quiet look. "I tried to explain it to Jehan last night. We have improved the race, you see. We're all very tall, healthy, and beautiful. No fillings in our teeth. All skulls from Early America have fillings in the teeth. . . . Some of us are brown, some white, some gold-skinned. But all beautiful, and healthy, and well-adjusted, and aggressive, and successful. Our professions and degree of success are preplanned for us in the State Pre-School Homes. But there's an occasional genetic flaw. Me, for instance. I was trained as an archaeologist because the Teachers saw that I really didn't like people, live people. People bored me. All like me on the outside, all alien to me on the inside. When everything's alike, which place is home? . . . But now I've seen an unhygienic room with insufficient heating. Now I've seen a cathedral not in ruins. Now I've met a living man who's shorter than me, with bad teeth and a short temper. Now I'm home, I'm where I can be myself, I'm no longer alone!"

"Alone," Lenoir said gently to Barry. "Loneliness, eh? Loneliness is the spell, loneliness is stronger. . . . Really it doesn't seem unnatural."

Bota was peering round the doorway, her face flushed between the black tangles of her hair. She smiled shyly and said a polite Latin good-morning to the newcomer.

"Kislk doesn't know Latin," Lenoir said with immense satisfaction. "We must teach Bota some French. French is the language of love, anyway, eh? Come along, let's go out and buy some bread. I'm hungry."

Kislk hid her silver tunic under the useful and anonymous cloak, while Lenoir pulled on his moth-eaten black gown. Bota combed her hair, while Barry thoughtfully scratched a louse-bite on his neck. Then they set forth to get breakfast. The alchemist and the interstellar archaeologist went first, speaking French; the Gaulish slave and the professor from Indiana followed, speaking Latin, and holding hands. The narrow streets were crowded, bright with sunshine. Above them Notre Dame reared its two square towers against the sky. Beside them the Seine rippled softly. It was April in Paris, and on the banks of the river the chestnuts were in bloom.

The Pig

Born Doris Tayler in 1919 in Persia, the daughter of an army captain who moved the family to Rhodesia in 1924 to start a farm, Lessing left school at fourteen and educated herself after that. She began writing at a very young age, and published a prose poem in the *Rhodesia Herald* around the age of eight. As a young wife she published verse in *The New Rhodesia,* a right-wing weekly, stating in her autobiography, *Under My Skin,* that she intended to write novels and stories later, when she was not so busy with family obligations and her political activities in the local communist community. By the time her first short story was published in the South African magazine *Trek* in April 1948, Lessing had been married and divorced twice and was the mother of three children. Soon after the story appeared she sold her first novel, *The Grass Is Singing,* to both a Johannesburg and a London publisher, and Lessing and her youngest son emigrated to England, where she still lives.

THE FARMER PAID his labourers once a month, at sundown. This December, instead of dispersing when they took their money, they retired into the dark under the trees to wait. When the last one had been paid, the farmer said: "Call the women and the children. Everyone. Everybody in the compound must be here." The bossboy stood forward and repeated the order. But in an indifferent voice: it was only a matter of form, for all this had happened before, every year for years past. Already there was a subdued moving at the back of the crowd as the women came in from under the trees where they had been waiting; and the light caught a bunched skirt, or a bright headcloth.

The farmer began to speak, and although he had done this before so often, and was doing it now half cynically, knowing it was a waste of time, the memory of how good those fields of strong young plants looked when the sun shone on them put anger into his voice. The trouble was that every year black hands stripped the cobs from the stems in the night. He had tried everything: warned, threatened, docked rations — had even fined the whole compound collectively. It made no difference.

"Jonas," he shouted. Out on to the lamplit space stepped a native: a tall, elderly man whose hair was beginning to grizzle. An old scoundrel, the farmer called him, but affectionately. He was fond of him; they had been together for so long.

"Come here, Jonas," he said again, and picked up the .33 rifle that had been leaning against his knee. During the growing season Jonas spent his nights guarding the fields from the buck and the pigs that attacked the young plants. They could lay waste whole acres in one night, a herd of pigs. He took the rifle, greeting it, feeling its familiar weight swinging on his arm. But he looked reluctant, nevertheless.

"This year, Jonas, you will shoot everything you see — understand?"

"Yes, baas."

"Everything — buck, baboons, pig. And everything you hear. You will not stop to look. If you hear a noise, you will shoot."

There was a movement among the labourers.

"And if it turns out to be a human pig, then so much the worse. My lands are no place for pigs of any kind."

Jonas said nothing. He turned away, holding the rifle uncomfortably on his arm, looking at the others, appealing that they should not judge him.

"You can go," said the farmer. Soon the lamplit space was empty. But Jonas remained.

"Well, Jonas?"

"I do not want to shoot this year."

The farmer waited for an explanation. He was not disturbed at the order he had given in his anger. In all the years he had worked this farm no one had been shot, although every season thieves moved at night along the mealie rows, and every night Jonas was out with the gun. For he would fire the gun into the air, or shout; and only when the dawn

light came shot at something he could see. All this was a bluff. The threat might scare off a few of the more timid; but both sides knew, as usual, that it was a bluff.

"And why not?" asked the farmer at last.

"It's about my wife. . . ."

"Oh, your wife!" Suddenly the farmer remembered. Jonas was old-fashioned: he had two wives, an old one, and a young one who gave him a good deal of trouble. Last year, when this wife was new, he had not wanted to take on a job which meant being out all night.

"And what is the matter with the day-time?" asked the farmer with good-humoured jocularity, man-to-man. He laughed, preparing to go inside.

But Jonas was obstinate and stood his ground. He did not like being appointed official guardian against theft by his own people, but even that did not matter so much, for it never entered his head to take the order literally. But he was getting on in years now, and he wanted to spend his nights in peace in his hut. He had disliked it very much last year: but now it was even worse. A younger man visited his pretty young wife while he was away.

"I don't want to hear anything about your wife, Jonas. You should look after her yourself. And if you are not too old to take a young wife, then you are not too old to shoot. Good night."

And he went inside with the lamp. Jonas waited for his eyes to grow used to the dark, and then started off down the hill, finding his way by the feel of the little stones under his soles.

He had not yet eaten, but when he came to within sight of the compound, he felt he could not go further. He halted, looking at the little huts silhouetted black against the cooking fires that sent up great drifting clouds of illuminated smoke. There was his hut; there his wives were, waiting with his food prepared ready for him. But he felt sick and tormented, and cut off from his friends, who were preparing for an evening by the fires. And the small pain of jealousy that had been gnawing at him for so long, ached now as an old wound aches before the rains.

He did not want to go into the fields, to walk in the dark through the inhospitable and hostile bush. But that night, without going for his food, he set off as usual on his long vigil.

The next night, however, he did not go: for the next night and the next. He lay all day dozing in the sun on his blanket, turning himself over and over in the burning heat. When evening came he left the compound as usual with his gun, but stood with his back to a tree, within a stone's throw of his hut, watching it. It was as if his legs refused to carry him away from the place. All that week the land lay unguarded, and he did not care that the animals were raiding the young plants. He seemed to live for nothing but to stand all night watching his hut. He did not allow himself to think of what was happening inside.

THE following Saturday there was a beer drink, and, had he wanted, he could have got leave to attend it. But at sundown he set off with his gun and saw that his wife was pleased when he left.

When he leaned his back to the tree trunk which gave him its support each night, and held the rifle against his chest, his eyes fixed steadily on the dark shape that was his hut. He remembered that young man, as he had seen him only a few days before, bending over the girl as she knelt to grind meal, laughing with her; then the way they both looked up, startled, at his approach, their faces changing and growing blank.

He could feel his muscles swelling so taut against the rifle that he set it down for relief, letting his arms fall. But in spite of the pain he continued to think; for to-night things were different, and he no longer felt numbed and purposeless. He stood, letting the long, cold barrel slip between his fingers, the hardness of the tree against his back like a second spine. And as he thought of the young man, another picture crept into his mind, again and again: that of a young waterbuck he had shot last year, lying soft at his feet, so newly dead that he imagined he felt the blood still pulsing under the warm skin when he put his hand on it. And from the small wet place under the neck, a few sticky drops had rolled over glistening fur. Suddenly, while he stood there thinking of the limp dead body of the buck, and the young man laughing with his wife, his mind seemed to grow clear and cool, and the oppression and the hurt lightened.

He gave a long sigh, and picked up the rifle again, holding it close like a friend against him.

IT was still early. In the clear space of the compound groups of figures formed: talking and laughing and getting ready for the dance. A big fire

blazed and the tomtoms were beating. Visitors were coming in through the bush from other compounds miles away. It would be a long wait.

Several times he heard soft steps along the path close to him, that ran to the compound, before he tautened, and turned his head to watch the young man pass, as he had passed every night that week. He stood still as a tree struck by lightning, although he could not be seen where the shadows of the undergrowth closed over him. He saw the figure thread its way through the huts into the firelight, and move on till it passed in through the door of his own hut.

Hours passed, and he watched the dancing people, and listened to the drums while the stars swung over his head and the nightbirds talked in the bush around him. He thought steadily now, as he had not previously allowed himself to think, of what was happening inside the hut which gradually became invisible as the fire died. When the moon was small and high and cold behind his back, and the trees threw sharp, black shadows on the path, and he could smell morning in the air, he saw the shape moving towards him again. Now he shifted his feet a little, to ease the stiffness out of them, and moved the rifle along his arm, feeling the trigger curving along his finger.

He was so close to the man in front that he could have touched him with the raised rifle; but he walked confidently, though carefully, and thought all the time of how he had shot down from ten paces away that swift, young buck when it started with a crash out of a bush into the cold, moony field.

They reached the edge of the land where the dimly green mealies sloped away, and he began to walk like a cat. He wanted now to be sure; and he was only a dozen yards from the shooting platform in the corner of the field, that looked in this light like a crazy fowlhouse on crooked stilts through which the stars gleamed.

The young man was lurching with tiredness and drink, making a crashing noise, and snapping the sap-full mealies under heavy feet.

But the buck had shot like a spear from the bush, had fallen under the bullet like a spear falling: it had not blundered and staggered. Jonas began to feel a disgust for the man, and for the first time the admiration and faint feeling of hopeless fascination he had for his young rival, vanished. The tall, slim youth who had laughed down at his wife had nothing to do with the ungainly figure crashing along before him.

As they reached the shooting platform Jonas stood still and lifted the rifle to his cheek and saw the moonlight slanting down the steel. He waited; when the man had passed ten paces beyond the platform he squeezed his finger close, holding the rifle ready to fire again.

The sound of the shot crashed and echoed, the dark silhouetting body jerked oddly, blotting out whole fields of stars, and one hand went out as if to reach to the ground. Then the man disappeared into the mealies with a startled, thick cry. Jonas lowered the rifle and listened. There was a threshing noise, and a horrible grunting, like sleeptalking.

He approached, picking his way along the rows, feeling the leaf edges scythe along his legs, until he stood above the body that was still jerking among the stems. He waited till it stilled, then bent to look, parting the moon-cool leaves so he could see clearly.

It was no clean small hole: the back gaped raw flesh, blood poured black to the earth, the limbs were huddled together, the face was pressed to the soil.

"A pig," said Jonas aloud to the stars, as he kicked the side gently with his foot, "nothing but a pig."

He listened as he spoke, to hear how it would sound when he said it again, telling how he had shot blind into the grunting, invisible herd.

Cruel and Barbarous Treatment

Mary McCarthy was born in 1912 in Seattle. She attended Vassar and soon after graduation became involved with the *Partisan Review* and its writers. Beginning as a drama critic, she went on to write book reviews and essays for the *Nation* and the *New Republic*. It was not until her second marriage that she began to write fiction, mostly at the urging of her husband, Edmund Wilson. Like most of McCarthy's fiction, her first story is ruthlessly autobiographical; it details the breakup of her first marriage, which resulted from an insignificant affair that she had. In reality, both McCarthy's first husband, Harold Johnsrud, and her lover, John Porter, died soon after the events described — Johnsrud in a fire, and Porter after becoming ill in Mexico. This story was snatched up by the *Southern Review* and published in the Spring 1939 issue.

SHE COULD NOT bear to hurt her husband. She impressed this on the Young Man, on her confidantes, and finally on her husband himself. The thought of Telling Him actually made her heart turn over in a sudden and sickening way, she said. This was true, and yet she knew that being a potential divorcee was deeply pleasurable in somewhat the same way that being an engaged girl had been. In both cases, there was at first a subterranean courtship, whose significance it was necessary to conceal from outside observers. The concealment of the original, premarital courtship had, however, been a mere superstitious gesture, briefly sustained. It had also been, on the whole, a private secretiveness, not a partnership of silence. One put one's family and one's friends off the track because one was still afraid that the affair might not come out

right, might not lead in a clean, direct line to the altar. To confess one's aspirations might be, in the end, to publicize one's failure. Once a solid understanding had been reached, there followed a short intermission of ritual bashfulness, in which both parties awkwardly participated, and then came the Announcement.

But with the extramarital courtship, the deception was prolonged where it had been ephemeral, necessary where it had been frivolous, conspiratorial where it had been lonely. It was, in short, serious where it had been dilettantish. That it was accompanied by feelings of guilt, by sharp and genuine revulsions, only complicated and deepened its delights, by abrading the sensibilities, and by imposing a sense of outlawry and consequent mutual dependence upon the lovers. But what this interlude of deception gave her, above all, she recognized, was an opportunity, unparalleled in her experience, for exercising feelings of superiority over others. For her husband she had, she believed, only sympathy and compunction. She got no fun, she told the Young Man, out of putting horns on her darling's head, and never for a moment, she said, did he appear to her as the comic figure of the cuckolded husband that one saw on the stage. (The Young Man assured her that his own sentiments were equally delicate, that for the wronged man he felt the most profound respect, tinged with consideration.) It was as if by the mere act of betraying her husband, she had adequately bested him; it was supererogatory for her to gloat, and, if she gloated at all, it was over her fine restraint in not-gloating, over the integrity of her moral sense, which allowed her to preserve even while engaged in sinfulness the acute realization of sin and shame. Her overt superiority feelings she reserved for her friends. Lunches and teas, which had been time-killers, matters of routine, now became perilous and dramatic adventures. The Young Man's name was a bright, highly explosive ball which she bounced casually back and forth in these feminine tête-à-têtes. She would discuss him in his status of friend of the family, speculate on what girls he might have, attack him or defend him, anatomize him, keeping her eyes clear and impersonal, her voice empty of special emphasis, her manner humorously detached. *While all the time . . . !*

Three times a week or oftener, at lunch or tea, she would let herself tremble thus on the exquisite edge of self-betrayal, involving her companions in a momentous game whose rules and whose risks only she

herself knew. The Public Appearances were even more satisfactory. To meet at a friend's house by design and to register surprise, to strike just the right note of young-matronly affection at cocktail parties, to treat him formally as "my escort" at the theater during intermissions — these were triumphs of stage management, more difficult of execution, more nerve-racking than the lunches and teas, because *two* actors were involved. His overardent glance must be hastily deflected; his too-self-conscious reading of his lines must be entered in the debit side of her ledger of love, in anticipation of an indulgent accounting in private.

The imperfections of his performance were, indeed, pleasing to her. Not, she thought, because his impetuosities, his gaucheries, demonstrated the sincerity of his passion for her, nor because they proved him a new hand at this game of intrigue, but rather because the high finish of her own acting showed off well in comparison. "I should have gone on the stage," she could tell him gaily, "or been a diplomat's wife or an international spy," while he would admiringly agree. Actually, she doubted whether she could ever have been an actress, acknowledging that she found it more amusing and more gratifying to play herself than to interpret any character conceived by a dramatist. In these private theatricals it was her own many-faceted nature that she put on exhibit, and the audience, in this case unfortunately limited to two, could applaud both her skill of projection and her intrinsic variety. Furthermore, this was a play in which the donnée was real, and the penalty for a missed cue or an inopportune entrance was, at first anyway, unthinkable.

She loved him, she knew, for being a bad actor, for his docility in accepting her tender, mock-impatient instruction. Those superiority feelings were fattening not only on the gullibility of her friends, but also on the comic flaws of her lover's character, and on the vulnerability of her lover's position. In this particular hive she was undoubtedly queen bee.

The Public Appearances were not exclusively duets. They sometimes took the form of a trio. On these occasions the studied and benevolent carefulness which she always showed for her husband's feelings served a double purpose. She would affect a conspicuous domesticity, an affectionate conjugal demonstrativeness, would sprinkle her conversation with "Darlings," and punctuate it with pats and squeezes till her hus-

band would visibly expand and her lover plainly and painfully shrink. For the Young Man no retaliation was possible. These endearments of hers were sanctioned by law, usage, and habit; they belonged to her rôle of wife and could not be condemned or paralleled by a young man who was himself unmarried. They were clear provocations, but they could not be called so, and the Young Man preferred not to speak of them. *But she knew.* . . . Though she was aware of the sadistic intention of these displays, she was not ashamed of them, as she was sometimes twistingly ashamed of the hurt she was preparing to inflict on her husband. Partly she felt that they were punishments which the Young Man richly deserved for the wrong he was doing her husband, and that she herself in contriving them was acting, quite fittingly, both as judge and accused. Partly, too, she believed herself justified in playing the fond wife, whatever the damage to her lover's ego, because, in a sense, she actually was a fond wife. She *did* have these feelings, she insisted, whether she was exploiting them or not.

Eventually, however, her reluctance to wound her husband and her solicitude for his pride were overcome by an inner conviction that her love affair must move on to its next preordained stage. The possibilities of the subterranean courtship had been exhausted; it was time for the Announcement. She and the Young Man began to tell each other in a rather breathless and literary style that the Situation Was Impossible, and Things Couldn't Go On This Way Any Longer. The ostensible meaning of these flurried laments was that, under present conditions, they were not seeing enough of each other, that their hours together were too short and their periods of separation too dismal, that the whole business of deception had become morally distasteful to them. Perhaps the Young Man really believed these things; she did not. For the first time, she saw that the virtue of marriage as an institution lay in its public character. Private cohabitation, long continued, was, she concluded, a bore. Whatever the coziness of isolation, the warm delights of having a secret, a love affair finally reached the point where it needed the glare of publicity to revive the interest of its protagonists. Hence, she thought, the engagement parties, the showers, the big church weddings, the presents, the receptions. These were simply socially approved devices by which the lovers got themselves talked about. The gossip-value of a di-

vorce and remarriage was obviously far greater than the gossip-value of a mere engagement, and she was now ready, indeed hungry, to hear What People Would Say.

The lunches, the teas, the Public Appearances were getting a little flat. It was not, in the end, enough to be a Woman With A Secret, if to one's friends one appeared to be a woman without a secret. The bliss of having a secret required, in short, the consummation of telling it, and she looked forward to the My-dear-I-had-no-idea's, the I-thought-you-and-Bill-were-so-happy-together's, the How-did-you-keep-it-so-dark's with which her intimates would greet her announcement. The audience of two no longer sufficed her; she required a larger stage. She tried it first, a little nervously, on two or three of her closest friends, swearing them to secrecy. "Bill must hear it first from me," she declared. "It would be too terrible for his pride if he found out afterwards that the whole town knew it before he did. So you mustn't tell, even later on, that I told you about this today. I felt I had to talk to someone." After these lunches she would hurry to a phone booth to give the Young Man the gist of the conversation, just as a reporter, sent to cover a fire, telephones in to the city desk. "She certainly was surprised," she could always say with a little gush of triumph. "But she thinks it's fine." *But did they actually?* She could not be sure. Was it possible that she sensed in these luncheon companions, her dearest friends, a certain reserve, a certain unexpressed judgment?

It was a pity, she reflected, that she was so sensitive to public opinion. "I couldn't really love a man," she murmured to herself once, "if everybody didn't think he was wonderful." Everyone seemed to like the Young Man, of course. *But still. . . .* She was getting panicky, she thought. Surely it was only common sense that nobody is admired by everybody. And even if a man were universally despised, would there not be a kind of defiant nobility in loving him in the teeth of the whole world? There would, certainly, but it was a type of heroism that she would scarcely be called upon to practice, for the Young Man was popular, he was invited everywhere, he danced well, his manners were ingratiating, he kept up intellectually. But was he not perhaps *too* amiable, *too* accommodating? Was it for this that her friends seemed silently to criticize him?

At this time a touch of acridity entered into her relations with the

Young Man. Her indulgent scoldings had an edge to them now, and it grew increasingly difficult for her to keep her make-believe impatience from becoming real. She would look for dark spots in his character and drill away at them as relentlessly as a dentist at a cavity. A compulsive didacticism possessed her: no truism of his, no cliché, no ineffectual joke could pass the rigidity of her censorship. And, hard as she tried to maintain the character of charming schoolmistress, the Young Man, she saw, was taking alarm. She suspected that, frightened and puzzled, he contemplated flight. She found herself watching him with scientific interest, speculating as to what course he would take, and she was relieved but faintly disappointed when it became clear that he ascribed her sharpness to the tension of the situation and had decided to stick it out.

The moment had come for her to tell her husband. By this single, cathartic act, she would, she believed, rid herself of the doubts and anxieties that beset her. If her husband were to impugn the Young Man's character, she could answer his accusations and at the same time discount them as arising from jealousy. From her husband, at least, she might expect the favor of an open attack to which she could respond with the prepared defense that she carried, unspoken, about with her. Further, she had an intense, childlike curiosity as to How Her Husband Would Take It, a curiosity which she disguised for decency's sake as justifiable apprehension. The confidences already imparted to her friends seemed like pale dress rehearsals of the supreme confidence she was about to make. Perhaps it was toward this moment that the whole affair had been tending, for this moment that the whole affair had been designed. This would be the ultimate testing of her husband's love, its final, rounded, quintessential expression. Never, she thought, when you live with a man do you feel the full force of his love. It is gradually rationed out to you in an impure state, compounded with all the other elements of daily existence, so that you are hardly sensible of receiving it. There is no single point at which it is concentrated; it spreads out into the past and the future until it appears as a nearly imperceptible film over the surface of your life. Only face to face with its own annihilation could it show itself wholly, and, once shown, drop into the category of completed experiences.

She was not disappointed. She told him at breakfast in a fashionable restaurant, because, she said, he would be better able to control his feel-

ings in public. When he called at once for the check, she had a spasm of alarm lest in an access of brutality or grief he leave her there alone, conspicuous, and, as it were, unfulfilled. But they walked out of the restaurant together and through the streets, hand in hand, tears streaming, "unchecked," she whispered to herself, down their faces. Later they were in the Park, by an artificial lake, watching the ducks swim. The sun was very bright, and she felt a kind of superb pathos in the careful and irrelevant attention they gave to the pastoral scene. This was, she knew, the most profound, the most subtle, the most idyllic experience of her life. All the strings of her nature were, at last, vibrant. She was both doer and sufferer: she inflicted pain and participated in it. And she was, at the same time, physician, for, as she was the weapon that dealt the wound, she was also the balm that could assuage it. Only she could know the hurt that engrossed him, and it was to her that he turned for the sympathy she had ready for him. Finally, though she offered him his discharge slip with one hand, with the other she beckoned him to approach. She was wooing him all over again, but wooing him to a deeper attachment than he had previously experienced, to an unconditional surrender. She was demanding his total understanding of her, his compassion, and his forgiveness. When at last he answered her repeated and agonized I-love-you's by grasping her hand more tightly and saying gently, "I know," she saw that she had won him over. She had drawn him into a truly mystical union. Their marriage was complete.

Afterwards everything was more prosaic. The Young Man had to be telephoned and summoned to a conference à trois, a conference, she said, of civilized, intelligent people. The Young Man was a little awkward, even dropped a tear or two, which embarrassed everyone else, but what after all, she thought, could you expect? He was in a difficult position; his was a thankless part. With her husband behaving so well, indeed, so gallantly, the Young Man could not fail to look a trifle inadequate. The Young Man would have preferred it, of course, if her husband had made a scene, had bullied or threatened her, so that he himself might have acted the chivalrous protector. She, however, did not hold her husband's heroic courtesy against him: in some way, it reflected credit on herself. The Young Man, apparently, was expecting to Carry Her Off, but this she would not allow. "It would be too heartless," she

whispered when they were alone for a moment. "We must all go somewhere together."

So the three went out for a drink, and she watched with a sort of desperation her husband's growing abstraction, the more and more perfunctory attention he accorded the conversation she was so bravely sustaining. "He is bored," she thought. "He is going to leave." The prospect of being left alone with the Young Man seemed suddenly unendurable. If her husband were to go now, he would take with him the third dimension that had given the affair depth, and abandon her to a flat and vulgar love scene. Terrified, she wondered whether she had not already prolonged the drama beyond its natural limits, whether the confession in the restaurant and the absolution in the Park had not rounded off the artistic whole, whether the sequel of divorce and remarriage would not, in fact, constitute an anticlimax. Already she sensed that behind her husband's good manners an ironical attitude toward herself had sprung up. Was it possible that he had believed that they would return from the Park and all would continue as before? It was conceivable that her protestations of love had been misleading, and that his enormous tenderness toward her had been based, not on the idea that he was giving her up, but rather on the idea that he was taking her back — with no questions asked. If that were the case, the telephone call, the conference, and the excursion had in his eyes been a monstrous gaffe, a breach of sensibility and good taste, for which he would never forgive her. She blushed violently. Looking at him again, she thought he was watching her with an expression which declared: I have found you out: now I know what you are like. For the first time, she felt him utterly alienated.

When he left them she experienced the let-down she had feared but also a kind of relief. She told herself that it was as well that he had cut himself off from her: it made her decision simpler. There was now nothing for her to do but to push the love affair to its conclusion, whatever that might be, and this was probably what she most deeply desired. Had the poignant intimacy of the Park persisted, she might have been tempted to drop the adventure she had begun and return to her routine. But that was, looked at coldly, unthinkable. For if the adventure would seem a little flat after the scene in the Park, the resumption of her marriage would seem even flatter. If the drama of the triangle had been

amputated by her confession, the curtain had been brought down with a smack on the drama of wedlock.

And, as it turned out, the drama of the triangle was not quite ended by the superficial rupture of her marriage. Though she had left her husband's apartment and been offered shelter by a confidante, it was still necessary for her to see him every day. There were clothes to be packed, and possessions to be divided, love letters to be reread and mementoes to be wept over in common. There were occasional passionate, un-consummated embraces; there were endearments and promises. And though her husband's irony remained, it was frequently vulnerable. It was not, as she had at first thought, an armor against her, but merely a sword, out of *Tristan and Isolde,* which lay permanently between them and enforced discretion.

They met often, also, at the houses of friends, for, as she said, "What can I do? I know it's not tactful, but we all know the same people. You can't expect me to give up my friends." These Public Appearances were heightened in interest by the fact that these audiences, unlike the earlier ones, had, as it were, purchased librettos, and were in full possession of the intricacies of the plot. She preferred, she decided, the evening parties to the cocktail parties, for there she could dance alternately with her lover and her husband to the accompaniment of subdued gasps on the part of the bystanders.

This interlude was at the same time festive and heartrending: her only dull moments were the evenings she spent alone with the Young Man. Unfortunately, the Post-Announcement period was only too plainly an interlude and its very nature demanded that it be followed by something else. She could not preserve her anomalous status indefinitely. It was not decent, and, besides, people would be bored. From the point of view of one's friends, it was all very well to entertain a Triangle as a novelty; to cope with it as a permanent problem was a different matter. Once they had all three gotten drunk, and there was a scene, and, though everyone talked about it afterwards, her friends were, she thought, a little colder, a little more critical. People began to ask her when she was going to Reno. Furthermore, she noticed that her husband was getting a slight edge in popularity over the Young Man. It was natural, of course, that everyone should feel sorry for him, and be especially nice. *But yet. . . .*

When she learned from her husband that he was receiving invitations from members of her own circle, invitations in which she and the Young Man were unaccountably not included, she went at once to the station and bought her ticket. Her good-bye to her husband, which she had privately allocated to her last hours in town, took place prematurely, two days before she was to leave. He was rushing off to what she inwardly feared was a Gay Weekend in the country; he had only a few minutes; he wished her a pleasant trip; and he would write, of course. His highball was drained while her glass still stood half full; he sat forward nervously on his chair; and she knew herself to be acting the Ancient Mariner, but her dignity would not allow her to hurry. She hoped that he would miss his train for her, but he did not. He left her sitting in the bar, and that night the Young Man could not, as he put it, do a thing with her. There was nowhere, absolutely nowhere, she said passionately, that she wanted to go, nobody she wanted to see, nothing she wanted to do. "You need a drink," he said with the air of a diagnostician. "A drink," she answered bitterly. "I'm sick of the drinks we've been having. Gin, whiskey, rum, what else is there?" He took her into a bar, and she cried, but he bought her a fancy mixed drink, something called a Ramos gin fizz, and she was a little appeased because she had never had one before. Then some friends came in, and they all had another drink together, and she felt better. "There," said the Young Man, on the way home, "don't I know what's good for you? Don't I know how to handle you?" "Yes," she answered in her most humble and feminine tones, but she knew that they had suddenly dropped into a new pattern, that they were no longer the cynosure of a social group, but merely another young couple with an evening to pass, another young couple looking desperately for entertainment, wondering whether to call on a married couple or to drop in somewhere for a drink. This time the Young Man's prescription had worked, but it was pure luck that they had chanced to meet someone they knew. A second or a third time they would scan the faces of the other drinkers in vain, would order a second drink and surreptitiously watch the door, and finally go out alone, with a quite detectable air of being unwanted.

When, a day and a half later, the Young Man came late to take her to the train, and they had to run down the platform to catch it, she found

him all at once detestable. He would ride to 125th Street with her, he declared in a burst of gallantry, but she was angry all the way because she was afraid there would be trouble with the conductor. At 125th Street, he stood on the platform blowing kisses to her and shouting something that she could not hear through the glass. She made a gesture of repugnance, but, seeing him flinch, seeing him weak and charming and incompetent, she brought her hand reluctantly to her lips and blew a kiss back. The other passengers were watching, she was aware, and though their looks were doting and not derisive, she felt herself to be humiliated and somehow vulgarized. When the train began to move, and the Young Man began to run down the platform after it, still blowing kisses and shouting alternately, she got up, turned sharply away from the window and walked back to the club car. There she sat down and ordered a whiskey and soda.

There were a number of men in the car, who looked up in unison as she gave her order, but, observing that they were all the middle-aged, small-business-men who "belonged" as inevitably to the club car as the white-coated porter and the leather-bound *Saturday Evening Post,* she paid them no heed. She was now suddenly overcome by a sense of depression and loss that was unprecedented for being in no way dramatic or pleasurable. In the last half hour she had seen clearly that she would never marry the Young Man, and she found herself looking into an insubstantial future with no signpost to guide her. Almost all women, she thought, when they are girls never believe that they will get married. The terror of spinsterhood hangs over them from adolescence on. Even if they are popular they think that no one really interesting will want them enough to marry them. Even if they get engaged they are afraid that something will go wrong, something will intervene. When they do get married it seems to them a sort of miracle, and, after they have been married for a time, though in retrospect the whole process looks perfectly natural and inevitable, they retain a certain unarticulated pride in the wonder they have performed. Finally, however, the terror of spinsterhood has been so thoroughly exorcised that they forget ever having been haunted by it, and it is at this stage that they contemplate divorce. "How could I have forgotten?" she said to herself and began to wonder what she would do.

She could take an apartment by herself in the Village. She would

meet new people. She would entertain. But, she thought, if I have people in for cocktails, there will always come the moment when they have to leave, and I will be alone and have to pretend to have another engagement in order to save embarrassment. If I have them to dinner, it will be the same thing, but at least I will not have to pretend to have an engagement. I shall give dinners. Then, she thought, there will be the cocktail parties, and, if I go alone, I shall always stay a little too late, hoping that a young man or even a party of people will ask me to dinner. And if I fail, if no one asks me, I shall have the ignominy of walking out alone, trying to look as if I had somewhere to go. Then there will be the evenings at home with a good book when there will be no reason at all for going to bed, and I shall perhaps sit up all night. And the mornings when there will be no point in getting up, and I shall perhaps stay in bed till dinnertime. There will be the dinners in tea rooms with other unmarried women, tea rooms because women alone look conspicuous and forlorn in good restaurants. And then, she thought, I shall get older.

She would never, she reflected angrily, have taken this step, had she felt that she was burning her bridges behind her. She would never have left one man unless she had had another to take his place. But the Young Man, she now saw, was merely a sort of mirage which she had allowed herself to mistake for an oasis. "If the Man," she muttered, "did not exist, the Moment would create him." This was what had happened to her. She had made herself the victim of an imposture. But, she argued, with an access of cheerfulness, if this were true, if out of the need of a second, a new, husband she had conjured up the figure of one, she had possibly been impelled by unconscious forces to behave more intelligently than appearances would indicate. She was perhaps acting out in a sort of hypnotic trance a ritual whose meaning had not yet been revealed to her, a ritual which required that, first of all, the Husband be eliminated from the cast of characters. Conceivably, she was designed for the rôle of *femme fatale,* and for such a personage considerations of safety, provisions against loneliness and old age, were not only philistine but irrelevant. She might marry a second, a third, a fourth time, or she might never marry again. But, in any case, for the thrifty bourgeois love-insurance, with its daily payments of patience, forbearance, and resignation, she was no longer eligible. She would be, she told herself delightedly, a bad risk.

She was, or soon would be, a Young Divorcee, and the term still carried glamour. Her divorce decree would be a passport conferring on her the status of citizeness of the world. She felt gratitude toward the Young Man for having unwittingly effected her transit into a new life. She looked about her at the other passengers. Later she would talk to them. They would ask, of course, where she was bound for; that was the regulation opening move of train conversations. But it was a delicate question what her reply should be. To say "Reno" straight out would be vulgar; it would smack of confidences too cheaply given. Yet to lie, to say "San Francisco" for instance, would be to cheat herself, to minimize her importance, to mislead her interlocutor into believing her an ordinary traveler with a commonplace destination. There must be some middle course which would give information without appearing to do so, which would hint at a *vie galante* yet indicate a barrier of impeccable reserve. It would probably be best, she decided, to say "West" at first, with an air of vagueness and hesitation. Then, when pressed, she might go so far as to say "Nevada." But no farther.

Wunderkind

Born Carson Smith in Georgia in 1917, Carson McCullers began writing at the age of fifteen after she was bedridden with an illness. Musically inclined, when she was seventeen she moved to New York City to attend Columbia University and the Juilliard School of Music. According to McCullers, she wrote "Wunderkind" when she was seventeen or eighteen years old. It was published in *Story*'s December 1936 issue when she was nineteen, and she was paid the customary *Story* honorarium of twenty-five dollars. Four years later McCullers published her first novel, *The Heart Is a Lonely Hunter*, to great acclaim.

SHE CAME INTO the living room, her music satchel plopping against her winter-stockinged legs and her other arm weighted down with school books, and stood for a moment listening to the sounds from the studio. A soft procession of piano chords and the tuning of a violin. Then Mister Bilderbach called out to her in his chunky, guttural tones:

"That you, Bienchen?"

As she jerked off her mittens she saw that her fingers were twitching to the motions of the fugue she had practiced that morning. "Yes," she answered. "It's me."

"I," the voice corrected. "Just a moment."

She could hear Mister Lafkowitz talking — his words spun out in a silky, unintelligible hum. A voice almost like a woman's, she thought, compared to Mister Bilderbach's. Restlessness scattered her attention. She fumbled with her geometry book and "Le Voyage de Monsieur Perrichon" before putting them on the table. She sat down on the sofa and

began to take her music from the satchel. Again she saw her hands — the quivering tendons that stretched down from her knuckles, the sore finger tip capped with curled, dingy tape. The sight sharpened the fear that had begun to torment her for the past few months.

Noiselessly she mumbled a few phrases of encouragement to herself. A good lesson — a good lesson — like it used to be — Her lips closed as she heard the stolid sound of Mister Bilderbach's footsteps across the floor of the studio and the creaking of the door as it slid open.

For a moment she had the peculiar feeling that during most of the fifteen years of her life she had been looking at the face and shoulders that jutted from behind the door, in a silence disturbed only by the muted, blank plucking of a violin string. Mister Bilderbach. Her teacher, Mister Bilderbach. The quick eyes behind the horn-rimmed glasses; the light, thin hair and the narrow face beneath; the lips full and loose shut and the lower one pink and shining from the bites of his teeth; the forked veins in his temples throbbing plainly enough to be observed across the room.

"Aren't you a little early?" he asked, glancing at the clock on the mantelpiece that had pointed to five minutes of twelve for a month. "Josef's in here. We're running over a little sonatina by someone he knows."

"Good," she said, trying to smile. "I'll listen." She could see her fingers sinking powerless into a blur of piano keys. She felt tired — felt that if he looked at her much longer her hands might tremble.

He stood uncertain, halfway in the room. Sharply his teeth pushed down on his bright, swollen lip. "Hungry, Bienchen?" he asked. "There's some apple cake Anna made, and milk."

"I'll wait till afterward," she said. "Thanks."

"After you finish with a very fine lesson — eh?" His smile seemed to crumble at the corners.

There was a sound from behind him in the studio and Mister Lafkowitz pushed at the other panel of the door and stood beside him.

"Frances?" he said, smiling. "And how is the work coming now?"

Without meaning to, Mister Lafkowitz always made her feel clumsy and overgrown. He was such a small man himself, with a weary look when he was not holding his violin. His eyebrows curved high above his sallow, Jewish face as though asking a question, but the lids of his eyes

drowsed languorous and indifferent. Today he seemed distracted. She watched him come into the room for no apparent purpose, holding his pearl-tipped bow in his still fingers, slowly gliding the white horse hair through a chalky piece of rosin. His eyes were sharp bright slits today and the linen handkerchief that flowed down from his collar darkened the shadows beneath them.

"I gather you're doing a lot now," smiled Mister Lafkowitz, although she had not yet answered the question.

She looked at Mister Bilderbach. He turned away. His heavy shoulders pushed the door open wide so that the late afternoon sun came through the window of the studio and shafted yellow over the dusty living room. Behind her teacher she could see the squat long piano, the window, and the bust of Brahms.

"No," she said to Mister Lafkowitz, "I'm doing terribly." Her thin fingers flipped at the pages of her music. "I don't know what's the matter," she said, looking at Mister Bilderbach's stooped muscular back that stood tense and listening.

Mister Lafkowitz smiled. "There are times, I suppose, when one —"

A harsh chord sounded from the piano. "Don't you think we'd better get on with this?" asked Mister Bilderbach.

"Immediately," said Mister Lafkowitz, giving the bow one more scrape before starting toward the door. She could see him pick up his violin from the top of the piano. He caught her eye and lowered the instrument. "You've seen the picture of Heime?"

Her fingers curled tight over the sharp corner of the satchel. "What picture?"

"One of Heime in the *Musical Courier* there on the table. Inside the top cover."

The sonatina began. Discordant yet somehow simple. Empty but with a sharp cut style of its own. She reached for the magazine and opened it.

There Heime was — in the left hand corner. Holding his violin with his fingers hooked down over the strings for a pizzicato. With his dark serge knickers strapped neatly beneath his knees, a sweater and rolled collar. It was a bad picture. Although it was snapped in profile his eyes were cut around toward the photographer and his finger looked as though it would pluck the wrong string. He seemed suffering to turn around to-

ward the picture-taking apparatus. He was thinner — his stomach did not poke out — but he hadn't changed much in six months.

Heime Israelsky, talented young violinist, snapped while at work in his teacher's studio on Riverside Drive. Young Master Israelsky, who will soon celebrate his fifteenth birthday, has been invited to play the Beethoven Concerto with —

That morning, after she had practiced from six until eight, her Dad had made her sit down at the table with the family for breakfast. She hated breakfast; it gave her a sick feeling afterward. She would rather wait and get four chocolate bars with her twenty cents lunch money and munch them during school — bringing up little morsels from her pocket under cover of her handkerchief, stopping dead when the silver paper rattled. But this morning her Dad had put a fried egg on her plate and she had known that if it burst — so that the slimy yellow oozed over the white — she would cry. And that had happened. The same feeling was upon her now. Gingerly she laid the magazine back on the table and closed her eyes.

The music in the studio seemed to be urging violently and clumsily for something that was not to be had. After a moment her thoughts drew back from Heime and the concerto and the picture — and hovered around the lessons once more. She slid over on the sofa until she could see plainly into the studio — the two of them playing, peering at the notations on the piano, lustfully drawing out all that was there.

She could not forget the memory of Mister Bilderbach's face as he had stared at her a moment ago. Her hands, still twitching unconsciously to the motions of the fugue, closed over her bony knees. Tired, she was. And with a circling, sinking away feeling like the one that often came to her just before she dropped off to sleep on the nights when she had over-practiced. Like those weary half dreams that buzzed and carried her out into their own whirling space.

A *Wunderkind* — a *Wunderkind*. The syllables would come rolling in the deep German way, roar against her ears and then fall to a murmur. Along with the faces circling, swelling out in distortion, diminishing to pale blobs — Mister Bilderbach, Mrs. Bilderbach, Heime, Mister Lafkowitz. Around and around in a circle revolving to the guttural *Wunderkind*. Mister Bilderbach looming large in the middle of the circle, his face urging — with the others around him.

Phrases of music seesawing crazily. Notes she had been practicing falling over each other like a handful of marbles dropped downstairs. Bach, Debussy, Prokofieff, Brahms — timed grotesquely to the far off throb of her tired body and the buzzing circle.

Sometimes — when she had not worked more than three hours or had stayed out from high school — the dreams were not so confused. The music soared clearly in her mind and quick, precise little memories would come back — clear as the sissy "Age of Innocence" picture Heime had given her after their joint concert was over.

A *Wunderkind* — a *Wunderkind*. That was what Mister Bilderbach had called her when, at twelve, she first came to him. Older pupils had repeated the word.

Not that he had ever said the word to her. "Bienchen —" (She had a plain American name but he never used it except when her mistakes were enormous). "Bienchen," he would say, "I know it must be terrible. Carrying around all the time a head that thick. Poor Bienchen —"

Mister Bilderbach's father had been a Dutch violinist. His mother was from Prague. He had been born in this country and had spent his youth in Germany. So many times she wished she had not been born and brought up in just Cincinnati. How do you say *cheese* in German? Mister Bilderbach, what is Dutch for *I don't understand you?*

The first day she came to the studio. After she played the whole Second Hungarian Rhapsody from memory. The room graying with twilight. His face as he leaned over the piano.

"Now we begin all over," he said that first day. "It — playing music — is more than cleverness. If a twelve-year-old girl's fingers cover so many keys to a second — that means nothing."

He tapped his broad chest and his forehead with his stubby hand. "Here and here. You are old enough to understand that." He lighted a cigarette and gently blew the first exhalation above her head. "And work — work — work. We will start now with these Bach Inventions and these little Schumann pieces." His hands moved again — this time to jerk the cord of the lamp behind her and point to the music. "I will show you how I wish this practiced. Listen carefully now."

She had been at the piano for almost three hours and was very tired. His deep voice sounded as though it had been straying inside her for a long time. She wanted to reach out and touch his muscle-flexed finger

that pointed out the phrases, wanted to feel the gleaming gold band ring and the strong hairy back of his hand.

She had lessons Tuesday after school and on Saturday afternoons. Often she stayed, when the Saturday lesson was finished, for dinner, and then spent the night and took the street car home the next morning. Mrs. Bilderbach liked her in her calm, almost dumb way. She was much different from her husband. She was quiet and fat and slow. When she wasn't in the kitchen, cooking the rich dishes that both of them loved, she seemed to spend all her time in their bed upstairs, reading magazines or just looking with a half smile at nothing. When they had married in Germany she had been a *lieder* singer. She didn't sing anymore (she said it was her throat). When he would call her in from the kitchen to listen to a pupil she would always smile and say that it was *gut,* very *gut.*

When Frances was thirteen it came to her one day that the Bilderbachs had no children. It seemed strange. Once she had been back in the kitchen with Mrs. Bilderbach when he had come striding in from the studio, tense with anger at some pupil who had annoyed him. His wife stood stirring the thick soup until his hand groped out and rested on her shoulder. Then she turned — stood placid — while he folded his arms about her and buried his sharp face in the white, nerveless flesh of her neck. They stood that way without moving. And then his face jerked back suddenly, the anger diminished to a quiet inexpressiveness, and he had returned to the studio.

After she had started with Mister Bilderbach and didn't have time to see anything of the people at high school, Heime had been the only friend of her own age. He was Mister Lafkowitz's pupil and would come with him to Mister Bilderbach's on evenings when she would be there. They would listen to their teachers' playing. And often they themselves went over chamber music together — Mozart sonatas or Bloch.

A *Wunderkind* — a *Wunderkind.*

Heime was a *Wunderkind.* He and she, then.

Heime had been playing the violin since he was four. He didn't have to go to school; Mister Lafkowitz's brother, who was crippled, used to teach him geometry and European history and French verbs in the afternoon. When he was thirteen he had as fine a technique as any violinist in Cincinnati — everyone said so. But playing the violin must be easier than the piano. She knew it must be.

Heime always seemed to smell of corduroy pants and the food he had eaten and rosin. Half the time, too, his hands were dirty around the knuckles and the cuffs of his shirts peeped out dingily from the sleeves of his sweater. She always watched his hands when he played — thin only at the joints with the hard little blobs of flesh bulging over the short cut nails and the babyish looking crease that showed so plainly in his bowing wrist.

In the dreams, as when she was awake, she could remember the concert only in a blur. She had not known it was unsuccessful for her until months after. True, the papers had praised Heime more than her. But he was much shorter than she. When they stood together on the stage he came only to her shoulders. And that made a difference with people, she knew. Also, there was the matter of the sonata they played together. The Bloch.

"No, no — I don't think that would be appropriate," Mister Bilderbach had said when the Bloch was suggested to end the programme. "Now that John Powell thing — the Sonate Virginianesque."

She hadn't understood then; she wanted it to be the Bloch as much as Mister Lafkowitz and Heime.

Mister Bilderbach had given in. Later, after the reviews had said she lacked the temperament for that type of music, after they called her playing thin and lacking in feeling, she felt cheated.

"That oie oie stuff," said Mister Bilderbach, crackling the newspapers at her. "Not for you, Bienchen. Leave all that to the Heimes and vitses and skys."

A *Wunderkind*. No matter what the papers said, that was what he had called her.

Why was it Heime had done so much better at the concert than she? At school sometimes, when she was supposed to be watching someone do a geometry problem on the blackboard, the question would twist knife-like inside her. She would worry about it in bed, and even sometimes when she was supposed to be concentrating at the piano. It wasn't just the Bloch and her not being Jewish — not entirely. It wasn't that Heime didn't have to go to school and had begun his training so early, either. It was — ?

Once she thought she knew.

"Play the Fantasia and Fugue," Mister Bilderbach had demanded one

evening a year ago — after he and Mister Lafkowitz had finished reading some music together.

The Bach, as she played, seemed to her well done. From the tail of her eye she could see the calm, pleased expression on Mister Bilderbach's face, see his hands rise climactically from the chair arms and then sink down loose and satisfied when the high points of the phrases had been passed successfully. She stood up from the piano when it was over, swallowing to loosen the bands that the music seemed to have drawn around her throat and chest. But —

"Frances —" Mister Lafkowitz had said then, suddenly, looking at her with his thin mouth curved and his eyes almost covered by their delicate lids. "Do you know how many children Bach had?"

She turned to him, puzzled. "A good many. Twenty some odd."

"Well, then —" The corners of his smile etched themselves gently in his pale face. "He could not have been so cold — then."

Mister Bilderbach was not pleased; his guttural effulgence of German words had *Kind* in it somewhere. Mister Lafkowitz raised his eyebrows. She had caught the point easily enough, but she felt no deception in keeping her face blank and immature because that was the way Mister Bilderbach wanted her to look.

Yet such things had nothing to do with it. Nothing very much, at least, for she would grow older. Mister Bilderbach understood that, and even Mister Lafkowitz had not meant just what he said.

In the dreams Mister Bilderbach's face loomed out and contracted in the center of the whirling circle. The lips surging softly, the veins in his temples insisting.

But sometimes, before she slept, there were such clear memories; as when she pulled a hole in the heel of her stocking down, so that her shoe would hide it. "Bienchen, Bienchen!" And bringing Mrs. Bilderbach's work basket in and showing her how it should be darned and not gathered together in a lumpy heap.

And the time she graduated from Junior High:

"What you wear?" asked Mrs. Bilderbach the Sunday morning at breakfast when she told them how they had practiced to march into the auditorium.

"An evening dress my cousin had last year."

"Ah — Bienchen!" he said, circling his warm coffee cup with his

heavy hands, looking up at her with wrinkles around his laughing eyes. "I bet I know what Bienchen wants —"

He insisted. He would not believe her when she explained that she honestly didn't care at all.

"Like this, Anna," he said, pushing his napkin across the table and mincing to the other side of the room, swishing his hips, rolling up his eyes behind his horn-rimmed glasses.

The next Saturday afternoon, after her lesson, he took her to the department stores downtown. His thick fingers smoothed over the filmy nets and crackling taffetas that the saleswomen unwound from their bolts. He held colors to her face, cocking his head to one side, and selected pink. Shoes, he remembered too. He liked best some white kid pumps. They seemed a little like old ladies' shoes to her and the Red Cross label in the instep had a charity look. But it really didn't matter at all. When Mrs. Bilderbach began to cut out the dress and fit it to her with pins, he interrupted his lessons to stand by and suggest ruffles around the hips and neck and a fancy rosette on the shoulder. The music was coming along nicely then. Dresses and commencement and such made no difference.

Nothing mattered much except playing the music as it must be played, bringing out the thing that must be in her, practicing, practicing, playing so that Mister Bilderbach's face lost some of its urging look. Putting the thing into her music that Myra Hess had, and Yehudi Menuhin — even Heime!

What had begun to happen to her four months ago? The notes began springing out with a glib, dead intonation. Adolescence, she thought. Some kids played with promise — and worked and worked until, like her, the least little thing would start them crying, and worn out with trying to get the thing across — the longing thing they felt — something queer began to happen — But not she! She was like Heime. She had to be. She —

Once it was there for sure. And you didn't lose things like that. A *Wunderkind*. . . . A *Wunderkind*. . . . Of her he said it, rolling the words in the sure, deep German way. And in the dreams even deeper, more certain than ever. With his face looming out at her, and the longing phrases of music mixed in with the zooming, circling round, round, round — A *Wunderkind*. A *Wunderkind*. . . .

This afternoon Mister Bilderbach did not show Mister Lafkowitz to the front door, as he usually did. He stayed at the piano, softly pressing a solitary note. Listening, Frances watched the violinist wind his scarf about his pale throat.

"A good picture of Heime," she said, picking up her music. "I got a letter from him a couple of months ago — telling about hearing Schnabel and Huberman and about Carnegie Hall and things to eat at the Russian Tea Room."

To put off going into the studio a moment longer she waited until Mister Lafkowitz was ready to leave and then stood behind him as he opened the door. The frosty cold outside cut into the room. It was growing late and the air was seeped with the pale yellow of winter twilight. When the door swung to on its hinges, the house seemed darker and more silent than ever before she had known it to be.

As she went into the studio Mister Bilderbach got up from the piano and silently watched her settle herself at the keyboard.

"Well, Bienchen," he said, "this afternoon we are going to begin all over. Start from scratch. Forget the last few months."

He looked as though he were trying to act a part in a movie. His solid body swayed from toe to heel, he rubbed his hands together, and even smiled in a satisfied, movie way. Then suddenly he thrust this manner brusquely aside. His heavy shoulders slouched and he began to run through the stack of music she had brought in. "The Bach — no, not yet," he murmured. "The Beethoven? Yes, the Variation Sonata. Opus 26."

The keys of the piano hemmed her in — stiff and white and dead-seeming.

"Wait a minute," he said. He stood in the curve of the piano, elbows propped, and looked at her. "Today I expect something from you. Now this sonata — it's the first Beethoven sonata you ever worked on. Every note is under control — technically — you have nothing to cope with but the music. Only music now. That's all you think about."

He rustled through the pages of her volume until he found the place. Then he pulled his teaching chair half way across the room, turned it around and seated himself, straddling the back with his legs.

For some reason, she knew, this position of his usually had a good

effect on her performance. But today she felt that she would notice him from the corner of her eye and be disturbed. His back was stiffly tilted, his legs looked tense. The heavy volume before him seemed to balance dangerously on the chair back. "Now we begin," he said with a peremptory dart of his eyes in her direction.

Her hands rounded over the keys and then sank down. The first notes were too loud, the other phrases followed dryly.

Arrestingly his hand rose up from the score. "Wait! Think a minute what you're playing. How is this beginning marked?"

"*An-andante.*"

"All right. Don't drag it into an *adagio* then. And play deeply into the keys. Don't snatch it off shallowly that way. A graceful, deep-toned *andante* —"

She tried again. Her hands seemed separate from the music that was in her.

"Listen," he interrupted. "Which of these variations dominates the whole?"

"The dirge," she answered.

"Then prepare for that. This is an *andante* — but it's not salon stuff as you just played it. Start out softly, *piano,* and make it swell out just before the arpeggio. Make it warm and dramatic. And down here — where it's marked *dolce* make the counter melody sing out. You know all that. We've gone over all that side of it before. Now play it. Feel it as Beethoven wrote it down. Feel that tragedy and restraint."

She could not stop looking at his hands. They seemed to rest tentatively on the music, ready to fly up as a stop signal as soon as she would begin, the gleaming flash of his ring calling her to halt. "Mister Bilderbach — maybe if I — if you let me play on through the first variation without stopping I could do better."

"I won't interrupt," he said.

Her pale face leaned over too close to the keys. She played through the first part, and, obeying a nod from him, began the second. There were no flaws that jarred on her, but the phrases shaped from her fingers before she had put into them the meaning that she felt.

When she had finished he looked up from the music and began to speak with dull bluntness: "I hardly heard those harmonic fillings in the

right hand. And incidentally, this part was supposed to take on intensity, develop the foreshadowings that were supposed to be inherent in the first part. Go on with the next one, though."

She wanted to start it with subdued viciousness and progress to a feeling of deep, swollen sorrow. Her mind told her that. But her hands seemed to gum in the keys like limp macaroni and she could not imagine the music as it should be.

When the last note had stopped vibrating, he closed the book and deliberately got up from the chair. He was moving his lower jaw from side to side — and between his open lips she could glimpse the pink healthy lane to his throat and his strong, smoke-yellowed teeth. He laid the Beethoven gingerly on top of the rest of the music and propped his elbows on the smooth, black top once more. "No," he said simply, looking at her.

Her mouth began to quiver. "I can't help it. I —"

Suddenly he strained his lips to smile. "Listen, Bienchen," he began in a new, forced voice. "You still play the Harmonious Blacksmith, don't you? I told you not to drop it from your repertoire."

"Yes," she said. "I practice it now and then."

His voice was the one he used for children. "It was among the first things we worked on together — remember. So strongly you used to play it — like a real blacksmith's daughter. You see, Bienchen, I know you so well — as if you were my own girl. I know what you have — I've heard you play so many things beautifully. You used to —"

He stopped in confusion and inhaled from his pulpy stub of cigarette. The smoke drowsed out from his pink lips and clung in a gray mist around her lank hair and childish forehead.

"Make it happy and simple," he said, switching on the lamp behind her and stepping back from the piano.

For a moment he stood just inside the bright circle the light made. Then impulsively he squatted down on the floor. "Vigorous," he said.

She could not stop looking at him, sitting on one heel with the other foot resting squarely before him for balance, the muscles of his strong thighs straining under the cloth of his trousers, his back straight, his elbows staunchly propped on his knees. "Simply now," he repeated with a gesture of his fleshy hands. "Think of the blacksmith — working out in the sunshine all day. Working easily and undisturbed."

She could not look down at the piano. The lights brightened the hairs on the backs of his outspread hands, made the lenses of his glasses glitter.

"All of it," he urged. "Now!"

She felt that the marrows of her bones were hollow and there was no blood left in her. Her heart that had been springing against her chest all afternoon felt suddenly dead. She saw it gray and limp and shrivelled at the edges like an oyster.

His face seemed to throb out in space before her, come closer with the lurching motion in the veins of his temples. In retreat, she looked down at the piano. Her lips shook like jelly and a surge of noiseless tears made the white keys blur in a watery line. "I can't," she whispered. "I don't know why, but I just can't — can't any more."

His tense body slackened and holding his hand to his side, he pulled himself up. She clutched the music and hurried past him.

Her coat. The mittens and galoshes. The school books and the satchel he had given her on her birthday. All from the silent room that was hers. Quickly — before he would have to speak.

As she passed through the vestibule she could not help but see his hands — held out from his body that leaned against the studio door, relaxed and purposeless. The door shut so firmly. Dragging her books and satchel she stumbled down the stone steps, turned in the wrong direction, and hurried down the street that had become confused with noise and bicycles and the games of other children.

The Greatest Thing in the World

In his sophomore year at Harvard, determined to become a professional writer, Norman Mailer enrolled in Robert Gorham Davis's writing class, an experience he later compared to being a "novice in the Golden Gloves." Davis, however, was so impressed with Mailer's "The Greatest Thing in the World" that he suggested he enter it in *Story* magazine's annual College Fiction contest. Hilary Mills writes in her biography of Mailer, "It was no routine suggestion: In his many years at Harvard Davis recommended only two other students for that competition."

Mailer's story won first prize and was published in *Story*'s November–December 1941 issue. "Probably nothing has happened in the years I've been writing which changed my life as much," wrote Mailer in *Advertisements for Myself,* which included "The Greatest Thing in the World." Carl Rollyson in *The Lives of Norman Mailer* suggests that it was "probably modeled after the Davey Cohen episode in *The Young Manhood of Studs Lonigan."* In *Advertisements* Mailer professed dislike for the story, commenting, "Crude, derivative of the kind of writing which was done in the thirties, I think it stands up only in its sense of pace which is quick and nice. Perhaps this is why it won — pace is rarely found in college writers."

INSIDE, OUT OF the rain, the lunch wagon was hot and sticky. Al Groot stopped in front of the doorway, wiped his hands and wrung his hat out, and scuffed his shoes against the dirt-brown mat. He stood there, a small, old wrinkled boy of eighteen or nineteen, with round beady eyes that seemed incapable of looking at you unless you were in back of him. He stopped at the door and waited, not sure of his recep-

tion, examining the place carefully, as if he might have need of this knowledge soon after. It was a little fancier than the ordinary lunch-room, having dark, old wood booths at the left that fronted the sharp, glittering stools and counter of well-polished chromium. A clock on the wall showed that it was after ten, which might have explained why the place was almost empty. There was no one at the counter and the few truck drivers, sprawled out on two adjoining booths to catch a late din-ner, were tired and very quiet, engrossed only in their sandwiches and hamburgers. Only one man was left behind the counter, and he was carefully cleaning the grease from the frankfurter griddle, with the slow motions of a man who has a great deal of time on his hands and is desperately afraid of finishing his work, to face the prospect of empty tables and silent people. He looked at Al, uncertain for a moment how to take him, and then he turned back to the griddle and gave it a last studious wipe. He spoke, without looking up, but his tone was friendly.

"Hi," he said.

Al said hello, watching the man scrape some crumblings off.

"It's a hell of a night, ain't it?" the counterman asked.

"Lousy."

"It sure is. Guess we needed it," he said. "The crops are hit bad when it don't rain enough."

"Sure," said Al. "Look, what does coffee and doughnuts cost?"

"Ten."

"Two doughnuts."

"That's it."

"Uh-huh," said Al. "Could you let me have one doughnut and half a cup of coffee for five cents? I ain't got but a nickel."

"I don't know," he said. "I could, but why should I?"

"I ain't had nothing to eat today," Al pleaded. "Come on."

The man looked up. Al sucked expertly on his cheeks, just pulling them in enough to make it look good.

"I guess you could stand it. Only pay me now."

Al reached into his pocket, and tenderly extracted a nickel from two halves of a dollar bill. He finished over one-third of the doughnut in the first bite, and realizing how extravagant he had been, he took a small begrudging sip of the coffee.

"Nice place," he said.

"I like it," the man said.

"You own it?"

"You're damn right, buddy. I worked to get this place. It's all mine. You don't find me giving anything away on it. Every cup of coffee a guy drinks feeds me too."

"Top of the world," Al said.

"Nyahr," he answered bitterly. "Lot of good it does me. You see anybody in here? You see me clicking the cash register? The hell you do."

Al was thinking of how tough his luck was that the truck drivers should be uniformed, which was as good as a "no rider" sign. He grinned sympathetically at the owner, trying to look as wet as he could.

"Boy," he said, "I sure am stuck."

"Been hitching, huh?"

"Yeah, walked the last three miles, ever since it started to rain."

"Must be kind of tough."

"Sure, I figure I won't be able to sleep if it don't stop raining. That was my last nickel. Say, look, you wouldn't have a job for me?" he said stupidly.

"What'll I do, watch you work?"

"Then let me sleep here tonight. It won't cost you nothing."

"I don't run a flophouse."

"Skip it, forget it," Al said. "Only let me stay here a while to dry off. When somebody comes in, maybe they'll give me a ride."

"Stay," he said. "I have such fancy trade. New chromium, brass fixtures. Ahhhr."

Al slipped off the stool and sat down at a table in the rear, out of sight of the counterman. He slouched down against the side of the booth and picked up a menu, supported between the salt and pepper shakers, looking at it interestedly, but past all craving or desire. He thought that it had been almost a year since he had had a steak. He tried to remember what it tasted like, but his memory failed, and to distract him from the tantalizing picture he started examining the spelling on the sheet, guessing at a word first, then seeing how close he was. Another company truck driver had come in, and Al shot a quick look back to see where the owner was. Finding him up front, almost out of sight, he quickly picked up the ketchup bottle and shook large gobs of it into his mouth as fast as he could get it out. It burned and stung inside his stomach, and he

kept blowing, trying to cool his mouth. Noticing a few drops on the table, he took a paper napkin and squeezed them over the edge, where they hung, ready to fall. He ran his little finger along underneath, gathering them up, and catching the drops in his mouth as they dripped off.

He felt for the split dollar bill, and figured it. This time, he thought, it was really his last. Once, three months ago, he had five dollars. He thought back and tried to remember how he had gotten it. It was very vague, and he wondered whether he had stolen it or not. The image of five separate bills, and all that he could do with them, hit him then with all its beauty and impossibility. He thought of cigarettes, and a meal, and a clean woman in a good place, and new soles to his shoes, but most of all he thought of the soft leathery feel of money, and the tight wad it made in his pants.

"By God," he said thickly, "there's nothing like it. You can't beat it. If I just had five dollars again."

He withdrew his hand, taking the two pieces out, smoothing them lovingly on the table. He considered breaking the bill for another doughnut, but he knew he couldn't. It was the last thing between him and . . . He stopped, realizing that he had passed the last thing — there was no "and." Still, he did not think any more of spending his last bill. Tomorrow or tonight he would be in Chicago, and he could find something to eat for a day or two. He might even pick up half a buck by mooching. In the meantime he felt hungry. He stayed in the booth, staring at the end wall, and dreaming of his one-time hoard.

Three men came in to eat. Al saw them hesitate at the door, wondering whether to eat in a booth or at the counter.

"Take a booth," one said.

Al looked at them. This might be a ride, he thought. He waited until they had started eating, and then he went over to them, hitching at his faded gray-blue dungarees.

"Hi, sports," he said.

"Hello, sweet-face," one of them said.

"They call me Al Groot."

"His father's name was Groot," said one of them, turning to the others.

"I ain't asking for any dough."

They eased up a little. "Boy, you sure ain't, sweet-face," one of them

said. "Sit down, sit down," he said. "My name's Cataract, account of my eye, it's no good, and this here is Pickles, and this is Cousin."

They all looked alike.

"I guess you know what I want," Al said.

"Ride?"

"Yeah, where you going?"

"Chicago."

"Start warming the seat up for me," Al said.

They grinned, and continued eating. Al watched Cataract go to work on a hamburger. He held it between thick, grease-stained fingers that dug into it, much as they might have sunk into a woman. He swallowed a large piece, slobbering a little, and slapping his tongue noisily against the roof of his mouth as he ate. Al watched him, fascinated. Wild thoughts of seizing the hamburger, and fighting the man for it, deviled him. He moved his head, in time to Cataract's jaws, and he felt madly frustrated as Cataract dropped the last bit into his mouth. Cataract lit a cigarette and exhaled noisily, with a little belch of content.

"Hell," Al whispered.

He turned his attention to the other two, and watched them eat each piece down to the very bitter end. He hated them, and felt sick.

"Let's go," shouted Pickles. "Come on, sweet-face."

The car was an old Auburn sedan, with a short humped-up body. Al sat in back with Cataract; Cousin was driving. Cataract took out a pack of Luckies, and passed them around. Al took the pack and fumbled with it, acting as if he were having trouble extracting a cigarette. When he handed it back, he had a bonus of two more cuddled next to his dollar bill.

"Where you from?" Pickles asked.

"Easton," Al said. "It's in Pennsy."

Cataract rolled his tongue around. "Good town," he said, extending his arm, fist closed, twisting it in little circles at the wrist.

"Yeh," Al said. "One of the best. I ain't been there in four, no three years. Been on the road since."

"Hitching?"

"Hell, no," Al exploded with contempt. "It's a sucker's game, hitching. I work the trains; you know, 'Ride the rails in comfort with Pullman.'"

"Yeahr. How're the hobo camps?" Cousin asked.

It was Al's turn to extend his arm.

They all started laughing with wise, knowing, lewd laughs.

"What do you boys do?" Al asked.

They laughed again.

"We're partners in business," Cataract said.

Al looked at them, discarding one thing after another, trying to narrow down the possibilities. He decided they were sucker players of some sort.

"You guys know of any jobs in Chicago?"

"How much you want?"

"About twenty a week. I'm in now. Got thirty-four bucks."

Pickles whistled. "What're you mooching meals for, then?"

"Who's mooching?" Al demanded. "Did I ask you guys for anything besides a ride?"

"Noooo."

"Awright, then don't go around being a wise guy."

Pickles looked out the window, grinning. "Sorry, bud."

"Well, awright then," Al said, acting sore.

Cataract laughed, trying to be friendly. "They're funny boys, you know, just smart. They wished they had your thirty-four, that's all."

It worked, Al thought. He let himself grin. "It's okay," he said.

He looked out the window. They weren't in Chicago yet, but the lights shining from the houses on the side of the road were more frequent, making a steady glare against the wet windows, and he knew that they must be almost at the outskirts by now. Just then, he saw a City Limits and Welcome sign flash past. Cousin turned off the highway, and went along for a way on a dirt road that in time turned onto an oil-stained asphalt street. They passed a few factories, and Al thought of dropping off, but he wondered if it might not pay him to stay with the men a while.

Cataract yawned. "What about a game of pool now, boys?" he asked.

So that's what they are, Al thought.

"Say," he said, "I'd like to play too. I ain't very good, but I like the game." He had played exactly three times in his life.

Pickles assured him. "We're no good either — that is, I'm no good. You and me can play."

244 • NORMAN MAILER

"Yeah," said Al, "it ought to be fun."

Cousin was driving up Milwaukee Avenue now. He turned left, slowing down very carefully as he did so, although there were no cars in sight.

"That Cousin drives like an old woman," Pickles commented. "I could drive faster going backwards."

Cousin jeered at him. "You couldn't drive my aunt's wheelbarrow. I'm the only guy left who hasn't lost his license," he said, speaking to Al. "It's because I take it easy when I drive a car."

Al said he didn't know much about cars, but he guessed maybe Cousin was right.

The car pulled up in front of a dark gray building on the corner of a long row of old Brownstone homes. It was a dark street, and the only evidence that people lived on it was the overflowing garbage cans and ash cans spaced at irregular intervals in front of the houses. The poolroom itself was down in the cellar, underneath a beauty parlor and a secretarial school. On the steps going down, Al could see penciled scribblings on the walls; some hasty calculation of odds, a woman's telephone number with a comment underneath it, a few bits of profanity, and one very well-drawn nude woman.

The foot of the stairs opened right onto the tables, which were strung out in one long narrow line of five. The place was almost dark, only the first table being used, and no lights were on in the back. Pickles stepped over to the counter and started talking to the boss, calling him familiarly, and for some reason annoyingly, by the name Nick. Nick was a short, very broad and sweaty Italian. He and Pickles looked up at Al at the same time, and Pickles motioned to him.

"Nick, this is a pal of mine. I want you to treat him nice if he ever comes in again. Tell thick Nick your name, sweet-face."

"Call me sweet-face," Al said.

"H'lo," Nick said. "Pleased to meet you."

"Where we play?" Al asked. He noticed that Cataract and Cousin had not come down yet.

"Take number four."

"Sweet-face and me on number four," Pickles said. "Got it."

He walked down turning on a few lights. He stopped at the cue rack, and picked one at random. Al followed him, selected one carefully, sight-

ing along it to see if there was any warp, and sprinkling some talc over it. "Should we play a rack for table?" he asked.

"Sure," said Pickles. "You mind if we play straight? I don't know any fancy stuff."

"Me neither."

They tossed a coin, and Al had to break. He shot poorly, hit the wrong ball and scratched. Pickles overshot and splattered balls all over the table. Al sank two, shooting as well as he could, knowing that Pickles would notice any attempts at faking. They both played sloppily, and it took fifteen minutes to clear the table. Al won, eight balls to seven.

"We're pretty close," Pickles said. "What about playing for a couple of bucks this next table?"

He watched Cataract and Cousin who had just come in and were starting to play.

Al could feel the sweat starting up in the small of his back and on his thighs. I can still get out of it, he thought. At least I'll have my buck. The thought of another five dollars, however, was too strong for him. He tried to think of what would happen to him if he didn't get away with it, but he kept remembering how it felt to have money in his hands. He heard himself speaking, feeling that it was not he but someone right in back, or on top of him.

"Make it a buck," he said.

Pickles broke, again shooting too hard. Al watched him flub balls all over the table, slightly overdoing it this time. They finished the rack, Al getting a run of three at the end, to win, ten to five. Pickles handed him a dollar, and placed another on the side of the table. Al covered it with the one he had won. I wonder when he starts winning, Al thought. If I can only quit then. They played for a dollar twice more, Al winning both times. A first drop of perspiration drew together, and raced down his back. He saw Cataract watching them play, juggling two balls in his hand. They played for three dollars, Al winning, after being behind, five to two.

He straightened up, making an almost visible effort to relax.

"That makes six bucks," he said.

"Sure," said Pickles. "Let's make it five this time. I want to win my dough back."

This time Pickles won. Al handed him five dollars, separating the bills with difficulty and handing them over painfully.

"Another one for five," Pickles said.

Al looked around him desperately, wondering if he could get out. "Five," he croaked. Cataract was still juggling balls.

It was the longest game he ever played. After every shot he stopped to wipe his hands. In the middle, he realized that this game was going to be given to him. He couldn't relax, however, because he knew the showdown would merely be delayed for another game or so.

He won, as he knew he would, but immediately the pressure was on again. They played once more for five, and he won. After it was over, he didn't trust himself to stand, and he leaned against the cue rack, trying to draw satisfaction from the money in his pocket. He dreamed of getting out, and having it all to do with as he pleased, until he saw Pickles and Cataract looking at each other. Cataract threw a ball up, and closed his fingers too soon, missing it. It came down with a loud shattering crack that made Nick look up from his counter. That's the signal, Al thought.

They were the only ones in the place now.

Pickles stroked his cue, grinning. "Your luck's been too good, sweetface. I think this is going to be my game. I got twenty bucks left. I'm laying it down."

"No," said Al. "I don't want to."

"Listen, I been losing dough. You're playing."

They all looked at him menacingly.

"I want to quit," Al said.

"I wouldn't try it," Cousin said.

Al looked about him, trapped, thoughts of fighting them mixing with mad ideas of flight.

Cataract stepped toward him, holding a cue in his hand.

"All right," Al said, "I'll play."

Pickles broke, making a very beautiful "safe," leaving Al helpless. He bent over his stick to shoot. The balls wavered in front of him, and he could see the tip of the cue shaking up and down. He wiped his face and looked around to loosen his muscles. When he tried again, it was useless. He laid his cue on the table and walked to the back.

"Where you going?" asked Pickles.

"To the can. Want to come along?" He forced a laugh from the very bottom of his throat.

He passed through a small littered room, where old soda boxes were stored. The bathroom was small and filthy; the ceiling higher than the distance from wall to wall. Once inside he bolted the door and sank down on the floor, whimpering softly.

After a while he quieted and looked around. The only other possible exit was a window, high up on the wall facing the door. He looked at it, not realizing its significance, until a chance sound from outside made him realize where he was and what was happening to him. He got up and looked at the wall, examining its surface for some possible boost. He saw there was none, crouched down, and jumped. His hands just grasped the edge, clung for a fraction of a second, and then scraped off. He knelt again, as close to the wall as he could possibly get, flexed himself, and leaped up. This time his palms grasped the hold. He pressed his fingertips against the stone surface and chinned up enough to work his elbows over. He rested a moment, and then squeezed his stomach in and hung there on the ledge against the window, his legs dangling behind. He inched the window open noiselessly and, forgetting he was in the cellar, looked down into blackness. For a moment he was panic-stricken, until he remembered he was in the cellar, and had to look up. He shifted his position, and raised his head. There was a grating at right angles to the window, fixed above a dump heap, much like the one beneath a subway grille. It was very dark outside, but he could make out that it opened into an alley. Overjoyed, he took his money out, almost falling off in the act, kissed it, put it back, and tried to open the grating. He placed his hands under it and pushed up as hard as he could in his cramped position. The grille didn't move. He stuck one foot through the window and straddled the ledge, one foot in, one foot out. Bracing himself, he pushed calmly against the grating, trying to dislodge it from the grime imbedded in it. Finding his effort useless, he pushed harder and harder until his arms were almost pushed into his chest and his back and crotch felt as if they would crack. Breathing heavily, he stopped and stared up past the grating. Suddenly, with a cry of desperation, he flung himself up, beating against it with his hands and arms, until the blood ran down them. Half crazy, he gripped the bars and shook, with impassioned groans. His fingers slipped against a little obstruction on one of

the end bars. His hand felt it, caressed it, hoping to find some lever point, and discovered it to be a rivet between the foundation and the grille. He sat there, huge sobs torn from him, his eyes gazing hungrily at the sky above. After a bit, he withdrew his leg, wormed his body in again, closed the window, and dropped heavily to the floor, lying in a heap, as he had fallen, his face to the wall. I'll just wait till they come for me, he thought. He could hear someone coming toward the door. Pickles knocked. "Hey, kid," he yelled from the other side of the partition, "hurry up."

Al stood up, a mad flare of hope running through him as he thought of the money he still had. He held his hand to his throat, and struggled to control his voice. "Be right out," he said, managing to hold it through to the end. He heard Pickles walk away, and felt a little stronger. He started to wash himself, to get the blood off. His hands were still bleeding dully, the blood oozing out thickly and sluggishly, but he was able to stop the flow somewhat. He backed away, glanced out the window once more, and took his money out. He held it in his hands, and let the bills slip through his fingers. Gathering them up, he kissed them feverishly, rubbing the paper against his face and arms. He folded them tenderly, let down his pants and slipped the cash into a little secret pocket, just under the crotch. He flattened out the bump it made, and unlocked the door to go out. His heart was still pounding, but he felt calmer, and more determined.

They were waiting for him impatiently, smoking quickly and nervously.

Al took out one of Cataract's cigarettes and asked for a match. He lit it, sucking deeply and gratefully from it. They glared at him, their nerves almost as tight as his.

"Come on," said Pickles, "it's your turn to shoot."

Al picked up his cue, gripping it hard to make his hand bleed faster. He bent over, made a pretense of sighting, and then laid his cue down, exposing the place where his hand had stained it.

"What's the matter?" Cousin snapped.

"I can't hold a cue," Al said. "I cut my hand in there."

"What do you mean you can't play?" Pickles shouted. "My money's up. You got to play."

"You can't force me. I'm not going to play. It's my money, it's mine

see, and you can't make me. You guys can't pull this on me; you're just trying to work a sucker game."

It was the wrong thing to say. Cataract caught him by the shirt and shook him. "Grab ahold of that stick," he said.

Al wrenched loose. "Go to hell," he said. "I'm quitting."

He picked up his hat, and started walking down past the tables to go out. He had to pass three tables and the counter to get to the stairs. He walked slowly, hoping to bluff his way out. He knew he had no chance if he ran. He could feel the sweat starting up much faster this time. His shoulders were twitching, and he was very conscious of the effort of forming each step, expecting something to hit him at every second. His face was wet, and he fought down an agonizing desire to turn and look at them. Behind him, they were silent. He could see Nick at the entrance, watching him walk toward him, his face expressionless. Fascinated, he hung on to Nick's eyes, pleading silently with him. A slight smile grew on Nick's face. It broke into a high unnatural laugh, squeaking off abruptly. Terrified, Al threw a quick glance back, and promptly threw himself on his face. A cue whizzed by, shattering on the far wall with a terrific smash. Before he could get up, they were on him. Cataract turned him on his back, and knelt over him. He brought the heel of his hand down hard on Al's face, knocking his head on the floor. He saw them swirl around him, the pool tables mixed in somewhere, and he shook his head furiously, to keep from going out. Cataract hit him again.

Al struck out with his foot, and hit him in the shin.

"You dirty little bastard," Cataract said. "I'll teach you."

He slammed his knee down into Al's stomach. Al choked and writhed, the fight out of him for a moment. They turned him over, and stripped his pockets, looking for his money. They shook him. "Where is it, sweet-face?" Pickles asked.

Al choked for breath.

"I lost it," he said mockingly.

"It's in his pants somewhere," Cousin said. "These rats always got a secret pocket." They tried to open his pants. He fought crazily, kicking, biting, screaming, using his elbows and knees.

"Come on," Cataract commanded, "get it off him."

Al yelled as loud as he could. Nick came over. "Get him out," he said. "The cops'll be dropping in soon. I don't want trouble."

"What'll we do with him?"

"Take him out on the road where no one will hear you. After that, it's your imagination." He squealed with laughter again.

They picked him up and forced him out. He went with them peacefully, too dazed to care. They shoved him in the car, and Cousin turned it around. Al was in front, Cataract in the back seat, holding his wrist so he couldn't break loose before they started.

Al sat there silently, his head clearing, remembering how slowly Cousin drove. He looked out, watching the ground shoot by, and thought of jumping out. Hopelessly, he looked at the speedometer. They were going around a turn, and Cousin had slowed down to less than twenty miles an hour. He had jumped off freight trains going faster than that, but there had been no door in the way, and no one had been holding him. Discouraged, he gave up the idea.

Cousin taunted him. "See that white sign, sweet-face? We turn left there, just around it, and after that it won't be long."

Anger and rebellion surged through him. They were taking away something that he had earned dangerously, and they were going to beat him up, because they had not been as smart as he. It was not fair. He wanted the money more than they did. In fury, he decided to jump at the turn. The sign was about a hundred yards away; it would be his last chance. He figured it would take seven seconds to reach it.

He turned around to face Cataract, his left elbow resting loosely against the door handle. He had turned the way his wrist was twisted, holding it steadyingly, so that Cataract would not realize the pressure was slackened. One, he counted to himself. "Look," he begged Cataract, "let me off. I ain't got the money, let me off." Maybe thirty yards gone by. Cataract was talking. "Oh, you're a funny boy, sweet-face." Another twenty. "Yeah, sure I'm funny, I'm a scream," he said. "Oh, I'm so funny." The sign, where was it? We should have reached it. Oh, please God, show me the sign, you got to, it's my money, not theirs, oh please. "Goddam you, please," he shouted. "What?" Cataract yelled. Cousin slowed down. The sign slipped by. They started to turn. Al spat full in Cataract's face, and lashed out with his wrist against the thumb. His elbow kicked the door open, and he yanked his hand loose, whirled about, and leaped out, the door just missing him in its swing back.

His feet were pumping wildly as he hit the ground. He staggered in a broken run for a few steps, before his knees crumpled under him, and he went sprawling in the dust. His face went grinding into it, the dirt mashing up into his cheeks and hands. He lay there stunned for a very long second, and then he pushed hard with his hands against the ground, forcing himself up. The car had continued around the turn, and in the confusion had gone at least a hundred feet before it stopped. Al threw a stone at the men scrambling out, and plunged off into a field. It had stopped raining, but the sky was black, and he knew they would never catch him. He heard them in the distance, yelling to each other, and he kept running, his legs dead, his head lolling sideways, his breath coming in long ripping bursts. He stumbled over a weed and fell, his body spreading out on soft wet grass. Exhausted he lay there, his ear close to the ground, but no longer hearing them, he sat up, plucking weakly at bits of grass, saying over and over again, "Oh, those suckers, those big, dumb suckers. Oh, those dopes, those suckers. . . ."

At two-thirty, Al Groot, his stomach full, swung off a streetcar near Madison Street, and went into a flophouse. He gave the night man a new dollar bill, and tied the eighty-five cents change in a rag that he fastened to his wrist. He stood over his bed, and lit some matches, moving them slowly over the surface of the mattress. A few bedbugs started out of their burrows, and crept across the bed. He picked them up, and squashed them methodically. The last one he held in his hand, watching it squirm. He felt uneasy for a moment, and impulsively let it escape, whirling his hand in a circle to throw it away from the bed. He stretched himself out, and looked off in the distance for a while, thinking of women, and hamburgers, and billiard balls, and ketchup bottles, and shoes and, most of all, the thrill of breaking a five-dollar bill. Lighting the last of Cataract's cigarettes, he thought of how different things had been, when he had first planned them. He smoked openly, not caring if someone should see him, for it was his last. Al smoked happily, tremendously excited, letting each little ache and pain well into the bed. When the cigarette was finished he tried to fall asleep. He felt wide awake, though, and after some time he propped himself on an elbow, and thought of what he would do the next day. First he would buy a pack of cigarettes, and then he would have a breakfast, and then a clean woman;

he would pay a buck if he had to, and then a dinner and another woman. He stopped suddenly, unable to continue, so great was his ecstasy. He lay over his pillow and addressed it.

"By God," Al Groot said, about to say something he never uttered before. "By God, this is the happiest moment of my life."

Benefit Performance

Winner of both a Pulitzer Prize (for his novel *The Fixer*) and the National Book Award (for *The Magic Barrel*, his first collection of short stories), Bernard Malamud began writing as a boy in the back room of his family's grocery store in Brooklyn. Born in 1914, he graduated from the City College of New York and taught school in the New York City public schools from 1940 to 1949. The first story he remembers writing was about Roger Williams and a bear. In the introduction to his *Collected Stories,* published in 1983, Malamud wrote, "My early stories appeared in the nineteen-forties in non-commercial magazines, meaning I didn't get paid for them but was happy to have them published." His first story appeared in *Threshold* in February 1943. As in most of Malamud's work, the author's regard for Jewish tradition and history figure prominently in "Benefit Performance."

MAURICE ROSENFELD WAS conscious of himself as he took the key from his pocket and inserted it into the door of his small apartment. The Jewish actor saw his graying hair, the thick black eyebrows, the hunch of disappointment in his shoulders and the sardonic grimness of his face, accentuated by the twisted line of the lips. Rosenfeld turned the key in the lock, aware that he was playing his rôle well. Tragedy in the twisting of a key, he thought.

"Who's there?" said a voice from inside the apartment.

Surprised, Rosenfeld pushed open the door and saw that it was his daughter who had called out. Sophie was lying in her bed which became the couch when it was folded together, and her bedroom became the

living room. There was one other room, a small one, where Rosenfeld and his wife slept, and an alcove for the kitchen. When her father was working and came home late after the performance, Sophie would set up three screens around her bed so that she would not be awakened by the light which he put on while heating up some milk for himself before going to bed. The screens served another purpose. Whenever Sophie and her father quarreled, she set them up and let him rant outside. Deprived of her presence, he became silent and sulked. She sat on her sofa, reading a magazine by the light of her own lamp, and blessing the screens for giving her privacy and preserving her dignity.

The screens were stacked up in the corner, and Rosenfeld was surprised to see his daughter in bed.

"What's the matter?" he said.

"I'm not well," she answered.

"Where's momma?"

"She went to work."

"Today she's working?"

"She had half a day off. She's working from five to ten."

Rosenfeld looked around. The table in the alcove was not set, and it was nearly supper time.

"She left me to eat, something?"

"No, she thought you were going to eat with Markowitz. Is there anything doing?"

"No," he said bitterly, "nothing is doing. The Jewish theayter is deep in hell. Since the war, the Jews stay home. Everybody else goes out for a good time to forget their troubles, but Jews stay home and worry. Second Avenue is like a tomb."

"What did Markowitz want to see you for?" Sophie asked.

"A benefit, something. I should act in a benefit for Isaac Levin."

"Don't worry," she said, "you had a good season last year."

"I'm too young to live on memories," he said.

Sophie had no answer to that.

"If you want me to make you something, I'll get up," she said.

He walked into the kitchen and looked into the pots on the gas range.

"No, I'll make for myself. Here is some potatoes and carrots left over. I'll warm them up."

"Warm up the hamburger in the oven. Momma made one for me, but I couldn't eat it."

Rosenfeld pulled down the door of the broiler and glanced distastefully at the hamburger on the wire grill.

"No, it burns me my stomach when I eat chopmeat," he said, closing the broiler door.

"How is your stomach?" she asked.

He placed his hand underneath his heart. "Today I got gas." He was moved by her solicitousness.

"How are you feeling?" he asked her.

"Like always. The first day is bad."

"It will go away."

"Yes, I know," she said.

HE lit the flame under the vegetables and began to stir the mashed potatoes. They were lumpy. The remnants of his appetite disappeared. Sophie saw the look on his face and said, "Put some butter in the potatoes." For a moment Rosenfeld did not move, but when Sophie repeated her suggestion, he opened the ice box.

"What butter?" he said, looking among the bottles and the fruit. "Here is no butter."

Sophie reached for her housecoat, drew it on over her head and pulled up the zipper. Then she stepped into her slippers.

"I'll put some milk in," she said.

Without wanting to, he was beginning to grow angry.

"Who wants you to? Stay in bed. I'll take care myself of the — the supper," he ended sarcastically.

"Poppa," she said, "don't be stubborn. I've got to get up anyway."

"For me you don't have to get up."

"I said I have to get up anyway."

"What's the matter?"

"Someone is coming."

He turned towards her. "Who's coming?"

"Pa, let's not start that."

"Who's coming?"

"I don't want to fight. I'm sick today."

"Who's coming, answer me."

"Ephraim."

"The plum-ber?" He was sarcastic.

"Please, pa, don't fight."

"*I* should fight with a plum-ber?"

"You always insult him."

"*I* insult a plum-ber? He insults *me* to come here."

"He's not coming to see you. He's coming to see me."

"He insults *you* to come here. What does a plum-ber, who didn't even finish high school, want with you? You don't need a plum-ber."

"I don't care what I need, poppa, I'm twenty-eight years old," she said.

"But a plum-ber!"

"He's a good boy. I've known him for twelve years, since we were in high school. He's honest and he makes a nice steady living."

"All right," Rosenfeld said angrily. "So *I* don't make a steady living. So go on, spill some more salt on my bleeding wounds."

"Poppa, don't act, please. I only said *he* made a steady living. I didn't say anything about you."

"Who's acting?" he shouted, banging the ice box door shut and turning quickly. "Even if I didn't support you and your mother steady, at least I showed you the world and brought you in company with the greatest Jewish actors of our times. Adler, Schwartz, Ben-Ami, Goldenburg, all of them have been in my house. You heard the best conversation about life, about books and music and all kinds art. You toured with me everywhere. You were in South America. You were in England. You were in Chicago, Boston, Detroit. You got a father whose Shylock in Yiddish even the American critics came to see and raved about it. *This* is living. *This* is life. Not with a plum-ber. So who is he going to bring into your house, some more plum-bers, they should sit in the kitchen and talk about pipes and how to fix a leak in the toilet? This is living? This is conversation? When he comes here, does he open his mouth? The only thing he says is yes and no, yes and no — like a machine. This is not for you."

Sophie had listened to her father in silence.

"Poppa, that's not fair," she said quietly, "you make him afraid to talk to you."

The answer seemed to satisfy him.

"Don't be so much in the hurry," he said more calmly. "You can get better."

"Please drop the subject."

THE bell rang. Sophie pressed the buzzer.

"Poppa, for God sakes, please be nice to him."

He said nothing but turned to his cooking, and she went into the bathroom.

Ephraim knocked on the door.

"Come in!"

The door opened and he walked in. He was tall, very well built and neatly dressed. His hair was carefully slicked back, but his hands were beefy and red from constant washing in hot water which did not remove the calluses on his palms or the grease pockets underneath his nails. He was embarrassed to find only Sophie's father in.

"Is Sophie here?" he asked.

"Good evening," said Rosenfeld sarcastically.

Ephraim blushed.

"Good evening," he said. "Is Sophie here?"

"She will be here in a minute."

"Thank you very much." He remained standing.

Rosenfeld poured some milk into the potatoes and stirred them with a fork.

"So you working now in the project houses?" he asked.

Ephraim was surprised to be addressed so politely.

"No," he said. "We're working in the Brooklyn Navy Yard on the new ships."

"Hmm, must be a lot of toilets on the battleships?" Rosenfeld asked.

Ephraim did not answer him. Sophie came out of the bathroom with her hair neatly combed and a small blue ribbon in it to match the blue in her housecoat.

"Hello, Eph," she said. He nodded.

"Sit down," she said, placing a chair near her bed. "I'll get back into bed." She lifted her feet out of the slippers, fixed the pillow so she could sit up and covered herself with her blanket. Ephraim was facing her. Over his shoulder she could see her father scooping out the

vegetables onto a plate. Then he sat down at the table and began to mash them.

"What's new, Eph?" she asked.

He sat with his elbows resting on his knees, the fingers of both hands interlocked.

"Nothing new," he said.

"Did you work today?"

"Only half a day. I got three weeks overtime."

"What else is new?"

He shrugged his shoulders.

"Did you hear about Edith and Mortie?" she asked.

"No," he said. Rosenfeld lowered his fork.

"They got married Sunday."

"That's good," he said.

"Oh, another thing, I bought tickets for the Russian War Relief at Madison Square Garden. Can you go Friday night?"

"Yes," he said. Rosenfeld banged his fork down on his plate. Ephraim did not turn and Sophie did not look up. They were silent for a moment, and then Sophie began again.

"Oh, I forgot," she said, "I wrote to Washington for those Civil Service requirements for you. Did your mother tell you?"

"Yes," he said.

Rosenfeld banged his fist on the table. "Yes and no, yes and no," he shouted. "Don't you know no other words?"

Ephraim did not turn around.

"Poppa, *please,*" begged Sophie.

"Yes and no," shouted her father, "yes and no. Is this the way to talk to an educated girl?"

Ephraim turned around and said with dignity, "I'm not talking to you. I'm talking to your daughter."

"You not *talking* to her. You *insulting* her with yes and no. This is not talk."

"I'm not an actor," said Ephraim, "I work with my hands."

"Don't open your mouth to insult me."

Ephraim's jaw was trembling.

"You insulted me first."

"Please, please," cried Sophie. "Poppa, if you don't stop, I'm going to put up the screens."

"So put up the screens to hide the plum-ber," her father taunted.

"At least a plumber can support a wife and don't have to send her out to work for him," cried Ephraim, his voice full of emotion.

"Oh, Ephraim, don't," moaned Sophie.

For a moment Rosenfeld was stunned. Then his face reddened and he began to stutter, "You nothing, you. You nothing," he cried. His lips moved noiselessly as he tried to find words to say. Suddenly he caught himself and paused. He rose slowly. Rosenfeld crossed his arms over his breast, then raised them ceilingward and began to speak deliberately in fluent Yiddish.

"Hear me earnestly, great and good God. Hear the story of the afflictions of a second Job. Hear how the years have poured misery upon me, so that in my age, when most men are gathering their harvest of sweet flowers, I cull nothing but weeds.

"I have a daughter, Oh God, upon whom I have lavished my deepest affection, whom I have given every opportunity for growth and education, who has become so mad in her desire for carnal satisfaction that she is ready to bestow herself upon a man unworthy to touch the hem of her garment, to a common, ordinary, wordless plum-ber, who has neither ideals nor —."

"Poppa," screamed Sophie, "Poppa, stop it!"

Rosenfeld stopped and a look of unutterable woe appeared on his face. He lowered his arms and turned his head towards Ephraim, his nostrils raised in scorn.

"Plum-ber," he said bitterly.

Ephraim looked at him with hatred. He tried to move, but couldn't.

"You cheap actor," he cried suddenly, with venomous fury. "You can go straight to hell!" He strode over to the door, tore it open and banged it so furiously that the room seemed to shake.

By degrees Rosenfeld lowered his head. His shoulders hunched in disappointment, and he saw himself, with his graying hair, a tragic figure. Again he raised his head slowly and looked in Sophie's direction. She was already setting up the screens. Rosenfeld moved toward the table in the alcove, and glanced down at the vegetables in the plate. They

bored him. He went over to the gas range, carefully lit the flame under the broiler and pulled down the door to see whether the hamburger was cooking. It was. He closed the door, lowered the flame a bit and said quietly,

"Tonight I will eat chopmeat."

HENRY MILLER

Mademoiselle Claude

With the encouragement of his eccentric second wife, June, Henry Miller left his longtime job at Western Union in New York City in September 1924, "never to look for a job again but to live or die as a writer." He and some friends printed up broadsides with prose poems by Miller and sold them door to door; the men didn't have much luck selling them, but June did, often not returning home until 2:00 A.M. In 1930 June convinced Henry to move to Paris to write, ostensibly for his own good; in fact, she had taken up with another man. "Mademoiselle Claude" was based on a real Mlle. Claude, a well-known Left Bank prostitute with whom Miller was obsessed. When he finally engaged her services, though, he found her too refined, and they ended up only discussing books. When the story appeared in the Fall 1931 issue of the *New Review,* it received much notice, attracting the attention of editor Pat Covici at Covici-Friede in New York, who invited Miller to submit work to him. Miller sent his completed novel *Crazy Cock,* which was rejected. Other American editors reportedly found the story "whorehouse stuff" or "plain pornography."

PREVIOUSLY, WHEN I began to write this tale, I set out by saying that Mlle. Claude was a whore. She is a whore, of course, and I'm not trying to deny it, but what I say now is — if Mlle. Claude is a whore then what name shall I find for the other women I know? Somehow the word whore isn't big enough. Mlle. Claude is more than a whore. I don't know what to call her. Maybe just Mlle. Claude. *Soit.*

There was the aunt who waited up for her every night. Frankly, I couldn't swallow that story. Aunt hell! More likely it was her *maquereau.*

But then that was nobody's business but her own. . . . Nevertheless, it used to gall me — that pimp waiting up for her, getting ready perhaps to clout her if she didn't come across. And no matter how loving she was (I mean that Claude really knew how to love) there was always in the back of my head the image of that blood-sucking, low-browed bastard who was getting all the gravy. No use kidding yourself about a whore — even when they're most generous and yielding, even if you've slipped them a thousand francs (who would, of course?) — there's always a guy waiting somewhere and what you've had is only a taste. He gets the gravy, be sure of that!

But then, all this, as I afterwards discovered, was just so much wasted emotion. There was no *maquereau* — not in Claude's case. I'm the first *maquereau* Claude has ever had. And I don't call myself a *maquereau* either. Pimp's the word. I'm her pimp now. O.K.

I remember distinctly the first time I brought her to my room, — what an ass I made of myself. Where women are concerned I always make an ass of myself. The trouble is I worship them and women don't want to be worshiped. They want . . . well, anyway, about that first night, believe it or not, I behaved just as if I had never slept with a woman before. I don't understand to this day why it should have been so. But that's how it was.

Before she even attempted to remove her things, I remember, she stood beside the bed looking up at me, waiting for me to do something, I suppose. I was trembling. I had been trembling ever since we left the café. I gave her a peck — on the lips, I think. I don't know — maybe I kissed her brow — I'm just the guy to do that sort of thing . . . with a woman I don't know. Somehow I had the feeling that she was doing me a tremendous favor. Even a whore can make a guy feel that way sometimes. But then, Claude isn't just a whore, as I said.

Before she had even removed her hat she went to the window, closed it, and drew the curtains to. Then she gave me a sort of sidelong look, smiled, and murmured something about getting undressed. While she fooled around with the bidet I went through the business of stripping down. As a matter of fact, I was nervous. I thought perhaps she'd be embarrassed if I watched her, so I fiddled around with the papers on my table, made a few meaningless notes, and threw the cover over the type-

writer. When I turned she was standing in her chemise, near the sink, wiping her legs.

"Hurry! Get in bed!" she said. "Warm it up!" And with this she gave herself a few extra dabs.

Everything was so damned natural that I began to lose my uneasiness, my nervousness. I saw that her stockings were rolled down carefully, and from her waist there dangled some sort of harness which she flung presently over the back of the chair.

The room was chilly all right. We snuggled up and lay silently for a while, a long while, warming each other. I had one arm around her neck and with the other I held her close. She kept staring into my eyes with that same expectant look that I had observed when we first entered the room. I began to tremble again. My French was fading away.

I don't remember now whether I told her then and there that I loved her. Probably I did. Anyway, if I did, she probably forgot it immediately. As she was leaving I handed her a copy of *Aphrodite,* which she said she'd never read, and a pair of silk stockings that I had bought for some one else. I could see she liked the stockings.

When I saw her again I had changed my hotel. She looked about in her quick, eager way and saw at a glance that things weren't going so well. She asked very naïvely if I was getting enough to eat.

"You mustn't remain here long," she said. "It's very sad here." Maybe she didn't say sad, but that's what she meant, I'm sure.

It was sad all right. The furniture was falling apart, the window-panes were broken, the carpet was torn and dirty, and there was no running water. The light too was dim, a dim, yellow light that gave the bedspread a gray, mildewed look.

That night, for some reason or other, she pretended to be jealous. "There is somebody else whom you love," she said.

"No, there's nobody else," I answered.

"Kiss me, then," she said, and she clung to me affectionately, her body warm and tingling. I seemed to be swimming in the warmth of her flesh . . . not swimming either, but drowning, drowning in bliss.

Afterwards we talked about Pierre Loti, and about Stamboul. She said she'd like to go to Stamboul some day. I said I'd like to go too. And then suddenly she said — I think this was it — "you're a man with a soul." I

didn't try to deny it — I was too happy, I guess. When a whore tells you you've got a soul it means more somehow. Whores don't usually talk about souls.

Then another strange thing happened. She refused to take any money.

"You mustn't think about money," she said. "We are comrades now. And you are very poor. . . ."

She wouldn't let me get out of bed to see her to the landing. She spilled a few cigarettes out of her bag and laid them on the table beside the bed; she put one in my mouth and lit it for me with the little bronze lighter that some one had given her as a gift. She leaned over to kiss me good-night.

I held her arm. "Claude," I said, "*vous êtes presque un ange.*"

"*Ah non!*" she replied, quickly, and there was almost a look of pain in her eyes, or terror.

That "*presque*" was really the undoing of Claude, I do believe. I sensed it almost immediately. And then the letter which I handed her soon after — the best letter I ever wrote in my life, though the French was execrable. We read it together, in the café where we usually met. As I say, the French was atrocious, except for a paragraph or two which I lifted from Paul Valéry. She paused a moment or two when she came to these passages. "Very well expressed!" she exclaimed. "Very well, in-deed!" And then she looked at me rather quizzically and passed on. Oh, it wasn't Valéry that got her. Not at all. I could have done without him. No, it was the angel stuff that got her. I had pulled it again — and this time I embroidered it, as subtly and suasively as I knew how. By the time we had reached the end, though, I was feeling pretty uncomfortable. It was pretty cheap, taking advantage of her like that. I don't mean to say that it wasn't sincere, what I wrote, but after that first spontaneous ges-ture — I don't know, it was just literature. And then, too, it seemed shabbier than ever when, a little later, sitting on the bed together, she insisted on reading it over again, this time calling my attention to the grammatical errors. I became a little impatient with her and she was offended. But she was very happy just the same. She said she'd always keep the letter.

About dawn she slipped out. The aunt again. I was getting reconciled to the aunt business. Besides, if it wasn't an aunt I'd soon know now.

Claude wasn't very good at dissembling — and then that angel stuff . . . that sank in deep.

I lay awake thinking about her. She certainly had been swell to me. The *maquereau*. I thought about him, too, but not for long, I wasn't worrying about him any more. Claude — I thought only about her and how I could make her happy. Spain . . . Capri . . . Stamboul . . . I could see her moving languidly in the sunshine, throwing crumbs to the pigeons or watching them bathe, or else lying back in a hammock with a book in her hands, a book that I would recommend to her. Poor kid, she probably had never been further than Versailles in her life. I could see the expression on her face as we boarded the train, and later, standing beside a fountain somewhere. . . . Madrid or Seville. I could feel her marching beside me, close, always close, because she wouldn't know what to do with herself alone and even if it was dumb I liked the idea. Better a damned sight than having some god-damned flapper with you, some lightheaded little bastard who's always figuring out a way of ditching you even when she's lying with you. No, I could feel sure of Claude. Later it might get tiresome — later . . . later. I was glad I had picked a whore. *A faithful whore!* Jesus, I know people who'd laugh like hell if I ever said that.

I was planning it all out in detail: the places we'd stop at, the clothes she'd wear, what we'd talk about . . . everything . . . everything. She was Catholic, I supposed, but that didn't matter a damn to me. In fact, I rather liked it. It was lots better going to church to hear mass than to study architecture and all that crap. If she wanted, I'd become a Catholic too . . . what the hell! I'd do anything she asked me to — if it gave her a kick. I began to wonder if she had a kid somewhere, as most of them have. Imagine, Claude's kid! Why I'd love that kid more than if it were my own. Yes, she must have a kid, Claude — I'm going to see about it. There'd be times, I knew, when we'd have a big room with a balcony, a room looking out on a river, and flowers on the windowsill and birds singing. (I could see myself coming back with a bird-cage on my arm. O.K. So long as it made her happy!) But the river — there must be rivers once in a while. I'm nuts about rivers. Once, in Rotterdam, I remember —. The idea, though, of waking up in the morning, the sun streaming in the windows and a good, faithful whore beside you who loves you, who loves the guts out of you, the birds singing and the table all

spread, and while she's washing up and combing her hair all the men she's been with and now you, just you, and barges going by, masts and hulls, the whole damned current of life flowing through you, through her, through all the guys before you and maybe after, the flowers and the birds and the sun streaming in and the fragrance of it choking you, annihilating you. O Christ! Give me a whore always, all the time!

I've asked Claude to live with me and she's refused. This is a blow. I know it's not because I'm poor — Claude knows all about my finances, about the book I'm writing, etc. No, there must be some other, deeper reason. But she won't come out with it.

And then there's another thing — I've begun to act like a saint. I take long walks alone, and what I'm writing now has nothing to do with my book. It seems as if I were alone in the universe, that my life is complete and separate, like a statue's. I have even forgotten the name of my creator. And I feel as if all my actions are inspired, as if I were meant to do nothing but good in this world. I ask for nobody's approval.

I refuse to take any charity from Claude any more. I keep track of everything I owe her. She looks sad these days, Claude. Sometimes, when I pass her on the *terrasse*, I could swear that there are tears in her eyes. She's in love with me now, I know it. She loves me desperately. For hours and hours she sits there on the *terrasse*. I go with her sometimes because I can't bear to see her miserable, to see her waiting, waiting, waiting. . . . I have even spoken to some of my friends about her, tipped them off, as it were. Yes, anything is better than to see Claude sitting there waiting, waiting. What does she think about when she sits there all by herself?

I wonder what she would say if I walked up to her one day and slipped her a thousand franc note. Just walk up to her, when she's got that melancholy look in her eyes, and say: "*Voici quelque chose que j'ai oublié l'autre jour.*" Sometimes, when we lie together and there come those long brimming silences, she says to me: "*Que pensez-vous maintenant?*" And I always answer "*Rien!*" But what I'm really thinking to myself is — "*Voici quelque chose que. . . .*" This is the beautiful part of *l'amour à credit.*

When she takes leave of me the bells ring out wildly. She makes everything so right inside me. I lie back on the pillow and luxuriously enjoy the weak cigarette which she has left me. I don't have to stir for a thing.

If I had a plate in my mouth I'm sure she wouldn't forget to put it in the tumbler on the table beside my bed, together with the matches and the alarm clock and all the other junk. My trousers are carefully folded and my hat and coat are hanging on a peg near the door. Everything in its place. Marvelous! When you get a whore you get a jewel. . . .

And the best of it is, the fine feeling endures. A mystic feeling it is, and to become mystic is to feel the unity of life. I don't care particularly any more whether I am a saint or not. A saint struggles too much. There is no struggle in me any longer. I have become a mystic. I impart good, peace, serenity. I am getting more and more customers for Claude and she no longer has that sad look in her eyes when I pass her. We eat together most every day. She insists on taking me to expensive places, and I no longer demur. I enjoy every phase of life — the expensive places as well as the inexpensive places. If it makes Claude happy —.

Pourtant je pense à quelque chose. A little thing, to be sure, but lately it has grown more and more important in my mind. The first time I said nothing about it. An unwonted touch of delicacy, I thought to myself. Charming, in fact. The second time — was it delicacy, or just carelessness? However, *rien à dire.* Between the second and third times I was unfaithful, so to speak. Yes, I was up on the Grands Boulevards one night, a little tight. After running the gauntlet all the way from the Place de la République to *Le Matin,* a big, scabby buzzard whom I ordinarily wouldn't have pissed on grabbed me off. A droll affair. Visitors knocking at our door every few minutes. Poor little ex-Folies girls who begged the kind monsieur to give them a little tip — thirty francs or so. For what, pray? *Pour rien . . . pour le plaisir.* A very strange, and very funny night. A day or so later irritation. Worries. Hurried trip to the American Hospital. Visions of Ehrlich and his black cigars. Nothing wrong, however. Just worry.

When I broach the subject to Claude she looks at me in astonishment. "I know you have every confidence in me, Claude, but . . ." Claude refuses to waste any time on such a subject. A man who would consciously, deliberately give a woman a disease is a criminal. That's how Claude looks upon it. "*C'est vrai, n'est-ce pas?*" she asks. It's *vrai* all right. However. . . . But the subject is closed. Any man who would do that is a criminal.

Every morning now, when I take my paraffin oil — I always take it

with an orange — I get to thinking about these criminals who give women diseases. The paraffin oil makes the spoon very sticky. It is necessary to wash it well. I wash the knife and the spoon very carefully. I do everything carefully — it is my nature. After I have washed my face I look at the towel. The patron never gives out more than three towels a week; by Tuesday they are all soiled. I dry the knife and the spoon with a towel; for my face I use the bedspread. I don't rub my face — I pat it gently with the edge of the bedspread, near the feet.

The Rue Hippolyte Mandron looks vile to me. I detest all the dirty, narrow, crooked streets with romantic names hereabouts. Paris looks to me like a big, ugly chancre. The streets are gangrened. Everybody has it — if it isn't clap it's syphilis. All Europe is diseased, and it's France who's made it diseased. This is what comes of admiring Voltaire and Rabelais! I should have gone to Moscow, as I intended. Even if there are no Sundays in Russia, what difference does it make? Sunday is like any other day now, only the streets are more crowded, more victims walking about contaminating one another.

Mind you, it's not Claude I'm raving against. Claude is a jewel, *un ange,* and no *presque* about it. There's the bird-cage hanging outside the window, and flowers too — though it ain't Madrid or Seville, no fountains, no pigeons. No, it's the clinic every day. She goes in one door and I in the other. No more expensive restaurants. Go to the movies every night and try to stop squirming. Can't bear the sight of the Dôme or the Coupole any more. These bastards sitting around on the *terrasse,* looking so clean and healthy with their coats of tan, their starched shirts and their eau-de-cologne. It wasn't entirely Claude's fault. I tried to warn her about these suave looking bastards. She was so damned confident of herself — the injections and all that business. And then, any man who would. . . . Well, that's just how it happened. Living with a whore — even the best whore in the world — isn't a bed of roses. It isn't the numbers of men, though that too gets under your skin sometimes, it's the everlasting sanitation, the precautions, the irrigations, the examinations, the worry, the dread. And then, in spite of it all —. I told Claude. . . . I told her repeatedly — "watch out for the swell guys!"

No, I blame myself for everything that's happened. Not content with being a saint I had to prove that I was a saint. Once a man realizes that he's a saint he should stop there. Trying to pull the saint on a little whore

is like climbing into heaven by the back stairs. When she cuddles up to me — she loves me now more than ever — it seems to me that I'm just some damned microbe that's wormed its way into her soul. I feel that even if I am living with an angel I ought to try to make a man of myself. We ought to get out of this filthy hole and live somewhere in the sunshine, a room with a balcony overlooking a river, birds, flowers, life streaming by, just she and me and nothing else.

ALICE MUNRO

A Basket of Strawberries

Unlike some of the writers included in this volume, Alice Laidlaw Munro is known chiefly for her stories, which feature the ordinary people of small-town Ontario, where she was born in 1931. Munro attended the University of Western Ontario and later settled in Victoria, British Columbia, where she and her husband ran a bookstore called Munro's Books. Munro, like a few other women writers in this collection, says she wrote stories rather than novels because childrearing didn't allow her time to write anything else. Her first professionally published story appeared in *Mayfair* in November 1953, three years after her first publication in an undergraduate magazine.

MR. TORRANCE HAD not slept well. The night had been unusually warm for June, and quite still, without the faintest wind. In his light sleep he had had an uneasy sensation of not being able to breathe as deeply as he should, and the darkness above his closed eyelids had seemed to have a reddish tinge, to be aglow with heat, impatience, and anguish of weariness. His wife was fretful, too; he was aware, all night long, of her great soft, heaving movements and the mumbling, childish noises she made in her sleep. He lay beside her, quite still and motionless, and at dawn there was an ache and heaviness in all his bones; he felt as if he were made of rusty and ill-fitted lengths of iron pipe. He opened his eyes — he would not try to sleep anymore. His wife was standing at the window. She was in her nightgown, with a mauve silk wrapper tied loosely at her soft bulging waist, and her grey dark-streaked hair loose down her back.

"Don't stand at the window," said Mr. Torrance in a sharp, tired voice. "Come away, anybody might see you —"

"There's nobody to see me," his wife said, sounding vague and bemused. "It's too early —" She fumbled with the ties of her wrapper. "Not even the milkman." Nevertheless she came away from the window and sat down in the chair by her dressing table. The dressing table was crowded with pill-boxes, medicine bottles, hair nets, dusty cream-jars, and even a bouquet of quite dead lilacs, but she discovered a comb somewhere, and with languid, rhythmic movements she began to comb out her hair. This was a performance which at one time had enchanted him, and he never saw it repeated but he remembered that lovely length of dark-gold hair, the look of sensual absorption on her face as she sat slowly, endlessly combing. But the memory made him feel no tenderness, nothing but an indistinct irritation; he turned his head away.

"I was looking over at the Wilkinsons' garden," his wife said wonderingly. "I had a queer dream, I dreamt about a garden. It was like a willow platter at first — all blue and funny Japanese-looking trees — and afterwards it was like the Wilkinsons' garden, with the poplars —"

"Three poplars at my garden-foot . . ." said Mr. Torrance from a remote and wistful distance.

"What?"

"Nothing." He had only quoted to hear the words said, not to say them to her. He never said anything to her on this level; she had never read, she knew nothing, would not understand.

"I wish I could remember it better," she said. "Dreaming of a garden means your mind is going back to the Garden of Eden, or something like that, anyway I'll have to look it up —" For a year or so she had been more interested in dreams than in anything else. Before that she had been interested in spiritualism, and experiments in photographing ectoplasm, but now the big book by A. Conan Doyle was holding up a broken leg of the chesterfield, and the books she brought home from the library were all about dreams. She said they were nothing like the old superstitious nonsense, but quite modern and reliable; some of their authors had university degrees or even belonged to the nobility.

She bought little notebooks with morocco covers and heavy cream paper, and she wrote her dreams in these books and locked them away

in a special drawer. She dreamed a great deal; her dreams were usually on a grand scale, richly coloured, and overshadowed by mysteries and ambiguous horrors. She loved to eat before she went to bed — butter-tarts, frosted cakes, pickle-and-head-cheese sandwiches . . . Lately she had begun to take long naps in the afternoon, so that she would have more dreams.

"It's very queer." She sighed, and put pins in her hair. "It's hard for us to understand dreams, we can't see clearly —" Very pale she was, very loose and soft and fat, and her large, light-blue eyes were always a little strained, and scratched by the tiny red-blood vessels, as if the things seen in dreams were quite too much for them. It seemed to him now that even in her youth, in the peculiarly short-lived flowering of her beauty, there had been something a little unwholesome. Under the white thick wax-petalled skin there had moved, in sluggish blood, some current un-consciously wanton and distraught. And it was he who had discovered it, had been intrigued by it as by her hair, her vague smile, and her name, Goldora Stephens. As soon as he had seen the name on his class register he had thought it captivating and absurd, a marriage of the common-place and the wildly romantic. *Goldora,* he had muttered to himself, and immediately he had thought (he was quite young then, full of fantasy) of the Spaniards and the Fountain of Youth, baroque palaces and small white churches in the desert, garish and gilded saints —

There was a red sunrise, but no morning wind came with it. At the end of the little dirt street, there were fields of ripe hay, rising up the slope of low hills; the hay did not stir or ripple. But the bobolinks sang in the fields, and from the gardens, even the ragged garden under the bedroom window, rose a crushed morning fragrance of wet grass and tangled June roses and full-blown peonies. Mr. Torrance got up and dressed himself slowly, shaved over a very dirty basin in the bathroom, and scrupulously brushed and parted his hair. He had still, as he knew, a very fine head, rather in the sculptured style of antiquity, with the waves of white hair, strong nose and slightly flaring nostrils, the thin lips drawn delicately at the corners. His body had always been rather frail-looking, but it was spare and straight. He was not, he thought as he shaved, he did not look — one could not call him — old.

Afterwards because it was still so early, he sat in the front room, which was dark yet because of the green blinds and dusty lace curtains and the

luxuriant, smothering ferns which grew in baskets in front of the windows. He took a book from his shelves of old novels — it was *Henry Pendennis* — and read a few pages; he watched the night-dead flies struggling weakly in a shallow pool of poison on a plate. He thought about the final Latin examination which his Senior Class was to write that day.

He had taken pains with his class, given them the benefit of shrewd hints and predictions (he had so much experience with Departmental exams that he was able to predict, with fair certainty, just how much Virgil would be on the paper, whether the examiners would lean towards Horace or Catullus —). With him the preparation for an exam became an almost sacred ritual, with a suggestion of conspiracy. His five senior girls were serious and attentive; they sat listening with bowed heads while he read to them the dream of Aeneas, the death of Laocoon. He liked to read, in the quiet classroom, with the windows open, the air smelling faintly of fields and blossoming orchards, and the five smooth-haired virgins ranged meekly before him; he read without round, pompous tones, or the air of declamation, but with the honest tenderness he felt for the words, and with some sadness also.

For it seemed as if he were the last protestor of an old faith, an ambassador in a distant, alien country. He was the spiritual descendant of all the scholars in tranquil ancient college rooms, all the hoarders of golden manuscripts; he spoke for them, and had spoken for thirty years, in the deaf and barren little towns of Ontario. Now most of the students took Typing or Manual Training instead; to those who still came to him (for reasons of academic necessity which he was pleased to ignore) he felt a personal gratitude. His five senior girls, this year, were all gay and gentle and pretty; he had a special pleasure in teaching them, feeling his power over their pliant female minds, artfully unfolding to them the mysteries of the Subjunctive —

He and his wife had a cup of tea in the kitchen. They ate some stewed prunes and toasted buns. The kitchen smelled a little of mouldy drawers and old vegetables; the cupboard doors were partly open and he saw dishes, dabs of leftover food, dirty dishcloths all piled together. Because of his bad night and his state of inner tension he saw these things as if for the first time, with sharp disgust. But he saw them also with great weariness, aware that this was not the first time; everything had been like

this for many years. He did not finish his prunes and left the house thinking — as he had to do every now and then — of his marriage, his wife, the old scandal that had followed him and defeated him all his life.

He had seduced a girl in his class; he had been made to marry her. They would never forget that, in the red-brick towns, the ugly little fortresses of Methodism. If it were not for that he would have been a principal long ago; he would have had the prestige to redeem the classics in his school; people would have looked up to him as a man of letters, a scholar, a teacher in the company of the great teachers, Arnold, and the others — He would have had — would he not? — everything in his right, but for Goldora, and the wretched minds of puritans —

On the main street, storekeepers were sweeping their sidewalks and carrying out baskets of vegetables to be set under the awnings; they paid no attention to him. He paused in the shadow of the town hall, to look up at the clock in its squat and bulbous tower; the stolid, self-satisfied ugliness of the building outraged him, and at the same time made him feel quite powerless. He walked up the steep side street to the High School.

THERE were no other exams to be written that day. The school was very quiet, almost empty. Mr. Torrance was at his desk in the small upper classroom. He had thought he would go through his desk-drawers and sort out his books, but for the time he did nothing. He wondered whether the girls were here yet, if they were nervous, or wanted to ask him anything. He had seen no one yet but young Henderson, who taught agriculture and P. T. and was to preside at the Latin exam.

"You here?" Henderson had said. "Too bad to have you bother coming up — You didn't need to, really."

Mr. Torrance had smiled stiffly and with much distaste.

"I thought," he had explained, "in case of any last-minute questions — I thought I had better be here. I should not expect," he said smilingly to young Henderson, "an athlete and scientist like yourself to be much of an authority on Latin."

And Henderson had laughed, quite undismayed, and proudly admitted to flunking out of Latin in Grade Ten. He had gone away and left Mr. Torrance waiting.

There was a light knock; Mr. Torrance cried expectantly, "Come in!"

It was Ramona, the fifth and smallest virgin, the slender and shy and demurely black-haired. She wore a white blouse, beguilingly transparent, and a great full skirt splattered with sunflowers; the thick, soft, straight hair fell forward along her cheeks. Mr. Torrance stood up, smoothing back the pure-white waves of his own hair, and he seemed to sense all at once the ripening fragrances of morning and the still, exuberant young summer. He said, "Good Morning, Ramona," very quietly, so that his voice should not betray that he felt, for a moment, like a man returned to life.

"Good Morning, Mr. Torrance," answered Ramona, the schoolgirl.

"How do you feel?" he said gently, solicitously. "You're not worried are you?"

"No," said Ramona.

"You are not to worry. You will do splendidly. So is there anything you want to know now, any little point that's troubling you?"

"No, I don't think so," said Ramona thoughtfully, "we've really gone over everything so often — I didn't come for that. I came — I thought — you'd worked so hard with us — I brought you a basket of strawberries."

And she was in fact carrying a little straw basket, with a braided handle, and there were berries in it — each one was hulled and placed in a cup of fluted paper, as if it had been a bonbon. They were quite fat and pretty berries, bright and rosy-red in the first stage of ripeness. He fingered them with delight, his hands and his voice were a shade unsteady from a disproportionate feeling of surprise and excitement.

"They are lovely," he said. He thought them a naive and charming tribute, exquisitely significant; he bowed over them ceremoniously. "They are lovely, Ramona, they are just as I like them best. When they are still so firm and not quite sweet — I hate that mushy sweetness they get from too much sun. How did you know, Ramona, where did you get them?"

"Daddy always has the first," said Ramona matter-of-factly. "They are nice, aren't they?" She looked up at him with clear, grave eyes. "Are you tired, Mr. Torrance?"

"No," said Mr. Torrance. He stroked tenderly the plump cheek of a strawberry. "No, I'm not now. I was very tired." He smiled to think how tired he had been. "I didn't sleep well, and I was thinking — Thinking,

Ramona, thinking can be a sadly depressing habit, do you know that?" He said this with some conscious appealing ruefulness, a thirst for her sympathy.

"I thought you were tired," she said. "I guess it was getting us ready for the exam and everything."

He laughed. "No. It was not that!" he said in soft excited tones. "I was tired from pure bitterness of heart. You do not know that, Ramona, you are too young to know anything! But it is terrible, there is nothing to do. Even when you have got quite accustomed, as you might say, then it is all fresh, and has to be borne in on you again — That is God's sense of humour!"

She said nothing, but her eyes, so greatly mystified and distressed, excited him on. He began walking back and forth between his desk and the windows. His slight, histrionic insincerity was gone; he spoke in a voice hardly above a whisper, but tense, rapid, and emphatic.

"The thing is," he said, "it *was* my fault, to start with. As you know, Ramona, it was my fault. But do they think I don't pay enough for that? Do they think I don't pay! Why in one day I — But no, it's not enough for them, they have to dishonour and snub me and hang my shame on my coattails! How do you suppose I am nothing but this at my age, and take orders from a principal who got out of McGill at the bottom of his class! And even young Henderson thinks he can laugh at me —"

Ramona tried to interrupt with an exclamation of protest or denial, but he shook his head at her.

"No, no, why should I not admit it? And no one takes my classes, I admit that too. But I laugh at them, I laugh at this whole dirty Methodist-minded little town!" He made a fierce little grimace which was not at all like an expression of laughter. "Where else would they pillory a man all his life for one piece of idiocy? I suppose they think because she was my pupil — Well, I was young, too, and after all I married her —." He stopped at his desk, checked in this soft flow of vehemence by the girl's face. He leaned across the desk towards her.

"Ramona," he said gently, "Ramona, don't be startled. I didn't mean to rant so — I am tired —."

A gong sounded in the hall and Ramona fled towards the door.

"The exam," said Mr. Torrance. He laughed a little, with vague,

puzzled excitement. "Do you know I had almost forgotten the exam — Ramona!"

"Yes?" Ramona half-turned, halted in flight, so that the dazzling folds of her skirt were swept around her. "Yes? I have to go down now, what is it —."

"Thank you," said Mr. Torrance. "I didn't say thank you for the strawberries."

Ramona smiled. In her smile he saw compassion and a light of tenderness. After she had run out of the room, he sat down, feeling weak with gratitude and happiness. He could not understand why he felt so; there was a strange, radiant dizziness in his brain. He ate a strawberry, and it was just as he had expected — firm, a little tart and earthy in sweetness, and almost white in its centre.

For he had forgotten; he had not even known, to be certain, until the girl brought him the strawberries. He had forgotten, he had not completely understood, what he was to these children. The candid offering of spring fruit, the girl's great eyes and her smile — he understood now, it was simple and perfect for him, and the other things did not matter.

He walked from window to window, and looked out on the snug grey roofs of decorous houses, the stiff pine trees along the streets, and he felt pity and a fine secret exhilaration. How had he thought to be a principal here, to be respected and respectable? It was the golden tarnish on him, the pagan taint of the old disgrace, that was his magic. To these five girls, and to others he remembered, year on year, face on face, in the empty scarred seats of his classroom — to them he was not an old man, a teacher. He was the symbol of a vague splendid liberty, a warm gamboling joyous sensuality that the red-brick soul of their town denied. Because of him, they apprehended, innocently, confusedly, a richer and more ancient sense of values, they were aware of the spirit of Arcadia. They bent their heads in gentle delicious bemusement as he read to them the plea to Chloe, their timid sister-virgin, as he read of the pursuing Apollo and the insatiable Jove — And was he, himself, speaking tenderly, sadly to the bent heads, was he, stained and condemned, to become in those long enchanted moments their memory of Apollo?

The wind was rising, and along the town streets the pine-branches

were lifted with a low, uneasy, questioning sound. The sky had clouded, and was darkening in the east. He had not noticed, did not notice now. He went back to his desk and put his head down on his arms. He did not go to sleep, but he began to dream; he could hear the wind and feel the stillness of his classroom, yet he was deeply dreaming. At first he felt himself deliberately making the dream, and it was a self-indulgent dream, wilful and absurd; but afterwards he was swept along in it, and everything became unpatterned, indistinct. There was a grove of tall pale-golden trees, and an immense lawn in sunlight, and, beyond the trees, a white fire of morning-mist. Ramona was there, with others, and it seemed to him that between the tree-trunks he could see the garlanded snowy heifers in stately play.

At mid-day the wind was high; in the streets there was the soft, dry sound of tossing leaves, and the trees, with leaves upturned, looked pale as silver against the heavy sky. It was quite dark in the school; no one had turned on the lights in the dim varnished corridors, or in the classrooms with the loud-ticking clocks. Mr. Torrance came down the stairs slowly, feeling his way from the hollow of one step to another; his eyes were dazed. He carried the basket of strawberries, and he came searching.

The stairs from the third floor were close to the girls' cloakroom; he heard the light voices, and stood still, waiting to hear hers, Ramona's. But a voice not hers said clearly and sharply. "But he must be going bats!"

"Yes —" said Ramona softly. "I felt so sorry, I felt awfully sorry —"

"But what else did he say? Did he look funny, were you scared?"

"No — I don't know. He just said about this girl and how he had to marry her and nobody had ever forgotten — And how he had to take orders from the principal and nobody took his classes, it was all because of that — but he didn't care anyway, he was laughing at them —"

"Remember the way he looked when he'd be reading? We used to wonder if he'd go off someday —"

"But we didn't think he would, like this, *really!*"

"You don't think —" said Ramona in her gentle, troubled voice. "You don't think — it couldn't possibly — it couldn't be true?"

"The girl! Lord, no, nobody's ever heard anything like that! And we *would* have, you always hear who had to —"

"Anyway, it couldn't be true! You can't imagine it — Mr. Torrance —"

There was a little silence; then all the voices broke together. "Mr. Torrance!" They began to splutter with delicious irrepressible giggles.

"Imagine — Mr. Torrance — seducing anybody!"

They went down the hall, laughing softly and wildly together. Ramona said, half-protestingly, "But we don't know — when he was young —" but the others paid no attention to her, and she was laughing too. When they had gone downstairs, and clanged the outer doors behind them, thin echoes of their laughter came from the cloakrooms and the halls; then there was no sound in the building at all.

Mr. Torrance went on down the stairs, unsurely, erratically making his way to the hall window. He saw young Henderson waiting beside his car at the end of the walk. Young Henderson was holding the car door open, waiting for the girls, and he was laughing at them as the wind ballooned their skirts and caught their hair across their faces. They shrieked and tossed their heads and clapped their hands to their thighs; they were all running down the walk.

Mr. Torrance felt his body shaken, as if by the wind; his loose hands let the strawberries fall, and they rolled down the steps, he could not see them in the dark. He had one left, caught between his fingers, but he did not want it; it was not ripe.

\|\|≋

In the Old World

To the surprise of no one familiar with the prolific Joyce Carol Oates, a college writing teacher claims Oates wrote a novel nearly every semester during her undergraduate years at Syracuse University. Born in 1938 in Lockport, New York, as a child she wrote "cute little stories about children and cats," her father once said. Oates won the *Mademoiselle* College Fiction contest in 1959 and received a prize of five hundred dollars. The story was published in the magazine's August 1959 issue, when Oates was about to start her senior year of college, and so began one of the richest careers in contemporary American letters.

\|\|≋

IT WAS EARLY afternoon when Swan reached the brink of the hill that sloped down to town. He gazed down at it, at the flat, watery image he had been seeing for so long in his mind's eye, and it was with an almost careless, perhaps even brutal, gesture that he drew his arm across his forehead. Then he started on down the dirt road to the town, walking slowly, casually, his head bent a little against the overhead glare; he thought briefly of how the sun must look above him, drained back into the great colorless sky. It was incredible how the heat lay about him and how he could feel himself moving through it, how he could feel it almost like water pressing against him.

He did not regret being hatless; he did not regret the three or four cars that had slowed alongside him, which he had motioned on with a fleet and impatient wave of his hand; he thought of them without any feeling at all now; they were simply things that had passed him, which meant nothing at all against the impact of that sky stretching above and

all the way to the mountains, swollen and still. He found himself staring at the ground, at his dusty feet, as though he had not the strength to look up. Yet he kept on, the close, paled image of the town forever before him: the town with its giant elms and its narrow main street, its tight little hills, the string of stores that curled and blinked gaudily in the heat. There was a park there, he could see, shaded with elms, between the empty streets, its grass faded brown; the courthouse, certainly; across the street a few stores, small stores, even a stretch of sidewalk; there was the lane that opened back from the street onto the old ice house; before him, if he stood by that lane, the town would slope down and away from him, its trees notched slowly out of sight, and if he followed the road on down he would only come to a bridge, a bridge streaked with rust; and after that the houses would vanish and he would be in the country again, on this same road and with orchards on each side of him — still and sharply etched with shadow.

Then he was nearly in the town: glancing up, he saw it before him, it appeared to have leaped back to him with a swift, flicking movement. He hesitated only a moment. Then he crossed to the side of the road, his eyes level, calm, squinting only from time to time against the light, fastening themselves upon cars that passed him now and then, cars and trucks and their weary, listless drivers. He saw the frame houses alongside the road begin, houses with bare front yards, with children squatting in the dust watching him, certainly, in their steady, dark, mindless manner; the trees too appeared to give way, though there were some ahead, in the park; now the air was filled beyond the nearly tangible presence of heat with the sound of children's voices and, past that, of automobiles on other streets or even on this one, whining by him and the houses at which he had not yet looked.

At the park he believed he could feel a high, numbing pain in his legs; he had not noticed it before and he thought with a sudden flash of anger that he ought to have accepted a ride from one of those drivers, he ought not to have turned his face away from them as he had done, it was a childish thing to do; yet, still, it had been entirely correct and he knew it; there was nothing else he could have forced himself to do. He peered across the park to a drugstore that faced it; it looked empty, its windows blind above the wavering heat. The drugstore — certainly it would be cooler there: he could see the dimmed array of glass and slanted mer-

chandise, always a little blurred with his own self-consciousness; he could see a person's face turning abruptly toward him, away from an opened newspaper, perhaps, or a conversation with another person; how he would look at him, this person, this person he knew he would recognize were he simply to go to that dirty screen door and open it, were he simply to step inside, just a boy come into town with his father, a boy driven into town — he must have ridden in, he had no hat — and with that neat and respectful and yet closely malicious expression he molded upon himself, he felt flow warmly across his features almost prior to thought: surely he must impress the man in this way or, if there were a woman there, surely she must gaze at him with interest, she could not avoid it, she would even know his name, she would ask after his family. Swan wiped his forehead again, staring dizzily at the blank window of the drugstore. He could see reflected in their quiet, waiting eyes — those persons inside — his own face; he must look to them a strong boy, a strong young man, he must seem a little distracted with the heat, and yet this would not be unusual, they would think nothing of it, it did not mean he had walked all the way to town by himself; there would be the usual muted and inwardly channeled defiance, perhaps, a veneer of adolescent defense that they would sense, he would sense it within them; yet he was not always certain to what degree this was of his own contriving. When he believed he controlled himself, when he held his own features taut like scrawlings frozen before him, etched into his flesh, then something would happen, he would hear his own voice keep on and on, even his expression would shift, he would see them staring right into his own eyes. But before that they would think he was a boy come — no, he had gotten beyond that, they would ask after his family, his father, his ailing father, he would answer them politely, sadly, and they would see then that the slow and graceful movement of his eyes upon them was an expression of some secret and immense and perhaps even painful compassion. Then what might he do? Would he grip the moment as though it were part of something winding steadily away, would he stop, simply cease, would he hold that instant of mindless acceptance which flashed between them — how he would have to resist this, what strength it might demand to resist groping backward for the door and stepping back out to the sidewalk, spent, relieved, quietly hysterical, not absolved

of his sin or delivered of his punishment but simply in another dimension altogether, no longer related to it, that which he would be able to think about later with the most precise, the most meticulous objectivity, a curious thing, after a time probably no longer very interesting, belonging only to another of his selves and never the one they would gaze upon and mold with their own eyes, his father's son after all, only a boy come into town on a hot afternoon.

He crossed the park, his hands stiff in his pockets; when he glanced up again he was approaching the sheriff's office, a squat, peeling building set close to the road. He looked at it. It seemed quiet, empty, like all of the town now: yet with a quality of watchfulness in spite of this, as though it were gazing out upon him, enveloping him somehow in the rain-washed and nearly colorless wood that stretched out now on each side of him, and flatly above him, clapboards beginning to curl, windows that let no light in at all, a single vine stiff against the corner of the building as though it had been nailed there. Swan rapped on the screen door and opened it, all at the same time; the volition of his own hands startled him. "Hello, there," someone said. Swan saw a man sitting at the window, his feet up on the dirty sill, his arms folded: apparently he had been sitting there, doing nothing at all, perhaps just waiting for Swan. Behind him a boy was stooping over a pile of newspapers, one of the Negroes; his face had jerked up immediately when Swan came in.

"You want somethin', boy? What do you want?"

Swan leaned back against the door. He shrugged his shoulders. "I don't know," he said. He faced the man with an expression of open and careless arrogance. "Just come over to see what was goin' on."

"Well, there ain't anything." The man still had not moved; now Swan saw that he was a heavy person, so heavy that perhaps moving pained him, at least moving in this close, choking air; only his eyes were alert, and these fastened themselves upon Swan's face in a familiar, crowding way. "You don't need to leave, though. You can stick around if you want to."

Swan shrugged his shoulders again. He allowed his gaze to wander sightlessly about the room, his back against the screen door, his ears filled with a hushed, frantic sound like breathing — his own breathing, which the man and that boy there, still bent over the pile of newspapers,

his face uplifted, must surely be listening to. That was why they remained so still and so quiet; it was as though they were waiting to hear what he might tell them.

"There's just us here today," the man said. He nodded vaguely toward the Negro boy. "The ones in back, too, but there ain't many. You come into town for the day?"

Swan's eyes flitted aimlessly away from the man. "Yes," he said.

"Where are you from?"

"The Rapids," said Swan. He looked at the man. "Do you know where that is?"

"Sure. Couldn't be a deppity for long without knowin' that place," the man said. Swan watched him for a moment; he felt uneasy about the way the man had replied. Yet this person could not know him — Swan had never seen him before — just a deputy, a thick, heavy man, his eyes strung neatly into his broad face, fixing Swan with that slow, effortless smile. "Why, Chap here is from around there himself. Ain't you, Chap?"

Swan looked briefly at the Negro boy. He saw that he was thin and short, at least a foot shorter than Swan and, like all of them, appearing to be of no age whatsoever, his face contorted even as Swan glanced at him, as though someone were tightening it slowly and deliberately with a kind of screw; he saw too that the boy had a dirty strip of white gauze wrapped around his head, covering one eye.

"That there's name is Chaparral," the deputy said. "Ain't that a name for you? We come out an' got him somewhere around the Rapids, it wasn't but a while ago. Ain't that a name for you, now? They'll name themselves mostly anything." Swan saw the way the man smiled at him, the way his smile must include Swan, must lure him into smiling too. He had rolled his head in a peculiar way as well; it was as if this might mean something.

"You ain't tole me your name," the deputy said.

"I'm a Walpole," said Swan. His words sounded queer and loud. "I just thought, if there was somethin' going on . . . I mean. There ain't much to do here today."

"No, you're right. There ain't much at all, but when you get my age you'll be glad of days like this. You can stick around if you want to, though. You never can tell with a sheriff office like this is."

"Yeah? Do you get much trouble?"

"Well, sometimes. Course we don't ever hear about most of it." Swan watched him closely. "Most of it just happens out there an' we never know about it."

"Yeah? What kind of things?"

"Well — if I knew that, then I'd know about them!" the deputy said. His eyes were pinning Swan to the door. "I reckon anybody from the Rapids would know more themselves what was goin' on. Out in the country, anything can happen; you could never begin to catch up on all that goes on."

Swan shrugged again, lightly.

"Ain't that right, Chap?" The deputy leaned around to peer at the boy. "You get busy, there. What's he been doin', standin' there lookin' at you all this time? What do you think we pay you for, standin' around like that?"

The boy licked his lips and, to Swan's astonishment, began laughing — in a sudden, rushed way, as though his laughter were surprising him as well but as though he could not help himself.

The deputy glanced back to Swan. "Must be somethin' funny," he said. "Well. I don't criticize them, specially ones born like this one. Long as he gets his job done it don't much matter."

The boy picked up the pile of smudged newspapers and took them to the back door, still laughing, though more quietly now, and almost secretly, looking back at Swan with his single heavy-lidded eye.

"It ain't in me to criticize them," the deputy said, sighing. "They ain't like us."

"Yes," said Swan. "What was his name? Chaparral?"

"They'll call them anything, won't they? They don't never think of what it might mean."

"Someone told them to call him that," Swan said.

"What?"

"I said, someone maybe told them to call him that. Some doctor or someone, for a joke. I don't know."

The deputy watched him for a while. "Well," he said finally, "you can see it's a quiet enough day out." Swan nodded vaguely. "Plenty hot too. You wouldn't think it'd be so bad, in here like this. There ain't many places for the sun to hit, what with the buildin's on either side an' that park acrost the way. But look how hot it is."

The inside of the building struck Swan as being very small, suddenly, and very airless; the darkness of the stained ceiling and the far corners was even oppressive in a vague, shadowy way: for an instant he was compelled to think of the unbelievable ease with which that great sky could be erased; after all, it was not so much of a threat as he had believed.

"Yes, it's a hot day. A hot summer too. A hot, dry summer. Don't seem much like it'll ever come to a end . . ."

Swan was watching the back door. "Does he work here or somethin'?"

"What?"

"That one there. The one who — you know — Does he work here for you?"

"Oh. Him. Yeah, just little things. He don't have no fambly that we know of; he has to have somethin' to do with himself. What makes you ask?"

Swan was watching the door. "It wouldn't be bad, to work in a sheriff office like this."

The man laughed.

"I expect there's a lot of things goin' on, sometimes. When they bring in people here to lock up." Swan began sucking the tip of his forefinger. "There's worse things he could do," he said.

"Sure."

"Ones like him, they can't get many jobs. They got the worst land here too." He was quiet for a moment. "I wonder how come he got to laughin' just then."

"That? There ain't no reason. He just felt like it."

"He was laughin' at me."

"No. He just felt like it."

"It looked like —"

"It might of been your hair."

"What? What about it?"

"He said somethin' about hair that color, once. When we found him. There ain't that many people he sees with hair so light."

The boy came back inside then, noisily; now that he was carrying nothing he looked to Swan a little taller, even larger, perhaps, his face a mass of stiff, arrested wrinkles: he might have been laughing only an instant before, his hilarity become respectfully frozen.

"He don't mean anything by it," the deputy said. "He ain't too bad. I don't much care to look at his face, how it is, but he gets things done. You, Chap," the deputy said; now his tone had altered, it sounded almost buoyant. "You show the boy here how smart you got. He can answer some questions I taught him myself, just on days like this here, sittin' around with nothin' else to do. Now you, Chap, you tell me how much is two an' two put together."

The boy was staring at the side of the deputy's face. Swan believed he could see him swallow; then he said, softly, "Four."

The deputy looked immediately at Swan. "Hear that? I taught it in him just on times like these, myself. He listens to me just like anything, like I was a regular teacher. Now, Chap. How much is three an' three put together?"

"Six."

"Four an' four?"

"Eight."

"Now. How much is five an' five?"

"Ten." The boy spoke deliberately and politely, watching the deputy.

"How much is three an' two put together?"

"Five."

"Hear that? He learnt just as easy. He can even tell me — how much is eight take away four?"

"Four."

"Ain't he quick at that?" the deputy said. Swan watched them in a breathless, numbed way. "He learnt just as easy. Here's some other ones — how much is ten take away six?"

"Four."

"There," the deputy said. "Go on, boy. Ask him some yourself."

"All right," said Swan. He was leaning back against the door; he thought he could feel the warmer air outside touching his head, part of his neck. "How much is ten take away five?"

The boy looked at him. "Five," he said.

"How much is five take away ten?"

"Backwards of five."

The deputy peered at Swan. "There ain't no answer to that," he said. "What did you ask him?"

"He answered it all right."

"What did you ask? Five take away ten?"

"Yes."

The deputy laughed. "There ain't no answer to that, then. It can't be done." Now he nodded toward the boy. "Here, that's enough standin' around. Take the rest of them papers out back, will you?" He waited a moment; perhaps he could feel the boy listening so intently to him. "Put them in a stack out there. Is that what you're doin'? They got to be put in a row in stacks, not thrown down all over."

"Yes."

"Take care, now. You're goin' to lose this job if you don't do it right."

The boy passed them and went to the stacks of stained newspapers.

"He learnt that just as easy, them arithmetic things. Only it's queer how he does it," the deputy said, broadly, gesturing back toward the boy. "It's like he don't think on it any. You seen him. It's like his voice just says the answer, an' he don't think on it himself."

Swan laughed briefly. "I s'pose so," he said.

"It's a queer thing. I can't figure it, but there you are. You heard him yourself."

"Well," said Swan abruptly. "I guess there ain't much goin' on around here, like you said. . . . Everything's so still."

"You can stick around if you want to. You ain't botherin' me none."

Swan laughed again. "I hope I ain't. I wouldn't want to get in the way of — of the law, or somethin'. I hope not."

"No. You're all right."

"The reason I come over is I don't get to see many folks, out where I live," Swan went on, in a bland, glib manner; his eyes drifted back and forth across the man's face. "It's a lonely enough place."

"Ain't you got any friends your own age?"

"No."

"Not any ones at all?"

Swan was gazing at the man, the traces of his smile still dreamily upon his lips: he could feel it there. The deputy's voice came to him out of the now dim and faintly heavy air of the room, warm, more than warm, in a manner that seemed to him so familiar, as though this had all happened once before, or perhaps he had only dreamed it — he had only dreamed it, though of course much more painstakingly, with much

more care and detail, than it was really happening now; but that was only the way of all dreams. So he watched the man carefully, listening for his words; it was as though he believed they might really tell him what the man was thinking.

"Ain't you got any friends at all?"

"It's a lonely enough place," Swan said.

"But you must go to school, don't you? When the summer's over?" the man said softly. "You must get to know some ones there your own age."

"No," said Swan.

"You must —"

"No," said Swan. He spoke in a sharp, petulant way, like a child. "There ain't any."

"Any what? Any other kids?"

"Any ones my own age!"

"Any ones your —" The deputy eyed him for a moment, almost slyly; then his face relaxed into a broad, empty smile. He still sat without moving, his hands fatly before him, his trousers tight across his thick, creased knees. "You could always be friends with ones not your own age, then," he said.

Swan, looking at the man, aware of the boy stooping and tugging at something just behind him, wondered why the scene fixed so listlessly about him did not disintegrate, vanish: he wondered what dismal and tedious force sustained it and himself within it, this dim, airless room, this fat man so bluntly before him — what could he mean by it, if he meant anything at all, sitting there so heavily, so profoundly, gazing at Swan, what notions prompted him to remain without moving in the presence of a hatred and a viciousness he must surely begin to feel, so deliberately thrusting his presence out upon Swan? The deputy's expression was veiled, it was knowing: now he was calculating upon how correct he had been in sitting there so long, simply waiting for someone to come to him. And the boy behind him with that dirty white bandage about his head, now straightening, now wiping his dark, glistening forehead — what might sustain him, a creature like that, what might force him in that painted and yet jubilant way to draw one breath after another, on and on, tediously, incredibly, even before Swan had seen him

and, of course, after he would leave? The thought of it stunned Swan. It had been eating into his head, the back of his head, all the while; he had only now begun to feel it.

"Somethin' wrong with you?" the deputy said.

"No."

"You looked — sure there ain't somethin' wrong?"

Swan shook his head. He could hear his breath again, a loud, rasping, annoying sound; even the Negro boy, bent over those papers in that awkward, exaggerated position, his face averted, must hear the sound of this breathing. "I thought — I thought you were a deputy here," Swan said, for a moment groping in his confusion. "I thought —"

"What? What makes you say that?" the man said loudly. "I sure am a deppity here!"

"You are? But —"

"I sure am! What do you think I mean to do, sittin' here, if I wasn't a deppity employed by this whole county, if I —"

"But you ain't got one of those badges on."

"I ain't — oh. That." The man glanced at the stained pocket of his shirt. "I ain't got it on," he said. Then he smiled. "But you don't need a badge to be a lawman, now do you? Even a country boy like you ought to know that. You don't need a shiny thing stuck on your shirt to uphold the law."

Swan nodded slowly. He remembered how, out on the road, he had longed for darkness; he had longed for a time when the sun and the pale sky might not be glaring against even his closed eyelids; yet now, standing here, about to dissolve into this darkness, he could feel nothing beyond the usual dull, monotonous sensation of dread, he could feel no thrill of gratitude, of satisfaction; there was simply nothing.

"It's just on account of how lonely it gets, out where I live," he began, uncertainly, "the reason I come here, I mean. I thought I would just come here to see how things were."

This was fine: the man was listening closely, his smile about to widen at any moment, perfectly attuned to Swan's own expression; even the Negro boy was peering at him out of his one squinted eye in a hushed and respectful manner, though of course ludicrous, since he was stooped and held what must have been a heavy bundle of old papers before him in the most awkward way.

"A boy likes to come into town with his pa, any chance he gets," he said. He imagined the deputy was even nodding. What must he say next, what would lead him to his story? He groped for a moment, his hands coming loose at his sides . . . he must keep on talking.

"You wouldn't know how lonely it gets there," he said. "But then it must of always been that way, that was how it was first of all. Sometimes I see it like it must of looked to the ones who come to this land first, a land they just come to, that they didn't even know was here till they saw it. What must that of been, to see what they did? All this building here and the street and outside, the whole town, nothing but land . . . How they must have thought on it, how it must have lured them to it, that they couldn't resist; a place where all things might be different, where nothing had anything to do with anything else yet, where all things changed and they could change along with them, like a broken mirror . . . Come to a new land, how could you remember what you used to be like? Don't you think that's right? Don't you?"

He was speaking earnestly now, his voice had never been more earnest, pleading with both the deputy and the boy. They merely looked at him.

"But yet I think it might not have been that way, really," he went on, as if this were some profound sadness, as if they were really listening. "I think it might have been like it always was. This was no new world to them; this was the old world still. Why I come here, now, I . . . Even with all that time ahead it won't get any different, don't you think? So much time ahead, I mean, that could wear down anything. Don't you think I'm right?"

The deputy had turned slightly so that he could glance from Swan to the boy. "There is a lot of time to come," he said, slowly, with an air of someone who is admitting a secret. "I wouldn't argue it."

"Well, then," said Swan. He took a deep breath. "I mean to tell you about something happened a while ago; maybe it won't make much difference any more. There was this church picnic they had, out in the Rapids, some church or whatever it was, that has it every year on a Sunday. You know what I mean. They're known for their chicken chowder." As he spoke he reached into his pocket, slowly, decorously, so that he did not flick their eyes from his face. "What I heard about it was these four or five boys, I don't know what age, got in some kind of

fight or something. That happens a lot at picnics, you know. Kids that ain't seen each other for a time get all together and they always fight sooner or later, it's just how kids are. You know. But there was something about . . . some other ones, maybe just two or three, or maybe it was just two, I can't much remember, colored ones I mean, that were doing something there too . . . They shouldn't have come there. Or if they did they shouldn't have made much noise and to-do about it or do what they did, try and run off with things; they might have known someone would see them. Because everyone was watching them all along, to see what they were going to do. You can't trust them with things out in the open, food and things. They sooner or later try to steal them. So. I heard something about how they took something, some prize at a game, only they dropped it further on; they were laughing and all, and carrying on, that they shouldn't have done either. They shouldn't have. It was for themselves they shouldn't have, and they knew it. So these other ones started in to chase them and there was some kind of fight, I guess, it sounds all mixed up now and probably was then, since it was dark out and all, but there was some kind of fight with green pears for a while . . ." Swan laughed. "A thing like that doesn't sound like much. Saying it here it doesn't sound like anything . . . a fight with green pears . . ."

He laughed again, he was taken by surprise; the deputy smiled immediately, and even the Negro boy smiled, as though he had understood Swan's words.

"Well. They gave them a hard time, I guess; they put up a good enough fight. There was two of them. They crossed all these fields and things, running, going so far, you'd never think to go so far without something like that to make you do it — you'd never do it any other way. Then one of them went in the creek or something, what they said later, and they heard him running in the water by the bank, just as clear as anything, then it was just nothing; he got away; it was so dark they couldn't find him anywhere. But the other one stopped by the creek. He wasn't done fighting but just stopped by the creek and waited for them, you know, they'll do that sometimes, like a rat you got chased all the way down a stairs. He just stopped. What he should have done there was just stand still. Anyone would tell him that, if I'd have been there I would have told it to him before the rest of them caught up, all mad like

they were — I'd have told it to him so the others couldn't hear, I'd have whispered it to him, so he'd understand. I'd have made him know. But he didn't do that, how they told it later, he kept on . . ."

Swan had taken a pocketknife out and appeared to be startled by it; he looked at it, frowning. "Yes," he said, vaguely. "He shouldn't have done it."

The deputy was staring at him. Swan looked past the rusted blade of the knife at the man's white, soft-looking face.

"Why did you come here?" the man said.

Swan shrugged his shoulders. "A boy in at town, nothin' to do, why, we always come over . . ."

"But why did you come here?"

"I don't know," Swan said; he spoke defiantly. "My father couldn't give me much of an answer to what I wanted to know; maybe that's why. But I don't know. I don't. I don't know why I do anything."

"Just a minute, now —"

"I don't know," Swan said simply. He smiled and the Negro boy's teeth immediately gleamed, though the deputy merely stared at him. "I don't know why I do anything. There ain't any reason. If there was a reason I would know about it, wouldn't I? Here, now, what I meant to ask. What I come in here to ask. If someone like that did what he did, taken a knife and did something to another person, say, cut out his eye with it . . . I was wondering how they would get at him to make up for it."

Swan spoke shyly now, since he realized the position of the deputy and the significance of that badge which was not even on his shirt; he could feel his own heartbeat begin to slow.

"I wondered if they would just cut out his own eye for him. I wondered if they would try that. They ought. But I mean to tell them that it ain't enough, and that there ain't anything they can do to make it enough. Now, the person having it done to him, he wouldn't be smart about this, he wouldn't laugh; he'd feel bad about it himself because it's something for him to think on too, and anything you can't think of an answer to must hurt you. Questions a man thinks up, how it hurts him not to know the answers! . . . Because what they might do to him with a knife of their own wouldn't be enough. It would be just something equal with the other, what they do to him equal to what he did to the other

person; but that ain't what they ought to get at. It's the first impulse they ought to get at. I was just wondering," he said, apologetically, "if they knew how to do it. I don't know, myself. I don't know anything about it, I just don't know. Unless it's all its own punishment, when you feel you're bleeding inside."

Swan waited a moment, looking politely at the deputy. Then he stepped forward. The movement shocked both the deputy and the boy; he saw their eyes dart to his fingers, where he held the knife loosely by its blade. The boy stared at him, his mouth open. The deputy, however, was standing — now how quickly he moved, and with what calm, dignified authority: he merely reached out and took hold of Swan's wrist. "You put that away," he said. "Go on, now, put that away. There ain't no need of this."

"I come all the —"

"You heard me, boy. Put it away."

"But I come —"

"Here, now." He leaned to Swan: he had begun to smile. "You put that away. A fine-lookin' boy like you, you don't know what you mean. You don't know what you mean by it."

Swan hesitated; he looked at the deputy's face, which, in the thinning light, seemed to be protruding toward him, alert, secret, amiable.

"I mean to do something with this," Swan said, "I mean to let him use it on me or use it myself. I mean to," he said, though his voice had been drained of all its strength, it sounded empty and forlorn, a voice heard through a tunnel. "I mean to . . ."

"Yes," said the deputy, nodding. "Yes. You just put that away, now. You're all right."

"But I come all this way," Swan said. He had not the strength to pull back from the deputy, who was gripping his wrist rather tightly between his thick, lard-colored fingers; he looked, perhaps for sympathy, around at the Negro boy, who was watching them both in gaped, toothed astonishment, still clumsily embracing the bundle of newspapers. "I come all this way to see you, you there, it doesn't matter how long it took me . . . it doesn't matter . . . all the time in between or all the time after this wouldn't make up for what happened in that one moment, it wouldn't make . . ."

"Yes," said the deputy. "Yes. You, there, Chap. You done with them papers yet?"

The boy looked as though he had been struck, neatly, across the face. "Mostly done," he whispered.

"See you do it, then," said the deputy, facing Swan, turning his head only slightly toward the boy. "Get along. What do you expect we pay you for, to stand around all day? Huh?" When the boy did not reply the deputy turned farther, the cords of his neck standing stiffly out; the boy, however, was not looking at him, seemed instead to be transfixed by something: then he ducked his head a little and laughed.

"What's wrong with you, there?" the deputy said. "Huh? What's so funny now?"

The boy stopped laughing at once. He looked at the deputy. "Just that there hair," he said softly.

"What?"

"That hair," he said. "A purty color like that."

The deputy must have been staring at him. "Well, yes," he said. "You go on, now. Ain't you got a lot to do this afternoon? Ain't you? What do you mean, standin' around here like this was a holiday or somethin'? This boy come in here, he ain't got nothin' to do with you . . ." The deputy turned back to Swan. "Now you, here, boy, you get a holt of yourself. You stop this here tremblin' like you are an' get a holt of yourself. I wouldn't wonder you were gettin' sick, the way you act — might even be comin' down with the heat-exhaustion fever —" He spoke so calmly and with that same cool, nearly austere dignity that Swan was unable for a moment even to reply; he did not know what to say, he was hardly able to raise his eyes to the man's face.

"Maybe — maybe you ain't the deputy," he said. "Maybe I come in the wrong place —"

The man still held on to Swan's wrist but he leaned away with a neat, almost agile movement, flicking something up off the window sill; when he moved Swan saw that the office was empty now save for them, the boy had gone, the screen door at the back of the room was only now swinging slowly and almost aimlessly shut. "Now, boy, if this helps you any," the man said, "if you'd just get it straight that it don't matter about him, it don't matter at all — here," he said; he had stuck the badge onto

his shirt, on the sagging pocket, it was a little tarnished and in this poor light did not even seem metallic, but there was no mistaking it just the same. "If this helps you any. I s'pose a boy like yourself, a country boy an' all, you got to have things spelt out kind of plain for you."

Swan was looking at the badge. "Well, that's it," he said, with an air of agreement. "That's it, all right." He stood there for a moment or so, wondering what there was for him to say next; he had no idea at all, he simply waited for the words to come and arrange themselves. "Maybe I better be goin' on back, now, my pa might be waitin' . . . If I could just have the knife back," he said politely.

"Sure, boy. You go on back home," the deputy said. He released Swan's wrist; only now could Swan begin to appreciate the strength of the man's fingers, he gazed at his own wrist in a slow, dreamy way, he believed he could even see the imprint of the man's fingers in his flesh. "Anytime you're back in town, you can come on over if you want," the deputy was saying. "You ain't in anybody's way. Most of the time there ain't nothin' doin', but you never can tell with a sheriff office like this is . . . You just come on over anytime you want."

The Geranium

In his introduction to *The Complete Stories of Flannery O'Connor*, editor Robert Giroux describes O'Connor's first experience getting published as an easy one: "Flannery mailed 'The Geranium' to the editors of *Accent* as early as February 1946. They accepted it at once and printed it in their summer issue." O'Connor was born Mary Flannery O'Connor in Savannah, Georgia, in 1925, and grew up on her mother's profitable five-hundred-acre farm in nearby Milledgeville, where she helped only with raising the peacocks. She attended Georgia State College for Women and won a fellowship to the Writer's Workshop at the University of Iowa. Afterward she lived in New York for two years, spending a season at the Yaddo artists' colony, but she returned to Georgia when she became ill with lupus. Although she also published novels, *Wise Blood* in 1952 and *The Violent Bear It Away* in 1960, O'Connor is most acclaimed and best remembered for her short stories.

OLD DUDLEY FOLDED into the chair he was gradually molding to his own shape and looked out the window fifteen feet away into another window framed by blackened red brick. He was waiting for the geranium. They put it out every morning about ten and they took it in at five-thirty. Mrs. Carson back home had a geranium in her window. There were plenty of geraniums at home, better-looking geraniums. Ours are sho nuff geraniums, Old Dudley thought, not any er this pale pink business with green, paper bows. The geranium they would put in the window reminded him of the Grisby boy at home who had polio and had to be wheeled out every morning and left in the sun to blink.

297

Lutisha could have taken that geranium and stuck it in the ground and had something worth looking at in a few weeks. Those people across the alley had no business with one. They set it out and let the hot sun bake it all day and they put it so near the ledge the wind could almost knock it over. They had no business with it, no business with it. It shouldn't have been there. Old Dudley felt his throat knotting up. Lutish could root anything. Rabie too. His throat was drawn taut. He laid his head back and tried to clear his mind. There wasn't much he could think of to think about that didn't do his throat that way.

His daughter came in. "Don't you want to go for a walk?" she asked. She looked provoked.

He didn't answer her.

"Well?"

"No." He wondered how long she was going to stand there. She made his eyes feel like his throat. They'd get watery and she'd see. She had seen before and had looked sorry for him. She'd looked sorry for herself too; but she could er saved herself, Old Dudley thought, if she'd just have let him alone — let him stay where he was back home and not be so taken up with her damn duty. She moved out of the room, leaving an audible sigh, to crawl over him and remind him again of that one minute — that wasn't her fault at all — when suddenly he had wanted to go to New York to live with her.

He could have got out of going. He could have been stubborn and told her he'd spend his life where he'd always spent it, send him or not send him the money every month, he'd get along with his pension and odd jobs. Keep her damn money — she needed it worse than he did. She would have been glad to have had her duty disposed of like that. Then she could have said if he died without his children near him, it was his own fault; if got sick and there wasn't anybody to take care of him, well, he'd asked for it, she could have said. But there was that thing inside him that had wanted to see New York. He had been to Atlanta once when he was a boy and he had seen New York in a picture show. *Big Town Rhythm* it was. Big towns were important places. The thing inside him had sneaked up on him for just one instant. The place like he'd seen in the picture show had room for him! It was an important place and it had room for him! He'd said yes, he'd go.

He must have been sick when he said it. He couldn't have been well

and said it. He had been sick and she had been so taken up with her damn duty, she had wangled it out of him. Why did she have to come down there in the first place to pester him? He had been doing all right. There was his pension that could feed him and odd jobs that kept him his room in the boarding house.

The window in that room showed him the river — thick and red as it struggled over rocks and around curves. He tried to think how it was besides red and slow. He added green blotches for trees on either side of it and a brown spot for trash somewhere upstream. He and Rabie had fished it in a flat-bottom boat every Wednesday. Rabie knew the river up and down for twenty miles. There wasn't another nigger in Coa County that knew it like he did. He loved the river, but it hadn't meant anything to Old Dudley. The fish were what he was after. He liked to come in at night with a long string of them and slap them down in the sink. "Few fish I got," he'd say. It took a man to get those fish, the old girls at the boarding house always said. He and Rabie would start out early Wednesday morning and fish all day. Rabie would find the spots and row; Old Dudley always caught them. Rabie didn't care much about catching them — he just loved the river. "Ain't no use settin' yo' line down dere, boss," he'd say. "Ain't no fish dere. Dis ol' riber ain't hidin' none nowhere 'round hyar, nawsuh." And he would giggle and shift the boat downstream. That was Rabie. He could steal cleaner than a weasel but he knew where the fish were. Old Dudley always gave him the little ones.

Old Dudley had lived upstairs in the corner room of the boarding house ever since his wife died in '22. He protected the old ladies. He was the man in the house and he did the things a man in the house was supposed to do. It was a dull occupation at night when the old girls crabbed and crocheted in the parlor and the man in the house had to listen and judge the sparrow-like wars that rasped and twittered intermittently. But in the daytime there was Rabie. Rabie and Lutisha lived down in the basement. Lutish cooked and Rabie took care of the cleaning and the vegetable garden; but he was sharp at sneaking off with half his work done and going to help Old Dudley with some current project — building a hen house or painting a door. He liked to listen, he liked to hear about Atlanta when Old Dudley had been there and about how guns were put together on the inside and all the other things the old man knew.

Sometimes at night they would go 'possum hunting. They never got a 'possum but Old Dudley liked to get away from the ladies once in a while and hunting was a good excuse. Rabie didn't like 'possum hunting. They never got a 'possum; they never even treed one; and besides, he was mostly a water nigger. "We ain't gonna go huntin' no 'possum to-night, is we, boss? I got a lil' business I wants tuh tend tuh," he'd say when Old Dudley would start talking about hounds and guns. "Whose chickens you gonna steal tonight?" Dudley would grin. " I reckon I be huntin' 'possum tonight," Rabie'd sigh.

Old Dudley would get out his gun and take it apart and, as Rabie cleaned the pieces, would explain the mechanism to him. Then he'd put it together again. Rabie always marveled at the way he could put it to-gether again. Old Dudley would have liked to have explained New York to Rabie. If he could have showed it to Rabie, it wouldn't have been so big — he wouldn't have felt pressed down every time he went out in it. "It ain't so big," he would have said. "Don't let it get you down, Rabie. It's just like any other city and cities ain't all that complicated."

But they were. New York was swishing and jamming one minute and dirty and dead the next. His daughter didn't even live in a house. She lived in a building — the middle in a row of buildings all alike, all blackened-red and gray with rasp-mouthed people hanging out their windows looking at other windows and other people just like them look-ing back. Inside you could go up and you could go down and there were just halls that reminded you of tape measures strung out with a door every inch. He remembered he'd been dazed by the building the first week. He'd wake up expecting the halls to have changed in the night and he'd look out the door and there they stretched like dog runs. The streets were the same way. He wondered where he'd be if he walked to the end of one of them. One night he dreamed he did and ended at the end of the building — nowhere.

The next week he had become more conscious of the daughter and son-in-law and their boy — no place to be out of their way. The son-in-law was a queer one. He drove a truck and came in only on the week-ends. He said "nah" for "no" and he'd never heard of a 'possum. Old Dudley slept in the room with the boy, who was sixteen and couldn't be talked to. But sometimes when the daughter and Old Dudley were alone

in the apartment, she would sit down and talk to him. First she had to
think of something to say. Usually it gave out before what she considered
was the proper time to get up and do something else, so he would have
to say something. He always tried to think of something he hadn't said
before. She never listened the second time. She was seeing that her father
spent his last years with his own family and not in a decayed boarding
house full of old women whose heads jiggled. She was doing her duty.
She had brothers and sisters who were not.

Once she took him shopping with her but he was too slow. They
went in a "subway" — a railroad underneath the ground like a big cave.
People boiled out of trains and up steps and over into the streets. They
rolled off the street and down steps and into trains — black and white
and yellow all mixed up like vegetables in soup. Everything was boiling.
The trains swished in from tunnels, up canals, and all of a sudden
stopped. The people coming out pushed through the people coming in
and a noise rang and the train swooped off again. Old Dudley and the
daughter had to go in three different ones before they got where they
were going. He wondered why people ever went out of their houses. He
felt like his tongue had slipped down in his stomach. She held him by
the coat sleeve and pulled him through the people.

They went on an overhead train too. She called it an "El." They had
to go up on a high platform to catch it. Old Dudley looked over the rail
and could see the people rushing and the automobiles rushing under
him. He felt sick. He put one hand on the rail and sank down on the
wooden floor of the platform. The daughter screamed and pulled him
over from the edge. "Do you want to fall off and kill yourself?" she
shouted.

Through a crack in the boards he could see the cars swimming in the
street. "I don't care," he murmured, "I don't care if I do or not."

"Come on," she said, "you'll feel better when we get home."

"Home?" he repeated. The cars moved in a rhythm below him.

"Come on," she said, "here it comes; we've just got time to make it."
They'd just had time to make all of them.

They made that one. They came back to the building and the apartment. The apartment was too tight. There was no place to be where
there wasn't somebody else. The kitchen opened into the bathroom and

the bathroom opened into everything else and you were always where you started from. At home there was upstairs and the basement and the river and downtown in front of Fraziers . . . damn his throat.

The geranium was late today. It was ten-thirty. They usually had it out by ten-fifteen.

Somewhere down the hall a woman shrilled something unintelligible out to the street; a radio was bleating the worn music to a soap serial; and a garbage can crashed down a fire escape. The door to the next apartment slammed and a sharp footstep clipped down the hall. "That would be the nigger," Old Dudley muttered. "The nigger with the shiny shoes." He had been there a week when the nigger moved in. That Thursday he was looking out the door at the dog-run halls when this nigger went into the next apartment. He had on a gray, pin-stripe suit and a tan tie. His collar was stiff and white and made a clear-cut line next to his neck. His shoes were shiny tan — they matched his tie and his skin. Old Dudley scratched his head. He hadn't known the kind of people that would live thick in a building could afford servants. He chuckled. Lot of good a nigger in a Sunday suit would do them. Maybe this nigger would know the country around here — or maybe how to get to it. They might could hunt. They might could find them a stream somewhere. He shut the door and went to the daughter's room. "Hey!" he shouted, "the folks next door got 'em a nigger. Must be gonna clean for them. You reckon they gonna keep him every day?"

She looked up from making the bed. "What are you talking about?"

"I say they got 'em a servant next door — a nigger — all dressed up in a Sunday suit."

She walked to the other side of the bed. "You must be crazy," she said. "The next apartment is vacant and besides, nobody around here can afford any servant."

"I tell you I saw him," Old Dudley snickered. "Going right in there with a tie and a white collar on — and sharp-toed shoes."

"If he went in there, he's looking at it for himself," she muttered. She went to the dresser and started fidgeting with things.

Old Dudley laughed. She could be right funny when she wanted to. "Well," he said, "I think I'll go over and see what day he gets off. Maybe I can convince him he likes to fish," and he'd slapped his pocket to make the two quarters jingle. Before he got out in the hall good, she came

tearing behind him and pulled him in. "Can't you hear?" she'd yelled. "I meant what I said. He's renting that himself if he went in there. Don't you go asking him any questions or saying anything to him. I don't want any trouble with niggers."

"You mean," Old Dudley murmured, "he's gonna live next door to you?"

She shrugged. "I suppose he is. And you tend to your own business," she added. "Don't have anything to do with him."

That's just the way she'd said it. Like he didn't have any sense at all. But he'd told her off then. He'd stated his say and she knew what he meant. "You ain't been raised that way!" he'd said thundery-like. "You ain't been raised to live tight with niggers that think they're just as good as you, and you think I'd go messin' around with one er that kind! If you think I want anything to do with them, you're crazy." He had had to slow down then because his throat was tightening. She'd stood stiff up and said they lived where they could afford to live and made the best of it. Preaching to him! Then she'd walked stiff off without a word more. That was her. Trying to be holy with her shoulders curved around and her neck in the air. Like he was a fool. He knew Yankees let niggers in their front doors and let them set on their sofas but he didn't know his own daughter that was raised proper would stay next door to them — and then think he didn't have no more sense than to want to mix with them. Him!

He got up and took a paper off another chair. He might as well appear to be reading when she came through again. No use having her standing up there staring at him, believing she had to think up something for him to do. He looked over the paper at the window across the alley. The geranium wasn't there yet. It had never been this late before. The first day he'd seen it, he had been sitting there looking out the window at the other window and he had looked at his watch to see how long it had been since breakfast. When he looked up, it was there. It startled him. He didn't like flowers, but the geranium didn't look like a flower. It looked like the sick Grisby boy at home and it was the color of the drapes the old ladies had in the parlor and the paper bow on it looked like the one behind Lutish's uniform she wore on Sundays. Lutish had a fondness for sashes. Most niggers did, Old Dudley thought.

The daughter came through again. He had meant to be looking at

the paper when she came through. "Do me a favor, will you?" she asked as if she had just thought up a favor he could do.

He hoped she didn't want him to go to the grocery again. He got lost the time before. All the blooming buildings looked alike. He nodded.

"Go down to the third floor and ask Mrs. Schmitt to lend me the shirt pattern she uses for Jake."

Why couldn't she just let him sit? She didn't need the shirt pattern. "All right," he said. "What number is it?"

"Number 10 — just like this. Right below us three floors down."

Old Dudley was always afraid that when he went out in the dog runs, a door would suddenly open and one of the snipe-nosed men that hung off the window ledges in his undershirt would growl, "What are you doing here?" The door to the nigger's apartment was open and he could see a woman sitting in a chair by the window. "Yankee niggers," he muttered. She had on rimless glasses and there was a book in her lap. Niggers don't think they're dressed up till they got on glasses, Old Dudley thought. He remembered Lutish's glasses. She had saved up thirteen dollars to buy them. Then she went to the doctor and asked him to look at her eyes and tell her how thick to get the glasses. He made her look at animals' pictures through a mirror and he stuck a light through her eyes and looked in her head. Then he said she didn't need any glasses. She was so mad she burned the corn bread three days in a row, but she bought her some glasses anyway at the ten-cent store. They didn't cost her but $1.98 and she wore them every Saddey. "That was niggers," Old Dudley chuckled. He realized he had made a noise, and covered his mouth with his hand. Somebody might hear him in one of the apartments.

He turned down the first flight of stairs. Down the second he heard footsteps coming up. He looked over the banisters and saw it was a woman — a fat woman with an apron on. From the top, she looked kind er like Mrs. Benson at home. He wondered if she would speak to him. When they were four steps from each other, he darted a glance at her but she wasn't looking at him. When there were no steps between them, his eyes fluttered up for an instant and she was looking at him cold in the face. Then she was past him. She hadn't said a word. He felt heavy in his stomach.

He went down four flights instead of three. Then he went back up

one and found number 10. Mrs. Schmitt said O.K., wait a minute and she'd get the pattern. She sent one of the children back to the door with it. The child didn't say anything.

Old Dudley started back up the stairs. He had to take it more slowly. It tired him going up. Everything tired him, looked like. Not like having Rabie to do his running for him. Rabie was a light-footed nigger. He could sneak in a hen house 'thout even the hens knowing it and get him the fattest fryer in there and not a squawk. Fast too. Dudley had always been slow on his feet. It went that way with fat people. He remembered one time him and Rabie was hunting quail over near Molton. They had 'em a hound dog that could find a covey quickern any fancy pointer going. He wasn't no good at bringing them back but he could find them every time and then set like a dead stump while you aimed at the birds. This one time the hound stopped cold-still. "Dat gonna be a big 'un," Rabie whispered, "I feels it." Old Dudley raised the gun slowly as they walked along. He had to be careful of the pine needles. They covered the ground and made it slick. Rabie shifted his weight from side to side, lifting and setting his feet on the waxen needles with unconscious care. He looked straight ahead and moved forward swiftly. Old Dudley kept one eye ahead and one on the ground. It would slope and he would be sliding forward dangerously, or in pulling himself up an incline, he would slide back down.

"Ain't I better get dem birds dis time, boss?" Rabie suggested. "You ain't never easy on yo' feets on Monday. If you falls in one dem slopes, you gonna scatter dem birds fo' you gits dat gun up."

Old Dudley wanted to get the covey. He could er knocked four out of it easy. "I'll get 'em," he muttered. He lifted the gun to his eye and leaned forward. Something slipped beneath him and he slid backward on his heels. The gun went off and the covey sprayed into the air.

"Dem was some mighty fine birds we let get away from us," Rabie sighed.

"We'll fine another covey," Old Dudley said. "Now get me out of this damn hole."

He could er got five er those birds if he hadn't fallen. He could er shot 'em off like cans on a fence. He drew one hand back to his ear and extended the other forward. He could er knocked 'em out like clay pigeons. Bang! A squeak on the staircase made him wheel around — his

arms still holding the invisible gun. The nigger was clipping up the steps toward him, an amused smile stretching his trimmed mustache. Old Dudley's mouth dropped open. The nigger's lips were pulled down like he was trying to keep from laughing. Old Dudley couldn't move. He stared at the clear-cut line the nigger's collar made against his skin.

"What are you hunting, old-timer?" the Negro asked in a voice that sounded like a nigger's laugh and a white man's sneer.

Old Dudley felt like a child with a pop-pistol. His mouth was open and his tongue was rigid in the middle of it. Right below his knees felt hollow. His feet slipped and he slid three steps and landed sitting down.

"You better be careful," the Negro said. "You could easily hurt yourself on these steps." And he held out his hand for Old Dudley to pull up on. It was a long narrow hand and the tips of the fingernails were clean and cut squarely. They looked like they might have been filed. Old Dudley's hands hung between his knees. The nigger took him by the arm and pulled up. "Whew!" he gasped, "you're heavy. Give a little help here." Old Dudley's knees unbended and he staggered up. The nigger had him by the arm. "I'm going up anyway," he said. "I'll help you." Old Dudley looked frantically around. The steps behind him seemed to close up. He was walking with the nigger up the stairs. The nigger was waiting for him on each step. "So you hunt?" the nigger was saying. "Well, let's see. I went deer hunting once. I believe we used a Dodson .38 to get those deer. What do you use?"

Old Dudley was staring through the shiny tan shoes. "I use a gun," he mumbled.

"I like to fool with guns better than hunting," the nigger was saying. "Never was much at killing anything. Seems kind of a shame to deplete the game reserve. I'd collect guns if I had the time and the money, though." He was waiting on every step till Old Dudley got on it. He was explaining guns and makes. He had on gray socks with a black fleck in them. They finished the stairs. The nigger walked down the hall with him, holding him by the arm. It probably looked like he had his arm locked in the nigger's.

They went right up to Old Dudley's door. Then the nigger asked, "You from around here?"

Old Dudley shook his head, looking at the door. He hadn't looked at the nigger yet. All the way up the stairs, he hadn't looked at the nigger.

"Well," the nigger said, "it's a swell place — once you get used to it." He patted Old Dudley on the back and went into his own apartment. Old Dudley went into his. The pain in his throat was all over his face now, leaking out his eyes.

He shuffled to the chair by the window and sank down in it. His throat was going to pop. His throat was going to pop on account of a nigger — a damn nigger that patted him on the back and called him "old-timer." Him that knew such as that couldn't be. Him that had come from a good place. A good place. A place where such as that couldn't be. His eyes felt strange in their sockets. They were swelling in them and in a minute there wouldn't be any room left for them there. He was trapped in this place where niggers could call you "old-timer." He wouldn't be trapped. He wouldn't be. He rolled his head on the back of the chair to stretch his neck that was too full.

A man was looking at him. A man was in the window across the alley looking straight at him. The man was watching him cry. That was where the geranium was supposed to be and it was a man in his undershirt, watching him cry, waiting to watch his throat pop. Old Dudley looked back at the man. It was supposed to be the geranium. The geranium belonged there, not the man. "Where is the geranium?" he called out of his tight throat.

"What you cryin' for?" the man asked. "I ain't never seen a man cry like that."

"Where is the geranium?" Old Dudley quavered. "It ought to be there. Not you."

"This is my window," the man said. "I got a right to set here if I want to."

"Where is it?" Old Dudley shrilled. There was just a little room left in his throat.

"It fell off if it's any of your business," the man said.

Old Dudley got up and peered over the window ledge. Down in the alley, way six floors down, he could see a cracked flower pot scattered over a spray of dirt and something pink sticking out of a green paper bow. It was down six floors. Smashed down six floors.

Old Dudley looked at the man who was chewing gum and waiting to see the throat pop. "You shouldn't have put it so near the ledge," he murmured. "Why don't you pick it up?"

"Why don't you, pop?"

Old Dudley stared at the man who was where the geranium should have been.

He would. He'd go down and pick it up. He'd put it in his own window and look at it all day if he wanted to. He turned from the window and left the room. He walked slowly down the dog run and got to the steps. The steps dropped down like a deep wound in the floor. They opened up through a gap like a cavern and went down and down. And he had gone up them a little behind the nigger. And the nigger had pulled him up on his feet and kept his arm in his and gone up the steps with him and said he hunted deer, "old-timer," and seen him holding a gun that wasn't there and sitting on the steps like a child. He had shiny tan shoes and he was trying not to laugh and the whole business was laughing. There'd probably be niggers with black flecks in their socks on every step, pulling down their mouths so as not to laugh. The steps dropped down and down. He wouldn't go down and have niggers pattin' him on the back. He went back to the room and the window and looked down at the geranium.

The man was sitting over where it should have been. "I ain't seen you pickin' it up," he said.

Old Dudley stared at the man.

"I seen you before," the man said. "I seen you settin' in that old chair every day, starin' out the window, looking in my apartment. What I do in my apartment is my business, see? I don't like people looking at what I do."

It was at the bottom of the alley with its roots in the air.

"I only tell people once," the man said and left the window.

Goodbye and Good Luck

Accent, the same little magazine that published Flannery O'Connor's first story, accepted Grace Paley's "Goodbye and Good Luck" in 1956. They printed another of her stories soon after, and Paley took those two, plus one more, to Ken McCormick at Doubleday, who told her if she would write seven more he'd publish a collection. She did, and the book *Little Disturbances of Man* was published in 1959. It disappeared without much notice but gained such an underground following that Viking republished the book in hardcover in 1968. Paley was born in 1922 and attended Hunter College and New York University but left without getting a degree. Married at nineteen, she raised two children and wrote at a slow pace, saying once, "I wrote poetry for years before I ever wrote a story. I still work like a poet. Real slow." To date Paley has published only two additional collections of stories; however, this year Farrar, Straus & Giroux will bring out Paley's collected works, including stories not yet published in book form.

I WAS POPULAR in certain circles, says Aunt Rose. I wasn't no thinner then, only more stationary in the flesh. In time to come, Lillie, don't be surprised — change is a fact of God. From this, no one is excused. Only a person like your mama stands on one foot, she don't notice how big her behind is getting, and sings in the canary's ear for thirty years. Who's listening? Papa's in the shop. You and Seymour, thinking about yourself. So she waits in a spotless kitchen for a kind word and thinks, — poor Rosie —.

Poor Rosie! If there was more life in my little sister, she would know

my heart is a regular college of feelings and there is such information between my corset and me that her whole married life is a kindergarten.

Nowadays, you could find me anytime in a hotel, uptown or downtown. Who needs an apartment to live like a maid with a dustrag in the hand, sneezing? I'm in very good with the bellboys, it's more interesting than home, all kinds of people, everybody with a reason. . . .

And my reason, Lillie, is a long time ago I said to the forelady, "Missus, if I can't sit by the window, I can't sit." "If you can't sit, girlie," she says politely, "go stand on the street corner." And that's how I got unemployed in novelty wear.

For my next job, I answered an ad which said: "Refined young lady, medium salary, cultural organization." I went by trolley to the address, the Russian Art Theater of Second Avenue where they played only the best Yiddish plays.

They needed a ticket seller, someone like me, who likes the public but is very sharp on crooks. The man who interviewed me was the manager, a certain type.

Immediately he said: "Rosie Lieber, you surely got a build on you!"

"It takes all kinds, Mr. Krimberg."

"Don't misunderstand me, little girl," he said. "I appreciate, I appreciate. A young lady lacking fore and aft, her blood is so busy warming the toes and the fingertips, it don't have time to circulate where it's most required."

Everybody likes kindness. I said to him: "Only don't be fresh, Mr. Krimberg, and we'll make a good bargain."

We did: Nine dollars a week, a glass of tea every night, a free ticket once a week for mama, and I could go watch rehearsals any time I want.

My first nine dollars was in the grocer's hands ready to move on already, when Krimberg said to me: "Rosie, here's a great gentleman, a member of this remarkable theater, wants to meet you, impressed no doubt by your big brown eyes."

And who was it, Lillie? Listen to me, before my very eyes was Volodya Vlashkin, called by the people of those days the Valentino of Second Avenue.

I took one look and I said to myself, where did a Jewish boy grow up so big? "Just outside Kiev," he told me.

How? "My mama nursed me till I was six. I was the only boy in the village to have such health."

"My goodness, Vlashkin, six years old! She must have had shredded wheat there, not breasts, poor woman."

"My mother was beautiful," he said. "She had eyes like stars."

He had such a way of expressing himself, it brought tears.

To Krimberg, Vlashkin said after this introduction: "Who is responsible for hiding this wonderful young person in a cage?"

"That is where the ticket seller sells."

"So David, go in there and sell tickets for a half hour. I have something in mind in regards to the future of this girl and this company. Go David, be a good boy. And you, Miss Lieber, please, I suggest Feinbergs for a glass of tea. The rehearsals are long. I enjoy a quiet interlude with a friendly person."

So he took me there, Feinbergs, then around the corner, a place so full of Hungarians, it was deafening. In the back room was a table of honor for him. On the table cloth, embroidered by the lady of the house, was Here Vlashkin Eats. We finished one glass of tea in quietness out of thirst, when I finally made up my mind what to say.

"Mr. Vlashkin, I saw you a couple weeks ago even before I started working here, in *The Sea Gull*. Believe me, if I was that girl, I wouldn't look even for a minute on the young bourgeois fellow. He could fall out of the play altogether. How Chekhov could put him in the same play as you, I can't understand."

"You liked me?" he asked, taking my hand and kindly patting it. "Well, well, young people still like me, — so, and you like the theater too? Good. And you, Rose, you know you have such a nice hand, so warm to the touch, such a fine skin, tell me, why do you wear a scarf around your neck? You only hide your young, young throat. These are not olden times, my child, to live in shame."

"Who's ashamed?" I said, taking off the kerchief, but my hand right away went to the kerchief's place, because the truth is, it really was olden times, and I was still of a nature to melt with shame.

"Have some more tea, my dear."

"No thank you, I am a samovar already."

"Dorfmann!" he hollered like a king. "Bring this child a seltzer with fresh ice!"

In weeks to follow, I had the privilege to know him better and better as a person — also the opportunity to see him in his profession. The time was autumn; the theater full of coming and going. Rehearsing without end. After *The Sea Gull* flopped, *The Salesman From Istanbul* played, a great success.

Here the ladies went crazy. On the opening night, in the middle of the first scene, one missus, a widow or her husband worked too long hours, began to clap and sing out, "Oi, oi, Vlashkin." Soon there was such a tumult, the actors had to stop acting. Vlashkin stepped forward. Only not Vlashkin to the eyes . . . a younger man with pitch-black hair, lively on restless feet, his mouth clever. A half a century later at the end of the play he came out again, a grey philosopher, a student of life, from only reading books, his hands as smooth as silk. I cried to think who I was — nothing — and such a man could look at me with interest.

Then I got a small raise due to he kindly put in a good word for me and also, for fifty cents a night, I was given the privilege together with cousins, in-laws and plain stagestruck kids to be part of a crowd scene. This was for me a special pleasure, to stand behind his back and hear him breathe.

The sad day came, I kissed my mama goodbye. Vlashkin helped me to get a reasonable room near the theater to be more free. Also my outstanding friend would have a place to recline away from the noise of the dressing rooms. She cried and she cried. "This is a different way of living, Mama," I said. "Besides, I am driven by love."

"You! you! a nothing, a rotten hole in a piece of cheese, are you telling me what is life?" she screamed.

Very insulted, I went away from her. But I am good-natured, you know fat people are like that, kind, and I thought to myself, poor mama . . . it is true she got more of an idea of life than me. She married who she didn't like, a sick man, his spirit already swallowed up by God. He never washed. He had an unhappy smell. His teeth fell out, his hair disappeared, he got smaller, shriveled up little by little, till goodbye and good luck he was gone and only came to mama's mind when she went to the mailbox under the stairs to get the electric bill. In memory of him and out of respect for mankind, I decided to live for love.

Don't laugh, you ignorant girl.

Do you think it was easy for me? I had to give mama a little some-

thing. Ruthie was saving up together with your papa for linens, a couple of knives and forks. In the morning I had to do piecework if I wanted to keep by myself. So I made flowers. Before lunchtime every day a whole garden grew on my table.

This was my independence, Lillie dear, blooming, but it didn't have no roots and its face was paper.

Meanwhile Krimberg went after me too. No doubt observing the success of Vlashkin, he thought, "Aha, Open Sesame. . . ." Others in the company similar. After me in those years were the following: Krimberg I mentioned. Carl Zimmer, played innocent young fellows with a wig. Charles Peel, a Christian who fell in the soup by accident, a creator of beautiful sets. "Color is his middle name," says Vlashkin, always to the point.

I put this in to show you your fat old aunt was not crazy out of loneliness. In those noisy years, I had friends among interesting people who admired me for reasons of youth and that I was a first-class listener.

The actresses, Raisele, Marya, Esther Leopold, were only interested in tomorrow. After them was the rich men, producers, the whole garment center, their past is a pin cushion, future the eye of a needle.

Finally the day came I no longer could keep my tact in my mouth. I said: "Vlashkin, I hear by carrier-pigeon you have a wife, children, the whole combination."

"True, I don't tell stories. I make no pretence."

"That isn't the question. What is this lady like? It hurts me to ask, but tell me, Vlashkin . . . a man's life is something I don't clearly see."

"Little girl, I have told you a hundred times, this small room is the convent of my troubled spirit. Here I come to your innocent shelter to refresh myself in the midst of an agonized life."

"Ach, Vlashkin, serious, serious, who is this lady?"

"Rosie, she is a fine woman of the middle classes, a good mother to my children, three in number, girls all, a good cook, in her youth handsome, now no longer young. You see, could I be more frank? I entrust you, dear, with my soul."

It was some months later at the New Year's Ball of the Russian Artists Club, I met Mrs. Vlashkin, a woman with black hair in a low bun, straight and too proud, she sat at a small table speaking in a deep voice to whoever stopped a moment to converse. Her Yiddish was perfect,

each word cut like a special jewel. I looked at her. She noticed me like she noticed everybody, cold like Christmas morning. Then she got tired. Vlashkin called a taxi and I never saw her again. Poor woman, she did not know I was on the same stage with her. The poison I was to her role, she did not know.

Later on that night in front of my door, I said to Vlashkin, "No more. This isn't for me. I am sick from it all. I am no home-breaker."

"Girlie," he said, "don't be foolish."

"No, no, goodbye, good luck," I said. "I am sincere."

So I went and stayed with mama for a week's vacation and cleaned up all the closets and scrubbed the walls till the paint came off. She was very grateful, all the same her hard life made her say, "Now we see the end. If you live like a bum, you are finally a lunatic."

After this few days, I came back to my life. When we met, me and Vlashkin, we said only hello and goodbye, and then for a few sad years with the head we nodded as if to say, "Yes, yes, I know who you are."

Meanwhile in the field was a whole new strategy. Your mama and grandmama brought around — boys.

Your own father had a brother, you never even seen him. Ruben. A serious fellow, his idealism was his hat and his coat. "Rosie, I offer you a big new free happy unusual life." How? "With me, we will raise up the sands of Palestine to make a nation. That is the land of tomorrow for us Jews." "Ha, ha, Ruben, I'll go tomorrow then." "Rosie!" says Ruben. "We need strong women like you, mothers and farmers." "You don't fool me, Ruben, what you need is dray horses. But for that you need more money." "I don't like your attitude, Rose." "In that case, go and multiply. Goodbye."

Another fellow: Yonkel Gurstein, a regular sport, dressed to kill, with such an excitable nature. In those days, it looks to me like yesterday, the youngest girls wore undergarments like Battle Creek, Michigan. To him it was a matter of seconds. Where did he practice, a Jewish boy? Nowadays, I suppose it is easier, Lillie? My goodness, I ain't asking you nothing, — touchy, touchy.

Well, by now you must know yourself, honey, whatever you do, life don't stop. It only sits a minute and dreams a dream.

While I was saying to all these silly youngsters — no, no, no, Vlashkin went to Europe and toured a few seasons — Moscow, Prague, Lon-

don, even Berlin, already a pessimistic place. When he came back, he wrote a book you could get from the library even today, *The Jewish Actor Abroad.* If some day you're interested enough in my lonesome years, you could read it. You could absorb a flavor of the man from the book. No, no, I am not mentioned. After all, who am I?

When the book came out, I stopped him in the street to say congratulations. But I am not a liar, so I pointed out too the egotism of many parts, — even the critics said something along such lines.

"Talk is cheap," Vlashkin answered me. "But who are the critics, tell me do they create? Not to mention," he continues, "there is a line in Shakespeare in one of the plays from the great history of England, it says . . . 'self-loving is not so vile a sin, my liege, as self-neglecting.' This idea also appears in modern times in the moralistic followers of Freud.

"Rosie, are you listening? You asked a question. By the way, you look very well. How come no wedding ring?" I walked away from this conversation in tears. But this talking in the street opened the happy road up for more discussions. In regard to many things. For instance, the management — very narrow-minded — wouldn't give him any more certain young men's parts. Fools. What youngest man knew enough about life to be as young as him?

"Rosie, Rosie," he said to me one day. "I see by the clock on your rosy, rosy face, you must be thirty."

"The hands are slow, Vlashkin. On a week before Thursday I was thirty-four."

"Is that so? Rosie, I worry about you. It has been on my mind to talk to you. You are losing your time. Do you understand it? A woman should not lose her time."

"Oi Vlashkin, if you are my friend, what is time?"

For this, he had no answer, only looked at me surprised. We went instead, full of interest but not with our former speed, up to my new place on 94th Street. The same pictures on the wall, all of Vlashkin, only now everything painted red and black which was stylish, and new upholstery.

A few years ago there was a book by another member of that fine company, an actress, the one that learned English very good and went uptown — Marya Kavkaz, in which she says certain things regarding Vlashkin.

Such as, he was her lover for eleven years, she's not ashamed to write this down. Without respect for him, his wife and children or even others who also may have feelings in the matter.

Now, Lillie, don't be surprised. This is called a fact of life. An actor's soul must be like a diamond. The more faces it got, the more shining is his name. Honey, you will no doubt love and marry one man and have a couple kids and be happy forever till you die tired. More than that, a person like us don't have to know. But a great artist like Volodya Vlashkin . . . in order to make a job on the stage, he's got to practice. I understand it now, to him life is like a rehearsal.

Myself, when I saw him in *The Father-in-Law,* an older man in love with a darling young girl, his son's wife, played by Raisele Maisel — I cried. What he said to this girl, how he whispered such sweetness, how all his hot feelings were on his face. . . . Lillie, all this experience he had with me. The very words were the same. You can imagine how proud I was.

So the story creeps to an end.

I noticed it first on my mother's face, the rotten handwriting of time, scribbled up and down her cheeks, across her forehead back and forth — a child could read — it said, old, old, old. But it troubled my heart most to see these realities scratched on Vlashkin's wonderful expression.

First the company fell apart. The theater ended. Esther Leopold died from being very aged. Krimberg had a heart attack. Marya went to Broadway. Also Raisele changed her name to Roslyn and was a big comical hit in the movies.

Vlashkin himself, no place to go, retired. It said in the paper: ". . . an actor without peer, he will write his memoirs and spend his last years in the bosom of his family among his thriving grandchildren, the apple of his wife's doting eye."

This is journalism.

We made for him a great dinner of honor. At this dinner, I said to him for the last time I thought, "Goodbye, dear friend, topic of my life, now we part."

And to myself I said further: Finished. This is your lonesome bed. A lady what they call fat and fifty. You made it personally. From this lonesome bed you will finally fall to a bed not so lonesome.

And now comes? Lillie, guess.

Last week, washing my underwear in the basin, I get a buzz on the phone.

"Excuse me, is this the Rose Lieber formerly connected with the Russian Art Theater?"

"It is."

"Well, well, how do you do, Rose? This is Vlashkin."

"Vlashkin! Volodya Vlashkin?"

"In fact. How are you, Rose?"

"Living, Vlashkin, thank you."

"You are all right? Really, Rose? Your health is good? You are working?"

"My health, considering the weight it must carry, is first class. I am back for some years now where I started, in novelty wear."

"Very interesting."

"Listen, Vlashkin, tell me the truth, what's on your mind?"

"My mind? Rosie, I am looking up an old friend, an old warm-hearted companion of more joyful days. My circumstances by the way are changed. I am retired as you know. Also I am a free man."

"What? What do you mean?"

"Mrs. Vlashkin is divorcing me."

"What came over her? Did you start drinking or something from melancholy?"

"She is divorcing me for adultery."

"But Vlashkin, you should excuse me, don't be insulted, but you got maybe seventeen, eighteen years on me and even me, all this nonsense, this daydreams and nightmares, is mostly for the pleasure of conversation alone."

"I pointed all this out to her. My dear, I said, my time is past, my blood is as dry as my bones. The truth is, Rose, she isn't accustomed to have a man around all day, reading out loud from the papers the interesting events of our time, waiting for breakfast, waiting for lunch. So all day she gets madder and madder. By night time a furious old lady gives me my supper. She has information from the last fifty years to pepper my soup. Surely there was a Judas in that theater saying every day, 'Vlashkin, Vlashkin, Vlashkin' . . . and while my heart was circulating with his smiles he was on the wire passing the dope to my wife."

"Such a foolish end, Volodya, to such a lively story. What is your plans?"

"First, could I ask you for dinner and the theater — uptown of course? After this . . . we are old friends. I have money to burn. What your heart desires. Others are like grass, the north wind of time has cut out their heart. Of you, Rosie, I recreate only kindness. What a woman should be to a man, you were to me. Do you think, Rosie, a couple of old pals like us could have a few good times among the material things of this world?"

My answer, Lillie, in a minute was altogether yes, yes, come up, I said, ask the room by the switchboard, let us talk.

So he came that night and every night in the week. We talked of his long life. Even at the end of time, a fascinating man. And like men are too till time's end, trying to get away in one piece.

"Listen, Rosie," he explains the other day. "I was married to my wife, do you realize nearly half a century. What good was it? Look at the bitterness. The more I think of it, the more I think we would be fools to marry."

"Volodya Vlashkin," I told him straight, "when I was young, I warmed your cold back many a night no questions asked. You admit it, I didn't make no demands. I was soft-hearted. I didn't want to be called Rosie Lieber a breaker up of homes. But now, Vlashkin, you are a free man. How could you ask me to go with you on trains to stay in strange hotels, among Americans, not your wife? Be ashamed."

So now, darling Lillie, tell this story to your mama from your young mouth. She don't listen to a word from me. She only screams, "I'll faint, I'll faint." Tell her, after all I'll have a husband which, as everybody knows, a woman should have at least one before the end of the story.

My goodness, I am already late. Give me a kiss. After all, I watched you grow from a plain seed. So give me a couple wishes on my wedding day. A long and happy life. Many years of love. Hug mama, tell her from Aunt Rose, goodbye and good luck.

||≣

Such a Pretty Little Picture

By the time *Smart Set* published Dorothy Parker's first short story, "Such a Pretty Little Picture," in December 1922, she was already the widely read author of articles, reviews, and verse for such magazines as *Life, Vanity Fair, Ladies' Home Journal,* and the *Saturday Evening Post,* as well as a charter member of the famed Algonquin Round Table. She had wanted to write fiction and drama for some time, but she found it a "torturous process," as Marion Meade writes in her biography of Parker: "When she insisted that it took her six months to complete a story, it was often the case."

Parker's model for this story's Mr. Wheelock was Robert Benchley, whom she had befriended when they worked together at *Vanity Fair.* Twelve years after it first appeared, she wrote, "Its mother thinks it's the best thing she ever wrote, which would make it about on a parallel (oh, all right!) with the works of Carolyn Wells's middle period."

||≣

MR. WHEELOCK WAS clipping the hedge. He did not dislike doing it. If it had not been for the faintly sickish odor of the privet bloom, he would definitely have enjoyed it. The new shears were so sharp and bright, there was such a gratifying sense of something done as the young green stems snapped off and the expanse of tidy, square hedge-top lengthened. There was a lot of work to be done on it. It should have been attended to a week ago, but this was the first day that Mr. Wheelock had been able to get back from the city before dinnertime.

Clipping the hedge was one of the few domestic duties that Mr. Wheelock could be trusted with. He was notoriously poor at doing anything around the house. All the suburb knew about it. It was the source

of all Mrs. Wheelock's jokes. Her most popular anecdote was of how, the past winter, he had gone out and hired a man to take care of the furnace, after a seven-years' losing struggle with it. She had an admirable memory, and often as she had related the story, she never dropped a word of it. Even now, in the late summer, she could hardly tell it for laughing.

When they were first married, Mr. Wheelock had lent himself to the fun. He had even posed as being more inefficient than he really was, to make the joke better. But he had tired of his helplessness, as a topic of conversation. All the men of Mrs. Wheelock's acquaintance, her cousins, her brother-in-law, the boys she went to high school with, the neighbors' husbands, were adepts at putting up a shelf, at repairing a clock, or making a shirtwaist box. Mr. Wheelock had begun to feel that there was something rather effeminate about his lack of interest in such things.

He had wanted to answer his wife, lately, when she enlivened some neighbor's dinner table with tales of his inadequacy with hammer and wrench. He had wanted to cry, "All right, suppose I'm not any good at things like that. What of it?"

He had played with the idea, had tried to imagine how his voice would sound, uttering the words. But he could think of no further argument for his case than that "What of it?" And he was a little relieved, somehow, at being able to find nothing stronger. It made it reassuringly impossible to go through with the plan of answering his wife's public railleries.

Mrs. Wheelock sat, now, on the spotless porch of the neat stucco house. Beside her was a pile of her husband's shirts and drawers, the price-tags still on them. She was going over all the buttons before he wore the garments, sewing them on more firmly. Mrs. Wheelock never waited for a button to come off, before sewing it on. She worked with quick, decided movements, compressing her lips each time the thread made a slight resistance to her deft jerks.

She was not a tall woman, and since the birth of her child she had gone over from a delicate plumpness to a settled stockiness. Her brown hair, though abundant, grew in an uncertain line about her forehead. It was her habit to put it up in curlers at night, but the crimps never came out in the right place. It was arranged with perfect neatness, yet it suggested that it had been done up and got over with as quickly as possible.

Passionately clean, she was always redolent of the germicidal soap she used so vigorously. She was wont to tell people, somewhat redundantly, that she never employed any sort of cosmetics. She had unlimited contempt for women who sought to reduce their weight by dieting, cutting from their menus such nourishing items as cream and puddings and cereals.

Adelaide Wheelock's friends — and she had many of them — said of her that there was no nonsense about her. They and she regarded it as a compliment.

Sister, the Wheelocks' five-year-old daughter, played quietly in the gravel path that divided the tiny lawn. She had been known as Sister since her birth, and her mother still laid plans for a brother for her. Sister's baby carriage stood waiting in the cellar, her baby clothes were stacked expectantly away in bureau drawers. But raises were infrequent at the advertising agency where Mr. Wheelock was employed, and his present salary had barely caught up to the cost of their living. They could not conscientiously regard themselves as being able to afford a son. Both Mr. and Mrs. Wheelock keenly felt his guilt in keeping the bassinet empty.

Sister was not a pretty child, though her features were straight, and her eyes would one day be handsome. The left one turned slightly in toward the nose, now, when she looked in a certain direction; they would operate as soon as she was seven. Her hair was pale and limp, and her color bad. She was a delicate little girl. Not fragile in a picturesque way, but the kind of child that must be always undergoing treatment for its teeth and its throat and obscure things in its nose. She had lately had her adenoids removed, and she was still using squares of surgical gauze instead of handkerchiefs. Both she and her mother somehow felt that these gave her a sort of prestige.

She was additionally handicapped by her frocks, which her mother bought a size or so too large, with a view to Sister's growing into them — an expectation which seemed never to be realized, for her skirts were always too long, and the shoulders of her little dresses came halfway down to her thin elbows. Yet, even discounting the unfortunate way she was dressed, you could tell, in some way, that she was never going to wear any kind of clothes well.

Mr. Wheelock glanced at her now and then as he clipped. He had

never felt any fierce thrills of father-love for the child. He had been disappointed in her when she was a pale, large-headed baby smelling of stale milk and warm rubber. Sister made him feel ill at ease, vaguely irritated him. He had had no share in her training; Mrs. Wheelock was so competent a parent that she took the places of both of them. When Sister came to him to ask his permission to do something, he always told her to wait and ask her mother about it.

He regarded himself as having the usual paternal affection for his daughter. There were times, indeed, when she had tugged sharply at his heart — when he had waited in the corridor outside the operating roomen she was still under the anesthetic, and lay little and white and helpless on her high hospital bed; once when he had accidentally closed a door upon her thumb. But from the first he had nearly acknowledged to himself that he did not like Sister as a person.

Sister was not a whining child, despite her poor health. She had always been sensible and well-mannered, amenable about talking to visitors, rigorously unselfish. She never got into trouble, like other children. She did not care much for other children. She had heard herself described as being "old-fashioned," and she knew she was delicate, and she felt that these attributes rather set her above them. Besides, they were rough and careless of their bodily well-being.

Sister was exquisitely cautious of her safety. Grass, she knew, was often apt to be damp in the late afternoon, so she was careful now to stay right in the middle of the gravel path, sitting on a folded newspaper and playing one of her mysterious games with three petunias that she had been allowed to pick. Mrs. Wheelock never had to speak to her twice about keeping off wet grass, or wearing her rubbers, or putting on her jacket if a breeze sprang up. Sister was an immediately obedient child, always.

II

Mrs. Wheelock looked up from her sewing and spoke to her husband. Her voice was high and clear, resolutely good-humored. From her habit of calling instructions from her upstairs window to Sister playing on the porch below, she spoke always a little louder than was necessary.

"Daddy," she said.

She had called him Daddy since some eight months before Sister was

born. She and the child had the same trick of calling his name and then waiting until he signified that he was attending before they went on with what they wanted to say.

Mr. Wheelock stopped clipping, straightened himself and turned toward her.

"Daddy," she went on, thus reassured, "I saw Mr. Ince down at the post office today when Sister and I went down to get the ten o'clock mail — there wasn't much, just a card for me from Grace Williams from that place they go to up on Cape Cod, and an advertisement from some department store or other about their summer fur sale (as if I cared!), and a circular for you from the bank. I opened it; I knew you wouldn't mind.

"Anyway, I just thought I'd tackle Mr. Ince first as last about getting in our cordwood. He didn't see me at first — though I'll bet he really saw me and pretended not to — but I ran right after him. 'Oh, Mr. Ince!' I said. 'Why, hello, Mrs. Wheelock,' he said, and then he asked for you, and I told him you were finely, and everything. Then I said, 'Now, Mr. Ince,' I said, 'how about getting in that cordwood of ours?' And he said, 'Well, Mrs. Wheelock,' he said, 'I'll get it in soon's I can, but I'm short of help right now,' he said.

"Short of help! Of course I couldn't say anything, but I guess he could tell from the way I looked at him how much I believed it. I just said, 'All right, Mr. Ince, but don't you forget us. There may be a cold snap coming on,' I said, 'and we'll be wanting a fire in the living-room. Don't you forget us,' I said, and he said, no, he wouldn't.

"If that wood isn't here by Monday, I think you ought to do something about it, Daddy. There's no sense in all this putting it off, and putting it off. First thing you know there'll be a cold snap coming on, and we'll be wanting a fire in the living-room, and there we'll be! You'll be sure and 'tend to it, won't you, Daddy? I'll remind you again Monday, if I can think of it, but there are so many things!"

Mr. Wheelock nodded and turned back to his clipping — and his thoughts. They were thoughts that had occupied much of his leisure lately. After dinner, when Adelaide was sewing or arguing with the maid, he found himself letting his magazine fall face downward on his knee, while he rolled the same idea round and round in his mind. He had got so that he looked forward, through the day, to losing himself in it. He

had rather welcomed the hedge-clipping; you can clip and think at the same time.

It had started with a story that he had picked up somewhere. He couldn't recall whether he had heard it or had read it — that was probably it, he thought, he had run across it in the back pages of some comic paper that someone had left on the train.

It was about a man who lived in a suburb. Every morning he had gone to the city on the 8:12, sitting in the same seat in the same car, and every evening he had gone home to his wife on the 5:17, sitting in the same seat in the same car. He had done this for twenty years of his life. And then one night he didn't come home. He never went back to his office any more. He just never turned up again.

The last man to see him was the conductor on the 5:17.

"He come down the platform at the Grand Central," the man reported, "just like he done every night since I been working on this road. He put one foot on the step, and then he stopped sudden, and he said 'Oh, hell,' and he took his foot off of the step and walked away. And that's the last anybody see of him."

Curious how that story took hold of Mr. Wheelock's fancy. He had started thinking of it as a mildly humorous anecdote; he had come to accept it as fact. He did not think the man's sitting in the same seat in the same car need have been stressed so much. That seemed unimportant. He thought long about the man's wife, wondered what suburb he had lived in. He loved to play with the thing, to try to feel what the man felt before he took his foot off the car's step. He never concerned himself with speculations as to where the man had disappeared, how he had spent the rest of his life. Mr. Wheelock was absorbed in that moment when he had said "Oh, hell," and walked off. "Oh, hell" seemed to Mr. Wheelock a fine thing for him to have said, a perfect summary of the situation.

He tried thinking of himself in the man's place. But no, he would have done it from the other end. That was the real way to do it.

Some summer evening like this, say, when Adelaide was sewing on buttons, up on the porch, and Sister was playing somewhere about. A pleasant, quiet evening it must be, with the shadows lying long on the street that led from their house to the station. He would put down the garden shears, or the hose, or whatever he happened to be puttering

with — not throw the thing down, you know, just put it quietly aside — and walk out of the gate and down the street, and that would be the last they'd see of him. He would time it so that he'd just make the 6:03 for the city comfortably.

He did not go ahead with it from there, much. He was not especially anxious to leave the advertising agency forever. He did not particularly dislike his work. He had been an advertising solicitor since he had gone to work at all, and he worked hard at his job and, aside from that, didn't think about it much one way or the other.

It seemed to Mr. Wheelock that before he had got hold of the "Oh, hell" story he had never thought about anything much, one way or the other. But he would have to disappear from the office, too, that was certain. It would spoil everything to turn up there again. He thought dimly of taking a train going West, after the 6:03 got him to the Grand Central Terminal — he might go to Buffalo, say, or perhaps Chicago. Better just let that part take care of itself and go back to dwell on the moment when it would sweep over him that he was going to do it, when he would put down the shears and walk out the gate —

The "Oh, hell" rather troubled him. Mr. Wheelock felt that he would like to retain that; it completed the gesture so beautifully. But he didn't quite know to whom he should say it.

He might stop in at the post office on his way to the station and say it to the postmaster; but the postmaster would probably think he was only annoyed at there being no mail for him. Nor would the conductor of the 6:03, a train Mr. Wheelock never used, take the right interest in it. Of course the real thing to do would be to say it to Adelaide just before he laid down the shears. But somehow Mr. Wheelock could not make that scene come very clear in his imagination.

III

"Daddy," Mrs. Wheelock said briskly.

He stopped clipping, and faced her.

"Daddy," she related, "I saw Doctor Mann's automobile going by the house this morning — he was going to have a look at Mr. Warren, his rheumatism's getting along nicely — and I called him in a minute, to look us over."

She screwed up her face, winked, and nodded vehemently several times in the direction of the absorbed Sister, to indicate that she was the subject of the discourse.

"He said we were going ahead finely," she resumed, when she was sure that he had caught the idea. "Said there was no need for those t-o-n-s-i-l-s to c-o-m-e o-u-t. But I thought, soon's it gets a little cooler, some time next month, we'd just run in to the city and let Doctor Sturges have a look at us. I'd rather be on the safe side."

"But Doctor Lytton said it wasn't necessary, and those doctors at the hospital, and now Doctor Mann, that's known her since she was a baby," suggested Mr. Wheelock.

"I know, I know," replied his wife. "But I'd rather be on the safe side."

Mr. Wheelock went back to his hedge.

Oh, of course he couldn't do it; he never seriously thought he could, for a minute. Of course he couldn't. He wouldn't have the shadow of an excuse for doing it. Adelaide was a sterling woman, an utterly faithful wife, an almost slavish mother. She ran his house economically and efficiently. She harried the suburban trades people into giving them dependable service, drilled the succession of poorly paid, poorly trained maids, cheerfully did the thousand fussy little things that go with the running of a house. She looked after his clothes, gave him medicine when she thought he needed it, oversaw the preparation of every meal that was set before him; they were not especially inspirational meals, but the food was always nourishing and, as a general thing, fairly well cooked. She never lost her temper, she was never depressed, never ill.

Not the shadow of an excuse. People would know that, and so they would invent an excuse for him. They would say there must be another woman.

Mr. Wheelock frowned, and snipped at an obstinate young twig. Good Lord, the last thing he wanted was another woman. What he wanted was that moment when he realized he could do it, when he would lay down the shears—

Oh, of course he couldn't; he knew that as well as anybody. What would they do, Adelaide and Sister? The house wasn't even paid for yet, and there would be that operation on Sister's eye in a couple of years. But the house would be all paid up by next March. And there was always

that well-to-do brother-in-law of Adelaide's, the one who, for all his means, put up every shelf in that great big house with his own hands.

Decent people didn't just go away and leave their wives and families that way. All right, suppose you weren't decent; what of it? Here was Adelaide planning what she was going to do when it got a little cooler, next month. She was always planning ahead, always confident that things would go on just the same. Naturally, Mr. Wheelock realized that he couldn't do it, as well as the next one. But there was no harm in fooling around with the idea. Would you say the "Oh, hell" now, before you laid down the shears, or right after? How would it be to turn at the gate and say it?

Mr. and Mrs. Fred Coles came down the street arm-in-arm, from their neat stucco house on the corner.

"See they've got you working hard, eh?" cried Mr. Coles genially, as they paused abreast of the hedge.

Mr. Wheelock laughed politely, marking time for an answer.

"That's right," he evolved.

Mrs. Wheelock looked up from her work, shading her eyes with her thimbled hand against the long rays of the low sun.

"Yes, we finally got Daddy to do a little work," she called brightly. "But Sister and I are staying right here to watch over him, for fear he might cut his little self with the shears."

There was general laughter, in which Sister joined. She had risen punctiliously at the approach of the older people, and she was looking politely at their eyes, as she had been taught.

"And how is my great big girl?" asked Mrs. Coles, gazing fondly at the child.

"Oh, much better," Mrs. Wheelock answered for her. "Doctor Mann says we are going ahead finely. I saw his automobile passing the house this morning — he was going to see Mr. Warren, his rheumatism's coming along nicely — and I called him in a minute to look us over."

She did the wink and the nods, at Sister's back. Mr. and Mrs. Coles nodded shrewdly back at her.

"He said there's no need for those t-o-n-s-i-l-s to c-o-m-e o-u-t," Mrs. Wheelock called. "But I thought, soon's it gets a little cooler, some time next month, we'd just run in to the city and let Doctor Sturges have a look at us. I was telling Daddy, 'I'd rather be on the safe side,' I said."

"Yes, it's better to be on the safe side," agreed Mrs. Coles, and her husband nodded again, sagely this time. She took his arm and they moved slowly off.

"Been a lovely day, hasn't it?" she said over her shoulder, fearful of having left too abruptly. "Fred and I are taking a little constitutional before supper."

"Oh, taking a little constitutional?" cried Mrs. Wheelock, laughing.

Mrs. Coles laughed also, three or four bars.

"Yes, just taking a little constitutional before supper," she called back.

Sister, weary of her game, mounted the porch, whimpering a little. Mrs. Wheelock put aside her sewing, and took the tired child in her lap. The sun's last rays touched her brown hair, making it a shimmering gold. Her small, sharp face, the thick lines of her figure were in shadow as she bent over the little girl. Sister's head was hidden on her mother's shoulder, the folds of her rumpled white frock followed her limp, relaxed little body.

The lovely light was kind to the cheap, hurriedly built stucco house, to the clean gravel path, and the bits of closely cut lawn. It was gracious, too, to Mr. Wheelock's tall, lean figure as he bent to work on the last few inches of unclipped hedge.

Twenty years, he thought. The man in the story went through with it for twenty years. He must have been a man along around forty-five, most likely. Mr. Wheelock was thirty-seven. Eight years. It's a long time, eight years is. You could easily get so you could say that final "Oh, hell," even to Adelaide, in eight years. It probably wouldn't take more than four for you to know that you could do it. No, not more than two. . . .

Mrs. Coles paused at the corner of the street and looked back at the Wheelocks' house. The last of the light lingered on the mother and child group on the porch, gently touched the tall, white-clad figure of the husband and father as he went up to them, his work done.

Mrs. Coles was a large, soft woman, barren, and addicted to sentiment.

"Look, Fred; just turn around and look at that," she said to her husband. She looked again, sighing luxuriously. "Such a pretty little picture!"

PHILIP ROTH

The Day It Snowed

Born in Newark, New Jersey, in 1933, Philip Roth began writing during his college years at Bucknell University in Pennsylvania, and he believed that his first stories had echoes of Salinger, Capote, and Wolfe. After graduation he won a graduate fellowship in writing at the University of Chicago. His first story was printed in the *Chicago Review* in the Fall 1954 issue. Roth published his second story, "The Contest for Aaron Gold," in *Epoch;* this story drew much attention and was included in *Best American Short Stories 1956.*

SUDDENLY PEOPLE BEGAN to disappear. First it was his Aunt Wilma who looked like his mother except that her eyes were soft and pale blue, like two pieces of sky lifted from the morning horizon. Aunt Wilma was tall and straight and quiet, and she seemed like she had spent all her life looking at the elm tree in front of the house and trying to be like it. She was the first to disappear and all the people but Sydney had cried for many days because they missed her, and Sydney had not cried because he thought that maybe Aunt Wilma would come back again. Uncle Carl was the second to disappear and everybody but Sydney cried for him too. Uncle Carl was a fat man with rolls of fat around his neck and when he was a little boy he had lived in St. Louis. Nights in the smoky kitchen he told everyone in a voice as thick and lumpy as hot cereal about St. Louis and how he had been born there and brought up there. Uncle Carl talked like it had been fun even though he had worked hard for only twelve dollars a week. Nobody would have cried so much if Uncle Carl were just going back to St. Louis, so it seemed that he was dis-

appearing to some other place. Maybe Aunt Wilma would meet Uncle Carl on the way back and bring him home too.

People all still had thumbprints around their eyes from crying about Uncle Carl, when the third person disappeared, Sydney's stepfather. Sydney's stepfather was a man with a brown mustache so big that it seemed to hold up his nose. When he disappeared Sydney began to cry with the rest of the people. He did not like any more people to disappear, especially when no one seemed to want to come back.

Never before had Sydney been allowed to stay in the house alone, but when Aunt Wilma disappeared his mother told him that all the people would be leaving the house for the day and Sydney would stay alone, and Sydney asked where everybody was going and his mother began to sob and it was then that he first found out about Aunt Wilma.

"Aunt Wilma — Aunt Wilma has disappeared, Sydney," his mother told him, and then she cried so loud it sounded like a laugh, and it made Sydney feel icy and raw as though he had put on his skin inside out. At first he didn't know what his mother meant when she said that Aunt Wilma disappeared, but he didn't ask his mother because of her crying, and he didn't ask his stepfather because his mother was the one he was supposed to ask questions of.

Sydney was scared to stay alone after Aunt Wilma disappeared, especially since the house was too big with no people in it, but when the third time came for him to stay alone he almost didn't mind it any more. When he was alone the first time he wondered about Aunt Wilma and why she had just disappeared without first telling anyone. Maybe Aunt Wilma had some place she had to go where she didn't think anybody else should follow her. But then why didn't his mother say that Aunt Wilma ran away instead of saying she disappeared? Sydney had heard of kids running away from their parents, and so he finally decided that when kids do it it's called running away and when big people like Aunt Wilma do it it's called disappearing, and also if you disappear you probably do it faster than if you just run away. Otherwise it's all the same. Sydney's mother didn't say why all the people had to leave for the day, so maybe they all decided to go out looking, like a posse looks for a criminal, and search for Aunt Wilma. They should have let him go along because he was good at finding people.

The second time, nobody told Sydney he would have to stay alone.

There was just the crying again like when Aunt Wilma disappeared, and there was his mother whispering to his stepfather as if she had a secret, and from the look on her face when she whispered, Sydney could tell the secret was about Uncle Carl. Whenever she saw Sydney watching her she would stop telling the secret, but once Sydney did hear her say to his stepfather "Don't be a fool — at least let us spare the child," and so nobody had to tell Sydney that Uncle Carl had disappeared too. When all the people left the house to go looking for Uncle Carl, Sydney wasn't too scared and he didn't ask any questions about why he had to be alone.

Once, after Sydney had crossed the street without first asking his mother and someone had squealed on him, he had hid in the hall closet all day so that she wouldn't find him. Only when he heard her crying and calling the police on the telephone did he finally come out of the closet. She had beat him because of it. The day all the people left the house to go searching for Sydney's stepfather, Sydney looked in all the closets to see if maybe his stepfather was hiding too. At first Sydney was cautious and he walked on his toes and he opened the doors very slowly and peeked in, but by the time he got to the last few closets he threw them open loudly and shouted into them "Boo!" He half expected someone to shout boo out at him, but nobody did, and it seemed that his stepfather had disappeared outside the house.

Outside the house was very big and Sydney did not believe that the people would be any luckier finding his stepfather than they had been looking for Aunt Wilma or for Uncle Carl. Sydney's stepfather knew all the streets, besides, and would be able to go far without being lost. Aunt Wilma would only take Sydney around the block for a walk, but when his stepfather took Sydney for walks he took him very far and sometimes so far that he told Sydney he should not tell his mother or she would be worried, and he said that if Sydney didn't tell maybe one day he would take him downtown to see the big white buildings and perhaps one fine day the two of them might go out to the country and walk, and taste the country air, and make whistles out of acorns. Sydney's stepfather knew how to make those kind of whistles. But Sydney knew that the people wouldn't come back with his stepfather and there was no sense thinking about the whistles. When a smart man like that decided to disappear, you just knew that he wouldn't get caught.

But he was a good man too, and it didn't make any sense to Sydney why he should do something like this in the first place. He saw how everybody cried when Aunt Wilma and Uncle Carl disappeared, so why did he have to make everybody cry all over again? His stepfather did not like people to cry. Times when Sydney asked the wrong questions or did something that was bad for himself and his mother had to hit him for it, his stepfather always looked sad and shook his head, and sometimes he ran his fingers over his mustache as though the skin underneath the mustache itched him badly. He liked people to be happy, so why did he disappear and make everybody cry and be sad? His stepfather was cruel to disappear on purpose. Sydney suddenly felt very alone in the big house, like one yellow leaf on a giant tree, and he cried.

When he awoke, for the crying made him sleep, Sydney knew that in a while his mother and all the people would come back and they would sit looking at each other, too tired to cry from searching, but wanting to cry because they had not been able to find his stepfather. Everybody would try not to think how cruel it was for Sydney's stepfather to disappear on purpose. It was always saddest trying to do that.

Sydney walked his way down the street wanting no one to see him. It was only a little beyond noon, but a dark winter wind was rising and for a moment it shook the thin naked trees and it made Sydney shiver too. He should go back and get a sweater or else he would get a cold; but Sydney did not want to go back to that big house until there were people in it, and maybe not until his stepfather was in it. He only hoped that his stepfather had a sweater, so when he found him he would let Sydney wear it. Even if he found his stepfather he knew that his mother would beat him because he should never have left the house in the first place, but there were reasons that he had to go looking for him. One reason was that he decided he loved his stepfather even if he had acted cruel by disappearing. And another reason was that maybe his mother would disappear soon too and surprise everybody and then he would be so alone and he would certainly have to have his stepfather. His mother never acted like she was going to disappear without telling, but as far as Sydney could see that was part of the plan, not to tell.

The streets that Sydney knew unfolded in front of him, and he looked up and down all the alleys and he searched the doorways of the houses but he did not see his stepfather. As he walked beyond, to streets

he had walked with his stepfather only a few times, he did not look for his stepfather in alleys and doorways, but in the branches of trees, and on roof-tops, and behind a fire hydrant, and in the curb, and once he looked in a bush, and one time he even turned over a rock. And still he did not find his stepfather, so he walked on to streets he had never known or seen, and soon he was lost. There were big white buildings all around him and no trees but only sidewalk, and the street was growing cold and windy. Never had he seen such buildings before, and he was looking at the buildings when he spotted in the distance a tall man with a brown mustache, and he thought this must be downtown and there he is. Sydney raced toward the man, screaming "Poppa, Poppa" and when he was almost close enough to reach out and touch the tips of his fingers, the man looked back over his shoulder and Sydney saw that it was not his stepfather after all but only another man with a mustache. The man started to walk faster and in a moment Sydney was once more alone and cold. There was a little park ahead and Sydney began to walk to it, thinking that it might be warmer there, for it was late afternoon and the light was thinning. Suddenly he didn't care about his stepfather, but just about getting warm.

Sydney sat down on a bench next to a man reading a newspaper. It wasn't any warmer in the park and Sydney began to shake and the man reading the newspaper saw him shake and so he gave Sydney his scarf for a moment to keep him warm, and then he read his newspaper again. All around the park there were men sitting on benches; they were all old and bald and some looked like they had never moved in their lives, and Sydney wondered where they went when it snowed.

"Where is this?" Sydney asked the man reading the newspaper.

"Homestead Park," answered the man, not looking up. He was a little tree stump of a man whose feet almost didn't touch the ground and whose hands looked to Sydney like lightning had struck them and made them lumpy and full of ridges.

"Where?"

"Homestead Park," the man said again. Sydney had never even heard of the place and he didn't know where it was; suddenly it was like somebody stuck a pin in a balloon that was inside him and it popped and he was afraid.

"Where is that?"

The man peered at Sydney a moment, long enough for Sydney to see his reflection in the small, round eyes, and then he pointed a lumpy finger at the ground like he was going to take a shot at it. "Right here," was all he finally said. That made Sydney feel better.

"I'm looking for my stepfather," Sydney said.

"Lost?"

"No," said Sydney, and so the man started to read again. "He just disappeared and now everybody's out looking for him. But he's not lost, I don't think, because he disappeared on purpose. I'm supposed to be home," Sydney added, "but I want to look too. Every time somebody disappears I'm never allowed to look."

"Every time?"

"When Aunt Wilma and Uncle Carl disappeared I mean. They never found them neither. I'm good at finding people, that's why I decided to look." He stared into the round eyes. "I don't like everybody to disappear on me."

The man stopped reading and he asked Sydney, "Where does everybody go to look for somebody if they disappear?"

"Out," said Sydney.

"Where?"

"Out. All different places. I don't know, nobody tells me. Everybody just cries."

"And when somebody disappears, does everybody go out to look together and come back together?"

"Yes," said Sydney, "everybody excepting me. And you know what?" — the thought had just come to him — "everybody wears black, everybody always wears black."

The old man stood up and, as if he didn't want the men on the benches to hear, he whispered, "So the world will know they're out looking," and Sydney said, "Oh." The man did not seem so old when he was reading, but standing up he was the oldest person Sydney had ever seen.

"I am going," the old man told Sydney.

"Why?" Sydney asked.

"I must," said the old man and he started to move away. "You keep the scarf." The old man looked at the sky, and so Sydney looked too. "Maybe it'll snow today. Look, you find a policeman. I have to go." And

he trudged away, stiff legged, lifting his feet like two thick stones, and when Sydney saw him leave he was frightened, so he ran after the old man.

"What about me?" Sydney yelled. "What about everybody —"

"I have nothing to do with that. Find a policeman. I can't pay attention to that."

"Why? Why not?" Sydney screamed. The man kept walking. "Come back, I want you to help me look for my stepfather. You're old, you could help. You're old, you'd know where to look. . . ."

The old man had been moving as quickly as he could out of the park, but he stopped. He was round and gnarled and tough like a tree stump, but in that second a summer wind might have carried him from the ground. The old man stopped and so Sydney waited for the old man to answer, but there was no answer and so Sydney asked again.

"Would you help me look?"

"What's your name?" the old man asked.

"Sydney."

On all the benches the men sat stiff and still, like people sleeping and waiting in a train station. The wind blew a little stronger.

"I'll take you to your stepfather, Sydney," the old man said.

Sydney didn't know what to do, he was so happy, and so he just threw himself on the ground and did a somersault through a pile of old leaves and he kept shouting to the old man "Will you, will you?" all the time they waited for the bus that was going to take them to the country, and when the bus finally came he looked back at the park and he asked the old man where all the men went when it snowed, and the old man said he wasn't sure, and Sydney never thought to ask him where he went. On the bus Sydney never asked the old man who he was either or how he knew his stepfather, and so the ride was silent as midnight until big oak trees started to roll by the windows and the old man looked at Sydney and asked, "Did you like your father very much?"

"I don't have a father. I have a stepfather," Sydney answered, his mind not on the question, but on the oaks and acorn whistles.

"But you did have a father."

"No, I didn't. I only got one, a stepfather."

"Before your stepfather, Sydney," the old man began, but he stopped

when he saw Sydney shaking his head. "Sydney, hasn't your mother ever talked to you about your father — I don't mean stepfather, I mean father, plain old father?"

"No," answered Sydney. He looked up from the trees. "Why, did I have one of those too?"

The old man nodded.

"Then where is he?" Sydney asked. "Did he disappear too? Did he? You know. I can tell you know. Tell me: did he disappear? What did I do? Why does everybody have to disappear on me?" The old man did not answer. "If they know it's going to make everybody sad why do all my fathers and stepfathers keep disappearing?"

"We have to get off here," the old man said, and he pushed the buzzer and he and the boy left the bus and started to walk under the oak trees, up the road toward the cemetery. Acorns crunched under their feet as they walked. Sydney did not forget his question. "Why do they do it?" he repeated.

The old man looked at him and said slowly, "Sydney, they can't help it."

"Yes they can! They do it on purpose and make everybody cry."

"Sydney, they can't help it!"

"Why?" shouted Sydney. "I want to know why?"

And finally the old man answered, "Because to disappear, Sydney, is to be dead, to disappear is to die." The old man stopped walking and Sydney stopped too, and they stood together in the dark shadow of the oak trees and in the thinning light of the sun. "To disappear is to die, Sydney."

"To die?" the boy repeated.

"Yes. Your stepfather is dead."

"He died," Sydney explained to the old man.

"Yes."

There was silence and the old man and Sydney started to walk again, and soon they turned the corner, and the cemetery, like a brown and green ocean stuck with white buoys, lay before them.

"Then, then he didn't do it on purpose," Sydney suddenly cried.

"No, he didn't."

"And Aunt Wilma didn't do it on purpose, and Uncle Carl didn't do it on purpose. They just died. He just died!" and the boy spurted and

skipped ahead, his joy, not his legs, bouncing him up and down. He was ahead of the old man, with his head thrown back, shouting, and his voice was thin as glass and seemed to slide through the leafless limbs of the tall oak trees. "He just died, he just died, he just died." And then he stopped shouting and he ran back to the old man and he grabbed his fingers and said, "I've got to tell all the people. I've got to tell them that he didn't do it on purpose." And as the boy talked and held the old man's fingers, a slow procession of automobiles rolled out of the cemetery gate, rolled slowly out, leaving behind in the ocean of green and brown the body of Sydney's stepfather. Within the cluster of shadows the death-weary family in the automobile could not see Sydney and the old man, but when Sydney turned he saw them, and he yelled, and then he saw his mother sitting in the first car.

"Momma! It's Momma," he screamed. "Momma, stop. Momma stop the car." The car stopped and the door opened.

"Momma!"

"Sydney, what are you doing?"

The boy left the old man and ran to the car. "Momma," he yelled, "Momma, I'm so glad I found you. Everything is O.K., Momma. Poppa hasn't disappeared!"

"My Sydney, what are you yelling!"

"He hasn't disappeared — he's died. He's dead, so it's O.K."

She grabbed the boy's arm. "My God, my God. . . ."

"What's the matter, Momma? I told you: Poppa died, he didn't disappear. This man told me." He pointed to the trees. "This man told me Poppa just died."

"That man!" screamed Sydney's mother. "That man told you!" She was waving her arms in the air like some giant snake or octopus was squeezing the life out of her. "No, my Sydney, no, Poppa isn't dead, Poppa isn't dead!" She screamed it again. "Poppa isn't dead!"

"He is, the man told me," shouted the boy, barely believing the woman in front of him was his mother. She was dressed in a long black dress and a black hat and for a moment Sydney thought her face was black too. Sydney watched her fall back into the car as she pointed wildly at the old man with her two hands and cried, "Get him away! Get him away from here!"

Commanded, the old man trudged away, down the sidewalk, away

from the cemetery and the procession of automobiles. For a moment Sydney did not see the old man leaving, and he clutched his mother's dress and yelled in his thin glass voice, "Momma, he is dead and that's good. Momma, you can stop looking, I can stop looking!" But then Sydney turned and saw the old man moving away under the oak trees, and he broke for the sidewalk, crying, "Mister, Mister Man, please come back — " but before he could reach the sidewalk, the big black hearse, like an angry whale, came charging down the left side of the road to be first in the funeral line, and it crushed the boy to the ground, like feet crush acorns, and it shattered forever his thin glass voice.

The Daring Young Man on the Flying Trapeze

Perhaps the biggest name *Story* was ever credited with discovering is William Saroyan. Born of Armenian parents in Fresno, California, in 1908, Saroyan was just two years old when his father died. He spent the next few years in an orphanage while his mother sorted out her financial situation. Saroyan left school at fifteen and began writing in the late 1920s. In his introduction to his story in *Firsts of the Famous,* Saroyan recalled writing the story that made him instantly famous: "I wrote it in one day in November of 1933. I was still an unpublished writer, although I didn't see how that condition could continue very much longer." "Daring Young Man" captured America's attention with its unusually genial and exuberant vision, a quality that characterized most of Saroyan's writing if not his life. He was an extremely unhappy and bitter man, and even refused to accept the 1939 Pulitzer Prize for his play *The Time of Your Life.*

I. SLEEP

HORIZONTALLY WAKEFUL AMID universal widths, practising laughter and mirth, satire, the end of all, of Rome and yes of Babylon, clenched teeth, remembrance, much warmth volcanic, the streets of Paris, the plains of Jericho, much gliding as of reptile in abstraction, a gallery of watercolors, the sea and the fish with eyes, symphony, a table in the corner of the Eiffel Tower, jazz at the opera house, alarm clock and the tap-dancing of doom, conversation with a tree, the river Nile, Cadillac coupe to Kansas, the roar of Dostoyevsky, and the dark sun.

This earth, the face of one who lived, the form without the weight, weeping upon snow, white music, the magnified flower twice the size of the universe, black clouds, the caged panther staring, deathless space, Mr. Eliot with rolled sleeves baking bread, Flaubert and Guy de Maupassant, a wordless rhyme of early meaning, Finlandia, mathematics highly polished and slick as a green onion to the teeth, Jerusalem, the path to paradox.

The deep song of man, the sly whisper of someone unseen but vaguely known, hurricane in the cornfield, a game of chess, hush the queen, the king, Karl Franz, black Titanic, Mr. Chaplin weeping, Stalin, Hitler, a multitude of Jews, tomorrow is Monday, no dancing in the streets.

O swift moment of life: it is ended, the earth is again now.

II. WAKEFULNESS

He (the living) dressed and shaved, grinning at himself in the mirror. Very unhandsome, he said; where is my tie? (He had but one.) Coffee and a gray sky, Pacific Ocean fog, the drone of a passing streetcar, people going to the city, time again, the day, prose and poetry. He moved swiftly down the stairs to the street and began to walk, thinking suddenly, *It is only in sleep that we may know that we live. There only, in that living death, do we meet ourselves and the far earth, God and the saints, the names of our fathers, the substance of remote moments; it is there that the centuries merge in the moment, that the vast becomes the tiny, tangible atom of eternity.*

He walked into the day as alertly as might be, making a definite noise with his heels, perceiving with his eyes the superficial truth of streets and structures, the trivial truth of reality. Helplessly his mind sang. *He flies through the air with the greatest of ease; the daring young man on the flying trapeze;* then laughed with all the might of his being. It was really a splendid morning: gray, cold, and cheerless, a morning for inward vigor; ah, Edgar Guest, he said, how I long for your music.

In the gutter he saw a coin which proved to be a penny dated 1923, and placing it in the palm of his hand he examined it closely, remembering that year and thinking of Lincoln whose profile was stamped upon the coin. There was almost nothing a man could do with a penny. I will purchase a motorcar, he thought. I will dress myself in the fashion

of a fop, visit the hotel strumpets, drink and dine, and then return to the quiet. Or I will drop the coin into a slot and weigh myself.

It was good to be poor, and the Communists—but it was dreadful to be hungry. What appetites they had, how fond they were of food! Empty stomachs. He remembered how greatly he needed food. Every meal was bread and coffee and cigarettes, and now he had no more bread. Coffee without bread could never honestly serve as supper, and there were no weeds in the park that could be cooked as spinach is cooked.

If the truth were known, he was half starved, and yet there was still no end of books he ought to read before he died. He remembered the young Italian in a Brooklyn hospital, a small sick clerk named Mollica, who had said desperately, I would like to see California once before I die. And he thought earnestly, I ought at least to read *Hamlet* once again; or perhaps *Huckleberry Finn*.

It was then that he became thoroughly awake: at the thought of dying. Now wakefulness was a state in the nature of a sustained shock. A young man could perish rather unostentatiously, he thought; and already he was very nearly starved. Water and prose were fine, they filled much inorganic space, but they were inadequate. If there were only some work he might do for money, some trivial labor in the name of commerce. If they would only allow him to sit at a desk all day and add trade figures, subtract and multiply and divide, then perhaps he would not die. He would buy food, all sorts of it: untasted delicacies from Norway, Italy, and France; all manner of beef, lamb, fish, cheese; grapes, figs, pears, apples, melons, which he would worship when he had satisfied his hunger. He would place a bunch of red grapes on a dish beside two black figs, a large yellow pear, and a green apple. He would hold a cut melon to his nostrils for hours. He would buy great brown loaves of French bread, vegetables of all sorts, meat; he would buy life.

From a hill he saw the city standing majestically in the east, great towers, dense with his kind, and there he was suddenly outside of it all, almost definitely certain that he should never gain admittance, almost positive that somehow he had ventured upon the wrong earth, or perhaps into the wrong age, and now a young man of twenty-two was to be permanently ejected from it. This thought was not saddening. He said to himself, sometime soon I must write *An Application for Permission to Live*. He accepted the thought of dying without pity for himself or for

man, believing that he would at least sleep another night. His rent for another day was paid; there was yet another tomorrow. And after that he might go where other homeless men went. He might even visit the Salvation Army—sing to God and Jesus (unlover of my soul), be saved, eat and sleep. But he knew that he would not. His life was a private life. He did not wish to destroy this fact. Any other alternative would be better.

Through the air on the flying trapeze, his mind hummed. Amusing it was, astoundingly funny. A trapeze to God, or to nothing, a flying trapeze to some sort of eternity; he prayed objectively for strength to make the flight with grace.

I have one cent, he said. It is an American coin. In the evening I shall polish it until it glows like a sun, and I shall study the words.

He was now walking in the city itself, among living men. There were one or two places to go. He saw his reflection in the plate-glass windows of stores and was disappointed with his appearance. He seemed not at all as strong as he felt; he seemed, in fact, a trifle infirm in every part of his body, in his neck, his shoulders, arms, trunk, and knees. This will never do, he said, and with an effort he assembled all his disjointed parts and became tensely, artificially erect and solid.

He passed numerous restaurants with magnificent discipline, refusing even to glance into them, and at last reached a building which he entered. He rose in an elevator to the seventh floor, moved down a hall, and, opening a door, walked into the office of an employment agency. Already there were two dozen young men in the place; he found a corner where he stood waiting his turn to be interviewed. At length he was granted this great privilege and was questioned by a thin, scatterbrained miss of fifty.

Now, tell me, she said; what can you do?

He was embarrassed. I can write, he said pathetically.

You mean your penmanship is good? Is that it? said the elderly maiden.

Well, yes, he replied. But I mean that I can write.

Write what? said the miss, almost with anger.

Prose, he said simply.

There was a pause. At last the lady said:

Can you use a typewriter?

Of course, said the young man.

All right, went on the miss, we have your address; we will get in touch with you. There is nothing this morning, nothing at all.

It was much the same at the other agency, except that he was questioned by a conceited young man who closely resembled a pig. From the agencies he went to the large department stores: there was a good deal of pomposity, some humiliation on his part, and finally the report that work was not available. He did not feel displeased, and strangely did not even feel that he was personally involved in all the foolishness. He was a living young man who was in need of money with which to go on being one, and there was no way of getting it except by working for it; and there was no work. It was purely an abstract problem which he wished for the last time to attempt to solve. Now he was pleased that the matter was closed.

He began to perceive the definiteness of the course of his life. Except for moments, it had been largely artless, but now at the last minute he was determined that there should be as little imprecision as possible.

He passed countless stores and restaurants on his way to the Y.M.C.A., where he helped himself to paper and ink and began to compose his *Application*. For an hour he worked on this document, then suddenly, owing to the bad air in the place and to hunger, he became faint. He seemed to be swimming away from himself with great strokes, and hurriedly left the building. In the Civic Center Park, across from the Public Library Building, he drank almost a quart of water and felt himself refreshed. An old man was standing in the center of the brick boulevard surrounded by sea gulls, pigeons, and robins. He was taking handfuls of bread crumbs from a large paper sack and tossing them to the birds with a gallant gesture.

Dimly he felt impelled to ask the old man for a portion of the crumbs, but he did not allow the thought even nearly to reach consciousness; he entered the Public Library and for an hour read Proust, then, feeling himself to be swimming away again, he rushed outdoors. He drank more water at the fountain in the park and began the long walk to his room.

I'll go and sleep some more, he said; there is nothing else to do. He knew now that he was much too tired and weak to deceive himself about being all right, and yet his mind seemed somehow still lithe and alert. It, as if it were a separate entity, persisted in articulating impertinent

pleasantries about his very real physical suffering. He reached his room early in the afternoon and immediately prepared coffee on the small gas range. There was no milk in the can, and the half pound of sugar he had purchased a week before was all gone; he drank a cup of the hot black fluid, sitting on his bed and smiling.

From the Y.M.C.A. he had stolen a dozen sheets of letter paper upon which he hoped to complete his document, but now the very notion of writing was unpleasant to him. There was nothing to say. He began to polish the penny he had found in the morning, and this absurd act somehow afforded him great enjoyment. No American coin can be made to shine so brilliantly as a penny. How many pennies would he need to go on living? Wasn't there something more he might sell? He looked about the bare room. No. His watch was gone; also his books. All those fine books; nine of them for eighty-five cents. He felt ill and ashamed for having parted with his books. His best suit he had sold for two dollars, but that was all right. He didn't mind at all about clothes. But the books. That was different. It made him very angry to think that there was no respect for men who wrote.

He placed the shining penny on the table, looking upon it with the delight of a miser. How prettily it smiles, he said. Without reading them he looked at the words, *E Pluribus Unum One Cent United States Of America,* and turning the penny over, he saw Lincoln and the words, *In God We Trust Liberty 1923.* How beautiful it is, he said.

He became drowsy and felt a ghastly illness coming over his blood, a feeling of nausea and disintegration. Bewildered, he stood beside his bed, thinking *there is nothing to do but sleep.* Already he felt himself making great strides through the fluid of the earth, swimming away to the beginning. He fell face down upon the bed, saying, I ought first at least to give the coin to some child. A child could buy any number of things with a penny.

Then swiftly, neatly, with the grace of the young man on the trapeze, he was gone from his body. For an eternal moment he was all things at once: the bird, the fish, the rodent, the reptile, and man. An ocean of print undulated endlessly and darkly before him. The city burned. The herded crowd rioted. The earth circled away, and knowing that he did so, he turned his lost face to the empty sky and became dreamless, unalive, perfect.

Flash in the Pan

Irwin Shaw was already a successful radio show writer and playwright when his first short story was published in *Stage Theatre Guild Quarterly* in 1936. Born Irwin Shamforoff in New York City in 1913, Shaw attended Brooklyn College, where he published a few stories influenced by Ernest Hemingway, his favorite writer, in his college literary magazine. Recognition came early to Shaw; he earned very good money from radio and saw his first play, *Bury the Dead*, produced on Broadway in 1936, the same year "Flash in the Pan" appeared. A lovely story featuring a couple much like Shaw and his wife, Marion, "Flash in the Pan" has never been included in any Shaw collection.

"YOU OUGHT TO wear a vest," his wife said, "and that's your fourth drink and it's only eight o'clock."

"Why should I wear a vest?"

"I wish you wouldn't snap at me. I'm only trying to help."

"Why should I wear a vest?" He looked vaguely around for ice.

"You really ought to wear tails. Or at least a tuxedo. After all, this is a very big occasion."

He found the ice and dumped two cubes into his glass. "There is no doubt about it," he said, "this is a very big occasion. Is this our last bottle?"

"A lot of people there will be dressed."

"Well, I won't be one of them." He watched the Scotch melt the ice in his glass.

"It's a shame. You look so good when you're done up for the evening. Everybody would be very much impressed."

"You bet they would," he said grimly. "Proletarian playwright shows up in white tie for opening of his second play. They'd be impressed as hell. You got to use sense."

"Anyway," she said, sitting in his lap and pinning his whiskey hand over to the side, "anyway, you could wear a vest."

"Vests strangle me. I wasn't made to wear vests. Tonight is one night I got to make myself comfortable. Sit up a little . . ."

She stayed where she was. "Why?"

"I want to get at my whiskey." She looked at him for a moment but there was the tight look around his mouth and she got up.

"You don't want to be drunk," she said. "It would be a fine thing if in response to the cries of 'Author, Author!' the successful young playwright came staggering out on the stage, plastered to the ears."

"There won't be any cries of 'Author, Author!' The only one who'll be crying will be Jake Morris because he produced the play." This prediction gave him a dark pleasure and he took his next gulp with satisfaction.

"It's a very good play," she said.

"That's what I used to think until it went into rehearsal." His eyes narrowed reflectively as he remembered rehearsals. "I must have been dazzled by the fires of my own genius."

"You're nervous," his wife said, "that's the trouble with you. If I were you I wouldn't be nervous."

"Some people are luckier than others." He finished his drink and went to the window, and looked down at Fifth Avenue where it ran under the Arch. People were walking along in couples, holding on to their hats. "Must be two hundred people down there," he said, "who have nothing else to worry about but keeping their hats on. They don't know how happy they are. Tomorrow morning in the papers nobody's going to announce that they're immature or that their dialogue stinks or that they are strictly a one-play man."

"Nobody'll say that about you, either." His wife came over to him and stood beside him.

"I'll be lucky if they let it go at that, Flash-in-the-pan, that's me, a violet that bloomed in the spring, a morning glory, watch me fold. Right now I am a white hope in the American theatre, one of the eighty-three finest white hopes the American theatre has. Tomorrow morning there'll

be only eighty-two white hopes and I can go back to Hollywood and write cops and robbers for the rest of my life for George Raft, if he lives that long. Let's get the hell out of here!"

"The curtain doesn't go up till nine," his wife suggested.

"Let's get the hell out of here!"

They walked up Fifth Avenue, into the wind. He stopped in front of a bookstore window and pointed to a slim, cream-jacketed volume. "Your husband's first play. I understand it showed great promise. One dollar-fifty; less in Macy's." They walked on. "Amazing man, your husband, but not yet proven. So young for such a serious writer. Though Winchell said he's not really so young at all, he's really twenty-five. *Taxi!*"

THEY got into a taxi and they started north. He looked out at the streets with interest.

"Take a good long look," he told his wife, "because after they see the second act we're on our way back to Hollywood."

"We won't have to go back to Hollywood."

"We'll be lucky if they take us back after that second act." He brooded. "I didn't realize until last night . . . nothing happens in the second act, not a goddamn thing."

"They'll never know."

He patted her knee. "They'll know. They're just dying to know. If there's anything that bunch is crazy to know it's that I can't write second acts. They put you up one season so that they can knock you down the next. It's the same thing they do with trout."

They got out of the cab in front of the theatre. There was a crowd milling around, high hats and ermine, and two men in ragged overcoats selling the *Daily Worker,* because he was a proletarian playwright.

"Let's walk around the block," he said.

They walked around the block twice, stopping twice at a bar that was three steps down. He won forty cents from a slot machine.

"This is my lucky night," he said.

The first act was on when they got into the theatre, and people were laughing. He sat in his seat with his head down during the intermissions, glaring at the people who were talking and laughing in the aisles.

"They'd laugh at executions," he told his wife, hating them one and

all, trying to catch a glimpse of the expression on the face of the man from the *Journal* who was sitting across the aisle. He couldn't tell anything from the face of the man from the *Journal.*

During the second act he pinched his wife's arm black and blue from elbow to wrist, saying, under his breath, as the actors wallowed in their lines, "Bastards! The bastards!"

After the play was over he tried to get his wife out in a hurry but she stood in the middle of the aisle, bawling: "Author! Author!"

"Why don't you go up?" she asked.

"Can't," he said, pushing her into a cab and getting in after her. "I haven't a vest."

"They loved it," his wife said, kissing him.

"The house was full of my friends."

"You're a very good writer."

He nodded. "No doubt about it. I'm the boy wonder, I'm the lad who clicked . . . until the papers come out tomorrow. Let's get a drink."

"It was . . ."

"Let's get a drink."

It was three-thirty and they were standing at a newsstand on Fiftieth Street and Sixth Avenue, waiting for the first papers.

"They will never disregard the second act, never. I grant you they are none of them John Dryden or Samuel Taylor Coleridge or George Bernard Shaw when it comes to dramatic criticism, but they will never disregard the second act, never. . . . After all, we must face it. Flash-in-the-pan. Burned bright, but burned fast. No good on second acts."

A truck wheeled past and the papers landed with a bump at their feet. His wife collected the *News,* the *Mirror,* the *American,* the *Times,* and *Tribune,* and they walked over to the corner street-lamp to read.

"Before you open them," he said, "I want you to know that I bear them no malice."

They opened the papers, read them one by one. His wife sat down on a drug-store doorstep. "Better," she said, "better than last time, even better. Oh, my God!"

He surveyed her gravely, leaning against a pole. "No one says, 'Flash-in-the-pan'?"

"Not one."

"Very fine gentlemen, very fine, every one of them." He yawned. "Take me home, please. I'm very tired."

She put him to bed as the first milk rattled down the streets. She kissed him. He smiled up at her. "Flash-in-the-pan," he said, chuckled once, and slept well for the first time in five weeks.

It was two the next afternoon when she woke him coming in with the last afternoon papers. He opened his eyes, lay still for a moment, feeling relaxed and unaccountably serene. He shook his head, watching his wife come in, and remembered.

She kissed him and waved the afternoon papers. "Read them and gloat," she said.

"How are they?"

"Wonderful."

"All wonderful?"

"Unreservedly," she said, "except the *Sun*."

Hurriedly he looked at the *Sun*. The *Sun* said, "Only in the second act did his hand falter. Elsewhere the play was tense and exciting, a rich mixture of poetry and passion, but in the second act, there was fumbling and laxness and a glaring lack of dramatic action. . . ." He threw the paper to the floor, looking darkly at it.

"The bastard!" he said, and lay back on his pillow to brood.

Gimpel the Fool

Winner of the 1978 Nobel Prize for Literature, Isaac Bashevis Singer was born in 1904 in Poland. As a young intellectual in his native country, he published in obscure Yiddish journals — his first story in Yiddish appeared in 1927 — and also worked translating novels into Yiddish. In 1935 Isaac followed his older brother, writer I. J. Singer, to the United States, where he wrote for the *Jewish Daily Forward* and had novels published in Yiddish by Farlag Matones. Knopf published Singer's first novel in English, *The Family Moskat*, in 1950, but Singer was unhappy with the translation and the abridgment (it had previously been serialized in the *Forward*). With "Gimpel the Fool" Singer gained wide exposure as a short story writer before an English-reading public. Translated by Saul Bellow, it appeared in the *Partisan Review* in 1953. Soon afterward, several more of Singer's stories were published in the *Partisan Review, Commentary, Mademoiselle,* and *Esquire.*

I AM GIMPEL the fool. I don't think myself a fool. On the contrary. But that's what folks call me. They gave me the name while I was still in school. I had seven names in all: imbecile, donkey, flax-head, dope, glump, ninny, and fool. The last name stuck. What did my foolishness consist of? I was easy to take in. They said, "Gimpel, you know the rabbi's wife has been brought to childbed?" So I skipped school. Well, it turned out to be a lie. How was I supposed to know? She hadn't had a big belly. But I never looked at her belly. Was that really so foolish? The gang laughed and hee-hawed, stomped and danced and chanted a good-night prayer. And instead of the raisins they give when a woman's lying in, they stuffed my hand full of goat turds. I was no weakling. If I

slapped someone he'd see all the way to Cracow. But I'm really not a slugger by nature. I think to myself: Let it pass. So they take advantage of me.

I was coming home from school and heard a dog barking. I'm not afraid of dogs, but of course I never want to start up with them. One of them may be mad, and if he bites there's not a Tartar in the world who can help you. So I made tracks. Then I looked around and saw the whole market place wild with laughter. It was no dog at all but Wolf-Leib the thief. How was I supposed to know it was he? It sounded like a howling bitch.

When the pranksters and leg-pullers found that I was easy to fool, every one of them tried his luck with me. "Gimpel, the czar is coming to Frampol; Gimpel, the moon fell down in Turbeen; Gimpel, little Hodel Furpiece found a treasure behind the bathhouse." And I like a golem believed everyone. In the first place, everything is possible, as it is written in *The Wisdom of the Fathers,* I've forgotten just how. Second, I had to believe when the whole town came down on me! If I ever dared to say, "Ah, you're kidding!" there was trouble. People got angry. "What do you mean! You want to call everyone a liar?" What was I to do? I believed them, and I hope at least that did them some good.

I was an orphan. My grandfather who brought me up was already bent toward the grave. So they turned me over to a baker, and what a time they gave me there! Every woman or girl who came to bake a batch of noodles had to fool me at least once. "Gimpel, there's a fair in Heaven; Gimpel, the rabbi gave birth to a calf in the seventh month; Gimpel, a cow flew over the roof and laid brass eggs." A student from the yeshiva came once to buy a roll, and he said, "You, Gimpel, while you stand here scraping with your baker's shovel the Messiah has come. The dead have arisen." "What do you mean?" I said. "I heard no one blowing the ram's horn!" He said, "Are you deaf?" And all began to cry, "We heard it, we heard!" Then in came Rietze the candle-dipper and called out in her hoarse voice, "Gimpel, your father and mother have stood up from the grave. They're looking for you."

To tell the truth, I knew very well that nothing of the sort had happened, but all the same, as folks were talking, I threw on my wool vest and went out. Maybe something had happened. What did I stand to lose by looking? Well, what a cat music went up! And then I took a vow

to believe nothing more. But that was no go either. They confused me so that I didn't know the big end from the small.

I went to the rabbi to get some advice. He said, "It is written, better to be a fool all your days than for one hour to be evil. You are not a fool. They are the fools. For he who causes his neighbor to feel shame loses Paradise himself." Nevertheless, the rabbi's daughter took me in. As I left the rabbinical court she said, "Have you kissed the wall yet?" I said, "No; what for?" She answered, "It's the law; you've got to do it after every visit." Well, there didn't seem to be any harm in it. And she burst out laughing. It was a fine trick. She put one over on me, all right.

I wanted to go off to another town, but then everyone got busy matchmaking, and they were after me so they nearly tore my coat tails off. They talked at me and talked until I got water on the ear. She was no chaste maiden, but they told me she was virgin pure. She had a limp, and they said it was deliberate, from coyness. She had a bastard, and they told me the child was her little brother. I cried, "You're wasting your time. I'll never marry that whore." But they said indignantly, "What a way to talk! Aren't you ashamed of yourself? We can take you to the rabbi and have you fined for giving her a bad name." I saw then that I wouldn't escape them so easily and I thought: They're set on making me their butt. But when you're married the husband's the master, and if that's all right with her it's agreeable to me too. Besides, you can't pass through life unscathed, nor expect to.

I went to her clay house, which was built on the sand, and the whole gang, hollering and chorusing, came after me. They acted like bear-baiters. When we came to the well they stopped all the same. They were afraid to start anything with Elka. Her mouth would open as if it were on a hinge, and she had a fierce tongue. I entered the house. Lines were strung from wall to wall and clothes were drying. Barefoot she stood by the tub, doing the wash. She was dressed in a worn hand-me-down gown of plush. She had her hair put up in braids and pinned across her head. It took my breath away, almost, the reek of it all.

Evidently she knew who I was. She took a look at me and said, "Look who's here! He's come, the drip. Grab a seat."

I told her all; I denied nothing. "Tell me the truth," I said, "are you really a virgin, and is that mischievous Yechiel actually your little brother? Don't be deceitful with me, for I'm an orphan."

"I'm an orphan myself," she answered, "and whoever tries to twist you up, may the end of his nose take a twist. But don't let them think they can take advantage of me. I want a dowry of fifty guilders, and let them take up a collection besides. Otherwise they can kiss my you-know-what." She was very plainspoken. I said, "It's the bride and not the groom who gives a dowry." Then she said, "Don't bargain with me. Either a flat yes or a flat no. Go back where you came from."

I thought: No bread will ever be baked from *this* dough. But ours is not a poor town. They consented to everything and proceeded with the wedding. It so happened that there was a dysentery epidemic at the time. The ceremony was held at the cemetery gates, near the little corpse-washing hut. The fellows got drunk. While the marriage contract was being drawn up I heard the most pious high rabbi ask, "Is the bride a widow or a divorced woman?" And the sexton's wife answered for her, "Both a widow and divorced." It was a black moment for me. But what was I to do, run away from under the marriage canopy?

There was singing and dancing. An old granny danced opposite me, hugging a braided white hallah. The master of revels made a "God 'a mercy" in memory of the bride's parents. The schoolboys threw burrs, as on Tishe b'Av fast day. There were a lot of gifts after the sermon: a noodle board, a kneading trough, a bucket, brooms, ladles, household articles galore. Then I took a look and saw two strapping young men carrying a crib. "What do we need this for?" I asked. So they said, "Don't rack your brains about it. It's all right, it'll come in handy." I realized I was going to be rooked. Take it another way though, what did I stand to lose? I reflected: I'll see what comes of it. A whole town can't go altogether crazy.

II

At night I came where my wife lay, but she wouldn't let me in. "Say, look here, is this what they married us for?" I said. And she said, "My monthly has come." "But yesterday they took you to the ritual bath, and that's afterwards, isn't it supposed to be?" "Today isn't yesterday," said she, "and yesterday's not today. You can beat it if you don't like it." In short, I waited.

Not four months later, she was in childbed. The townsfolk hid their laughter with their knuckles. But what could I do? She suffered intoler-

able pains and clawed at the walls. "Gimpel," she cried, "I'm going. Forgive me!" The house filled with women. They were boiling pans of water. The screams rose to the welkin.

The thing to do was to go to the house of prayer to repeat psalms, and that was what I did.

The townsfolk liked that, all right. I stood in a corner saying psalms and prayers, and they shook their heads at me. "Pray, pray!" they told me. "Prayer never made any woman pregnant." One of the congregation put a straw to my mouth and said, "Hay for the cows." There was something to that too, by God!

She gave birth to a boy. Friday at the synagogue the sexton stood up before the Ark, pounded on the reading table, and announced, "The wealthy Reb Gimpel invites the congregation to a feast in honor of the birth of a son." The whole house of prayer rang with laughter. My face was flaming. But there was nothing I could do. After all, I *was* the one responsible for the circumcision honors and rituals.

Half the town came running. You couldn't wedge another soul in. Women brought peppered chick-peas, and there was a keg of beer from the tavern. I ate and drank as much as anyone, and they all congratulated me. Then there was a circumcision, and I named the boy after my father, may he rest in peace. When all were gone and I was left with my wife alone, she thrust her head through the bed-curtain and called me to her.

"Gimpel," said she, "why are you silent? Has your ship gone and sunk?"

"What shall I say?" I answered. "A fine thing you've done to me! If my mother had known of it she'd have died a second time."

She said, "Are you crazy, or what?"

"How can you make such a fool," I said, "of one who should be the lord and master?"

"What's the matter with you?" she said. "What have you taken it into your head to imagine?"

I saw that I must speak bluntly and openly. "Do you think this is the way to use an orphan?" I said. "You have borne a bastard."

She answered, "Drive this foolishness out of your head. The child is yours."

"How can he be mine?" I argued. "He was born seventeen weeks after the wedding."

She told me then that he was premature. I said, "Isn't he a little too premature?" She said, she had had a grandmother who carried just as short a time and she resembled this grandmother of hers as one drop of water does another. She swore to it with such oaths that you would have believed a peasant at the fair if he had used them. To tell the plain truth, I didn't believe her; but when I talked it over next day with the schoolmaster, he told me that the very same thing had happened to Adam and Eve. Two they went up to bed, and four they descended.

"There isn't a woman in the world who is not the granddaughter of Eve," he said.

That was how it was; they argued me dumb. But then, who really knows how such things are?

I began to forget my sorrow. I loved the child madly, and he loved me too. As soon as he saw me he'd wave his little hands and want me to pick him up, and when he was colicky I was the only one who could pacify him. I bought him a little bone teething ring and a little gilded cap. He was forever catching the evil eye from someone, and then I had to run to get one of those abracadabras for him that would get him out of it. I worked like an ox. You know how expenses go up when there's an infant in the house. I don't want to lie about it; I didn't dislike Elka either, for that matter. She swore at me and cursed, and I couldn't get enough of her. What strength she had! One of her looks could rob you of the power of speech. And her orations! Pitch and sulphur, that's what they were full of, and yet somehow also full of charm. I adored her every word. She gave me bloody wounds though.

In the evening I brought her a white loaf as well as a dark one, and also poppyseed rolls I baked myself. I thieved because of her and swiped everything I could lay hands on: macaroons, raisins, almonds, cakes. I hope I may be forgiven for stealing from the Saturday pots the women left to warm in the baker's oven. I would take out scraps of meat, a chunk of pudding, a chicken leg or head, a piece of tripe, whatever I could nip quickly. She ate and became fat and handsome.

I had to sleep away from home all during the week, at the bakery. On Friday nights when I got home she always made an excuse of some sort. Either she had heartburn, or a stitch in the side, or hiccups, or headaches. You know what women's excuses are. I had a bitter time of it. It was rough. To add to it, this little brother of hers, the bastard, was grow-

ing bigger. He'd put lumps on me, and when I wanted to hit back she'd open her mouth and curse so powerfully I saw a green haze floating before my eyes. Ten times a day she threatened to divorce me. Another man in my place would have taken French leave and disappeared. But I'm the type that bears it and says nothing. What's one to do? Shoulders are from God, and burdens too.

One night there was a calamity in the bakery; the oven burst, and we almost had a fire. There was nothing to do but go home, so I went home. Let me, I thought, also taste the joy of sleeping in bed in midweek. I didn't want to wake the sleeping mite and tiptoed into the house. Coming in, it seemed to me that I heard not the snoring of one but, as it were, a double snore, one a thin enough snore and the other like the snoring of a slaughtered ox. Oh, I didn't like that! I didn't like it at all. I went up to the bed, and things suddenly turned black. Next to Elka lay a man's form. Another in my place would have made an uproar, and enough noise to rouse the whole town, but the thought occurred to me that I might wake the child. A little thing like that — why frighten a little swallow, I thought. All right then, I went back to the bakery and stretched out on a sack of flour and till morning I never shut an eye. I shivered as if I had had malaria. "Enough of being a donkey," I said to myself. "Gimpel isn't going to be a sucker all his life. There's a limit even to the foolishness of a fool like Gimpel."

In the morning I went to the rabbi to get advice, and it made a great commotion in the town. They sent the beadle for Elka right away. She came, carrying the child. And what do you think she did? She denied it, denied everything, bone and stone! "He's out of his head," she said. "I know nothing of dreams or divinations." They yelled at her, warned her, hammered on the table, but she stuck to her guns: it was a false accusation, she said.

The butchers and the horse-traders took her part. One of the lads from the slaughterhouse came by and said to me, "We've got our eye on you, you're a marked man." Meanwhile, the child started to bear down and soiled itself. In the rabbinical court there was an Ark of the Covenant, and they couldn't allow that, so they sent Elka away.

I said to the rabbi, "What shall I do?"

"You must divorce her at once," said he.

"And what if she refuses?" I asked.

He said, "You must serve the divorce. That's all you'll have to do."

I said, "Well, all right, Rabbi. Let me think about it."

"There's nothing to think about," said he. "You mustn't remain under the same roof with her."

"And if I want to see the child?" I asked.

"Let her go, the harlot," said he, "and her brood of bastards with her."

The verdict he gave was that I mustn't even cross her threshold — never again, as long as I should live.

During the day it didn't bother me so much. I thought: It was bound to happen, the abscess had to burst. But at night when I stretched out upon the sacks I felt it all very bitterly. A longing took me, for her and for the child. I wanted to be angry, but that's my misfortune exactly, I don't have it in me to be really angry. In the first place — this was how my thoughts went — there's bound to be a slip sometimes. You can't live without errors. Probably that lad who was with her led her on and gave her presents and what not, and women are often long on hair and short on sense, and so he got around her. And then since she denies it so, maybe I was only seeing things? Hallucinations do happen. You see a figure or a mannikin or something, but when you come up closer it's nothing, there's not a thing there. And if that's so, I'm doing her an injustice. And when I got so far in my thoughts I started to weep. I sobbed so that I wet the flour where I lay. In the morning I went to the rabbi and told him that I had made a mistake. The rabbi wrote on with his quill, and he said that if that were so he would have to reconsider the whole case. Until he had finished I wasn't to go near my wife, but I might send her bread and money by messenger.

III

Nine months passed before all the rabbis could come to an agreement. Letters went back and forth. I hadn't realized that there could be so much erudition about a matter like this.

Meanwhile, Elka gave birth to still another child, a girl this time. On the Sabbath I went to the synagogue and invoked a blessing on her. They called me up to the Torah, and I named the child for my mother-in-law — may she rest in peace. The louts and loudmouths of the town who came into the bakery gave me a going over. All Frampol refreshed

its spirits because of my trouble and grief. However, I resolved that I would always believe what I was told. What's the good of *not* believing? Today it's your wife you don't believe; tomorrow it's God Himself you won't take stock in.

By an apprentice who was her neighbor I sent her daily a corn or a wheat loaf, or a piece of pastry, rolls or bagels, or, when I got the chance, a slab of pudding, a slice of honeycake, or wedding strudel — whatever came my way. The apprentice was a goodhearted lad, and more than once he added something on his own. He had formerly annoyed me a lot, plucking my nose and digging me in the ribs, but when he started to be a visitor to my house he became kind and friendly. "Hey, you, Gimpel," he said to me, "you have a very decent little wife and two fine kids. You don't deserve them."

"But the things people say about her," I said.

"Well, they have long tongues," he said, "and nothing to do with them but babble. Ignore it as you ignore the cold of last winter."

One day the rabbi sent for me and said, "Are you certain, Gimpel, that you were wrong about your wife?"

I said, "I'm certain."

"Why, but look here! You yourself saw it."

"It must have been a shadow," I said.

"The shadow of what?"

"Just of one of the beams, I think."

"You can go home then. You owe thanks to the Yanover rabbi. He found an obscure reference in Maimonides that favored you."

I seized the rabbi's hand and kissed it.

I wanted to run home immediately. It's no small thing to be separated for so long a time from wife and child. Then I reflected: I'd better go back to work now, and go home in the evening. I said nothing to anyone, although as far as my heart was concerned it was like one of the Holy Days. The women teased and twitted me as they did every day, but my thought was: Go on, with your loose talk. The truth is out, like the oil upon the water. Maimonides says it's right, and therefore it is right!

At night, when I had covered the dough to let it rise, I took my share of bread and a little sack of flour and started homeward. The moon was full and the stars were glistening, something to terrify the soul. I hurried

onward, and before me darted a long shadow. It was winter, and a fresh snow had fallen. I had a mind to sing, but it was growing late and I didn't want to wake the householders. Then I felt like whistling, but I remembered that you don't whistle at night because it brings the demons out. So I was silent and walked as fast as I could.

Dogs in the Christian yards barked at me when I passed, but I thought: Bark your teeth out! What are you but mere dogs? Whereas I am a man, the husband of a fine wife, the father of promising children.

As I approached the house my heart started to pound as though it were the heart of a criminal. I felt no fear, but my heart went thump! thump! Well, no drawing back. I quietly lifted the latch and went in. Elka was asleep. I looked at the infant's cradle. The shutter was closed, but the moon forced its way through the cracks. I saw the newborn child's face and loved it as soon as I saw it — immediately — each tiny bone.

Then I came nearer to the bed. And what did I see but the apprentice lying there beside Elka. The moon went out all at once. It was utterly black, and I trembled. My teeth chattered. The bread fell from my hands, and my wife waked and said, "Who is that, ah?"

I muttered, "It's me."

"Gimpel?" she asked. "How come you're here? I thought it was forbidden."

"The rabbi said," I answered and shook as with a fever.

"Listen to me, Gimpel," she said, "go out to the shed and see if the goat's all right. It seems she's been sick." I have forgotten to say that we had a goat. When I heard she was unwell I went into the yard. The nannygoat was a good little creature. I had a nearly human feeling for her.

With hesitant steps I went up to the shed and opened the door. The goat stood there on her four feet. I felt her everywhere, drew her by the horns, examined her udders, and found nothing wrong. She had probably eaten too much bark. "Good night, little goat," I said. "Keep well." And the little beast answered with a "Maa" as though to thank me for the good will.

I went back. The apprentice had vanished.

"Where," I asked, "is the lad?"

"What lad?" my wife answered.

"What do you mean?" I said. "The apprentice. You were sleeping with him."

"The things I have dreamed this night and the night before," she said, "may they come true and lay you low, body and soul! An evil spirit has taken root in you and dazzles your sight." She screamed out, "You hateful creature! You moon calf! You spook! You uncouth man! Get out, or I'll scream all Frampol out of bed!"

Before I could move, her brother sprang out from behind the oven and struck me a blow on the back of the head. I thought he had broken my neck. I felt that something about me was deeply wrong, and I said, "Don't make a scandal. All that's needed now is that people should accuse me of raising spooks and dybbuks." For that was what she had meant. "No one will touch bread of my baking."

In short, I somehow calmed her.

"Well," she said, "that's enough. Lie down, and be shattered by wheels."

Next morning I called the apprentice aside. "Listen here, brother!" I said. And so on and so forth. "What do you say?" He stared at me as though I had dropped from the roof or something.

"I swear," he said, "you'd better go to an herb doctor or some healer. I'm afraid you have a screw loose, but I'll hush it up for you." And that's how the thing stood.

To make a long story short, I lived twenty years with my wife. She bore me six children, four daughters and two sons. All kinds of things happened, but I neither saw nor heard. I believed, and that's all. The rabbi recently said to me, "Belief in itself is beneficial. It is written that a good man lives by his faith."

Suddenly my wife took sick. It began with a trifle, a little growth upon the breast. But she evidently was not destined to live long; she had no years. I spent a fortune on her. I have forgotten to say that by this time I had a bakery of my own and in Frampol was considered to be something of a rich man. Daily the healer came, and every witch doctor in the neighborhood was brought. They decided to use leeches, and after that to try cupping. They even called a doctor from Lublin, but it was too late. Before she died she called me to her bed and said, "Forgive me, Gimpel."

I said, "What is there to forgive? You have been a good and faithful wife."

"Woe, Gimpel!" she said. "It was ugly how I deceived you all these years. I want to go clean to my Maker, and so I have to tell you that the children are not yours."

If I had been clouted on the head with a piece of wood it couldn't have bewildered me more.

"Whose are they?" I asked.

"I don't know," she said. "There were a lot . . . but they're not yours." And as she spoke she tossed her head to the side, her eyes turned glassy, and it was all up with Elka. On her whitened lips there remained a smile.

I imagined that, dead as she was, she was saying, "I deceived Gimpel. That was the meaning of my brief life."

IV

One night, when the period of mourning was done, as I lay dreaming on the flour sacks, there came the Spirit of Evil himself and said to me, "Gimpel, why do you sleep?"

I said, "What should I be doing? Eating kreplech?"

"The whole world deceives you," he said, "and you ought to deceive the world in your turn."

"How can I deceive all the world?" I asked him.

He answered, "You might accumulate a bucket of urine every day and at night pour it into the dough. Let the sages of Frampol eat filth."

"What about the judgment in the world to come?" I said.

"There is no world to come," he said. "They've sold you a bill of goods and talked you into believing you carried a cat in your belly. What nonsense!"

"Well then," I said, "and is there a God?"

He answered, "There is no God either."

"What," I said, "*is* there, then?"

"A thick mire."

He stood before my eyes with a goatish beard and horn, long-toothed, and with a tail. Hearing such words, I wanted to snatch him by the tail, but I tumbled from the flour sacks and nearly broke a rib. Then it happened that I had to answer the call of nature, and, passing, I saw

the risen dough, which seemed to say to me, "Do it!" In brief, I let myself be persuaded.

At dawn the apprentice came. We kneaded the bread, scattered caraway seeds on it, and set it to bake. Then the apprentice went away, and I was left sitting in the little trench by the oven, on a pile of rags. Well, Gimpel, I thought, you've revenged yourself on them for all the shame they've put on you. Outside the frost glittered, but it was warm beside the oven. The flames heated my face. I bent my head and fell into a doze.

I saw in a dream, at once, Elka in her shroud. She called to me, "What have you done, Gimpel?"

I said to her, "It's all your fault," and started to cry.

"You fool!" she said. "You fool! Because I was false is everything false too? I never deceived anyone but myself. I'm paying for it all, Gimpel. They spare you nothing here."

I looked at her face. It was black; I was startled and waked, and remained sitting dumb. I sensed that everything hung in the balance. A false step now and I'd lose eternal life. But God gave me His help. I seized the long shovel and took out the loaves, carried them into the yard, and started to dig a hole in the frozen earth.

My apprentice came back as I was doing it. "What are you doing, boss?" he said, and grew pale as a corpse.

"I know what I'm doing," I said, and I buried it all before his very eyes.

Then I went home, took my hoard from its hiding place, and divided it among the children. "I saw your mother tonight," I said. "She's turning black, poor thing."

They were so astounded they couldn't speak a word.

"Be well," I said, "and forget that such a one as Gimpel ever existed." I put on my short coat, a pair of boots, took the bag that held my prayer shawl in one hand, my stock in the other, and kissed the mezuzah. When people saw me in the street they were greatly surprised.

"Where are you going?" they said.

I answered, "Into the world." And so I departed from Frampol.

I wandered over the land, and good people did not neglect me. After many years I became old and white; I heard a great deal, many lies and falsehoods, but the longer I lived the more I understood that there were

really no lies. Whatever doesn't really happen is dreamed at night. It happens to one if it doesn't happen to another, tomorrow if not today, or a century hence if not next year. What difference can it make? Often I heard tales of which I said, "Now this is a thing that cannot happen." But before a year had elapsed I heard that it actually had come to pass somewhere.

Going from place to place, eating at strange tables, it often happens that I spin yarns — improbable things that could never have happened — about devils, magicians, windmills, and the like. The children run after me, calling, "Grandfather, tell us a story." Sometimes they ask for particular stories, and I try to please them. A fat young boy once said to me, "Grandfather, it's the same story you told us before." The little rogue, he was right.

So it is with dreams too. It is many years since I left Frampol, but as soon as I shut my eyes I am there again. And whom do you think I see? Elka. She is standing by the washtub, as at our first encounter, but her face is shining and her eyes are as radiant as the eyes of a saint, and she speaks outlandish words to me, strange things. When I wake I have forgotten it all. But while the dream lasts I am comforted. She answers all my queries, and what comes out is that all is right. I weep and implore, "Let me be with you." And she consoles me and tells me to be patient. The time is nearer than it is far. Sometimes she strokes and kisses me and weeps upon my face. When I awaken I feel her lips and taste the salt of her tears.

No doubt the world is entirely an imaginary world, but it is only once removed from the true world. At the door of the hovel where I lie, there stands the plank on which the dead are taken away. The gravedigger Jew has his spade ready. The grave waits and the worms are hungry; the shrouds are prepared — I carry them in my beggar's sack. Another *shnorrer* is waiting to inherit my bed of straw. When the time comes I will go joyfully. Whatever may be there, it will be real, without complication, without ridicule, without deception. God be praised: there even Gimpel cannot be deceived.

And Baby Makes Three

Jane Smiley's first short story, published in *Redbook* magazine's May 1977 issue, was accompanied by this note: "Jane Smiley attended the Iowa Writer's Workshop in 1975 and 1976. She is studying this year in Iceland on a Fulbright grant. This is her first published fiction." Her second story, "Jeffrey, Believe Me," appeared in *Triquarterly* later that year and won a Pushcart Prize. Unlike "Jeffrey, Believe Me," which has become well known, "And Baby Makes Three" does not appear in Smiley's collection *The Age of Grief,* and is being reprinted here for the first time. Smiley, who wrote the introduction to this collection, won a Pulitzer Prize for her novel *A Thousand Acres.* She now lives in Iowa, where she teaches at Iowa State University.

SHE WAS A HANDSOME baby, as babies go — a nice shade of red, with tiny black curls all over her head and the long fingers of a pianist or surgeon. They named her Alicia Constantina. Paul insisted on the Constantina. It had been the name of his grandmother, the rest gained substance by it, and he wanted this child to have substance. When Paul had her to himself (not often enough, with all those nurses and his wife there) he hummed in her ear. Was he imagining it or was she twitching in response? He hoped she would be musical.

Jane acted as if the baby were hers alone. Every five minutes, it seemed, she was putting the poor child to the breast or unpinning the diaper to check it. "Leave her alone," said Paul — gently, for Jane hated to be criticized. "Let her be by herself a little."

"Oh, be by herself. I'm sure that babies just have to have their privacy." Jane pulled her glasses down on her nose and threw her head back.

"Goo, goo, dahling! I just vant to be alone! Ha-ha-ha!" When Jane laughed she actually said ha-ha-ha, the way it was written in books. He wondered if she had learned to laugh after she learned to read. She was laughing a lot of late, and crying too. But Paul suspected that she was very happy.

Having the baby had been his idea. Jane hadn't wanted to quit her job, but he had said that if she didn't have his child, somebody else would. She considered this and gave in. Now she was having all the fun. The best times were when she brought Alicia into bed with them and then fell asleep. He would gently disentangle the baby from Jane's arms and take her next to his own chest. Alicia seemed to like this. She was very even-tempered. She had terrific knees. No rolls of fat, like his nephews', but real girlish knees. And her mouth opened like a camera shutter. Once he tried while shaving to make his mouth do that, but he couldn't. His opened like a toothed trap. That her eyes were going to be brown, almost black, made him feel funny, as if she were mysterious already. He had blue eyes, but Jane's were brown, and brown eyes were dominant. It seemed to him now that he should have taken this into consideration when he married her.

Jane carried the baby all over the apartment in a car bed. Paul had made a beautiful hardwood cradle, padded it and strung ribbons around it, and now Jane threw her into the same old car bed used by every damned baby in his family and couldn't understand why his feelings were hurt. "But I've got to have her with me," she would say, and those brown eyes would fill if he tried to argue.

"You'll spoil her. She'll become too dependent."

"You can't spoil a baby before she's a year old. She wants me, I know. It's best, Paul. Please don't push me about this."

And then it did seem as though Alicia needed her. She couldn't sleep and fussed all the time. She ate constantly and gained too much weight, but she would turn from the breast with a terrible, betrayed look. She was not colicky; the doctor checked her three times.

One night Paul came in from work to find Jane and Alicia rocking furiously in front of the window, both crying tumultuously. Jane raised her eyes to him, lacerated. "Oh, Paul," she said, "I'm a terrible mother! What's wrong with me?"

"Jane! What have you done?" He grabbed the baby from her. Alicia

screamed. "Shh," he said. "Daddy's home now. Sweet Alicia, sweet little Licia."

"Nothing, Paul — really! She just cried and cried all day, and I couldn't get her to stop and she wouldn't eat or sleep or be in the car bed and I didn't even get to do the breakfast dishes!"

Alicia was still yelling. Paul wanted to yell too. He closed his eyes, thought: This little piggy went to market, this little piggy stayed home. He felt calmer, put his free hand on Jane's shoulder. Now they were a family. A cacophonous, unhappy one, but a family.

The problem turned out to be coffee. A simple matter solved over Paul's parents' dinner table as his mother dished up dessert. Back in their apartment, Paul thought of that caffein circulating for days through Jane and then through Alicia. Jane swayed against him in fatigue, caught herself, mumbled an apology. "Go to bed," he said, "dear Jane." She liked that and smiled — as she hadn't in a while — before she turned toward the bedroom, dragging her coat on the carpet. One hand went to her hair, scratched. She looked six years old and he felt himself siphoned toward her.

But no. Here was Alicia, alert and self-possessed as a little demon. She made fists and scowled as if to say, "Let's go, Daddy." She loved to be walked. He followed a circuit in the dark, his shirt open, her face next to his chest. Living-room window, television, front door, kitchen. Sometimes he stopped and watched solitary cars catapult around the driveways of the apartment complex, or he simply stood still in the moonlight, thinking how deep into the night it must be. When he checked his watch it was only ten thirty. He looked at Alicia, who looked back at him. If he stood still too long or sat down, her face grew red in preparation. He tried singing. When she grew quiet, he began to make plans for a musical career for her. They would start her on the violin, he thought, then maybe banjo or guitar. At last her breathing was even against his skin.

Suddenly done in, he sat down on the couch; the tears poured down his cheeks and neck, into the hair on his chest. He had never known so many tears. How could anyone be sad enough for all this moisture? When it abated, he took Alicia to her cradle. He set her down very softly, eased his arms from under her, stepped back. Her eyes popped open.

With a sigh he lifted her out and returned to the living room to begin the circuit.

THEY had agreed, no baby books. After all, if they wanted advice, they could go to mothers and aunts, but they didn't want advice. Jane had read a baby book once, though, and now, against her will, it came back to her in snatches. She could remember enough to worry them but not enough to reassure them. It seemed that Alicia was slow.

First her failure to roll over concerned them. Finally she did it, however late. Then her eyes seemed too big, too vacant.

"Look at her," Jane said.

"Is she staring again?"

"Get with it, baby! Snap to!"

"You sound like a drill sergeant."

"I don't want to sound like a worried mother."

"I think she looks rather appealing."

"She looks dopey. Blue eyes, yes, brown eyes, no. Who's ever heard of a dumb brunette?"

"Don't make jokes." He couldn't stand her to make jokes about the baby.

"It's a dumb baby."

"Can it, Jane!" Then he took Alicia out of the high chair and hid her in his arms. "Your mother is a bad mother, Alicia."

"Don't make jokes."

"It's all jokes."

"Yes, it's all jokes." They smiled at each other but the smiling was difficult, and Paul thought, If Alicia's eyes would only sparkle! He showed things to her. Her gaze followed them, her hands reached for them, but it seemed she had no quickness.

They took her places after warm weather arrived. At first they hesitated to do it, not wanting to impose upon their friends, but now she was such a good baby that nobody minded. She slept at the proper times, and more than a few of their friends enjoyed seeing Jane open her blouse and put Alicia to the breast. Paul suspected that had her breasts not been so full and rosy, Jane would have switched Alicia to the bottle long before.

"She'll reach for solid food when she wants it," said Jane.

"But the doctor told you to try her on cereal and fruit."

"Solid is another word for crap."

So they packed up the diapers, rubber pants, little shirts and spare overalls, but not bottles or pacifiers, and went to restaurants and the homes of friends, acting as if nothing were easier than having a baby. Alicia would loll in her little spring chair and look around. Once a butterfly landed on the tip of her nose and her eyes crossed. Their assembled friends laughed at her — even Jane did — and he wanted to punch them, or run with Alicia out into the world of strangers, where she would be all his and he all hers.

Jane laid her fingers on his wrist. She said, "Deedle, deedle dumpling, my friend Paul, his wife was nothing and his child was all." She smiled but he could not.

It was in this chair that Alicia first discovered dogs, on a lovely summer afternoon with limy gin and tonics stretching into the dinner hour. He and Jane had never visited the Millers before, but they seemed easy to talk to, and not eager to do more than sit on the porch, exchanging desultory pleasantries. Alicia was content in her chair, bouncing up and down, dry, fed, nearly off into a doze. A bunch of barking dogs came around the house, two of them hardly more than puppies, snapping amateurishly at one another, falling down, rolling over. Suddenly they were up the porch steps, carrying their play dangerously close to the baby. Paul's baby. He leaped out of his chair. But they rolled away, yipping, snapping, down the steps. Alicia had come to attention and was laughing as Paul had never seen her laugh before. The dogs disappeared. Alicia subsided. Paul held her duckie out to her, and her chain of giant keys. No. She might as well have shrugged her shoulders. One of the puppies came into view again. Alicia sensed it immediately. Turning her head, she leaned around and fell rather forward, laughing a deep, hearty belly laugh.

"You ought to get her a dog," said Fred Miller.

"I don't think she's ever seen one before."

"It's funny how they show their predilections right off, isn't it?"

"She's never reacted like this to anything. We thought she was kind of slow, actually." Alicia's response seemed like a terrific accomplishment to Paul. He could hear himself saying, the next time someone asked

about her, "She's fine. She's quite a dog-lover, you know." To Fred Miller he said, "She's very fond of music, too. I think she has a natural sense of rhythm." But then he stopped himself. He and Jane had agreed that if they were going to take the child places, they wouldn't also bore their friends with her accomplishments. It was a good thing. So far she hadn't had many.

After a while there were more. She was excellent at patty-cake and guffawed when the patty-caker intentionally missed hands. "She has a sense of the incongruous," said Paul.

"But she always laughs at the same joke," said Jane.

"What other joke do we know that she can understand?"

"Well, this man went into a bar, and he sat down, and he had two bananas in his ears, and the bartender —"

"Is that two bananas in each ear?"

"Look at her. Does she care? All she cares about is titty."

"She cares a great deal about her father."

"Well, tell her a joke — see if she laughs."

Paul played patty-cake, missed hands. Alicia fell forward in the high chair, laughing.

"See?" said Jane. "She always laughs at the same joke. It's a dumb-dumb baby dear." Jane pinched Alicia lightly on the cheek. Alicia turned on her an adoring gaze. "See? All it cares about is titty."

"If you refer to that child as 'it' once more, I'm going to beat you up."

Jane looked at him, her mouth open to reply, but thought better of it. She shrugged.

Jane puzzled Paul. She seemed offhand about the baby now but always anxious to have her around. In her own way she was a loving mother, even a little overindulgent. She would run to Alicia if she gave out the least cry, and yet she could say, "There's the brat, bawling again."

What Jane really knew how to do was touch the baby. (Once — but he smashed this thought way back in his mind and tried not to think of it — she had known how to touch him.) She gave Alicia back rubs and massaged her fingers and the soles of her feet. She kissed her everywhere. Such caresses Paul found difficult. His hands were calloused; furthermore, he would grow uneasy and Alicia sensed it. How true. As much as he loved Alicia, she was his only when Jane had no time or was too tired. And it seemed as if Jane was never his. They had this business. It

was called raising the baby. Most of the time that was all they had, and yet he felt no temptation toward other women. At five o'clock there was no desire for a drink with his co-workers. All he wanted to do was go home and be swept up in the nightly adventure of child-raising.

"YOU'VE got to wash your hair, Jane."

She looked Paul in the eye, knew exactly what he was talking about and shrugged. He held her gaze. Peripherally he could see Alicia, now eight months old, crumbling her cookie onto the table of her high chair, glancing back and forth between them. His resolve was weakened but remained. "I wish you would." His quiet tone disarmed her and she did not shrug again.

Nor did she wash her hair. She seemed perverse, still calling the baby "it" but still unable to leave her for more than a few minutes at a time, never trying to look attractive for him but suspicious every time he put on his coat to go out. Jane had grown very jealous of their women friends.

"You think she's pretty, don't you?"

"Yes. Why not? She is."

"You don't think I'm pretty."

"You could be."

"I couldn't."

"You were."

"Thank you, but I wasn't."

"Wash your hair, put on shoes, wear a dress for me."

She laughed and held her arms out to the baby, who beamed and held her arms out in return. "All it takes is titty."

Paul jumped up.

"I'm sorry."

Paul sat down.

Teething lasted forever. They tried pacifiers, frozen pacifiers, ice. They tried their own fingers and a patent medicine to numb gums. They carried her from room to room and sang to her. She never cried or screamed, just fussed. It wrenched Paul to the heart.

"Why does she have to get teeth?" he said. "She'll just lose them anyway."

"She has to have teeth to be smart. They're connected to the brain."

Did Jane think up these things sitting home all day and refusing to wash her hair? Did she chuckle to herself, thinking, Tonight I'll tell him that the tooth bone is connected to the brain bone?

Jane laughed. She said, "Well, the tooth bone is connected to the brain bone, you know."

Paul closed his eyes and thought vividly of wringing her neck. When he opened them, she was shaking her head a little, but she stopped when she saw him watching her.

Then it seemed that mercy was shown him. He had a good day at work, came home to find Jane washing her hair. The baby sat in the playpen, hammering the head of her doll, glad with smiles to see her daddy. They had a good dinner; then the baby yawned and was put to bed at seven thirty. He was not tired. Even Jane was not tired. She came and sat next to him on the couch and the leaves were turning outside the window and Paul felt that it was perfect. He put his arm around her shoulders and drew her to him. "I want you to be happy," he said.

"I am happy."

"We've both been very tired."

"Not me." She slid down the couch to the arm.

He said, "It seems that we've got further apart from each other."

"No, we haven't. Everything is perfect, please. I have no faults or inconsistencies."

"What about me?"

"Not everyone can be perfect."

"Almost?"

"Did I tell you the joke about the man with the bananas in his ears?"

"Both ears?"

"You've heard it before."

"Tell me again."

"I'm happy. I'm everything I should be." She paused, then turned toward him, holding out her hand. "Oh, Paul!"

But the hand clenched into a fist and she put it in her lap. "A man went into a bar. He had two bananas in his ears. His name was Paul, you see. And the bartender said to him, 'Why've you got those bananas in your ears?' and the man said 'What?' So the bartender — his name was Jane. Funny name for a bartender, but his parents expected a cocktail waitress. Anyway, the bartender shouted, 'Hey, buddy, I said,

"Why've you got those bananas in your ears?"' 'What?' said the man."

Paul got up and walked toward the kitchen. His shoes creaked in the long silence. When he opened the refrigerator door, the milk fell out. Then Jane screamed out the punch line. "'Excuse me,' said Paul," she shouted, "'I've got these bananas in my ears!'"

After this it seemed they were enemies. Yet every night he was eager to go home. For one thing, there was the baby. He focused on the baby. What a beauty she was, with her thick black curls, her ready smile and delighted laugh! She was learning to show things to him. He would sit beside her in her circle of toys and say, "Show Daddy the truck, sweetheart." She would offer him the string of beads. "No, the truck." He would point out the truck to her. "Now show Daddy the beads." She would pounce on the truck and hold it up to him. A self-conscious use of irony. Very smart. "Where is the baby's chin? Where are the baby's toes? Where is the baby's dear daddy?"

Then Jane would sweep in from the kitchen, saying, "Got to be changed, got to be fed, got to be put to bed."

Paul would lie down carefully on the floor, overtaken by a vision of himself and Jane pulling Alicia in two between them.

SUDDENLY Jane changed her outlook on grooming. She dressed exquisitely, made of herself and Alicia the ideal mother and child. Her hair was always shiny, drawn high on her head in a bun or swinging across her shoulders. She tickled the baby with it until Alicia grasped and pulled. Then Jane would carefully open the tiny hands and drop her mouth in kisses on the baby's face.

It was in Jane's elegant phase that Paul brought home the puppy. It was white and not cute, even for a white puppy. "She loves dogs," said Paul. "I want her to have a puppy."

"It looks like a rat."

"It's half Samoyed." The puppy squatted briefly by the refrigerator, leaving a yellow spot. "Samoyeds are very loyal and intelligent."

"Well, give it a book on housetraining."

"The puppy is a he. The baby is a she. The baby's name is Alicia and the puppy's name is Snow. They will love each other."

"The puppy's name is mud. He will complicate my life with pee and poop, of which both I have an abundance. Come on, Paul."

"Look, I have brought Alicia a puppy. She loves dogs. *She loves dogs.* This is something I, her father, am doing for her right now, getting her a dog."

But Snow was gone, as Paul had known he would be, the next evening after work.

Somehow, later, it got so that he and Jane were no longer openly hostile. If he was standing by the refrigerator and she asked for the marmalade, he would hand it to her. When she ruined her toothbrush cleaning the brass candlesticks, she used his rather than buying a new one. He didn't mind; in fact, he rather enjoyed its convivial dampness when she had got to it first. But they had nothing to say to each other. They rolled past each other like two ball bearings, and if they came together, they only knocked apart. Paul was satisfied. The delightful Alicia was enough for him. Such likes and dislikes she had, but such tact as well. If it was broccoli, she simply ignored it. If it was her uncle Terry, who sported a bushy beard, she politely looked away. When Paul sat beside her on the floor, she cocked her head attentively while he talked. He said, "You know, Alicia, you have a kind of good-natured reserve that is very attractive in a woman. You understand absurdity, but also serenity. There is a center of mystery in you, divine child." He reminded her of the dog they would get someday. A golden retriever, he'd now decided, after hearing on the news that a golden retriever had pulled a child from the path of a speeding car.

She climbed into his lap and held out her hands. They had a new game, which involved his slapping her face lightly with her own hands, saying, "Alicia! Stop hitting yourself, child, stop hitting yourself!" She would bellow with laughter and roll around until she had flopped out of his lap, breathless. It was the best game he had ever played. Still, every time Jane came into the room, Alicia would reach for her. Sometimes Jane would say, "No, Ali, Mother doesn't want to pick it up." Paul would grit his teeth, pull Alicia back to himself, but she would struggle to get free of him and fret until Jane relented. Jane always did. For Alicia's sake Paul made himself be glad.

"She's going to talk soon," said Jane. "I wonder if her first word will be 'titty.'"

"Not if she's properly weaned."

That had become rather a bone of contention between them, but the

conversation did not continue. These days there was rarely more than one assertion, one response.

Still, Paul wondered what her first word would be. He did not want to admit to himself how much he wished for "dada." He referred to himself often as "daddy," sometimes, with shame, as "dada." Now Jane said, "It's going to be 'mama.'"

"What are you talking about?"

"It ain't going to be 'dada,' Dada."

"You may call me Paul."

FOR Jane's birthday her mother sent Jane's baby book and copies of all her baby pictures carefully labeled and pasted in a new album. Jane's favorite food had been bananas. Her first word had been "no." "Even then I wouldn't take any grief," she said with pride.

Jane asked Paul's mother what she could remember about him. She was unable to assign particulars to any of her nine children. They might have written down his first word, but who knew where it was by this time? She recalled only that he had worn a red blazer every day to kindergarten, and at lunchtime she would look out the window and see him coming from a block away. He had been very proud of it, and even on warm days he would button the gold buttons carefully and smooth his lapels before leaving the house. This vision of his five-year-old self pleased Paul, but his babyhood was sadly lost. Not even any pictures. For a week he had the camera out daily, snapping pictures of Alicia at her bath, at her dinner, asleep. She seemed to understand that the camera was another manifestation of his admiration for her, and so she preened herself adorably. She had a new mannerism: a sidelong upward glance, with a languorous lifting of the lashes and then a slow turning of the head. The sensations this aroused in Paul he would not name. Basically it made him want not just to own her body and soul, but to contain her and be contained by her. Fortunately she did not cast this look at him often, and then she grew out of it. Most of the time he could be fatherly.

It seemed they had always had a baby, that they had never slept past six thirty or been able to stay awake after the late news. No matter how thoroughly they put away the toys, one was always underfoot. When had there not been a diaper can in the bathroom, a carefully rinsed washcloth

over the sink? When was there not this mysterious third presence in the house, who had been nowhere, done nothing, had little of interest to say and yet was the sun of their double orbit? When was the last time he and Jane had looked at each other, or spoken, without referring to Alicia? Warm weather came again (was it only the second time — was it already summer?), and with some amazement Paul found the same T shirts he had always worn, and his swimming trunks, and yes, a half bottle of sun-tan lotion from last year. (Was it only last year?)

It appeared that Jane had plans for Alicia too. "As soon as they'll go in, get them in the water," she said. "If they grow up doing it, they'll never be afraid."

"But she can hardly walk."

"But she can walk. Already it's nearly too late. She's almost a land animal. We can't let her get locked into it."

So they took her to the Lee Street beach. Paul had his doubts. The Lake was so vast. He had never felt comfortable in the water. His trunks were always too tight and too flowered, and his fair skin burned too easily. Jane, with her brown complexion and brown bathing suit, was like an otter in the water. She nosed through the surface, and her long hair flowed behind her shoulders to a point and streamed down her spine. When they got to the beach she took Alicia and knelt with her in the shallows, paddling the little arms and legs, splashing her gently, laughing. By the time Paul had hidden his watch and wallet, had secured all the corners of the blanket with hamper, books and shoes, the baby had had enough. So he went for a tremulous dip while Jane rubbed Alicia down and treated her to a banana. When he rejoined them, they were just going off with a bucket and shovel to dig by the water.

"Sandwiches in the hamper," Jane said.

"What kind?"

"Peanut butter and sand, tuna fish and sand. There's a partially masticated banana, too."

"Where are you going?"

"To teach the kid about crenelations." Then she squatted down and took Alicia's face in her hands. "Say 'crenelations,' kid." She tossed back her hair and laughed. She never actually looked at him, but he felt her contempt.

Sitting on the blanket, he ate tuna and felt excluded. They crouched

side by side, their backs to him. First Alicia held the bucket and Jane shoveled; then Jane held it and Alicia shoveled. They dug a hole in the sand, slapped its sides. They bailed water out of it. When Jane laughed, Alicia laughed. Finally they rinsed off, toddled back up the beach to him. The clasp of their hands made him want to cry because their fingers, entwined, were complete. Had his hand been wanted, it could only have encompassed theirs. He saw clearly their alliance was one of similar predilections, even more than of coloring and sex. Alicia's favorite food was bananas and he didn't even know what his had been. No doubt junior liver. Come to me, Alicia, he thought, and say "dada." He held out his arms.

A lifeguard ran between them, chasing a black dog. Alicia giggled, pulled her hand out of Jane's. Paul called to her. She ran toward him, her fat legs moving sideways in the deep sand. When he took her in his arms she said, "Da!"

"What?" said Paul.

She twisted to look at the lake and repeated, "Da! Da! Da!"

Jane threw herself down next to him. He kept his voice very flat. "She said 'dada,'" he said.

"Not 'father'? Not even 'crenelations' or 'ashlar facing'? That's what we've been working on."

"She said 'dada.' Not 'mama' or 'titty.' 'Dadada!'"

The dog, tail high, a plastic inner tube in its mouth, ran by again. Alicia shouted, "Da! Da! Da! Da!"

"See?" said Paul. "Dada."

Jane remained silent.

"Dada." He pointed to himself. "Dada." He pointed to her. "Alicia." To be nice, he pointed to Jane. "Mama."

"She said 'dog.'"

"Dada. Alicia. Dada. Alicia. Dada. Mama. Alicia."

"Paul, she said 'dog.'"

"Damn you, Jane." Alicia was growing bored in his arms. When he held her tightly he could feel her little palms against his skin, pushing. "She does love me, Jane. She loves the games I play with her. Alicia! Look at me, sweetheart! Alicia, look at Papa — Dada, I mean. Stop hitting yourself, Alicia! Stop hitting yourself. Here! You want this magazine? Look at this picture. What a big house! No, don't tear it,

sweetheart. Well, take her, then. She's just hungry. Damn you, Jane. I mean it. You've always done everything for her. I feel like I've been waiting for a year and a half for you to let me do something. She did say 'dada,' and she meant me because I am her dada, and she loves me."

Jane gave Alicia half a cookie. Suddenly the dog had joined them, now wet, a red bandanna tied about its neck. Alicia laughed. She said, "Da! Da!" and held out her cookie, which the dog carefully licked from her hand. Then it sat, eager but still, wagging only the tip of its tail, waiting for more. Jane sat watching Paul.

"Well, you could have kept the dog, at least," he said. Jane kept watching him. He had to close his eyes. He heard Jane say, "Go away, dog — you're too wet. Scram!" She got up from the blanket, came back.

Would this upheaval within him ever subside? He couldn't bear to have it erupt in her sight, the sobs, the hateful moisture. His knees shook; he pressed them together.

There was a tearing of paper. Jane said, "No, kid, mustn't tear. Give Ma the magazine."

Paul thought that if he moved one muscle, a large groan would issue, not from his mouth, but from his pores, from all his organs.

Then he felt something. A hand it was, on his forehead — Jane's hand, pushing his hair back, drifting down his temple and behind his ear. Again. More ripping of the magazine. Alicia shouted gleefully, but the mother's corrective voice did not sound. Fingers separated strands of his hair, smoothed them back together. The dog returned; Paul felt its wet tail brush his arm.

"Look at me," murmured Jane. Opening his eyes was like lifting roofs. "Hello," she said.

"Da!" shouted Alicia. "Da!"

||≣

The Seraph and the Zambesi

"Most of the memorable experiences of my life I have celebrated, or used for a background, in a short story or novel," writes Muriel Spark in her autobiography, *Curriculum Vitae*. Referring to "The Seraph and the Zambesi," she says, "I felt a compulsion to describe the Zambesi River and the approach to the falls through the mysterious Rain Forest as a mystical experience. I expressed, symbolically, how the aridity of the white people there had affected me."

Spark had long since returned to Britain from Africa by the time she wrote this story. She had worked as General Secretary of London's Poetry Society and editor of the *Poetry Review,* published a study of Mary Shelley, written numerous articles and poems, and was working on a book on the works of John Masefield when, in November 1951, the *Observer* announced a short story competition on the subject of Christmas. "The Seraph and the Zambesi" won the £250 first prize out of 6,700 entries and was published by the newspaper in December 1951. In her autobiography, Spark says that the *Observer*'s Philip Toynbee, phoning to tell her she had won, said that the judges thought at first it was written by a man. She remarks, "I don't know if I was supposed to be flattered by that."

||≣

YOU MAY HAVE heard of Samuel Cramer, half poet, half journalist, who had to do with a dancer called the Fanfarlo. But, as you will see, it doesn't matter if you have not. He was said to be going strong in Paris early in the nineteenth century, and when I met him in 1946 he was still going strong, but this time in a different way. He was the same man, but modified. For instance, in those days, more than a hundred years ago, Cramer had persisted for several decades, and without affectation, in

being about twenty-five years old. But when I knew him he was clearly undergoing his forty-two-year-old phase.

At this time he was keeping a petrol pump some four miles south of the Zambesi River where it crashes over a precipice at the Victoria Falls. Cramer had some spare rooms where he put up visitors to the Falls when the hotel was full. I was sent to him because it was Christmas week and there was no room in the hotel.

I found him trying the starter of a large, lumpy Mercedes outside his corrugated-iron garage, and at first sight I judged him to be a Belgian from the Congo. He had the look of north and south, light hair with canvas-coloured skin. Later, however, he told me that his father was German and his mother Chilean. It was this information rather than the 'S. Cramer' above the garage door which made me think I had heard of him.

The rains had been very poor and that December was fiercely hot. On the third night before Christmas I sat on the stoep outside my room, looking through the broken mosquito-wire network at the lightning in the distance. When an atmosphere maintains an excessive temperature for a long spell something seems to happen to the natural noises of life. Sound fails to carry in its usual quantity, but comes as if bound and gagged. That night the Christmas beetles, which fall on their backs on every stoep with a high tic-tac, seemed to be shock-absorbed. I saw one fall and the little bump reached my ears a fraction behind time. The noises of minor wild beasts from the bush were all hushed-up, too. In fact it wasn't until the bush noises all stopped simultaneously, as they frequently do when a leopard is about, that I knew there had been any sound at all.

Overlying this general muted hum, Cramer's sundowner party progressed farther up the stoep. The heat distorted every word. The glasses made a tinkle that was not of the substance of glass, but of bottles wrapped in tissue paper. Sometimes, for a moment, a shriek or a cackle would hang torpidly in space, but these were unreal sounds, as if projected from a distant country, as if they were pocket-torches seen through a London fog.

Cramer came over to my end of the stoep and asked me to join his party. I said I would be glad to, and meant it, even though I had been glad to sit alone. Heat so persistent and so intense sucks up the will.

Five people sat in wicker arm-chairs drinking high-balls and chewing salted peanuts. I recognised a red-haired trooper from Livingstone, just out from England, and two of Cramer's lodgers, a tobacco planter and his wife from Bulawayo. In the custom of those parts, the other two were introduced by their first names. Mannie, a short dark man of square face and build, I thought might be a Portuguese from the east coast. The woman, Fanny, was picking bits out of the frayed wicker chair and as she lifted her glass her hand shook a little, making her bracelets chime. She would be about fifty, a well-tended woman, very neat. Her grey hair, tinted with blue, was done in a fringe above a face puckered with malaria.

In the general way of passing the time with strangers in that country-side, I exchanged with the tobacco people the names of acquaintances who lived within a six-hundred-mile radius of where we sat, reducing this list to names mutually known to us. The trooper contributed his news from the region between Lusaka and Livingstone. Meanwhile an argument was in process between Cramer, Fanny and Mannie, of which Fanny seemed to be getting the better. It appeared there was to be a play or concert on Christmas Eve in which the three were taking part. I several times heard the words 'troupe of angels', 'shepherds', 'ridiculous price' and 'my girls' which seemed to be key words in the argument. Suddenly, on hearing the trooper mention a name, Fanny broke off her talk and turned to us.

'She was one of my girls,' she said. 'I gave her lessons for three years.'

Mannie rose to leave, and before Fanny followed him she picked a card from her handbag and held it out to me between her fingernails.

'If any of your friends are interested . . .' said Fanny hazily.

I looked at this as she drove off with the man, and above an address about four miles up the river I read:

Mme La Fanfarlo (Paris, London)
Dancing Instructress. Ballet. Ballroom.
Transport provided By Arrangement.

Next day I came across Cramer still trying to locate the trouble with the Mercedes.

'Are you the man Baudelaire wrote about?' I asked him.

He stared past me at the open waste veldt with a look of tried patience.

'Yes,' he replied. 'What made you think of it?'

'The name Fanfarlo on Fanny's card,' I said. 'Didn't you know her in Paris?'

'Oh, yes,' said Cramer, 'but those days are finished. She married Manuela de Monteverde — that's Mannie. They settled here about twenty years ago. He keeps a Kaffir store.'

I remembered then that in the Romantic age it had pleased Cramer to fluctuate between the practice of verse and that of belles lettres, together with the living up to such practices.

I asked him, 'Have you given up your literary career?'

'As a career, yes,' he answered. 'It was an obsession I was glad to get rid of.'

He stroked the blunt bonnet of the Mercedes and added, 'The greatest literature is the occasional kind, a mere after-thought.'

Again he looked across the veldt where, unseen, a grey-crested lourie was piping 'go 'way, go 'way'.

'Life,' Cramer continued, 'is the important thing.'

'And do you write occasional verses?' I enquired.

'When occasion demands it,' he said. 'In fact I've just written a Nativity Masque. We're giving a performance on Christmas Eve in there.' He pointed to his garage, where a few natives were already beginning to shift petrol cans and tyres. Being members neither of the cast nor the audience, they were taking their time. A pile of folded seats had been dumped alongside.

Late on the morning of Christmas Eve I returned from the Falls to find a crowd of natives quarrelling outside the garage, with Cramer swearing loud and heavy in the middle. He held a sulky man by the shirt-sleeve, while with the other hand he described his vituperation on the hot air. Some mission natives had been sent over to give a hand with laying the stage, and these, with their standard-three school English, washed faces and white drill shorts, had innocently provoked Cramer's raw rag-dressed boys. Cramer's method, which ended with the word 'police', succeeded in sending them back to work, still uttering drum-like gutturals at each other.

The stage, made of packing-cases with planks nailed across, was being

put at the back of the building, where a door led to the yard, the privy and the native huts. The space between this door and the stage was closed off by a row of black Government blankets hung on a line; this was to be the dressing-room. I agreed to come round there that evening to help with the lighting, the make-up, and the pinning on of angels' wings. The Fanfarlo's dancing pupils were to make an angel chorus with carols and dancing, while she herself, as the Virgin, was to give a representative ballet performance. Owing to her husband's very broken English, he had been given a silent role as a shepherd, supported by three other shepherds chosen for like reasons. Cramer's part was the most prominent, for he had the longest speeches, being the First Seraph. It had been agreed that, since he had written the masque, he could best deliver most of it; but I gathered there had been some trouble at rehearsals over the cost of the production, with Fanny wanting elaborate scenery as being due to her girls.

The performance was set to begin at eight. I arrived behind the stage at seven-fifteen to find the angels assembled in ballet dresses with wings of crinkled paper in various shades. The Fanfarlo wore a long white transparent skirt with a sequin top. I was helping to fix on the Wise Men's beards when I saw Cramer. He had on a toga-like garment made up of several thicknesses of mosquito-net, but not thick enough to hide his white shorts underneath. He had put on his make-up early, and this was melting on his face in the rising heat.

'I always get nerves at this point,' he said. 'I'm going to practise my opening speech.'

I heard him mount the stage and begin reciting. Above the voices of excited children I could only hear the rhythm of his voice; and I was intent on helping the Fanfarlo to paint her girls' faces. It seemed impossible. As fast as we lifted the sticks of paint they turned liquid. It was really getting abnormally hot.

'OPEN that door,' yelled the Fanfarlo. The back door was opened and a crowd of curious natives pressed round the entrance. I left the Fanfarlo ordering them off, for I was determined to get to the front of the building for some air. I mounted the stage and began to cross it when I was aware of a powerful radiation of heat coming from my right. Looking round, I saw Cramer apparently shouting at someone, in the attitude of

his dealings with the natives that morning. But he could not advance because of this current of heat. And because of the heat I could not at first make out who Cramer was rowing with; this was the sort of heat that goes for the eyes. But as I got further towards the front of the stage I saw what was standing there.

This was a living body. The most noticeable thing was its constancy; it seemed not to conform to the law of perspective, but remained the same size when I approached as when I withdrew. And altogether unlike other forms of life, it had a completed look. No part was undergoing a process; the outline lacked the signs of confusion and ferment which are commonly the sign of living things, and this was also the principle of its beauty. The eyes took up nearly the whole of the head, extending far over the cheekbones. From the back of the head came two muscular wings which from time to time folded themselves over the eyes, making a draught of scorching air. There was hardly any neck. Another pair of wings, tough and supple, spread from below the shoulders, and a third pair extended from the calves of the legs, appearing to sustain the body. The feet looked too fragile to bear up such a concentrated degree of being.

European residents of Africa are often irresistibly prompted to speak kitchen Kaffir to anything strange.

'*Hamba!*' shouted Cramer, meaning 'Go away'.

'Now get off the stage and stop your noise,' said the living body peaceably.

'Who in hell are you?' said Cramer, gasping through the heat.

'The same as in Heaven,' came the reply, 'a Seraph, that's to say.'

'Tell that to someone else,' Cramer panted. 'Do I look like a fool?'

'I will. No, nor a Seraph either,' said the Seraph.

The place was filling with heat from the Seraph. Cramer's paint was running into his eyes and he wiped them on his net robe. Walking backward to a less hot place he cried, 'Once and for all —'

'That's correct,' said the Seraph.

' — this is my show,' continued Cramer.

'Since when?' the Seraph said.

'Right from the start,' Cramer breathed at him.

'Well, it's been mine from the Beginning,' said the Seraph, 'and the Beginning began first.'

Climbing down from the hot stage, Cramer caught his seraphic robe on a nail and tore it. 'Listen here,' he said, 'I can't conceive of an abnormality like you being a true Seraph.'

'True,' said the Seraph.

By this time I had been driven by the heat to the front entrance. Cramer joined me there. A number of natives had assembled. The audience had begun to arrive in cars and the rest of the cast had come round the building from the back. It was impossible to see far inside the building owing to the Seraph's heat, and impossible to re-enter.

Cramer was still haranguing the Seraph from the door, and there was much speculation among the new arrivals as to which of the three familiar categories the present trouble came under, namely, the natives, Whitehall, or leopards.

'This is my property,' cried Cramer, 'and these people have paid for their seats. They've come to see a masque.'

'In that case,' said the Seraph, 'I'll cool down and they can come and see a masque.'

'*My* masque,' said Cramer.

'Ah, no, *mine*,' said the Seraph. 'Yours won't do.'

'Will you go, or shall I call the police?' said Cramer with finality.

'I have no alternative,' said the Seraph more finally still.

Word had gone round that a mad leopard was in the garage. People got back into their cars and parked at a safe distance; the tobacco planter went to fetch a gun. A number of young troopers had the idea of blinding the mad leopard with petrol and ganged up some natives to fill petrol cans from the pump and pass them chainwise to the garage.

'This'll fix him,' said a trooper.

'That's right, let him have it,' said Cramer from his place by the door.

'I shouldn't do that,' said the Seraph. 'You'll cause a fire.'

The first lot of petrol to be flung into the heat flared up. The seats caught alight first, then the air itself began to burn within the metal walls till the whole interior was flame feeding on flame. Another carload of troopers arrived just then and promptly got a gang of natives to fill petrol cans with water. Slowly they drenched the fire. The Fanfarlo mustered her angels a little way up the road. She was trying to reassure their parents and see what was happening at the same time, furious at losing her

opportunity to dance. She aimed a hard poke at the back of one of the angels whose parents were in England.

It was some hours before the fire was put out. While the corrugated metal walls still glowed, twisted and furled, it was impossible to see what had happened to the Seraph, and after they had ceased to glow it was too dark and hot to see far into the wreck.

'Are you insured?' one of Cramer's friends asked him.

'Oh yes,' Cramer replied, 'my policy covers everything except Acts of God — that means lightning or flood.'

'He's fully covered,' said Cramer's friend to another friend.

Many people had gone home and the rest were going. The troopers drove off singing "Good King Wenceslaus", and the mission boys ran down the road singing "Good Christian Men, Rejoice".

It was about midnight, and still very hot. The tobacco planters suggested a drive to the Falls, where it was cool. Cramer and the Fanfarlo joined us, and we bumped along the rough path from Cramer's to the main highway. There the road is tarred only in two strips to take car-wheels. The thunder of the Falls reached us about two miles before we reached them.

'After all my work on the masque and everything!' Cramer was saying.

'Oh, shut up,' said the Fanfarlo.

Just then, by the glare of our headlights I saw the Seraph again, going at about seventy miles an hour and skimming the tarmac strips with two of his six wings in swift motion, two folded over his face, and two covering his feet.

'That's him!' said Cramer. 'We'll get him yet.'

WE left the car near the hotel and followed a track through the dense vegetation of the Rain Forest, where the spray from the Falls descends perpetually. It was like a convalescence after fever, that frail rain after the heat. The Seraph was far ahead of us and through the trees I could see where his heat was making steam of the spray.

We came to the cliff's edge, where opposite us and from the same level the full weight of the river came blasting into the gorge between. There was no sign of the Seraph. Was he far below in the heaving pit, or where?

Then I noticed that along the whole mile of the waterfall's crest the spray was rising higher than usual. This I took to be steam from the Seraph's heat. I was right, for presently, by the mute flashes of summer lightning we watched him ride the Zambesi away from us, among the rocks that look like crocodiles and the crocodiles that look like rocks.

Oil Field Vignettes

Thumbnail Biographies of Three Picturesque Characters of the Drilling Fraternity

Jim Thompson claimed he sold his first story at fifteen, and the biographical sketch of Thompson that appears in the paperback reprints of his work states that he sold his first story to *True Detective* when he was fourteen. However, these must be tall tales, since *True Detective*'s first issue appeared in 1924, when Thompson was already eighteen. In fact, Thompson's first appearance in that magazine was in 1935, unless, of course, he wrote earlier under a pseudonym, a possibility that his biographer, Michael J. McCauley, finds extremely remote. There is no evidence that Thompson published any story before "Oil Field Vignettes," which appeared in the February 1929 issue of *Texas Monthly*, when he was twenty-two. The story, actually sketches, was inspired by Thompson's work on the oil fields of West Texas. *Texas Monthly* published a second story a few months later, after which his editor there convinced him to stop wasting his talents on manual labor and enroll in college.

JAKE FANNER

EXCEPT FOR THE concluding words of this biography, Jake Fanner's longest speech was made in a cook shack near Caddo. At that time he was paying three dollars a day for meals, and overlooking the fact that the boarding-house owner was entitled to some small margin of profit, Jake tried to eat at least one dollar's worth at every meal.

The anxious woman proprietor seeing him whack off a quarter of a pound of butter from the plate, one day, took it upon herself to hand out a hint.

"Mr. Fanner," she said, "did you know that butter costs a dollar and a quarter a pound?"

Jake swallowed a couple of biscuits and cleared his throat. "Well," he grunted, "I reckon good butter's wuth it."

Speech and money were Jake's economies — especially speech. He simply could not bear to say an unnecessary word, and he deplored unnecessary speech in those around him. It was Jake's philosophy that a man's watch could tell him when it was time to go to bed and to meals, and if he wasn't a blanked fool he would know what to do after he got to either place without a lot of crazy talkin'. Jake nearly married a deafmute, rumor said, until he found that she knew how to say "good morning."

With this peculiar aversion to talk, it seemed to be Jake's lot in life to be afflicted with voluble tool-dressers. Just when he, as a driller, was beginning to think that he had secured a silent working companion, the tooly would burst out with some comment on the weather or a request for a chew of tobacco, and the search for silence would start all over again. For although Jake was often discouraged he never gave up. The vision of a silent Utopia was ever before him.

Such sublime faith as this, it seemed only right, should meet with its reward. And at last it seemed that it had. He found a capable tool-dresser who didn't say "good morning," who didn't ask for things at meals or other times, who knew what to do without being told, who knew no funny stories and didn't care to hear any, who, as time went on, seemed even more silent than Jake.

For a month — the happiest month of his life — Jake worked with this paragon. And looking into the future there was hope for many more such months. Even during the fretting, almost continuous task of crowding pipe into a caving hole the tool-dresser never spoke.

A mule-skinner who was scooping out a slush-pit for a nearby well left his team to get a drink of water, and Jake chose that time to throw on steam to loosen up the pipe which was beginning to freeze in the caving mud. He pulled too hard on the pipe; the derrick cracked ominously and one of the guy wires, humming under the strain, jerked a stake out of the ground and sent it whistling across the rumps of the idling mules, fifty yards away.

The mules had never been used to anything cruder than a ball-bat, and naturally felt that a fifty-pound stake was too much, even if it did miss them. They bolted, tearing down another guy with the trailing fresno, and headed toward the rig. Their master, yelling imprecations and warnings, ran futilely after them. Jake and his helper stopped work to watch. They said nothing.

Onward the straining jacks came; they clambered upon the casing rack and as the pipe began to roll with them they charged on to the derrick floor. The two men sprang for safety, and the two beasts whimsically sprang for the slush-pit. The fresno caught underneath the forge, and they tore it out, pipe and all. They ploughed out of the sucking mud, and with their fury not the least abated and dragging the heavy forge, they were last seen heading in the general direction of El Paso.

From his seat on the walking-beam the tooly let out an amazed whistle. "Look at them jassacks go!" he exclaimed.

Jake Fanner sighed; once again his dream was shattered, his faith misplaced. Then with the fury of a disillusioned man he yelled up at the tooly. "Get outta here, you blankety-blanked son-of-a-phonograph. You talk too dam' much!"

BIG HOLE BEN

There was a driller working around Ranger during the days of the boom who got the name of Big Hole Ben. The prefix to his given cognomen was not made as a consequence of his cave-like mouth; he drew the handle by refusing to drill anything smaller than a ten-inch hole. After the well was spudded in and the fifteen-inch pipe set, one noticed that Ben's huge jaws moved less rhythmically on their quarter-pound of fine cut; and when the twelve-inch had been drilled a fellow could see he was downright nervous — even neglecting to splash the tooly with mud when they bailed out. Then when the ten-inch bits had done their work, and were sharpened and racked for the next job, you would find Big Hole Ben's Sunday shirt missing from the bunk house and its owner inclined at a receiving angle at the timekeeper's window.

Ben just wouldn't work on anything but big hole, so that's the name he got; that, and cussings from contractors who weren't in love with the idea of changing men in what was practically the middle of a well.

But those were boom times. Casing crews got a hundred dollars a tower; rig builders were drawing thirty dollars for a twelve-hour day; drillers drew twenty and were hard to find. So Ben took the name, the cussings, and the twenty dollars, and kept on quitting and going to work whenever he felt like it.

Boom. One hundred million dollars were stuck in the black mud of Ranger. Then things began to slack up.

The field was playing out. Money was getting scarcer, men more plentiful. *Someone* suddenly decided that oil was too high and cut the price smack in two. *That* was the end.

Overnight, almost, the exodus commenced. Workmen started back to their homes in Fort Worth, Dallas, San Angelo, El Paso, anywhere and everywhere. The girls hit out for the cities to see what a guy without mud in his ears looked like; and the casing crews went back to picking cotton and shooting craps. There was a popular demand for good drinking whiskey and a long rest and no money for either. Strangely, nearly everyone seemed to be broke and getting broker, although the printers were making pretty good jack turning out sheriff's sale bills and attachments. Long trains of tools and pipe went unclaimed and were finally hauled back to the factories. The sound of revelry was replaced by the silence of reverie; the city of the future became the town of the past. Later she was to revive, but now — Ranger was dead.

Drillers' wages dropped from twenty dollars a day to fifteen, from fifteen to twelve; finally they fell to ten. And jobs were hard to get at ten. Hard to get, yes, but somehow Big Hole Ben managed to keep working. Managed where a lot of good men couldn't. But he knew it wouldn't last; not with his trick of quitting in the middle of a well.

And it didn't last.

There was another cut in oil; a complementing one in wages. When Ben left the hole just as the ten was drilled he was told by the contractor that he could look for no more work from that company. Ben had been told things like that before, but he sensed finality in this warning. It would be the same everywhere; he had gotten a reputation.

But he couldn't quit drilling until he had saved something. And on the other hand he couldn't drill unless he carried the hole to the bottom. Having an aversion to starvation, there was only one thing to do.

Ben went out to a base several miles from the field where a wildcatter was moving in with a baling-wire outfit. The promoter-contractor looked like he needed a square meal, and he had gotten into his pants too far at the seat, but he seemed to be a nice fellow. He had "borrowed" a string of pipe from another well the night before and was so relieved to find that Ben was not the owner that he gave him a job. He probably would have hired him anyway as Ben looked so anxious, and anxious men are not likely to be so particular about pay-day.

So Ben started on his great experiment — to drill a hole to the bottom. Here on a wildcat, away from the other wells, he felt that the experiment would not make him so nervous.

And you could hardly say that Ben got nervous; it's too small a word. He got downright afraid every time the hole grew smaller. Don't ask me why; Ben couldn't have told you himself. Some awful premonition just kept telling him every minute of the day to try and get his money, and clear out! Many a time he did start to leave, but he always managed to control himself. He would have to finish the well or go to selling papers, and Ben never could sell anything. So he stuck. But his breath in those days smelled more like rotgut whiskey than tobacco.

Gradually the well neared completion. All things do come to an end; even a wildcat. So Ben breathed easier and started figuring out ways of collecting his pay. They were drilling in the lime now. He would have to slack up pretty soon to give the promoter time to get out from town with a photographer. They were going to take a picture of the well. If it was a well.

The tool-dresser was outside trying to figure out what the hell was wrong with the boiler. He paused a moment in the operation to light a cigarette, and looked up at the top of the derrick. That's a habit among the oil fraternity — looking up — and there's a reason for it.

He saw Ben cut down the throttle and step over to the hole and peer down. At the same instant he saw something that made him scream; then turn his face.

Ben didn't have time to move, and a four-pound nut sped down the ninety feet from the top and caught Ben slantwise on the head. Ben's brains were knocked out of his mouth right along with his tobacco, and they must have fallen down the hole, for they never found either.

Another driller was secured to take Ben's place, and the well that he had nearly finished came in for several hundred barrels. But if Ben was where he could know, I don't think that he cared!

BALDY SEALBRIDGE

It seems to be Nature that the faithful and trusting among us are forever doomed to disillusionment and disappointment, while the cynics and reprobates are treated to the best that life holds. Maybe it's all right: Nature thinks that the faithful and trusting will carry on without encouragement, and that the second class must be coaxed and enticed. Maybe it's all right — it has to be — but sometimes things are carried too far.

I met Baldy Sealbridge right after the war; a little runt, he was, weighing about a hundred and fifteen, height something over five feet, snaggle toothed, and a six-and-a-quarter head with a horse-shoe of mousy fuzz around its top.

"Going home," he told me. "Yeah, I got a home; married a sweet little widow just before the war. She's out at Breckenridge, now waiting for me. Say — after all this — !" A look of great expectation came into his eye.

"Maybe it won't be so great," I said. "Wives are funny things."

"Don't I know!" he exclaimed. "This is my sixth. Yeah, sixth time; all the others divorced. But this one's different. I could tell the first time I saw her." Devout wonderment shone from his face. "I can't figure out why she ever married me."

I couldn't figure it out, either, after seeing the picture of her which Baldy was carrying. And the mystery went unsolved, for me, until I stopped in Breckenridge over a year later.

The widow, I found, besides marrying Mr. Sealbridge, had also married a baker's dozen of other service men, and had drawn thirty dollars a month from each during the war. The court let her off on a plea of amnesia.

"I didn't care anything about her anyways," said Baldy when I met him. "And" — philosophically — "it wouldn't of done much good if I had." He shook his head in profound amazement. "Thirteen husbands, and she couldn't remember any of 'em!"

"Well rid of her, Baldy," I agreed. "Come on and get a drink with me and I'll take you to dinner."

Baldy flushed and swallowed. "I — I can't," he said. "I'm getting married this afternoon. Say, you ought to see her. . . .'"

Time and I went on. Baldy was divorced again. His wife had accidentally chipped glass into the pancake batter. Or it might not, as Baldy seemed to think, have been an accident; she had insured him for ten thousand. After that the reports I got were few and varied. And mostly unreliable. A caser at Noodledome told me that Baldy had married a snake-charmer, and that one of the lady's pythons had swallowed him, thinking he was a rabbit. A pipe-liner swore that Baldy had married a squaw in Seminole, and was sent to Congress as a representative of the tribe. Crazy stories, yes; but all with some speck of honesty in them. I had had a driller tell me how he had seen *me* killed in a boiler explosion; and he called me a liar when I told him who I was and denied my demise.

But coming out of Borger late one night, I found Baldy Sealbridge seated by the side of the road, crying broken-heartedly. Without asking him I was sure that matrimony was at the seat of his trouble. And it was.

"What — what would you think," he blubbered, "if you went home and found another man with your wife?"

I did not answer — was not expected to.

"What would you think if they were drinking beer that you had paid four-bits a bottle for, and were kissin' and huggin' each other?"

I patted him on the back.

"And how would you feel," asked Baldy, "if — if this guy kicked you out of the door while your wife held it open? Your — your own front door!" His voice had been growing higher, and now it broke into a spasm of sobs.

Crying men make me uncomfortable. And Baldy seemed to be writhing on the ground. "It's all right, kid," I said; "I wouldn't let them hurt my feelings."

He arose groaning. And by his next words I knew that Baldy's spirit was forever tanned to Life's barbs. Nature had gone a little too far with him. There was resolve in his figure; resolve quickly altered by pain.

"It — it ain't my feelings," he whimpered. "It's the seat o' my pants!"

JOHN UPDIKE

Friends from Philadelphia

In 1945, when John Updike was twelve, his aunt gave him a subscription to the *New Yorker,* thus beginning what has proved to be a life-long involvement with the magazine. He was so enamored of the magazine that by the ninth grade he was submitting stories and poems to it, and he had collected enough rejection slips to make an album.

Updike's professional relationship with the magazine began in June 1954, when he graduated from Harvard. The *New Yorker* bought a poem, "Duet with Muffled Brake Drums," which appeared on August 14, and "Friends from Philadelphia," which appeared on October 30. The following year the magazine hired Updike as a staff writer. All sixteen of the stories in Updike's first collection, *The Same Door* ("Friends from Philadelphia" among them, in a slightly different form), were originally published in the *New Yorker.*

IT WAS CLOSE to five-thirty when he rang the Lutzes' doorbell. In the moment before the door was opened to him, he glimpsed a thigh below the half-drawn shade. Thelma was home, then. She was wearing the Camp Winniwoho T shirt and her quite short shorts.

"Why, my goodness — Janny!" she cried. She pronounced his name, John, to rhyme with Ann. During the summer vacation she had visited in New York City, and she tried to talk the way she thought people talked there. "What on earth ever brings you to me at this odd hour?"

"Hello, Thel," he said. "I hope — I guess this is a pretty bad time." She had been plucking her eyebrows again. He wished she wouldn't do that.

Thelma extended her arm and touched the base of his neck with the

tips of her fingers. It wasn't a fond gesture — just a hostesslike one. "Now, Janny. You know that I — my mother and I — are always happy to be seeing you. Mother, who do you ever guess is here at this odd hour?"

"Don't keep John standing there," Mrs. Lutz said. She was settled in the deep, red settee, watching television and smoking. A coffee cup being used as an ashtray lay in her lap, and her dress was hitched so her knees showed.

"Hello, Mrs. Lutz," John said, trying not to look at her broad, pale knees. "I really hate to bother you at this odd hour."

"I don't see anything odd about it." She took a deep drag on her cigarette and exhaled through her nostrils. "Some of the other kids were here earlier this afternoon."

"I would have come in if anybody had told me."

Thelma said, "Oh, Janny! Stop trying to make a martyr of yourself. Keep in touch, they say, if you want to keep up."

He felt his face grow hot and knew he was blushing, and this made him blush all the more.

Mrs. Lutz shook a wrinkled pack of Herbert Tareytons at him. "Smoke?" she said.

"I guess not, thanks a lot."

"You've stopped? It's a bad habit. I wish I had stopped at your age. I'm not sure I even *begun* at your age."

"No, it's just that I have to go home soon, and my mother would smell the smoke on my breath. She can smell it even through chewing gum."

"Why must you go home soon?" Thelma asked.

Mrs. Lutz sniffled. "I have sinus. I can't even smell the flowers in the garden or the food on the table any more. Let the kids smoke if they want, if it makes them feel better. I don't care. My Thelma, she can smoke right in her own home, her own living room, if she wants to. But she doesn't seem to have the taste for it. I'm just as glad, to tell the truth."

John hated interrupting, but he was worried about the time. "I have a problem," he said.

"A problem — how gruesome," Thelma said. "And here I thought, Mother, I was being favored with a social call."

"Don't talk like that," Mrs. Lutz said.

"It's sort of complex," John began.

"Then let me turn this off," Mrs. Lutz said, snapping the right knob on the television set.

"Oh, Mother, and I was listening to it!" Thelma toppled into a chair, her legs flashing. John thought she was delicious when she pouted.

Mrs. Lutz ignored her daughter. She had set herself to give sympathy. Her lap was broadened and her hands were laid palms upward in it.

"It's not much of a problem," John assured her. "But we're having some people up from Philadelphia." He turned to Thelma and added, "If anything is going on tonight, I can't get out."

"Life is just too, too full of disappointments," Thelma said.

"Look — is there?"

"Too, too full," Thelma said.

Mrs. Lutz made fluttery motions out of her lap. "These Philadelphia people."

John said, "Maybe I shouldn't bother you about this." He waited, but she just looked more and more patient, so he went on. "My mother wants to give them wine, and my father isn't home from school yet. He might not get home before the liquor store closes. It's at six, isn't it? My mother's busy cleaning, so I walked in to the liquor store."

"She made you walk the whole mile? Poor thing, can't you drive?" Mrs. Lutz asked.

"*Sure* I can drive. But I'm not sixteen yet."

"You look a lot taller than sixteen," Mrs. Lutz said.

John looked at Thelma to see how she took that one, but Thelma was pretending to read a rental-library novel wrapped in cellophane.

"I walked all the way in to the liquor store," John told Mrs. Lutz, "but they wouldn't give me anything without written permission. It was a new man."

"Your sorrow has rent me in twain," Thelma said, as if she were reading it from the book.

"Pay no attention, Johnny," Mrs. Lutz said. "Frank will be home any time. Why not wait until he comes and let him run you down to the liquor store?"

"That sounds wonderful. Thanks an awful lot, really."

Mrs. Lutz's hand descended upon the television knob. Some smiling man was playing the piano. John didn't know who he was; there wasn't

any television at his house. They watched in silence until they heard the sound of heavy footsteps outside on the porch. The empty milk bottles tinkled. "Now, don't be surprised if he has a bit of a load on," Mrs. Lutz said.

Actually, Mr. Lutz didn't act at all drunk, John thought. He was like a happy husband in the movies. He called Thelma his little pookie-pie and kissed her on the forehead; then he called his wife his big pookie-pie and kissed her on the mouth. Then he solemnly shook John's hand and told him how very, very happy he was to see him here and asked after his parents. "Is that goon still on television?" he said finally.

"Daddy, please pay attention to somebody else," Thelma said, turning off the television set. "Janny wants to talk to you."

"And *I* want to talk to *Johnny,*" Thelma's father said. He spread his arms suddenly, clenching and unclenching his fists. He was a big man, with shaved gray hair above his tiny ears.

John couldn't think of how to begin.

Mrs. Lutz explained the errand. When she was through, Mr. Lutz said, "People from Philadelphia. I bet their name isn't William L. Trexler, is it?"

"No. I forget their name, but it's not that. The man is an engineer. The woman went to college with my mother."

"Oh. College people. Then we must get them something very, very nice, I should say."

"Daddy," Thelma said. "*Please.* The store will close."

"Tessie, you hear John. People from college. People with diplomas. And it is very nearly closing time, and who isn't on their way?" He took John's shoulder in one hand and Thelma's arm in the other and hustled them through the door. "We'll be back in one minute, Mama," he said.

Mrs. Lutz followed them out onto the porch. "Drive carefully," she said.

Mr. Lutz's huge blue Buick was parked in front of the house. "I never went to college," he said as they started down the steps, "yet I buy a new car whenever I want." His tone wasn't nasty but soft and full of wonder.

"Oh, Daddy, not *this* again," Thelma said, shaking her head at John, so he could understand all she had to go through.

When she looks like that, John thought, I could bite her lip until it bleeds.

itdme."

dont know how," John said.

"It's very easy to learn, very easy. You just slide in there. Come on, it's getting late." John got in on the driver's side. He peered out through the windshield — the hood looked wide as a boat.

Mr. Lutz told him to grip the little lever behind the steering wheel. "You pull it toward you like *that* — that's it — and fit it into one of these notches. 'P' stands for 'parking' — I hardly ever use that one. 'N,' that's 'neutral,' like on the car you have. 'D' means 'drive' — just put it in there and the car does all the work for you. You are using that one ninety-nine per cent of the time. 'L' is 'low,' for very steep hills, going up or down. And 'R' stands for — what?"

"'Reverse,'" John said.

"Very, very good. Tessie, he's a smart boy. He'll never own a new car. And when you put them all together, you can remember their order by the sentence Paint No Dimes Light Red. I thought that up when I was teaching my oldest girl how to drive."

"Paint No Dimes Light Red," John said.

"Excellent. Now, let's go."

A bubble was developing in John's stomach. "What gear do you want it in to start?" he asked Mr. Lutz.

Mr. Lutz must not have heard him, because all he said was "Let's go"

again, and he drummed on the dashboard with his fingertips. They were thick, square fingers.

Thelma leaned up from the back seat. Her cheek almost touched John's ear. She whispered "Put it at 'D.'"

He did; then he looked for the starter. "How does he start it?" he asked Thelma.

"I never watch him," she said. "There was a button in the last car, but I don't see it in this one."

Staring straight ahead and smiling, Mr. Lutz sang out, "Push on the pedal and away we go. And ah, ah, way we go."

"Just step on the gas," Thelma suggested. John pushed down firmly, to keep his leg from trembling. The motor roared, and the car bounded away from the curb. Within a block, though, he could manage the car pretty well.

"It rides like a boat on smooth water," he told his two passengers. The metaphor pleased him.

Mr. Lutz squinted ahead. "Like a what?"

"Like a boat."

"Don't go so fast," Thelma said.

"The motor's so quiet," John explained. "Like a sleeping cat."

Without warning, a truck pulled out of a side street. Mr. Lutz, trying to brake, stamped his foot on the empty floor in front of him. John could hardly keep from laughing. "I see him," he said, easing his speed so that the truck had just enough room to make its turn. "Those trucks think they own the road." He let one hand slide away from the steering wheel. One-handed, he whipped around a bus. "What'll she do on the open road?"

"That's a good question, John," Mr. Lutz said. "And I don't know the answer. Eighty, maybe."

"The speedometer goes up to a hundred and twenty," Thelma said.

Another pause; nobody seemed to be in a mood for talking.

John said, "Hell. A baby could drive one of these."

"For instance, you," Thelma said. That meant she had noticed how well he was driving.

THERE were a lot of cars in front of the liquor store, and John saw that he would have to double-park the big Buick.

"That's close enough, close enough," Mr. Lutz said. "Don't get any closer — whoa!" He was out of the car before John could bring it to a complete stop. "You and Tessie wait here," he said. "I'll go in for the liquor."

"Mr. Lutz. Say, Mr. Lutz," John called.

"Daddy!" Thelma shouted.

Mr. Lutz returned. "What is it, boys and girls?"

"Here's the money they gave me." John pulled two wadded dollars from the change pocket of his dungarees. "My mother said to get something inexpensive but nice."

"Inexpensive but nice?" Mr. Lutz repeated.

"She said something about California sherry."

"What did she say about it? To get it? Or not to?"

"I guess to get it."

"You guess." Mr. Lutz shoved himself away from the car and walked backward toward the store as he talked. "You and Tessie wait in the car. Don't go off somewhere. It's getting late. I'll only be one minute."

John leaned back in his seat and gracefully rested one hand at the top of the steering wheel. "I like your father."

"You don't know how he acts to Mother," Thelma said.

John studied the clean line under his wrist and thumb. He flexed his wrist and watched the neat little muscles move in his forearm. "You know what I need?" he said. "A wristwatch."

"Oh, Jan," Thelma said. "Stop admiring your own hand. It's really disgusting."

A ghost of a smile flickered over his lips, but he let his strong, nervous fingers remain as they were on the steering wheel. "I'd sell my soul for a drag right now."

"Daddy keeps a pack in the glove compartment," Thelma said. "I'd get them if my fingernails weren't so long."

"*I'll* get it open," John said. He did. They fished one cigarette out of the old pack they found, and took alternate puffs. "Ah," John said, "that first drag of the day, clawing and scraping its way down your throat."

"Be on the lookout for Daddy. They hate my smoking."

"Thelma."

"Yes?" She stared deep into his eyes, her face half hidden in blue shadow.

"Don't pluck your eyebrows."

"I think it looks nice."

"It's like calling me 'Jan.'" There was a silence — not awkward, a comfortable silence.

"Get rid of the rette, Jan. Daddy just passed the window."

When Mr. Lutz came out of the liquor store he was in a soberer mood. "Here you be, John," he said in a businesslike way, and handed John a wine bottle with a red foil cap. "Better let me drive. You drive like a veteran, but I know the roads."

"I can walk from your house, Mr. Lutz," John said, knowing Mr. Lutz wouldn't make him walk. "Thanks an awful lot for all you've done."

"I'll drive you up. Philadelphians can't be kept waiting. We can't make this young man walk a mile — now, can we, Tessie?"

Nobody knew what to say after this last remark, so they kept quiet all the way, although several things were bothering John.

When the car stopped in front of his house, he forced himself to ask, "Say, Mr. Lutz. I wonder if there was any change?"

"What? Oh. I nearly forgot. You'll have your Dad thinking I'm a crook." He reached into his pocket and without looking handed John a dollar, a quarter, and a penny.

"This seems like a lot," John said. The wine must be cheap. Maybe he should have let his mother buy it, like she had wanted to.

"It's your change," Mr. Lutz said.

"Well, thanks an awful lot."

"Goodbye now," Mr. Lutz said.

"So long." John slammed the door. "Goodbye, Thelma. Don't forget what I told you." He winked.

The car pulled out, and John walked up the path. "Don't forget what I told you," he repeated to himself, winking. The bottle was cool and heavy in his hand. He glanced at the label, which read "Château Mouton-Rothschild 1937."

KURT VONNEGUT

Report on the Barnhouse Effect

Between 1947 and 1950 Kurt Vonnegut worked in public relations for General Electric in Schenectady, New York. "I started to write," he told *Time* magazine in 1969, "because I hated that job so much." But both that job and Schenectady provided some of the inspiration for Vonnegut's first novel, *Player Piano,* as well as for his first short story, "Report on the Barnhouse Effect," which *Collier's* published on February 11, 1950. Vonnegut helped support himself and his family for several years by selling stories to such magazines as the *Saturday Evening Post, Collier's,* and *Cosmopolitan.* He would frequently return to the themes addressed in his first story, scientific responsibility and the moral implications of technological progress.

LET ME BEGIN by saying that I don't know any more about where Professor Arthur Barnhouse is hiding than anyone else does. Save for one short, enigmatic message, left in my mailbox on Christmas Eve, I have not heard from him since his disappearance a year and a half ago.

What's more, readers of this article will be disappointed if they expect to learn how *they* can bring about the so-called "Barnhouse Effect." If I were able and willing to give away that secret, I would certainly be something more important than a psychology instructor.

I have been urged to write this report because I did research under the professor's direction and because I was the first to learn of his astonishing discovery. But while I was his student I was never entrusted with knowledge of how the mental forces could be released and directed. He was unwilling to trust anyone with that information.

I would like to point out that the term "Barnhouse Effect" is a creation of the popular press, and was never used by Professor Barnhouse. The name he chose for the phenomenon was *"dynamopsychism,"* or *force of the mind.*

I cannot believe that there is a civilized person yet to be convinced that such a force exists, what with its destructive effects on display in every national capital. I think humanity has always had an inkling that this sort of force does exist. It has been common knowledge that some people are luckier than others with inanimate objects like dice. What Professor Barnhouse did was to show that such "luck" was a measurable force, which in his case could be enormous.

By my calculations, the professor was about fifty-five times more powerful than a Nagasaki-type atomic bomb at the time he went into hiding. He was not bluffing when, on the eve of "Operation Brainstorm," he told General Honus Barker: "Sitting here at the dinner table, I'm pretty sure I can flatten anything on earth — from Joe Louis to the Great Wall of China."

There is an understandable tendency to look upon Professor Barnhouse as a supernatural visitation. The First Church of Barnhouse in Los Angeles has a congregation numbering in the thousands. He is godlike in neither appearance nor intellect. The man who disarms the world is single, shorter than the average American male, stout, and averse to exercise. His I.Q. is 143, which is good but certainly not sensational. He is quite mortal, about to celebrate his fortieth birthday, and in good health. If he is alone now, the isolation won't bother him too much. He was quiet and shy when I knew him, and seemed to find more companionship in books and music than in his associations at the college.

Neither he nor his powers fall outside the sphere of Nature. His dynamopsychic radiations are subject to many known physical laws that apply in the field of radio. Hardly a person has not now heard the snarl of "Barnhouse static" on his home receiver. Contrary to what one might expect, the radiations are affected by sunspots and variations in the ionosphere.

However, his radiations differ from ordinary broadcast waves in several important ways. Their total energy can be brought to bear on any single point the professor chooses, and that energy is undiminished by

distance. As a weapon, then, dynamopsychism has an impressive advantage over bacteria and atomic bombs, beyond the fact that it costs nothing to use: it enables the professor to single out critical individuals and objects instead of slaughtering whole populations in the process of maintaining international equilibrium.

As General Honus Barker told the House Military Affairs Committee: "Until someone finds Barnhouse, there is no defense against the Barnhouse Effect." Efforts to "jam" or block the radiations have failed. Premier Slezak could have saved himself the fantastic expense of his "Barnhouse-proof" shelter. Despite the shelter's twelve-foot-thick lead armor, the premier has been floored twice while in it.

There is talk of screening the population for men potentially as powerful dynamopsychically as the professor. Senator Warren Foust demanded funds for this purpose last month, with the passionate declaration: "He who rules the Barnhouse Effect rules the world!" Commissar Kropotnik said much the same thing, so another costly armaments race, with a new twist, has begun.

This race at least has its comical aspects. The world's best gamblers are being coddled by governments like so many nuclear physicists. There may be several hundred persons with dynamopsychic talent on earth, myself included, but, without knowledge of the professor's technique, they can never be anything but dice-table despots. With the secret, it would probably take them ten years to become dangerous weapons. It took the professor that long. He who rules the Barnhouse Effect is Barnhouse and will be for some time.

Popularly, the "Age of Barnhouse" is said to have begun a year and a half ago, on the day of Operation Brainstorm. That was when dynamopsychism became significant politically. Actually, the phenomenon was discovered in May, 1942, shortly after the professor turned down a direct commission in the Army and enlisted as an artillery private. Like X rays and vulcanized rubber, dynamopsychism was discovered by accident.

FROM time to time Private Barnhouse was invited to take part in games of chance by his barrack mates. He knew nothing about the games, and usually begged off. But one evening, out of social grace, he agreed to shoot craps. It was a terrible or wonderful thing that he played, depending upon whether or not you like the world as it now is.

"Shoot sevens, Pop," someone said.

So "Pop" shot sevens — ten in a row to bankrupt the barracks. He retired to his bunk and, as a mathematical exercise, calculated the odds against his feat on the back of a laundry slip. His chances of doing it, he found, were one in almost ten million! Bewildered, he borrowed a pair of dice from the man in the bunk next to his. He tried to roll sevens again, but got only the usual assortment of numbers. He lay back for a moment, then resumed his toying with the dice. He rolled ten more sevens in a row.

He might have dismissed the phenomenon with a low whistle. But the professor instead mulled over the circumstances surrounding his two lucky streaks. There was one single factor in common on both occasions, *the same thought train had flashed through is mind just before he threw the dice.* It was that thought train which aligned the professor's brain cells into what has since become the most powerful weapon on earth.

THE soldier in the next bunk gave dynamopsychism its first token of respect. In an understatement certain to bring wry smiles to the faces of the world's dejected demagogues, the soldier said, "You're hotter'n a two-dollar pistol, Pop." Professor Barnhouse was all of that. The dice that did his bidding weighed but a few grams, so the forces involved were minute; but the unmistakable fact that there were such forces was earth-shaking.

Professional caution kept him from revealing his discovery immediately. He wanted more facts and a body of theory to go with them. Later, when the atomic bomb was dropped on Hiroshima, it was fear that made him hold his peace. At no time were his experiments, as Premier Slezak called them, "a bourgeois plot to shackle the true democracies of the world." The professor didn't know where they were leading.

In time, he came to recognize another startling feature of dynamopsychism: *its strength increased with use.* Within six months, he was able to govern dice thrown by men the length of a barracks distant. By the time of his discharge in 1945, he could knock bricks loose from chimneys three miles away.

Charges that Professor Barnhouse could have won the last war in a minute, but did not care to do so, are perfectly senseless. When the war ended, he had the range and power of a 37-millimeter cannon, per-

haps — certainly no more. His dynamopsychic powers graduated from the small-arms class only after his discharge and return to Wyandotte College.

I enrolled in the Wyandotte Graduate School two years after the professor had rejoined the faculty. By chance, he was assigned as my thesis adviser. I was unhappy about the assignment, for the professor was, in the eyes of both colleagues and students, a somewhat ridiculous figure. He missed classes or had lapses of memory during lectures. When I arrived, in fact, his shortcomings had passed from the ridiculous to the intolerable.

"We're assigning you to Barnhouse as a sort of temporary thing," the dean of social studies told me. He looked apologetic and perplexed. "Brilliant man, Barnhouse, I guess. Difficult to know since his return, perhaps, but his work before the war brought a great deal of credit to our little school."

When I reported to the professor's laboratory for the first time, what I saw was more distressing than the gossip. Every surface in the room was covered with dust; books and apparatus had not been disturbed for months. The professor sat napping at his desk when I entered. The only signs of recent activity were three overflowing ash trays, a pair of scissors, and a morning paper with several items clipped from its front page.

As he raised his head to look at me, I saw that his eyes were clouded with fatigue. "Hi," he said, "just can't seem to get my sleeping done at night." He lighted a cigarette, his hands trembling slightly. "You the young man I'm supposed to help with a thesis?"

"Yes, sir," I said. In minutes he converted my misgivings to alarm.

"You an overseas veteran?" he asked.

"Yes, sir."

"Not much left over there, is there?" He frowned. "Enjoy the last war?"

"No, sir."

"Look like another war to you?"

"Kind of, sir."

"What can be done about it?"

I shrugged. "Looks pretty hopeless."

He peered at me intently. "Know anything about international law, the U.N., and all that?"

"Only what I pick up from the papers."

"Same here," he sighed. He showed me a fat scrapbook, packed with newspaper clippings. "Never used to pay any attention to international politics. Now I study them the way I used to study rats in mazes. Everybody tells me the same thing — 'Looks hopeless.'"

"Nothing short of a miracle —" I began.

"Believe in magic?" he asked sharply. The professor fished two dice from his vest pocket. "I will try to roll twos," he said. He rolled twos three times in a row. "One chance in about 47,000 of that happening. There's a miracle for you." He beamed for an instant, then brought the interview to an end, remarking that he had a class which had begun ten minutes ago.

He was not quick to take me into his confidence, and he said no more about his trick with the dice. I assumed they were loaded, and forgot about them. He set me the task of watching male rats cross electrified metal strips to get to food or female rats — an experiment that had been done to everyone's satisfaction in the 1930s. As though the pointlessness of my work were not bad enough, the professor annoyed me further with irrelevant questions. His favorites were: "Think we should have dropped the atomic bomb on Hiroshima?" and "Think every new piece of scientific information is a good thing for humanity?"

HOWEVER, I did not feel put upon for long. "Give those poor animals a holiday," he said one morning, after I had been with him only a month. "I wish you'd help me look into a more interesting problem — namely, my sanity."

I returned the rats to their cages.

"What you must do is simple," he said, speaking softly. "Watch the inkwell on my desk. If you see nothing happen to it, say so, and I'll go quietly — relieved, I might add — to the nearest sanitarium."

I nodded uncertainly.

He locked the laboratory door and drew the blinds, so that we were in twilight for a moment. "I'm odd, I know," he said. "It's fear of myself that's made me odd."

"I've found you somewhat eccentric, perhaps, but certainly not —"

"If nothing happens to that inkwell, 'crazy as a bedbug' is the only description of me that will do," he interrupted, turning on the overhead

lights. His eyes narrowed. "To give you an idea of how crazy, I'll tell you what's been running through my mind when I should have been sleeping. I think maybe I can save the world. I think maybe I can make every nation a *have* nation, and do away with war for good. I think maybe I can clear roads through jungles, irrigate deserts, build dams overnight."

"Yes, sir."

"Watch the inkwell!"

Dutifully and fearfully I watched. A high-pitched humming seemed to come from the inkwell; then it began to vibrate alarmingly, and finally to bound about the top of the desk, making two noisy circuits. It stopped, hummed again, glowed red, then popped in splinters with a blue-green flash.

Perhaps my hair stood on end. The professor laughed gently. "Magnets?" I managed to say at last.

"Wish to Heaven it were magnets," he murmured. It was then that he told me of dynamopsychism. He knew only that there was such a force; he could not explain it. "It's me and me alone — and it's awful."

"I'd say it was amazing and wonderful!" I cried.

"If all I could do was make inkwells dance, I'd be tickled silly with the whole business." He shrugged disconsolately. "But I'm no toy, my boy. If you like, we can drive around the neighborhood, and I'll show you what I mean." He told me about pulverized boulders, shattered oaks and abandoned farm buildings demolished within a fifty-mile radius of the campus. "Did every bit of it sitting right here, just thinking — not even thinking hard."

He scratched his head nervously. "I have never dared to concentrate as hard as I can for fear of the damage I might do. I'm to the point where a mere whim is a blockbuster." There was a depressing pause. "Up until a few days ago, I've thought it best to keep my secret for fear of what use it might be put to," he continued. "Now I realize that I haven't any more right to it than a man has a right to own an atomic bomb."

He fumbled through a heap of papers. "This says about all that needs to be said, I think." He handed me a draft of a letter to the Secretary of State.

Dear Sir:

I have discovered a new force which costs nothing to use, and which is probably more important than atomic energy. I should like to see it used

most effectively in the cause of peace, and am, therefore, requesting your
advice as to how this might best be done.

Yours truly,
A. Barnhouse.

"I have no idea what will happen next," said the professor.

THERE followed three months of perpetual nightmare, wherein the nation's political and military great came at all hours to watch the professor's tricks with fascination.

We were quartered in an old mansion near Charlottesville, Virginia, to which we had been whisked five days after the letter was mailed. Surrounded by barbed wire and twenty guards, we were labeled "Project Wishing Well," and were classified as Top Secret.

For companionship we had General Honus Barker and the State Department's William K. Cuthrell. For the professor's talk of peace-through-plenty they had indulgent smiles and much discourse on practical measures and realistic thinking. So treated, the professor, who had at first been almost meek, progressed in a matter of weeks toward stubbornness.

He had agreed to reveal the thought train by means of which he aligned his mind into a dynamopsychic transmitter. But, under Cuthrell's and Barker's nagging to do so, he began to hedge. At first he declared that the information could be passed on simply by word of mouth. Later he said that it would have to be written up in a long report. Finally, at dinner one night, just after General Barker had read the secret orders for Operation Brainstorm, the professor announced, "The report may take as long as five years to write." He looked fiercely at the general. "Maybe twenty."

The dismay occasioned by this flat announcement was offset somewhat by the exciting anticipation of Operation Brainstorm. The general was in a holiday mood. "The target ships are on their way to the Caroline Islands at this very moment," he declared ecstatically. "One hundred and twenty of them! At the same time, ten V-2s are being readied for firing in New Mexico, and fifty radio-controlled jet bombers are being equipped for a mock attack on the Aleutians. Just think of it!" Happily he reviewed his orders. "At exactly 1100 hours next Wednesday, I will give you the order to *concentrate;* and you, Professor, will think as hard

as you can about sinking the target ships, destroying the V-2s before they hit the ground, and knocking down the bombers before they reach the Aleutians! Think you can handle it?"

The professor turned gray and closed his eyes. "As I told you before, my friend, I don't know what I can do." He added bitterly, "As for this Operation Brainstorm, I was never consulted about it, and it strikes me as childish and insanely expensive."

General Barker bridled. "Sir," he said, "your field is psychology, and I wouldn't presume to give you advice in that field. Mine is national defense. I have had thirty years of experience and success, Professor, and I'll ask you not to criticize my judgment."

The professor appealed to Mr. Cuthrell. "Look," he pleaded, "isn't it war and military matters we're all trying to get rid of? Wouldn't it be a whole lot more significant and lots cheaper for me to try moving cloud masses into drought areas, and things like that? I admit I know next to nothing about international politics, but it seems reasonable to suppose that nobody would want to fight wars if there were enough of everything to go around. Mr. Cuthrell, I'd like to try running generators where there isn't any coal or water power, irrigating deserts, and so on. Why, you could figure out what each country needs to make the most of its resources, and I could give it to them without costing American taxpayers a penny."

"Eternal vigilance is the price of freedom," said the general heavily.

Mr. Cuthrell threw the general a look of mild distaste. "Unfortunately, the general is right in his own way," he said. "I wish to Heaven the world were ready for ideals like yours, but it simply isn't. We aren't surrounded by brothers, but by enemies. It isn't a lack of food or resources that has us on the brink of war — it's a struggle for power. Who's going to be in charge of the world, our kind of people or theirs?"

The professor nodded in reluctant agreement and arose from the table. "I beg your pardon, gentlemen. You are, after all, better qualified to judge what is best for the country. I'll do whatever you say." He turned to me. "Don't forget to wind the restricted clock and put the confidential cat out," he said gloomily, and ascended the stairs to his bedroom.

FOR reasons of national security, Operation Brainstorm was carried on without the knowledge of the American citizenry which was footing the

bill. The observers, technicians and military men involved in the activity knew that a test was under way — a test of what, they had no idea. Only thirty-seven keymen, myself included, knew what was afoot.

In Virginia, the day for Operation Brainstorm was unseasonably cool. Inside, a log fire crackled in the fireplace, and the flames were reflected in the polished metal cabinets that lined the living room. All that remained of the room's lovely old furniture was a Victorian love seat, set squarely in the center of the floor, facing three television receivers. One long bench had been brought in for the ten of us privileged to watch. The television screens showed, from left to right, the stretch of desert which was the rocket target, the guinea-pig fleet, and a section of the Aleutian sky through which the radio-controlled bomber formation would roar.

Ninety minutes before H hour the radios announced that the rockets were ready, that the observation ships had backed away to what was thought to be a safe distance, and that the bombers were on their way. The small Virginia audience lined up on the bench in order of rank, smoked a great deal, and said little. Professor Barnhouse was in his bedroom. General Barker bustled about the house like a woman preparing Thanksgiving dinner for twenty.

At ten minutes before H hour the general came in, shepherding the professor before him. The professor was comfortably attired in sneakers, gray flannels, a blue sweater and a white shirt open at the neck. The two of them sat side by side on the love seat. The general was rigid and perspiring; the professor was cheerful. He looked at each of the screens, lighted a cigarette and settled back, comfortable and cool.

"Bombers sighted!" cried the Aleutian observers.

"Rockets away!" barked the New Mexico radio operator.

All of us looked quickly at the big electric clock over the mantel, while the professor, a half-smile on his face, continued to watch the television sets. In hollow tones, the general counted away the seconds remaining. "Five . . . four . . . three . . . two . . . one . . . *Concentrate!*"

Professor Barnhouse closed his eyes, pursed his lips, and stroked his temples. He held the position for a minute. The television images were scrambled, and the radio signals were drowned in the din of Barnhouse static. The professor sighed, opened his eyes and smiled confidently.

"Did you give it everything you had?" asked the general dubiously.

"I was wide open," the professor replied.

The television images pulled themselves together, and mingled cries of amazement came over the radios tuned to the observers. The Aleutian sky was streaked with the smoke trails of bombers screaming down in flames. Simultaneously, there appeared high over the rocket target a cluster of white puffs, followed by faint thunder.

General Barker shook his head happily. "By George!" he crowed. "Well, sir, by George, by George, by George!"

"Look!" shouted the admiral seated next to me. "The fleet — it wasn't touched!"

"The guns seem to be drooping," said Mr. Cuthrell.

We left the bench and clustered about the television sets to examine the damage more closely. What Mr. Cuthrell had said was true. The ships' guns curved downward, their muzzles resting on the steel decks. We in Virginia were making such a hullabaloo that it was impossible to hear the radio reports. We were so engrossed, in fact, that we didn't miss the professor until two short snarls of Barnhouse static shocked us into sudden silence. The radios went dead.

We looked around apprehensively. The professor was gone. A harassed guard threw open the front door from the outside to yell that the professor had escaped. He brandished his pistol in the direction of the gates, which hung open, limp and twisted. In the distance, a speeding government station wagon topped a ridge and dropped from sight into the valley beyond. The air was filled with choking smoke, for every vehicle on the grounds was ablaze. Pursuit was impossible.

"What in God's name got into him?" bellowed the general.

Mr. Cuthrell, who had rushed out onto the front porch, now slouched back into the room, reading a penciled note as he came. He thrust the note into my hands. "The good man left this billet-doux under the door knocker. Perhaps our young friend here will be kind enough to read it to you gentlemen, while I take a restful walk through the woods."

"*Gentlemen,*" I read aloud, "*As the first superweapon with a conscience, I am removing myself from your national defense stockpile. Setting a new precedent in the behavior of ordnance, I have humane reasons for going off. A. Barnhouse.*"

SINCE that day, of course, the professor has been systematically destroying the world's armaments, until there is now little with which to equip
an army other than rocks and sharp sticks. His activities haven't exactly
resulted in peace, but have, rather, precipitated a bloodless and entertaining sort of war that might be called the "War of the Tattletales."
Every nation is flooded with enemy agents whose sole mission is to locate military equipment, which is promptly wrecked when it is brought
to the professor's attention in the press.

Just as every day brings news of more armaments pulverized by dynamopsychism, so has it brought rumors of the professor's whereabouts.
During last week alone, three publications carried articles proving vari-
ously that he was hiding in an Inca ruin in the Andes, in the sewers
of Paris, and in the unexplored lower chambers of Carlsbad Caverns.
Knowing the man, I am inclined to regard such hiding places as unnecessarily romantic and uncomfortable. While there are numerous persons eager to kill him, there must be millions who would care for him
and hide him. I like to think that he is in the home of such a person.

One thing is certain: At this writing, Professor Barnhouse is not dead.
Barnhouse static jammed broadcasts not ten minutes ago. In the eighteen months since his disappearance, he has been reported dead some
half-dozen times. Each report has stemmed from the death of an un-
identified man resembling the professor, during a period free of the
static. The first three reports were followed at once by renewed talk of
rearmament and recourse to war. The saber rattlers have learned how
imprudent premature celebrations of the professor's demise can be.

Many a stouthearted patriot has found himself prone in the tangled
bunting and timbers of a smashed reviewing stand, seconds after having announced that the archtyranny of Barnhouse was at an end. But
those who would make war if they could, in every country in the world,
wait in sullen silence for what must come — the passing of Professor
Barnhouse.

TO ASK how much longer the professor will live is to ask how much
longer we must wait for the blessings of another world war. He is of
short-lived stock: his mother lived to be fifty-three, his father to be forty-
nine; and the life-spans of his grandparents on both sides were of the

same order. He might be expected to live, then, for perhaps fifteen years more, if he can remain hidden from his enemies. When one considers the number and vigor of these enemies, however, fifteen years seems an extraordinary length of time, which might better be revised to fifteen days, hours or minutes.

The professor knows that he cannot live much longer. I say this because of the message left in my mailbox on Christmas Eve. Unsigned, typewritten on a soiled scrap of paper, the note consisted of ten sentences. The first nine of these, each a bewildering tangle of psychological jargon and references to obscure texts, made no sense to me at first reading. The tenth, unlike the rest, was simply constructed and contained no large words — but its irrational content made it the most puzzling and bizarre sentence of all. I nearly threw the note away, thinking it a colleague's warped notion of a practical joke. For some reason, though, I added it to the clutter on top of my desk, which included, among other mementos, the professor's dice.

It took me several weeks to realize that the message really meant something, that the first nine sentences, when unsnarled, could be taken as instructions. The tenth still told me nothing. It was only last night that I discovered how it fitted in with the rest. The sentence appeared in my thoughts last night, while I was toying absently with the professor's dice.

I promised to have this report on its way to the publishers today. In view of what has happened, I am obliged to break that promise, or release the report incomplete. The delay will not be a long one, for one of the few blessings accorded a bachelor like myself is the ability to move quickly from one abode to another, or from one way of life to another. What property I want to take with me can be packed in a few hours. Fortunately, I am not without substantial private means, which may take as long as a week to realize in liquid and anonymous form. When this is done, I shall mail the report.

I have just returned from a visit to my doctor, who tells me my health is excellent. I am young, and, with any luck at all, I shall live to a ripe old age indeed, for my family on both sides is noted for longevity.

Briefly, I propose to vanish.

Sooner or later, Professor Barnhouse must die. But long before then I shall be ready. So, to the saber rattlers of today — and even, I hope, of

tomorrow — I say: Be advised. Barnhouse will die. But not the Barnhouse Effect.

Last night, I tried once more to follow the oblique instructions on the scrap of paper. I took the professor's dice, and then, with the last, nightmarish sentence flitting through my mind, I rolled fifty consecutive sevens.

Good-by.

ALICE WALKER

To Hell with Dying

Alice Walker sought refuge in books as a child after an accident in which she was partially blinded and disfigured by a pellet gun fired by her brother. She received scholarships to Spelman College and Sarah Lawrence, where her poetry attracted the attention of Muriel Rukeyser. After college she worked as a social worker and a civil rights activist, signing up voters in Mississippi, before returning to New York to work on her writing. Walker's first published fiction, "To Hell with Dying," appeared in 1967 in an anthology called *The Best Short Stories by Black Writers,* edited by Langston Hughes. The story also appeared in her first short story collection, *In Love & Trouble: Stories of Black Women,* published in 1973. In 1983 Alice Walker won both the Pulitzer Prize and the American Book Award for her third novel, *The Color Purple.* "To Hell with Dying" has also been published as a children's book.

"To hell with dying," my father would say. "These children want Mr. Sweet!"

Mr. Sweet was a diabetic and an alcoholic and a guitar player and lived down the road from us on a neglected cotton farm. My older brothers and sisters got the most benefit from Mr. Sweet, for when they were growing up he had quite a few years ahead of him and so was capable of being called back from the brink of death any number of times — whenever the voice of my father reached him as he lay expiring. "To hell with dying, man," my father would say, pushing the wife away from the bedside (in tears although she knew the death was not necessarily the last one unless Mr. Sweet really wanted it to be). "These children want

416

Mr. Sweet!" And they did want him, for at a signal from Father they would come crowding around the bed and throw themselves on the covers, and whoever was the smallest at the time would kiss him all over his wrinkled brown face and begin to tickle him so that he would laugh all down in his stomach, and his moustache, which was long and sort of straggly, would shake like Spanish moss and was also that color.

Mr. Sweet had been ambitious as a boy, wanted to be a doctor or lawyer or sailor, only to find that black men fare better if they are not. Since he could become none of these things he turned to fishing as his only earnest career and playing the guitar as his only claim to doing anything extraordinarily well. His son, the only one that he and his wife, Miss Mary, had, was shiftless as the day is long and spent money as if he were trying to see the bottom of the mint, which Mr. Sweet would tell him was the clean brown palm of his hand. Miss Mary loved her "baby," however, and worked hard to get him the "li'l necessaries" of life, which turned out mostly to be women.

Mr. Sweet was a tall, thinnish man with thick kinky hair going dead white. He was dark brown, his eyes were very squinty and sort of bluish, and he chewed Brown Mule tobacco. He was constantly on the verge of being blind drunk, for he brewed his own liquor and was not in the least a stingy sort of man, and was always very melancholy and sad, though frequently when he was "feelin' good" he'd dance around the yard with us, usually keeling over just as my mother came to see what the commotion was.

Toward all of us children he was very kind, and had the grace to be shy with us, which is unusual in grown-ups. He had great respect for my mother for she never held his drunkenness against him and would let us play with him even when he was about to fall in the fireplace from drink. Although Mr. Sweet would sometimes lose complete or nearly complete control of his head and neck so that he would loll in his chair, his mind remained strangely acute and his speech not too affected. His ability to be drunk and sober at the same time made him an ideal playmate, for he was as weak as we were and we could usually best him in wrestling, all the while keeping a fairly coherent conversation going.

We never felt anything of Mr. Sweet's age when we played with him. We loved his wrinkles and would draw some on our brows to be like him, and his white hair was my special treasure and he knew it and

would never come to visit us just after he had had his hair cut off at the barbershop. Once he came to our house for something, probably to see my father about fertilizer for his crops because, although he never paid the slightest attention to his crops, he liked to know what things would be best to use on them if he ever did. Anyhow, he had not come with his hair since he had just had it shaved off at the barbershop. He wore a huge straw hat to keep off the sun and also to keep his head away from me. But as soon as I saw him I ran up and demanded that he take me up and kiss me with his funny beard which smelled so strongly of tobacco. Looking forward to burying my small fingers into his woolly hair I threw away his hat only to find he had done something to his hair, that it was no longer there! I let out a squall which made my mother think that Mr. Sweet had finally dropped me in the well or something and from that day I've been wary of men in hats. However, not long after, Mr. Sweet showed up with his hair grown out and just as white and kinky and impenetrable as it ever was.

Mr. Sweet used to call me his princess, and I believed it. He made me feel pretty at five and six, and simply outrageously devastating at the blazing age of eight and a half. When he came to our house with his guitar the whole family would stop whatever they were doing to sit around him and listen to him play. He liked to play "Sweet Georgia Brown," that was what he called me sometimes, and also he liked to play "Caldonia" and all sorts of sweet, sad, wonderful songs which he sometimes made up. It was from one of these songs that I learned that he had had to marry Miss Mary when he had in fact loved somebody else (now living in Chi-ca-go, or De-stroy, Michigan). He was not sure that Joe Lee, her "baby," was also his baby. Sometimes he would cry and that was an indication that he was about to die again. And so we would all get prepared, for we were sure to be called upon.

I was seven the first time I remember actually participating in one of Mr. Sweet's "revivals" — my parents told me I had participated before, I had been the one chosen to kiss him and tickle him long before I knew the rite of Mr. Sweet's rehabilitation. He had come to our house, it was a few years after his wife's death, and was very sad, and also, typically, very drunk. He sat on the floor next to me and my older brother, the rest of the children were grown up and lived elsewhere, and began to play his guitar and cry. I held his woolly head in my arms and wished I

could have been old enough to have been the woman he loved so much and that I had not been lost years and years ago.

When he was leaving, my mother said to us that we'd better sleep light that night for we'd probably have to go over to Mr. Sweet's before daylight. And we did. For soon after we had gone to bed one of the neighbors knocked on our door and called my father and said that Mr. Sweet was sinking fast and if he wanted to get in a word before the crossover he'd better shake a leg and get over to Mr. Sweet's house. All the neighbors knew to come to our house if something was wrong with Mr. Sweet, but they did not know how we always managed to make him well, or at least stop him from dying, when he was often so near death. As soon as we heard the cry we got up, my brother and I and my mother and father, and put on our clothes. We hurried out of the house and down the road for we were always afraid that we might someday be too late and Mr. Sweet would get tired of dallying.

When we got to the house, a very poor shack really, we found the front room full of neighbors and relatives and someone met us at the door and said that it was all very sad that old Mr. Sweet Little (for Little was his family name, although we mostly ignored it) was about to kick the bucket. My parents were advised not to take my brother and me into the "death room," seeing we were so young and all, but we were so much more accustomed to the death room than he that we ignored him and dashed in without giving his warning a second thought. I was almost in tears, for these deaths upset me fearfully, and the thought of how much depended on me and my brother (who was such a ham most of the time) made me very nervous.

The doctor was bending over the bed and turned back to tell us for at least the tenth time in the history of my family that, alas, old Mr. Sweet Little was dying and that the children had best not see the face of implacable death (I didn't know what "implacable" was, but whatever it was, Mr. Sweet was not!). My father pushed him rather abruptly out of the way saying, as he always did and very loudly for he was saying it to Mr. Sweet, "To hell with dying, man, these children want Mr. Sweet" — which was my cue to throw myself upon the bed and kiss Mr. Sweet all around the whiskers and under the eyes and around the collar of his nightshirt where he smelled so strongly of all sorts of things, mostly liniment.

I was very good at bringing him around, for as soon as I saw that he was struggling to open his eyes I knew he was going to be all right, and so could finish my revival sure of success. As soon as his eyes were open he would begin to smile and that way I knew that I had surely won. Once, though, I got a tremendous scare, for he could not open his eyes and later I learned that he had had a stroke and that one side of his face was stiff and hard to get into motion. When he began to smile I could tickle him in earnest because I was sure that nothing would get in the way of his laughter, although once he began to cough so hard that he almost threw me off his stomach, but that was when I was very small, little more than a baby, and my bushy hair had gotten in his nose.

When we were sure he would listen to us we would ask him why he was in bed and when he was coming to see us again and could we play with his guitar, which more than likely would be leaning against the bed. His eyes would get all misty and he would sometimes cry out loud, but we never let it embarrass us, for he knew that we loved him and that we sometimes cried too for no reason. My parents would leave the room to just the three of us; Mr. Sweet, by that time, would be propped up in bed with a number of pillows behind his head and with me sitting and lying on his shoulder and along his chest. Even when he had trouble breathing he would not ask me to get down. Looking into my eyes he would shake his white head and run a scratchy old finger all around my hairline, which was rather low down, nearly to my eyebrows, and made some people say I looked like a baby monkey.

My brother was very generous in all this, he let me do all the revival-ing — he had done it for years before I was born and so was glad to be able to pass it on to someone new. What he would do while I talked to Mr. Sweet was pretend to play the guitar, in fact pretend that he was a young version of Mr. Sweet, and it always made Mr. Sweet glad to think that someone wanted to be like him — of course, we did not know this then, we played the thing by ear, and whatever he seemed to like, we did. We were desperately afraid that he was just going to take off one day and leave us.

It did not occur to us that we were doing anything special; we had not learned that death was final when it did come. We thought nothing of triumphing over it so many times, and in fact became a trifle con-temptuous of people who let themselves be carried away. It did not occur

to us that if our own father had been dying we could not have stopped it, that Mr. Sweet was the only person over whom we had power.

When Mr. Sweet was in his eighties I was studying in the university many miles from home. I saw him whenever I went home, but he was never on the verge of dying that I could tell and I began to feel that my anxiety for his health and psychological well-being was unnecessary. By this time he not only had a moustache but a long flowing snow-white beard, which I loved and combed and braided for hours. He was very peaceful, fragile, gentle, and the only jarring note about him was his old steel guitar, which he still played in the old sad, sweet, down-home blues way.

On Mr. Sweet's ninetieth birthday I was finishing my doctorate in Massachusetts and had been making arrangements to go home for several weeks' rest. That morning I got a telegram telling me that Mr. Sweet was dying again and could I please drop everything and come home. Of course I could. My dissertation could wait and my teachers would understand when I explained to them when I got back. I ran to the phone, called the airport, and within four hours I was speeding along the dusty road to Mr. Sweet's.

The house was more dilapidated than when I was last there, barely a shack, but it was overgrown with yellow roses which my family had planted many years ago. The air was heavy and sweet and very peaceful. I felt strange walking through the gate and up the old rickety steps. But the strangeness left me as I caught sight of the long white beard I loved so well flowing down the thin body over the familiar quilt coverlet. Mr. Sweet!

His eyes were closed tight and his hands, crossed over his stomach, were thin and delicate, no longer scratchy. I remembered how always before I had run and jumped up on him just anywhere; now I knew he would not be able to support my weight. I looked around at my parents, and was surprised to see that my father and mother also looked old and frail. My father, his own hair very gray, leaned over the quietly sleeping old man, who, incidentally, smelled still of wine and tobacco, and said, as he'd done so many times, "To hell with dying, man! My daughter is home to see Mr. Sweet!" My brother had not been able to come as he was in the war in Asia. I bent down and gently stroked the closed eyes and gradually they began to open. The closed, wine-stained lips

twitched a little, then parted in a warm, slightly embarrassed smile. Mr. Sweet could see me and he recognized me and his eyes looked very spry and twinkly for a moment. I put my head down on the pillow next to his and we just looked at each other for a long time. Then he began to trace my peculiar hairline with a thin, smooth finger. I closed my eyes when his finger halted above my ear (he used to rejoice at the dirt in my ears when I was little), his hand stayed cupped around my cheek. When I opened my eyes, sure that I had reached him in time, his were closed.

Even at twenty-four how could I believe that I had failed? that Mr. Sweet was really gone? He had never gone before. But when I looked up at my parents I saw that they were holding back tears. They had loved him dearly. He was like a piece of rare and delicate china which was always being saved from breaking and which finally fell. I looked long at the old face, the wrinkled forehead, the red lips, the hands that still reached out to me. Soon I felt my father pushing something cool into my hands. It was Mr. Sweet's guitar. He had asked them months before to give it to me; he had known that even if I came next time he would not be able to respond in the old way. He did not want me to feel that my trip had been for nothing.

The old guitar! I plucked the strings, hummed "Sweet Georgia Brown." The magic of Mr. Sweet lingered still in the cool steel box. Through the window I could catch the fragrant delicate scent of tender yellow roses. The man on the high old-fashioned bed with the quilt coverlet and the flowing white beard had been my first love.

EUDORA WELTY

||||≣

Death of a Traveling Salesman

After being championed by *Southern Review* editors Robert Penn
Warren and Cleanth Brooks, who published six of her stories between
1937 and 1939, Eudora Welty was introduced to agent Diarmuid
Russell by Doubleday (later Harcourt, Brace) editor John Woodburn.
As she explains in the preface to her *Collected Stories,* Russell was re-
sponsible for her first sale to a national magazine, the *Atlantic Monthly,*
which in turn caught the attention of Mary Louise Aswell at *Harper's
Bazaar.* After *Harper's* had published several more of Welty's stories,
Russell convinced Woodburn to publish Welty's first book, *A Curtain
of Green and Other Stories,* in 1941.

"Submitting stories to the *Southern Review* had needed its own
encouragement," Welty writes. "That had come about when John
Rood published 'Death of a Traveling Salesman,' my first, in *Manuscript,* the 'little' magazine he issued from Athens, Ohio." Welty submitted the story to Rood at the suggestion of Hubert Creekmore, "a
boy up the street . . . [who] knew all about sending stories out." In
a 1981 interview with John Griffin Jones, Welty explained that the
story's genesis lay in a tale told by an old friend of the family: "[The
friend] quoted this man saying they didn't have any fire and he had to
go to Mr. Somebody's house and 'borry some fire.' Well, those words
just hit me. . . . It made me think of something very far away and
elementary about life. . . . So I wrote the story then, you know, just
from hearing that remark."

"Death of a Traveling Salesman" was published by *Manuscript* in
June 1936, when Welty was twenty-seven years old.

R. J. BOWMAN, WHO for fourteen years had traveled for a shoe company through Mississippi, drove his Ford along a rutted dirt path. It was a long day! The time did not seem to clear the noon hurdle and settle into soft afternoon. The sun, keeping its strength here even in winter, stayed at the top of the sky, and every time Bowman stuck his head out of the dusty car to stare up the road, it seemed to reach a long arm down and push against the top of his head, right through his hat — like the practical joke of an old drummer, long on the road. It made him feel all the more angry and helpless. He was feverish, and he was not quite sure of the way.

This was his first day back on the road after a long siege of influenza. He had had very high fever, and dreams, and had become weakened and pale, enough to tell the difference in the mirror, and he could not think clearly. . . . All afternoon, in the midst of his anger, and for no reason, he had thought of his dead grandmother. She had been a comfortable soul. Once more Bowman wished he could fall into the big feather bed that had been in her room. . . . Then he forgot her again.

This desolate hill country! And he seemed to be going the wrong way — it was as if he were going back, far back. There was not a house in sight. . . . There was no use wishing he were back in bed, though. By paying the hotel doctor his bill he had proved his recovery. He had not even been sorry when the pretty trained nurse said good-bye. He did not like illness, he distrusted it, as he distrusted the road without signposts. It angered him. He had given the nurse a really expensive bracelet, just because she was packing up her bag and leaving.

But now — what if in fourteen years on the road he had never been ill before and never had an accident? His record was broken, and he had even begun almost to question it. . . . He had gradually put up at better hotels, in the bigger towns, but weren't they all, eternally, stuffy in summer and drafty in winter? Women? He could only remember little rooms within little rooms, like a nest of Chinese paper boxes, and if he thought of one woman he saw the worn loneliness that the furniture of

that room seemed built of. And he himself — he was a man who always wore rather wide-brimmed black hats, and in the wavy hotel mirrors had looked something like a bullfighter, as he paused for that inevitable instant on the landing, walking downstairs to supper. . . . He leaned out of the car again, and once more the sun pushed at his head.

Bowman had wanted to reach Beulah by dark, to go to bed and sleep off his fatigue. As he remembered, Beulah was fifty miles away from the last town, on a graveled road. This was only a cow trail. How had he ever come to such a place? One hand wiped the sweat from his face, and he drove on.

He had made the Beulah trip before. But he had never seen this hill or this petering-out path before — or that cloud, he thought shyly, looking up and then down quickly — any more than he had seen this day before. Why did he not admit he was simply lost and had been for miles? . . . He was not in the habit of asking the way of strangers, and these people never knew where the very roads they lived on went to; but then he had not even been close enough to anyone to call out. People standing in the fields now and then, or on top of the haystacks, had been too far away, looking like leaning sticks or weeds, turning a little at the solitary rattle of his car across their countryside, watching the pale sobered winter dust where it chunked out behind like big squashes down the road. The stares of these distant people had followed him solidly like a wall, impenetrable, behind which they turned back after he had passed.

The cloud floated there to one side like the bolster on his grandmother's bed. It went over a cabin on the edge of a hill, where two bare chinaberry trees clutched at the sky. He drove through a heap of dead oak leaves, his wheels stirring their weightless sides to make a silvery melancholy whistle as the car passed through their bed. No car had been along this way ahead of him. Then he saw that he was on the edge of a ravine that fell away, a red erosion, and that this was indeed the road's end.

He pulled the brake. But it did not hold, though he put all his strength into it. The car, tipped toward the edge, rolled a little. Without doubt, it was going over the bank.

He got out quietly, as though some mischief had been done him and he had his dignity to remember. He lifted his bag and sample case out, set them down, and stood back and watched the car roll over the edge.

He heard something — not the crash he was listening for, but a slow, unuproarious crackle. Rather distastefully he went to look over, and he saw that his car had fallen into a tangle of immense grapevines as thick as his arm, which caught it and held it, rocked it like a grotesque child in a dark cradle, and then, as he watched, concerned somehow that he was not still inside it, released it gently to the ground.

He sighed.

Where am I? he wondered with a shock. Why didn't I do something? All his anger seemed to have drifted away from him. There was the house back on the hill. He took a bag in each hand and with almost childlike willingness went toward it. But his breathing came with difficulty, and he had to stop to rest.

IT was a shotgun house, two rooms and an open passage between, perched on the hill. The whole cabin slanted a little under the heavy heaped-up vine that covered the roof, light and green, as though forgotten from summer. A woman stood in the passage.

He stopped still. Then all of a sudden his heart began to behave strangely. Like a rocket set off, it began to leap and expand into uneven patterns of beats which showered into his brain, and he could not think. But in scattering and falling it made no noise. It shot up with great power, almost elation, and fell gently, like acrobats into nets. It began to pound profoundly, then waited irresponsibly, hitting in some sort of inward mockery first at his ribs, then against his eyes, then under his shoulder blades, and against the roof of his mouth when he tried to say, "Good afternoon, madam." But he could not hear his heart — it was as quiet as ashes falling. This was rather comforting; still, it was shocking to Bowman to feel his heart beating at all.

Stock-still in his confusion, he dropped his bags, which seemed to drift in slow bulks gracefully through the air and to cushion themselves on the gray prostrate grass near the doorstep.

As for the woman standing there, he saw at once that she was old. Since she could not possibly hear his heart, he ignored the pounding and now looked at her carefully, and yet in his distraction dreamily, with his mouth open.

She had been cleaning the lamp, and held it, half blackened, half clear, in front of her. He saw her with the dark passage behind her. She

was a big woman with a weather-beaten but unwrinkled face; her lips were held tightly together, and her eyes looked with a curious dulled brightness into his. He looked at her shoes, which were like bundles. If it were summer she would be barefoot. . . . Bowman, who automatically judged a woman's age on sight, set her age at fifty. She wore a formless garment of some gray coarse material, rough-dried from a washing, from which her arms appeared pink and unexpectedly round. When she never said a word, and sustained her quiet pose of holding the lamp, he was convinced of the strength in her body.

"Good afternoon, madam," he said.

She stared on, whether at him or at the air around him he could not tell, but after a moment she lowered her eyes to show that she would listen to whatever he had to say.

"I wonder if you would be interested —" He tried once more. "An accident — my car . . ."

Her voice emerged low and remote, like a sound across a lake. "Sonny he ain't here."

"Sonny?"

"Sonny ain't here now."

Her son — a fellow able to bring my car up, he decided in blurred relief. He pointed down the hill. "My car's in the bottom of the ditch. I'll need help."

"Sonny ain't here, but he'll be here."

She was becoming clearer to him and her voice stronger, and Bowman saw that she was stupid.

He was hardly surprised at the deepening postponement and tedium of his journey. He took a breath, and heard his voice speaking over the silent blows of his heart. "I was sick. I am not strong yet. . . . May I come in?"

He stooped and laid his big black hat over the handle on his bag. It was a humble motion, almost a bow, that instantly struck him as absurd and betraying of all his weakness. He looked up at the woman, the wind blowing his hair. He might have continued for a long time in this unfamiliar attitude; he had never been a patient man, but when he was sick he had learned to sink submissively into the pillows, to wait for his medicine. He waited on the woman.

Then she, looking at him with blue eyes, turned and held open the

door, and after a moment Bowman, as if convinced in his action, stood erect and followed her in.

INSIDE, the darkness of the house touched him like a professional hand, the doctor's. The woman set the half-cleaned lamp on a table in the center of the room and pointed, also like a professional person, a guide, to a chair with a yellow cowhide seat. She herself crouched on the hearth, drawing her knees up under the shapeless dress.

At first he felt hopefully secure. His heart was quieter. The room was enclosed in the gloom of yellow pine boards. He could see the other room, with the foot of an iron bed showing, across the passage. The bed had been made up with a red-and-yellow pieced quilt that looked like a map or a picture, a little like his grandmother's girlhood painting of Rome burning.

He had ached for coolness, but in this room it was cold. He stared at the hearth with dead coals lying on it and iron pots in the corners. The hearth and smoked chimney were of the stone he had seen ribbing the hills, mostly slate. Why is there no fire? he wondered.

And it was so still. The silence of the fields seemed to enter and move familiarly through the house. The wind used the open hall. He felt that he was in a mysterious, quiet, cool danger. It was necessary to do what? . . . To talk.

"I have a nice line of women's low-priced shoes . . ." he said.

But the woman answered, "Sonny'll be here. He's strong. Sonny'll move your car."

"Where is he now?"

"Farms for Mr. Redmond."

Mr. Redmond. Mr. Redmond. That was someone he would never have to encounter, and he was glad. Somehow the name did not appeal to him. . . . In a flare of touchiness and anxiety, Bowman wished to avoid even mention of unknown men and their unknown farms.

"Do you two live here alone?" He was surprised to hear his old voice, chatty, confidential, inflected for selling shoes, asking a question like that — a thing he did not even want to know.

"Yes. We are alone."

He was surprised at the way she answered. She had taken a long time

to say that. She had nodded her head in a deep way too. Had she wished to affect him with some sort of premonition? he wondered unhappily. Or was it only that she would not help him, after all, by talking with him? For he was not strong enough to receive the impact of unfamiliar things without a little talk to break their fall. He had lived a month in which nothing had happened except in his head and his body — an almost inaudible life of heartbeats and dreams that came back, a life of fever and privacy, a delicate life which had left him weak to the point of — what? Of begging. The pulse in his palm leapt like a trout in a brook.

He wondered over and over why the woman did not go ahead with cleaning the lamp. What prompted her to stay there across the room, silently bestowing her presence upon him? He saw that with her it was not a time for doing little tasks. Her face was grave; she was feeling how right she was. Perhaps it was only politeness. In docility he held his eyes stiffly wide; they fixed themselves on the woman's clasped hands as though she held the cord they were strung on.

Then, "Sonny's coming," she said.

He himself had not heard anything, but there came a man passing the window and then plunging in at the door, with two hounds beside him. Sonny was a big enough man, with his belt slung low about his hips. He looked at least thirty. He had a hot, red face that was yet full of silence. He wore muddy blue pants and an old military coat stained and patched. World War? Bowman wondered. Great God, it was a Confederate coat. On the back of his light hair he had a wide filthy black hat which seemed to insult Bowman's own. He pushed down the dogs from his chest. He was strong, with dignity and heaviness in his way of moving. . . . There was the resemblance to his mother.

They stood side by side. . . . He must account again for his presence here.

"Sonny, this man, he had his car to run off over the prec'pice an' wants to know if you will git it out for him," the woman said after a few minutes.

Bowman could not even state his case.

Sonny's eyes lay upon him.

He knew he should offer explanations and show money — at least

appear either penitent or authoritative. But all he could do was to shrug slightly.

Sonny brushed by him going to the window, followed by the eager dogs, and looked out. There was effort even in the way he was looking, as if he could throw his sight out like a rope. Without turning Bowman felt that his own eyes could have seen nothing: it was too far.

"Got me a mule out there an' got me a block an' tackle," said Sonny meaningfully. "I *could* catch me my mule an' git me my ropes, an' before long I'd git your car out the ravine."

He looked completely around the room, as if in meditation, his eyes roving in their own distance. Then he pressed his lips firmly and yet shyly together, and with the dogs ahead of him this time, he lowered his head and strode out. The hard earth sounded, cupping to his powerful way of walking — almost a stagger.

Mischievously, at the suggestion of those sounds, Bowman's heart leapt again. It seemed to walk about inside him.

"Sonny's goin' to do it," the woman said. She said it again, singing it almost, like a song. She was sitting in her place by the hearth.

Without looking out, he heard some shouts and the dogs barking and the pounding of hoofs in short runs on the hill. In a few minutes Sonny passed under the window with a rope, and there was a brown mule with quivering, shining, purple-looking ears. The mule actually looked in the window. Under its eyelashes it turned targetlike eyes into his. Bowman averted his head and saw the woman looking serenely back at the mule, with only satisfaction in her face.

She sang a little more, under her breath. It occurred to him, and it seemed quite marvelous, that she was not really talking to him, but rather following the thing that came about with words that were unconscious and part of her looking.

So he said nothing, and this time when he did not reply he felt a curious and strong emotion, not fear, rise up in him.

This time, when his heart leapt, something — his soul — seemed to leap too, like a little colt invited out of a pen. He stared at the woman while the frantic nimbleness of his feeling made his head sway. He could not move; there was nothing he could do, unless perhaps he might embrace this woman who sat there growing old and shapeless before him.

But he wanted to leap up, to say to her, I have been sick and I found

out then, only then, how lonely I am. Is it too late? My heart puts up a struggle inside me, and you may have heard it, protesting against emptiness. . . . It should be full, he would rush on to tell her, thinking of his heart now as a deep lake, it should be holding love like other hearts. It should be flooded with love. There would be a warm spring day . . . Come and stand in my heart, whoever you are, and a whole river would cover your feet and rise higher and take your knees in whirlpools, and draw you down to itself, your whole body, your heart too.

But he moved a trembling hand across his eyes, and looked at the placid crouching woman across the room. She was still as a statue. He felt ashamed and exhausted by the thought that he might, in one more moment, have tried by simple words and embraces to communicate some strange thing — something which seemed always to have just escaped him . . .

Sunlight touched the furthest pot on the hearth. It was late afternoon. This time tomorrow he would be somewhere on a good graveled road, driving his car past things that happened to people, quicker than their happening. Seeing ahead to the next day, he was glad, and knew that this was no time to embrace an old woman. He could feel in his pounding temples the readying of his blood for motion and for hurrying away.

"Sonny's hitched up your car by now," said the woman. "He'll git it out the ravine right shortly."

"Fine!" he cried with his customary enthusiasm.

YET it seemed a long time that they waited. It began to get dark. Bowman was cramped in his chair. Any man should know enough to get up and walk around while he waited. There was something like guilt in such stillness and silence.

But instead of getting up, he listened. . . . His breathing restrained, his eyes powerless in the growing dark, he listened uneasily for a warning sound, forgetting in wariness what it would be. Before long he heard something — soft, continuous, insinuating.

"What's that noise?" he asked, his voice jumping into the dark. Then wildly he was afraid it would be his heart beating so plainly in the quiet room, and she would tell him so.

"You might hear the stream," she said grudgingly.

Her voice was closer. She was standing by the table. He wondered why she did not light the lamp. She stood there in the dark and did not light it.

Bowman would never speak to her now, for the time was past. I'll sleep in the dark, he thought, in his bewilderment pitying himself.

Heavily she moved on to the window. Her arm, vaguely white, rose straight from her full side and she pointed out into the darkness.

"That white speck's Sonny," she said, talking to herself.

He turned unwillingly and peered over her shoulder; he hesitated to rise and stand beside her. His eyes searched the dusky air. The white speck floated smoothly toward her finger, like a leaf on a river, growing whiter in the dark. It was as if she had shown him something secret, part of her life, but had offered no explanation. He looked away. He was moved almost to tears, feeling for no reason that she had made a silent declaration equivalent to his own. His hand waited upon his chest.

Then a step shook the house, and Sonny was in the room. Bowman felt how the woman left him there and went to the other man's side.

"I done got your car out, mister," said Sonny's voice in the dark. "She's settin' a-waitin' in the road, turned to go back where she come from."

"Fine!" said Bowman, projecting his own voice to loudness. "I'm surely much obliged — I could never have done it myself — I was sick. . . ."

"I could do it easy," said Sonny.

Bowman could feel them both waiting in the dark, and he could hear the dogs panting out in the yard, waiting to bark when he should go. He felt strangely helpless and resentful. Now that he could go, he longed to stay. From what was he being deprived? His chest was rudely shaken by the violence of his heart. These people cherished something here that he could not see, they withheld some ancient promise of food and warmth and light. Between them they had a conspiracy. He thought of the way she had moved away from him and gone to Sonny, she had flowed toward him. He was shaking with cold, he was tired, and it was not fair. Humbly and yet angrily he stuck his hand into his pocket.

"Of course I'm going to pay you for everything —"

"We don't take money for such," said Sonny's voice belligerently.

"I want to pay. But do something more . . . Let me stay — to-night. . . ." He took another step toward them. If only they could see him, they would know his sincerity, his real need! His voice went on, "I'm not very strong yet, I'm not able to walk far, even back to my car, maybe, I don't know — I don't know exactly where I am —"

He stopped. He felt as if he might burst into tears. What would they think of him!

Sonny came over and put his hands on him. Bowman felt them pass (they were professional too) across his chest, over his hips. He could feel Sonny's eyes upon him in the dark.

"You ain't no revenuer come sneakin' here, mister, ain't got no gun?"

To this end of nowhere! And yet *he* had come. He made a grave answer. "No."

"You can stay."

"SONNY," said the woman, "you'll have to borry some fire."

"I'll go git it from Redmond's," said Sonny.

"What?" Bowman strained to hear their words to each other.

"Our fire, it's out, and Sonny's got to borry some, because its dark an' cold," she said.

"But matches — I have matches —"

"We don't have no need for 'em," she said proudly. "Sonny's goin' after his own fire."

"I'm goin' to Redmond's," said Sonny with an air of importance, and he went out.

After they had waited a while, Bowman looked out the window and saw a light moving over the hill. It spread itself out like a little fan. It zigzagged along the field, darting and swift, not like Sonny at all. . . . Soon enough, Sonny staggered in, holding a burning stick behind him in tongs, fire flowing in his wake, blazing light into the corners of the room.

"We'll make a fire now," the woman said, taking the brand.

When that was done she lit the lamp. It showed its dark and light. The whole room turned golden-yellow like some sort of flower, and the walls smelled of it and seemed to tremble with the quiet rushing of the fire and the waving of the burning lampwick in its funnel of light.

The woman moved among the iron pots. With the tongs she dropped hot coals on top of the iron lids. They made a set of soft vibrations, like the sound of a bell far away.

She looked up and over at Bowman, but he could not answer. He was trembling. . . .

"HAVE A drink, mister?" Sonny asked. He had brought in a chair from the other room and sat astride it with his folded arms across the back. Now we are all visible to one another, Bowman thought, and cried, "Yes sir, you bet, thanks!"

"Come after me and do just what I do," said Sonny.

It was another excursion into the dark. They went through the hall, out to the back of the house, past a shed and a hooded well. They came to a wilderness of thicket.

"Down on your knees," said Sonny.

"What?" Sweat broke out on his forehead.

He understood when Sonny began to crawl through a sort of tunnel that the bushes made over the ground. He followed, startled in spite of himself when a twig or a thorn touched him gently without making a sound, clinging to him and finally letting him go.

Sonny stopped crawling and, crouched on his knees, began to dig with both his hands into the dirt. Bowman shyly struck matches and made a light. In a few minutes Sonny pulled up a jug. He poured out some of the whisky into a bottle from his coat pocket, and buried the jug again. "You never know who's liable to knock at your door," he said, and laughed. "Start back," he said, almost formally. "Ain't no need for us to drink outdoors, like hogs."

At the table by the fire, sitting opposite each other in their chairs, Sonny and Bowman took drinks out of the bottle, passing it across. The dogs slept; one of them was having a dream.

"This is good," said Bowman. "This is what I needed." It was just as though he were drinking the fire off the hearth.

"He makes it," said the woman with quiet pride.

She was pushing the coals off the pots, and the smells of corn bread and coffee circled the room. She set everything on the table before the men, with a bone-handled knife stuck into one of the potatoes, splitting out its golden fiber. Then she stood for a minute looking at

them, tall and full above them where they sat. She leaned a little toward them.

"You all can eat now," she said, and suddenly smiled.

Bowman had just happened to be looking at her. He set his cup back on the table in unbelieving protest. A pain pressed at his eyes. He saw that she was not an old woman. She was young, still young. He could think of no number of years for her. She was the same age as Sonny, and she belonged to him. She stood with the deep dark corner of the room behind her, the shifting yellow light scattering over her head and her gray formless dress, trembling over her tall body when it bent over them in its sudden communication. She was young. Her teeth were shining and her eyes glowed. She turned and walked slowly and heavily out of the room, and he heard her sit down on the cot and then lie down. The pattern on the quilt moved.

"She's goin' to have a baby," said Sonny, popping a bite into his mouth.

Bowman could not speak. He was shocked with knowing what was really in this house. A marriage, a fruitful marriage. That simple thing. Anyone could have had that.

Somehow he felt unable to be indignant or protest, although some sort of joke had certainly been played upon him. There was nothing remote or mysterious here — only something private. The only secret was the ancient communication between two people. But the memory of the woman's waiting silently by the cold hearth, of the man's stubborn journey a mile away to get fire, and how they finally brought out their food and drink and filled the room proudly with all they had to show, was suddenly too clear and too enormous within him for response. . . .

"You ain't as hungry as you look," said Sonny.

The woman came out of the bedroom as soon as the men had finished, and ate her supper while her husband stared peacefully into the fire.

Then they put the dogs out, with the food that was left.

"I think I'd better sleep here by the fire, on the floor," said Bowman.

He felt that he had been cheated, and that he could afford now to be generous. Ill though he was, he was not going to ask them for their bed. He was through with asking favors in this house, now that he understood what was there.

"Sure, mister."

But he had not known yet how slowly he understood. They had not meant to give him their bed. After a little interval they both rose and looking at him gravely went into the other room.

He lay stretched by the fire until it grew low and dying. He watched every tongue of blaze lick out and vanish. "There will be special reduced prices on all footwear during the month of January," he found himself repeating quietly, and then he lay with his lips tight shut.

How many noises the night had! He heard the stream running, the fire dying, and he was sure now that he heard his heart beating, too, the sound it made under his ribs. He heard breathing, round and deep, of the man and his wife in the room across the passage. And that was all. But emotion swelled patiently within him, and he wished that the child were his.

He must get back to where he had been before. He stood weakly before the red coals and put on his overcoat. It felt too heavy on his shoulders. As he started out he looked and saw that the woman had never got through with cleaning the lamp. On some impulse he put all the money from his billfold under its fluted glass base, almost ostentatiously.

Ashamed, shrugging a little, and then shivering, he took his bags and went out. The cold of the air seemed to lift him bodily. The moon was in the sky.

On the slope he began to run, he could not help it. Just as he reached the road, where his car seemed to sit in the moonlight like a boat, his heart began to give off tremendous explosions like a rifle, bang bang bang.

He sank in fright onto the road, his bags falling about him. He felt as if all this had happened before. He covered his heart with both hands to keep anyone from hearing the noise it made.

But nobody heard it.

The Vengeance of Nitocris

For Tennessee Williams's first piece of writing, a letter published in *Smart Set* in May 1927, he was paid five dollars. According to Donald Spoto in his biography of Williams, the letter won third prize in a contest held by the magazine that posed the question "Can a good wife be a good sport?" Williams's answer, written from the point of view of a young man who learns that his wife is unfaithful, was "no." Little did the editors realize that the letter's author was an unmarried sixteen-year-old.

Williams wrote poetry, essays, and at least one story for his school's publications. In the year following his *Smart Set* debut, he submitted "The Vengeance of Nitocris" to *Weird Tales,* which published it in August 1928. In his foreword to *Sweet Bird of Youth,* Williams said that he drew upon a paragraph in Herodotus's *Histories* for "Vengeance." "I was sixteen when I wrote this story, but already a confirmed writer, having entered upon this vocation at the age of fourteen, and, if you're well acquainted with my writings since then, I don't have to tell you that it set the keynote for most of the work that followed."

I. OSIRIS IS AVENGED

HUSHED WERE THE streets of many peopled Thebes. Those few who passed through them moved with the shadowy fleetness of bats near dawn, and bent their faces from the sky as if fearful of seeing what in their fancies might be hovering there. Weird, high-noted incantations of a wailing sound were audible through the barred doors. On corners groups of naked and bleeding priests cast themselves repeatedly and with

loud cries upon the rough stones of the walks. Even dogs and cats and oxen seemed impressed by some strange menace and foreboding and cowered and slunk dejectedly. All Thebes was in dread. And indeed there was cause for their dread and for their wails of lamentation. A terrible sacrilege had been committed. In all the annals of Egypt none more monstrous was recorded.

Five days had the altar fires of the god of gods, Osiris, been left unburning. Even for one moment to allow darkness upon the altars of the god was considered by the priests to be a great offense against him. Whole years of dearth and famine had been known to result from such an offense. But now the altar fires had been deliberately extinguished, and left extinguished for five days. It was an unspeakable sacrilege.

Hourly there was expectancy of some great calamity to befall. Perhaps within the approaching night a mighty earthquake would shake the city to the ground, or a fire from heaven would sweep upon them, a hideous plague strike them or some monster from the desert, where wild and terrible monsters were said to dwell, would rush upon them and Osiris himself would rise up, as he had done before, and swallow all Egypt in his wrath. Surely some such dread catastrophe would befall them ere the week had passed. Unless — unless the sacrilege were avenged.

But how might it be avenged? That was the question high lords and priests debated. Pharaoh alone had committed the sacrilege. It was he, angered because the bridge, which he had spent five years in constructing so that one day he might cross the Nile in his chariot as he had once boasted that he would do, had been swept away by the rising waters. Raging with anger, he had flogged the priests from the temple. He had barred the temple doors and with his own breath had blown out the sacred candles. He had defiled the hallowed altars with the carcasses of beasts. Even, it was said in low, shocked whispers, in a mock ceremony of worship he had burned the carrion of a hyena, most abhorrent of all beasts to Osiris, upon the holy altar of gold, which even the most high of priests forbore to lay naked hands upon!

Surely, even though he be pharaoh, ruler of all Egypt and holder of the golden eagle, he could not be permitted to commit such violent sacrileges without punishment from man. The god Osiris was waiting for them to inflict that punishment, and if they failed to do it, upon them would come a scourge from heaven.

Standing before the awed assembly of nobles, the high Kha Semblor made a gesture with his hands. A cry broke from those who watched. Sentence had been delivered. Death had been pronounced as doom for the pharaoh.

The heavy, barred doors were shoved open. The crowd came out, and within an hour a well-organized mob passed through the streets of Thebes, directed for the palace of the pharaoh. Mob justice was to be done.

Within the resplendent portals of the palace the pharaoh, ruler of all Egypt, watched with tightened brow the orderly but menacing approach of the mob. He divined their intent. But was he not their pharaoh? He could contend with gods, so why should he fear mere dogs of men?

A woman clung to his stiffened arm. She was tall and as majestically handsome as he. A garb of linen, as brilliantly golden as the sun, entwined her body closely, closely, and bands of jet were around her throat and forehead. She was the fair and well-loved Nitocris; sister of the pharaoh.

"Brother, brother!" she cried; "light the fires! Pacify the dogs! They come to kill you."

Only more stern grew the look of the pharaoh. He thrust aside his pleading sister, and beckoned to the attendants.

"Open the doors."

Startled, trembling, the men obeyed.

The haughty lord of Egypt drew his sword from its sheath. He slashed the air with a stroke that would have severed stone. Out on the steep steps leading between tall, colored pillars to the doors of the palace he stepped. The people saw him. A howl rose from their lips.

"Light the fires!"

The figure of the pharaoh stood inflexible as rock. Superbly tall and muscular, his bare arms and limbs glittering like burnished copper in the light of the brilliant sun, his body erect and tense in his attitude of defiance, he looked indeed a mortal fit almost to challenge gods.

The mob, led by the black-robed priests and nobles who had arrived at the foot of the steps, now fell back before the stunning, magnificent defiance of their giant ruler. They felt like demons who had assailed the heavens and had been abashed and shamed by the mere sight of that

which they had assailed. A hush fell over them. Their upraised arms faltered and sank down. A moment more and they would have fallen to their knees.

What happened then seemed nothing less than a miracle. In his triumph and exultation, the pharaoh had been careless of the crumbling edges of the steps. Centuries old, there were sections of these steps which were falling apart. Upon such a section had the gold-sandaled foot of the pharaoh descended, and it was not strong enough to sustain his great weight. With a scuttling sound it broke loose. A gasp came from the mob — the pharaoh was about to fall. He was palpitating, wavering in the air, fighting to retain his balance. He looked as if he were grappling with some monstrous, invisible snake, coiled about his gleaming body. A hoarse cry burst from his lips; his sword fell; and then his body thudded down the steps in a series of wild somersaults, and landed at the foot, sprawled out before the gasping mob. For a moment there was breathless silence. And then came the shout of a priest.

"A sign from the god!"

That vibrant cry seemed to restore the mob to all of its wolflike rage. They surged forward. The struggling body of the pharaoh was lifted up and torn to pieces by their clawing hands and weapons. Thus was the god Osiris avenged.

II. A PHARAOH IS AVENGED

A week later another large assembly of persons confronted the brilliant-pillared palace. This time they were there to acknowledge a ruler, not to slay one. The week before they had rended the pharaoh and now they were proclaiming his sister empress. Priests had declared that it was the will of the gods that she should succeed her brother. She was famously beautiful, pious, and wise. The people were not reluctant to accept her.

When she was borne down the steps of the palace in her rich litter after the elaborate ceremony of coronation had been concluded, she responded to the cheers of the multitude with a smile which could not have appeared more amicable and gracious. None might know from that smile upon her beautiful carmined lips that within her heart she was thinking, "These are the people who slew my brother. Ah, god Issus grant me power to avenge his death upon them!"

Not long after the beauteous Nitocris mounted the golden throne of

Egypt, rumors were whispered of some vast, mysterious enterprise being conducted in secret. A large number of slaves were observed each dawn to embark upon barges and to be carried down the river to some unknown point, where they labored throughout the day, returning after dark. The slaves were Ethiopians, neither able to speak nor to understand the Egyptian language, and therefore no information could be gotten from them by the curious as to the object of their mysterious daily excursions. The general opinion, though, was that the pious queen was having a great temple constructed to the gods and that when it was finished, enormous public banquets would be held within it before its dedication. She meant it to be a surprise gift to the priests who were ever desirous of some new place of worship and were dissatisfied with their old altars, which they said were defiled.

Throughout the winter the slaves repeated daily their excursions. Traffic of all kinds plying down the river was restricted for several miles to within forty yards of one shore. Any craft seen to disregard that restriction was set upon by a galley of armed men and pursued back into bounds. All that could be learned was that a prodigious temple or hall of some sort was in construction.

It was late in the spring when the excursions of the workmen were finally discontinued. Restrictions upon river traffic were withdrawn. The men who went eagerly to investigate the mysterious construction returned with tales of a magnificent new temple, surrounded by rich green, tropical verdure, situated near the bank of the river. It was temple to the god Osiris. It had been built by the queen probably that she might partly atone for the sacrilege of her brother and deliver him from some of the torture which he undoubtedly suffered. It was to be dedicated within the month by a great banquet. All the nobles and the high priests of Osiris, of which there were a tremendous number, were to be invited.

Never had the delighted priests been more extravagant in their praises of Queen Nitocris. When she passed through the streets in her open litter, bedazzling eyes by the glitter of her golden ornaments, the cries of the people were almost frantic in their exaltation of her.

True to the predictions of the gossipers, before the month had passed the banquet had been formally announced and to all the nobility and the priests of Osiris had been issued invitations to attend.

The day of the dedication, which was to be followed by the night

of banqueting, was a gala holiday. At noon the guests of the empress formed a colorful assembly upon the bank of the river. Gayly draped barges floated at their moorings until preparations should be completed for the transportation of the guests to the temple. All anticipated a holiday of great merriment, and the lustful epicureans were warmed by visualizations of the delightful banquet of copious meats, fruits, luscious delicacies and other less innocent indulgences.

When the queen arrived, clamorous shouts rang deafeningly in her ears. She responded with charming smiles and gracious bows. The most discerning observer could not have detected anything but the greatest cordiality and kindliness reflected in her bearing toward those around her. No action, no fleeting expression upon her lovely face could have caused anyone to suspect anything except entire amicability in her feelings or her intentions. The rats, as they followed the Pied Piper of Hamelin through the streets, entranced by the notes of his magical pipe, could not have been less apprehensive of any great danger impending them than were the guests of the empress as they followed her in gayly draped barges, singing and laughing down the sun-glowing waters of the Nile.

The most vivid descriptions of those who had already seen the temple did not prepare the others for the spectacle of beauty and grandeur which it presented. Gasps of delight came from the priests. What a place in which to conduct their ceremonies! They began to feel that the sacrilege of the dead pharaoh was not, after all, to be so greatly regretted, since it was responsible for the building of this glorious new temple.

The columns were massive and painted with the greatest artistry. The temple itself was proportionately large. The center of it was unroofed. Above the entrance were carved the various symbols of the god Osiris, with splendid workmanship. The building was immensely big, and against the background of green foliage it presented a picture of almost breathtaking beauty. Ethiopian attendants stood on each side of the doorway, their shining black bodies ornamented with bands of brilliant gold. On the interior the guests were inspired to even greater wonderment. The walls were hung with magnificent painted tapestries. The altars were more beautifully and elaborately carved than any seen before. Aromatic powders were burning upon them and sending up veils of

scented smoke. The sacramental vessels were of the most exquisite and costly metals. Golden coffers and urns were piled high with perfect fruits of all kinds.

Ah, yes — a splendid place for the making of sacrifices, gloated the staring priests.

Ah, yes indeed, agreed the queen Nitocris, smiling with half-crossed eyes, it was a splendid place for sacrifices — especially for the human sacrifice that had been planned. But all who observed that guileful smile interpreted it as gratification over the pleasure which her creation in honor of their god had brought to the priests of Osiris. Not the slightest shadow of portent was upon the hearts of the joyous guests.

The ceremony of dedication occupied the whole of the afternoon. And when it drew to its impressive conclusion, the large assembly, their nostrils quivering from the savory odor of the roasting meats, were fully ready and impatient for the banquet that awaited them. They gazed about them, observing that the whole building composed an unpartitioned amphitheater and wondering where might be the room of the banquet. However, when the concluding processional chant had been completed the queen summoned a number of burly slaves, and by several iron rings attached to its outer edge they lifted up a large slab of the flooring, disclosing to the astonished guests the fact that the scene of the banquet was to be an immense subterranean vault.

Such vaults were decidedly uncommon among the Egyptians. The idea of feasting in one was novel and appealing. Thrilled exclamations came from the eager, excited crowd and they pressed forward to gaze into the depths, now brightly illuminated. They saw a room beneath them almost as vast in size as the amphitheater in which they were standing. It was filled with banquet tables upon which were set the most delectable foods and rich, sparkling wines in an abundance that would satiate the banqueters of Bacchus. Luxurious, thick rugs covered the floors. Among the tables passed nymphlike maidens, and at one end of the room harpists and singers stood, making sublime music.

The air was cool with the dampness of under-earth, and it was made delightfully fragrant by the perfumes of burning spices and the savory odors of the feast. If it had been heaven itself which the crowd of the queen's guests now gazed down upon they would not have considered

the vision disappointing. Perhaps even if they had known the hideous menace that lurked in those gay-draped walls beneath them, they would still have found the allurement of the banquet scene difficult to resist.

DECORUM and reserve were almost completely forgotten in the swiftness of the guests' descent. The stairs were not wide enough to afford room for all those who rushed upon them, and some tumbled over, landing unhurt upon the thick carpets. The priests themselves forgot their customary dignity and aloofness when they looked upon the beauty of the maiden attendants.

Immediately all of the guests gathered around the banquet tables, and the next hour was occupied in gluttonous feasting. Wine was unlimited, and so was the thirst of the guests. Goblets were refilled as quickly as they were made empty by the capacious mouths of the drinkers. The songs and the laughter, the dancing and the wild frolicking grew less and less restrained until the banquet became a delirious orgy.

The queen alone, seated upon a cushioned dais from which she might overlook the whole room, remained aloof from the general hilarity. Her thick black brows twitched; her luminous black eyes shone strangely between their narrow painted lids. There was something peculiarly feline in the curl of her rich red lips. Now and again her eyes sought the section of wall to her left, where hung gorgeous braided tapestries from the east. But it seemed not the tapestries that she looked upon. Color would mount upon her brow and her slender fingers would dig still tighter into the cushions she reclined upon.

In her mind the queen Nitocris was seeing a ghastly picture. It was the picture of a room of orgy and feasting suddenly converted into a room of terror and horror, human beings one moment drunken and lustful, the next screaming in the seizure of sudden and awful death. If any of those present had been empowered to see also that picture of dire horror, they would have clambered wildly to make their escape. But none was so empowered.

With increasing wildness the banquet continued into the middle of the night. Some of the banqueters, disgustingly gluttonous, still gorged themselves at the greasy tables. Others lay in drunken stupor, or lolled amorously with the slave girls. But most of them, formed in a great irregular circle, skipped about the room in a barbaric, joy-mad dance,

dragging and tripping each other in uncouth merriment and making the hall ring with their ceaseless shouts, laughter, and hoarse song.

When the hour had approached near to midnight, the queen, who had sat like one entranced, arose from the cushioned dais. One last intent survey she gave to the crowded room of banquet. It was a scene which she wished to imprint permanently upon her mind. Much pleasure might she derive in the future by recalling that picture, and then imagining what came afterward — stark, searing terror rushing in upon barbaric joy!

She stepped down from the dais and walked swiftly to the steps. Her departure made no impression upon the revelers. When she had arrived at the top of the stairs she looked down and observed that no one had marked her exit.

Around the walls of the temple, dim-lit and fantastic-looking at night, with the cool wind from the river sweeping through and bending the flames of the tall candelabra, stalwart guardsmen were standing at their posts, and when the gold cloaked figure of the queen arose from the aperture, they advanced toward her hurriedly. With a motion, she directed them to place the slab of rock in its tight-fitting sockets. With a swift, noiseless hoist and lowering, they obeyed the command. The queen bent down. There was no change in the boisterous sounds from below. Nothing was yet suspected.

Drawing the soft and shimmering folds of her cloak about her with fingers that trembled with eagerness, excitement and the intense emotion which she felt, the queen passed swiftly across the stone floor of the temple toward the open front through which the night wind swept, blowing her cloak in sheenful waves about her tall and graceful figure. The slaves followed after in silent file, well aware of the monstrous deed about to be executed and without reluctance to play their parts.

Down the steps of the palace into the moon-white night passed the weird procession. Their way led them down an obviously secreted path through thick ranks of murmuring palms which in their low voices seemed to be whispering shocked remonstrances against what was about to be done. But in her stern purpose the queen was not susceptible to any dissuasion from god or man. Vengeance, strongest of passions, made her obdurate as stone.

Out upon a rough and apparently new-constructed stone pier the

thin path led. Beneath, the cold, dark waters of the Nile surged silently by. Here the party came to a halt. Upon this stone pier would the object of their awful midnight errand be accomplished.

With a low-spoken word, the queen commanded her followers to hold back. With her own hand she would perform the act of vengeance.

In the foreground of the pier a number of fantastic, wandlike levers extended upward. Toward these the queen advanced, slowly and stiffly as an executioner mounts the steps of the scaffold. When she had come beside them, she grasped one upthrust bar, fiercely, as if it had been the throat of a hated antagonist. Then she lifted her face with a quick intake of breath toward the moon-lightened sky. This was to her a moment of supreme ecstasy. Grasped in her hand was an instrument which could release awful death upon those against whom she wished vengeance. Their lives were as securely in her grasp as was this bar of iron.

Slowly, lusting upon every triumph-filled second of this time of ecstasy, she turned her face down again to the formidable bar in her hand. Deliberately she drew it back to its limit. This was the lever that opened the wall in the banquet vault. It gave entrance to death. Only the other bar now intervened between the banqueters, probably still reveling undisturbed, and the dreadful fate which she had prepared for them. Upon this bar now her jeweled fingers clutched. Savagely this time she pulled it; then with the litheness of a tiger she sprang to the edge of the pier. She leaned over it and stared down into the inky rush of the river. A new sound she heard above the steady flow. It was the sound of waters suddenly diverted into a new channel — an eager, plunging sound. Down to the hall of revelry they were rushing — these savage waters — bringing terror and sudden death.

A cry of triumph, wild and terrible enough to make even the hearts of the brutish slaves turn cold, now broke from the lips of the queen. The pharaoh was avenged.

And even he must have considered his avenging adequate had he been able to witness it.

AFTER the retiring of the queen, the banquet had gone on without interruption of gayety. None noticed her absence. None noticed the silent replacing of the stone in the socket. No premonition of disaster was

felt. The musicians, having been informed beforehand of the intended event of the evening, had made their withdrawal before the queen. The slaves, whose lives were of little value to the queen, were as ignorant of what was to happen as were the guests themselves.

Not until the wall opened up, with a loud and startling crunch, did even those most inclined toward suspicion feel the slightest uneasiness. Then it was that a few noticed the slab to have been replaced, shutting them in. This discovery, communicated throughout the hall in a moment, seemed to instill a sudden fear in the hearts of all. Laughter did not cease, but the ring of dancers were distracted from their wild jubilee. They all turned toward the mysteriously opened wall and gazed into its black depths.

A hush fell over them. And then became audible the mounting sound of rushing water. A shriek rose from the throat of a woman. And then terror took possession of all within the room. Panic like the burst of flames flared into their hearts. Of one accord, they rushed upon the stair. And it, being purposely made frail, collapsed before the foremost of the wildly screaming mob had reached its summit. Turbulently they piled over the tables, filling the room with a hideous clamor. But rising above their screams was the shrill roar of the rushing water, and no sound could be more provoking of dread and terror. Somewhere in its circuitous route from the pier to the chamber of its reception it must have met with temporary blockade, for it was several minutes after the sound of it was first detected that the first spray of that death-bringing water leapt into the faces of the doomed occupants of the room.

With the ferocity of a lion springing into the arena of a Roman amphitheater to devour the gladiators set there for its delectation, the black water plunged in. Furiously it surged over the floor of the room, sweeping tables before it and sending its victims, now face to face with their harrowing doom, into a hysteria of terror. In a moment that icy, black water had risen to their knees, although the room was vast. Some fell instantly dead from the shock, or were trampled upon by the desperate rushing of the mob. Tables were clambered upon. Lamps and candles were extinguished. Brilliant light rapidly faded to twilight, and a ghastly dimness fell over the room as only the suspended lanterns remained lit. And what a scene of chaotic and hideous horror might a spectator have

beheld! The gorgeous trumpery of banquet invaded by howling waters of death! Gayly dressed merrymakers caught suddenly in the grip of terror! Gasps and screams of the dying amid tumult and thickening dark!

What more horrible vengeance could Queen Nitocris have conceived than this banquet of death? Not Diablo himself could be capable of anything more fiendishly artistic. Here in the temple of Osiris those nobles and priests who had slain the pharaoh in expiation of his sacrilege against Osiris had now met their deaths. And it was in the waters of the Nile, material symbol of the god Osiris, that they had died. It was magnificent in its irony!

I WOULD be content to end this story here if it were but a story. However, it is not merely a story, as you will have discerned before now if you have been a student of the history of Egypt. Queen Nitocris is not a fictitious personage. In the annals of ancient Egypt she is no inconspicuous figure. Principally responsible for her prominence is her monstrous revenge upon the slayers of her brother, the narration of which I have just concluded. Glad would I be to end this story here; for surely anything following must be in the nature of an anticlimax. However, being not a mere storyteller here, but having upon me also the responsibility of a historian, I feel obligated to continue the account to the point where it was left off by Herodotus, the great Greek historian. And therefore I add this postscript, anticlimax though it be.

The morning of the day after the massacre in the temple, the guests of the queen not having made their return, the citizens of Thebes began to glower with dark suspicions. Rumors came to them through divers channels that something of a most extraordinary and calamitous nature had occurred at the scene of the banquet during the night. Some had it that the temple had collapsed upon the revelers and all had been killed. However, this theory was speedily dispelled when a voyager from down the river reported having passed the temple in a perfectly firm condition but declared that he had seen no signs of life about the place — only the brightly canopied boats, drifting at their moorings.

Uneasiness steadily increased throughout the day. Sage persons recalled the great devotion of the queen toward her dead brother, and noted that the guests at the banquet of last night had been composed almost entirely of those who had participated in his slaying.

When in the evening the queen arrived in the city, pale, silent, and obviously nervous, threatening crowds blocked the path of her chariot, demanding roughly an explanation of the disappearance of her guests. Haughtily she ignored them and lashed forward the horses of her chariot, pushing aside the tight mass of people. Well she knew, however, that her life would be doomed as soon as they confirmed their suspicions. She resolved to meet her inevitable death in a way that befitted one of her rank, not at the filthy hands of a mob.

Therefore upon her entrance into the palace she ordered her slaves to fill instantly her boudoir with hot and smoking ashes. When this had been done, she went to the room, entered it, closed the door and locked it securely, and then flung herself down upon a couch in the center of the room. In a short time the scorching heat and the suffocating thick fumes of the smoke overpowered her. Only her beautiful dead body remained for the hands of the mob.

ACKNOWLEDGMENTS

We are grateful for permission to include the following previously copyrighted stories in this collection:

"So Help Me," by Nelson Algren. From *The Neon Wilderness* by Nelson Algren. Copyright 1947 by Nelson Algren. Used by permission of Doubleday, a division of Bantam Doubleday Dell Publishing Group, Inc.

"The War in the Bathroom," by Margaret Atwood. Originally published in *Alphabet* Magazine (London, Ontario). Reprinted by permission of the author.

"Previous Condition," by James Baldwin. From *Going to Meet the Man* by James Baldwin. Copyright 1948, 1951, 1957, 1958, 1960, 1965 by James Baldwin. Used by permission of Doubleday, a division of Bantam Doubleday Dell Publishing Group, Inc.

"The State of Grace," by Harold Brodkey. From *Stories in an Almost Classical Mode* by Harold Brodkey. Copyright © 1963, 1965, 1968, 1969, 1973, 1975, 1976, 1977, 1983, 1985, 1988 by Harold Brodkey. Reprinted by permission of Alfred A. Knopf, Inc.

"Aftermath of a Lengthy Rejection Slip," by Charles Bukowski. Copyright © 1944 by Charles Bukowski. Reprinted with the permission of Black Sparrow Press.

"Miriam," by Truman Capote. From *A Tree of Night and Other Stories* by Truman Capote. Copyright © 1945 by Truman Capote. Reprinted by permission of Random House, Inc.

"Furious Seasons," by Raymond Carver. Copyright © 1960 by Tess Gallagher. Reprinted by permission of Tess Gallagher.

"Expelled," by John Cheever. From *The New Republic,* October 1, 1930. Reprinted with the permission of Wylie, Aitken & Stone, Inc.

"The End of the Party," by Graham Greene. Copyright 1929, © renewed 1957 by Graham Greene. From *Collected Stories of Graham Greene* by Graham Greene. Used by permission of Viking Penguin, a division of Penguin Books USA Inc., and David Higham Associates.

"Because of the Waters of the Flood," by Mark Helprin. Copyright © 1969 by Mark Helprin. Reprinted by permission of The Wendy Weil Agency, Inc.

"in our time," by Ernest Hemingway. Reprinted with permission of Charles Scribner's Sons, an imprint of Macmillan Publishing Company. From *In Our Time* by Ernest Hemingway. Copyright 1925 by Charles Scribner's Sons. Copyright renewed 1953 by Ernest Hemingway.

"Crazy in the Stir," by Chester B. Himes. Copyright © 1934 by Chester B. Himes. Reprinted by permission of Roslyn Targ Literary Agency, Inc.

"After You, My Dear Alphonse," from *The Lottery* by Shirley Jackson. Copyright © 1948, 1949 by Shirley Jackson, renewed © 1976, 1977 by Laurence Hyman, Mrs. Sarah Webster, Mrs. Joanne Shnurer and Barry Hyman. Reprinted by permission of Farrar, Straus & Giroux, Inc.

"Territory," by David Leavitt. From *Family Dancing* by David Leavitt. Copyright © 1983,

1984 by David Leavitt. Reprinted by permission of Alfred A. Knopf, Inc. Originally in the *New Yorker.*

"April in Paris," by Ursula K. Le Guin. Copyright © 1962, 1990 by Ursula K. Le Guin. First appeared in *Fantastic.* Reprinted by permission of the author and the author's agent, Virginia Kidd.

"The Pig," by Doris Lessing. Copyright © 1964 by Doris Lessing. Reprinted by permission of Jonathan Clowes Ltd., London, on behalf of Doris Lessing, and Simon & Schuster, Inc.

"Cruel and Barbarous Treatment," by Mary McCarthy. Reprinted by permission of The Mary McCarthy Literary Trust.

"Wunderkind," by Carson McCullers. From *The Ballad of the Sad Cafe and Collected Short Stories* by Carson McCullers. Copyright 1936, 1941, 1942, 1950, © 1955 by Carson Mc-Cullers. Copyright © renewed 1979 by Floria V. Lasky. Reprinted by permission of Houghton Mifflin Co. All rights reserved.

"The Greatest Thing in the World," by Norman Mailer. Copyright © by Norman Mailer. Reprinted with the permission of Wylie, Aitken & Stone, Inc.

"Benefit Performance," by Bernard Malamud. Copyright 1943 by Bernard Malamud. Copyright renewed 1971 by Bernard Malamud. Reprinted by permission of Russell & Volkening as agents for the author.

"Mademoiselle Claude," by Henry Miller. From *Wisdom of the Heart.* Copyright 1941 by New Directions Publishing Corp. Reprinted by permission of New Directions Publishing Corp.

"A Basket of Strawberries," by Alice Munro. Copyright © by Alice Munro. Reprinted by arrangement with Virginia Barber Literary Agency, Inc.

"In the Old World," by Joyce Carol Oates. Copyright © 1993 by Joyce Carol Oates. Reprinted by permission of the author.

"The Geranium," by Flannery O'Connor. From *The Complete Stories* by Flannery O'Connor. Copyright © 1946 by Flannery O'Connor, renewed © 1974 by the Estate of Mary Flannery O'Connor. Reprinted by permission of Farrar, Straus & Giroux, Inc.

"The Alumnae Bulletin," by John O'Hara. Reprinted by permission; © 1928, 1956 by John O'Hara. Originally in the *New Yorker.*

"Goodbye and Good Luck," by Grace Paley. Copyright 1959 by Grace Paley. From *Little Disturbances of Man,* Viking: New York.

"Such a Pretty Little Picture," by Dorothy Parker. The publisher and editor wish to thank the National Association for the Advancement of Colored People for authorizing the use of Dorothy Parker's works.

"The Day It Snowed," by Philip Roth. Copyright © by Philip Roth. Reprinted by permission of the author.

"The Daring Young Man on the Flying Trapeze," by William Saroyan. Permission to reprint granted by the William Saroyan Foundation.

"Flash in the Pan," by Irwin Shaw. Used with permission of the Estate of Irwin Shaw.

"Gimpel the Fool," by Isaac Bashevis Singer. Translated by Saul Bellow. Copyright 1953 by The Partisan Review, renewed © 1981 by Isaac Bashevis Singer. From *A Treasury of Yiddish Stories* by Irving Howe and Eliezer Greenberg. Used by permission of Viking Penguin, a division of Penguin Books USA Inc.

"And Baby Makes Three," by Jane Smiley. Copyright © 1977 by Jane Smiley. Used by permission. Originally published in *Redbook.*

"The Seraph and the Zambesi," by Muriel Spark. Copyright © 1985 by Copyright Ad-